Let's Review Regents:
English Revised Edition

Carol Chaitkin, M.S.
Former Director of American Studies
Lycée Français de New York
New York, New York

Former English Department Head
Great Neck North High School
Great Neck, New York

Acknowledgments

Page 75: "Pitcher" from *The Orb Weaver* by Robert Francis © 1960, by Robert Francis and reprinted by permission of Wesleyan University Press.

Page 79: "Old Photograph of the Future" by Robert Penn Warren © 1985. Reprinted by permission of Random House, Inc.

Page 81: "Child on Top of a Greenhouse," copyright © 1946 by Editorial Publications, Inc.; from COLLECTED POEMS by Theodore Roethke. Used by permission of Doubleday, an imprint of Knopf Doubleday Publishing Group, a division of Random House LLC. All rights reserved.

Page 81: "The Sleeping Giant" from OLD AND NEW POEMS by Donald Hall. Copyright © 1990 by Donald Hall. Reprinted by permission of Houghton Mifflin Harcourt Publishing Company. All rights reserved.

© Copyright 2021, 2020, 2018, 2017, 2016, 2015, 2013, 2012, 2011, 2008, 2007, 2006, 2005, 2004, 2003, 2002, 2001, 1999, 1995 by Kaplan, Inc., d/b/a Barron's Educational Series

All rights reserved.
No part of this book may be reproduced or distributed in any form or by any means without the written permission of the copyright owner.

Published by Kaplan, Inc., d/b/a Barron's Educational Series
750 Third Avenue
New York, NY 10017
www.barronseduc.com

ISBN: 978-1-5062-6481-3

10 9 8 7 6 5 4 3 2 1

Kaplan, Inc., d/b/a Barron's Educational Series print books are available at special quantity discounts to use for sales promotions, employee premiums, or educational purposes. For more information or to purchase books, please call the Simon & Schuster special sales department at 866-506-1949.

TABLE OF CONTENTS

INTRODUCTION		**1**
	A Guide to the New York State Standards in Literacy (ELA)	1
	Terms to Help You Understand the State Standards	2
	The Regents ELA (Common Core) Exam	3
	Ways to Use *Let's Review: English*	4
CHAPTER 1	**READING COMPREHENSION**	**5**
	Close Reading	5
	Questions to Keep in Mind As You Read	6
	Reading Comprehenshion Passages and Questions for Review	7
CHAPTER 2	**WRITING FROM SOURCES**	**23**
	Step One—Reading for Information and Understanding	23
	Looking at the Texts	30
	Step Two—Composing a Source-based Argument	31
	Planning the Essay	32
	Looking at a Variety of Effective Claims	32
CHAPTER 3	**READING AND WRITING TO ANALYZE TEXT**	**35**
	Text Analysis: Exposition	35
	Sample Text and Expository Response	35
	Additional Texts for Analysis and Review	38
CHAPTER 4	**READING PROSE**	**45**
	What Writers Do: A List of Useful Terms	45
	Reading Fiction	46
	Reading Nonfiction	53
	A Glossary of Literary Terms and Techniques	66

Table of Contents

CHAPTER 5	**READING POETRY**	**75**
	Introduction	75
	Structure and Language in Poetry	78
	Theme in Poetry	83
	Tone	86
	Writing About Poetry/Explication	86
	Poetry on Examinations	87
	A Handful of Poems for Further Reading	87
	A Glossary of Poetic Terms and Techniques	94
CHAPTER 6	**WRITING ABOUT LITERATURE: A GENERAL REVIEW**	**101**
	Topics for Literary Essays	101
	Topic and Focus	102
	Selection of Significant Details	102
	Developing the Topic	102
	Looking at Key Terms in Literature Questions	104
	Using Fluent and Precise Language	104
	Choosing Your Own Topic: Representative Literary Subjects and Themes	105
	Audience and Literature Essays	108
	A Note on Conclusions	108
CHAPTER 7	**WRITING ON DEMAND**	**109**
	Writing to Inform or Persuade	109
	Writing from a Prompt	115
	Evaluating Composition	118
	Preparing for Essay Exams	119
	Writing on Timed Examinations	119
	Using Synonymies to Enhance Your Writing	121
	A Glossary of Terms for Writing	124
CHAPTER 8	**VOCABULARY**	**127**
	Academic Language	128
	Unfamiliar and Archaic Language	133
	Studying New Words	135

	Roots and Prefixes from Latin and Greek	136
	A Note on Synonyms and Using a Thesaurus	142
	Organizing Vocabulary Study	143
	Vocabulary for Study	149

CHAPTER 9   GRAMMAR AND USAGE FOR THE CAREFUL WRITER: A GUIDE TO STANDARD WRITTEN ENGLISH   161

	Reviewing the Fundamentals	161
	Avoiding Common Errors in Writing	165
	Expressions Often Confused, Misused, and Overused	174

CHAPTER 10   PUNCTUATION: GUIDELINES AND REMINDERS   183

	End Punctuation	183
	Internal Punctuation	187
	Titles of Works of Literature	196
	A Final Note on Punctuation	196

CHAPTER 11   SPELLING   197

	Spelling on Writing Exams	197
	Spelling Rules and Patterns	197
	Words Commonly Confused	206
	Words Commonly Misspelled	207

RECOMMENDED READING   215

	Novels	215
	Autobiography, Essays, and Other Nonfiction	217
	Poetry	218
	Short Stories	220
	Plays	220

APPENDICES: THE NEW YORK STATE COMMON CORE LEARNING STANDARDS FOR ENGLISH LANGUAGE ARTS   223

Table of Contents

REGENTS ELA (COMMON CORE) EXAMINATIONS

June 2019 Examination — 233

INDEX — 261

INTRODUCTION

Let's Review is designed as a handbook for high school English courses, including those aligned with the new Common Core Standards, and as a review book for students preparing to take the Regents Exam in English Language Arts (Common Core). Because the English Regents Exam is not a test of specific curriculum but an assessment of skills in reading comprehension, literary analysis, and composition, *Let's Review* offers a comprehensive guide to essential language, literature, and critical reading and writing skills all high school students should seek to demonstrate as they prepare for college and the workplace.

A GUIDE TO THE NEW YORK STATE STANDARDS IN LITERACY (ELA)

Most middle school and high school students in New York State should already be familiar with some key shifts in curriculum and instruction in their English courses. These shifts in emphasis include the following:

- Students will read more informational texts and perhaps fewer literary texts than in the past. Alignment with the Common Core requires a balancing of the two.
- In all academic subjects, students will be expected to build their knowledge primarily through engaging directly with text.
- Throughout secondary school, students will read texts of increasing complexity and will be expected to develop skills in **close reading** in all academic subjects.
- Students will be expected to engage in rich and rigorous **evidence-based** conversations/class discussions about text.
- Student writing will emphasize **use of evidence** from sources to express their understanding and to form and develop argument.
- Students will acquire the **academic vocabulary** they need to comprehend and respond to grade level complex texts. This vocabulary is often relevant to more than one subject.

Introduction

TERMS TO HELP YOU UNDERSTAND THE STATE STANDARDS

- **ELA/LITERACY**—**English Language Arts** refers to skills in reading, writing, speaking, and listening. Courses and exams once identified as English may also be identified as ELA. **Literacy** refers to the ability to read and write and to use language proficiently. The term also identifies the quality of being knowledgeable in a particular subject or field. For example, we often refer to "digital" or "computer literacy."
- **COMMON CORE LEARNING STANDARDS (CCLS)***—These are the learning standards in ELA and math, also known as **CCSS** (Common Core State Standards), developed and adopted by a consortium of over 40 states. New York State adopted the CCLS in 2010 and continues to implement them in curriculum and assessments (testing).
- **CCR**—The phrase **"college and career ready"** is widely used in discussion of new curriculum and assessments. This refers to the fundamental principle of the Common Core Standards: to reflect the knowledge and skills that all students need for success in college and careers.
- **ASSESSMENT**—You may hear teachers and other educators using the term **assessment** instead of test or examination. An **assessment** is more than a simple test (in vocabulary, say) because it seeks to measure a number of skills at one time. Although we continue to refer to the English Regents as an exam or test, its goal is to be a valid **assessment** of a broad range of reading, thinking, language, and writing skills outlined in the Standards.
- **TEXT**—Broadly, the term text refers to any written material. The Common Core standards use the term to refer to the great variety of material students are expected to be able to read, understand, analyze, and write about. Texts may include **literary** works of fiction, drama, and poetry; and **informational**, or nonfiction, including essays, memoirs, speeches, and scientific and historical documents. The Common Core also emphasizes the use of **authentic texts;** that is, students will read actual historical documents or scientific essays rather than simply read articles about them.
- **CLOSE READING**—Skill in close, analytic reading is fundamental to the CCLS and to the new Regents exam. The Common Core curriculum focuses student attention on the text itself in order to understand not only what the text says and means but also how that meaning is constructed and revealed. Close reading enables students to understand central ideas and key supporting details. It also enables students to reflect on the meanings of individual words and sentences, the order in which sentences unfold, and the development of ideas over the course

of the text, which ultimately leads students to arrive at an understanding of the text as a whole.
- **ARGUMENT**—What is an argument? In academic writing, an argument is usually a central idea, often called a **claim** or **thesis statement,** which is backed up with evidence that supports the idea. Much of the writing high school students do in their English courses constitutes essays of argument, in addition to personal essays, descriptive pieces, and works of imagination.
- **SOURCE-BASED/EVIDENCE-BASED**—The ability to compose sound arguments using relevant and specific evidence from a given text is central to the expectations of the Common Core Standards.
- **WRITING STRATEGY**—This is the general term for a literary element, literary technique, or rhetorical device. Examples include characterization, conflict, denotation/connotation, metaphor, simile, irony, language use, point of view, setting, structure, symbolism, theme, and tone. In class discussions and on examinations, students are expected to understand and explain how literary elements and writing strategies contribute to the meaning of a text.

*The Anchor (Common Core) Standards for Grades 11–12 Reading, Writing, and Language are found in the Appendices, pages 223–227.

THE REGENTS ELA (COMMON CORE) EXAM

This 3-hour examination requires students to read, analyze, and write about both literary and informational texts.

PART I—READING COMPREHENSION

This part requires close reading of three texts and will contain at least one literature text, one poem, and one informational text, followed by 24 multiple-choice questions.

PART II—WRITING FROM SOURCES: ARGUMENT

This part includes close reading of four informational texts and may contain some information in graphics; students will compose an essay of argument with a claim based on the sources.

Part III—Text Analysis: Exposition

Students will perform a close reading of one informational or one literature text and write a two to three paragraph expository response that identifies a central idea in the text and analyzes how the author's use of one writing strategy develops that central idea.

Note: The ACT and the new SAT (2015) include similar assessments of close reading, text analysis, the rhetoric of arguments, and the use of academic vocabulary.

WAYS TO USE *LET'S REVIEW: ENGLISH*

As a handbook for literature study in high school and college courses, see especially

    Chapter 4—Reading Prose
    Chapter 5—Reading Poetry
    Chapter 6—Writing About Literature: A General Review

As a handbook for reading comprehension and language skills, see especially

    Chapter 1—Reading Comprehension
    Chapter 3—Reading and Writing to Analyze Text
    Chapter 4—Reading Prose
    Chapter 5—Reading Poetry
    Chapter 8—Vocabulary

As a handbook for writing and proofreading, see especially

    Chapter 2—Writing from Sources
    Chapter 3—Reading and Writing to Analyze Text
    Chapter 6—Writing About Literature: A General Review
    Chapter 9—Grammar and Usage for the Careful Writer
    Chapter 10—Punctuation: Guidelines and Reminders

As a review text for the ELA (Common Core) Regents exam, the SAT, and the ACT, see especially

    Chapter 1—Reading Comprehension
    Chapter 2—Writing from Sources
    Chapter 3—Reading and Writing to Analyze Text
    Chapter 8—Vocabulary
    Appendices—The New York State Common Core Learning Standards for English Language Arts

Chapter 1

READING COMPREHENSION

Throughout your schooling, you have been developing skills in the ability to read and comprehend works of literature as well as informational texts in nearly every subject, including history and social studies, science, and technical studies. Because the ability to understand, interpret, and make use of a wide range of texts is central to learning, it is a skill students are regularly asked to demonstrate. Assessment of students' reading comprehension skills may be informal or indirect, as in a class discussion or short quiz, or through formal testing.

Students at Regents level—11th and 12th grades—are expected to have the ability to understand and interpret both literary and informational texts of significant complexity: that is, Regents-level students understand literary texts with multiple levels of meaning, with structures that may be complex or unconventional, and with elements of figurative or deliberately ambiguous language that are integral to its meaning. The expectations for reading informational texts include the ability to interpret and analyze personal essays, speeches, opinion pieces, and memoir and autobiographical works as well as official documents and historical, scientific, and technical material for subject courses other than English. This increased emphasis on a wide range of informational texts is one of the key shifts in high school curriculum and should already be familiar to most students. It is also helpful to know that both the ACT and new SAT (2015) exams include a similar variety of texts and primary source documents.

CLOSE READING

One useful way to think about what we mean by "close reading" is to think about what you are doing when you can annotate something you are reading; that is, what do you underline? circle? check in the margins? You are probably checking off main ideas and conclusions, underlining the most important details, and circling significant or unfamiliar words. Whether or not you actually mark up a text, that process of checking, underlining, and circling is the thinking process of close reading.

In-class discussions of literary works are often exercises in what is meant by close reading—Where are we? Which details give us an image of the setting? What just happened? What is this character thinking now? What does the story lead us to expect? What is surprising? How were we prepared? How does the author/narrator guide our understanding of characters and their actions? Why is this incident important in the plot? What does this character's remark really mean? Was the ending convincing?

The most satisfying "close reading," however, is what we are doing when our imaginations are fully engaged in a story, a play, a poem, or a film(!) Then it is not an academic exercise or assessment but the pleasure of experiencing a good story.

Reading for information in history, social studies, or science requires careful attention to the sequence of ideas, to how general statements are supported with relevant details. This kind of reading may also require familiarity with specialized language. (See Academic Language in Chapter 8—Vocabulary.)

On exams, you will exercise this same kind of thinking and engagement with the text on your own. The multiple-choice questions are designed to assess your close reading skills and the depth of your understanding.

QUESTIONS TO KEEP IN MIND AS YOU READ

If you are reading a literary passage, ask yourself

What is this piece about? What is the narrative point of view?
What do we understand about the setting?
What do we understand about the narrator? Other characters?

In reading a poem, consider

What experience, memory, or dramatic situation is the poem about?
Who and where is the narrator/speaker?
How does the organization of lines and stanzas affect the meaning?
How are language and imagery used?

In passages of memoir and personal essay, ask

What experience is meant to be shared and understood?
What does the author say? Describe? Suggest? Reveal?

If you are reading an informational text, ask yourself

What is the subject? What do I already know about this subject?
What main idea or theme is being developed? What phrases or terms signal that?
What is the purpose? To inform? To persuade? To celebrate? To guide? To show a process? To introduce a new or unfamiliar subject?

READING COMPREHENSION PASSAGES AND QUESTIONS FOR REVIEW

The following passages and questions are from actual tasks on Regents ELA exams.

PASSAGE ONE — LITERATURE

This passage is from a classic Sherlock Holmes story by Sir Arthur Conan Doyle. Many of the expressions are unfamiliar but can be understood in context. High school students may already be familiar with the character of Sherlock Holmes, both through reading of the original stories and through modern retelling in popular American and British television series. On the Regents ELA exam, you are expected to read and analyze texts from works of American literature as well as works from British and world literatures.

    It was upon the 4th of March, as I have good reason to remember, that I rose somewhat earlier than usual, and found that Sherlock Holmes had not yet finished his breakfast. The landlady had become so accustomed to my late habits that my place had not been laid nor my coffee prepared. With the unreasonable petulance[1] of
(5) mankind I rang the bell and gave a curt intimation that I was ready. Then I picked up a magazine from the table and attempted to while away the time with it, while my companion munched silently at his toast. One of the articles had a pencil-mark at the heading, and I naturally began to run my eye through it. ...
    "From a drop of water," said the writer, "a logician could infer the possibility
(10) of an Atlantic or a Niagara without having seen or heard of one or the other. So all life is a great chain, the nature of which is known whenever we are shown a single link of it. Like all other arts, the Science of Deduction and Analysis is one which can only be acquired by long and patient study, nor is life long enough to allow any mortal to attain the highest possible perfection in it. Before turning to those
(15) moral and mental aspects of the matter which present the greatest difficulties, let the inquirer begin by mastering more elementary problems. Let him, on meeting a fellow-mortal, learn at a glance to distinguish the history of the man and the trade or profession to which he belongs. Puerile[2] as such an exercise may seem, it sharpens the faculties of observation and teaches one where to look and what to look for. By
(20) a man's fingernails, by his coat-sleeve, by his boot, by his trouser-knees, by the callosities of his forefinger and thumb, by his expression, by his shirt-cuffs—by each of these things a man's calling is plainly revealed. That all united should fail to enlighten the competent inquirer in any case is almost inconceivable."

    [1]petulance — a quality or state of being rude
    [2]puerile — childish

"What ineffable twaddle!" I cried, slapping the magazine down on the table; "I (25) never read such rubbish in my life."

"What is it?" asked Sherlock Holmes.

"Why, this article," I said, pointing at it with my egg-spoon as I sat down to my breakfast. "I see that you have read it, since you have marked it. I don't deny that it is smartly written. It irritates me, though. It is evidently the theory of some arm- (30) chair lounger who evolves all these neat little paradoxes in the seclusion of his own study. It is not practical. I should like to see him clapped down in a third-class car- riage on the Underground and asked to give the trades of all his fellow-travellers. I would lay a thousand to one against him."

"You would lose your money," Sherlock Holmes remarked, calmly. "As for the (35) article, I wrote it myself."

"You?"

"Yes, I have a turn both for observation and for deduction. The theories which I have expressed there, and which appear to you to be so chimerical, are really extremely practical—so practical that I depend upon them for my bread-and- (40) cheese."

"And how?" I asked, involuntarily.

"Well, I have a trade of my own. I suppose I am the only one in the world. I'm a consulting detective, if you can understand what that is. Here in London we have lots of government detectives and lots of private ones. When these fellows are at (45) fault they come to me, and I manage to put them on the right scent. They lay all the evidence before me, and I am generally able, by the help of my knowledge of the history of crime, to set them straight. There is a strong family resemblance about misdeeds, and if you have all the details of a thousand at your finger-ends, it is odd if you can't unravel the thousand and first. Lestrade is a well-known detective. He (50) got himself into a fog recently over a forgery case, and that was what brought him here."

"And these other people?"

"They are mostly sent out by private inquiry agencies. They are all people who are in trouble about something, and want a little enlightening. I listen to their story, (55) they listen to my comments, and then I pocket my fee."

"But do you mean to say," I said, "that without leaving your room you can unravel some knot which other men can make nothing of, although they have seen every detail for themselves?"

"Quite so. I have a kind of intuition that way. Now and again a case turns up (60) which is a little more complex. Then I have to bustle about and see things with my own eyes. You see, I have a lot of special knowledge which I apply to the problem, and which facilitates matters wonderfully. Those rules of deduction laid down in that article which aroused your scorn are invaluable to me in practical work. Observation with me is second nature. You appeared to be surprised when I told you, on our first meeting, that you had come from Afghanistan."

"You were told, no doubt."

"Nothing of the sort. I *knew* you came from Afghanistan. From long habit the train of thought ran so swiftly through my mind that I arrived at the conclusion without being conscious of intermediate steps. There were such steps, however. The train of reasoning ran: 'Here is a gentleman of a medical type, but with the air of a military man. Clearly an army doctor, then. He has just come from the tropics, for his face is dark, and that is not the natural tint of his skin, for his wrists are fair. He has undergone hardship and sickness, as his haggard face says clearly. His left arm has been injured. He holds it in a stiff and unnatural manner. Where in the tropics could an English army doctor have seen much hardship and got his arm wounded? Clearly in Afghanistan.' The whole train of thought did not occupy a second. I then remarked that you came from Afghanistan, and you were astonished." ...

I was still annoyed at his bumptious style of conversation. I thought it best to change the topic.

"I wonder what that fellow is looking for?" I asked, pointing to a stalwart, plainly dressed individual who was walking slowly down the other side of the street, looking anxiously at the numbers. He had a large, blue envelope in his hand, and was evidently the bearer of a message.

"You mean the retired sergeant of marines," said Sherlock Holmes.

"Brag and bounce!" thought I to myself. "He knows that I cannot verify his guess." The thought had hardly passed through my mind when the man whom we were watching caught sight of the number on our door, and ran rapidly across the roadway. We heard a loud knock, a deep voice below, and heavy steps ascending the stair.

"For Mr. Sherlock Holmes," he said, stepping into the room and handing my friend the letter.

Here was an opportunity of taking the conceit out of him. He little thought of this when he made that random shot. "May I ask, my lad," I said, blandly, "what your trade may be?"

"Commissionnaire, sir," he said, gruffly. "Uniform away for repairs."

"And you were?" I asked, with a slightly malicious glance at my companion. "A sergeant, sir, Royal Marine Light Infantry, sir. No answer? Right, sir." He clicked his heels together, raised his hand in a salute, and was gone.

—A. Conan Doyle
excerpted from *A Study in Scarlet*, 1904
Harper & Brothers Publishers

Questions for Comprehension

This passage, narrated by the character of Dr. Watson, reveals the differences in character and personality of the two men. The discussion of the magazine article leads to a dramatic demonstration of Holmes's powers of observation and deduction. At the end, Watson's doubts are erased, and he is left speechless.

1 The phrase "with the unreasonable petulance of mankind" (lines 4–5) emphasizes the narrator's

   (1) frustration with himself for missing sleep
   (2) irritation about not finding his breakfast ready
   (3) concern regarding the pencil-mark on the newspaper
   (4) impatience with Sherlock Holmes's silence   1____

2 How do the words "logician" (line 9), "deduction" (lines 12, 37, and 62), and "analysis" (line 12) advance the author's purpose?

   (1) by indicating the relationship between science and art
   (2) by suggesting the reasons why private inquiry agencies seek outside help
   (3) by highlighting the complexity of the crimes encountered by Sherlock Holmes
   (4) by emphasizing the systematic nature of Sherlock Holmes's approach to solving crimes   2____

3 What is the effect of withholding the identity of Sherlock Holmes as the author of the article (lines 9 through 35)?

   (1) It creates a somber mood.
   (2) It foreshadows an unwelcome turn of events.
   (3) It allows the reader to learn the narrator's true feelings.
   (4) It leads the reader to misunderstand who the writer is.   3____

4 In this passage, the conversation between Holmes and the narrator (lines 24 through 40) serves to

  (1) reinforce the narrator's appreciation for deduction
  (2) establish a friendship between the narrator and Holmes
  (3) reveal how Holmes makes his living
  (4) expose some of Holmes's misdeeds   4_____

5 As used in line 38, the word "chimerical" most nearly means

  (1) unfair   (3) aggravating
  (2) unrealistic   (4) contradictory   5_____

6 Which analysis is best supported by the details in lines 45 through 58 of the text?

  (1) Private detectives base their analyses on an understanding of human nature.
  (2) Sherlock Holmes's association with other well-known detectives improves his crime-solving abilities.
  (3) Government detectives are mostly ineffective at solving complicated crimes.
  (4) Sherlock Holmes's intuition relies on his ability to detect similarities among various crimes.   6_____

Reading Comprehension Passages and Questions for Review

Looking at the Questions and the Standards

- Questions 1, 2, and 5 ask you to determine the meaning of words and phrases as they are used in context and to understand how they contribute to the meaning of the text.
- Question 3 asks you to recognize how the author uses one element or detail to structure the plot. Holmes deliberately allows Watson to think someone else wrote the article, which then creates the situation in which he can show how skilled and clever he is.
- Questions 4 and 6 ask you to recognize how specific details contribute to character development and plot structure.

Answers

(1) **2**   (2) **4**   (3) **3**   (4) **3**   (5) **2**   (6) **4**

(See Chapter 4—Reading Prose for a detailed review of the elements of fiction.)

PASSAGE TWO—POEM

Money Musk

      Listen, you upstate hillsides (nothing
      Like the herb-strewn fields of Provence[1])
      Which I have loved
      So loyally, your wood lots
 (5) And trailers and old farmhouses,
      Your satellite dishes—

      Haven't I driven
      Past the strip malls and country airports,
      The National Guard armories and even
(10) That abandoned missile depot
      Clutched in the lake's fingers
      Past the tattered billboards.
      The barns spray-painted with praise,

---

[1]Provence—a region of southern France

Past the farm tools, fiddles,
(15) And fishing lures, the sprung bellows
Of accordions on the tables of flea markets,
Just to catch a glimpse of you as you once were,
Like the brass showing, raw and dull,
Where the silver plate has worn off
(20) The frame around this mirror, and the silver
Gone too, the only reflection as faint

As light on dusty glass,
And beyond it, tarnished, dim, the rafters
And beams of the attic where I climbed
(25) To take out my grandmother's mandolin
And play on the three or four unbroken strings
With a penny for a pick.   Listen,
Wasn't that offering enough, a life
(30) Of playing half-badly on an antique instrument,
Trying to catch a tune you'd long ago
Forgotten even the name of, *Money Musk*
Or *Petronella*.[2] Wasn't it enough
To take my vows of poverty of spirit
(35) Before the plain geometry of a 19th-century
Farmhouse, and praise no other goods
Than this rectitude,[3] this stillness,
This clarity you have spurned now, oh
Landscape I have sung
(40) Despite my voice, despite the stubborn
Silence behind your tawdry,[4] best intentions.

—Jordan Smith
from *The Cortland Review*
Issue Eight, August 1999

---

[2]Money Musk or Petronella—classic old American dances
[3]rectitude—honesty
[4]tawdry—cheap

Questions for Comprehension

The opening line establishes the dramatic situation and the speaker in this poem: we hear the voice of someone who once lived in the area he is now driving through and who now regrets the changes he sees. The poem is a song to the landscape he has loved and been loyal to.

1 The details presented in lines 4 through 13 emphasize the landscape's

   (1) historical significance
   (2) beauty
   (3) economic possibilities
   (4) transformation   1____

2 What shift in focus occurs from lines 7 through 27?

   (1) from social conflict to personal conflict
   (2) from external description to childhood memory
   (3) from the narrator's feelings to his family's feelings
   (4) from the narrator's thoughts to the narrator's actions   2____

3 What is the effect of the simile used in lines 21 and 22?

   (1) It suggests how the narrator has changed.
   (2) It conveys the narrator's lack of awareness.
   (3) It indicates the darkness of the setting.
   (4) It emphasizes the diminishing of the past.   3____

4 Which word best describes the narrator's tone in lines 28 through 38 of the poem?

   (1) frustrated   (3) contentment
   (2) embarrassed   (4) respectful   4____

5 Lines 33 through 37 contribute to a central theme in the poem by describing the narrator's

  (1) wish to live in a suburban setting
  (2) obligation to continue a past tradition
  (2) commitment to the values of a past era
  (4) reluctance to accept different points of view   5____

Looking at the Questions and the Standards

- Questions 1 and 3 focus on the significance of key details. The importance of the landscape to the narrator is the central theme of the poem. The simile in these lines reflects the changes in the landscape the narrator so regrets.
- Question 4 asks you to recognize how the meaning of a word or phrase establishes tone, that is, the attitude of the narrator is revealed throughout the poem.
- Questions 2 and 5 ask you to recognize key elements in the structure of the poem, through a shift in focus and in the narrator's final address to the landscape.

Answers

(1) **4**   (2) **2**   (3) **4**   (4) **1**   (5) **3**

(See Chapter 5—Reading Poetry for a detailed review of the elements of poetry.)

PASSAGE THREE — INFORMATIONAL

This passage is an engaging and effective presentation for a general reader of a challenging question in modern physics and cosmology: Is there "a theory of everything"? Readers familiar with the highly successful film *The Theory of Everything* (2014) will recognize some of the ideas explored in the article.

A few years ago the City Council of Monza, Italy, barred pet owners from keeping goldfish in curved fishbowls. The sponsors of the measure explained that it is cruel to keep a fish in a bowl because the curved sides give the fish a distorted view of reality. Aside from the measure's significance to the poor goldfish, the story raises
(5) an interesting philosophical question: How do we know that the reality we perceive is true?

The goldfish is seeing a version of reality that is different from ours, but can we be sure it is any less real? For all we know, we, too, may spend our entire lives staring out at the world through a distorting lens.

(10) In physics, the question is not academic. Indeed, physicists and cosmologists are finding themselves in a similar predicament to the goldfish's. For decades we have strived to come up with an ultimate theory of everything—one complete and consistent set of fundamental laws of nature that explain every aspect of reality. It now appears that this quest may yield not a single theory but a family of intercon-
(15) nected theories, each describing its own version of reality, as if it viewed the universe through its own fishbowl.

This notion may be difficult for many people, including some working scientists, to accept. Most people believe that there is an objective reality out there and that our senses and our science directly convey information about the material world.
(20) Classical science is based on the belief that an external world exists whose properties are definite and independent of the observer who perceives them. In philosophy, that belief is called realism.

Do Not Attempt to Adjust the Picture

The idea of alternative realities is a mainstay of today's popular culture. For example, in the science-fiction film *The Matrix* the human race is unknowingly liv-
(25) ing in a simulated virtual reality created by intelligent computers to keep them pacified and content while the computers suck their bioelectrical energy (whatever that is). How do we know we are not just computer-generated characters living in a Matrix-like world? If we lived in a synthetic, imaginary world, events would not necessarily have any logic or consistency or obey any laws. The aliens in control
(30) might find it more interesting or amusing to see our reactions, for example, if everyone in the world suddenly decided that chocolate was repulsive or that war was not

an option, but that has never happened. If the aliens did enforce consistent laws, we would have no way to tell that another reality stood behind the simulated one. It is easy to call the world the aliens live in the "real" one and the computer-generated (35) world a false one. But if—like us—the beings in the simulated world could not gaze into their universe from the outside, they would have no reason to doubt their own pictures of reality.

The goldfish are in a similar situation. Their view is not the same as ours from outside their curved bowl, but they could still formulate scientific laws governing (40) the motion of the objects they observe on the outside. For instance, because light bends as it travels from air to water, a freely moving object that we would observe to move in a straight line would be observed by the goldfish to move along a curved path. The goldfish could formulate scientific laws from their distorted frame of reference that would always hold true and that would enable them to make predictions (45) about the future motion of objects outside the bowl. Their laws would be more complicated than the laws in our frame, but simplicity is a matter of taste. If the goldfish formulated such a theory, we would have to admit the goldfish's view as a valid picture of reality.

Glimpses of the Deep Theory

In the quest to discover the ultimate laws of physics, no approach has raised (50) higher hopes—or more controversy—than string theory. String theory was first proposed in the 1970s as an attempt to unify all the forces of nature into one coherent framework and, in particular, to bring the force of gravity into the domain of quantum[1] physics. By the early 1990s, however, physicists discovered that string theory suffers from an awkward issue: there are five different string theories. For (55) those advocating that string theory was the unique theory of everything, this was quite an embarrassment. In the mid-1990s researchers started discovering that these different theories—and yet another theory called supergravity—actually describe the same phenomena, giving them some hope that they would amount eventually to a unified theory. The theories are indeed related by what physicists call duali- (60) ties, which are a kind of mathematical dictionaries for translating concepts back and forth. But, alas, each theory is a good description of phenomena only under a certain range of conditions—for example at low energies. None can describe every aspect of the universe.

String theorists are now convinced that the five different string theories are just (65) different approximations to a more fundamental theory called M-theory. (No one seems to know what the "M" stands for. It may be "master," "miracle" or "mystery," or all three.) People are still trying to decipher the nature of M-theory, but it seems that the traditional expectation of a single theory of nature may be untenable[2]

---

[1]quantum—a small, indivisible unit of energy
[2]untenable—indefensible

and that to describe the universe we must employ different theories in different situations. Thus, M-theory is not a theory in the usual sense but a network of theories. It is a bit like a map. To faithfully represent the entire Earth on a flat surface, one has to use a collection of maps, each of which covers a limited region. The maps overlap one another, and where they do, they show the same landscape. Similarly, the different theories in the M-theory family may look very different, but they can all be regarded as versions of the same underlying theory, and they all predict the same phenomena where they overlap, but none works well in all situations.

Whenever we develop a model of the world and find it to be successful, we tend to attribute to the model the quality of reality or absolute truth. But M-theory, like the goldfish example, shows that the same physical situation can be modeled in different ways, each employing different fundamental elements and concepts. It might be that to describe the universe we have to employ different theories in different situations. Each theory may have its own version of reality, but according to model-dependent realism, that diversity is acceptable, and none of the versions can be said to be more real than any other. It is not the physicist's traditional expectation for a theory of nature, nor does it correspond to our everyday idea of reality. But it might be the way of the universe.

—Stephen Hawking and Leonard Mlodinow
excerpted from "The (Elusive) Theory of Everything,"
Scientific American, October 2010

Questions for Comprehension

The topic is highly complex, but the narrative of description and explanation is composed in language that is highly readable and developed through a series of vivid images and analogies, beginning with the anecdote about goldfish in curved bowls.

1 The authors' anecdote about pet owners in Monza, Italy, serves to introduce a

 (1) proof of a universal world view
 (2) measure that is objectionable to scientists
 (3) central question about the way we see
 (4) philosophical question about what we value   1_____

2 The primary purpose of lines 10 through 16 is to clarify the

(1) need for a single theory
(2) role of the senses in understanding
(3) possibility of other life in the universe
(4) origin of alternative theories   2____

3 How do lines 17 through 22 develop a claim?

(1) by providing details about a philosophical challenge faced by scientists
(2) by showing how scientists should handle alternate realities
(3) by arguing for an approach that scientists have always followed
(4) by explaining how scientists should view a philosophical approach   3____

4 The reference to *The Matrix* in lines 24 through 28 is used to emphasize the questioning of our

(1) virtues
(2) perception
(3) education
(4) ideals   4____

5 The references to goldfish in lines 39 through 49 contribute to the authors' purpose by suggesting that

(1) people's theories are influenced by their viewpoints
(2) nature's mysteries are best left undiscovered
(3) reality can only be determined by an outside perspective
(4) light must be viewed under similar circumstances   5____

6 As used in lines 51 and 52 of the text, what does the word "coherent" mean?

(1) balanced
(2) indisputable
(3) popular
(4) understandable   6____

7 The authors' reference to "a collection of maps" (line 72) is used to help clarify

   (1) a complex theory
   (2) a historical concept
   (3) the representation of space
   (4) the limitations of previous theories   7____

8 The function of lines 77 through 84 is to

   (1) argue for a specific theory
   (2) suggest that theories relate to expectations
   (3) describe the way differing theories should co-exist
   (4) evaluate theories based on specific needs   8____

9 With which statement would the authors most likely agree?

   (1) The perception of the universe can never be questioned.
   (2) There is a single, agreed upon theory of reality.
   (3) There are multiple realities that are possible to prove.
   (4) The understanding of the universe continues to change.   9____

10 The authors attempt to engage the audience through the use of

   (1) absolute statements
   (2) real-world examples
   (3) detailed descriptions
   (4) simple questions   10____

Looking at the Questions and the Standards

- Questions 1 and 10 call your attention to how rhetorical elements are part of the structure.
  The anecdote at the beginning and the real-world examples used throughout the article help the reader understand key ideas.
- Question 6 is an example of determining the meaning of a term in context, and question 7 calls attention to how a specific image clarifies the meaning of a central idea.
- Questions 2–5 and 7–9 focus on the need to determine the central ideas and analyze how they are developed over the course of a text.

Answers

(1) **3**   (4) **2**   (7) **1**   (10) **2**
(2) **4**   (5) **1**   (8) **3**
(3) **1**   (6) **4**   (9) **4**

(See Chapter 4—Reading Prose for a detailed review of elements of nonfiction.)

Chapter 2

WRITING FROM SOURCES

Most high school students already have experienced writing essays of opinion and personal experience; these are likely to have been on topics the writer was interested in. The shift in the new standards is to source-based argument, where the writer must first do research to understand a topic before trying to develop an opinion.

In the second part of the Regents ELA exam, you will demonstrate your ability to comprehend and analyze several documents on a substantive, even controversial topic. The topics raise questions that have a variety of legitimate answers or present problems with alternative solutions. You then must take a position on that topic and develop a coherent essay of argument, which is supported by specific evidence in the texts; the final essay must include references to at least three of the sources. These are, in fact, the skills you use when you do any kind of research and writing project.

Close reading in this part means first reading to understand the issue and then to analyze the information in the texts to understand how they support various points of view. As you read the following documents, keep in mind the process of annotation: note central ideas and themes, key details, and important terms and phrases. On an actual exam, you are permitted to take notes in the margins, and you will have scrap paper to plan your essay.

STEP ONE—READING FOR INFORMATION AND UNDERSTANDING

Here are the texts from a recent Regents ELA Exam.

> **Topic:** Should companies be allowed to track consumers' shopping or other preferences without their permission?

Text 1

Cell Phone Carrier Marketing Techniques: An Invasion of Privacy?

BOSTON (CBS) – Your cell phone may be spying on you.
Every time you download an app, search for a website, send a text, snap a QR code or drive by a store with your GPS on, you are being tracked by your cell phone company.

(5) "They know you were playing Angry Birds. They know that you drove by Sears. They know you drove by Domino's Pizza. They can take that and take a very unique algorithm[1] that can focus on your behavior," explained marketing expert Mark Johnson. "It's very impactful."

According to Johnson, your data trail is worth big money to the cell phone com-
(10) panies.

Details about your habits, your age and gender are compiled and can be sold to third parties. The information is predominantly used as a marketing tool so advertisers can target you with products or services that you are more likely to use or want.

(15) The idea does not sit well with smartphone user Harrine Freeman. "It does seem creepy that companies are collecting all this information about consumers," she said.

Freeman is so uneasy; she turns off her GPS when she is not using it. She also clears her browser history.

(20) "I think it is an invasion of privacy," she said.

All of the major cell phone carriers admit to collecting information about its customers. Some in the industry argue it benefits consumers because they get ads that are relevant to them. Cell phone companies do notify customers about the data they collect, but critics say the notices are often hard to understand and written in
(25) fine print.

Rainey Reitman of the Electronic Frontier Foundation doesn't like the fact that those who don't want to be tracked have to go out of their way to get the company to stop.

"This is something that consumers are automatically opted into," Reitman said.
(30) To find out how your cell phone company might be monitoring you, be sure to carefully read the privacy policy.

---

[1]algorithm — process or set of rules followed in calculations

Also, make sure you read all of the updates your carrier might send you because this tracking technology keeps changing.

—Paula Ebben
http://boston.cbslocal.com, January 16, 2012

Text 2

**EyeSee You and the Internet of Things:
Watching You While You Shop**

...Even the store mannequins have gotten in on the gig. According to the *Washington Post*, mannequins in some high-end boutiques are now being outfitted with cameras that utilize facial recognition technology. A small camera embedded in the eye of an otherwise normal looking mannequin allows storekeepers to keep (5) track of the age, gender and race of all their customers. This information is then used to personally tailor the shopping experience to those coming in and out of their stores. As the *Washington Post* report notes, "a clothier introduced a children's line after the dummy showed that kids made up more than half its mid-afternoon traffic... Another store found that a third of visitors using one of its (10) doors after 4 p.m. were Asian, prompting it to place Chinese-speaking staff members by the entrance."

At $5,072 a pop, these EyeSee mannequins come with a steep price tag, but for store owners who want to know more—*a lot more*—about their customers, they're the perfect tool, able to sit innocently at store entrances and windows, leaving (15) shoppers oblivious to their hidden cameras. Itaian mannequin maker Almax SpA, manufacturer of the EyeSee mannequins, is currently working on adding ears to the mannequins, allowing them to record people's comments in order to further tailor the shopping experience. ...

It's astounding the amount of information—from the trivial to the highly per-(20) sonal—about individual consumers being passed around from corporation to corporation, all in an effort to market and corral potential customers. Data mining companies collect this wealth of information and sell it to retailers who use it to gauge your interests and tailor marketing to your perceived desires.

All of the websites you visit collect some amount of information about you, (25) whether it is your name or what other sites you have visited recently. Most of the time, we're being tracked without knowing it. For example, most websites now include Facebook and Twitter buttons so you can "like" the page you are viewing or "Tweet" about it. Whether or not you click the buttons, however, the companies can still determine which pages you've visited and file that information away for (30) later use. ...

As the EyeSee mannequins show, you no longer even have to be in front of your computer to have your consumer data accessed, uploaded, stored and tracked. In August 2012, for example, data mining agency Redpepper began testing a service known as Facedeals in the Nashville, Tennessee area. Facial recognition cameras set
(35) at the entrances of businesses snap photos of people walking in, and if you've signed up to have a Facedeals account via your Facebook, you receive instant coupons sent to your smartphone. Similarly, a small coffee chain in San Francisco, Philz Coffee, has installed sensors at the front door of their stores in order to capture the Wi-Fi signal of any smartphone within 60 yards. Jacob Jaber, president of Philz Coffee,
(40) uses the information gleaned from these sensors to structure his stores according to the in-store behavior of customers. ...

Not even politicians are immune to the lure of data mining. In the run-up to the 2012 presidential election, the Romney and Obama campaigns followed voters across the web by installing cookies on their computers and observing the
(45) websites they visited in an attempt to gather information on their personal views. CampaignGrid, a Republican affiliated firm, and Precision Network, a Democratic affiliated firm, both worked to collect data on 150 million American Internet users, or 80% of the registered voting population. ...

—John W. Whitehead
excerpted *https://www.rutherford.org*, December 17, 2012

Text 3

Where Will Consumers Find Privacy Protection from RFIDs?: A Case for Federal Legislation

What Are RFIDs? How Do RFIDs Work?

...RFID [Radio Frequency Information Device] technology is an automatic identification system that identifies objects, collects data, and transmits information about the object through a "tag." A device called a reader extracts and processes the information on the tag. Experts characterize RFIDs as devices "that can be sensed
(5) at a distance by radio frequencies with few problems of obstruction or misorientation."[1] In essence, RFIDs are wireless barcodes. However, unlike typical barcodes, which are identical for all common products, each RFID has a unique identification. Therefore, every individually tagged item has a different barcode sequence.

---

[1] KATHERINE ALBRECHT & LIZ MCINTRYE, SPYCHIPS 13 (Nelson Current 2005) quoting Raghu Das, *RFID Explained: An Introduction to RFID and Tagging Technologies*, ID TECHEX (2003).
[2] *Id.*

Typical barcodes also require unobstructed paths for scanning, whereas RFIDs can be scanned through solid objects.[2] RFIDs have communication signals that facilitate data storage on RFID tags and enable the stored information to be gathered electronically—hypothetically permitting, for example, Coca-Cola to have a database storing information about the life cycle of a Coke can. The database would contain tracking details from the moment the can is manufactured through its processing at a garbage dump—since RFID readers can be attached to garbage trucks. Between the birth and death of a customer's Coke can, the RFID tags would tell the Coca-Cola Company where and when the Coke was purchased, what credit card the Coke was purchased with, and, in turn, the identity of the purchaser. Even if the customer did not purchase the Coke with a credit card, state issued ID cards equipped with RFID technology could relay the customer's identity to RFID readers as he or she leaves the store. Coca-Cola's final product of the RFIDs' communications is a database of the life cycles of individual cans of Coke and personal information about their purchasers. With this myriad of information, Coca-Cola has the ability to individually market to each of the 1.3 billion daily Coca-Cola consumers. ...

How Are RFIDs Used?

RFIDs are currently used in many ways, including, "livestock management[,] 24 hour patient monitoring[,] authentication of pharmaceuticals[,] tracking consignments in a supply chain[,] remote monitoring of critical components in aircraft [, and] monitoring the safety of perishable food."[3] Advocates of RFID technology, including retailers and manufacturers, praise the increased functionality and efficiency that will likely ensue from using RFIDs. Once all products are individually tagged, shoppers are expected to be able to purchase items without checking-out. This should be possible since RFID readers will be able to scan every item as the customer exits the store and charge an RFID credit card, thereby simultaneously increasing efficiency and possibly reducing shoplifting. Other RFID uses include easy monitoring of product recalls, tracking lobsters for conservation purposes, and purchasing products with transaction-free payment systems.[4] Additionally, in October 2003, the Department of Defense set standards mandating suppliers to place RFID tags on all packaging for the Department of Defense.[5] Thus, RFIDs can be used to increase efficiency and safety. ...

---

[2]*Id.*
[3]Viviane Reding, Member of the European Commission responsible for Information Society and Media, Address at EU RFID 2006 Conference: Heading for the Future, RFID: WHY WE NEED A EUROPEAN POLICY, 1,3 (Oct. 16, 2006).
[4]David Flint, *Everything with Chips!*, BUS. L. REV., Mar. 2006, 73, 73.
[5]PRESS RELEASE, US DEP. OF DEFENSE, DOD ANNOUNCES RADIO FREQUENCY IDENTIFICATION POLICY, UNITED STATES DEPARTMENT OF DEFENSE NEWS RELEASE (Oct. 23, 2003).

Do Consumers Have a Right to Privacy from RFIDs under Tort Law?[6]

(40) ...In the context of RFIDs, there are some situations where gathering information from RFID tags violates consumers' privacy expectations. For example, a consumer does not have a reasonable expectation of privacy when carrying RFID equipped items in a transparent shopping cart. However, once the items are placed in an opaque bag, a right to privacy immediately arises. If a business or third-party
(45) gathers data about the items once the items are no longer visible to the naked eye, there is an objective invasion of privacy. Gathering information stored in the RFID tag in a winter jacket worn in public is also not an invasion of privacy, yet pulling data off undergarments is intrusive. However, since the home is always considered a private place, once an active RFID tag enters the home, any information gathered,
(50) including information from the winter jacket, immediately offends the principles of privacy. Protecting consumers from unreasonably intrusive actions of businesses requires that RFID tags become unreadable once they enter private places. However, the fundamental nature of the technology does not harmonize with this privacy goal because RFID readers do not scrutinize whether the information is
(55) considered private before it gathers data from the tag. ...

With new technologies come new methods of consumer tracking and changing parameters for what may be considered highly offensive. These new methods of tracking are not considered intrusive simply because the nature of the technology requires consumer purchases to be recorded. If individuals make active decisions to
(60) use a credit card instead of cash—a voluntary act—their purchases can be tracked. Similarly, the gathering of information stored on RFID technology in consumer goods may not be deemed highly offensive depending on changing consumer expectations. ...

—Serena G. Stein excerpted and adapted
Duke Law & Technology Review, 2007, No.3

---

[6]Tort Law — covers civil wrongs resulting in an injury or harm constituting the basis for a claim by the injured person

Text 4

RFID Consumer Applications and Benefits

...One of the first consumer applications of RFID was automated toll collection systems, which were introduced in the late 1980s and caught on in the 1990s. An active transponder is typically placed on a car's or truck's windshield. When the car reaches the tollbooth, a reader at the booth sends out a signal that wakes up the
(5) transponder on the windshield, which then reflects back a unique ID to the reader at the booth. The ID is associated with an account opened by the car owner, who is billed by the toll authority. Consumers spend less time fumbling for change or waiting on lines to pay their toll fee.

In the late 1990s, ExxonMobil (then just Mobil) introduced Speedpass, an RFID
(10) system that allows drivers who have opened an account to pay for gas automatically. Drivers are given a small, passive 13.56 MHz transponder in a small wand or fob that can be put on a key chain. To pay for gas, they just wave the key fob by a reader built into the gas pump. Seven million people in the United States use the system, and it has increased the number of cars each gas station can serve during
(15) rush periods. ...

RFID has other consumer applications, besides being a convenient payment system. One is the recovery of lost or stolen items. A company called Snagg in Palo Alto, Calif., has created an electronic registry for musical instruments. It provides an RFID tag that can be affixed to a classic guitar or priceless violin and keeps a
(20) record of the serial number in the tag. If the instrument is recovered by the police after being lost or stolen, they can call Snagg, which can look up the rightful owner. ...

Merloni Elettrodomestici, an Italian appliance maker, has created a smart washing machine. When you drop your clothes in the machine, an RFID reader in the
(25) appliance can read the tags in the clothes (if your clothes have tags) and wash the clothes based on instructions written to the tag.

Whether smart appliances with RFID readers catch on depends on how long it takes for RFID tags to become cheap enough to be put into packaging for items. It also depends on whether consumers find RFID-enabled products convenient
(30) enough to accept the potential invasion of privacy that comes with having RFID tags in products. But RFID will certainly have a positive impact on people's lives in less direct ways.

One area of importance is product recalls. Today, companies often need to recall all tires, meat or drugs if there is a problem to ensure people's safety. But
(35) they can never be sure they recovered all the bad goods that were released into the supply chain. With RFID, companies will be able to know exactly which items are bad and trace those through to stores. Customers that register their products

could be contacted individually to ensure they know something they bought has been recalled. ...

(40) And RFID should enable consumers to get more information about the products they want to purchase, such as when the items were made, where, whether they are under warrantee and so on. When RFID tags are eventually put on the packaging of individual products, consumers will be able to read the tag with a reader embedded in a cell phone or connected to a computer and download data *(45)* from a Web site. They'll be able to learn, for example, whether the steak they are about to buy is from an animal that was raised organically in the United States. Some companies will be reluctant to share this information, but smart companies will provide it to their customers to build trust and loyalty.

RFID could also have an [sic] positive impact on our environment by greatly *(50)* reducing waste. The main reason many companies want to use RFID is to better match supply and demand and to make sure that products are where they are supposed to be. If successful, there should be fewer products that are thrown away because no one wants to buy them or they pass their sell-by date (it's estimated that 50 percent of all food harvested in the United States is never eaten).

(55) RFID tags could also help improve our environment by identifying hazardous materials that should not be dumped in landfills. One day, robots at landfills might be equipped with RFID tags, and they might be able to quickly sort through garbage to locate batteries and other items that contain toxic materials. ...

—Bob Violino
excerpted *http://www.rfidjournal.com*, January 16, 2005

LOOKING AT THE TEXTS

Text 1—*Cell Phone Carrier Marketing Techniques: An Invasion of Privacy?*

This document opens with a dramatic assertion: "Your cell phone may be spying on you." The rest of the short article, from a television news report, gives a general description of data collection by cell phone companies and provides a useful introduction to the issue.

Text 2—*EyeSee You and the Internet of Things: Watching You While You Shop*

This article, from a website devoted to issues of civil liberties, presents several detailed examples of how retailers, Internet providers, and political campaigns make use of data mining. This text is an excellent source of material to support an argument opposed to tracking consumers' behavior without their permission.

Text 3—*Where Will Consumers Find Privacy Protection from RFIDs?: A Case for Federal Legislation*

This article, from a university law review, is the most challenging: The article offers a detailed technical description of what RFIDs are and how they operate. It also offers an analysis of the complex legal issues they raise. Finally, the last paragraph seems to suggest that if consumers are aware of this new technology, its use might not be considered intrusive.

Text 4—*RFID Consumer Applications and Benefits*

The title of this document, from a journal that promotes development and use of RFIDs, is a clear statement of the content and point of view. What follows is a list of various applications of RFID technology in language that is technical but readily understood, and the examples are presented as only beneficial for consumers.

STEP TWO—COMPOSING A SOURCE-BASED ARGUMENT

Because the issues presented for argument will be relevant and may already be familiar to high school students, you should be able to choose a position (claim) that you can make convincing. Here are the Guidelines for Part 2 of the Regents ELA (Common Core) Exam:

BE SURE TO:

- Establish your claim regarding companies being allowed to track consumers' shopping or other preferences without their permission
- Distinguish your claim from alternate or opposing claims
- Use specific, relevant, and sufficient evidence from at least **three** of the texts to develop your argument
- Identify each source that you reference by text number and line number(s) or graphic (for example: Text 1, line 4 or Text 2, graphic)
- Organize your ideas in a cohesive and coherent manner
- Maintain a formal style of writing
- Follow the conventions of standard written English

PLANNING THE ESSAY

First, consider **who your audience is**. You should assume a reader who is interested in the subject but who has not yet formed a strong opinion about the issue. Your reader is interested in what you have to say and can be convinced by a sound and well-documented argument.

Establishing a claim and distinguishing it from an alternate or opposing claim means that you are taking a particular position on the issue, you are not just offering a description or explanation of the subject. In each of the following examples, there is a reference to at least one of the issues the topic raises, and there is an indication of how the writer's argument is going to be developed.

Supporting the claim with specific and relevant evidence is part of any effective argument; supporting the claim with **sufficient** evidence means the writer has included not only several examples from different sources but has also used analysis of the texts to determine which evidence **best supports** the argument. Remember, too, that showing faulty or weak reasoning in examples from documents with opposing views is one of the most effective strategies in argument. Identifying references is, of course, part of any source-based writing.

The organization (structure) of the essay should be determined by the logic of the argument. An effective essay moves from establishing the claim through a series of examples (evidence) to a persuasive conclusion. In a **coherent** essay, the reader should understand how each new section extends the ideas that have come before and leads to the ideas that follow and to a convincing conclusion. **Cohesive** writing means that the connection of your ideas within each sentence and at the paragraph level is clear and that the writing follows the conventions of standard written English.

LOOKING AT A VARIETY OF EFFECTIVE CLAIMS

Here are several examples of how students established effective claims for arguments on the topic of data mining and consumer privacy:

> *Technology is changing, allowing companies and other interests . . . to track our location any given time and collect information about what we buy, all without our consent. There should be a limit to what these entities can gather on us . . .*

Companies should be permitted to have access to consumers' spending habits without their permission. The companies may seem like they are invading our privacy, but they are simply finding better and more efficient ways to help their customers and profit their businesses.

Under most circumstances, consumers should not be tracked without permission for sole benefit of companies. However, if the consumer does authorize its use by way of contract, companies should have right to track them.

Companies should not be permitted to track consumers' shopping and other activities without their consent. Without informing people of new tracking devices and methods and letting them decide, companies invade people's personal privacy . . .

Technology has made major improvements all over the world; however, these improvements have made it much easier for companies to track consumers without their permission. I support the view that the tracking of a customer's habits and preferences is an invasion of privacy.

New innovations in technology have enabled companies to monitor cell phone usage, the goods bought by consumers, or the places that people travel. In some cases, this is seen as an invasion of privacy. However, for the majority of the time, this new technology should be seen as a benefit to both consumers and the companies involved.

(See also Chapter 7—Writing on Demand for more discussion.)

Chapter 3

READING AND WRITING TO ANALYZE TEXT

TEXT ANALYSIS: EXPOSITION

   Text analysis requires first doing a close reading of a passage to identify a central idea and then analyzing how the author develops that central idea. This means understanding the author's purpose and seeing how the author's choice of literary techniques or a specific rhetorical strategy serves that purpose. In this part of the Regents ELA exam, you may read a literary passage of autobiography or memoir, a speech of historical significance, or a personal essay on a historical or scientific subject or on a philosophical idea.

SAMPLE TEXT AND EXPOSITORY RESPONSE

   ...It turned out to be true. The face of the water [Mississippi River], in time, became a wonderful book—a book that was a dead language to the uneducated passenger, but which told its mind to me without reserve, delivering its most cherished secrets as clearly as if it uttered them with a voice. And it was not a book to be
(5) read once and thrown aside, for it had a new story to tell every day. Throughout the long twelve hundred miles there was never a page that was void of interest, never one that you could leave unread without loss, never one that you would want to skip, thinking you could find higher enjoyment in some other thing. There never was so wonderful a book written by man; never one whose interest was
(10) so absorbing, so unflagging, so sparklingly renewed with every reperusal. The passenger who could not read it was charmed with a peculiar sort of faint dimple on its surface (on the rare occasions when he did not overlook it altogether); but to the pilot that was an *italicized* passage; indeed, it was more than that, it was a legend of the largest capitals, with a string of shouting exclamation points at
(15) the end of it, for it meant that a wreck or a rock was buried there that could tear the life out of the strongest vessel that ever floated. It is the faintest and simplest expression the water ever makes, and the most hideous to a pilot's eye. In truth, the passenger who could not read this book saw nothing but all manner of pretty pictures in it, painted by the sun and shaded by the clouds, whereas to the trained

eye these were not pictures at all, but the grimmest and most dead-earnest of reading matter.

Now when I had mastered the language of this water, and had come to know every trifling feature that bordered the great river as familiarly as I knew the letters of the alphabet, I had made a valuable acquisition. But I had lost something, too. I had lost something which could never be restored to me while I lived. All the grace, the beauty, the poetry, had gone out of the majestic river! I still kept in mind a certain wonderful sunset which I witnessed when steamboating was new to me. A broad expanse of the river was turned to blood; in the middle distance the red hue brightened into gold, through which a solitary log came floating, black and conspicuous; one place a long, slanting mark lay sparkling upon the water; in another the surface was broken by boiling, tumbling rings, that were as many-tinted as an opal; where the ruddy flush was faintest, was a smooth spot that was covered with graceful circles and radiating lines, ever so delicately traced; the shore on our left was densely wooded, and the sombre shadow that fell from this forest was broken in one place by a long, ruffled trail that shone like silver; and high above the forest wall a clean-stemmed dead tree waved a single leafy bough that glowed like a flame in the unobstructed splendor that was flowing from the sun. There were graceful curves, reflected images, woody heights, soft distances; and over the whole scene, far and near, the dissolving lights drifted steadily, enriching it every passing moment with new marvels of coloring.

I stood like one bewitched. I drank it in, in a speechless rapture. The world was new to me, and I had never seen any thing like this at home. But as I have said, a day came when I began to cease from noting the glories and the charms which the moon and the sun and the twilight wrought upon the river's face; another day came when I ceased altogether to note them. Then, if that sunset scene had been repeated, I should have looked upon it without rapture, and should have commented upon it, inwardly, after this fashion: "This sun means that we are going to have wind to-morrow; that floating log means that the river is rising, small thanks to it; that slanting mark on the water refers to a bluff reef which is going to kill somebody's steamboat one of these nights, if it keeps on stretching out like that; those tumbling 'boils' show a dissolving bar and a changing channel there; the lines and circles in the slick water over yonder are a warning that that troublesome place is shoaling up dangerously; that silver streak in the shadow of the forest is the 'break' from a new snag, and he has located himself in the very best place he could have found to fish for steamboats; that tall dead tree, with a single living branch, is not going to last long, and then how is a body ever going to get through this blind place at night without the friendly old landmark?"

No, the romance and the beauty were all gone from the river. All the value any feature of it had for me now was the amount of usefulness it could furnish toward compassing the safe piloting of a steamboat. Since those days, I have pitied doctors from my heart. What does the lovely flush in a beauty's cheek mean to a doctor but a "break" that ripples above some deadly disease? Are not all her visible charms sown thick with what are to him the signs and symbols of hidden decay? Does he ever see her beauty at all, or doesn't he simply view her professionally, and comment *(65)* upon her unwholesome condition all to himself? And doesn't he sometimes wonder whether he has gained most or lost most by learning his trade?

—Mark Twain
excerpted and adapted from *Life on the Mississippi*, 1901
Harper & Brothers Publishers

RESPONSE

In this excerpt, Twain introduces the central idea as a metaphor: "The face of the water {Mississippi River}...became a wonderful book."

Throughout the passage he uses vivid imagery to convey the beauty of the river and to convey how the acquisition of knowledge means losing that beauty. Before the author learned to see the signs of danger in navigating the river, he saw only beauty. When Twain was new to steam boating, he witnessed a particularly magnificent sunset. The sky was red, which reflected on the water and slowly transitioned to gold. He noticed delicate rings growing from a spot in the water. He noticed a dead tree rising above the wall of forest, with a bough of leaves that shone with brightness of flames. He was in a state of "speechless rapture."

Later on, the beauty faded as he learned the signals behind what he saw. Twain tells us that the river was a "wonderful book"; but it was also "the grimmest and most dead-earnest of reading matter." That beautiful red hue in his surroundings would mean wind the next day. The growing ripples marked a dangerous obstacle that could kill a steamboat. The dead tree, whose leaves were like fire, was a "friendly landmark" and would be lost after it fell. In learning to read the book of the river, Twain loses forever the ability to see the beauty and grace of the Mississippi and regrets what he has lost in learning his trade: "No, the romance and beauty were all gone from the river... all it had for me now was the amount of usefulness it could furnish...."

This is an excellent example of an expository response: In the opening sentence, this writer expresses the central idea of the passage and identifies Twain's use of vivid imagery as key to understanding its meaning. The analysis is developed in two paragraphs, each of which cites several specific and relevant examples from the text. In the first paragraph, the images recall Twain's delight in the beauty of the river; in the second, these images become examples of how the knowledge Twain acquires destroys his ability to see beauty in them. This organization in parallel details is both sophisticated and effective. The incorporation of quoted phrases enhances development of the central idea and meets the requirement for an evidence-based analysis.

ADDITIONAL TEXTS FOR ANALYSIS AND REVIEW

Passage One

This passage is an excerpt from a speech given by Red Jacket, Chief of the Seneca Nation, to the United States acting secretary of war in Washington, D.C., on February 10, 1801.

...Brother, the business on which we are now come is to restore the friendship that has existed between the United States and the Six Nations, agreeably to the direction of the commissioner from the fifteen fires[1] of the United States. He assured us that whensoever, by any grievances, the chain of friendship should (5) become rusty, we might have it brightened by calling on you. We dispense with the usual formality of having your speech again read, as we fully comprehended it yesterday, and it would therefore be useless to waste time in a repetition of it.

Brother, yesterday you wiped the tears from our eyes, that we might see clearly; you unstopped our ears that we might hear; and removed the obstructions (10) from our throats that we might speak distinctly. You offered to join with us in tearing up the largest pine-tree in our forests, and under it to bury the tomahawk. We gladly join with you, brother, in this work, and let us heap rocks and stones on the root of this tree that the tomahawk may never again be found. ...

---

[1] fires—fires refers to states

Brother, we observe that the men now in office are new men, and, we fear, not fully informed of all that has befallen us. In 1791 a treaty was held by the commissioners of Congress with us at Tioga Point, on a similar occasion. We have lost seven of our warriors, murdered in cold blood by white men, since the conclusion of the war. We are tired of this mighty grievance and wish some general arrangement to prevent it in future. The first of these was murdered on the banks of the Ohio, near Fort Pitt. Shortly after two men belonging to our first families were murdered at Pine Creek; then one at Fort Franklin; another at Tioga Point; and now the two that occasion this visit, on the Big Beaver. These last two had families. The one was a Seneca; the other a Tuscarora. Their families are now destitute of support, and we think that the United States should do something toward their support, as it is to the United States they owe the loss of their heads.

Brother, these offences are always committed in one place on the frontier of Pennsylvania. In the Genesee country we live happy and no one molests us. I must therefore beg that the President will exert all his influence with all officers, civil and military, in that quarter, to remedy this grievance, and trust that he will thus prevent a repetition of it and save our blood from being spilled in future.

Brother, let me call to mind the treaty between the United States and the Six Nations, concluded at Canandaigua. At that treaty Colonel Pickering, who was commissioner on behalf of the United States, agreed that the United States should pay to the Six Nations four thousand five hundred dollars per annum, and that this should pass through the hands of the superintendent of the United States, to be appointed for that purpose. This treaty was made in the name of the President of the United States, who was then General Washington; and, as he is now no more, perhaps the present President would wish to renew the treaty. But if he should think the old one valid and is willing to let it remain in force we are also willing. The sum above mentioned we wish to have part of in money, to expend in more agricultural tools and in purchasing a team, as we have some horses that will do for the purpose. We also wish to build a sawmill on the Buffalo creek. If the President, however, thinks proper to have it continue as heretofore, we shall not be very uneasy. Whatever he may do we agree to; we only suggest this for his consideration.

Brother, I hand you the above-mentioned treaty, made by Colonel Pickering, in the name of General Washington, and the belt that accompanied it; as he is now dead we know not if it is still valid. If not, we wish it renewed—if it is, we wish it copied on clean parchment. Our money got loose in our trunk and tore it. We also show you the belt which is the path of peace between our Six Nations and the United States. ...

Brother, the business that has caused this our long journey was occasioned by some of your bad men; the expense of it has been heavy on us. We beg that as so

great a breach has been made on your part, the President will judge it proper that
(55) the United States should bear our expenses to and from home and whilst here.

Brother, three horses belonging to the Tuscarora Nation were killed by some men under the command of Major Rivardi, on the plains of Niagara. They have made application to the superintendent and to Major Rivardi, but get no redress. You make us pay for our breaches of the peace, why should you not pay also? A white
(60) man has told us the horses were killed by Major Rivardi's orders, who said they should not be permitted to come there, although it was an open common on which they were killed. Mr. Chapin has the papers respecting these horses, which we request you to take into consideration.

—Red Jacket
excerpted from *Orations from Homer to William McKinley,*
Vol. VII, 1902
P.F. Collier and Son

Looking at the Text

The repetition of "Brother, . . ." at the beginning of each point is the most obvious rhetorical element in this speech. Careful analysis will show how that not only establishes the speaker's attitude toward his audience (the tone of the speech) but also structures the various examples as reminders of past history and treaty obligations and establishes the legitimacy of the Chief's demands for compensation and justice.

Passage Two

Here is an example of a classic essay form, in which a specific aspect of human nature or conduct is explored. First made popular by the French writer Michel de Montaigne in the 16th century, this kind of essay is relatively brief, offers intellectual insight, and often includes anecdotes or analogies as illustrations. In "Of Suspicion," Sir Francis Bacon, a contemporary of Shakespeare, first offers his observations on how suspicion clouds the mind and then suggests ways to avoid its corrosive effects.

Of Suspicion

SUSPICIONS amongst thoughts are like bats amongst birds, they ever fly by twilight. Certainly they are to be repressed, or at least well guarded: for they cloud the mind; they leese [lose] friends; and they check with [hinder, restrain] business, whereby business cannot go on currently and constantly. They dispose [lead] *(5)* kings to tyranny, husbands to jealousy, wise men to irresolution [indecisiveness] and melancholy. They are defects, not in the heart, but in the brain; for they take place in the stoutest [bravest] natures; as in the example of Henry the Seventh of England. There was not a more suspicious man, nor a more stout. And in such a composition they do small hurt. For commonly they are not admitted, but [unless] *(10)* with examination, whether they be likely or no. But in fearful natures they gain ground too fast. There is nothing makes a man suspect much, more than to know little; and therefore men should remedy suspicion by procuring to know more, and not to keep their suspicions in smother [suppressed]. What would men have? Do they think those they employ and deal with are saints? Do they not think they will *(15)* have their own ends, and be truer to themselves than to them? Therefore there is no better way to moderate suspicions, than to account upon such suspicions as true and yet to bridle them as false. For so far a man ought to make use of suspicions, as to provide, as if that should be true that he suspects, yet it may do him no hurt. Suspicions that the mind of itself gathers are but buzzes; but suspicions that are *(20)* artificially nourished, and put into men's heads by the tales and whisperings of others, have stings. Certainly, the best mean [strategy] to clear the way in this same wood of suspicions is frankly to communicate them with the party that he suspects; for thereby he shall be sure to know more of the truth of them than he did before; and withal shall make that party more circumspect not to give further cause of sus- *(25)* picion. But this would not be done to men of base [dishonorable, corrupt] natures; for they, if they find themselves once suspected, will never be true. . . . (c 1625)

Looking at the Text

This is a passage that requires careful, slow reading. The essay begins with a simile that establishes the tone of what is to follow: suspicions are creatures of twilight; they are elusive, ambiguous, and potentially dangerous. Bacon then insists that suspicions must be kept under control and offers guidance on how best to "clear the way in...the wood of suspicions." Note how condensed the development of ideas is and how each sentence balances two or three assertions. The meanings of some unfamiliar terms have been inserted here, but the language of Bacon is also the language of Shakespeare and should be accessible to high school students at Regents level.

(There is a list of Archaic and Unfamiliar terms in Chapter 8—Vocabulary.)

Passage Three

In 1858, Abraham Lincoln and Stephen Douglas were campaigning in Illinois for the U.S. Senate seat then held by Douglas. They held a series of debates throughout the state, which were widely and often raucously attended. Douglas argued that it was an absolute right of self-government for residents of a territory to permit or to prohibit slavery. Here is a passage from an eyewitness account of the seventh and final of the Lincoln-Douglas debates.

. . . Douglas had been theatrical and scholarly, but this tall, homely man [Lincoln] was creating by his very looks what the brilliant lawyer and experienced Senator had failed to make people see and feel. The Little Giant [Douglas] had assumed striking attitudes, played tricks with his flowing white hair, mimicking
(5) the airs of authority, with patronizing allusions; but these affectations, usually so effective when he addressed an audience alone, went for nothing when brought face to face with realities. Lincoln had no genius for gesture and no desire to produce a sensation. The failure of Senator Douglas to bring conviction to critical minds was caused by three things: a lack of logical sequence in argument, a lack of
(10) intuitional judgment, and a vanity that was caused by too much intellect and too little heart. Douglas had been arrogant and vehement, Lincoln was now logical and penetrating. . . .

The enthusiasm created by Douglas was wrought out of smart epigram thrusts and a facile, superficial eloquence. . . . His weight in the political balance was
(15) purely materialistic; his scales of justice tipped to the side of cotton, slavery, and popular passions, while the man who faced him now brought to the assembly cold logic in place of wit, frankness in place of cunning, reasoned will and judgment in place of chicanery and sophistry. . . . His looks, his words, his voice, his attitude, were like a magical essence dropped into the seething cauldron of politics, reacting
(20) against the foam, calming the surface and letting the people see to the bottom. It did not take him long:

> "Is it not a false statesmanship," he asked, "that undertakes to build up a system of policy upon the basis of caring nothing about the very thing that everybody does care the most about? Judge Douglas may say
> (25) he cares not whether slavery is voted up or down, but he must have a choice between a right thing and a wrong thing. He contends that whatever community wants slaves has a right to have them. So they have, if it is not a wrong; but if it is a wrong he cannot say people have a right to do wrong. He says that upon the score of equality slaves should be
> (30) allowed to go into a new Territory like other property. This is strictly logical if there is no difference between it [slaves] and other property.

If it and other property are equal his argument is entirely logical; but if you insist that one is wrong and the other right there is no use to institute a comparison between right and wrong."

(35) This was the broadside. The great duel on the high seas of politics was over. The Douglas ship of State Sovereignty was sinking. The debate was a triumph that would send Lincoln to Washington as President in a little more than two years from that date.

—Francis Grierson, *The Valley of Shadows*

Looking at the Text

In this passage, the observer uses various rhetorical elements to recreate the experience of hearing the two famous men, and within this account, we are shown how Lincoln himself revealed the morally flawed logic in Douglas's position on slavery.

The observer sets the stage with a series of balanced and contrasting images: Douglas is theatrical and vain, a man of "too much intellect and too little heart." Lincoln "had no genius for gesture" or sensational language; Lincoln was ". . . now logical and penetrating." He introduces Lincoln's words with a vivid image of an alchemist calming intense passions—the seething cauldron of politics—with the "magical essence" of clear, moral argument.

Lincoln attacks Douglas for "caring nothing about" slavery, that is, for being neutral on the issue, when it is the issue the nation most cares about. Douglas contends that slavery is an issue of property and rights of States, but Lincoln says that is a logical fallacy: the issue is not about property, it is about right and wrong; " . . . *he cannot say people have a right to do wrong."* The passage ends with another strong metaphor: Douglas's ship of State Sovereignty has been sunk in a battle on the [political] high seas by the cannon shot of Lincoln's words.

(The Lincoln-Douglas Debates, Twain's memoir, and Red Jacket's speech are examples of what is meant by "seminal U.S. texts" in the State Standards. Analyzing and evaluating the reasoning in these and other "foundational U.S. documents of historical and literary significance" can be expected on the Regents ELA exam and on the new SAT (2015). See the Appendices, pages 223–227, to review the standards.)

Chapter 4

READING PROSE

One of the characters in Moliere's satire *Le Bourgeois Gentilhomme* (*The Bourgeois Gentleman*) makes an astonishing discovery: "For over forty years I have been speaking prose without knowing it!" Prose writing is composed in the rhythms and patterns of spoken discourse. When we read novels and short stories, essays and reports, journals and letters, we are usually reading prose. In our daily lives and as students, we read prose that varies widely in purpose, in method of development, and in tone. Prose serves the purposes of personal expression, persuasion, literary effect, and information.

WHAT WRITERS DO: A LIST OF USEFUL TERMS

A group of high school juniors recently was asked to list all the verbs they could think of to denote what writers *do*. Here is the list they came up with:

address	declare	imply	refine
affirm	defend	infer	reflect
alert	define	influence	refute
amuse	delineate	inform	remind
analyze	depict	inspire	reveal
appraise	describe	interpret	revise
argue	discern	invent	scrutinize
assert	discover	judge	see
assess	dramatize	note	select
capture	edit	observe	shock
caution	emphasize	offer	show
censure	enhance	persuade	suggest
cite	enrich	play	summarize
clarify	establish	ponder	support
classify	evaluate	portray	symbolize
comment	examine	present	teach
conclude	explain	probe	theorize
condemn	explore	produce	uncover
conjecture	expose	propose	view
convey	expound	provoke	work(!)
create	forewarn	question	
create images	formulate	reassure	
criticize	illustrate	recreate	

45

As you consider these terms, you will note that they are not separated by categories; many of them denote both purpose and tone, and many suggest a method of development as well. While this list may not include everything writers "do," it is a useful reminder of the great variety in written expression. (Because command of this vocabulary will also help you to express your understanding and appreciation of what you read, you will find examples showing how many of these words are applied to discussions of nonfiction and, in Chapter 6, writing about literature. Note also that most of these terms are part of the vocabulary that is considered Academic Language. (See Chapter 8—Vocabulary.)

To read well you must be listening actively to the narrator's voice, thinking with the author. If you are reading a piece for information or direction, ask questions; expect them to be answered. If you are reading a work of argument or persuasion, question it; actively agree or disagree; follow how the argument is developed. If you are reading a piece of personal expression, try to imagine, even share, the experience. If you are reading a piece of vivid description, recreate the images and feelings for yourself. Reading well offers us the entire range of human history and experience expressed in language.

Works of fiction are usually narrative in form. They tell us stories of what *happened* in the lives of the characters and, more important, *why it happened*. Nonfiction takes many forms, and its subjects touch on nearly everything in the human and natural worlds.

READING FICTION

When we speak of fiction, we are generally referring to narrative works—works in which events are recounted, are *told,* and have been imagined and structured by the author. (Although not narrative in form, drama shares many of the essential characteristics of fiction.) The subjects of fiction, however, are no less real than those of history or of what we call the actual or real world. In *Aspects of the Novel*, E. M. Forster shows how "fiction is truer than history." He reminds us that only in narrative fiction and drama can we truly know what is in a character's heart or mind; that is, only in a novel, short story, or play can we fully understand the motives, desires, and reasons for characters' actions. The historian draws conclusions from records of the past; the psychologist interprets interviews and tests; a jury weighs evidence and testimony; and our experience indicates that these are highly reliable ways to understand people and their lives. But only the author of a fictional work can offer an absolutely reliable account of what a character feels, believes, and desires, of why things happen as they do.

Plot and Story

The primary pleasure for most readers of narrative fiction is the story. The reason we become involved in a novel or short story is that we want to know how it turns out; we want to know what is going to happen to those characters. An author creates a **plot*** when he or she gives order and structure to the action: in a plot, the incidents, or episodes, of the story have meaningful relationships to one another. A story becomes a plot when we understand not only *what happened* but also *why*. In good fiction we are *convinced* of the causal relationship among incidents, and we are convinced by the relationship of characters' motives and feelings to the action.

For most readers of fiction, the first response is to keep track of the plot. We do this spontaneously. If you are preparing a novel or story for class discussion, one of the first things your instructor will expect you to know is, "What happens in . . . ?" This is not a trivial question, because you cannot fully understand the significance of character, theme, or structure if you do not first understand the action as it is presented. Understanding plot, of course, requires memory, and remembering the major incidents of a plot is usually a natural and relatively easy response. The more extensively you read, however, the more skilled you become in remembering and relating the key incidents in a complex plot and in recalling details when their full significance becomes evident—sometimes well after the incidents themselves occur. Keeping notes on the development of a complex plot is very useful, especially for students whose reading of a novel is broken up over days or weeks.

For a class, or as part of your preparation for the Regents exam questions on literature, practice summarizing the plots of works you know or are reading. Be able to tell the story of a novel or play to someone who does not know it in a narrative of your own words, including all the major incidents and their consequences. Be able to tell the story in the same way you would retell a familiar children's story or narrate a significant experience of your own.

Plot and Conflict

At the end of any meaningful story, something has *happened;* something is significantly different in the world and lives of the characters from what it was at the beginning. **Conflict** in the most general sense refers to the forces that move the action in a plot. Conflict in plot may be generated from a search or pursuit, from a discovery, from a deception or misunderstanding, from opportunities to make significant choices, or from unexpected consequences of an action. Although the term *conflict* connotes an active struggle

---

*Terms in bold are featured in A Glossary of Literary Terms and Techniques at the end of the chapter.

between opposing or hostile forces, conflict in fiction may refer to any progression, change, or discovery. The resolution of conflict in a plot may be subtle and confined to the inner life of a character or it may be dramatic and involve irreversible change, violent destruction, or death.

This term may identify an actual struggle between characters, anything from dominance or revenge to simple recognition or understanding. A plot may also focus on conflict between characters and the forces of nature or society. These are essentially **external conflicts**. A work may also center on **internal conflicts**, characters' struggle to know or change themselves and their lives. Most works of fiction and drama contain more than one aspect of conflict.

In Shakespeare's *Romeo and Juliet*, the most dramatic conflicts are external, vivid, and literal: the street brawls between followers of the rival Capulets and Montagues, the fatal fight with Tybalt that leads to Romeo's banishment, and the tragic deaths of the young lovers. In *Macbeth,* however, the primary interest is in the internal conflict between Macbeth's ambitious desires and his understanding of the moral consequences of the actions he takes to achieve those desires. The action in Edith Wharton's most famous story, "Roman Fever," is ironically serene and pleasant: two middle-aged women, longtime friends now both widowed, sit on a terrace overlooking the splendors of Rome and reflect on their common experiences and life-long friendship. At the end of the conversation—and the story—their actual feelings of rivalry have surfaced, and one of the two learns something that reveals how little she truly knew her husband or understood her marriage or the life of her friend. The conflict between the two women emerges almost imperceptibly, and its meaning is fully understood only in the completely unexpected revelation of the last line.

Plot and Chronology

Narrative is not necessarily presented in chronological order, but it does have a chronology. In other words, incidents may be presented out of the order in which they actually occurred, but by the end of the work the reader understands their order and relationship and appreciates why the story was structured as it was. Plots that are narrated in flashback or from different points of view are common examples.

The Great Gatsby, by F. Scott Fitzgerald, and *Ethan Frome,* by Edith Wharton, are novels in which the narrators first introduce themselves and their interest in the story, then tell the story in a narrative flashback whose full significance to the narrator (and reader) is revealed only at the end. Tennessee Williams's play *The Glass Menagerie* has a similar structure, in which the character of Tom serves both as a narrator in the present and as a principal character in the series of memory scenes that make up the drama. The memory scenes in Arthur Miller's play *Death of a Salesman,* however, are not flashbacks in the same way. Willy Loman relives incidents from the past while the other characters and the action of the play continue in the present. As the play progresses, the shifts in time occur only within Willy's mind.

Shakespeare's tragedies are dramas in which normal chronology is preserved, as it is in such familiar novels as William Golding's *Lord of the Flies* and Mark Twain's *Huckleberry Finn*.

Plot and Time

Related to understanding of chronology is appreciation of how an author creates understanding of *elapsed time*. In the several hours required to read a novel, the two to three hours for a full-length play, and the half-hour to an hour for a one-act play or short story, how much time in the lives of the characters has been accounted for? In one-act plays and many short stories, the time covered by the action is equal to the time to read them. In Wharton's "Roman Fever," for example, the action of the story is contained in a few hours of one afternoon—little more time than it takes to read the story. That conversation, however, completely transforms the women's, and the reader's, understanding of their lives over twenty-five years. The time required for the action in Shirley Jackson's widely read story "The Lottery" is also roughly equal to the time required to read it, yet the plot accounts indirectly for events that have taken place for longer than anyone in the story can even remember. Miller's play *Death of a Salesman* takes place over a period of only twenty-four hours, but the plot and Willy's memories tell us the story of an entire lifetime. Awareness of how an author uses and accounts for time adds considerably to the reader's appreciation of a work.

Narrative Point of View

The **narrator** of a work is the character or author's **persona** that tells a story. **Point of view** is the standpoint, perspective, and degree of understanding from which the narrator speaks. For many students and scholars, how a story is told is one of the most interesting questions. What is the narrative point of view? Is the narration **omniscient**, essentially the point of view of the author? If not, who is the narrator? What is the narrator's relationship to the story? What is the narrator's understanding of the story? How much does the narrator really know? Appreciating how, or by whom, a story is told is often essential to understanding its meaning.

One of the most easily discerned narrative points of view is the first person (*I*), in which either the central character or another directly involved in the action tells the story. J. D. Salinger's novel *The Catcher in the Rye* is a vivid and popular example of such narration. Fitzgerald's *The Great Gatsby* is also told in the first person. In each of these works, the fundamental meaning of the novel becomes apparent only when the reader understands the character of the narrator. In each of these works, what the narrator experiences and what he learns about himself and the world are the novel's most important themes.

In first-person narration, the incidents of the plot are limited to those that the narrator himself experiences. First-person narrators can, however, report what they learn from others. In Wharton's *Ethan Frome,* the engineer who narrates tells us that he has "pieced together the story" from the little he has been able to learn in the town of Starkfield, from his limited conversations with Frome himself, and from his brief visit to the Frome house. Wharton's method, of course, dramatizes Frome's inability to express or fulfill the desires of his heart and reveals the reluctance of the people of Starkfield to fully understand the lives of those around them.

Authors may also use first-person narration to achieve an ironic or satiric effect. In Ring Lardner's well-known story "Haircut," a barber in a small midwestern town narrates a story about a local fellow who kept the town entertained with his practical jokes on people. As the story progresses, the reader understands how cruel and destructive the fellow's pranks were, but the barber does not. The narrative method in this story reveals, indirectly, a story of painful ignorance and insensitivity in the "decent" citizens of a small town. Mark Twain's masterpiece, *Huckleberry Finn*, is told by Huck himself. Through the morally naive observations of Huck, Twain satirizes the evils of slavery, fraud, hypocrisy, and virtually every other kind of corrupt human behavior. Edgar Allan Poe's story "The Tell-Tale Heart" is the confession of a cunning madman.

In third-person narration (*he, she, it, they*) a story is reported. The narrative voice may be *omniscient* and, therefore, able to report everything from everywhere in the story; this voice can also report on the innermost thoughts and feelings of the characters themselves. In many novels of the eighteenth and nineteenth centuries, the omniscient narrator even speaks directly to the reader, as if taking him or her into the storyteller's confidence. In Nathaniel Hawthorne's *The Scarlet Letter,* the narrator pauses from time to time to share personal feelings with the reader, as does Nick Carraway, the narrator of *The Great Gatsby*.

A widely used narrative method is the **limited omniscient** point of view. The narrative is in the third person but is focused on and even may represent the point of view of a central character. The actions and feelings of other characters are presented from the perspective of that character. Hawthorne's short story "Young Goodman Brown" is an excellent example.

Some third-person narration is dramatically **objective** and detached; it simply reports the incidents of the plot as they unfold. This narrative method, too, can be used for intensely **ironic** effect. Jackson's "The Lottery" is one of the best examples. The real horror of the story is achieved through the utterly detached, nonjudgmental unfolding of the plot.

In some plays, too, there is a character who serves a narrative role: the Chorus in Shakespeare's *Henry V*, the character of Tom in Williams's *The Glass Menagerie,* and the Stage Manager in Thornton Wilder's *Our Town* are familiar examples.

In each of the works discussed here, the narrative method is not simply a literary device; it is an intrinsic part of the meaning of the work.

Setting

The setting of a work includes the time and places in which the action is played out; setting may also include a significant historical context. In drama, setting may be presented directly in the set, costumes, and lighting. In narrative fiction, it is usually presented directly through description. In some works, the physical setting is central to the plot and developed in great detail; in other works, only those details necessary to anchor the plot in a time or place will be developed. Regardless of detail, responsive readers recreate images of setting as they read.

In addition to the physical and natural details of the fictional world, setting also includes mood and **atmosphere**. In some works, social or political realities constitute part of the setting. *The Scarlet Letter* is not only set in Puritan Boston, it is also *about* that society; and *The Great Gatsby* presents a vivid picture of life in New York during Prohibition and the roaring twenties.

For some works, the author may create specific details of setting to highlight a theme. In Golding's novel *Lord of the Flies*, the island on which the story takes place has everything essential for basic survival: food and water are available, and the climate is temperate. In order to explore the moral questions of the boys' regression into savagery, Golding carefully establishes a setting in which survival itself is not a primary issue. In *Ethan Frome,* details of the harsh winter and of the isolation of a town "bypassed by the railroad" intensify the story of a man's desperately cold and isolated life.

Character

We understand characters in fiction and drama, as we do the people in our own lives, by what they say and do and by what others say about them. Because characters are imagined and created by an author, we can even understand them more reliably and fully than we can many of the people around us. Many students find their greatest satisfaction in reading works about characters to whom they can relate, characters whose struggles are recognizable and whose feelings are familiar.

Understanding character in fiction means understanding a person's values and **motivation**, beliefs and principles, moral qualities, strengths and weaknesses, and degree of self-knowledge and understanding. To fully appreciate a work, the reader must understand what characters are searching for and devoting their lives to.

Literature also seeks to account for the forces outside individuals that influence the directions and outcomes of their lives. These "forces" range from those of nature and history to the demands of family, community, and society. The response of characters to inner and outer forces is what literature depicts and makes comprehensible.

Any meaningful or convincing plot stems from human thought, motive, and action. Depending on the narrative point of view (see page 49), a character's thoughts and feelings may be presented directly through omniscient narrative or first-person commentary. In "Young Goodman Brown," the narrator tells us directly what the title character is thinking and feeling; in "Roman Fever," the reader discovers the most important revelations of character simultaneously with the two central characters. Character in drama is revealed directly in dialogue and action, but it may be expanded through soliloquies and asides. In Shakespeare's *Othello,* for example, the full extent of Iago's evil is revealed through the variety of methods Iago uses to manipulate different characters and through his **soliloquies**.

In some works, the author's primary purpose is to reveal character gradually through plot; in others, the author establishes understanding of character from the beginning in order to account for what happens. In the opening pages of *The Great Gatsby,* the narrator, Nick, who is also a character in the novel, introduces himself and declares his judgment of the moral quality of the people and events he is about to narrate. With Nick's own character and motives clearly established, the reader then shares his *gradual* discovery of the truth about Gatsby and his life.

Theme

The subjects of literature may come from any aspect of human experience: love, friendship, growing up, ambition, family relationships, conflicts with society, survival, war, evil, death, and so on. **Theme** in a work of literature is the understanding, insight, observation, and presentation of such subjects. Theme is what a work *says about* a subject. Themes are the central ideas of literary works.

One way to think about theme is to consider it roughly analogous to the topic or thesis of an expository essay. If the author of a novel, story, or play had chosen to examine the subjects of the work in an essay, what might be the topic assertions of such an essay? The student is cautioned, however, not to overinterpret the analogy. Themes in literature are rarely "morals," such as those found at the end of a fable, but neither are they "hidden meanings." Although scholars and critics often express thematic ideas in phrases, students are often required to state themes in full sentences. In the next paragraph are some examples of statements about theme.

Macbeth is a play about the temptation to embrace evil forces and about the power of ambition to corrupt; Macbeth himself makes one of the most important statements of theme in the play when he says, "I do all that becomes a man/who does more is none." *Ethan Frome* and Lardner's "Haircut" both illustrate that people in small towns may not truly understand the innermost needs and desires of other people they *think* they know. William Golding's novel *Lord of the Flies* illustrates the bleak view that supposedly "civilized" people will become savage and brutal without external forces of authority, that human beings are not civilized in their fundamental natures. In contrast, in *Adventures of Huckleberry Finn,* Twain presents civilization as the source of corruption and finds truly moral behavior only in the runaway slave, Jim, and the ignorant boy, Huck.

In Chapter 6 you will find an extensive list of literature topics, many of which are expressed in terms of theme.

READING NONFICTION

Fiction and nonfiction share many common elements; they also make similar demands and offer comparable rewards to the thoughtful reader. In broad contrast to fiction, where characters and plot are imaginative creations of the author, nonfiction is about actual persons, experiences, and phenomena. The texts reviewed in Chapter 3 are good examples of how nonfiction speculates on abstract and philosophical questions of history and politics, ethics and religion, culture and society, as well as the natural world. In biography and autobiography, the writer focuses on what is meaningful and interesting in the life of an individual. The purpose of this section is to review some of the distinctive features of formal and informal essays and to illustrate some of the methods authors use to develop arguments in persuasive writing. The glossary at the end of the chapter also features extended definitions and examples of many important terms.

Questions for the Critical Reader

Here again are the questions you are urged to keep in mind as you prepare for the reading comprehension and text analysis sections of the Regents ELA exam:

> What is the purpose of this piece? Its tone or mood? Its overall effect?
>
> What does the author say? believe? recall? value? assert?

What does the author mean? imply? suggest? agree with? disagree with?

How are language and imagery used?

What conclusions or inferences is the reader led to?

What experience is meant to be shared and understood?

Purpose

In speaking of fiction, the central ideas of a work are identified as its themes. In essays, purpose refers both to the central ideas and to their intended effect on the reader. For example, many authors of essays develop a thesis with a view to influencing opinion or urging action. We encounter such writing daily on the editorial and Op-Ed pages of a newspaper. Many of the verbs on the list of "what writers do" (page 45) identify such purposes: *affirm, alert, argue, assert, caution, censure, condemn, criticize, declare, defend, evaluate, expose, forewarn, imply, inspire, judge, persuade, propose, provoke, reveal, scrutinize, support.*

Much nonfiction, of course, has as its purpose to explain and inform. The verbs used to identify informative writing include *analyze, assess, clarify, define, describe, explore, formulate, illustrate, interpret, recreate, summarize.*

Other purposes may be likened to conversations between the author and the reader; these "conversations" may be about anything from the most personal experiences to reflections on the nature of life and the universe. Some useful verbs here might be *address, amuse, capture, comment, conjecture, depict, discover, enhance, enrich, examine, explore, invent, observe, offer, ponder, probe, propose, question, recreate, reflect, shock.*

Methods of Development and Patterns of Organization

The ability to use a variety of methods to organize and express ideas is one of the most important skills a student writer learns, and the thoughtful reader should also be able to appreciate how a writer develops material. Informational texts are part of the reading comprehension and text analysis parts of the Regents ELA exam and the new SAT (2015); reviewing the following methods of organization is also useful preparation for composing essays of argument.

From Abstract to Concrete/From General to Specific

Going from the general to the specific is the most common and natural pattern for explanation, illustration, and reasoning. A passage by author and playwright Sandy Asher is an especially good example:

> **As a child, I sensed there was something I desperately needed from books. As a writer for young readers, I've tried to figure out what that something was. It turned out to be a combination of three things: companionship, a sense of control, and magic.**

In her essay, Asher goes on to develop a paragraph about each of the three things that make up the "something" she is explaining.

Here is how journalist Ernie Pyle begins his explanation of what "The awful waste and destruction of war" really means:

> **I walked for a mile and a half along the water's edge of our many-miled invasion beach. I walked slowly, for the detail on the beach was infinite.**
>
> **The wreckage was vast and startling. The awful waste and destruction of war, even aside from the loss of human life, has always been one of its outstanding features to those who are in it. Anything and everything is expendable. And we did expend on our beachhead in Normandy during those first few hours.**
>
> **For a mile out from the beach there were scores of tanks and trucks and boats that were not visible, for they were at the bottom of the water—swamped by overloading, or hit by shells, or sunk by mines.**

His description of a Normandy beach following the D-Day invasion in 1944 is developed in a series of vivid images and poignant details that make the waste and destruction of war comprehensible to those who have not experienced it.

From Concrete to Abstract/From Specific to General

Reversing the more common pattern, going from the specific to the general can also be a very effective way to develop understanding of a general concept. This is the pattern author William Kittredge uses in the **anecdote** about his boyhood encounter with a sage grouse. The passage recounts a specific experience, which leads to the closing general observation:

> **For that childhood moment I believed the world to be absolutely inhabited by an otherness which was utterly demonic and natural, not of my own making. But soon as that bird was enclosed in a story which defined it as a common-place prairie chicken, I was no longer frightened. It is a skill we learn early, the art of inventing stories to explain away the fearful sacred strangeness of the world. Storytelling and make-believe, like war and agriculture, are among the arts of self-defense, and all of them are ways of enclosing otherness and claiming ownership.**

Here is how the passage by Stephen Hawking in Chapter 1 (page 16) begins:

> **A few years ago the City Council of Monza, Italy, barred pet owners from keeping goldfish in curved fishbowls. The sponsors of the measure explained that it is cruel to keep a fish in a bowl because the curved sides give the fish a distorted view of reality. Aside from the measure's significance to the poor goldfish, the story raises an interesting philosophical question: How do we know that the reality we perceive is true?**
>
> **The goldfish is seeing a version of reality that is different from ours, but can we be sure it is any less real? For all we know, we, too, may spend our entire lives staring out at the world through a distorting lens.**

FROM QUESTION TO ANSWER

Another method of developing **argument** and explanation is to pose a question, which the paragraph or essay then answers. Here is an example from the conclusion of Thoreau's *Walden:*

> **Why should we be in such desperate haste to succeed, in such desperate enterprises? If a man does not keep pace with his companions, perhaps it is because**

he hears a different drummer. Let him step to the music which he hears, however measured or far away.

And here is a passage from "The Almost Perfect State," an essay by Don Marquis:

> You have seen the tall towers of Manhattan, wonderful under the stars. How did it come about that such growths come from such soil—that a breed lawless and prosaic has written such a mighty hieroglyphic against the sky? How is it that this hideous, half-brute city is also beautiful and a fit habitation for demi-gods? How come? ... It comes about because the wise and subtle deities permit nothing worthy to be lost. It was with no thought of beauty that the builders labored ... the baffled dreams and broken visions and the ruined hopes and the secret desires of each one labored with him ... the rejected beauty, the strangled appreciation, the inchoate art, the submerged spirit—these groped and found each other and gathered themselves together and worked themselves into the tiles and mortar of the edifice and made a town that is a worthy fellow of the sunrise and the sea winds.

This passage by Sandy Asher is also an example of this method; the final paragraph reveals that the essay is an answer to the question, "Why do I write for children?"

> Magic, companionship, a sense of control. The wonder of ourselves, of each other, and of life—this is the true subject matter of all novels. The best children's literature speaks not only to children but to the human condition. Writing for children simply means writing for human beings in the beginning, when you can still take part in creation, before habit, cynicism and despair have set in, and while there is still hope and energy, a willingness to learn, and a healthy sense of humor. These qualities I find irresistible in the young people I write about and for, qualities I want

Reading Nonfiction

to hang onto and to cultivate in myself. So I write for children, not just for their sakes—but for my own.

CHRONOLOGICAL ORDER/NARRATION

Although narration is the primary mode of development for fiction, it is also widely used in **exposition** and argument. The historian uses narration and chronology in recounting significant events; the scientific writer may use narration to explain a process. Narration is also an essential part of biography and the personal essay. The passage from *Life on the Mississippi* (page 60) is a classic example of personal narrative. Here, author Annie Dillard, in a passage that appeared on a past Regents exam, uses narration to explain what she means by the "unwrapped gifts and free surprises" of Nature.

I walked up to a tree, an Osage orange, and a hundred birds flew away. They simply materialized out of the tree. I saw a tree, then a whisk of color, then a tree again. I walked closer and another hundred blackbirds took flight. Not a branch, not a twig budged: the birds were apparently weightless as well as invisible. Or, it was as if the leaves of the Osage orange had been freed from a spell in the form of red-winged blackbirds; they flew from the tree, caught my eye in the sky, and vanished. When I looked again at the tree, the leaves had reassembled as if nothing had happened. Finally I walked directly to the trunk of the tree and a final hundred, the real diehards, appeared, spread, and vanished. How could so many hide in the tree without my seeing them? The Osage orange, unruffled, looked just as it had looked from the house, when three hundred red-winged blackbirds cried from its crown. I looked upstream where they flew, and they were gone. Searching, I couldn't spot one. I wandered upstream to force them to play their hand, but they'd crossed the creek and scattered. One show to customer. These appearances catch at my throat; they are the free gifts, the bright coppers at the roots of trees.

CAUSE AND EFFECT

Formal development of cause and effect arguments is essential to the historian, the scientist, and the lawyer. It also serves as a basic method for much of the expository writing students do. This paragraph from a speech by former governor Madeleine Kunin offers a good example of explanation through cause and effect:

> **In my own case, most essential to my political evolution was a strong desire to have an effect on events around me, whether that was a flashing red light at the railroad crossing in my neighborhood, to protect my children on their way to school, or whether it was a new environmental law for the state of Vermont. The fact that I succeeded in obtaining the flashing red light, as a private citizen, enabled me to change the environmental laws as governor. Each step builds a new self-image, enabling us to move from the passive to the active voice.**

Here is a brief example from the Text on RFID technology (page 26) in Chapter 2:

> **All of the websites you visit collect some amount of information about you, whether it is your name or what other sites you have visited recently. Most of the time, we're being tracked without knowing it. For example, most websites now include Facebook and Twitter buttons so you can "like" the page you are viewing or "Tweet" about it. Whether or not you click the buttons, however, the companies can still determine which pages you've visited and file that information away for later use. . . .**

COMPARISON AND CONTRAST

In these paragraphs, historian Bruce Catton in "Lee and Grant: A Study in Constrasts," brings to a close his extended discussion of the contrasts between Ulysses S. Grant and Robert E. Lee and introduces the discussion of how the two men were alike:

> So Grant and Lee were in complete contrast, representing two diametrically opposed elements in American life. Grant was the modern man emerging; beyond him, ready to come on the stage, was the great age of steel and machinery, of crowded cities and a restless burgeoning vitality. Lee might have ridden down from the old age of chivalry, lance in hand, silken banner fluttering over his head. Each man was the perfect champion of his cause, drawing both his strengths and his weaknesses from the people he led.
>
> Yet it was not all contrast, after all. Different as they were—in background, in personality, in underlying aspiration—these two great soldiers had much in common. Under everything else, they were marvelous fighters. Furthermore, their fighting qualities were really very much alike.

Here, from *Life on the Mississippi* (1883), is Mark Twain's comparison of how the North and South treated the Civil War as a topic of conversation, years after it ended:

> In the North one hears the war mentioned, in social conversations, once a month; sometimes as often as once a week; but as a distinct subject for talk, it has long ago been relieved of duty. There are sufficient reasons for this. Given a dinner company of six gentlemen to-day, it can easily happen that four of them—and possibly five—were not in the field at all. So the chances are four to two, or five to one, that the war will at no time during the evening become the topic of conversation; and the chances are still greater that if it becomes the topic it will remain so but a little while. If you add six ladies to the company, you have added six people who saw so little of the dread realities of the war that they ran out of talk concerning them years ago, and now would soon weary of the topic if you brought it up.
>
> The case is very different in the South. There, every man you meet was in the war; and every lady you meet saw the war. The war is the great chief topic of

conversation. The interest in it is vivid and constant; the interest in other topics is fleeting. Mention of the war will wake up a dull company and set their tongues going, when nearly any other topic would fail. In the South, the war is what A.D. is elsewhere: they date from it . . . . It shows how intimately every individual was visited, in his own person, by the tremendous episode. It gives the inexperienced stranger a better idea of what a vast and comprehensive calamity invasion is than he can ever get by reading books at the fireside.

DEVELOPMENT THROUGH EXTENDED METAPHOR

An extended metaphor or **analogy** is a very effective way to develop an argument or illustrate a concept. It uses the known and familiar to explain the unfamiliar. The excerpt from *Life on the Mississippi* is also a vivid example of how a writer relates an experience through extended metaphor. Here is the introduction to an essay written by a student on the topic "All the World's a Stage."

All the world is indeed a stage. And we are the performers. Everything we do in life is a production, and we must constantly perform our best because, in life, there are no rehearsals. Each of us performs on a separate stage, some for a larger audience than others. But each performance, regardless of the size of the audience, is of equal importance, and each performer must meet the standard of life's most important critic—himself.

Here is a passage from Stephen Crane's novel *The Red Badge of Courage:*

The ground was cluttered with vines and bushes, and the trees grew close and spread out like bouquets. The creepers, catching against his legs, cried out harshly as their sprays were torn from the barks of trees. The swishing saplings tried to make known his presence to the world. He could not conciliate the forest. As he made his way, it was always calling out protestations. When he separated embraces of trees and vines the disturbed foliage waved their arms and turned their face leaves toward him.

Here is an illustrative passage from *The Education of Henry Adams*, published in 1918:

For convenience as an image, the [dynamic theory of history] may liken man to a spider in its web, watching for chance prey. Forces of nature dance like flies before the net, and the spider pounces on them when it can; but it makes many fatal mistakes, though its theory of force is sound. The spider-mind acquires a faculty of memory, and, with it, a singular skill of analysis and synthesis, taking apart and putting together in different relations the meshes of its trap. Man had in the beginning no power of analysis or synthesis approaching that of the spider, or even of the honey-bee; he had acute sensibility to the higher forces. Fire taught him secrets that no other animal could learn; running water probably taught him even more, especially in his first lessons of mechanics; the animals helped to educate him, trusting themselves into his hands merely for the sake of their food, and carrying his burdens or supplying his clothing; the grasses and grains were academies of study. With little or no effort on his part, all these forces formed his thought, induced his action, and even shaped his figure.

DEFINITION OR CLASSIFICATION

In this paragraph from a speech by Madeleine Kunin, she develops a key term by classifying its component parts:

Political courage stems from a number of sources: anger, pain, love, hate. There is no lack of political motivation within women. We feel it all. Anger at a world which rushes toward saber-rattling displays of power. Pain at a world which ignores the suffering of its homeless, its elderly, its children. Hatred toward the injustice which occurs daily as the strong overpower the weak. And love for the dream of peace on earth.

Here is a brief passage from *The Federalist #10* by James Madison:

> ... The two great points of difference between a democracy and a republic are: first, the delegation of the government, in the latter, to a small number of citizens elected by the rest; secondly, the greater number of citizens, and greater sphere of country, over which the latter may be extended.
> The effect of the first difference is, on the one hand, to refine and enlarge the public views, by passing them through the medium of a chosen body of citizens, whose wisdom may best discern the true interest of their country, and whose patriotism and love of justice will be least likely to sacrifice it to temporary or partial considerations. Under such a regulation, it may well happen that the public voice, pronounced by the representatives of the people, will be more consonant to the public good than if pronounced by the people themselves, convened for the purpose.

EXAMPLES IN ORDER OF IMPORTANCE

The most persuasive arguments are those in which the reasoning has a cumulative effect. The skilled writer does not present the supporting details of a thesis in random order; rather, the skilled writer presents details in an order that stresses importance and significance. Here is how Abraham Lincoln concluded his speech marking the celebration of Independence Day in 1858:

> ... So I say in relation to the principle that all men are created equal, let it be as nearly reached as we can. If we cannot give freedom to every creature, let us do nothing that will impose slavery upon any other creature. Let us then turn this government back into the channel in which the framers of the Constitution originally placed it.

Reading Nonfiction

> ... Let us discard all this quibbling about this man and the other man—this race and that race and the other race being inferior, and therefore they must be placed in an inferior position—discarding our standard that we have left us. Let us discard all these things, and unite as one people throughout this land, until we shall once more stand up declaring that all men are created equal.

This excerpt is from one of the best-known speeches in Shakespeare's *Hamlet*. The character of Polonius is advising his son on how to conduct himself honorably as a university student in Paris:

> ... Give thy thoughts no tongue,
> Nor any unproportioned thought his act.
> Be thou familiar, but by no means vulgar.
> Those friends thou hast, and their adoption tried,
> Grapple them to thy soul with hoops of steel;
> But do not dull thy palm with entertainment
> Of each new-hatch'd, unfledged comrade. Beware
> Of entrance to a quarrel, but being in,
> Bear't that the opposed may beware of thee.
> Give every man thy ear, but few thy voice;
> Take each man's censure, but reserve thy
>   judgment.
> Costly thy habit as thy purse can buy,
> But not express'd in fancy; rich, not gaudy;
> For the apparel oft proclaims the man,
> And they in France of the best rank and station
> Are of a most select and generous chief in that.
> Neither a borrower nor a lender be;
> For loan oft loses both itself and friend,
> And borrowing dulls the edge of husbandry.
> This above all: to thine ownself be true,
> And it must follow, as the night the day,
> Thou canst not then be false to any man.
> Farewell: my blessing season this in thee!

These models offer examples of only some of the ways in which writers develop ideas. As you read more widely, you will appreciate the extent to which every writer, especially the writer of essays, creates a form best suited to the subject and purpose. When you find a piece of writing you especially admire or find convincing, note how the author developed the ideas.

Tone

When we speak of **tone** in writing we are referring to the attitude of the writer toward the subject and/or toward the reader. It is closely related to what we mean when we refer to someone's "tone of voice." Tone may range from *harsh* and *insistent* to *gentle* and *reflective*. There is as much variety of tone in writing as there is in human feeling. Some pieces—essays of opinion, for example—usually have a very distinct tone; other works, especially in fiction or personal expression, may have a more subtle and indirect tone.

Here is a list of adjectives to help you identify the tone or mood of a prose passage. Many have been gathered by students in their reading of Op-Ed page essays. These terms are part of the academic language you are expected to comprehend in reading and to use appropriately in discussing works of nonfiction. Each reflects a distinctive feeling; be sure to look up in a dictionary any that you are not sure about.

admiring	cautious	informed	provocative
advisory	challenging	inquiring	questioning
affectionate	concerned	instructive	reasoned
alarmed	credible	intense	reflective
amused	critical	ironic	sad
anguished	curious	knowledgeable	sarcastic
appalled	cynical	melancholy	satirical
apprehensive	defensive	mocking	sentimental
argumentative	disappointed	mysterious	skeptical
arrogant	dismayed	nonchalant	surprised
assured	eerie	nostalgic	thoughtful
(with) awe	frank	objective	troubled
bewildered	grateful	offended	understanding
bitter	haughty	optimistic	whimsical
boastful	humorous	outraged	wondering
candid	indifferent	peaceful	
cautionary	indignant	probing	

The Op-Ed pages of most newspapers offer daily examples of essays on current topics, representing widely varied methods of argument, style, and tone. *Ploughshares, McSweeneys, Zoetrope, Harper's Magazine, The*

Atlantic Monthly, and *The New Yorker* include excellent selections of essays and other examples of literary nonfiction. National magazines such as *Time* and *Sports Illustrated* also offer examples of feature writing and reporting on current issues. The list of Recommended Reading on page 215 also offers titles of books of nonfiction available in paperback.

A GLOSSARY OF LITERARY TERMS AND TECHNIQUES

abstract In contrast to the *concrete,* abstract language expresses general ideas and concepts apart from specific examples or instances. Very formal writing is characterized by abstract expression. An *abstract* (n.) is a brief summary of the key ideas in a scientific, legal, or scholarly piece of writing.

analogy An expression of the similarities between things that are not wholly alike or related. (See, for example, the student essay on page 61.) See *metaphor* in A Glossary of Poetic Terms and Techniques, Chapter 5.

anecdote A very brief, usually vivid, story or episode. Often humorous, anecdotes offer examples of typical behavior or illustrate the personality of a character. Writers of biography and autobiography make extensive use of anecdote to reveal the lives of their subjects.

antithesis In formal argument, a statement that opposes or contrasts with a *thesis* statement. Informally, we use the term to refer to any expression or point of view completely opposed to another. In literature, even an experience or feeling may be expressed as the *antithesis* of another. See also *thesis*.

argument In persuasive writing or speaking, the development of reasons to support the writer's position; also the method of reasoning used to persuade. Informally, we may use the term to describe the development of a topic in any piece of exposition. Historically, it has also denoted a summary of a literary work's plot or main ideas.

atmosphere Closely related to *tone* or mood, it refers to a pervasive feeling in a work. Atmosphere often stems from setting and from distinctive characters or actions. For example, the atmosphere in many of Poe's stories is mysterious, troubling, even sinister, and Hawthorne's "Young Goodman Brown" reflects the threatening and ambiguous world of its Puritan setting.

autobiography A formally composed account of a person's life, written by that person. While we must trust, or be skeptical of, the reliability of the account, we often appreciate the firsthand narration of experience. Autobiography is also a rich source of information and insight into an historical period or into literary or artistic worlds. Autobiography, like the novel, has *narrative* and chronology. (See also *journal.*) We describe literary works that are closely based on the author's life as "autobiographical." Eugene O'Neill's *Long Day's Journey into Night* and Tennessee Williams's *The Glass Menagerie* are plays that reflect many details of their authors' lives.

biography A narrative, historical account of the life, character, and significance of its subject. Contemporary biography is usually researched in detail and may not always paint an admiring portrait of its subject. A critical biography of a literary figure includes discussion of the writer's works to show the writer's artistic development and career. Biographies of figures significant in history or public affairs also offer commentary on periods and events of historical importance.

character Characters are the imagined persons, created figures, who inhabit the worlds of fiction and drama. E. M. Forster distinguished between *flat* and *round* characters: Flat are those, like stereotypes, who represent a single and exaggerated human characteristic; round are those whose aspects are complex and convincing, and who change or develop in the course of a work. In good fiction, plot must develop out of character. The desires, values, and motives of characters account for the action and conflict in a plot.

characterization The method by which an author establishes character; the means by which personality, manner, and appearance are created. It is achieved directly through description and dialogue and indirectly through observations and reactions of other characters.

concrete Refers to the particular, the specific, in expression and imagery. That which is concrete can be perceived by the senses. Concrete also refers to that which is tangible, real, or actual, in contrast to the *abstract*, which is intangible and conceptual.

conflict In the most general sense, it identifies the forces that give rise to a plot. This term may identify an actual struggle between characters, anything from revenge to simple recognition or understanding. A plot may focus on conflict between characters and the forces of nature or society. These are essentially **external conflicts**. A work may also center on **internal conflicts**, characters' struggles to know or change themselves and their lives. Most works of fiction and drama contain more than one aspect of conflict. (See the discussion on page 47.)

denouement A French term meaning "untying a knot," it refers to the way the complications or conflict of a plot are finally resolved. It also refers to what is called the "falling action" in a drama, that part of the play that follows the dramatic climax and reveals the consequences of the main action for minor characters; it also accounts briefly for what happens in the world of the play after the principal drama is resolved. In Arthur Miller's *Death of a Salesman*, the "Requiem" may be considered a denouement; it accounts for the response to Willy's death by his wife, sons, and only friend. In Shakespeare's *Macbeth*, the climax is in the scene following the death of Lady Macbeth in which Macbeth understands that he has destroyed all capacity for feeling and has rendered his life meaningless; the denouement includes the battle in which Macbeth understands that he cannot escape the witches' prophecy and is killed by MacDuff, thus restoring the throne to the rightful heir, Malcolm.

determinism The philosophical view that human existence is determined by forces over which humans have little or no control. The concept that fate predestines the course of a character's life or a tragic figure's downfall is a form of determinism.

episode A series of actions or incidents that make up a self-contained part of a larger narrative. Some novels are structured so that each chapter is a significant episode. Fitzgerald's *The Great Gatsby* and Mark Twain's *Huckleberry Finn* are good examples of this structure. A *scene* in a play is often analogous to an episode in a narrative. Many television series are presented in weekly episodes.

essay A general term (from French *essai,* meaning an attempt, a trying out of something) to denote an extended composition, usually expository, devoted to a single topic. Essays may be composed to persuade, to reflect on philosophical questions, to analyze a subject, to express an opinion, or to entertain. As a literary form, the essay dates from the sixteenth century and remains a popular and widely practiced form. The essay by Francis Bacon on page 41 is a classic example. See *formal/informal* essay.

exposition Writing whose purpose is to inform, illustrate, and explain. In literature, exposition refers to those passages or speeches in which setting, offstage or prior action, or a character's background is revealed. In *The Great Gatsby,* Nick Carraway pauses in the narrative to give the reader additional information about Gatsby's background. The prologue to Shakespeare's *Romeo and Juliet* is an example of exposition.

flashback A presentation of incidents or episodes that occurred prior to the beginning of the narrative itself. When an author or filmmaker uses flashback, the "present" or forward motion of the plot is suspended. Flashback may be introduced through the device of a character's memory or through the narrative voice itself. William Faulkner's "Barn Burning" and *Light in August* include vivid passages of memory and narrative flashback. Jack Burden's recounting of the Cass Mastern story in Robert Penn Warren's *All the King's Men* is also a form of flashback.

foreshadowing A technique in which an author establishes details or mood that will become more significant as the plot of a work progresses. Thoughtful readers usually sense such details and accumulate them in their memories. In one of the opening scenes of *Ethan Frome*, Ethan and Mattie talk about the dangers of sledding down Starkfield's steepest hill; and, in the second paragraph of "The Lottery," the boys are stuffing their pockets with stones or making piles of them on the edge of the square.

form The organization, shape, and structure of a work. Concretely, form may refer to *genre* (see below), for example, the sonnet form, the tragic form. More abstractly, form also refers to the way we sense inherent structure and shape.

formal/informal essay The formal essay emphasizes organization, logic, and explanation of ideas, whereas the informal essay emphasizes the voice and perspective of the writer. In the latter, also called a *personal essay*, the reader is aware of the author's *persona* and is asked to share the author's interest in the subject.

genre A type or form of literature. Examples include *novel, short story, epic poem, essay, sonnet, tragedy.*

image Although the term suggests something that is visualized, an image is an evocation through language of *any* experience perceived directly through the senses. See also A Glossary of Poetic Terms and Techniques, Chapter 5.

irony In general, a tone or figure of speech in which there is a discrepancy (a striking difference or contradiction) between what is expressed and what is meant or expected. Irony achieves its powerful effect indirectly: in satire, for example, which often uses *understatement* or *hyperbole* to express serious criticism of human behavior and social institutions. We also speak of *dramatic irony* when the narrator or reader understands more than the characters do.

journal A diary or notebook of personal observations. Many writers use journals to compose personal reflection and to collect ideas for their works; the journals of many writers have been published. Students are often urged to keep journals as a way to reflect on their reading, compose personal pieces, and practice writing free of concern for evaluation.

melodrama A plot in which incidents are sensational and designed to provoke immediate emotional responses. In such a plot, the "good" characters are pure and innocent and victims of the "bad" ones, who are thoroughly evil. The term refers to a particular kind of drama popular in the late nineteenth century and, later, in silent films and early Westerns. A work becomes melodramatic when it relies on improbable incidents and unconvincing characters for strong emotional effect.

memoir A form of autobiographical writing that reflects on the significant events the writer has observed and on the interesting and important personalities the writer has known.

monologue In a play, an extended expression or speech by a single speaker that is uninterrupted by response from other characters. A monologue is addressed to a particular person or persons, who may or may not actually hear it. Ring Lardner's short story "Haircut" is an example of monologue as a method of narration. In it, a barber tells the story to a customer (the reader) who is present but does not respond. See also *dramatic monologue* in A Glossary of Poetic Terms and Techniques, Chapter 5.

motivation The desires, values, needs, or impulses that move characters to act as they do. In good fiction the reader understands, appreciates, and is convinced that a character's motivation accounts for the significant incidents and the outcome of a plot.

narrative point of view The standpoint, perspective, and degree of understanding from which a work of narrative fiction is told. See *omniscient point of view, objective point of view.*

narrator The character or author's *persona* that tells a story. It is through the perspective and understanding of the narrator that the reader experiences the work. In some works, the narrator may inhabit the world of the story or be a character in it. In other works, the narrator is a detached but knowledgeable observer.

naturalism Closely related to *determinism,* naturalism depicts characters who are driven not by personal will or moral principles but by natural forces that they do not fully understand or control. In contrast to other views of human experience, the naturalistic view makes no moral judgments on the lives of the characters. Their lives, often bleak or defeating, simply *are* as they are, determined by social, environmental, instinctive, and hereditary forces. Naturalism was in part a reaction by writers against the nineteenth century Romantic view of humans as the masters of their own fate. It is important to note, however, that none of the Naturalistic writers in America (Crane, Dreiser, London, Anderson, and Norris chief among them) presented a genuinely deterministic vision. Several of these authors began their careers in journalism and were drawn to the Naturalistic view of life as a result of their own experience and observation of life in the United States. See also *realism.*

objective point of view In fiction or nonfiction, this voice presents a story or information, respectively, without expressed judgment or qualification. A fundamental principle of journalism is that news *reports* should be objective. Ernest Hemingway's short story "The Killers" is an example of fiction rendered in a completely detached, objective point of view.

omniscient point of view Spoken in third person (*she, he, it, they*), this is the broadest narrative perspective. The omniscient narrator speaks from outside the story and sees and knows everything about the characters and incidents. Omniscient narration is not limited by time or place. In **limited omniscient** point of view, the author may choose to reveal the story through full understanding of only one character and limit the action to those incidents in which this character is present.

persona A term from the Greek meaning "mask," it refers in literature to a narrative voice created by an author and through which the author speaks. A narrative persona usually has a perceptible, even distinctive, personality that contributes to our understanding of the story. In Nathaniel Hawthorne's *The Scarlet Letter,* the omniscient narrator has a distinctive persona whose attitudes toward Puritan society and the characters' lives are revealed throughout the novel.

plot The incidents and experiences of characters selected and arranged by the author to create a meaningful narrative. A good plot is convincing in terms of what happens and why.

poetic justice The concept that life's rewards and punishments should be perfectly appropriate and distributed in just proportions. In Ring Lardner's short story "Haircut," Jim Kendall's ironic fate is an example of poetic justice: He is a victim of one of his own crude and insensitive practical jokes.

point of view In nonfiction, this denotes the attitudes or opinions of the writer. In narrative fiction, it refers to how and by whom a story is told: the perspective of the narrator and the narrator's relationship to the story. Point of view may be *omniscient,* where the narrator knows everything about the characters and their lives; or it may be *limited* to the understanding of a particular character or speaker. Point of view may also be described as *objective* or *subjective. Third-person* narrative refers to characters as "he, she, it, they." *First-person* narrative is from the "I" point of view. J. D. Salinger's *The Catcher in the Rye* and Twain's *Huckleberry Finn* are told in the first person. *Second-person* narrative, the "you" form, is rare but is found in sermons addressed to a congregation or in essays of opinion addressed directly to a leader or public figure: "You, Mr. Mayor (Madame President), should do the following . . ." Thomas Friedman and Gail Collins occasionally write pieces in the second-person voice for the Op-Ed page of *The New York Times*.

prologue An introductory statement of the dramatic situation of a play or story. Shakespeare's *Romeo and Juliet* begins with a brief prologue. The first two pages of Fitzgerald's *The Great Gatsby* are a prologue to the story Nick Carraway will tell.

prose Most of what we write is prose, the expression in sentences and phrases that reflect the natural rhythms of speech. Prose is organized by paragraphs and is characterized by variety in sentence length and rhythm.

protagonist A term from Ancient Greek drama, it refers to the central character, the hero or heroine, in a literary work.

realism The literary period in the United States following the Civil War is usually called the Age of Realism. Realism depicts the directly observable in everyday life. Realistic writers seek to *present* characters and situations as they would appear to a careful observer, not as they are imagined or created by the author. After 1865, American writers became increasingly interested in the sources of power and force, and in the means to survival and success, in an increasingly materialistic society. For writers of this period, realism was a literary mode to express a *naturalistic* philosophy. See also *naturalism, verisimilitude*.

rhetoric From Ancient Greece, the art of persuasion in speech or writing achieved through logical thought and skillful use of language.

rhetorical question A question posed in the course of an *argument* to provoke thought or to introduce a line of reasoning.

romance A novel or tale that includes elements of the supernatural, heroic adventure, or romantic passion. Hawthorne's *The Scarlet Letter* is a romance, not because it is a love story but because it goes beyond *verisimilitude* in dramatizing elements of demonic and mystical forces in the characters and their lives.

satire A form or style that uses elements of irony, ridicule, exaggeration, understatement, sarcasm, humor, or absurdity to criticize human behavior or a society. All satire is **ironic** (see above) in that meaning or theme is conveyed in the discrepancy between what is said and what is meant, between what is and what should be, between what appears and what truly is. While satire is often entertaining, its purpose is serious and meant to provoke thought or judgment. The verses of Alexander Pope are often extended satire, and many poems by e. e. cummings are satiric. In prose, much of the writing of Mark Twain is satire; *Huckleberry Finn* is the most striking example. Other American writers of satire include Sinclair Lewis, Dorothy Parker, Edith Wharton, Joseph Heller, and Tom Wolfe. On television, *Saturday Night Live*, and *The Simpsons* are good examples of contemporary satire, as was *The Colbert Report*.

short story This form is distinguished from most novels not simply by length but by its focus on few characters and on a central, revealing incident. In short stories, however, there is as much variety in narrative point of view, subject, and technique as there is in novels. Edgar Allan Poe characterized the short story as "a short prose narrative, requiring from a half-hour to one or two hours in its perusal."

soliloquy A form of *monologue* in which a character expresses thoughts and feelings aloud but does not address them to anyone else or intend other characters in the work to hear them. In essence, the audience for a play is secretly listening in on a character's innermost thoughts. Macbeth's reflection on "Tomorrow, and tomorrow, and tomorrow . . ." is the best-known soliloquy in the play.

speaker The narrative voice in a literary work (see *persona*). Also, the character who speaks in a *dramatic monologue*.

symbol Most generally, anything that stands for or suggests something else. Language itself is symbolic; sounds and abstract written forms may be arranged to stand for virtually any human thought or experience. In literature, symbols are not codes to crack—they are not "hidden meanings." Symbols are real objects and *concrete* images that lead us to *think about* what is suggested. They organize a wide variety of ideas into single acts of understanding. They embody not single "meanings" but suggest whole areas of meaning.

theme Roughly analogous to thesis in an essay, this is an observation about human experience or an idea central to a work of literature. The *subject* of a work is in the specific setting, characters, and plot. Theme in a work of fiction is what is meaningful and significant to human experience generally; themes are the ideas and truths that transcend the specific characters and plot. Shakespeare's *Macbeth* is about an ambitious nobleman who, encouraged by his equally ambitious wife, murders the king of Scotland in order to become king himself. The themes in *Macbeth* include the power of ambition to corrupt even those who are worthy and the mortal consequences of denying what is fundamental to one's nature.

thesis The central point, a statement of position in a formal or logical argument. Also used to refer to the topic, or controlling, idea of an essay. Use of the term *thesis* implies elaboration by reasons and examples. See *antithesis*.

tone The attitude of the writer toward the subject and the reader. See also A Glossary of Poetic Terms and Techniques, Chapter 5.

transition A transition is a link between ideas or sections in a work. In prose arguments, single words such as *first, second . . . moreover,* and *therefore* or phrases such as *in addition, on the other hand,* and *in conclusion* serve as transitions. In fiction, a brief passage or chapter may serve as a transition. In *The Great Gatsby,* the narrator pauses from time to time to "fill in" the reader and to account for the passage of time between the dramatic episodes that make up the novel's main plot.

turning point In drama and fiction, the moment or episode in a plot when the action is moved toward its inevitable conclusion.

verisimilitude A quality in fiction and drama of being "true to life," of representing that which is real or actual. Verisimilitude in fiction is often achieved through specific, vivid description and dialogue; first-person narration also creates the effect of verisimilitude. In drama it may be enhanced through means of set, costumes, and lighting that are realistic in all their details.

(See also, in Chapter 5—A Glossary of Poetic Terms and Techniques.)

Chapter 5

READING POETRY

INTRODUCTION

How to Read a Poem

How should you read a poem? Aloud. Several times. And never quickly. Here is a short poem about baseball. As you read, pay attention first to what the poem by Robert Francis says.

Pitcher

His art is eccentricity, his aim
How not to hit the mark he seems to aim at,
His passion how to avoid the obvious,
His technique how to vary the avoidance.
The others throw to be comprehended. He
Throws to be a moment misunderstood.
Yet not too much. Not errant, arrant, wild,
But every seeming aberration willed.
Not to, yet still, still to communicate
Making the batter understand too late.

Now, read the poem again, with particular attention to the varied length of the statements; read from comma to comma or period to period as you would in prose. When you reach the end of the first and fifth lines, for example, pause very slightly—but do not stop. After several readings, you will not only appreciate what Robert Francis undertands about the art of pitching but also feel the way in which the rhythm of the poem is also the rhythm of pitching.

In poetry we are meant to sense a structure and to feel the rhythm. (See **meter*** and **rhythm**.) The structure and rhythm of poetry may be formal, informal, even "free." Poetry is also characterized by its directness of effect and by its concentration—ideas and feelings are expressed in relatively few words. Karl Shapiro says, "Poems are what ideas *feel like*." Robert Francis's poem is about what good pitching *feels like*.

---

*Terms in bold type are defined in A Glossary of Poetic Terms and Techniques at the end of the chapter.

Introduction

This poem, by Emily Dickinson (1830–1886), recalls the feeling of mourning:

> After great pain, a formal feeling comes—
> The nerves sit ceremonious, like Tombs—
> The stiff Heart questions was it He, that bore,
> and Yesterday, or Centuries before?
>
> The Feet, mechanical, go round—
> Of Ground, or Air or Ought—
> A Wooden way
> Regardless grown,
> A Quartz contentment, like a stone—
>
> This is the Hour of Lead—
> Remembered, if outlived,
> As Freezing persons, recollect the Snow—
> First—Chill—then Stupor—then the letting go—

In this poem, Dickinson recreates what it feels like suddenly to encounter a snake in the grass:

> A narrow Fellow in the Grass
> Occasionally rides—
> You may have met Him—did you not
> His notice sudden is—
> The Grass divides as with a Comb—
> A spotted shaft is seen—
> And then it closes at your feet
> And opens further on—
>
> He likes a Boggy Acre
> A Floor too cool for corn—
> Yet when a boy, and Barefoot—
> I more than once at Noon
> Have passed, I thought, a Whip lash
> Unbraiding in the Sun
> When stooping to secure it
> It wrinkled, and was gone—

**Several of Nature's People
I know, and they know me—
I feel for them a transport
Of cordiality—**

**But never met this Fellow
Attended, or alone
Without a tighter breathing
And Zero at the Bone—**

Where the writer of prose may seek immediate clarity of meaning above all, the poet often seeks **ambiguity**, not to create "confusion," but to offer multiplicity of meaning, in single words, in images, in the meaning of the poem itself. Look again at "Pitcher." Might this poem also be a reflection on the art of poetry itself? It is because of such richness in meaning that poems often require several readings.

The experience of poetry is conveyed in vivid **imagery**, which appeals to the mind and to the senses. It is often expressed in **figurative language**, that is, words and comparisons that are not literal but that imaginatively create original, vivid, and often unexpected images and associations. (See **metaphor** and **simile**.) Finally, in poetry there is particular significance in the way words and lines sound. The story or experience is enhanced through musical effects. A poem should be heard or felt!

In this poem by Laurence Binyon, a boy kept home from school with a fever, is dazzled by the light of the sun as it comes out after rain, and he no longer regrets being "…a captive/Apart from his schoolfellows."

The rain was ending, and light

**THE rain was ending, and light
Lifting the leaden skies.
It shone upon ceiling and floor
And dazzled a child's eyes.**

**Pale after fever, a captive
Apart from his schoolfellows,
He stood at the high room's window
With face to the pane pressed close,**

**And beheld an immense glory
Flooding with fire the drops
Spilled on miraculous leaves
Of the fresh green lime-tree tops.**

> Washed gravel glittered red
> To a wall, and beyond it nine
> Tall limes in the old inn yard
> Rose over the tall inn sign.
>
> And voices arose from beneath
> Of boys from school set free,
> Racing and chasing each other
> With laughter and games and glee.
>
> To the boy at the high room-window,
> Gazing alone and apart,
> There came a wish without reason,
> A thought that shone through his heart.
>
> I'll choose this moment and keep it,
> He said to himself, for a vow,
> To remember for ever and ever
> As if it were always now.

A note on reading this poem: do not read to emphasize regular meter and rhyming pattern; remember, read from comma to comma, period to period. For example, the second and third stanzas should be read with only slight pauses at the commas and through the third stanza, where there is no end punctuation, in as few breaths as possible. The fourth stanza completes the vivid image of the "immense glory" the boy sees as he looks out the window.

STRUCTURE AND LANGUAGE IN POETRY

All the traditional poetic forms stem from an oral tradition, in which poetry was sung or recited. The **epic** and the **ballad** are the oldest forms of **narrative poetry**, but modern poets also tell stories in narrative verse. (Robert Frost's "Out, Out—" is a well-known example.) Most of the poetry we read today, however, is **lyric** poetry.

Think of the lyric poem as a song; in the Ancient Greek tradition, the lyric poem was meant to be sung to the accompaniment of a lyre, a small harplike instrument. Indeed, we speak of the words for a song as its lyrics. The ancient form is evident in the songs for Shakespeare's plays, in the tradition of the nineteenth-century art song, and in the twentieth-century ballads and songs. The ancient form is evident in the songs for Shakespeare's plays, in the tradition of the nineteenth-century art song, and in the twentieth-century ballads and songs we associate, for example, with Rodgers and Hart, Cole Porter, and Stephen Sondheim and sung by Frank Sinatra, Barbra Streisand, among many others, including Tony Bennett in his duets with Lady Gaga.

Lyric poems are relatively brief and are expressed in the voice (that is, from the point of view) of a single speaker. They express a powerful emotion, usually captured in a significant experience or dramatic situation. A lyric poem, like a song, often tells a story, but it does so in nonnarrative form. The **speaker** (or "poet") may recall an experience, or render it directly, in order to understand its meaning and then reveal it to the reader. Thus, many lyric poems are *meditations, reflections,* or *recollections* of experience that lead to a *discovery*, to an emotionally powerful *recognition* of the meaning of the experiences. The effect of the poem is to convey that meaning directly, to engage readers in such a way that they share the experience, feel the emotion, with the speaker. The poems by Robert Francis, Emily Dickinson, and Laurence Binyon on the previous pages are examples of lyrics.

This poem by Robert Penn Warren appeared on a past Regents ELA exam.

Old Photograph of the Future

That center of attention—an infantile face
That long years ago showed, no doubt, pink and white—
Now faded, and in the photograph only a trace
Of grays, not much expression in sight.

(5) That center of attention, swathed in a sort of white dress,
Is precious to the woman who, pretty and young,
Leans with a look of surprised blessedness
At the mysterious miracle forth-sprung.

In the background somewhat, the masculine figure
(10) Looms, face agleam with achievement and pride.
In black coat, derby at breast, he is quick to assure
You the world's in good hands—lay your worries aside.

The picture is badly faded. Why not?
Most things show wear around seventy-five,
(15) And that's the age this picture has got.
The man and woman no longer, of course, live.

**They lie side by side in whatever love survives
Under green turf, or snow, and that child, years later,
stands there
While old landscapes blur and he in guilt grieves**
(20) **Over nameless promises unkept, in undefinable despair.**

In this poem, the speaker expresses the profound feelings of guilt and despair he feels in looking at an old photograph of himself and his parents when he was an infant. The **tone** of the poem is reflective, that of an elegy. The mood at the end is one of regret and loss as the speaker recalls his dead parents, confronts his own age, "the age this picture has got," and grieves at the "nameless promises unkept." Although the narrator speaks of "that child, years later" who "stands there . . . and . . . in guilt grieves," the intensity and privacy of feeling at the end indicate that the speaker is that child. The narrative voice and the lack of specific identification of the characters serve to emphasize the passage of time and underscore the fact that looking at the photograph leads the "child," now old, to reflect on his entire life.

The structure is simple and easy to observe: five **quatrains** with alternating **rhyme**; each quatrain is self-contained—ends with a period—and tells a part of the story. The first fifteen lines of the poem describe the picture and the "characters" in it. Note that the final section of the poem begins with the last line of the fourth quatrain, the description having concluded in line 15. Line 16 both ends the narrator's rendering of the photograph and also begins the "conclusion," which is the significance of the experience of looking at the photograph.

The rhythm within lines is varied and often broken by dashes or other pauses; this rhythm allows us to share the speaker's questions and reflections. The rhythm of the fourth stanza slows as each line completes a thought. In contrast, the final stanza flows into a single, long gesture of recognition and regret.

The experience of looking at the picture—in which he is the "center of attention"—leads the speaker to reflect on whether he has satisfied the "promises" that the "mysterious miracle" of his birth meant to his awed and proud parents. The photograph also leads the speaker to reflect on the unfulfilled promises of his own life.

There is little in the way of figurative language in this poem. The imagery, however, reveals more than a description of a photograph, and the paradox in the title reveals one of the poem's central **themes**, the cycle of birth, life, and death. On rereading Warren's poem, with our appreciation of the poet's experience in mind, we perceive how the third and fourth lines are more than a description of the photograph—they also suggest the speaker's age. He sees himself (in the photo and metaphorically) as "faded . . . only a trace of grays, not much expression in sight." The repetition of the fact that he was the "center of attention" (in the photograph and in his parents' lives) makes more poignant the grief over "promises unkept" at the end.

The poet offers only a few details of the photograph, but they are the details many of us will recognize from our own photographs of grandparents and great-grandparents: the father "In the background somewhat" and in formal pose—"in black coat, derby at breast"—the child (girl or boy) in "a sort of white dress." It is, of course, such widely shared experience that is both the poem's form and its theme.

In this poem by Theodore Roethke, the speaker recalls a significant experience from childhood:

Child on Top of a Greenhouse

The wind billowing out of the seat of my britches,
My feet crackling splinters of glass and dried putty,
The half-grown chrysanthemums staring up like accusers,
Up through the streaked glass, flashing with sunlight,
A few white clouds all rushing eastward,
A line of elms plunging and tossing like horses,
And everyone, everyone pointing up and shouting!

Try repeating just the verbs of this poem, feeling their dramatic energy. The repetition of "-ing" forms also creates what is called **internal rhyme**, while the words "like," "sunlight," "white," "line" form the pattern of sound called **assonance**.

In this poem by Donald Hall the speaker also recalls an important childhood experience:

The Sleeping Giant
(A Hill, So Named, in Hamden, Connecticut)

The whole day long, under the walking sun
That poised an eye on me from its high floor,
Holding my toy beside the clapboard house
I looked for him, the summer I was four.

I was afraid the waking arm would break
From the loose earth and rub against his eyes
A fist of trees, and the whole country tremble
In the exultant labor of his rise;

> Then he with giant steps in the small streets
> Would stagger, cutting off the sky, to seize
> The roofs from house and home because we had
> Covered his shape with dirt and planted trees;
>
> And then kneel down and rip with fingernails
> A trench to pour the enemy Atlantic
> Into our basin, and the water rush,
> With the streets full and the voices frantic.
>
> That was the summer I expected him.
> Later the high and watchful sun instead
> Walked low behind the house, and school began,
> And winter pulled a sheet over his head.

In this poem, a child's fearful and vivid imagination is sparked by **personification** of the hill near his house. This poem is particularly effective because it recalls for us the fact that small children are literal and that they tend to give names and human character to inanimate things. This child actually sees—and fears—the sleeping giant. Note too how the images of the sun in the first and last stanzas both unify the poem and denote the passage of time. Finally, there is a gentle **irony** in the final line that suggests that the child, no longer fearful, can now "play" with the metaphor of the sleeping giant, as "winter pulled a sheet over his head."

Shakespeare's Sonnet 30 illustrates several of the formal aspects of verse:

When to the sessions of sweet silent thought

> When to the sessions of sweet silent thought
> I summon up remembrance of things past
> I sigh the lack of many a thing I sought
> And with old woes new wail my dear time's waste:
>
> (5) Then can I drown an eye, unused to flow,
> For precious friends hid in death's dateless night,
> And weep afresh love's long-since-canceled woe,
> And moan th'expense of many a vanished sight;

(10)   Then can I grieve at grievances forgone,
And heavily from woe to woe tell o'er
The sad account of fore-bemoaned moan,
Which I new pay as if not paid before.
  But if the while I think on thee, dear friend,
  All losses are restored and sorrows end.

The structure of the Shakespearean **sonnet** is three **quatrains** and a closing **couplet**. The **rhyme scheme** is *abab/cdcd/efef/gg*. This pattern allows us to feel the structure of the poem, to track the development of the ideas. The couplet, with its similar end rhyme and self-contained thought, contrasts the feelings expressed in the previous 12 lines and concludes the poem.

We find in this Shakespearean sonnet, as well, examples of **alliteration** and assonance: The first quatrain features alliteration in the many words that begin with "s." Lines 7 through 12 offer assonance in the repetition of "oh" sounds, which are also examples of **onomatopoeia**—that is, the sounds reflect the meanings of the words. Lines 4 and 10 also illustrate what is called internal rhyme.

THEME IN POETRY

Some lyric poems may assert a belief. Others may be a comment on the nature of human experience—love, death, loss or triumph, mystery and confusion, conflict and peace, on the humorous and the ironic, on the imagined and the unexpected in all its forms. Some poems reflect on the nature of time, of existence. Many lyrics are about poetry itself. These aspects of human experience are what we refer to as the themes of poetry.

In this well-known sonnet, Number 55, Shakespeare asserts that poetry confers immortality, that it can prevail over the most powerful forces of time. Note how the central idea is developed in the three quatrains and how the couplet—in its thought and its rhyme—concludes the development of that idea.

Not marble, nor the gilded monuments

Not marble, nor the gilded monuments
Of princes, shall outlive this pow'rful rhyme;
But you shall shine more bright in these contents
Than unswept stone besmeared with sluttish time.

When wasteful war shall statues overturn,
And broils root out the work of masonry,
Nor Mars his sword nor war's quick fire shall burn
The living record of your memory.

'Gainst death and all-oblivious enmity
Shall you pace forth; your praise shall still find room
Even in the eyes of all posterity
That wear this world out to the ending doom.
  So, till the judgment that yourself arise,
  You live in this, and dwell in lovers' eyes.

In this lyric by Carl Sandburg, the poet suggests that poetry is "about" the meaning in life itself.

Last Answers

I WROTE a poem on the mist
And a woman asked me what I meant by it.
I had thought till then only of the beauty of the mist,
    how pearl and gray of it mix and reel,
And change the drab shanties with lighted lamps
    at evening into points of mystery quivering with
    color.
  I answered:
The whole world was mist once long ago and some
    day it will all go back to mist,
Our skulls and lungs are more water than bone and
    tissue
And all poets love dust and mist because all the last
    answers
Go running back to dust and mist.

The best-known lyrics, however, are probably love poems—Sonnet 116 of Shakespeare, for example:

Let me not to the marriage of true minds

Let me not to the marriage of true minds
Admit impediments. Love is not love
which alters when it alteration finds,
Or bends with the remover to remove.

O, no, it is an ever-fixed mark
That looks on tempests and is never shaken;
It is the star to every wand'ring bark,
Whose worth's unknown, although his height be taken.

Love's not Time's fool, though rosy lips and cheeks
Within his bending sickle's compass come;
Love alters not with his brief hours and weeks,
But bears it out even to the edge of doom.
  If this be error and upon me proved,
  I never writ, nor no man ever loved.

In this lyric by Claude McKay, the poet is overcome with longing for his homeland on the island of Jamaica.

The Tropics in New York

Bananas ripe and green, and ginger-root,
  Cocoa in pods and alligator pears,
And tangerines and mangoes and grape fruit,
  Fit for the highest prize at parish fairs,

Set in the window, bringing memories
  Of fruit-trees laden by low-singing rills,
And dewy dawns, and mystical blue skies
  In benediction over nun-like hills.

My eyes grew dim, and I could no more gaze;
  A wave of longing through my body swept,
And, hungry for the old, familiar ways,
  I turned aside and bowed my head and wept.

TONE

Tone in poetry, as in prose and all forms of human communication, expresses the *attitude* of the speaker toward the reader or listener and toward the subject. Tone in literature is as varied as the range of human experience and feeling it reflects. When we speak of the *mood* of a piece of writing, we are also speaking of tone, of an overall feeling generated by the work.

Here are some terms to help you recognize and articulate tone or mood:

ambiguous*	insistent	reconciled
amused	ironic*	reflective
angry	melancholy	regretful
bitter	mournful	reminiscent
celebratory	mysterious	satiric*
elegiac (from elegy*)	nostalgic	sorrowful
grateful	optimistic	thoughtful
harsh	paradoxical*	understated*
humorous	questioning	

WRITING ABOUT POETRY/EXPLICATION

When you are asked to *explicate* a poem, you are being asked to look closely at it and "unfold" its meaning, line by line, idea by idea. Explication combines paraphrase with close reading of form. You are explaining both the content *and* the form: the ideas and meaning as well as the structure and poetic elements.

To begin an explication, read the poem several times to discover what it says. Who is the speaker? What is the subject? the dramatic situation? What theme or experience is central to the poem? What is the tone or mood? Try to summarize or paraphrase the poem as a whole. Then note the formal details: What is the pattern of organization? What is the movement of ideas and feeling? of images and metaphors? How do stanzas or arrangement of lines reveal that? How do rhyme, meter, and rhythm contribute to the experience, to the meaning of the poem? (The commentary that follows Robert Penn Warren's "Old Photograph of the Future" on page 79 is an example of explication.)

---

*These terms are defined in A Glossary of Poetic Terms and Techniques at the end of the chapter.

POETRY ON EXAMINATIONS

On examinations, such as the Regents ELA exam and the AP Literature and Composition exam, the multiple-choice questions are designed to measure your skill at close reading and *explication*. You are expected to recognize and identify the elements of poetry. (See A Glossary of Poetic Terms and Techniques.) In addition, you are usually required to compose an essay/explication of a poem on the AP Literature and Composition exam, and such essays are commonly assigned in high school and college literature courses. *Analysis,* which requires detailed examination of particular elements of a poem or passage, is usually reserved for course assignments. The thoughtful student will, of course, develop skill in both explication and analysis.

A HANDFUL OF POEMS FOR FURTHER READING

In this excerpt from an extended essay in verse, Alexander Pope reflects on how poets express meaning through sound and rhythm.

An Essay on Criticism

True ease in writing comes from art, not chance,
As those move easiest who have learned to dance.
'Tis not enough no harshness gives offense,
The sound must seem an echo to the sense:
Soft is the strain when Zephyr gently blows,
And the smooth stream in smoother numbers flows;
But when loud surges lash the sounding shore,
The hoarse, rough verse should like the torrent roar.

The horror and loss of war are often expressed through irony. Here is Stephen Crane's reflection on war:

Do Not Weep, Maiden, for War Is Kind

Do not weep, maiden, for war is kind.
Because your lover threw wild hands against the sky
And the affrighted steed ran on alone,
Do not weep.
War is kind.

    Hoarse, booming drums of the regiment
    Little souls who thirst for fight
    These men were born to drill and die.
    The unexplained glory flies above them,
    Great is the battle-god, great, and his kingdom—
    A field where a thousand corpses lie.

Do not weep, babe, for war is kind.
Because your father tumbled in the yellow trenches,
Raged at his breast, gulped and died,
Do not weep.
War is kind.

    Swift blazing flag of the regiment,
    Eagle with crest of red and gold,
    These men were born to drill and die.
    Point for them the virtue of slaughter,
    Make plain to them the excellence of killing
    And a field where a thousand corpses lie.

Mother whose heart hung humble as a button
On the bright splendid shroud of your son,
Do not weep.
War is kind.

In this poem, by Walt Whitman (1819–1892), the speaker moves from the observation of a spider to a reflection on the soul's search to understand all existence.

A Noiseless Patient Spider

A noiseless patient spider,
I mark'd where on a little promontory it stood isolated,
Mark'd how to explore the vacant vast surrounding,
It launch'd forth filament, filament, filament, out of itself,
Ever unreeling them, ever tirelessly speeding them.

And you O my soul where you stand,
Surrounded, detached, in measureless oceans of space,
Ceaselessly musing, venturing, throwing, seeking the
    spheres to connect them,
Till the bridge you will need be form'd, till the ductile
    anchor hold,
Till the gossamer thread you fling catch somewhere,
    O my soul.

In this brief poem by Alfred, Lord Tennyson (1809–1892) the language and imagery convey the experience of both the observer and of the eagle itself.

The Eagle

He clasps the crag with crooked hands;
Close to the sun in lonely lands,
Ringed with the azure world, he stands.

The wrinkled sea beneath him crawls;
He watches from his mountain walls,
And like a thunderbolt he falls.

Here, in free verse, is Whitman's vision of eagles:

The Dalliance of Eagles

Skirting the river road, (my forenoon walk, my rest,)
Skyward in air a sudden muffled sound, the dalliance
    of the eagles,
The rushing amorous contact high in space together,
The clinching interlocking claws, a living, fierce,
    gyrating wheel,
Four beating wings, two beaks, a swirling mass tight
    grappling,
In tumbling turning clustering loops, straight downward
    falling,
Till o'er the river pois'd, the twain yet one, a moment's
    lull,
A motionless still balance in the air, then parting, talons
    loosing,
Upward again on slow-firm pinions slanting, their
    separate diverse flight,
She hers, he his, pursuing.

And here is a poet, Katharine Lee Bates, who takes delight in playing with the names and characters of various fish; the result is a collection of puns, wordplay, and forms of internal and external rhyme.

Don't You See?

THE day was hotter than words can tell,
So hot the jelly-fish wouldn't jell.
The halibut went all to butter,
And the catfish had only force to utter
A faint sea-mew—aye, though some have doubted,
The carp he capered and the horn-pout pouted.
The sardonic sardine had his sly heart's wish
When the angelfish fought with the paradise fish.
'T was a sight gave the bluefish the blues to see,
But the seal concealed a wicked glee—
The day it went from bad to worse,
Till the pickerel picked the purse-crab's purse.

And the crab felt crabedder yet no doubt,
Because the oyster wouldn't shell out.
The sculpin would sculp, but hadn't a model,
And the coddlefish begged for something to coddle.
But to both the dolphin refused its doll,
Till the whale was obliged to whale them all.

In the first of these two poems by Robert Browning (1812–1889) the rich and varied imagery recreates the journey of a lover to his beloved and, in the second, his return to the "world of men."

Meeting at Night

The grey sea and the long black land;
And the yellow half-moon large and low;
And the startled little waves that leap
In fiery ringlets from their sleep,
As I gain the cove with pushing prow,
And quench its speed i' the slushy sand.

Then a mile of warm sea-scented beach;
Three fields to cross till a farm appears;
A tap at the pane, the quick sharp scratch
And spurt of a lighted match,
And a voice less loud, through its joys and fears,
Than the two hearts beating each to each.

Parting at Morning

Round the cape of a sudden came the sea,
And the sun looked over the mountain's rim:
And straight was a path of gold for him,
And the need of a world of men for me.

In this sonnet, George Meredith (1828–1909) imagines the desire of this fallen angel, now Satan, to return to the heavens he once inhabited.

Lucifer in Starlight

On a starred night Prince Lucifer uprose.
Tired of his dark dominion swung the fiend
Above the rolling ball in cloud part screened,
Where sinners hugged their spectre of repose.
Poor prey to his hot fit of pride were those.
And now upon his western wing he leaned,
Now his huge bulk o'er Afric's sands careened,
Now the black planet shadowed Arctic snows.
Soaring through wider zones that pricked his scars
With memory of the old revolt from Awe,
He reached a middle height, and at the stars,
Which are the brain of heaven, he looked, and sank.
Around the ancient track marched, rank on rank,
The army of unalterable law.

In this well-known sonnet by Percy Bysshe Shelley (1792–1822) we experience the ironic fate of a once proud and arrogant king.

Ozymandias

I met a traveler from an antique land
Who said: Two vast and trunkless legs of stone
Stand in the desert. Near them, on the sand,
Half sunk a shattered visage lies, whose frown,
And wrinkled lip, and sneer of cold command,
Tell that its sculptor well those passions read
Which yet survive, stamped on these lifeless things,
The hand that mocked them and the heart that fed;
And on the pedestal these words appear:
"My name is Ozymandias, king of kings:
Look on my works, ye Mighty, and despair!"
Nothing beside remains. Round the decay
Of that colossal wreck, boundless and bare,
The lone and level sands stretch far away.

Romantic poets and painters were fond of celebrating sunsets. Here is an excerpt from "Enough Has Been Said of Sunset," by Iris Barry.

> **LIGHT—imperceptible as**
> **One thin veil drawn across blackness:**
> **Is it dawn? . . .**
> **Comes the twitter-whistle of sleepy birds**
> **Crescendo . . .**
> **Now bright grayness creeping**
> **Drowns the dark; and waves of sea-wind**
> **Rock the thin leaves . . .**
> **A door bangs; sharp barks from dogs released,**
> **   scampering.**
> **After some silence, footsteps.**
> **And the rising bustle of people**
> **Roused by the day-break.**

Here is what dawn "feels like" to William Carlos Williams:

Metric Figure

> **THERE is a bird in the poplars—**
> **It is the sun!**
> **The leaves are little yellow fish**
> **Swimming in the river;**
> **The bird skims above them—**
> **Day is on his wings.**
> **Phoenix!**
> **It is he that is making**
> **The great gleam among the poplars.**
> **It is his singing**
> **Outshines the noise**
> **Of leaves clashing in the wind.**

These poems represent only a few examples of the great variety of expression in verse. Your own textbooks and anthologies offer many more examples; and the list of Recommended Reading at the end of the book includes titles of collections readily available in paperback. You will also find the addresses of some excellent websites devoted to poetry. You should read as widely as possible, and always read aloud!

A GLOSSARY OF POETIC TERMS AND TECHNIQUES

allegory A narrative, in prose or verse, in which abstract ideas, principles, human values or states of mind, are *personified*. The purpose of the allegory is to illustrate the signficance of the ideas by dramatizing them. *Parable* and *fable* are particular kinds of allegory, in which a moral is illustrated in the form of a story.

alliteration The repetition of initial consonant sounds in words and syllables. This is one of the first patterns of sound a child creates (for instance "ma-ma," "pa-pa"). The children's stories of Dr. Seuss use alliteration and assonance. Poets use alliteration for its rich musical effect: "Fish, flesh, and fowl commend all summer long/Whatever is begotten, born, and dies" (Yeats); for humor: "Where at, with blade, with bloody, blameful blade/He bravely broached his boiling bloody breast" (Shakespeare); and to echo the sense of the lines: "The iron tongue of midnight hath told twelve" (Shakespeare).

allusion A reference to a historical event, to Biblical, mythological, or literary characters and incidents with which the reader is assumed to be familiar. Allusion may, with few words, enrich or extend the meaning of a phrase, idea, or image. Allusion may also be used for ironic effect. In his poem "Out, out . . ." Robert Frost expects the reader to recall from Macbeth's final soliloquy the line, "Out, out brief candle!" Such expressions as "a Pandora's box" or "Achilles heel" are also forms of allusion.

ambiguity Denotes uncertainty of meaning. In literature, however, especially in poetry, we speak of *intentional* ambiguity, the use of language and images to suggest more than one meaning at the same time.

assonance The repetition of vowel sounds among words that begin or end with different consonants. Sonnet 30 of Shakespeare (page 82) and "Child on Top of a Greenhouse" by Theodore Roethke (page 81), for example, are rich in assonance. Some poets may vary end rhymes with assonance; for example, Emily Dickinson (page 76) does it here: "The Feet, mechanical, go round—Of Ground, or Air, or Ought—."

ballad Narrative poem, sometimes sung, that tells a dramatic story.

blank verse Unrhymed *iambic pentameter,* usually in "paragraphs" of verse instead of stanzas. Shakespeare's plays are composed primarily in blank verse. For example, from *Macbeth* (Act I, Scene 5):

>Your face, my Thane, is as a book where men
>May read strange matters. To beguile the time,
>Look like the time; bear welcome in your eye,
>Your hand, your tongue; look like the innocent flower,
>But be the serpent under't . . .

connotation The feelings, attitudes, images, and associations of a word or expression. Connotations are usually said to be "positive" or "negative." See also discussion on page 148 in Chapter 8—Vocabulary.

couplet Two lines of verse with similar meter and end rhyme. Couplets generally have self-contained ideas as well, so they may function as stanzas within a poem. In the English (Shakespearean) *sonnet,* the couplet concludes the poem. (See the sonnets on pages 82–84.) Also many scenes in Shakespeare's plays end with rhymed couplets: "Away, and mock the time with fairest show/False face must hide what the false heart doth know" (*Macbeth* Act I, Scene 7).

denotation That which a word actually names, identifies, or "points to." Denotation is sometimes referred to as "the dictionary definition" of a word.

dramatic monologue A poem in which a fictional character, at a critical or dramatic point in life, addresses a particular "audience," which is identifiable but silent. In the course of the monologue, we learn a great deal, often ironically, about the character, who is speaking and the circumstances that have led to the speech. Robert Browning is the best-known nineteenth-century poet to compose dramatic monologues; "My Last Duchess" is a famous example. In the twentieth century, such poets as Kenneth Fearing, E. A. Robinson, T. S. Eliot ("The Love Song of J. Alfred Prufrock"), Robert Frost, and Amy Lowell have composed well-known dramatic monologues.

elegy A meditative poem mourning the death of an individual.

epic A long narrative poem often centering on a heroic figure who represents the fate of a great nation or people. *The Iliad* and *The Odyssey* of Homer, *The Aeneid* of Vergil, and the Anglo-Saxon *Beowulf* are well-known epics. Milton's *Paradise Lost* and Dante's *The Divine Comedy* are examples of epic narratives in which subjects of great human significance are dramatized. *Omeros,* by Derek Walcott, is a contemporary example of an epic poem.

figurative language The intentional and imaginative use of words and comparisons that are not literal but that create original, vivid, and often unexpected images and associations. Figurative language is also called *metaphorical language.* See *metaphor* and *simile.*

free verse A poem written in free verse develops images and ideas in patterns of lines without specific metrical arrangements or formal rhyme. Free verse is distinguished from prose, however, because it retains such poetic elements as assonance, alliteration, and figurative language. The poetry of Walt Whitman offers striking examples.

hyperbole An exaggerated expression (also called overstatement) for a particular effect, which may be humorous, satirical, or intensely emotional. Hyperbole is the expression of folk tales and legends and, of course, of lovers: Romeo says to Juliet, "there lies more peril in thine eye/Than twenty of their swords." Hyperbole is often the expression of any overwhelming feeling. After he murders King Duncan, Macbeth looks with horror at his bloody hands: "Will all great Neptune's ocean wash this blood/Clean from my hand . . . ?" In her sleepwalking scene, Lady Macbeth despairs that "All the perfumes of Arabia will not sweeten this little hand." And every one of us has felt, "I have mountains of work to do!"

iambic pentameter The basic meter of English speech: "I think I know exactly what you need/and yet at times I know that I do not." Formally, it identifies verse of ten syllables to the line, with the second, fourth, sixth, eight, and tenth syllables accented. There is, however, variation in the stresses within lines to reflect natural speech—and to avoid a "sing-song" or nursery rhyme effect. Most of the dialogue in Shakespeare's plays is composed in this meter. See *blank verse*.

image Images and imagery are the heart of poetry. Although the term suggests only something that is visualized, an image is the recreation through language of *any* experience perceived directly through the senses. For example, Tennyson's "The Eagle" (page 89) is composed of striking visual images. The feelings of fear and of mourning in Emily Dickinson's poems are also images. In "Pitcher" (page 75) we feel the motion of pitching.

internal rhyme A pattern in which a word or words within a line rhyme with the word that ends it. Poets may also employ internal rhyme at irregular intervals over many lines. The verbs in Theodore Roethke's poem "Child on Top of a Greenhouse" (page 81) create the effect of internal rhyme.

irony In general, a tone or figure of speech in which there is a discrepancy—(a striking difference or contradiction)—between what is expressed and what is meant or expected. Irony may be used to achieve a powerful effect indirectly. In satire, for example, it may be used to ridicule or criticize. Stephen Crane's poem "Do Not Weep, Maiden, for War Is Kind" (page 88) is intensely ironic, both in the stanzas apparently seeking to comfort those whose lovers, fathers, and sons have died and in the contrasting stanzas of apparent celebration of the glories of war. We also speak of *dramatic irony* in fiction in which the reader understands more than the characters do. Ring Lardner's short story "Haircut" is an excellent example.

lyric A general term used to describe poems that are relatively brief and expressed in the voice of a single *speaker* (narrative voice). Lyric poems express a powerful emotion revealed in a significant experience or observation. (See discussion on page 78.)

metaphor A form of analogy. Through metaphor, a poet discovers and expresses a similarity between dissimilar things. The poet use metaphors to imaginatively find common qualities between things we would not normally or literally compare. As a figure of speech, metaphor is said to be implicit or indirect. This contrasts to *simile* (see page 98), where the comparison is expressed directly. In his final soliloquy, Macbeth uses a series of metaphors to express the meaninglessness of his own life: "Life's but a walking shadow, a poor player . . . it is a tale told by an idiot . . . ."

meter and **rhythm**   Rhythm refers to the pattern of movement in a poem. As music has rhythm, so does poetry. Meter refers to specific patterns of stressed and unstressed syllables. See *iambic pentameter.*

ode   A meditation or celebration of a specific subject. Traditional odes addressed "elevated" ideas and were composed in elaborate stanza forms. Keats's "Ode to a Nightingale" and "Ode to Autumn" are particularly fine examples. Modern odes may address subjects either serious or personal. One well-known contemporary ode is Pablo Neruda's "Ode to My Socks."

onomatopoeia   The use of words whose sound reflects their sense. "Buzz," "hiss," and "moan" are common examples. Shakespeare's Sonnet 30 shows how the sounds and rhythm of whole lines may be onomatopoetic.

oxymoron   Closely related to *paradox,* oxymoron is a figure of speech in which two contradictory or sharply contrasting terms are paired for emphasis or ironic effect. Among students' favorite examples are "jumbo shrimp" and "army intelligence." Poets have written of the "wise fool," a "joyful sadness," or an "eloquent silence."

paradox   An expression, concept, or situation whose literal statement is contradictory, yet which makes a truthful and meaningful observation. Consider the widely used expression "less is more," for example. Shakespeare's play *Macbeth* opens with a series of paradoxes to establish the moral atmosphere in which "foul is fair." John Donne's famous poem "Death Be Not Proud" ends with the paradox "Death thou shalt die," and the title of Robert Penn Warren's poem "Old Photograph of the Future" is a paradox.

personification   A form of metaphor or simile in which nonhuman things—objects, plants and animals, forces of nature, abstract ideas—are given human qualities; for example, "The half-grown chrysanthemums staring up like accusers" (Roethke, page 81), "the walking sun/that poised an eye on me from its high floor" (Hall, page 81), "Time . . . the thief of youth" (Milton), and "Blow winds, and crack your cheeks! Rage! Blow!" (Shakespeare).

prose poem   This form appears on the page in the sentences and paragraphs of prose yet its effect is achieved through rhythm, images, and patterns of sound associated with poetry.

quatrain   Stanza of four lines. The quatrain is the most commonly used stanza form in English poetry. Quatrains may be rhymed, *abab, aabb, abba,* for example, or they may be unrhymed. The sonnets of Shakespeare (pages 82–83), the poem by Laurence Binyon (page 77), "Old Photograph of the Future" (page 79), and "The Sleeping Giant" (page 81) are also composed in quatrains.

rhyme In general, any repetition of identical or similar sounds among words that are close enough together to form an audible pattern. Rhyme is most evident when it occurs at the ends of lines of metrical verse. The *quatrains* of Shakespeare's Sonnet 55 (pages 83–84) have alternating rhyme as do those of Robert Penn Warren's poem "Old Photograph of the Future" (page 79).

rhyme scheme A regular pattern of end rhyme in a poem. The rhyme scheme in Shakespeare's sonnets, for example, is *abab/cdcd/efef/gg*.

satire A form or style that uses elements of irony, ridicule, exaggeration, understatement, sarcasm, humor, or absurdity to criticize human behavior or a society. All satire is *ironic* (see page 96) in that meaning or theme is conveyed in the discrepancy between what is said and what is meant, between what is and what should be, between what appears and what truly is. While satire is often entertaining, its purpose is serious and meant to provoke thought or judgment. The verse of Alexander Pope is often extended satire, and many poems by e. e. cummings are satiric.

simile An expression that is a direct comparison of two things. It uses such words as *like, as, as if, seems, appears*. For instance: "A line of elms plunging and tossing like horses" (Theodore Roethke); "Mind in its purest play is like some bat" (Richard Wilbur); "I wandered lonely as a cloud" (William Wordsworth).

soliloquy A form of monologue found most often in drama. It differs from a dramatic monologue in that the speaker is alone, revealing thoughts and feelings to or for oneself that are intentionally unheard by other characters. In Shakespeare's plays, for example, the principal characters' reflections on how to act or questions of conscience are revealed in their soliloquies. Hamlet's "To be, or not to be . . ." is probably the most famous dramatic soliloquy in English.

sonnet A poem of fourteen lines in *iambic pentameter* that may be composed of different patterns of stanzas and rhyme schemes. The most common forms are the English, or Shakespearean, sonnet, which consists of three quatrains and a closing couplet, and the Italian sonnet, which consists of an *octave* of eight lines and a *sestet* of six lines.

speaker The narrative voice in a poem. Also, the character who speaks in a *dramatic monologue*. The poems "The Sleeping Giant" and "Old Photograph of the Future" have distinctive speakers who are also the central characters in the dramatic experience of the poem.

stanza The grouping of lines within a poem. A stanza provides the basic organization and development of ideas, much as a paragraph does in an essay. Many stanza patterns have a fixed number of lines and a regular pattern of rhyme; the poems of Robert Penn Warren (page 79) and Donald Hall (page 81) are good examples. Poets, however, often create stanzas of varying length and form within a single poem. A stanza that ends with a period, completing an idea or image, is considered "closed," while a stanza that ends with a comma or with no punctuation, is called "open," indicating that there should be very little pause in the movement from one stanza to another. Roethke's poem "Child on Top of a Greenhouse" (page 81) is an example of a poem composed in a single stanza.

symbol Most generally, anything that stands for or suggests something else. Language itself is symbolic; sounds and abstract written forms may stand for almost any human thought or experience. Symbols are real objects and *concrete* images that lead us to think about what is suggested. Symbols organize a wide variety of ideas into single acts of understanding. They embody not single "meanings" but suggest whole areas of meaning.

tone The attitude or feeling of the speaker toward the subject. Tone may also refer to the dominant mood of a poem. (See discussion of *tone* on page 86.)

understatement Expression in which something is presented as less important or significant than it really is. The first and third stanzas of Stephen Crane's "Do Not Weep, Maiden" (page 88) ironically understate the horror of death in battle and the loss for those who mourn. Understatement is often used for humorous, *satiric,* or *ironic* effect. Much of the satire in *Huckleberry Finn* stems from Huck's naive and understated observations. One particular form of understatement, actually a double negative, includes such expressions as "I was not uninterested," which really means "I was interested," or "He was not without imagination," which really means "He had some imagination."

Chapter 6

WRITING ABOUT LITERATURE: A GENERAL REVIEW

For most students, writing papers and responding to essay questions on exams are the most challenging aspects of their course work. Writing requires that you articulate and focus your understanding of what you read. Like all good writing, writing about literature not only demonstrates to others what you understand and think but also obliges you to clarify *for yourself* what you truly know. That process is sometimes hard, but it is worthwhile. Writing is essential to developing your critical reading and thinking skills.

TOPICS FOR LITERARY ESSAYS

Much of your writing about literature is done in response to assignments and exam questions. Students are also urged to maintain notes and journals. For essays, instructors may assign very specific topics, or they may offer general subjects that require you to develop your own topic and controlling idea.

In your literature courses and exams you will find that the majority of the questions focus on **character**. Because essay topics may apply to many works of nonfiction you read—personal essay, memoir, and autobiography in particular—the term *character* should be understood to refer to any persons, not exclusively to those of fiction and drama.

As you think about characters in the literature you read, keep the following questions in mind: What are a character's values and motives? beliefs and principles? moral qualities? strengths and weaknesses? illusions or delusions? For what is a character searching? striving? devoting his or her life? What significant decisions and actions does a character take? What are the consequences of those decisions and actions? To what extent does a character "succeed" or "fail"? understand or fail to understand?

Literature also seeks to account for the forces outside individuals, that is, the external forces that influence the direction and outcome of their lives. These "forces" range from those of nature and history to the demands of family, community, and society. The response of individuals to inner and outer forces is what literature considers and dramatizes. (See Chapters 4 and 5 for discussions of reading literature and for glossaries of important terms and techniques.)

Developing the Topic

TOPIC AND FOCUS

As any essay must, your paper must have a clear purpose, a controlling idea; moreover, the development of the purpose must be convincing to the reader. *Focus* means in writing, as it does in a photograph, that the subject is clear! We can see it, even recognize it. And, if the photographer/writer has "framed" the material properly, we can perceive the relationship of the background details to the principal subject. When you take a picture of your best friend at camp, or of the place you most want to remember from a vacation trip, you keep the lens of your camera directed at what is most important—not at the tree next to your friend, not at the bus that took you to Niagara Falls.

SELECTION OF SIGNIFICANT DETAILS

One of the most widely observed characteristics of short stories is that they are very selective in detail. The author of a short story includes only those elements of setting, character, and plot that reveal the significance of the central incident. In "The Lottery," for example, we do not know when the story takes place, we do not even know the name of the town or where it is located, and we know little about the lives of individual characters. Those details are not *significant*—they do not matter—to the story Shirley Jackson tells; comparable details *are* significant in "Haircut," and, therefore, Ring Lardner includes them.

To achieve focus in your essays about works of literature, you must exercise the same rigorous process of selection. However interesting you may find a particular incident or aspect of a character, do not include those details if they do not directly explain or clarify your topic.

DEVELOPING THE TOPIC

Many of the common methods of developing arguments are discussed in Chapter 4—Reading Prose. Here are some of those methods as they might be used to develop essays on works of literature:

Comparison/Contrast

Although *compare* means to identify similarities, and *contrast* means to identify differences, the term *comparison* is often used for a discussion that examines both similarities and differences among the items being compared. This is one of the most useful approaches, and one of the most commonly used, because the process of comparing helps sharpen thought. To compose a meaningful comparison, the writer must understand the objects of comparison in detail.

Any literary aspect found in two or more works may serve as a basis for comparison. For example, one could compare the effective use of first-person narration in *The Great Gatsby* and *Ethan Frome,* or in *The Catcher in the Rye* and *Huckleberry Finn.* Although the circumstances of their lives are vastly different, the fact that both Ethan Frome and Jay Gatsby fail to achieve what they most desire—a life with the women they love—offers a rich possibility for comparison and contrast. "Haircut" and "The Lottery" share common elements of setting and irony. *Othello* and *Romeo and Juliet* have a common theme—the tragic destruction of great love.

Comparison may, of course, focus on much narrower topics and be confined to a single work. The best way to develop notes for a comparison is first to list the aspects common to the items under comparison, then to list for each all the specific details that differentiate them. Finally, as you do in preparation for any essay, you select those that are most significant.

Analysis

Analysis requires detailed examination of a particular aspect of a literary work. The purpose of an analytic paper is to show the significance of that aspect to the meaning of the work as a whole. Examples of analytic topics include the use of time in Miller's *Death of a Salesman,* the imagery of light and dark in *Othello,* and the extended metaphor in Emily Dickinson's poem "I Taste a Liquor Never Brewed."

Classification

Classification organizes objects, people, and other living things into categories; it is a process of identifying and relating. In discussions of literature, classification may be an important part of an essay, or it may constitute a topic in its own right. An essay in which the writer shows how a particular work exemplifies a **genre** is considered classification: *The Scarlet Letter* as a **romance**; Shakespeare's *Macbeth* as Elizabethan **tragedy**; Dreiser's *Sister Carrie* as **naturalism**.

Cause and Effect

Many of the topics for writing and discussion of literature may be developed by showing how circumstances or actions have direct and observable consequences. Demonstrating actual cause and effect, however, requires careful thinking and attention to detail. Cause and effect are more easily demonstrated in logic and chemistry than in human experience.

Literary topics that focus on **plot** often lend themselves to cause and effect development because essentially any plot is built on cause and effect: specific circumstances, actions, or decisions lead to others and have consequences in the lives of the characters. Plot summary alone does *not* establish cause and effect; it simply relates "what happened." Cause-and-effect argument requires the writer to show how and why incidents are related.

Exemplification

Whenever you cite specific details to support a thesis, and when you choose the works you will use to answer the literature question in Part B of Session Two, you are using exemplification. *To exemplify* means to illustrate the meaning of a general concept through use of specific examples. This method is fundamental to the development of nearly any essay or literary topic.

LOOKING AT KEY TERMS IN LITERATURE QUESTIONS

identify   To name and also to characterize and to place in context; sometimes you may be required to state the significance of what you are identifying. Often identification includes linking characters to the theme or experience that serves as the topic.

describe   To give the essential characteristics of a person, object, or experience. If you are asked to describe, your choice of details or characteristics must reveal your understanding of a larger question. Why are these details relevant to the topic? Description alone will not be the focus of a literature topic.

explain/show/discuss   These terms indicate the most important parts of a question, which will be developed in the body of an essay. Once you have identified and described your subject, you must interpret and demonstrate the significance of your examples and details; you must offer evidence, using specific references, to support your argument.

USING FLUENT AND PRECISE LANGUAGE

Effective writing is characterized by interesting and vivid language, and "use of precise and engaging language" is among the criteria for evaluation of Regents essays. From the list of what writers *do,* here are some terms to help you articulate your observations about creation of plot:

> *convey, create, delineate, depict, describe, dramatize, foreshadow, illustrate, invent, portray, present, recreate, reveal, select, shock, show, symbolize*

The following terms offer precision and variety in discussing details of a plot:

> *affair, circumstance, climax, development, episode, event, experience, incident, instance, juncture, moment, occasion, occurrence, opportunity, scene, situation*

Terms useful in referring to *character* include:

> *disposition, identity, individuality, makeup, mettle, nature, persona, personality, self, spirit, temperament*

Finally, here is a list of adjectives collected by students to describe some of the many relationships and attitudes among characters in literature (and in our own lives!):

> *admiring, affectionate, bitter, cautious, compassionate, curious, deceitful, disapproving, disdainful, dishonest, distant, envious, false, fearful, generous, hostile, indifferent, loving, optimistic, reluctant, resentful, reserved, respectful, scornful, sincere, skeptical, stern, suspicious, sympathetic, treacherous, watchful*

(See also Using Synonymies to Enhance Your Writing in Chapter 7.)

CHOOSING YOUR OWN TOPIC: REPRESENTATIVE LITERARY SUBJECTS AND THEMES

In many high school and college literature courses, students must select their own topics for writing. The subjects of literature are as varied as human experience itself, and below are some of the many themes authors dramatize. You will encounter these as topics in class discussion and as topics for essays and examination questions. These topics may, of course, serve for discussion of more than one work in an essay.

Topics That Focus on Character

- In many works of literature, an important theme is an **individual's achievement of self-knowledge as a result of undergoing an ordeal**. This self-knowledge may be a recognition of the individual's own strengths, weaknesses, values, prejudices, aspirations, or fears. Identify the individual and the self-knowledge he or she achieves. Using specific references from the work, explain how the ordeal led the individual to the self-knowledge.
- **Nature** can have different effects on different people. It can defeat someone with its power; it can inspire someone with its beauty. Identify the character; using specific references, show how he or she was either defeated or inspired by nature.
- It has been said that to live with **fear** and not be overcome by it is the final **test of maturity**. Explain what fear a character lives with; show how the character "passes" or "fails" the test of maturity on the basis of his or her response to that fear.
- A commonly held belief is that **suffering strengthens an individual's character**. The suffering can be physical, mental, or emotional. Identify the individual; describe the nature of the suffering; explain how the suffering did or did not strengthen the individual's character.
- Sometimes a person **struggles to achieve a goal** only to discover that, once the goal is achieved, the results are not what was expected.
- In many works of literature there are characters who are **troubled by injustice** in society, such as poverty, discrimination, or lawlessness, and **who try to correct** the injustice. Identify the character and the injustice, explain what actions the character takes; discuss whether or not the efforts are successful.
- In many works, characters who love one another or share a special friendship often face **obstacles to their relationship**. Sometimes characters overcome the obstacle; sometimes they are defeated by it. Identify the characters and the obstacle; explain how the characters overcome or are defeated by the obstacle; discuss the effect this outcome (the success or failure, not the obstacle) has on the relationship.
- In many works of literature, **a character sacrifices something of value** in order to achieve something of greater value.
- Sometimes a character faces a **conflict between his or her conscience** and the standards of behavior expected by others. Identify the character; explain the specific nature of the conflict; discuss how the character was affected by this conflict.
- In many works of literature, a character reaches a **major turning point** in his or her life. From that point onward, the character undergoes a significant change.
- Characters in works of literature frequently **learn about life or themselves** by taking risks.

- The phrase **"rite of passage"** describes a situation in which a young person is faced with an experience that results in his or her becoming mature. Explain the experience; discuss how the young person matures as a result of the way in which he or she deals with the experience.
- In many works of literature, characters are **challenged by unfamiliar environments**. Show how the character was or was not successful in meeting the challenge.
- Some individuals in literature **try to do what they believe is right**, even though they face opposition.
- In some works of literature, an important character **makes a mistake that advances the reader's understanding of that individual**.
- Confusion, danger, or tragedy sometimes results when **one character misunderstands the words or actions of another character**.
- In many works of literature, a character **struggles against circumstances that seem to be beyond his or her control**. Sometimes the character is victorious, sometimes not.

Topics That Focus on Literary Elements and Techniques

While topics that focus on character may be the most common in literature courses or on exams, various literary elements also provide topics for essays. The AP literature exam, for example, often features a question based on a literary element or technique.

- Some authors are especially successful at creating **a memorable visual image** that contributes to the reader's understanding of a work. Identify the image and its importance; show how the image contributes to the meaning of the work.
- In many works of literature, the **setting** contributes to the reader's understanding of the central conflict in the plot. Describe the setting; show how it contributes to the reader's understanding of the conflict on which the plot hinges.
- Authors often create a **predominant mood** in a work of literature. Using specific references, discuss incidents that convey that mood and explain the importance of mood to the work.
- Authors sometimes use **foreshadowing** to help develop the plot of a work. Foreshadowing usually takes the form of incidents that seem to be unimportant at first, but take on added significance later. Discuss examples of foreshadowing and show how they contribute to the overall effect and meaning of the work.
- A work of literature may be defined as **a classic** because it promotes deep insight into human behavior, presents a universal theme, or uses

language in an exceptional way. Show how a particular work meets the above definition of the term *classic*.
- Through their work, some **authors reveal their acceptance or rejection of values** held by society. Identify the value; state whether the author accepts or rejects it; using specific references, show how the author reveals his or her attitude toward that value.
- In literature, **symbols** are used to reinforce the central idea or to represent characters. Using specific references, explain how the symbol in a particular work enriches the reader's understanding of either the central idea or a character.
- The **narrative point of view** is significant to the effect and meaning of a literary work. Illustrate the truth of this statement by specific references to a work of literature.

AUDIENCE AND LITERATURE ESSAYS

Most teachers mention audience in the assignments they give; if it is not clear for whom you are writing, it is a good idea to ask before you complete an assignment. For most outside examinations, including the Regents, assume that you are writing for a reader who is familiar with the works of literature but who has not considered the topic; background discussion and *detailed* explanation of plot are not needed.

A NOTE ON CONCLUSIONS

No essay, however brief, should simply stop. Even if you run out of time or things to say, try not to telegraph that information to the reader. A conclusion must come back to the topic, must complete the discussion, in a way that leaves the reader feeling convinced by what you have written. On examinations, most students close with a brief, summative conclusion that highlights the relationship of the literary work or works to the topic or restates the thesis of the essay. Even if the reader of a short essay does not really *need* the conclusion to appreciate your argument, the obligation to compose a conclusion keeps you focused on the topic.

Student writers are urged to avoid the following in their conclusions: the expression "what this paper has shown . . ." or "As you can see . . ."; a reminder that Shakespeare was a great playwright or that Mark Twain was an important figure in American literature; a confession that the reader *really* liked or did not like a particular work. Above all, the conclusion is not the place to introduce a new topic or tack on an idea that properly belongs in the body of the essay.

Chapter 7

WRITING ON DEMAND

Writing has always been an important part of a student's education as well as an essential skill for a successful professional life. The National Commission on Writing is only one of the more recent initiatives in American education to emphasize the importance of good writing among our students. American colleges and universities also seek independent assessment of students' writing skills as part of the admissions process. In this chapter you will find some guidelines for effective writing on demand.

WRITING TO INFORM OR PERSUADE

A General Review

Much of the work you do in high school or college requires writing to demonstrate your ability to understand, analyze, and organize information and ideas. On exams and essays for science and social studies courses, as well as in English and writing courses, you are expected to do many of the following:

- Tell your audience (readers) what they need to know
- Use specific, accurate, and relevant information
- Use a tone and level of language appropriate for the task and audience
- Organize your ideas in a logical and coherent manner
- Follow the conventions of standard written English

These guidelines are also reminders of what your teachers mean when they direct you to compose a "well-written essay" on a given topic.

Personal Narrative

Here is an example of an informal essay written in response to a specific task. It is a good example of what is meant by **tone and level of language** appropriate for the audience. The essay is also organized in a logical and coherent manner.

Writing to Inform or Persuade

> **Task:** A representative of a middle school in your district has invited you to speak at the middle school graduation ceremonies on the topic "Getting Off to a Good Start in High School." Write a brief speech that you would give to the students, stating your recommendations for a successful start in high school. Use specific reasons, examples, or details to support your recommendations.

Sample Student Response

Not so long ago, I too was sitting where you are now, thinking and worrying about what my life in high school would be like. Will I stand out? Will I make friends? How should I approach people? Will my classes be too difficult? Will I be able to cope with the stress? These questions kept badgering me throughout the summer before ninth grade. I was especially nervous about starting school because I had just moved to a new neighborhood and did not know a single person.

By the end of the summer, the thought that especially frustrated me was that I would have no one to eat lunch with on the first day of school. This does not seem like such a big deal but it bothered me a lot. I knew that at the high school people went out to eat with a group of friends. I had no one to go out with. I told myself that I still had a week before school started and did not need to worry.

The first day of school finally arrived. As I neared the high school, I felt helpless and lonely. I wanted to plead with my mom to turn the car around and go back home. But I reluctantly got out of the car and slowly approached the front entrance of the school.

Luckily, I found my first class and quickly took a seat in the front. I felt as if all eyes were on me. The new kid. The freak. While everyone was talking and laughing about their summer, I sat in my seat trying to look as though I was busy fiddling with my notebook. I couldn't wait to get out of the classroom. I wanted to run home and hide, for this was one of the most difficult experiences of my life.

Things started to look better around fifth period. I got up the courage and started talking to people. I even went out to lunch with a few girls and had a comfortable time. I was not totally relaxed but knew that I would adapt and soon make more friends.

I have just finished my junior year in high school. I have many friends and am very happy in my school. I will be a senior this coming September and expect to experience new ideas and challenges. I am now starting to think about what I want to do with my life and what colleges I might want to attend. Soon I will be leaving high school and will again feel the nervousness and anxiety that all of you are going through in preparing for high school. I guess what we are experiencing is not trepidation but life, and what to expect in the future. You may be scared now, but be confident that you will overcome those fears and the experiences will only make you stronger.

Analysis

Although this speech is more a personal narrative than a list of recommendations, the writer/speaker clearly understands the purpose of the task and understands her audience:
"Not so long ago, I too was sitting where you are now. . . ." The diction is informal, the tone is conversational, and first-person narrative is highly appropriate for the occasion.

The theme is established in the opening sentence, but the speaker's main point is not stated until the very end: "You may be scared now, but . . . you will overcome those fears . . . and [be] stronger." She leads her audience to this conclusion by narrating her own feelings and experiences, starting with a series of "fears" she knows her listeners have.
The narrative covers a period of many weeks, but it is made coherent by specific references to time: "throughout the summer . . . by the end of summer . . . on the first day of school . . . my first class . . . around fifth period . . . lunch." She also uses a reference to time to come back to the present and bring the speech to a close: "I have just finished my junior year. . . ."

The ideas are well expressed; and the paragraph in which the writer describes what it was like to sit in her first class — "The new kid." "The freak." — pretending to be busy with her notebook is especially vivid and convincing. We also trust the speaker when she tells us that she had "a comfortable time" at lunch but that she "was not totally relaxed" either. If she had claimed that after lunch all her fears had disappeared, we would not believe her. This is also a good example of what is meant by honesty in writing: it rings true in our ears. This piece would be even better if the writer had included more specific examples of how she overcame her fears.

Writing to Inform or Persuade

Persuasive Writing

Here are two examples of what is called persuasive writing, pieces that develop and support an opinion on a particular topic. In contrast to the essay of argument in Part 2 of the Regents ELA exam, which must be based on evidence from given sources, these essays are developed with the writer's own reasoning and examples. Note what makes each a successful argument.

Task: The students in your science class have been invited to submit essays on topics of current interest or controversy for possible publication on the Op-Ed page of the school newspaper.

Sample Student Response

Using Animals for Scientific Research

The question of whether or not to use animals as subjects for scientific research is a difficult one. Those in opposition claim that using animals in research is inhumane, while those holding a diametrically opposing view maintain that it is a necessary evil whose long-term benefits far outweigh the sacrifice of a handful of animals. I am an ardent supporter of the latter view. I feel that the use of animals is justified by the benefits that are reaped by all of mankind, and that halting the use of animals as subjects would greatly impede advancements in the field of medicine.

One example of the tremendous benefits that animal research can bring about is the case of the discovery of insulin by Dr. William Banting and his assistant, Charles Best. Before this amazing discovery, diabetes mellitus was a devastating and inevitably fatal disease. The extent of treatment that doctors could offer afflicted patients was a starvation diet, which prolonged life only for a short time and caused the obviously detrimental and painful effects of virtual starvation.

When Dr. Banting came up with a unique idea that linked the cause of the disease to a hormonal secretion of the pancreas, a potential way to control this deadly disease arose. But the idea had to be tested and proven successful before it could be offered to human patients. Dr. Banting proceeded with his experiments, using fifteen dogs as his subjects. Although several of the dogs did die as a result of the experiment, the benefits that society gained because of the tests are infinitely greater. If those opposed to utilizing animals in testing had their way, the concept would have died prematurely because there would have been no way to test the idea. Fortunately for the field of science and for the millions of diabetics that have lived in the past few decades, Dr. Banting was able to find this treatment.

As a diabetic, I am greatly indebted to the work of Dr. Banting and the studies he conducted using animals as subjects. Today, I am not only alive, but healthy and active. I cannot help but be a supporter of animal testing because I owe my life to it. I understand how one may object to senseless cruelty to animals and the wasting of their lives worthlessly. But using animals strictly for scientific use is not "senseless cruelty" and it is clearly justified.

Analysis

This is a good example of a short essay of opinion because the student has chosen a subject that he could develop with expertise and compelling personal experience; it also demonstrates his skill in organizing and presenting an argument.

One of the most effective ways to approach a controversial topic is to "acknowledge the opposition." Indicate that you recognize, and even respect, the opposing view. This writer agrees that the question "is a difficult one," but goes on to say he is "an ardent supporter" of animal testing. Note that he skillfully saves his personal reasons for the end, first developing a factual but dramatic example of the benefits of testing for millions of people. Introducing his personal reasons earlier would have made the argument less persuasive because he would have appeared less objective. The conclusion is emotionally effective when he says, "I cannot help but be a supporter of animal testing because I owe my life to it." More importantly, the writer demonstrates skillful argument when he says, "I understand how one may object. . ." and closes with a distinction between scientific experiment and "senseless cruelty." This essay would be a good contribution to an Op-Ed page.

Task: The editor of your local newspaper has proposed that businesses that hire high school graduates pay them salaries in proportion to their grades from the last two years of high school; that is, the higher a graduate's grades for the last two years of high school, the higher the salary. Write a letter to the editor in which you state your opinion of the proposal. Use specific reasons, examples, or details.

Sample Student Response

I vehemently oppose the proposal that graduates be paid salaries in proportion to their grades for the last two years of high school.

First, grades should not affect the equal opportunity of all workers to receive the same paycheck for the same work. It must be taken into account that there are many factors that influence a student's grades in high school. For example, one student may have a harder course load than another student with higher grades. It is unfair to compare grades from different level classes. Perhaps a student does not do well on tests, but is an excellent student in class. Participation and the ability to speak one's mind are very beneficial in a career, yet that is not reflected by grades. Furthermore, if a student has an inborn proficiency in a subject (and gets good grades), it is unfair to assume that that student works hard to achieve his or her scores. An average student works harder and may still not get the same scores. Hard work and dedication are important factors in choosing an employee, but these factors cannot always be relayed by a report card.

There are other factors besides grades that play a role in whether a student is right for a job. The applicant may have experience in the field of interest, but the proposed system would not take this into account. Perhaps a student has been a volunteer or has been active in clubs and organizations outside of school. By looking at his or her track record with reference to involvement in organizations, the student's ability to follow through would be noted. This is an important factor to take into account when hiring a worker.

Also, grades do not indicate strength of personal character, an important determinant in the selection of an employee. One must not make the generalization that a student with good grades is also a good person, and that a student with poor grades is not a good person. Only a personal interview can give the employer some sense of personal character of the worker. Positive interactions with other workers are vital to the success of a business.

Finally, by locking in different salaries and pay rates based on high school grades, the employer is creating unnecessary competition and tension in the workplace. A worker with a lower salary may not work as hard, as a result. The worker with the lower salary might be treated differently, or unfairly, by the employer by not being encouraged to work up to potential.

Thank you for your attention to this matter. Perhaps now an employee will be viewed as a person, and not as a report card. Everyone deserves a fair chance.

> **Analysis**
>
> This essay would receive a relatively good evaluation because it expresses a clear and thoughtful opinion, it is well organized, and it is excellent in its development; on the other hand, the essay is not always focused on the specific topic. The letter begins well, with a clear statement of position, and the first section makes several important points about the limited significance of grades. Note, however, that the argument shifts from a discussion of how workers should be paid to how they should be hired in the first place. The second section makes several good points, but it too refers to *hiring* workers. The writer comes back to the topic of differentiated pay only in the third full paragraph.
>
> If the writer had followed her statement of opinion with a *because* statement and a summary of her main points, she could have established the focus needed. This writer clearly took time to gather good examples and reasons, but she did not always show how they related to the topic. The task directed the student to write a letter to an editor and to write *the body of the letter only*, but such letters are really essays of argument and must have focus and coherence to be effective. Composing "letters" of this kind is a very good way to practice writing persuasive essays.

WRITING FROM A PROMPT

On many examinations and in high school or college courses, you will encounter the term *prompt*. This term is used to refer in general to any set of directions for a writing task. In the theater, the prompter is the one who gives an actor or singer in danger of forgetting his or her lines the phrase that he or she needs to remember to continue the performance. In writing, a prompt serves to recall ideas or stimulate discussion. A prompt is also meant to inspire, or even provoke. A prompt may be in the form of a task and directions, as in the examples above, or it may be in the form of a quote or even a photograph—anything that offers the writer a subject and a reason to produce a piece of writing.

Here are two examples of persuasive writing where the prompt was in the form of a quote only; the writers had to establish controlling ideas and develop the examples on their own.

"All the World's a Stage"

William Shakespeare once wrote, "all the world's a stage and all the people players . . ." This well-known phrase has stuck in people's minds through time because theater is a prominent medium in society; whether it's an amphitheater in ancient Rome or Broadway in New York City, crowds of people are drawn to the theater every day.

The theater appeals to people for many different reasons. Some attend the theater to escape from the harsh realities of life for a little while. While sitting in a dark auditorium and watching trials and disputes played by live actors in front of you, it is very easy to forget your own problems. Other people find the theater simply entertaining. Plays and musicals involve audiences because they stimulate the senses and the mind. And some people go to the theater as a social event.

But theater is not only something to be watched. For many people, theater is their life. Every day, more and more people are becoming actors and actresses in hopes of becoming rich and famous. And for some people, that dream actually comes true. Many actors join the world of theater for their love of expressing themselves through their bodies, the tools of the trade. Nothing can compare to that adrenaline rush an actor gets just before he or she steps on stage in front of hundreds of people who all have their eyes focused on him or her, and the applause of an audience is all the gratitude some actors need to feel appreciated.

Many people don't realize that theater goes beyond the actors though, and that is where they are deceived. Sometimes the technical aspect of a production is more interesting than the acting is. A Broadway production can have a set with more complicated plans than a skyscraper building. Shows like "Phantom of the Opera" can have over twenty major trap doors and more than ninety minor ones. There are dozens of people in charge of sound, lighting, props, and costumes that no one ever sees or thinks about when sitting in the audience. There is just that wonderful feeling that these things just magically happen; no one seems to be responsible.

The theater is an art that will live on for a long time to come, as long as people take the time to support it. The magic of a show that enthralls most viewers, though, is a culmination of the hard work, time, and dedication of many people who never get credit for their actions. But Shakespeare was right because, for many people in the theater, all the world _is_ a stage.

"All the World's a Stage"

All the world is indeed a stage. And we are the performers. Everything we do in life is a production, and we must constantly perform our best because, in life, there are no rehearsals. Each of us performs on a separate stage, some for a larger audience than others. But each performance, regardless of the size of the audience, is of equal importance, and each performer must meet the standard of life's most important critic—himself.

As a high school student, I often find that there exists much pressure to perform: pressure to perform academically, pressure to perform in sports, pressure to perform in social situations, and countless others. Furthermore, there are many individuals for whom I constantly must perform. At this juncture in life, parents, teachers, friends, and others comprise what I often perceive as an overwhelmingly large audience, which is sometimes overly critical.

As I grow older, I am learning to accept new responsibilities, and I find that my role in life is changing. Often in life, we cannot constantly adhere to a routine performance; sometimes we must improvise. The improvisation, or adjustment to new responsibility, is often difficult though of critical importance to a successful production. In life, I have come to expect the unexpected and have done my best to deal with new situations. As performers, we must not allow tragedy, depression, and self-doubt to unnerve us. Instead, we must cope, adjust, and continue to perform.

Throughout my performance I have received evaluation from many critics, some of which I have taken better than others. No matter how many critics we have, we should remind ourselves that <u>we</u> are our most important critics, for of life's performance we will make the ultimate evaluation. Even though all the world's a stage, each of us need be concerned with only one performance.

> **Analysis**
>
> The first essay stumbles at the beginning: The introduction has a central idea, but it is not well expressed and there is no coherence in the reference to ancient Rome. This essay reads like a first draft, and perhaps the writer was pressed for time. It would be improved not only in revision of the opening paragraph but also in the transitions. This writer begins too many sentences with *and* or *but*, and the language is not always fluent or precise. The writer, however, does establish organization and some unity in the opening of the second paragraph: "The theater appeals to people for many different reasons."
>
> The writer also shows skill in development by moving from the role of theater for audiences to its importance for participants. The concluding sentence also works well because it relates the major part of the essay to a fresh meaning of the quote. In this case, a good conclusion rescues an essay with a weak introduction.
>
> The second essay is effective because of the exceptional way in which the writer developed the topic as an extended metaphor. The essay is brief, but it is absolutely focused; every detail supports the central idea, the comparison of one's life to a dramatic performance. The writer has maintained a consistent point of view and has developed the topic in a creative way.

EVALUATING COMPOSITION

Every student has seen on a paper or an essay test the comment "develop this point more." The Regents rubric on page 229 is a reminder that one of the most important criteria in evaluating essays for class or for an exam is the extent to which <u>the topic has been developed</u> to achieve the writer's purpose. Simply to announce a subject and say that you have thoughts on that subject is not enough.

For any topic, the student must show skill in establishing a central idea and in creating an effective way to develop it. All compositions must be unified and expressed in fluent and precise language, and they must follow the conventions of standard written English. (See Guide to Standard Written English beginning on page 161.)

PREPARING FOR ESSAY EXAMS

Nearly all the writing you have done, both personal and for school, serves as preparation. Just as an athlete or musician practices regularly in order to have the skills to draw on in a performance, high school students are developing their skills whenever they compose written responses. Reflect on what you know your strengths and weaknesses are. To review, go over the essays and exams you have written in high school; note what is consistently strong and what needs revision; review carefully your teachers' comments.

Good writers are also readers. Read good writing, observe what makes it effective, emulate it, and imitate for practice what you admire. In serious magazines and in the editorial pages, letters to the editor, and Op-Ed sections of newspapers you can often find good essays of argument on current topics. (See also Recommended Reading on page 215 for suggested works and authors of nonfiction.)

To succeed in any assigned task, you need to know what is expected and how you will be evaluated. Review the Regents exam scoring guides, which describe the criteria for scoring the written responses.

WRITING ON TIMED EXAMINATIONS

If you are writing an essay for an examination, you do not have time for extensive preparation, but you can learn to condense the kind of thinking and notetaking you do for course assignments into a process for planning an examination response. How to begin?

Gather Your Ideas

First, be sure you understand the task or the meaning of the topic. One way to do that is to rephrase the question into a topic assertion. This may not be original, but if a restatement of the question serves as a topic sentence for your introduction and gets you started—use it! You may not use such statements in your final essay, but the fact that you can express them for yourself means you understand what the question expects or that you have something to say about the topic

If you are creating your own topic, be sure you know what you want to say about it. This may seem obvious, but only when you sketch or outline can you be sure you have sufficient material for an essay. Use the brainstorming techniques you have learned in class or workshops. For example, if you have practiced "freewriting" in the past or have written journal entries as a way of developing ideas, take a few minutes to address the topic in that way, without regard to organization or "getting it absolutely right." Similarly, you can just note down in words or phrases everything the prompt brings to mind. It is better to note more ideas than you can use than to discover after twenty-five minutes that you have too few.

Organize

Second, take a few minutes to make a plan or outline. All essay writing requires this step. Do not leave it out, even on the SAT, in which you have only 25 minutes for the essay. The outline may consist of only phrases or a brief list to remind you of the points you want to make. Consider possible lines of argument. That is, answer for yourself the questions "How can I prove that? What information in the text (if given) can I quote or paraphrase as evidence? How can I show or persuade someone who is interested in what I have to say? What do I know or believe that will make my discussion convincing?" Finally, decide on the order that is best: chronological? sequence of cause and effect? order of importance or intensity? (Common methods of developing ideas in essays are reviewed, with examples, in Reading Nonfiction, Chapter 4.)

Compose

The essays you write for the Regents exam and for the SAT are, of course, "tests." You are not being asked to demonstrate acquired knowledge so much as you are to demonstrate how well you can communicate in standard written English what you understand about the given subjects and texts or what you think about a particular issue. What is being assessed is your ability to articulate a controlling idea and support it with reasons and appropriate examples. On the Regents exam, you must also be able to work from given texts and write for clearly defined purposes and audiences.

Concentrate on good development—not a finished product. An essay that reveals critical thinking and coherence and effectively develops several appropriate examples or reasons with command of sentence variety and language will receive a high score even if it remains somewhat unfinished or lacks a formal conclusion. Remember, on the SAT optional essay you are writing what will be evaluated as a first draft. Regents essays are viewed as somewhat more "finished," but those too are understood to have been written in only one sitting.

Edit as You Go

The time you take in planning is also well spent because on-demand writing requires you to edit and revise as you compose your response. If you still make spelling errors in commonly used words, make a deliberate effort to look for those errors and correct them on the exams. A few neatly corrected spelling or usage errors are not only acceptable, they reveal the writer's ability to edit his or her own work. (See Chapter 9 on Grammar and Usage and Chapter 10 on Punctuation.)

USING SYNONYMIES TO ENHANCE YOUR WRITING

Included in the expectations for any well-written essay is use of language that is vivid and appropriate; the rubrics for scoring Regents essays include "use of original, fluent, and precise language." The term *synonymy* refers to words that can be grouped according to general meaning; that is, they all denote or describe a specific instance of a general concept. Reviewing and creating synonymies will help you develop the vivid and precise language characteristic of good writing. Below are some examples of synonymies for commonly used but often vague or overused expressions.

to cause
bring about	generate	originate	raise
create	give rise to	persuade	spawn
effect	incite	produce	
engender	invent	promote	
excite	lead to	provoke	

to change
adapt	develop	grow	revise
adjust	deviate	mature	rework
alter	differ	metamorphose	transform
amend	digress	modify	turn (into)
become	diverge	modulate	vary
convert	diversify	mutate	
correct	edit	progress	
depart	evolve	remake	

to look upon someone/something
analyze	discern	judge	scrutinize
appraise	dismiss	observe	stereotype
censure	distinguish	perceive	summarize
classify	esteem	ponder	typecast
conclude	evaluate	reckon	value
condemn	honor	regard	view
consider	hypothesize	review	watch
deem	infer	ruminate	

Using Synonymies to Enhance Your Writing

to look down upon someone/something

belittle	diminish	frown upon	ridicule
censure	discredit	have disdain for	scorn
condescend	disfavor	hold inferior	shame
condemn	disgrace	humiliate	shun
degrade	disparage	ignore	taunt
demote	disregard	jeer	vilify
depreciate	show disrespect	mock	
deride	embarrass	rebuke	
devalue	find fault with	reject	

bad

abhorrent	detrimental	inequitable	scandalous
atrocious	devilish	infamous	scurrilous
awful	dirty	inferior	shameless
base	disquieting	loathsome	sinful
belittling	evil	malevolent	sinister
blemished	false	malign	slanderous
calumnious	fiendish	marred	sour
catastrophic	foul	mean	spiteful
contemptible	fraudulent	merciless	spoiled
corrupt	grotesque	monstrous	squalid
counterfeit	hateful	nefarious	tasteless
criminal	heinous	negative	terrible
cruel	hellish	notorious	unethical
damaged	hideous	odious	unscrupulous
deceptive	horrible	ominous	vile
defective	horrid	perverse	villainous
defiled	horrific	putrid	wicked
delinquent	immoral	rotten	
depraved	imperfect	ruthless	
despicable	impish	scabrous	

effective

capable	dazzling	forceful	persuasive
cogent	dramatic	impressive	potent
commanding	effectual	influential	powerful
compelling	efficacious	lively	strong
convincing	emotional	moving	telling

caring
affectionate	devoted	giving	selfless
benevolent	doting	goodhearted	sympathetic
bountiful	empathetic	humane	tender
compassionate	empathic	kind	thoughtful
concerned	fond	loving	warm
courteous	generous	philanthropic	warmhearted

due to
as a consequence of	because of	from	on account of
as a result of	by reason of	in light of	resulting from
because	caused by	in view of	
	following from	induced by	

hard/difficult
arduous	fatiguing	intricate	strong
bitter	galling	labyrinthine	tiresome
challenging	grievous	mighty	toilsome
complex	grim	oppressive	tough
daunting	harsh	relentless	unattainable
demanding	Herculean	resistant	unbending
enigmatic	impenetrable	rigorous	uncompromising
esoteric	impossible	serious	unyielding
exacting	impregnable	severe	wearisome
exhausting	inflexible	sharp	
exigent	insurmountable	strenuous	

sad/depressing (depressed)
abject	dejected	forsaken	somber
aching	desolate	gloomy	sorrowful
aggrieved	despairing	joyless	tormenting
bereaved	disconsolate	lugubrious	tragic
bereft	discontent	melancholy	unhappy
bleak	distraught	miserable	upset
blue	distressing	morose	wretched
cheerless	down	painful	
dark	forlorn	saddening	

same

akin	compatible	generic	parallel
alike	conformable	homogeneous	photocopy
allied	conforming	identical	related
analogous	congruent	imitation	replica
associated	consonant	indiscernible	same
clone	copy	inseparable	shared
cognate	correspondent	interchangeable	similar
collective	corresponding	joint	synonymous
common	duplicate	like	tantamount
comparable	equal	matching	twin
comparative	equivalent	mutual	

A GLOSSARY OF TERMS FOR WRITING*

anecdote   A brief story or account of a single experience, often biographical, which illustrates something typical or striking about a person. Anecdotes, like parables, are effective as vivid, specific examples of a general observation or quality.

argument   The development of reasons, examples to support a thesis; narrowly, to outline a position on an issue or problem with the intent to clarify or persuade. Argument is also used in a broad sense to refer to the way a writer develops any topic.

audience   For the writer this term refers to the intended reader. Awareness of an audience determines, for example, what the writer may assume a reader already knows, level of diction, and tone.

coherence   A piece of writing has coherence when the logical relationship of ideas is evident and convincing. In a coherent discussion, statements and sections follow one another in a natural, even inevitable way. A coherent discussion hangs together; an incoherent one is scattered and disorganized.

cohesion   This refers to the grammatical and usage aspects of writing. **Cohesive** writing means that the connection of ideas within each sentence and at the paragraph level is clear and that the writing follows the conventions of standard written English.

controlling idea   This refers to the writer's thesis or main idea. It asserts what the writer has to say <u>about</u> the topic or question.

conventions   These are the "rules" or common guidelines for punctuation, spelling, and usage.

description   The expression in words of what is experienced by the senses. Good description recreates what is felt, seen, heard—sensed in

---

*Many of the terms in this glossary are also discussed in Chapter 4, Reading Prose.

any way. We also use the term describe to mean *identify, classify, characterize,* even for abstract ideas. Description permits readers to recreate the subject in their own imaginations.

development This refers to the choice and elaboration of examples, reasons, or other details that support an argument or illustrate a controlling idea. (See also the rubric for scoring Regents essays in Appendix D.)

diction This refers to word choice. Diction may be formal or informal, complex or simple, elegant or modest, depending on the occasion and the audience. The language we use in casual conversation is different from the language we use in formal writing. The good writer uses language that is varied, precise, and vivid; the good writer has resources of language to suit a wide range of purposes.

exposition The development of a topic through examples, reasons, details, which explain, clarify, show, instruct—the primary purpose of exposition is to convey information. Much of the writing assigned to students is referred to as expository writing: Through exposition you can demonstrate what you have learned, discovered, understood, appreciated.

focus This refers to the way a writer contains and directs all the information, examples, ideas, reasons in an essay on the specific topic.

narrative Because it tells a story, narrative has chronological order. Narrative method is commonly used in exposition when examples are offered in a chronological development.

position paper A form of persuasive writing, a position paper is meant to generate support for an issue or cause; the essay is based on specific evidence that can be cited to support the writer's argument. A position paper may also evaluate solutions or suggest courses of action.

prompt This refers to a set of directions for a writing task; may also be a quote or passage meant to stimulate a piece of writing.

tone In writing, tone refers to the attitude of the writer toward the subject and/or toward the reader. Tone may range from *harsh and insistent* to *gentle and reflective*. There is as much variety of tone in writing as there is in human feeling. Some pieces, essays of opinion, for example, usually have a very distinct tone; other works, especially in fiction or personal expression, may have a more subtle and indirect tone. (See discussion of Tone on page 65 in Reading Prose and on page 86 in Reading Poetry.)

transition Words or phrases used to link ideas and sections in a piece of writing. Common transitions include *first, second . . . in addition . . . finally; on the other hand, moreover, consequently, therefore*. Transitions make the development of an argument clear.

unity In the narrowest sense, unity refers to focus: The ideas and examples are clearly related to the topic and to one another. In the largest sense, unity refers to a feature of our best writing: All elements—ideas, form, language, and tone—work together to achieve the effect of a complete and well-made piece.

Chapter 8

VOCABULARY

Formal vocabulary study may begin as early as kindergarten; associating meaning with different sounds begins virtually at birth. As all students have discovered, however, there always seem to be new words to learn. Every novel, essay, or newspaper article we read is likely to include some new expressions or unfamiliar words. Deliberately studying new words and preparing for tests on them is certainly one way to expand our vocabularies, and every serious student has developed a method for such study. But if you do not continue to use those new words—that is, read, speak, and write with them—they may be forgotten soon after the test.

The thousands of words you *know* were acquired through repeated use over time and through association with their contexts, that is, through reading and listening. As you study vocabulary words associated with a course in English, social studies, or science, you are learning them in a context, and you are also expanding your reading and writing vocabularies. Every word you study should create some kind of image for you: try to associate it with a phrase, an experience or feeling, an object or person, an action or incident. If you have no image, you do not truly know the word yet.

The vocabulary you are expected to know and use, and that will be assessed on the Regents ELA, the SAT, and the ACT exams, is the language of literary authors, essayists, historians, and scientists. On the Regents ELA exam, this means that your mastery of relevant vocabulary will be assessed through questions about the meanings of words within the extended reading comprehension passages. You will also be expected to understand how particular words or expressons establish tone and clarify an author's meaning in the texts for analysis. This shift in how vocabulary is assessed represents a shared goal of the Common Core aligned state exams (Regents, PARCC, SBAC) and the SAT and ACT. For high school students, this means less need to study exotic and unfamiliar vocabulary in isolation; rather, students will need to be able to understand—and use—what is called academic language.

In the next section, you will find examples of what is meant by academic language. At the end of the chapter, you will find three collections of words to review as well. The first represents words that have been tested on Regents exams over several years. The second is a list compiled by high school students from their reading of the Op-Ed pages of *The New York Times* and other sources. The third, from published book reviews, was also compiled by students. Each list offers the thoughtful reader and writer a rich source of vocabulary in current use.

ACADEMIC LANGUAGE

Academic language is the language you use to express understanding of texts in class discussion, lecture, and writing. It is the language of interpretation, analysis, evaluation, and explanation. This term also refers to the language of a particular subject or discipline: literature, history, biology, economics, art, and so on. Reviewing the glossaries of literary and poetic terms and the terms for writing is another way of strengthening your command of academic language.

Here is a list of **verbs**, followed by their noun and adjective forms, commonly used to express how nonfiction texts are written and how arguments are developed. You will recognize many of these terms from the list of What Writers Do at the beginning of Chapter 4.

allege	allegation	alleged, allegedly
analyze	analysis	analytic, analytically
apply	application	
argue	argument	argumentative
arrange	arrangement	
articulate		
assemble		
assert	assertion	assertive
assess	assessment	
associate	association	
assume	assumption	
categorize	category	categorical
cite	citation	
characterize	characterization	
claim	(a/the) claim	
clarify	clarification	
classify	classification	
compare	comparison	
compile	compilation	
complement	(a/the) complement	complementary
compose	composition	
comprehend	comprehension	comprehensive
conclude	conclusion	conclusive
construct	construct, construction	
contend	contention	contentious
contradict	contradiction	contradictory
contrast	contrast	contrasting
correlate	correlation	correlative
criticize	criticism	critical, critically
critique	(a/the) critique	

debate	(a/the) debate	debatable
deduce	deduction	deductive, deductively
defend	defense	defensive
define	definition	definitive
demonstrate	demonstration	demonstrative
derive	derivation	derivative
design	(a/the) design	
develop	development	
differentiate	differentiation	
discern	discernment	discerning
discover	discovery	
discuss	discussion	
distinguish	distinction	distinguished
elaborate	elaboration	elaborate, elaborately
emphasize	emphasis	
estimate	estimation	
evaluate	evaluation	
exaggerate	exaggeration	
examine	examination	
exclude	exclusion	
explain	explanation	
explore	exploration	exploratory
focus	(a/the) focus	
form	(a/the) form	formal, formally
formulate	formulation	
frame		
generalize	generalization	
highlight	highlight	
hypothesize	hypothesis	hyhpothetical
identify	identification	
illustrate	illustration	
imply	implication	
include	inclusion	inclusive
infer	inference	inferential, inferentially
influence	influence	influential
inquire	inquiry	
integrate	integration	
interpret	interpretation	interpretive
introduce	introduction	
investigate	investigation	
judge	judgment	judgmental, judgmentally
mean	meaning	meaningful
modify	modification	
observe	observation	
oppose	opposition	

Academic Language

organize	organization	
originate	origin	original
outline	(a/the) outline	
paraphrase	paraphrase	
persuade	persuasion	persuasive
predict	prediction	predictive
presume	presumption	presumptive
project	projection	
propose	proposition	
recall	recollection	
refer	reference	referential
report	report	
represent	representation	
respond	response	responsive
review	review	
select	(a/the) selection	selective, selectively
sequence	(a/the) sequence	sequential, sequentially
specify	specification	
speculate	speculation	speculative
state	statement	
structure	(a/the) structure	structural, structurally
suggest	suggestion	suggestive
summarize	summary	summarily
support	support	supportive
suppose	supposition	supposed, supposedly
symbolize	symbol	symbolic
synthesize	synthesis	
translate	translation	
utilize	utilization	
vary	variation	
verify	verification	

Note: The *-ed* (past participle) forms of all these verbs are also used as modifiers: *assembled, classified, identified*, and so on. The adjective/adverb forms listed previously are widely used as separate forms and some have differences in meaning from the verb and noun forms.

Here is a list of **nouns and adjectives** used to identify and describe rhetorical methods as well as a writer's tone and purpose:

abstraction	abstract
analogy	analogous
approach	
	appropriate
	approximate

argument	argumentative
aspect	
audience	
authenticity	authentic
background	
chronology	chronological
coherence	coherent
concision	concise
	concrete
consequence	consequentially
consistency	consistent, consistently
constancy	constant
context	contextually
credibility	credible
criterion/criteria	
detail	
diction	
dimension	
direction	direct
effect	effective
element	elemental
equivalence	equivalent
	essential
evidence	evident
example	
excerpt	
exercise	
expository	exposition
extract	extraction
fact	factual
factor	
feature	
	figurative, figuratively
fragment	
frequence	frequent
general	generally
graph	graphic
highlight	
image	
inclination	
indirection	indirect
intention	intentional
irony	ironic
irrelevance	irrelevant

131

Academic Language

literalness	literal, literally
logic	logical, logically
metaphor	metaphorical
method	*methodical
motivation	motivating
narration	narrative
narrator	
objectivity	objective
opinion	opinionated
order	ordered
origin	original
pattern	
perspective	
plagiarism	plagiarized
plan	
plausibility	plausible
point of view	
possibility	possible
primary	
priority	*prior
probability	probable
process	
profile	
prompt	
proposition	
purpose	purposeful
relevance	relevant
revision	revised
sequence	sequential
series	
signal	
significance	significant
source	
speaker	
specificity	specific
strategy	strategic
structure	
style	stylistic
subject	*subjective
subsequence	subsequent
substitution	substitute
succinctness	succinct
summary	
survey	

technique	technical
theme	
thesis	
tone	
topic	*topical
transition	
uniqueness	unique
validity	valid
variation, variety	varied
viewpoint	
voice	

*Note: As in the list of verbs, some nouns and adjectives with a common derivation may have differences in meaning.

Throughout *Let's Review*, you will find sources of what is meant by academic language, along with glossaries of terms for fiction, nonfiction, poetry, and writing. Your ability to recognize examples of various literary and rhetorical elements strengthens your comprehension; you will also be expected to use them appropriately when you write essays of argument and text analysis.

UNFAMILIAR AND ARCHAIC LANGUAGE

Here is some of the vocabulary you will encounter as you read and discuss what are considered authentic or historically significant texts. Some of the words are familiar in their current use; but, the meanings offered here are from texts as early as the 16th century, including works of Shakespeare, and are also found in 18th, 19th, and early 20th century writings in English.

Verbs

address	to consider, think about, speak to
apprise	to give verbal or written notice
behold	to observe with care, witness
breach	to break through
discover	to learn, to disclose
dispose	to be inclined
divine	to guess, figure out, foresee
endeavor	to try, attempt a task or challenge
fashion	to form or make something

forbear	to pause, delay, avoid voluntarily or decline to do something
have	to prefer, think, believe, consider, think about
peruse	to read or examine with care
relish	to enjoy, take delight in
smart	to cause pain
suffer	to put up with, tolerate
thirst	to have an intense desire for something
thwart	to oppose, frustrate or defeat
want	to fail, be deficient or lacking
witness	to see by personal presence, observe directly
wreak	to revenge, throw or dash with violence

Nouns

appendages	arms and legs
appetite	desire, interest
ardor	passion
aught, naught	anything, nothing
conveyance	vehicle
countenance	look, appearance
dominion	area of authority, knowledge or power
eloquence	artful, expressive speech
faculties	senses, aptitudes, abilities
fashion	a distinctive or habitual manner
forebearance	patience, tolerance
grievance	suffering, distress; grudge, resentment
humor	temperament
idleness	unimportance, uselessness, emptiness
infirmity	weakness, disorder; personal failing
justice	accuracy, wisdom
labors	efforts
nature	disposition, inherent quality
perusal	reading, consideration
petulance	irritability, contrariness
rapture	extreme joy or pleasure; passionate intensity
sensibility	acuteness of perception; capacity to feel or perceive
temper	disposition of mind
vanity	emptiness, untruth, unfruitful labor
virtue	strength of character, bravery, valor; moral excellence

Adjectives

base	corrupt, vile
bumptious	arrogant, brash
clever	intelligent, skilled
familiar	agreeable in conversation, not formal or distant
idle	unimportant, trivial
imbued	tinged, affected with
infirm	weak of mind, body, or will
petulant	pert, wanton, sour in temper
prevailing	having effect; persuading, succeeding
puerile	childish, trifling, weak
rough	coarse in manners, uncivil; terrible, dreadful
sensible	having perception by the mind or the senses
sober	serious, calm, subdued
stout	bold, intrepid, brave
sublime	high in excellence, lofty, grand
wholesome	contributing to health of mind, conducive to good

STUDYING NEW WORDS

Learning in Context

Even the most diligent student cannot reasonably expect simply to memorize—out of context—the hundreds, even thousands, of words on Regents and SAT lists. Recent studies also confirm that vocabulary study confined to lists of words without a context or pattern of association—as with a particular work of literature, for example—does not result in long-term retention. Moreover, the practice of recording dictionary definitions alone gives only general and sometimes misleading information about the meaning and correct use of words. Learning words means learning their precise meanings, connotations, and appropriate context.

Unless you are working with an unabridged dictionary, which often includes illustrative examples in sentences or phrases, you are likely to find in a desk dictionary only brief definitions, general in nature, and possibly a list of synonyms. This limited information is valuable as a *reference,* especially if you are reading a passage and need to know a word's meaning in order to understand the passage. Learning the full meaning of unfamiliar words, however, requires more active study. In the sections below you will find recommendations for ways to prepare and organize your vocabulary study.

ROOTS AND PREFIXES FROM LATIN AND GREEK

Although English is certainly not derived from Greek and Latin only, familiarity with the Greek or Latin forms in English words is often useful to students taking vocabulary tests. Recognition of root meanings in particular may help you determine the correct answer for a word you may not be sure of. Even more important, however, is the value of knowing the Latin and Greek origins of English when you are first studying new words. When you are aware of the meanings of the individual parts of a word you often can form an image for it. Think of the Latin root *spect*, for example. This root means *look into, observe, behold* and, with variations in spelling *spec* and *spic*, is the base of many English words: *inspect, introspect, expect, respect, speculate, spectacle, spectacular, conspicuous*—and many others. Even the word *spy* is related to this Latin root.

When you are looking up words in the dictionary, do not skip over the etymology—the section that shows you in abbreviated form the origin and history of a word. Grouping words by related origin can be a very useful way to organize when you are studying large groups of new words; by using their common origin, you will learn to associate a new word with others you already know. It is the process of forming associations in meaning, forming images, and knowing contexts that permits you to learn efficiently—and to remember—the words you study. (Familiarity with roots and prefixes is also very helpful in understanding spelling patterns, as you will see in Chapter 11.)

Listed below, with examples, are many of the Latin and Greek roots found in English. (As you review the meanings of these roots, provide additional examples from your own knowledge; you should also guess about possible examples—then look them up in a dictionary to confirm your guess.) This process is a demonstration of what is meant by *active* vocabulary study. It means you are thinking about a word and associating it with others you know.

As you examine the list of Greek and Latin roots common in English, you should be struck by how familiar many of these forms are. You should also note that all these roots denote specific actions or ideas. Knowing the meanings of these elements as you study new words, or review familiar ones, will give you specific images or experiences to associate with them. This in turn will make the meaning of many words more vivid and easier to remember than will an abstract definition or list of synonyms alone.

LATIN ROOTS

Forms	Meaning	Examples
alter	other	altercation, alternative
ami (amicus)	friend	amiable, amicable, amity
amor	love	amorous, enamored
anima	breath, mind, spirit	animation, unanimous, inanimate, animosity
bell (bellum)	war	bellicose, belligerent, antebellum
cad (cadere), cid	to fall	decay, decadence, deciduous
cap, cip	contain	captivate, capacity, capable
capit (caput)	head	capital, capitol, recapitulate
cede, ceed, cess (cedere)	to move, yield	proceed, accede, exceed, precede, excess, success, procession
cept (capere)	to take, seize, hold	intercept, reception, accept
cid, cis (caedere)	to cut, kill	precise, incisive, homicide
clam, claim (clamare)	to cry, call out	exclaim, proclaim, clamor
clud, clus (claudere)	to shut, close	include, exclusion, recluse
cred (credere)	to believe, loan, trust	creditable, incredible, credulous
culp (culpa)	fault, guilt	culpable, exculpate
cur, curs (currere)	to run	course, cursor, current, incur, precursor, recur
dict (dicere)	to say, tell	dictator, diction, edict, predict
doc (docere)	to teach	doctor, docile, indoctrinate
duc, duct (ducere)	to lead	deduce, induction, conduct
err (errare)	to go, lead astray	error, erroneous, erratum
err (errer)	to travel, wander	errand, arrant, erratic
fac, fact, fect, fic (facere)	to make, do	affect, defect, effect, facsimile, factor, artificial, deficit
fer (ferre)	to bear, carry	inference, offer, reference
fid (fidelitas)	faith, loyalty	infidel, perfidious, diffident
flect, flex (flectere)	to bend	reflex, reflection, flexibility
flu, fluct, flux (fluere)	to flow	affluent, fluctuation, fluent, influence, influx
fund (fundare) (fundus)	to base, bottom	(to) found, fundamental, profundity
fus (fundere)	pour	effusive, foundry, fusion
gen (genus) (genare)	kind, sort, birth, to beget	genre, heterogenous, genetic, generate, progenitor, genocide
grad, gress (gradus)	to walk, go, stage or step	digress, graduate, progress, grade, gradient, retrograde
greg (gregis)	flock, herd, group	egregious, gregarious, integrate
her, hes (haerere)	to cling, stick	adhesive, coherence, inherently
ject, jet (jacere)	to throw	inject, projection, jettison
jud, jur, jus (jus)	to judge; to swear just, right; law	abjure, adjudicate, prejudge, jury, justification, perjury
lat (latus)	borne, carried	correlative, related, superlative
leg (legis, lex)	law	legality, legislative
locus	place	location, locale, locomotive

Roots and Prefixes from Latin and Greek

locu, loqu (loqui)	to speak	eloquent, loquacious, soliloquy,
locutor	speaker	interlocutor, locution, obloquy
lude (ludere)	to play	interlude, ludicrous, prelude
mit, mitt, mis, miss (mittere)	to dispatch, send, to let go	emit, permit, remit, submissive, commission, missile, permission
mob, mot (movere)	to move	demote, motivate, promote, commotion, mobility
mor, mort (mortis)	death	immortal, mortality, mortified
ped (pedis)	foot	expeditious, impede, pedestrian
pel, puls (pellere)	to drive, push	compel, dispel, impulse, repel, compulsive, repellent
pend, pens (pendere)	to hang, weigh, pay	append, compensate, dependent, impending, pension, pensive
ple, plet (plere)	to fill	complete, complement, deplete
plen (plenus)	full	plentiful, replete
pon, pos, posit (ponere)	to place, put	component, depose, propose, juxtapostion, impose, opponent
port (portare)	to carry	comport, deportment, purport, portable, portfolio
pot, poten, poss (posse)	to be able	impossibility, omnipotent, potential
rad (radius)	root, spoke (wheel)	eradicate, radical, radiation
rect, reg (regula) (regire)	right, straight to guide, rule	direction, rectified, regal regimen, regime
rupt (rumpere)	to break, burst	disrupt, corrupt, interruption
sat (satis)	enough	dissatisfy, insatiable, saturated
sci (scire)	to know	conscience, omniscient, prescience, scientific
scrib, script (scribere)	to write	describe, inscription, scripture
sect (sectare)	to cut	dissect, intersection
secu, sequ (sequi)	to follow	consequence, obsequious, sectarian, sequel
sed, sid, sess (sedere)	to sit	dissidence, possess, residual, sedation, sedentary
sent, sens (sentire)	to feel	consensus, insensitive, sentient
son (sonus)	sound	consonant, dissonance, sonic, sonogram, sonority, unison
spec, spect, spic (spectare)	to look at, observe	auspicious, conspicuous, expect, inspect, respect, spectacular
spir, spirit	to breathe	inspiration, respiratory, spirit
sta, state, stit (stare)	to stand	constitute, instability, obstacle, stability, status
strict, string (stringere)	to draw tight	constrict, restriction, stringent
sume, sump (sumere)	to take	assume, consume, presumption
tact, tang, ting, tig (tangere)	to touch	contact, contiguous, intangible, tactile, tangential

ten, tain (tenere)	to hold, keep	abstain, pertain, restrain, tenacious, untenable
tend, tens (tendere)	to reach, stretch	contend, intensity, portent, pretentious, tendency
tort (torque)	to twist	contortion, extort, tortuous
tract (trahere)	to draw, pull	distract, intractible, protracted, retraction
ver (veritas)	truth	aver, veracity, verification
vers, vert (vertere)	to turn	adverse, aversion, diversity, inadvertent, reversion, subvert, version, versification
vid, vis (videre) (video)	to see	evident, improvident, supervise, revision, visage, visionary
vit, viv (vivere) (viva)	to live; life	revival, survive, vivacious, unviable
vinc, vict (vincere)	to conquer	conviction, eviction, invincible
voc, voke (vocare)	to call	advocate, equivocal, invocation, provocative, revoke, vocation
volv, volu (volvere)	to roll, turn	convoluted, evolution, revolving

GREEK ROOTS

Forms	Meaning	Examples
anthrop	man, humankind	anthropocentric, misanthropist, philanthropy
arch	rule, ruler	anarchy, patriarchal
astr, astron	star	astronomical, disastrous
bio	life, living things	biography, microbiology
chron	time	anachronistic, chronic
cosm (kosmos)	order, universe	cosmic, microcosm
demo	among the people	democratic, demography
gen	birth, race	genesis, progeny
gno, gnosis	know	agnostic, diagnosis, gnomic
gram, graph	write, writing	epigrammatic, biography
log, logue	word, reason	analogy, illogical, prologue
lect, lex	language, speak	dialect, lexical
lysis	dissolution, destruction	catalyst, paralysis
metr	measure	diametric, metrical
morph	form, shape	amorphous, metamorphose
mne, mnes	memory, remember	amnesty, mnemonic
onym	a name	eponymous, synonym
opti, optic	eye, sight	optical, synopsis
path (pathos)	feeling, suffering	apathy, empathetic, pathetic
ped	child	pediatrician, pedagogy, pedantic
phon	sound	euphony, phonetic, symphonic

Roots and Prefixes from Latin and Greek

Prefixes are units of one or two syllables that are not words in themselves but that have distinct meanings. The addition of a prefix to the beginning of an existing word (what is called a *stem* or *root*) creates a word with an additional meaning. The spelling variations for many of the prefixes listed below are reminders that in English the spelling of a prefix will be altered to match the root to which it is attached. For example, *ad,* which means *to* or *toward*, is attached to many words in English; the *d* often changes to the first letter of the word to which it is added, making the resulting new forms easier to pronounce. (See the examples below as well as those in Chapter 11 — Spelling.)

LATIN PREFIXES

Forms	Meaning	Examples*
a, ab, abs	away, from	abdicate, absence, abstraction
a, ad (ac, af, al, etc.)	to, toward	absent, acclimate, adherent, alliteration, assign, attribution
ambi	both, around	ambiance, ambiguous, ambidextrous, ambivalent
ante	before	antebellum, antecedent
bene, ben	good, well	beneficial, beneficent, benign
circum	around	circumnavigate, circumstances, circumlocution
co (col, com, cor)	together	coincidence, collaboration, commiserate, correspondence
contra, contro, counter	against, opposite	contradiction, controversy, counterfeit, counteract
de	away, down, from	deduction, deterrence, deviate
dis (di, dif)	apart, away; not; separate	disavow, disdain, disappear, disregard, disperse, discern
en (var. of in)	make, put into	enable, enhance, encourage
equ, equi	equal, even	equable, equanimity, equivalence, equivocate
ex (e, ef)	away from, out	efface, effective, ejection, exodus, expiration
in (il, im, ir)	in, within	immersion, impending, innate
in (il, im, ir)	not, without	illegible, imprudent, incognito
inter	among, between	intercede, intermediary, interim
magn	great	magnificence, magnanimous
mal	bad, evil	malevolent, malice, malefactor, malign, malignant
ob (oc, of, op)	to, toward; against; over; totally	objection; obdurate, obnoxious; obfuscate; obsolete, obliterate
omni	all	omnipotent, omniscient
per	completely; through	perceive, perdurable, pervasive
post	after	posterity, posthumous

pre	before, in advance	pre-empt, preclude, premonition
pro	before, forward	proclivity, prodigy, profane
re	again	reiterate, reverberate, retort, revise, remember
retro	backward	retrogression, retroactive
se	apart, aside	secession, sedition, select
sub (suf, sup, sus)	from below, under	subsidize, substandard, suffuse, suppress, sustenance
super	above, over	supercilious, superfluous, supervise, supersede
tra, trans	across, beyond	transgression, transcend

GREEK PREFIXES

Forms	Meaning	Examples
a, an	not, without	agnostic, anarchy, apathetic
ana	back, backward according to; through	anagram, anachronistic, anapest analogy, analysis
ant, anti	against, opposite	antipathy, antithesis, antipodes
auto	self	autonomous, autocracy
cata	down	cataclysm, catalyst, catastrophe
dia	through, between	dialect, dialogue, diameter
dys	bad, ill, difficult	dysfunctional, dyspeptic
epi	upon	epicenter, epigram, epilogue
eu	good, well	euphemism, euphoria, eugenics
hetero	different	heterodox, heterogeneous
homo	alike, same	homogeneous, homonym
macro	large, long duration	macrocosm, macroscopic
meta, met	after, beyond; changed	metaphor, metaphysical, metamorphosis
micro	small	microscope, microbe
mon, mono	one, single	monotheism, monolith
pan	all, complete	panacea, pandemonium
pro	before; favorable	prophecy; propitiate
proto	first, primary	protagonist, prototype
sym, syn	together, with	symmetry, synergy, synopsis

* When you review the lists for study at the end of the chapter you will notice how many words in English are formed with these prefixes. Use those lists to add to the examples offered here.

Here is the first group of vocabulary words from the Regents exams list on page 149. Note how many are formed from the Greek or Latin prefixes reviewed on the previous pages.

abdicate	**ad**monish	**a**morphous	**as**pire
aberrant	**ad**versity	**ana**chronistic	assay
abhorrent	**af**flict	**an**ecdotes	astute
abridgment	agrarian	animation	**a**sylum
absolve	**al**lot	**ap**pease	atrocious
acclaim	**al**lure	**ap**prehend	audacity
accost	**al**ly	arbitrator	**auto**nomous
accredit	**alter**cation	archaic	avarice
acme	amass	ardent	**a**verse
acquiesce	**ambi**ance	armistice	**a**version
acquittal	**ambi**dextrous	**ar**ray	avidly
adage	**ambi**guous	**ar**rogantly	azure
adhere	**ambi**valent	**a**scendancy	
adjunct	amnesty	ashen	

In many of these examples, the meaning of the original prefix has been absorbed into the meaning of the entire word, in **adage** and **allot**, for example. The highlighted prefixes illustrate, however, how extensively Greek and Latin forms are found in English.

A NOTE ON SYNONYMS AND USING A THESAURUS

As thoughtful students and careful writers know, synonyms are rarely equivalents. Synonyms are words closely related in meaning to a given word, but they should not be considered equally interchangeable with it.

Here is a list of synonyms for **acquiesce** that you might gather from a thesaurus:

accede	capitulate	concur	permit
accept	come to terms	conform	submit
agree to	with	consent	surrender
allow	comply with	give in	yield
assent	concede	grant	

This list is very helpful in enriching your understanding of the word, especially because it includes several terms that emphasize that there is a sense of giving in, of reluctance, in **acquiesce**. The closest synonyms in this list are *accede, come to terms with, conform, give in, yield. Capitulate, submit,* and *surrender* accurately reflect the connotation of the word, but they denote a more forceful sense of defeat than does *acquiesce*. The others, *accept, agree to, concur, consent, permit*, are less precise because they reflect only the general meaning and do not denote the sense of reluctance and the lack of enthusiam inherent in **acquiesce**.

Learning to distinguish among variations in meaning and context is an important part of developing your vocabulary. It is also essential to the craft of good writing. In Chapter 6, Writing About Literature, and Chapter 7, Writing on Demand, you will find several *synonymies,* which are words grouped by general meaning or connotation. The purpose of the *synonymies* is to help you develop precision and variety in your own writing. You should review those as part of your vocabulary study as well.

ORGANIZING VOCABULARY STUDY

Another way to work with lists such as the ones at the end of this chapter is to *sort* them, much as you would sort playing cards. Depending on the card game you are playing, you might sort a hand by suit, by numerical sequence, or by kind. You can sort a group of words in various ways as well: by part of speech, by connotation, by human or abstract qualities, and so on. Many students create their own flash cards for the words they study, which makes sorting in various ways easy.

Here are some suggestions for how you might sort the first group of words from the Regents list (page 149). First, sort by part of speech. In the list below, the *verbs* are printed in bold type:

VERBS

abdicate	adversity	anecdote	asylum
aberrant	**afflict**	animation	atrocious
abhorrent	agrarian	**appease**	audacity
abridgment	**allot**	**apprehend**	autonomous
absolve	allure	arbitrator	avarice
acclaim	**ally**	archaic	averse
accost	altercation	ardent	aversion
accredit	**amass**	armistice	avidly
acme	ambiance	**array**	azure
acquiesce	ambidextrous	arrogantly	
acquittal	ambiguous	ascendancy	
adage	ambivalent	ashen	
adhere	amnesty	**aspire**	
adjunct	amorphous	**assay**	
admonish	anachronistic	astute	

Then classify the group of verbs further as either *transitive* or *intransitive;* that is, according to the nature of the action they denote and the nature of the objects, if any, they take. When you look up these words in a dictionary, they will be identified as *v.i.* or *v.t. Transitive verbs* (*v.t.*) take a direct object; the action is directed from the subject to an object. For example, "She *admonished* (scolded, warned) the unruly child" and "King Midas *amassed* (accumulated) a fortune in gold." *Direct objects,* of course, may be persons and living creatures, or they may be things, even abstractions: "She quickly *apprehended* the danger she was in."

Intransitive verbs (*v.i.*) denote actions that are contained within the subject or that signify what we call states of being: "He *adhered* strictly to his ethical principles." *Adhere* connotes a state of mind, an attitude.

The distinction between transitive and intransitive action is not always easily made, but one way to demonstrate the difference is to make an active statement passive. For example, we can reverse the statement "She admonished the child" and turn it into "The child was admonished by her." The statement above about King Midas can be expressed in the passive as "A fortune in gold was amassed by King Midas." Although transitive actions may be reversed in this way, intransitive actions do not reverse. For example, the sentence "The principles were adhered by him" has no meaning. Some verbs may function both as transitive and intransitive. A simple example is the verb *to sink*: "The small sailboat sank during the heavy storm" (*v.i.*), but "The submarine fired a torpedo that sank the enemy battleship." (*v.t.*).

Most verbs in this first group are transitive, so it would be useful to sort them by the kinds of objects they take; that is, whether they denote actions directed at persons or at things and abstractions. You would, of course, note this information as you look up each unfamiliar word in a dictionary. Here is the list of verbs further sorted:

ACTIONS DIRECTED AT PERSONS

to **absolve** (free from, relieve) someone of guilt or responsibility

to **acclaim** (praise, honor) a person's performance, action, or work

to **accost** (approach, confront) someone

to **admonish** (caution, scold) someone for misbehavior or inaction

to **afflict** (burden, attack) someone with suffering or illness

to **appease** (conciliate) a person, a nation, or a government

to **apprehend** (catch, capture) a suspect or a criminal

ACTIONS DIRECTED AT THINGS OR ABSTRACTIONS

to **abdicate** (relinquish, abandon) a throne, a responsibility

to **accredit** (certify, recognize) a school or university, the value of an idea

to **allot** (distribute, assign) funds, resources

to **amass** (gather, accumulate) a fortune, an army

to **append** (add, match) a section, passage, body of information

to **apprehend** (understand, comprehend, capture) an idea, a concept

to **articulate** (verbalize, clarify, explain) ideas, feelings, understanding

to **array** (arrange) a display, a number of objects

to **assay** (measure, evaluate) a task, a situation

to **assert** (declare, claim, affirm, profess) ideas, an opinion, a judgment

INTRANSITIVE ACTIONS

to **acquiesce** (give in to, agree reluctantly) in demands of others

to **adhere** (hold, cling to, comply) to demands or to principles

to **ally** (join, support) with another person, group, or nation

to **aspire** (strive, seek) to a goal, an achievement

For purposes of study, these verbs could be shuffled, and then resorted, by *connotation*. Which are generally positive in feeling and association, and which are negative? There are many words for which this is not a useful distinction, but appreciation of connotation is often essential to fully understanding the meaning of a word.

POSITIVE

| absolve | accredit | ally |
| acclaim | adhere | aspire |

NEGATIVE

| abdicate | acquiesce | afflict |
| accost | admonish | appease |

Organizing Vocabulary Study

As you make your notes or compose your flash cards, be sure to include connotation if it is relevant. A dictionary usually does not define a word by its connotation; you must infer it from the meanings and examples offered.

NOUNS

The *nouns* are in bold type:

abdicate	**adversary**	anachronistic	aspire
aberrant	**adversity**	**anecdote**	**assay**
abhorrent	afflict	**animation**	assert
abridgment	affluent	appease	astute
absolve	agrarian	append	**asylum**
acclaim	allot	apprehend	atrocious
accost	**allure**	apprehensive	**audacity**
accredit	**ally**	**arbitrator**	autonomous
acme	**altercation**	archaic	**avarice**
acquiesce	amass	ardent	averse
acquittal	**ambiance**	**armistice**	**aversion**
adage	ambidextrous	**array**	avidly
adamant	ambiguous	arrogant	azure
adhere	ambivalent	articulate	
adjunct	**amnesty**	**ascendancy**	
admonish	amorphous	ashen	

As you look at a collection of nouns, try to group them in various ways based on the kinds of things or persons they name. Note that in this group only two, **adversary** and **arbitrator,** name persons. This list, however, includes several political or legal terms that would form a useful group for study:

acquittal
adversary (adversarial)
ally
amnesty

arbitrator (arbitration)
armistice
ascendancy
asylum

A small group of terms is related to literature:

abridgment **adage** **anecdote**

Other terms name attitudes or feelings. (Note the contrast in connotation here.)

Positive

acclaim　　　animation

Negative

audacity　　　aversion　　　avarice

Finally, there are nouns that name forces, situations, conditions, and other concepts.

acme　　　**ambiance**　　　**allure**　　　**array**

Adjectives

The *adjectives* are in bold type:

abdicate	adversary	**anachronistic**	aspire
aberrant	adversity	anecdote	assay
abhorrent	afflict	animation	assert
abridgment	**affluent**	appease	**astute**
absolve	**agrarian**	append	asylum
acclaim	allot	apprehend	**atrocious**
accost	allure	**apprehensive**	audacity
accredit	ally	arbitrator	autonomous
acme	altercation	**archaic**	avarice
acquiesce	amass	**ardent**	**averse**
acquittal	ambiance	armistice	aversion
adage	**ambidextrous**	array	avidly
adamant	**ambiguous**	**arrogant**	**azure**
adhere	**ambivalent**	articulate	
adjunct	amnesty	ascendancy	
admonish	**amorphous**	**ashen**	

Because adjectives modify—that is, qualify, limit, or describe—nouns, a useful way to group them is by the nature of what they describe. For example, some of the adjectives in the list above describe human behavior or *actions*:

aberrant　　　**abhorrent**　　　**atrocious**

(all strongly negative in connotation)

Several adjectives describe human *attitudes, feelings, aspects of character:*

NEGATIVE

adamant   **ambivalent**   **arrogant**

POSITIVE

ardent   **astute**   **avid**

Still others characterize *the way people appear or express themselves:*

ambiguous   **ambivalent**   **apprehensive**   **averse**

Language may be:

ambiguous   **anachronistic**   **archaic**

Two adjectives relate to color:

ashen   **azure**

One term, **ambidextrous,** describes a physical characteristic.

This particular group contains no adverb forms, but for many of the adjectives in the list, the adverb is formed by adding *-ly*. For example:

aberrantly	**apprehensively**	**avidly**
adamantly	**astutely**	
ambiguously	**atrociously**	

Reminder: If you prepare your own note cards for study, be sure to include all forms of the word. For example, your notes for **ambivalent** (adj.) would also include **ambivalence** (n.). This is how the lists of academic vocabulary on page 128 are organized.

These groups overlap and should be combined in different ways as you work through larger numbers of words. The process of sorting, or reshuffling, as new categories and associations occur to you is a very effective way to learn new words. Each time you sort, you are actively thinking about a word in a particular context and are associating it with other words; this process is essential to making a word a permanent part of your reading and writing vocabulary.

VOCABULARY FOR STUDY

Below are lists of words that have been collected from past Regents exams, Op-Ed pages, and book reviews. You will recognize many of them from the section on academic language.

Vocabulary from Regents Exams

abdicate	admonish	amorphous	aspire
aberrant	adversity	anachronistic	assay
abhorrent	afflict	anecdotes	astute
abridgment	agrarian	animation	asylum
absolve	allot	appease	atrocious
acclaim	allure	apprehend	audacity
accost	ally	arbitrator	autonomous
accredit	altercation	archaic	avarice
acme	amass	ardent	averse
acquiesce	ambiance	armistice	aversion
acquittal	ambidextrous	array	avid
adage	ambiguous	arrogantly	azure
adhere	ambivalent	ascendancy	
adjunct	amnesty	ashen	
badger	belied	blatant	breach
barrage	bemused	bleary	brevity
bask	benevolent	boisterous	
beguile	berate	brazen	
cache	charisma	commencement	converse
carnage	chasm	commiserate	convivial
celebrated	clandestine	conception	craven
chafe	clique	congeal	credence
chagrin	coalition	consecrate	crestfallen
charade	collate	constrict	cringe
dauntless	deified	desist	discreet
de facto	deluge	desolate	dissidence
debonair	delve	deter	dissuade
decrepit	demeaning	detest	divulge
deduce	denizen	diffuse	domain
deferred	depict	dilemma	dredge
deflect	deride	diminutive	dynamic
defunct	derogatory	discord	

Vocabulary for Study

eccentric	encore	envoy	euphoric
edify	endorse	equanimity	eviction
eject	endow	equilibrium	exemplary
elicit	enfeeble	equitable	exodus
elude	enhance	equivocal	exonerate
elusive	ensnare	eradicate	expedite
embroil	entail	erratic	exploitation
eminence	entreaty	escapade	exulted
facet	feasible	flail	fortitude
fallible	fiasco	fleeting	fortuitous
fanatic	fidelity	forage	fracas
fanfare	finesse	foreboding	frugal
farcical	finite	formidable	futility
garish	genuine	grate	guise
garrulous	geriatric	gratuity	guttural
gaudy	gesticulate	grievously	
genial	grapple	grisly	
hallowed	harrowing	heretical	homage
harangue	heinous	hinder	humid
idiosyncrasies	impertinent	indisputably	insomnia
ignoble	imprudent	induce	insubordinate
illuminate	inadvertent	infernal	insurgent
immutable	inaugural	infringe	inundated
impartial	incensed	ingenuity	invoked
impending	incessant	inherent	irate
imperative	incognito	inimitable	irksome
imperceptible	incompetent	innocuous	irrational
imperiled	incorrigible	insatiable	itinerant
imperious	indignant	insolent	
jeer	jovial	jut	
jocular	juncture		
lacerated	latent	lesion	lucrative
lackluster	lateral	lineage	lugubrious
lament	lavish	liquidate	lull
languorously	laxity	loquacious	

madcap	marauding	meticulous	mollify
maim	martial	militant	morose
malefactor	meager	misconstrue	mortify
malice	mediate	misgivings	mundane
malleable	melancholy	mitigate	muzzle
nefarious	niche	nostalgia	nuptial
negligible	nimble	notorious	nurture
nepotism	nonentity	nullification	
obliquely	omnipotent	optimum	override
obliterate	omniscient	oscillate	
obstinate	onslaught	oust	
oligarchy	opportune	ouster	
pacifism	perplexity	poise	profoundly
palatable	philanthropic	precariously	proponent
pandemonium	piety	precipice	protrude
parable	pinnacle	precludes	prowess
paraphrase	placid	prestige	proxy
penchant	plague	prevail	putrid
perjury	plausible	procrastinate	
perpetual	plight	prodigious	
qualms	quandary		
ramification	recalcitrant	reparation	revulsion
rampant	reciprocal	repercussion	roster
ramshackle	recoil	repress	rouse
rancid	recrimination	resolute	rue
rant	rectify	retort	ruinous
rapport	refute	revamped	russet
ravenous	reminiscent	reverberate	
sacrosanct	sheen	squalor	substantiate
salve	shortcomings	stalwart	subtlety
sanction	shrewd	stark	sullen
sanctity	singularly	stealthily	sumptuous
saunter	skeptical	strew	superfluous
scandalous	skulk	strut	suppress
scathing	sleek	subliminal	surcease
scrupulous	slipshod	submissive	surreptitious
scrutiny	smolder	subside	swagger
seedy	sporadic	subsidize	synopsis

Chapter Eight VOCABULARY

Vocabulary for Study

tainted	throng	transient	trudge
tally	token	trauma	tumult
tawny	topple	traverse	
tenacity	transcend	trifling	

unassuming	unnerve	unpalatable	utilitarian
uncanny	unobtrusive	unscrupulous	

vanquish	verbatim	viable
variance	verbose	vigilance
vehement	veritable	virtually

waive	whack	wrangle
warily	wield	wrath
weather (vb.)	wily	writhe

yield

zenith

Vocabulary from Op-Ed Pages

a priori	ad hoc	amiss	arcane
abdicate	adamant	amorphous	archetype
aberration	addled	androgyny	archive
abrogation	aegis	annals	ardent
abysmal	affidavit	annotate	artifice
abyss	affront	anoint	ascribe
accede	aggrieved	antidote	assessment
acclimate	agnostics	antipathy	assimilate
accolade	albeit	apathy	assuage
accrue	alleviate	append	asylum
acrimonious	allude (to)	arbiter	au courant
actuary	amalgamation	arbitrage	audit
acumen	ambivalence	arbitrary	autonomous

barrage	berth	blighted	bureaucrats
beguile	besmirch	blunder	burgeoning
beleaguered	bias	brass (slang def.)	
benighted	bipartisan	brute (vb.)	
bereft	blatant	budgetary	

cacophony	civics	concubine	convocation
cajole	clandestine	condone	covet
callous	clerical	confrere	crafty
canard	coda	conspiratorial	craven
candor	coffer	constituent	credibility
canonical/canon	collusion	contemporaries	cul-de-sac
capitulate	compliant	contend	cupidity
cataclysmic	complicit	contender	curtail
caveat	compound (vb.)	contingent	cushy
censure	compulsion	conundrum	cynical
chasm	concede	convene	cynicism
chimera	conciliate	conversant	
circumspect	conciliatory	conversely	

daunting	demur	despot	dispirit
debase	demystify	deter	disposition
decadence	denounce	detract	disquieting
decibel	denuded	didactic	dissemble
decree	denunciation	disavow	disseminate
decry	deplorable	discernible	dissident
deferment	depredation	discourse	dissipate
defrocked	deprivation	discretion	diversity
defunct	derail	discretionary	don (vb.)
deluded	derangement	disenchantment	doting
demagogue	deregulation	disingenuous	Draconian
demise	deride	disjointed	
demonize	derisive	dispel	

earmark	enclave	equivocate	exorbitant
egregious	enfranchise	eradicate	expenditure
electorate	enmesh	erode	expostulate
elixir	ennobling	ethos	expunge
eminence	ennui	eugenics	exude
empathetic	envoy	eviscerate	
empathy	epitomize	exhort	
encapsulate	equanimity	exonerate	

fallacious	firebrand	forlorn	frothing
farcical	fiscal	formidable	furor
fedora	flounder (vb.)	formulate	fusillade (fig.)
feint	flummoxed	fray (n.)	futility
fiasco	fodder (fig.)*	frenetic	
finagle	folly	fritter (vb.)	

*In this case, consider the figurative meaning of the words.

Vocabulary for Study

gaffe	gaudy	gouging	gubernatorial
gag rule	gauge	grapple	guffaw
galvanize	gerrymander	grim	
garner	glut	grotesque	

habeus corpus	hapless	hectoring	hubris
hackneyed	harbor (vb.)	heresy	hyperbole
hamlet	heckle	hoosegow (slang)	

iconography	importune	indignity	insular
ideological	impunity	ineptitude	integrity
idiosyncratic	incendiary	infiltrate	interlocking
idyllic	incessant	infirmity	intransigence
ignominious	incipient	inflationary	inure
ilk	incite	infuse	invaluable
impede	incontrovertible	inherent	inviolate
imperil	incumbent	innuendo	irk
implement (vb.)	indefatigable	inquisitorial	irredentism
implicit	indigenous	insignia	

lacerate	largess	leery	lout
laconic	latent	leitmotif	lucid
lambaste	laureate	levitate	
languish	lebensraum	litany	

malady	maudlin	molder	mortar
malaise	megalomaniac	monolith	murky
malign	meritorious	morass	myopic
manifestation	meticulous	moratorium	
mantra	milieu	moribund	
martyr	mimesis	morose	

nadir	nexus	nuance
nascent	nomadic	

obfuscate	odious	oppression	overweening
obsolescence	ominous	outlay	
obstreperous	omnipresent	overhaul	
oddity	oncology	overt	

palliative	perennial	plunder	prohibitive
panacea	peripheral	pogrom	proliferate
pandering	pernicious	polarization	proliferation
paradox	peroration	polemic	propensity
paramount	perpetuate	polyglot	protocol
parochial	perquisite	portend	provocation
parsimonious	perversion	pragmatism	prurience
partisan (adj.)	pillage	prattle	psyche
passel	pinnacle	preeminent	pugnacity
pathology	pious	preempt	pundit
patrician	pique	preclude	purport
pedantic	placable/placate	presage	purvey/purveyor
peevish	plaudits	probity	pusillanimous
pejorative	plight	profound	pyrotechnics
penchant	plummet	progeny	

quagmire	quaver	quintessential	
qualm	quibble		

rabid (fig.)	recidivism	resolute	rhetoric
rakish	reconcile	resonance	rifle (vb.)
rancor	rectitude	restorative	rogue
rapacious	rejoinder	retributive	rudimentary
rapprochement	relegate	reverberate	ruse
raucous	reparations	reverence	
realpolitik	replete	revile	

salve (vb.)	siphon	staid	sullen
sartorial	snare	stark	summarily
sashay	snide	staunch	sumptuary
scion	sobriquet	steely eyed	sunder
scoff	sophomoric	stint	supersede
scourge	sordid	stipend	supplant
seamy	sorghum	strident	surfeit
self-effacing	sovereignty	stringent	swindle
sham	spate	stymie	sword of
shaman	speculative	subsidize	Damocles
shore up	staggering	substantive	sycophant
shudder	stagnation	subterfuge	synergy

temporal	throng	tout	troupe
temporize	thwart	transgression	tsunami
tenacity	torpor	transitory	turbulent
tendentious	totter	treacherous	

Vocabulary for Study

undergird	unduly	unilateral	unrelenting
undermine	unencumbered	universality	unscrupulous
undiluted	unfettered	unprecedented	usurp
vagaries	vestige	vigilante	volatile
venality	vexing	vilify	voyeurs
veracity	viable	visceral	
verdant	victimize	vituperation	
waffling	welter	writ	
wallow	wheedling	writhe	
wastrels	winnow	wrongheaded	

xenophobia

zeal   zeitgeist

Vocabulary from Book Reviews

accolade	adumbrate	animus	arduous
accretion	adversity	annotate	arsenal
accrue	aesthetic	antipodes	ascetic
acerbic	albeit	aphrodisiac	asinine
acolyte	alluring	aplomb	aspire
acrimonious	amatory	apotheosis	attenuate
acumen	amiable	arbiter	austere
adage	amok	arbitrary	authorial
adduce	anapest	archaic	
adherent	ancillary	ardor	
banal	bemused	blight	boulevardier
barren	bestiality	blithe	bowdlerize
bathetic	bevy	bohemian	Byzantine
bedraggled	bifurcation	boorish	
cache	chic	compendium	credo
cadence	clandestine	complicity	cribbed
canny	cleric	congenial	crotchety
catharsis	cloying	consign	cupidity
caveat	coffer	contend	curmudgeon
chafe	cohere	contrivance	cursory
charisma	coherence	copious	
chastening	colloquial	counterpoise	
chastise	compendious	covert	

dash	demigod	dichotomy	divagation
daunting	denouement	didactic	divergence
debunk	deploy	discursive	droll
deft	despotic	dispense	duplicity
delineate	detritus	dispossess	dysfunctional
delude	devolve	dither	dystopia
eccentric	ensconce	esoteric	exigency
eclectic	entreaty	espouse	existential
edify	envisage	esthetic	expansive
egregious	epigraph	ethereal	expatriate
elegy	epitomize	ethos	expurgate
elocution	equanimity	evangelical	exultant
elucidate	eradicate	evocative	
enclave	Eros	exacerbate	
encomium	eschew	exhort	
fabulist	farce	foray	fruition
facsimile	fervid	forbearance	furtive
faction	florid	formulaic	
galvanize	gorgon	guile	
gamut	grapple	gustatory	
hackneyed	harrowing	hewn (details)	
hagiography	hedonism		
iconoclast	implacable	ineffable	intercede
iconography	impresario	ineffectual	intractable
idiosyncratic	incoherent	inept	inured
idyll/idyllic	incongruous	inextricably	invidious
ignite (fig.)	incur	insidious	irreverent
imminent	indelible	insinuation	itinerant
imperative	indeterminate	insouciance	
impetus	indigenous	intelligentsia	
jarring	jettison	jostle	Joycean
kamikaze			
lacuna	largess	loquacious	lyricism
lament	libertine	Lothario	
languish	lilting	lucid	
lapidary	litigious	lucrative	

Chapter Eight VOCABULARY

Vocabulary for Study

macabre	mawkish	minutiae	mosaic
malaise	melodrama	misogyny	muddle
malevolent	mendacious	mogul	murky
malign	mercurial	moldering	musing
manifold (adj.)	mien	mordant	muster
matrix	milieu	moribund	myopia

naiveté	natter	nonpareil	nuance
narcissistic	nihilism	non sequitur	
nascent	nimble	noxious	

obfuscation	opprobrium	ostensible	ostracize

palatable	penumbra	portent	prevaricate
pantheon	perdurable	portentous	prodigious
paradigm	peregrination	practitioner	prosaic
pathos	perennial	pragmatic	protean
paucity	petulance	prattle	punitive
pedagogical	piety	precocious	purport
pelt (vb.)	placebo	premonition	
penchant	plodding	prescient	

querulous	quintessential	quotidian
query	quixotic	

rancor	recalcitrant	reverence	riveting
rapacious	recapitulate	revile	rudimentary
rapture	relegate	rhetorical	ruminate
rancor	repatriation	ricochet	
raucous	replete	riff	
reap	repository	risible	

sagacity	sedentary	stanch	sunder
salacious	self-effacement	standoffish	supercilious
sally forth	sepulchral	staunch	surreptitious
sap (vb.)	shaman	stilted	surrogate
savor	shenanigans	stultifying	symbiosis
scatological	snippet	sublimate	symmetry
scourge	solicitous	sublime	synoptic
scuttlebutt	spurn	subterfuge	
searing	squander	succumb	

taut	titillating	transient	trenchant
teeter	torpid	transitory	trilogy
temporal	tortuous	transmogrify	truism
thrall	traffic (vb.)	travail	tweak
throng	transcendent	treatise	
unabashed	uncanny	unfathomable	unflinching
vacillate	venality	vignette	vitriol
valediction	verisimilitude	vindictiveness	voluminous
vapid	vernacular	virtuosity	vortex
venal	vicissitude	vis à vis	votary
waft	wend	withal	
welter	whimsy		

Chapter 9

GRAMMAR AND USAGE FOR THE CAREFUL WRITER: A GUIDE TO STANDARD WRITTEN ENGLISH

The grammar of a language is its logic. We observe the conventions of standard usage in order to write and speak clearly, in order to communicate precisely what we mean. This section reviews those aspects of grammar and usage you are expected to know and to apply.

On the Regents ELA exam, your command of the conventions—standard written English—is evaluated by how well you write the essay of argument and the text analysis. On the SAT, your command of the grammar and usage is assessed in the writing and language section and on the optional essay; the ACT exam includes a specific section on grammar and usage, sentence structure, and mechanics (see Chapter 10 for Punctuation Guidelines and Reminders).

None of these exams requires you to identify errors in usage by name, but a review of the essential terms and structures will help you to recognize errors and to understand how to correct them. What are the essentials?

REVIEWING THE FUNDAMENTALS

The Parts of Speech

Below are the parts of speech that you should review. These include the noun, pronoun, adjective, verb, and adverb, as well as conjunction, preposition, and interjection.

Noun

Names or identifies persons, creatures, objects, ideas. The articles *the, a, an* usually precede and signal a noun. For example:

> book   education   history
> child   English   politics
> climate   happiness   woman

Pronoun

Replaces or "stands in for" nouns or other pronouns already stated; the noun or pronoun referred to (replaced) is the **antecedent**.

Subject Forms: I, you, he/she/it, we, you, they
Object Forms: me, you, him/her/it, us, you, them
Possessive Forms: mine, yours, his/hers/its, ours, yours, theirs
Relatives: that, which, who, whom, whose, whoever, whomever

Adjective

Modifies nouns, that is, it describes, limits, specifies, what a noun names. For instance:

> *tall* woman   *young* child   *illustrated* book
> *temperate* climate   *American* history   *public* education

Verb

Denotes any *action*: run, talk, think, intend, suggest, play, strike, have, do; or *state of being*: appear, seem, be, feel. The principal parts of a verb are as follows:

Infinitive: to run, to talk, to think, to intend, to appear, to seem
Simple past: ran, talked, thought, intended, appeared, seemed
Present participle: running, talking, thinking, intending, appearing, seeming
Past participle: (has) run, (has) talked, (has) thought, intended, appeared, seemed

Adverb

Modifies verbs; it indicates the manner, quality, or degree of an *action*.

run *swiftly*   talk *loudly*   think *clearly*
play *well*   strike *suddenly*

Adverbs also function as *intensifiers*; that is, they indicate the degree or intensity of modifiers, both adjectives and adverbs.

rather tall woman   *very* young child
talk *too* loudly   *nearly* complete project

Conjunction

A word that connects two or more words or groups of words.

Coordinating conjunctions: and, but, yet, so, for
Subordinating conjunctions: because, although, since, while, if, until, when, unless, before, after

There are a tall woman *and* a young child.
We will stay home *if* it rains.
Because he trains regularly, he plays well.

Preposition

Expresses relationships of time, space, or position.

above	behind	in	under
across	beside	into	within
after	between	on	without
at	except	over	
before	for	to	

Interjection

An expression that begins or interrupts a sentence to express a particular feeling.

Ouch!, that hurts.   *Oh,* how interesting!   *Bravo!*

Phrases, Clauses, and Sentences

While we may express feelings and give commands with single words, our most useful expression is in words grouped in phrases, clauses, and sentences.

PHRASE

A meaningful group of words. There are many kinds of phrases in English. Here are some common examples:

A noun and its modifiers:

   the large brick building   the tall young woman

A verb and its auxiliaries (to show different tenses):

   has run   will arrive
   should have been done

A preposition and its object:

   across the room   in the final chapter
   down the hill   on the roof

A participle and its object or modifiers:

   opening the door carefully   sensing danger
   returning after many years*   walking slowly

CLAUSE

A meaningful group of words that contains a verb and its subject.

Clauses are *dependent* when they form only part of a complex sentence of more than one clause:

   Because he was late, ...   If it rains tomorrow, ...
   ... when the plane arrives   ... that you requested

Each of these expressions contains a verb and *its* subject, but you will notice that the sentence will not be complete—that is, the assertion will not be fully expressed or understood—until at least one additional clause is added.

---

* Note that prepositional phrases, which are modifiers because they function as adjectives and adverbs do, may be part of a larger participial phrase.

In these examples, one *independent* clause has been added to form a *complete sentence:*

[Because he was late], his appointment was canceled.

I will call you [when the plane arrives].

The book [that you requested] is now available.

A *sentence,* then, may be made up of a few words—a subject, and a predicate verb that establishes the action or state of being of the subject, and modifiers:

She ran.

The dog barked.

He was late.

The crowd cheered enthusiastically.

Or a sentence may be made up of more than one clause and contain several phrases as modifiers.

Because he was late, his appointment was canceled and had to be rescheduled for the following week.

The large crowd in the bleachers cheered enthusiastically as the home team took the field in the last inning.

Tests of standard usage are tests of how well you understand and can compose the many relationships of words, phrases, clauses, and sentences that make up standard written English.

Most of the problems in grammar and usage you are expected to recognize and be able to correct are considered "errors" because they result in a lack of clarity, even confusion, in the writer's expression.

Although writing that contains minor errors in standard usage may still be understood, careful writers seek expression that is precise and clear—even elegant—and that demonstrates their ability to use variety in language and structure. It is only through mastery of a wide range of expression that students may fully reveal their ideas, insights, and feelings.

AVOIDING COMMON ERRORS IN WRITING

When we refer to errors in writing, we are referring to expressions that are illogical, inconsistent, vague, or imprecise. The elements of usage reviewed here are those that high school students should be able to recognize.

Agreement of Subject and Verb

Agreement is a form of consistency and is one of the most basic elements of grammar. When you learn to conjugate verbs, for example, you are applying the concept of agreement. Singular subjects take singular verbs; plural subjects take plural verbs.

He speaks/they speak; One is/many are

Errors in agreement commonly occur in sentences where the subject follows the verb:

On the desk *are* my notebook, a few pencils, and the assignments for tomorrow.

"Desk" is not the subject of the verb; "notebook, pencils, assignments" is the subject, *they* are on the desk. In such inverted word order, the writer must think ahead to choose the correct form of the verb. Similarly:

There *seems* to be only *one answer*.

There *seem* to be *several ideas* worth considering.

Here *are* the *pieces* you have been looking for.

Agreement errors may also occur when a subject followed by a phrase precedes the verb:

New York with its many historical sites and tourist attractions *is* a fascinating city to visit.

His *many talents* in sports, academics, and student leadership *make* him a popular candidate.

Subjects may be expanded by such prepositional phrases as *along with, in addition to, as well as, together with*. These phrases, however, do not form part of the *grammatical* subject; they modify the subject:

English, as well as math, science, and social studies, *is* a required subject for most high school students.

Evan, along with several of his friends, *is* planning to visit colleges in the fall.

In some sentences, the subject may be modified by one or more clauses before the predicate verb is stated. In such sentences the writer must "remember" the actual subject before composing the correct form of the verb:

The *fact* that Americans must now compete in a global economy and must recognize the necessity for higher standards in our schools *has led* to educational reform in many states.

Many common pronouns are singular and must take a singular verb:

Each one of these books *is* worth reading.
Every one of us *is* prepared to contribute.
None of these solutions *is* acceptable. (No *one* is)

Note how agreement with correlatives *either/or, neither/nor* is achieved:

Either Susan or her brother *is* home now.
(Either Susan is . . . or her brother is)
Neither rain, nor sleet, nor snow *deters* us . . . .

When the correlative contains both a singular and plural expression, the verb agrees with the one closest:

Neither Susan nor her sisters *are* at home.
Either the members of the legislature or the governor *is* authorized to submit a budget.

Do not be confused when the predicate is completed with a plural expression:

His most reliable *source* of encouragement *is* friends and family.

To avoid the correct but awkward-sounding expression above, rewrite as follows:

His *friends and family are* his most reliable source of encouragement.

Collective nouns take singular verbs because all the "members" are understood to act as a single unit:

The *jury was* unanimous in its decision to acquit.
A school *board has* extensive responsibilities.
Our *family has agreed* on plans for the vacation.
The *team practices* for two hours every day.

When there is not such unity of action, you may use a plural verb:

The jury are not in unanimous agreement.

The family are expected to arrive at different times.

It is better, however, to avoid such awkward-sounding expressions by rewriting to make the plural idea clear:

The members of the jury are not in agreement.

Players on the team are required to keep their uniforms and equipment in good order.

Family members are expected to arrive at different times.

Agreement of Pronoun and Antecedent

Because pronouns replace nouns or other pronouns, they must agree with their singular or plural antecedents.

Evelyn is very grateful to *her parents* for *their* constant support and encouragement.

Most pronoun/antecedent errors arise when we use the indefinite pronouns *anyone, anybody, everyone, everybody, someone, somebody, no one*, and so on. These pronouns are singular because they refer to *individuals:*

Everybody is responsible for *his* own work.

Someone has left *her* books on the floor.

If *anyone* calls while I am out, please tell *him* or *her* I will call back after lunch.

The common practice of replacing *him/her* with *them*, or *her/his* with *their,* solves the problem of choosing gender, but it is ungrammatical and illogical. The careful writer (and speaker) avoids these errors or rewrites:

Please tell *anyone who calls* that I will return at noon.

Someone's books have been left on the floor.

Everyone has individual responsibility for the assignments.

Form of Pronouns

Use the subject forms when pronouns are *subjects* of verbs or identify the subject after a linking verb:

> *He and I* received the information we needed.
>
> *She* is the favorite candidate of the party.
>
> *He* is the head baseball coach.
>
> The head baseball coach is *he*.
>
> (Think of the verb *is* as an = sign.)

It is easy to avoid the awkward sound of the last sentence by choosing the preceding expression, which uses the pronoun first.

Pronouns as *objects* of verbs or prepositions must be in the object form:

> Please give *him* the information.
>
> Give the information to *them*.
>
> *Whom* did you see yesterday?

Errors often occur when we have pronouns preceded by a noun; the writer no longer "hears" the preposition and is reluctant to use the object form. But,

> Please give the information to Ellen and *him*. (to Ellen . . . to him)
>
> The host was very gracious to Ellen and *me*.
> (to Ellen . . . to me; *not* to Ellen and I)
>
> Just between you and me, this is simple.

We also use the object form with infinitives:

> We understand *her to be* the favorite candidate.
>
> We understand the favorite candidate *to be her*.

Remember to use the possessive form with *gerunds* ("-ing" verb forms that function as nouns):

> I do not approve of *your staying* out so late.
> (of your "late hours")
>
> She was concerned about *his working* too hard.
> (about his excessive work)

Note the following:

> Mark's mother saw *him* [*running* after the bus].
>
> Mark's mother encouraged [*his running* on the cross-country team].

In the first example, *running* is a participle describing *him*, which is the object of the verb *saw*. In the second example, *running* is a noun; it is the object of the verb *encouraged*.

Parallelism

Parallelism is used for consistency and clarity. Parallel ideas and expressions in a series should be composed in the same form:

> He wants to spend the summer *reading, sleeping, and traveling*.
>
> He plans *to read, to sleep, and to travel*.

Use parallel phrases and clauses:

> She is known *for* her talent and *for* her generosity.
>
> We expect our presidents to be skilled *not only in* domestic affairs *but also in* foreign policy.
>
> Our state senator was reelected *because* she is honest, *because* she works hard for the district, *and because* she has an important leadership position in the senate.

Use parallel construction when you use correlatives: *either, or; not only, but also:*

> *Either* you will complete the work now, *or* he will complete it in the morning.
>
> We will *either take* a train this afternoon *or take* a plane this evening.

Consistency of active and passive voice is also a form of parallelism:

> The research team *formulated* its ideas and *developed* its proposal.
>
> Ideas *were formulated* and a proposal *was developed* by the research team.

Verbs: Using the Correct Tense

Use the simple past tense for actions completed in the past:

> The train *arrived* at 6:30.
> He *retired* in 1993.
> The Nobel prizes *were announced* in January.

Use the present perfect tense to establish facts, to assert that something *has occurred, has happened, has been done*, without reference to a specific time.

> *Have you done* your homework yet?
> The renovation of our house *has been completed*.
> I *have read Macbeth* several times.

Note the correct *sequence of tenses* in the following:

> The novelist *completed* the book in 1993, two years after he *had begun* it.
> She *recorded* the names of everyone who *had called* the day before.

> In the Middle Ages, most people *believed* that the earth *is* round.
> Copernicus *demonstrated* that the earth *orbits* the sun.

> If I *were* you, I *would accept* the offer.
> If the congressman *were indicted*, he *would* lose the support of many constituents.

> If we *had taken* more time to plan, our trip *would have been* more pleasant.
> If you *had trained* harder, you *would have* made the team.

If you would have called earlier is sometimes said but this is not an acceptable construction in standard English.

Finally, you are generally expected to write about works of literature in the *present tense*.

> Macbeth *is driven* by ambition.
> Jay Gatsby *believes* he can recreate the past.
> Willy Loman *dies* believing his son will achieve great success.

Aspects of character, themes, plot, and setting remain constant—they *are* what they are—regardless of how the plot concludes or when we finish reading the work.

Logical Comparisons

> My sister is *taller* than I [am].
> She is *more* clever than he [is].
> Josh is the *tallest* member of the team.
> Among all of Miller's plays, *Death of a Salesman* is the *best* known.

Avoid incomplete comparisons in your writing:

> Dreiser's novels are *more* popular now [than they were when they were first published].
> Shakespeare's plays are *harder* to read [than modern works are].

The passages in brackets should be fully stated.
In informal speech we may use *so* as an intensifier:

> I was *so* tired. He was *so* angry.

In writing, however, be sure every *so* is followed by a *that,* every *more* by a *than.*
Comparisons must be parallel and logical:

> *The paintings of Monet are more popular than Goya* **should read**:
> *The paintings* of Monet are more popular than *the paintings* of Goya.

You must compare paintings to paintings, not inadvertently compare paintings to a man.
And,

> Anne is a better player than anyone on her team. **should read**:
> Anne is a *better* player *than any other* [player] on her team.

or,

> Anne is the *best player* on the team.

It is illogical to suggest Anne is better than she herself is.

172

Clear and Logical Modification

The careful writer must also be aware of errors in modification and in the logical relationships of ideas. Many such errors are corrected simply, with commas; others may require revision or reorganization of sentences.

Introductory subordinate (dependent) clauses must be set off by a comma:

> *After the lights had come back on,* the children were no longer frightened by the thunderstorm.
>
> *When it rains,* cats and dogs prefer not to go outside.

Without the comma, such sentences would be ambiguous.
Nonrestrictive (nonessential) phrases and clauses are set off by commas:

> My aunt, *who lives in Milwaukee,* will be flying in for a weekend visit to New York.
>
> Several stranded passengers, *feeling restless and impatient,* demanded flights on another airline.

When such phrases or clauses are restrictive* (essential to the meaning of the sentence), do not set them off with commas:

> Passengers *traveling with small children* will be permitted to board the plane first.
>
> My cousin *who lives in Milwaukee* will have to fly, but the cousins *who live in the New York area* will be able to drive to my brother's wedding.

A common error occurs when we begin a sentence with a participial phrase:

> Feeling restless and impatient, seats were demanded on other airlines' flights [by many travelers].
> (The seats are not restless . . .)
>
> *Barking loudly,* we were afraid the dog would wake our neighbors.
> (We are not barking, the dog is . . .)
>
> *Tired and hungry,* even cold leftovers looked good to us.
> (The leftovers are not hungry, we are . . .)

---

*For additional examples, see *which/that/who* on page 181.

The *subject* of the participle must also be stated as the subject of the clause that follows:

> *Feeling restless and impatient, many stranded travelers* sought seats on other airlines' flights.
> *Barking loudly, the dog* wakened our neighbors.
> *Tired and hungry, we* were satisfied with the cold leftovers.

You may also recompose sentences to make the modification clear:

> We were afraid our dog, *barking loudly,* would wake the neighbors.
> *Because we were tired and hungry,* even cold leftovers looked good to us.

EXPRESSIONS OFTEN CONFUSED, MISUSED, AND OVERUSED*

accept/except

> To **accept** is to receive, take willingly, agree to:
>
> > I **accept** your offer, apology, invitation
>
> To **except** is to exclude, to separate out:
>
> > I will **except** you from the requirement.
>
> **Except** is also a preposition:
>
> > Everyone **except** him will be leaving on Tuesday.

affect/effect

> To **affect** (vb.) means to move, influence, or change. It also means to put on an artificial quality of personality or character; such an exaggerated or artificial person may be called **affected**.
>
> An **effect** (n.) is a consequence or result.
>
> To **effect** (vb.) means to put into action, to complete—a plan or a change, for example.

---

*See also Words Commonly Confused/Misspelled in Chapter 11, Spelling.

aggravate

> To **aggravate** means to make worse. Do not use it when you really mean to irritate or annoy.

allusion/illusion

> An **allusion** is a reference (see Glossary of Poetic Terms and Techniques, Chapter 5); an **illusion** is a false or deceptive idea or vision.

among/between

> Use **between** for two, **among** for three or more:
>
> **between** you and me
>
> **among** all the members of the family

amount/number

> One has an **amount** of something (the quantity as a whole) and a **number** of things (that can be counted):
>
> an **amount** of time/a **number** of hours, days
>
> a large **amount** of work/a **number** of tasks

See also **fewer/less** for the same distinction.

as far as . . . is/are concerned

> The expression **as far as** used by itself creates an incomplete and illogical statement; it must be completed with **is/are concerned.** The expression as **far as . . . goes/go** is also widely used and correct as completed.
>
> *Faulty:* **As far as** plans for school construction in the future, we expect the legislature to take action in the next session.
>
> **As far as** the weather, it will be sunny and pleasant tomorrow.
>
> *Correct:* **As far as** plans for school construction in the future are concerned, we expect the legislature to take action in the next session
>
> **As far as** the weather goes, it will be sunny and pleasant.

bad/badly, good/well

> Use **bad** and **good** (adjectives) to describe how one feels; use **badly** and **well** (adverbs) to describe how one does something.
>
> He felt **bad** (sorry, regretful) because he caused the team to lose.

The team lost the game because he played so **badly**.

She feels **good** (in good spirits, positive) when her work is going **well**.

She is feeling **well** (no longer ill) now after a long bout with the flu.

The team lost because he did not play **well**.

being as, being that

These expressions are not standard speech. Use *because* or *since* instead.

compare to, compare with

Use **compare to** when you are expressing an analogy or similarity; use **compare with** when you are showing similarities and differences between two things.

He compared his small room **to** a closet.

The critics compared the movie **with** the book.

could of/ should of

Do not make this unfortunate confusion in the way words sound! You mean **could have/should have**.

different from (not **than**)

You should use the preposition **from** with **different** because you are making a distinction, a separation. Use **than** for comparisons, to show degrees of the same quality:

She is only slightly older **than** her sister, but her personality is very different **from** her sister's.

due to

This expression is popularly used for almost any cause and effect relationship. Avoid its overuse in your writing:

Absence **due to** illness is excused.

Delays **due to** bad weather are common in winter.

It is more precise to say:

The road was closed **because of** an accident.

The defendant was acquitted **by reason of** insanity.

There were many landslides **caused by** the heavy rains.

everybody, somebody, someone, nobody

> These are *singular* forms; they may refer to many people, but they refer to *each one individually*. Singular antecedents take singular pronouns:
>
> **Everybody** has *his/her* books, lunch, opinions.
>
> **Someone, a person** has *his/her* opinions.

farther/further

> In general, you may use **farther** or **further** for actual or figurative distance:
>
> The nearest town is ten miles **farther** from here.
>
> The latest agreements move us **further** toward a full peace.
>
> Use **further** when you mean more:
>
> We have nothing **further** to discuss.
>
> A final agreement requires **further** negotiations.

fewer/less

> One has **fewer** things and **less** something.
>
> **fewer** hours/**less** time
>
> **fewer** dollars/**less** money
>
> **fewer** ideas/**less** content

first, second, . . .

> To show transition and to enumerate examples, use these terms instead of *firstly, secondly*, . . .

hang/hanged/hung

> When we use this verb in the past tense to denote an execution, we use **hanged**; for such things as clothes and pictures, we use **hung**.
>
> The condemned man was **hanged** at dawn.
>
> We **hung** our winter coats in the hall closet.

hopefully

> This expression is popularly used to mean we hope, it is hoped, and so on. The careful writer should use it only as an adverb:
>
> The cat looked **hopefully** at the leftover chicken.

But:

> We **hope** the situation will improve.
>
> **It is hoped** that research will lead to a cure.

however

> Along with its cousins *therefore, moreover,* and *consequently,* **however** should be placed *within the sentence*, close to the verb it modifies; think of it as a conjunction, not as a transition at the beginning of a sentence.

if/whether

> Use **if** to introduce conditional expressions; use **whether** (or not) for choices, decisions, questions:
>
> **If** it rains, our game will be postponed.
>
> **If** you work hard, you will succeed.
>
> I do not know **whether** we will play or not.

infer/imply

> To **infer** is to conclude, to draw an inference from evidence; to **imply** is to suggest or hint.
>
> We can **infer** from his comments that he is pleased.
>
> She **implied** in her speech that she is planning to run for public office.

its/it's

> *it's* = a contraction* for it is.
>
> *its* = a possessive form; do not add an apostrophe.

if . . . were/if . . . was

> Use the **if . . . were** construction for *hypothetical* conditions and situations:
>
> **If you were** president, what would you do?
>
> **If I were you,** I would accept the offer.

---

*Contractions should be avoided in formal writing, unless you are quoting someone. Contractions are features of spoken language.

Use **if ... was** for situations that *were possible*:

If that really **was** Linda who called yesterday, she should have left a message.

incredible/incredulous

Incredible means unbelievable, beyond belief or understanding. In formal writing, avoid using it as *hyperbole*. Use instead such terms as *astonishing* or *extraordinary*.

A person is **incredulous** when he/she utterly cannot believe what is being said.

kind of/sort of/type of

Avoid using *a* or *an* with these expressions:

That type of character is popular in children's books.

Those types of characters are . . .

This kind of fabric is best for the new sofa.

Also avoid using **kind of** or **sort of** when you mean *a little, rather, somewhat*.

lie/lay

These verbs are often confused. Note their principal parts and distinctions in meaning: to **lie (down)** means to recline, be situated, rest:

You **lie** on your bed to take a nap.

The mail **has lain** on your desk since yesterday.

Last winter the snow **lay** on the ground for weeks.

Note that to **lay** means to put or place something. (It is a transitive verb and always takes a direct object.):

You can **lay** your hat and gloves on the hall table.

Masons **lay bricks** and hens **lay eggs**.

He cannot remember where he **laid** his car keys.

like/as/as if

Use **like** as a preposition, use **as** and **as if** as conjunctions:

He looks just **like** his father.

A talent **like** hers is rare.

It looks **as if** it will rain this afternoon.

You should do the assignments **as** you were instructed to.

"Do **as** I say, not **as** I do!"

only/just

These modifiers should be placed as close as possible to the expressions they actually limit:

I have **only** two dollars for lunch.

He has time for **only** a brief conversation.

I have **just** one thing to say.

presently

This should be used to denote the immediate future; it means right *away* or in *a little while:*

I will answer your question **presently**.

He is expected to arrive **presently**.

The meeting will begin **presently**.

For current time, use **at present** or **currently**:

He is **currently** a junior at North High.

At present, she is working on her master's degree.

purposely/purposefully

Use **purposely** to mean intentionally, knowingly, deliberately, that is, to describe an action done "on purpose" and not by accident.

purposefully is best used to mean decisively, firmly, resolutely, with determination, and with a specific purpose or goal in mind.

so

Try to avoid the casual use of "so" just to introduce an idea or an explanation. "So" is widely used in informal speech to begin the answer to almost any question, but it should be avoided in your formal writing. Use *so* as a conjunction to show a consequence:

We were hungry, **so** we went to lunch early.

Our plane was delayed, **so** we spent several hours waiting at the airport.

toward/towards

Either is acceptable; **toward** is more formal.

when/where

These are terms of time and place; do not use them to introduce definitions.

which/that/who

These relative *pronouns* introduce *clauses* that describe or define. Use **that** for clauses that are *restrictive* (defining, limiting):

The books **that** you ordered will arrive tomorrow; the ones **that** Sam ordered will come next week. (those particular books . . .)

He likes the car **that** he bought last year better than any other he has owned. (that particular car)

Basketball is the game **that** he plays best.

Use **which** for clauses that are *nonrestrictive* (descriptive):

The house on the corner, **which** was built in the 1880s, will be restored to its original design.

Shakespeare's plays, **which** were written nearly 400 years ago, remain popular in theaters and movies as well as in English courses.

Use **who** for people. (**That** is sometimes used when the identification is distant or impersonal.) Do not use **which** for people:

Lady Macbeth is a character **that** (**who**) remains fascinating to many students.

Use **whom** when the pronoun is an object:

To **whom** should I give the information? (obj. of prep.)

Whom did you ask? (obj. of verb)

who/whom/whoever/whomever

When these *pronouns* introduce *clauses,* their form is determined *solely* by their function in the clause:

The new coach, **who** led the team to a county title, gave all the credit to her players.
(**Who** is the subject of the verb *led;* therefore, it is in the subject form.)

Please give the information to (**whoever** needs it.)

(**Whoever** is the subject in the clause; the *entire* clause is the object of *give to*.)

Please give the award to (**whomever** you choose.)
(**Whomever** is the object of the verb *choose;* the *entire* clause is the object of *give to*.)

Careful attention to the conventions of usage and style outlined in this chapter will enhance your ability to express ideas and discuss information clearly and persuasively. When you have command of the language you use, you have command of the relationship between thought and expression.

Chapter 10

PUNCTUATION: GUIDELINES AND REMINDERS

When is the semicolon or colon used? Are there any rules for commas? Do I underline titles of books and poems or put them in quotation marks? Where do I put the period when a sentence ends with quotation marks? Even experienced writers need to consult a usage handbook for the answers to some of these questions.

In conversation we use pauses, stresses, and tone of voice to make our meaning clear. The printed page, however, does not readily show what voice and gesture can reveal, so the writer uses punctuation to achieve absolute clarity. Below, you will find a review of the elements of punctuation high school students should know and use in their own writing. Featured are answers to those questions most often raised about how to punctuate. (Many of the examples from the writing of specific authors come from the passages reprinted elsewhere in the book.)

END PUNCTUATION

The period, exclamation mark, and question mark bring statements and expressions to a close; they signal a full stop.

The Period

Use a **period** to indicate the end of a sentence or of a group of words having the emphasis of a sentence.

Declarative sentences (make a statement):

Good writers are also good readers.

"Camp fires, like red, peculiar blossoms, dotted the night."
(Stephen Crane, *The Red Badge of Courage*)

Imperative sentences (give an order or direction):

>Be sure to proofread.
>
>Come to practice on time or leave the team.
>
>Tell me how much I owe you.

Fragments for emphasis:

>"No doubt my younger brother and sister were in the house and warm. *Eating cookies*." (William Kittredge)
>
>"Much of their [whales'] behavior seems to be recreational: they sing, they play. *And so on*." (Robert Finch)

The Exclamation Mark

Use an **exclamation mark** to show intensity and emphasis in sentences or fragments.

>Come to practice!
>
>Be sure to proofread!
>
>Look out!
>
>Congratulations!

CAUTION: *Do not overuse the **exclamation mark** in expository writing; use effective language and sentence structure to achieve emphasis.*

The Question Mark

Use a **question mark** to signal interrogative forms in complete sentences, fragments, or series.

>Can you explain how to do this?
>
>Do you understand what he said?
>
>Can you recommend a good restaurant in the theater district?
>
>What was that all about? a joke? a mistake?
>
>Where should we meet? at home? at school?
>
>Ask questions as you read an essay: What is the author's purpose? tone? conclusion? Do you agree? disagree? feel convinced?

Question marks may also be used with single words or phrases as needed:

When?
Leave the team?
You did?
What homework?

Special Considerations

Periods are used in many abbreviations. For example:

U.S. government	Dipl. B.A. M.A. Ph.D.
U.N. Security Council	D.D.S. M.D. Esq.
N.Y.S. Board of Regents	A.M. P.M.

Some abbreviations take no periods:

CIA	mph
MTV	rpm
WCBS	

A sentence may end with more than one kind of punctuation. If it ends with an abbreviation using a period, do not add a second period.

Please report to my office promptly at 10:00 A.M.

In order to apply for a teaching position, you must have completed your M.A.

If it ends with a quotation or expression in quotation marks, place the final period *inside* the quotation marks.

Most high school students have read Poe's short story "The Cask of Amontillado."

When told his wife is dead, Macbeth remarks, "She should have died hereafter."

If the **entire sentence** requires a question mark, place it outside the quotation marks:

Have you read Poe's story "The Cask of Amontillado"?

Why does Macbeth say, "She should have died hereafter"?

End Punctuation

If the quotation at the end of a sentence requires a question mark, keep it within the quotes. (Do not add an additional period.)

> The title of a recent editorial in *The New York Times* was "Where do we go from here?"

If a statement within the quotes is a question, the question mark within the quote is sufficient.

> Did you read the editorial entitled "Where do we go from here?"

Similarly, if an exclamation point is part of a quoted expression, place it within the quote. An additional period is not required.

> One of my favorite pieces by James Thurber is called "Excelsior!"

To make the above into a question, however:

> Have you read Thurber's story "Excelsior!"?

If a sentence ends with a passage in parentheses, put the period outside the closing parenthesis:

> We did not leave on time because Sally was late (as usual).

Even if the expression is a complete sentence, do not punctuate within the parentheses:

> We did not leave on time because Sally was late (she always is).

If, however, the expression within the parentheses requires quotation marks, a question mark, or an exclamation point, include them:

> We did not leave on time because Sally was late (isn't she always?).

In such cases, a better solution would be to separate the parenthetical statement:

> We did not leave because Sally was late. (Isn't she always?)

What is the logic to all this? When sentences or passages are made up of a variety of elements, punctuation should make the structure of each element clear. If the end of a sentence becomes cluttered by the need to bring several individual pieces to a close at the same time, punctuate from the inside out—smaller pieces first, then larger. But do not double the end punctuation unless it is required for accuracy. If you have a question within a question, one question mark will do. If a closing quotation ends with a "strong" piece of punctuation, don't add a modest and redundant period to the whole sentence. Close with the strength of the quote.

INTERNAL PUNCTUATION

Internal punctuation includes the comma, the semicolon, the colon, and the dash. The single purpose of internal punctuation is to prevent confusion, to achieve clarity. The comma indicates brief pauses between separate elements in a sentence; the semicolon establishes a direct connection between two independent statements to form a single sentence; the colon serves to introduce things; and the dash permits you to digress or emphasize.

The Comma

Use the comma in compound sentences with coordinating conjunctions *and, but, yet, so, or, for*. A compound sentence joins two or more independent clauses that could be expressed separately as simple sentences. *Note that the comma precedes the conjunction:*

> "I walked slowly, *for* the detail on the beach was infinite." (Ernie Pyle)
>
> "The luncheon hour was long past; *and* the two had their end of the vast terrace to themselves." (Edith Wharton, "Roman Fever")
>
> "I was not going to talk about Whitewater today, *but* then I thought that if I didn't you'd think I know something about it, *and* the only way for me to prove that I don't is to talk about it at length, *so* I will." (Garrison Keillor)

In sentences where the clauses are short and the meaning is clear, you may omit a comma:

> The team tied the score in the last seconds of the game and the crowd cheered wildly.

If there is any possibility of misreading, you must use a comma:

> I went to the movies with Roger and Sally stayed home.
>
> I went to the movies with Roger, and Sally stayed home.

WHAT IS A COMMA SPLICE?

One of the most common errors in writing is the use of a comma alone to join independent clauses. This is the error familiar to students as the "run-on" sentence.

Run on: The crowd cheered wildly, the game was tied in the last few seconds.

   I went to the movies with Roger, Sally stayed home.

   The novel was riveting, I did not want it to end.

Correct: The crowd cheered wildly when the game was tied in the final seconds.

   I went to the movies with Roger, and Sally stayed home.

   The novel was riveting, so I did not want it to end.

DO I USE A COMMA BEFORE THE LAST ITEM IN A SERIES?

Some editors and instructors insist that all items in a series be set off by a comma; others prefer that you omit the last one, especially in a series of single words:

   You can find models of style in books, newspapers, and magazines.

   You can find models of style in books, newspapers and magazines.

SUGGESTION: *For sentences like the one above, the second comma needlessly slows down the sentence and makes no contribution to clarity. In a series of longer expressions, however, or in a series without a conjunction, set off each with a comma.*

   For class you are expected to bring a notebook, a pen or pencil, and the text we are reading.

   "He was white-headed as a mountain, bowed in the shoulders, and faded in general aspect." (Thomas Hardy)

   Writing has many purposes: personal expression, persuasion, literary effect, information.

USE A COMMA AFTER INTRODUCTORY CLAUSES

As the crowd cheered them on, the home team scored the winning touchdown.

If you are hungry, please help yourself to a sandwich.

"As the bell sounded the hour, there came a knocking at the street door." (Edgar Allan Poe)

Do not use a comma if the main clause is followed by a dependent clause:

Please help yourself to a sandwich whenever you get hungry.

The home team scored the winning touchdown as the crowd cheered them on.

USE A COMMA AFTER AN INTRODUCTORY PHRASE ONLY WHEN NEEDED

At last, the rain began to ease, and the sun came through breaks in the clouds.

The son of a tanner, Grant was everything Lee was not.

After the Labor Day recess, Congress will reconvene.

Feeling ill and confused, he left the dinner table without speaking.

These sentences require no comma:

On the desk you will find your final check and a letter of recommendation.

"For a long time they continued to sit side by side without speaking." (Edith Wharton)

USE COMMAS TO SET OFF DESCRIPTIVE AND NONESSENTIAL CLAUSES OR PHRASES WITHIN SENTENCES

"They were two strong men, these oddly different generals, and they represented the strengths of two conflicting currents that, through them, had come into final collision." (Bruce Catton)

The house on the corner, which was built in the 1880s, will be restored to its original design.

Shakespeare's plays, written nearly four hundred years ago, remain popular in theaters and movies as well as in English courses.

USE COMMAS WITH SOME SINGLE WORDS AND EXPRESSIONS

"Well, Jim's habits and his jokes didn't appeal to Julie . . ." (Ring Lardner, "Haircut")

"Now, I'll read the names—heads of families first." (Shirley Jackson, "The Lottery")

USE COMMAS WITH PARENTHETIC AND TRANSITIONAL EXPRESSIONS

Use commas to set off such expressions as *however, moreover, therefore, nevertheless, after all, by the way, of course, on the other hand, I think.*

"Yet it was not all contrast, after all . . . Furthermore, their fighting qualities were really very much alike." (Bruce Catton)

After all, what you learn is what really matters.

You must, of course, always proofread a paper before handing it in.

COMMAS IN DATES

For expressions of day, month, and year:

July 4, 1776, marks the beginning of the American Revolution.

Registration will take place on September 9, 1994, for the fall semester and on January 12, 1995, for the spring semester.

Do not use commas for expressions of month and year only.

Joan completed graduate school in June 1987, began her legal work in September 1987, and joined our firm in January 1993.

COMMAS WITH ADJECTIVES IN A SERIES

Use a comma when it means *and:*

The little room in Appomattox was "the scene of one of the poignant, dramatic contrasts in American history." (Bruce Catton)

The Regents examinations require you to write thoughtful, well-organized essays.

Do not use a comma if the adjective is part of the meaning of the noun:

She greeted her guests in the large sitting room.

USE COMMAS TO SET OFF QUOTES

"I always used to think," Mrs. Slade continued, "that our mothers had a much more difficult job than our grandmothers." (Edith Wharton, "Roman Fever")

"It isn't fair, it isn't right," Mrs. Hutchinson screamed, and then they were upon her. (Shirley Jackson, "The Lottery")

ADDITIONAL ILLUSTRATIONS OF COMMA USE

If you must sing, sing quietly.

These incidents took place a long, long time ago.

That's not what you meant, is it?

You have everything you need, don't you?

First come, first served.

Now you see it, now you don't.

Shakespeare's tragedy, *Macbeth*, is one of his best-known plays.

Verdi's only comic opera, *Falstaff,* is the last work he composed.

My sister Anne lives in Seattle; my sister Julia lives in New York.

My only sister, Anne, lives in Seattle.

COMMON ERRORS IN COMMA USE

Do not separate compound elements or isolate essential elements with commas.

Correct: "They greeted one another and exchanged bits of gossip as they went to join their husbands." (Shirley Jackson, "The Lottery")

Faulty: They greeted one another, and exchanged bits of gossip as they went to join their husbands.

Internal Punctuation

Alternative: *They greeted* one another, and *they exchanged* bits of gossip as they went to join their husbands.

Correct: "Whales possess a highly complex language and have developed sophisticated communications systems that transmit over long distances." (Robert Finch)

Faulty: Whales possess a highly complex language, and have developed sophisticated communications systems, that transmit over long distances.

Alternative: *Whales possess* a highly complex language, *and they have developed* sophisticated communications systems that transmit over long distances.

In the faulty examples, the first comma may *look* necessary, but it improperly separates the subject from the second verb; the final clause in each case is essential description and should not be separated from the rest of the sentence. The alternative versions are accurately punctuated and show how the original, correct sentences could be revised into compound sentences.

SUGGESTION: *In all the examples and explanations above, the commas serve one purpose: to make the expression clear on first reading. Insert commas in your own writing as you compose, as you hear the need for them. When you revise, do not be tempted to add commas simply because they look right—chances are, they do not belong.*

The Semicolon

A comma indicates a brief pause between separate elements in a sentence, whereas a semicolon indicates a longer pause between independent statements that form a single sentence. The semicolon may replace *and* or *but* in compound sentences. Here are some of the examples used earlier now revised with semicolons.

> I walked slowly; the detail on the beach was infinite.
>
> The luncheon hour was long past; the two had their end of the vast terrace to themselves.
>
> I was not going to talk about Whitewater today; then I thought that if I didn't, you'd think I know something about it; the only way for me to prove that I don't is to talk about it at length; so I will.

In each of these revisions, you will note that the effect of the semicolon is to indicate a cause and effect relationship or to show consequence without stating it directly. This results in forceful and emphatic sentences.

The semicolon also has a formal quality; it creates a feeling of balance and equivalence among statements.

> ". . . with a semicolon . . . you get a pleasant little feeling of expectancy; there is more to come; read on; it will get clearer." (Lewis Thomas)

The Colon

Use the colon to introduce something: a list, the body of a letter, a quotation, or an explanation.

> "Political courage stems from a number of sources: anger, pain, love, hate." (Madeleine Kunin)

> "Mrs. Slade began again: 'I suppose I did it as a sort of joke'—" (Edith Wharton)

> "The purpose of life is to be useful. It is, above all, to *matter:* to have it make some difference that you lived at all." (Leo Rosten)

The Dash

The dash permits you to pause without notice and insert an idea too interesting to delay and too important to put in parentheses—but don't overdo it!

> "At some gut level, the art of politics—combative, competitive, self-asserting—is sometimes difficult to integrate with our feminine selves." (Madeleine Kunin)

> "Different as they were—in background, in personality, in underlying aspiration—these two great soldiers had much in common." (Bruce Catton)

> "The wonder of ourselves, of each other, and of life—this is the true subject matter of all novels." (Sandy Asher)

The Ellipsis

The ellipsis is used in quoted passages to show that something has been omitted.

> "The purpose of life is to be useful . . . above all, to *matter*." (Rosten)

Internal Punctuation

When an ellipsis comes at the end of a sentence, the final period must be retained; that is, you will use four periods, not three. The following example shows the use of three ellipses: one in the middle of a sentence and two, each with a fourth period added, at the ends of sentences:

> Mark Van Doren asserts that "Iago's cynicism consists of believing that . . . the passions of men are toys for him to play with . . . . He likes nothing better than to make plans which other men's emotions will execute . . . ."

The Bracket

Brackets indicate where the writer has added a word or phrase to a quoted passage. Such additions are sometimes necessary to make connections in extended quotes where you have used ellipsis.

> "The persons of the tale were long since types [to Hawthorne], as were their souls' predicaments. The broken law, the hidden guilt, the hunger for confession, the studious, cold heart that watches and does not feel . . ." (Mark Van Doren)

> Men's passions should lead them to "more and better feeling . . . ," but Iago's knowledge of men's hearts transforms those passions into destructive forces, into "toys . . . tools to use." Iago contrives malign "plans which other men's [benign] emotions will execute."

The Apostrophe

The apostrophe has many important uses: to form contractions, to show possession, and to form the plural of numbers, symbols, and letters. Apostrophes are also easily misused. Below are examples of the most common uses.

CONTRACTIONS

The apostrophe takes the place of a missing letter or letters in a contraction:

> It's very warm today. = It is very warm today.

> You don't have to return the book right now. = You do not . . .

Remember that contractions are characteristic of spoken language and are not generally used in formal writing.

The apostrophe is also used to abbreviate dates:

June '82

The Class of '98

Possessive Forms of Nouns and Proper Names

You form the possessive of a singular noun or name by adding an apostrophe and an *s*:

The novel's major themes (= The major themes of the novel)

My neighbor's house

Charles's notebook

Dickens's novels

In general, you form the possessive of a plural noun by adding the apostrophe alone:

My neighbors' yards

the jurors' verdict

the witnesses' statements

The Smiths' house

the Davises' horse

Note: Be sure to avoid the common error of confusing the possessive form with the plural.

Mark Twain wrote several novels; he did not write "novel's."

The local nursery sells plants; it does not sell "plant's."

Some Plurals

Use the apostrophe to form the plurals of letters and some abbreviations:

There were sixteen A's on the last exam.

"Dot your *i*'s and cross your *t*'s."

Mark has earned two Ph.D.'s, each in a different discipline.

TITLES OF WORKS OF LITERATURE

Titles of books and other full-length, separately published works should be set in italics. If you are composing on a typewriter or writing by hand, *underline* such titles. Movies and plays are also set in italics.

The Great Gatsby   *Death of a Salesman*
Huckleberry Finn   *The Glass Menagerie*
To Kill a Mockingbird   *Macbeth*

The names of newspapers and magazines should also be in italics.

The New York Times   *Harper's*   *Newsweek*

Titles of poems, essays, and short stories are set off in quotes.

"The Tell-Tale Heart"   "The Sleeping Giant"
"Roman Fever"   "The Road Not Taken"
"The Lottery"   "Old Photograph of the Future"

A title should not be underlined *and* set in quotes; this is redundant and confusing.

Your own title for an essay or paper should not be underlined; use quotes only for names or phrases actually quoted within the title.

A FINAL NOTE ON PUNCTUATION

The topics reviewed here are meant to offer fundamental guidelines and to illustrate how accurate punctuation helps make writing clear. Review some of the prose passages in other parts of the book for vivid examples of how different authors use punctuation to make their meaning and tone clear.

Chapter 11

SPELLING

We know how to spell many words because we recognize them from our reading and because we have, from childhood or as English language learners, developed awareness of the conventions of English spelling. Even though English spelling may seem confusing at times, most of the troublesome sounds or patterns reflect the history of English pronunciation and the fact that the English language developed after the forces of William the Conqueror, a Frenchman from Normandy, had invaded and settled in what is now the island of Great Britain. The resulting language is a fusion of Anglo-Saxon, French, and Latin.

SPELLING ON WRITING EXAMS

Does spelling count? The rubrics for the essays on the English Regents ELA exam include the "conventions" as a quality to be assessed. These are defined as ". . . conventional spelling, punctuation, paragraphing, capitalization, grammar and usage"; and on the SAT essay, frequent errors in grammar, usage, and mechanics are considered significant weaknesses in a student's writing.

If you know you have difficulties in spelling, use this chapter to review the common patterns of English spelling and to study the list of words commonly misspelled.

A word misspelled is a word misused, and egregious spelling errors may affect the scoring of your essay. You would also be expected to observe conventional spelling in preparing a college essay, a resume, or cover letter, and would avoid the spelling "shortcuts" we sometimes find useful in composing e-mail or text messages.

SPELLING RULES AND PATTERNS

As you review spelling rules and patterns, you need to be familiar with the following terms:

vowels The letters *a, e, i o, u,* and occasionally *y* signal the vowel, or sustained, sounds in English. The variations in these vowel sounds are spelled as combinations of more than one letter or as combinations with consonants.

consonants In English, the consonant letters and sounds are composed by the following: *b, c, d, f, g, h, j, k, l, m, n, p, q, r, s, t, v, w, x, z*. In contrast to vowels, consonant sounds do not sustain.

syllable A vowel sound or a combination of a vowel and consonant sounds that makes up a single impulse, or "beat," in a word. Words of one syllable: *think, read, act*. Words of two syllables: *reflect, insist, review*. We regularly use words of six or more syllables: *unintentionally, coincidentally*.

endings Single letters or syllables that indicate grammatical forms, such as noun plurals or verb conjugations. English, in contrast to other languages high school students may study, has relatively few "endings." Among them are *-s* or *-es* to form plural nouns or to indicate third-person *singular* verb forms, and the verb endings *-ing* and *-ed*.

suffixes Endings used to form new words and different parts of speech: *love, lovely, loveliness; occur, occurrence*. The addition of endings and suffixes to words often alters their spelling. (See next page.)

prefixes Units of one or two syllables that, like suffixes, are not "words" in themselves but have distinct meanings. They are placed at the beginning of existing words, or of what are called *stems* or *roots*. (See the section "Roots and Prefixes from Latin and Greek," Chapter 8, for many examples in English of Latin and Greek roots.) Words formed in this way are spelled to show their meanings: *illogical, overreact, misspell*.

Although most spelling "rules" have exceptions, there are many common patterns for spelling in English. The first group (pages 198–202) involves adding endings or suffixes.

Words That End in Silent *e*

➤ Drop the *e* before adding a suffix or ending that begins with a vowel:

dare + -ing	➔	= daring	➔	+ -ed	= dared
hope + -ing	➔	= hoping	➔	+ -ed	= hoped
amuse + -ing	➔	= amusing	➔	+ -ed	= amused
revise + -ion	➔	= revision	➔	+ -ed	= revised
advise + -able	➔	= advisable,	➔	+ -ed	= advised
reverse + -ible	➔	= reversible	➔	+ -ed	= reversed

➤ When adding *s* or a suffix that begins with a consonant, retain the *e*:

amuse	➔	amuses	➔	amusement
arrange	➔	arranges	➔	arrangement
hope	➔	hopes	➔	hopeless
huge	➔	hugeness	➔	hugely
place	➔	places	➔	placement
spite	➔	spiteful		
sure	➔	surely		

➤ When the word ends in *ce* or in *ge,* retain the *e* when adding *able* or *ous:*

change	➤	changeable
peace	➤	peaceable
service	➤	serviceable
advantage	➤	advantageous
courage	➤	courageous
outrage	➤	outrageous

➤ But drop the silent *e* before adding *ing:*

change	➤	changing
rage	➤	raging
service	➤	servicing
trace	➤	tracing

➤ Note the following **exceptions:**

argue	➤	argument
true	➤	truly
judge	➤	judgment
nine	➤	ninety
whole	➤	wholly

Words That End in y

➤ For words preceded by a consonant, change the *y* to an *i* before adding a suffix:

accompany	➤	accompaniment					
busy	➤	business	➤	busily			
easy	➤	easily					
funny	➤	funnier	➤	funniest			
happy	➤	happiness	➤	happily			
lonely	➤	loneliness					
silly	➤	silliness	➤	sillier	➤	silliest

➤ The same pattern applies when we add *s* to form plural nouns or third-person-singular verb forms:

army	➤	armies
baby	➤	babies
city	➤	cities
marry	➤	marries
try	➤	tries
worry	➤	worries

Spelling Rules and Patterns

▶ But retain the *y* before adding *ing, ism, ish*:

baby	→	babyish → babying
copy	→	copying
crony	→	cronyism
marry	→	marrying
try	→	trying
worry	→	worrying

▶ For words that end in *y* preceded by a vowel, retain *y*:

annoy	→	annoys	→	annoyance	→	annoyed	→	annoying
boy	→	boys	→	boyish				
day	→	days						
destroy	→	destroys	→	destroyed	→	destroying		
monkey	→	monkeys						
play	→	plays	→	played	→	playing	→	player → playful
valley	→	valleys						

▶ However:

say	→	says	→	**said**
pay	→	pays	→	**paid**

Double Letters

In writing, we must often stop to think whether to double letters in adding suffixes to words. Here are guidelines to follow.

▶ For one-syllable words that end in a single consonant preceded by a single vowel, *double* the final consonant before a suffix beginning with a vowel:

bat	→	batter	→	batting			
big	→	bigger	→	biggest			
fit	→	fitted	→	fitting	→	fittest
sit	→	sitter	→	sitting			
spot	→	spotty	→	spotted			

As you look at the examples, you will notice that the effect of the double consonant is to retain the pronunciation of the base word.

➤ Words formed by adding prefixes to one-syllable words follow the same pattern:

    outfit → outfitted → outfitter
    unwrap → unwrapped

➤ For one-syllable words that have double vowels or that end in more than one consonant, do *not* double the final consonant:

    beat → beating
    neat → neatest
    mail → mailing → mailed
    read → reading → reader
    fail → failure
    list → listed
    faint → fainted

➤ However:

    quit → quitting

Because *u* must follow the *q*, *-ui* is considered a single vowel.

➤ Do not double the final consonant for words ending in *w, x,* or *y:*

    draw → drawing
    mix → mixing
    play → playing → player

It is when we add endings to words of more than one syllable that spelling errors commonly occur.

➤ For words of more than one syllable ending in one vowel and one consonant, double the final consonant before an ending that begins with a vowel *if the last syllable of the base word is accented*:

    confer → conferred
    infer → inferred
    refer → referred
    begin → beginning
    deter → deterrence
    omit → omitted
    commit → committed
    occur → occurrence
    equip → equipped

Spelling Rules and Patterns

➤ If the accent is *not* on the syllable to which the ending is added, *do not* double the final consonant:

benefit	➤	benefited		
credit	➤	credited		
open	➤	opening		
happen	➤	happening		
develop	➤	developing	➤	developed
deliver	➤	delivered	➤	delivering

➤ Note how the shift in accent determines spelling:

confer	➤	conference
infer	➤	inference
prefer	➤	preference
refer	➤	reference

Note the following exceptions:

➤ The following words double the final consonant:

program	➤	programmed	➤	programmer
question	➤	questionnaire		
excel	➤	excellence	➤	excellent

➤ Either form is considered acceptable for the following, but the first form, with a single *-l*, is preferred:

canceled	➤	cancelled
traveled	➤	travelled
traveling	➤	travelling

Adding Prefixes and Suffixes

With the exception of the patterns reviewed on the previous pages, which reflect how we pronounce the words, most words formed by adding prefixes and suffixes retain the spelling of each separate part. As a result, the full meaning of the word is reflected in its spelling:

mis + spell + ed	➤	= misspelled (both *s*'s are required)
mis + understand + ing	➤	= misunderstanding
dis + agree + able	➤	= disagreeable
dis + taste + ful	➤	= distasteful
dis + appear + ance	➤	= disappearance
dis + satisfaction	➤	= dissatisfaction

un + necessary	➤	= unnecessary
un + ending	➤	= unending
cool + ly	➤	= coolly
moral + ly	➤	= morally
co + operate	➤	= cooperate
de + emphasize	➤	= de-emphasize
re + entry	➤	= reentry
mean + ness	➤	= meanness
amuse + ment	➤	= amusement

➤ Note that words ending in *c* add a *k* as follows:

panic, panics	➤	panicky, panicked, panicking
mimic, mimics	➤	mimicked, mimicking
picnic, picnics	➤	picnicking, picnickers

Words That Include *ie* or *ei*

➤ Is it *i* before *e* or *e* before *i*? This is the spelling pattern everyone remembers.

i before *e*:

chief	thief	relief	yield

➤ Except after *c*:

receive	ceiling	conceit

➤ Or, when *ei* sounds long *a*:

sleigh	neighbor	weigh	veil

There are, however, several **exceptions** to this pattern. They must be memorized:

caffeine	foreign	plebeian	sovereign
counterfeit	forfeit	protein	surfeit
either	leisure	seize	weird
financier	neither	sheik	

Noun Plurals

▶ Noun *plurals* are generally formed by adding *s*:

cat	→	cats
house	→	houses
delay	→	delays
piano	→	pianos

▶ Nouns ending in *s*, *sh*, *ch*, *x*, and *z*, add *es* to form the plural:

watch	→	watches
brush	→	brushes
waltz	→	waltzes

▶ Nouns ending in the consonant *y*: drop the *y* and add *ies*:

spy	→	spies
lady	→	ladies
quantity	→	quantities

▶ However, do *not* alter the spelling of proper names:

There are two "Sallys" in the junior class.

Shakespeare wrote plays about the "Henrys" of England.

▶ Some words ending in *o* add *es* to form the plural:

echo	→	echoes
tomato	→	tomatoes
potato	→	potatoes
hero	→	heroes
veto	→	vetoes

▶ Some nouns ending in *f* or *fe* form the plural with *ves*:

calf	→	calves
elf	→	elves
knife	→	knives
life	→	lives
self	→	selves
thief	→	thieves
wife	→	wives

▶ Other nouns change their form internally:

man	→	men
woman	→	women
child	→	children
mouse	→	mice

▶ In compound expressions, the principal noun is made plural:

sisters-in-law

passers-by

spoonsful

Homophones

Many spelling problems occur because words have syllables whose sounds are alike but could be spelled in more than one way: for example, *cede, ceed, sede*. These are called homophones.

▶ The most common form is *cede:*

precede	antecede
concede	intercede

▶ A few forms are spelled *ceed:*

exceed   proceed   succeed

▶ Only one form is spelled *sede:*

supersede

▶ For *able, ible,* the more common form is *able:*

curable	lovable	peaceable
imaginable	movable	

▶ Though fewer in number, there are many common words ending in *ible*:

admissible	horrible	possible
compatible	intelligible	visible
credible	legible	
eligible	perceptible	

▶ There are also words ending in *ance, ant,* or *ence, ent:*

assistant	extravagant	ignorance
attendant	fragrant	relevance
dominant	hesitance	resistance

▶ Note, however:

adolescent	current	permanence
competent	frequent	vehemence
correspondent	negligence	

▶ Many nouns end in *-er*:

consumer	interpreter	philosopher
defender	organizer	

▶ Note, however:

actor	counselor	professor
creator	governor	tailor

NOTE: *The careful writer must memorize the most common spellings. We cannot always use a dictionary or a spellcheck program!*

On the following pages you will find a list of words often confused and an extensive list of words commonly misspelled.

WORDS COMMONLY CONFUSED

Many words in English sound or look very similar to one another. Such words are often "misspelled" as a result of the writer's confusion about them. Here are some of the most commonly confused words; *all are correctly spelled*. Be sure you know their respective meanings.

accept/except	breath/breathe
access/excess	choose/chose/chosen
adapt/adopt	cite/sight/site
advice/advise	cloths/clothes
affect/effect	coarse/course
allusion/illusion	complement/compliment
already/all ready	desert/dessert
altogether/all together	device/devise

discreet/discrete
dyeing/dying
elicit/illicit
elude/allude
envelop/envelope
formally/formerly
fourth/forth
hear/here
holy/wholly
hoping/hopping
idle/idol
imminent/eminent/emanate
its/it's
loath/loathe
local/locale
loose/lose
medal/meddle/metal/mettle
moral/morale
night/knight

principal/principle
quite/quiet
rain/reign/rein
right/rite
shone/shown
sight/site
stationary/stationery
than/then
their/there/they're
thorough/through
though/thought
threw/through
throne/thrown
to/too/two
vain/vane/vein
weather/whether
which/witch
who's/whose
your/you're

WORDS COMMONLY MISSPELLED

You will recognize the most familiar and the most notorious spelling demons in this list.

absence	acquire	against	analysis
absolutely	across	aggravate	analyze
academic	actually	aggravation	ancient
accept	address	aggressive	angrily
acceptance	adequately	alleviate	announcement
accessory	adherence	alliance	annually
accidentally	adjournment	ally	antagonist
accommodate	adjustment	almanac	antibiotic
accompanying	admittance	already	anticipation
accomplish	adolescent	altitude	antique
accuracy	advantage	amateur	anxious
achievement	advantageous	ambassador	apologetically
acknowledge	advertisement	amendment	apologies
acquaintance	advising	among	apologize

Words Commonly Misspelled

apology	argument	assumption	authority
apostrophe	arising	assurance	auxiliary
apparently	arrangement	atheist	availability
appreciate	article	athlete	avalanche
appropriate	artistically	athletic	average
approximate	ascend	attempt	awfully
aptitude	ascent	attendance	awkward
architecture	assassin	attractive	
Arctic	assent	audience	
argue	assistance	authoritative	
bachelor	before	boring	bruise
baggage	beginning	boundary	budget
banana	belief	breakfast	buoy
bankruptcy	believing	breath	buoyant
bargain	beneficial	breathe	bureau
barrel	benefit	bribery	burglar
basement	benefited	brief	burglarize
basically	bibliography	brilliant	business
beautify	bicycle	Britain	businesslike
becoming	biscuit	brittle	busy
cafeteria	cemetery	client	compatible
caffeine	censor	closet	compel
calculator	censure	clustered	compelled
calendar	century	coalition	competitive
calorie	certainly	coherence	competitor
campaign	challenge	collar	comprehensible
candidate	changeable	college	conceivable
cannibal	changing	colonel	conceive
canoe	channel	column	concentrate
capable	characterize	combustible	conception
capacity	chauffeur	comfortable	condemn
captain	chief	coming	condescend
career	chimney	commencement	conference
carrying	chivalry	commercial	conferred
cashier	chloride	commission	confidence
catastrophe	cholera	commit	confidential
category	choose	committee	connotation
caucus	choosing	communal	connote
carefully	choral	community	conqueror
cease	chose	companies	conscience
ceiling	chuckle	comparative	conscious
cellar	cite	comparison	consequence

consequently	controlled	corrode	cruel
considerable	controlling	corrupt	cruelly
considerably	controversial	counterfeit	cupola
consistency	convenience	courteous	curiosity
consistent	convenient	courtesy	curious
conspicuous	convertible	cousin	current
contemporary	convocation	credible	curriculum
contempt	cool	creditor	curtain
contemptible	coolly	credulous	customary
contemptuous	cooperate	crisis	customer
continual	corollary	critical	cyclical
continuous	corps	criticism	cylinder
contribution	correlate	criticize	
dangerous	deliberately	diameter	dissatisfied
debris	deodorant	different	dissent
debt	dependable	difficult	dissimilar
debtor	dependent	dilemma	dissipate
deceit	depth	diligent	divinity
deceitful	deputy	dining	divisible
deceived	descend	disappearance	division
decency	descendant	disappointment	doesn't
decent	descent	disapprove	dominant
deception	desert	disaster	dominate
decide	desirable	disastrous	dormitory
decision	despair	discern	dough
default	despite	disciple	dramatize
defendant	dessert	disciplinary	drunkenness
defense	destroy	discipline	due
defer	detriment	discomfort	dully
deference	devastate	discriminate	duly
deferred	developed	discriminatory	during
define	development	disease	dye
definitely	deviate	disillusion	dyeing
definition	device	dispatch	dying
deity	devise	disposal	
delegate	dexterity	disregard	
earnest	edgy	eight	eliminate
easily	edition	eighth	eloquent
economically	editor	eighty	elude
economy	effect	electoral	emanate
ecstasy	efficiency	elicit	embarrass
edge	efficient	eligible	embassy

Chapter Eleven **SPELLING**

209

Words Commonly Misspelled

emigrant	entirely	evidently	existence
emigrate	envelop	exaggerate	expedite
emphasis	envelope	exaggeration	expedition
emphasize	environment	exceed	experience
emphatic	equality	excellence	experiment
empirical	equally	exceptional	explanation
employee	equipment	excessive	explanatory
encouragement	equipped	excitable	exploit
encouraging	equivalent	excitement	explore
endeavor	erroneous	exclusive	extension
enough	escapade	exclusively	extraordinary
entangle	especially	excursion	extravagant
enterprise	essential	exhibit	extremely
entertain	everything	exhibition	
facility	feminine	forbidden	frequently
fallacious	feminist	forehead	fried
fallacy	feud	foreign	friendless
familiar	fictitious	forewarn	friendliness
fantasy	fidelity	forgetting	friendly
fascinate	fiend	formally	friendship
fashion	fiery	formerly	fulfill
fatality	filial	forth	fulfillment
faulty	finally	forty	fundamental
favorable	financial	fourth	furious
favorite	financier	fraternity	furthermore
February	flair	freight	
felicity	fluent	frequency	
gaiety	genetics	governor	grievous
gallant	genius	gradually	grocery
gardener	genuine	grammar	guarantee
gaseous	global	grandeur	guidance
gasoline	glorious	graphics	guilt
generally	glossary	grief	gymnasium
generation	goddess	grievance	
generic	government	grieve	
hammer	headache	hereditary	hopeful
handkerchief	heard	heroes	hopeless
handsome	heathen	heroic	hoping
happiness	heavily	heroine	hopping
harassment	height	hindrance	humidity
harpoon	heir	honorable	humor

humorous	hybrid	hypnotize	hysteria
hundredth	hygiene	hypocrisy	
hungrily	hypnosis	hypocrite	
hurrying	hypnotism	hypothesis	
icicle	incidentally	infancy	interaction
ignorant	incompetent	inferiority	intercede
illegal	inconvenience	infinite	interrelated
illicit	incredible	ingenious	interrupt
illusion	indebted	ingenuity	intimate
illusory	indecisive	ingenuous	introduce
imaginary	indefinite	inhabitant	invisible
imagine	independence	initiative	ironic
immaculate	indispensable	innocence	irony
immediately	indivisible	inquiry	irrelevant
immense	indulge	insistent	irresistible
immigrant	interference	inspiration	irritable
immoderate	inertia	intelligence	island
impressionable	inevitable	intentionally	isle
jealousy	journey	junction	
jewelry	judge	justifiable	
journal	judgment	justify	
kerosene	knight	kowtow	
kindergarten	knowledge		
laboratory	leisure	limb	losing
laborer	leisurely	literary	lottery
launch	lenient	literature	lovable
lawyer	library	liveliness	loveless
league	license	loathe	luncheon
legacy	lighten	loneliness	luscious
legible	lightning	lonely	luxurious
legislator	likelihood	loose	lying
legitimate	likely	lose	
macaroni	management	meanness	memorable
machinery	managing	medical	merchandise
magazine	maneuver	medicinal	merchant
magnificent	marriage	medicine	merger
maintenance	massacre	medieval	meteor
malaria	mathematics	medley	mettle
manageable	maximum	melancholy	miniature

Words Commonly Misspelled

minimum	misdemeanor	monogram	mosquitoes
minister	misfit	monopoly	mountain
miracle	missile	moral	movable
mirror	missionary	morale	muffle
mischief	misspell	mortgage	muscle
mischievous	monarch	mortified	mysterious
naturally	neighborly	ninth	nuisance
necessary	nickel	noticeable	
necessity	niece	notorious	
negligent	ninety	nuclear	
obedience	occasionally	opinion	originally
oblige	occur	opportunity	outrageous
obnoxious	occurred	opposite	overrated
obscure	occurrence	optimism	owing
observant	official	orchard	
obstacle	omission	ordinarily	
obtuse	omitted	organize	
package	pennant	pierce	predominant
pageant	perceive	pigeon	preference
paid	percentage	pillar	preferred
pamphlet	perception	planned	prejudice
parachute	perilous	plausible	preoccupied
paradox	permanence	playwright	preparation
paradoxical	permanent	pleasant	presence
paragraph	permissible	pledge	presidency
parallel	perplex	plentiful	prestige
paralysis	persistence	politeness	prevail
parcel	persistent	politician	prevalence
parenthesis	personally	popularity	priest
parliament	personnel	portable	primitive
partial	persuade	possess	principal
particle	persuasion	possession	principles
particularly	persuasive	possibility	priority
pastime	pertinent	possibly	privilege
patient	philosophy	potatoes	probability
patriotic	physical	practicality	probable
patriotism	physician	prairie	procedural
patron	pianos	prayer	procedure
peaceable	picnic	precede	proceed
peasant	picnicking	precedent	professional
peculiar	piece	precious	professor

prohibitive	propel	psychologist	purgatory
prologue	propeller	psychosomatic	purity
promenade	prophecy	publicity	pursue
prominent	proprietor	punctuation	pursuit
promising	psychiatrist	purchase	
pronunciation	psychoanalysis	purchasing	
qualified	quandary	query	quiet
qualitative	quantity	questionable	quite
radiant	recruit	repetitious	rhapsody
ratify	recur	requirement	rhetoric
realize	reference	requisition	rheumatism
really	referred	residence	rhyme
recede	reign	resistance	rhythm
receipt	rein	resolving	ridiculous
receive	reliable	resourceful	rigidity
recessive	relieve	responsible	routine
recognizable	reluctance	restaurant	
recollect	remembrance	reveille	
recommend	reminisce	rewrite	
sacrifice	sensible	solemn	studying
safety	sensitive	solicit	submission
salary	separate	soliloquy	subsidy
satellite	sergeant	solos	substantial
satisfactory	several	sophomore	substitute
savage	shadowy	source	subtle
scandal	shady	sovereign	succeed
scarcely	shepherd	spaghetti	successful
scary	sheriff	specimen	successive
scenery	shield	spectacles	sufficient
scent	shining	spectacular	suffix
schedule	shoulder	spirited	summary
schism	siege	sponsor	superb
scissors	sieve	squirrel	surgeon
scold	significant	statue	surprise
sculptor	simile	stifle	susceptible
secede	simultaneous	stomach	suspense
secrecy	sincerely	straight	suspicion
secretary	singular	strategy	suspicious
seize	siphon	strength	sustained
seniority	skillful	strenuous	syllable
senseless	society	stressful	syllabus

Chapter Eleven SPELLING

Words Commonly Misspelled

symbol	sympathize	symptom	
symmetrical	symphonic	synonym	
tableau	thematic	traction	treachery
tailor	theoretical	traffic	treason
technique	therefore	trafficked	treasury
temperament	thorough	tragedy	truant
temperature	tireless	tragic	truly
temporary	tobacco	transfer	turmoil
tendency	tolerance	transferred	twelfth
terrific	tomato	transistor	twilight
terrifying	tomatoes	transitive	typical
territory	tomorrow	transparent	tyranny
testimony	tournament	traveler	tyrant
umbrella	unison	urban	utterance
unanimous	unnecessary	urgent	
unconscious	unprecedented	usually	
undoubtedly	unveil	utensil	
vacuum	varying	vicinity	vinegar
valleys	vegetable	victim	volcano
valuable	vehicle	village	volunteer
variety	vengeance	villain	
various	vengeful	villainous	
warrant	weird	wholly	writing
warrior	whereabouts	woolen	written
wary	whimsical	wrangle	
weapon	whistle	wrestle	
weather	wholesome	write	
yacht	yield		

RECOMMENDED READING

The titles listed below, readily available in paperback, represent many of the classic and contemporary works most widely read and studied in comprehensive high school English courses; the emphasis is on works written in English, primarily by American writers. These titles are recommended to the student seeking to supplement regular course assignments or to prepare independently for the Regents exam. All would be suitable choices for an essay on the AP English Literature and Composition exam. These works also represent valuable additions to a student's personal library.

NOVELS

1984	George Orwell
A Death in the Family	James Agee
A Farewell to Arms	Ernest Hemingway
A Separate Peace	John Knowles
A Star Called Henry	Roddy Doyle
A Tale of Two Cities	Charles Dickens
All the King's Men	Robert Penn Warren
Americanah	Chimamanda Ngozi Adichie
Arrowsmith	Sinclair Lewis
Babbitt	Sinclair Lewis
Beloved	Toni Morrison
Billy Budd	Herman Melville
Brave New World	Aldous Huxley
Catch-22	Joseph Heller
Catcher in the Rye	J. D. Salinger
Cold Mountain	Charles Frazier
Daisy Miller	Henry James
Deliverance	James Dickey
Ethan Frome	Edith Wharton
Farenheit 451	Ray Bradbury
Felicia's Journey	William Trevor
Great Expectations	Charles Dickens
Huckleberry Finn	Mark Twain
Invisible Man	Ralph Ellison
Light in August	William Faulkner
Lord of the Flies	William Golding
Main Street	Sinclair Lewis

Recommended Reading

Native Son	Richard Wright
Netherland	Joseph O'Neill
Oliver Twist	Charles Dickens
One Hundred Years of Solitude	Gabriel Garcia Marquez
Ordinary People	Judith Guest
Rabbit, Run	John Updike
Ragtime	E. L. Doctorow
Rebecca	Daphne DuMaurier
Red Badge of Courage	Stephen Crane
Rumors of Peace	Ella Leffland
Sister Carrie	Theodore Dreiser
Slaughterhouse Five	Kurt Vonnegut
So Long, See You Tomorrow	William Maxwell
Summer	Edith Wharton
That Night	Alice McDermott
The Age of Innocence	Edith Wharton
The Assistant	Bernard Malamud
The Awakening	Kate Chopin
The Bean Trees	Barbara Kingsolver
The Bonfire of the Vanities	Tom Wolfe
The Caine Mutiny	Herman Wouk
The Centaur	John Updike
The Color Purple	Alice Walker
The Crying of Lot 49	Thomas Pynchon
The Grapes of Wrath	John Steinbeck
The Great Fire	Shirley Hazzard
The Great Gatsby	F. Scott Fitzgerald
The Heart Is a Lonely Hunter	Carson McCullers
The Human Stain	Philip Roth
The Joy Luck Club	Amy Tan
The Known World	Edward P. Jones
The Natural	Bernard Malamud
The Old Man and the Sea	Ernest Hemingway
The Secret Agent	Joseph Conrad
The Scarlet Letter	Nathaniel Hawthorne
The Time Machine	H. G. Wells
Things Fall Apart	Chinua Achebe
Things Invisible to See	Nancy Willard
To Kill a Mockingbird	Harper Lee
Underworld	Don DeLillo
Washington Square	Henry James
White Teeth	Zadie Smith
Wolf Hall	Hilary Mantel
World's Fair	E. L. Doctorow

AUTOBIOGRAPHY, ESSAYS, AND OTHER NONFICTION

A Civil Action	Jonathan Harr
A Hole in the Sky	Robert Finch
An American Childhood	Annie Dillard
Angela's Ashes	Frank McCourt
Black Boy	Richard Wright
Blood Dark Track	Joseph O'Neill
Cities on a Hill	Francis Fitzgerald
Dreams from My Father	Barack Obama
Growing Up	Russell Baker
Hiroshima	John Hersey
Hunger of Memory	Richard Rodriguez
I Know Why the Caged Bird Sings	Maya Angelou
Into Thin Air	Jon Krakauer
Iron and Silk	Mark Salzman
King of the World	David Remnick
Late Innings	Roger Angell
Nickel and Dimed	Barbara Ehrenreich
Night	Elie Wiesel
Notes of a Native Son	James Baldwin
Out of Africa	Isak Dinesen
Pilgrim at Tinker Creek	Annie Dillard
Stop-Time	Frank Conroy
Such, Such Were the Joys	George Orwell
The Art of Fiction	David Lodge
The Color of Water	James McBride
The Courage of Turtles	Edward Hoagland
The Crack-Up	F. Scott Fitzgerald
The Devils of Loudon	Aldous Huxley
The Duke of Deception	Geoffrey Wolff
The Last Cowboy	Jane Kramer
The Lives of a Cell	Lewis Thomas
The Mismeasure of Man	Stephen Jay Gould
The Solace of Open Spaces	Gretel Ehrlich
The Way to Rainy Mountain	N. Scott Momaday
The Warmth of Other Suns	Isabel Wilkerson
The White Album	Joan Didion
This Boy's Life	Tobias Wolff
This House of Sky	Ivan Doig
Travels with Charley	John Steinbeck
Up from Slavery	Booker T. Washington
Walden	Henry David Thoreau

Recommended Reading

There are many excellent collections of essays and literary nonfiction available. Here are some recommended classic and contemporary authors whose works are available in paperback editions:

Roger Angell	Stephen Jay Gould	Cynthia Ozick
Joan Didion	Garrison Keillor	David Remnick
Ralph Waldo Emerson	Tracy Kidder	Richard Rodriguez
	Verlyn Klinkenborg	Roger Rosenblatt
M. F. K. Fisher	Jane Kramer	Gore Vidal
Ian Frazier	Peter Mathiesson	Eudora Welty
Atul Gawande	Jane Mayer	E. B. White
Malcolm Gladwell	John McPhee	
Adam Gopnik	H. L. Mencken	

Recommended anthologies include:

The Art of the Personal Essay, by Philip Lopate; Anchor Books
The Best American Essays of the Century, Joyce Carol Oates, ed.; Houghton Mifflin Co.
The Best American Essays, compiled from essays written for magazines and journals and published annually by Houghton Mifflin Co.

Other volumes in the Best American Series, also published annually, include:

The Best American Sports Writing
The Best American Travel Writing
The Best American Science and Nature Writing
The Best American Nonrequired Reading

POETRY

Readers are urged to seek out collections of work by poets whom they encounter in class readings and whom they especially admire. *Dover Publications* offers nicely produced and very inexpensive paperback collections of poetry, including works of Shakespeare and other major British poets, as well as major American poets of the nineteenth and twentieth centuries. They are available from Dover online and in bookstores. Among the many poets introduced to high school students and whose work is widely available in paperback collections are the following:

W. H. Auden	Donald Hall	Adrienne Rich
Elizabeth Bishop	Langston Hughes	Theodore Roethke
Louise Bogan	Denise Levertov	Carl Sandburg
Gwendolyn Brooks	W. S. Merwin	Vijay Seshadri
Billy Collins	Edna St. Vincent Millay	Charles Simic
e. e. cummings		*May Swenson
Emily Dickinson	Marianne Moore	William Stafford
*Rita Dove	Howard Nemerov	Richard Wilbur
T. S. Eliot	*Sharon Olds	Nancy Willard
Carolyn Forché	*Marge Piercy	William Carlos Williams
Robert Frost	Robert Pinsky	
Louise Glück	Sylvia Plath	

* denotes a poet whose work has appeared on a New York State English Regents exam

Some currently available paperback anthologies of poetry include:

Poetry 180, An Anthology of Contemporary Poems, Billy Collins, ed.; Random House
Good Poems, selected and introduced by Garrison Keillor; Penguin Books
Poetry Daily, 366 Poems, selected from the Poetry Daily website; Sourcebooks Inc.
The Best American Poetry, annual series, David Lehman, ed.; Scribner
Contemporary American Poetry, Donald Hall, ed.; Viking
The Mentor Book of Major American Poets, Oscar Williams and Edwin Honig, eds.; New American Library
The Vintage Book of Contemporary American Poetry, J. D. McClatchy, ed.

Websites for the interested reader:

Poetry Daily: *www.poems.com*
Poetry Foundation: *www.poetryfoundation.org*
Academy of American Poets: *www.poets.org*
Poet's House: *www.poetshouse.org*
www.poemhunter.com

Recommended Reading

SHORT STORIES

Some recommended authors whose stories are available in paperback:

Sherwood Anderson	Nathaniel Hawthorne	Edgar Allan Poe
John Barth	Ernest Hemingway	Isaac Bashevis Singer
Ambrose Bierce	Bernard Malamud	William Trevor
Willa Cather	Bharati Mukherjee	John Updike
Isak Dinesen	Alice Munro	Kurt Vonnegut
William Faulkner	Joyce Carol Oates	Edith Wharton
F. Scott Fitzgerald	Tim O'Brien	Eudora Welty
Mavis Gallant	Flannery O'Connor	John Edgar Wideman

Collections available in paperback include:

Annual publications:
The O. Henry Prize Stories
The Best American Short Stories
The Pushcart Prize: Best of the Small Presses

Anthologies:
American Short Story Masterpieces, Raymond Carver and Tom Jenks, eds.
The Norton Anthology of Short Fiction, R. V. Cassill, ed.
The Oxford Book of American Short Stories, Joyce Carol Oates, ed.
The Oxford Book of Short Stories, V. S. Pritchett, ed.
   (includes British and American writers)
The Vintage Book of Contemporary American Short Stories, Tobias Wolff, ed.

PLAYS

Shakespeare	*Macbeth, Julius Caesar, Othello, As You Like It, Hamlet, King Lear, Much Ado About Nothing, The Tempest, Henry V*
Paddy Chayevsky	*Marty*
Anton Chekov	*Three Sisters, The Cherry Orchard, Uncle Vanya*
Henrik Ibsen	*A Doll's House, The Master Builder*
Edward Albee	*Who's Afraid of Virginia Woolf?, Zoo Story*
David Auburn	*Proof*
Samuel Beckett	*Waiting for Godot*
Robert Bolt	*A Man for All Seasons*
Noel Coward	*Blithe Spirit, Private Lives*
Mart Crowley	*The Boys in the Band*

Plays

Horton Foote	*Dividing the Estate, The Trip to Bountiful, The Young Man from Atlanta*
William Gibson	*The Miracle Worker*
Susan Glaspell	*Trifles*
John Guare	*Six Degrees of Separation*
A. R. Gurney	*The Dining Room*
Lorraine Hansberry	*A Raisin in the Sun*
Lillian Hellman	*The Little Foxes*
Beth Henley	*Crimes of the Heart*
William Inge	*Come Back, Little Sheba; Picnic; Bus Stop*
Eugene Ionesco	*The Lesson, The Bald Soprano, Rhinoceros*
George S. Kaufman/Moss Hart	*You Can't Take It With You, The Man Who Came to Dinner*
Jerome Lawrence/ Robert Lee	*Inherit the Wind*
Terrence McNally	*Master Class*
Arthur Miller	*All My Sons, Death of a Salesman, The Crucible, The Price, A View From the Bridge*
Clifford Odets	*Waiting for Lefty, The Country Girl*
Eugene O'Neill	*Long Day's Journey into Night*
Harold Pinter	*The Caretaker*
Terrence Rattigan	*The Winslow Boy, The Browning Version*
Yasmina Reza	*Art*
Rod Serling	*Requiem for a Heavyweight*
Peter Shaffer	*Equus, Black Comedy, The Royal Hunt of the Sun, Amadeus*
George Bernard Shaw	*Pygmalion*
Neil Simon	*The Odd Couple, Brighton Beach Memoirs*
Tom Stoppard	*Rosenkrantz and Guildenstern Are Dead, Arcadia, The Real Thing, Jumpers, The Coast of Utopia*
Alfred Uhry	*Driving Miss Daisy*
Wendy Wasserstein	*The Heidi Chronicles*
Oscar Wilde	*The Importance of Being Earnest*
Thornton Wilder	*Our Town, The Matchmaker, The Skin of Our Teeth*
Tennessee Williams	*The Glass Menagerie, A Streetcar Named Desire, Cat on a Hot Tin Roof, Sweet Bird of Youth*
August Wilson	*Fences, The Piano Lesson, Ma Rainey's Black Bottom, Jitney, Joe Turner's Come and Gone*

Appendices

The New York State Common Core Learning Standards for English Language Arts

The following 11/12 grade-specific standards define end-of-year expectations and a cumulative progression designed to enable students to meet college and career readiness (CCR) expectations no later than the end of high school. The new ELA/Common Core Regents Exam is designed to assess many (but not all) of the standards in each of the categories: Reading Literature, Reading Informational Texts, Writing, and Language. Note that the 2017 Revised Standards now include reading for Literature and reading for Informational Texts in a single set of standards (RL and RI).

2017 REVISED ELA STANDARDS FOR READING–LITERATURE AND INFORMATIONAL TEXTS (RL AND RI)

11-12R1: Cite strong and thorough textual evidence to support analysis of what the text says explicitly/implicitly and make logical inferences, including determining where the text is ambiguous; develop questions for deeper understanding and for further exploration. (RI&RL)

11-12R2: Determine two or more themes or central ideas in a text and analyze their development, including how they emerge and are shaped and refined by specific details; objectively and accurately summarize a complex text. (RI&RL)

11-12R3: In literary texts, analyze the impact of author's choices. (RL) In informational texts, analyze a complex set of ideas or sequence of events and explain how specific individuals, ideas, or events interact and develop. (RI)

11-12R4: Determine the meaning of words and phrases as they are used in a text, including figurative and connotative meanings. Analyze the impact of specific word choices on meaning, tone, and mood, including words with multiple meanings. Analyze how an author uses and refines the meaning of technical or key term(s) over the course of a text. (RI&RL)

11-12R5: In literary texts, analyze how varied aspects of structure create meaning and affect the reader. (RL) In informational texts, analyze the impact and evaluate the effect structure has on exposition or argument in terms of clarity, persuasive/rhetorical technique, and audience appeal. (RI)

11-12R6: Analyze how authors employ point of view, perspective, and purpose to shape explicit and implicit messages (e.g., persuasiveness, aesthetic quality, satire, sarcasm, irony, or understatement). (RI&RL)

11-12R7: In literary texts, analyze multiple adaptations of a source text as presented in different formats (e.g., works of art, graphic novels, music, film, etc.), specifically evaluating how each version interprets the source. (RL) In informational texts, integrate and evaluate sources on the same topic or argument in order to address a question or solve a problem. (RI)

11-12R8: Delineate and evaluate an argument in applicable texts, applying a lens (e.g., constitutional principles, logical fallacy, legal reasoning, belief systems, codes of ethics, philosophies, etc.) to assess the validity or fallacy of key arguments, determining whether the supporting evidence is relevant and sufficient. (RI&RL)

11-12R9: Choose and develop criteria to evaluate the quality of texts. Make connections to other texts, ideas, cultural perspectives, eras, and personal experiences. (RI&RL)

WRITING STANDARDS
GRADES 11/12 (W)

1. Write arguments to support claims in an analysis of substantive topics or texts, using valid reasoning and relevant and sufficient evidence.

2. Write informative/explanatory texts to examine and convey complex ideas and information clearly and accurately through the effective selection, organization, and analysis of content.

3. Write narratives to develop real or imagined experiences or events using effective technique, well-chosen details, and well-structured event sequences.

4. Produce clear and coherent writing in which the development, organization, and style are appropriate to task, purpose, and audience.

5. Develop and strengthen writing as needed by planning, revising, editing, rewriting, or trying a new approach.

6. Use technology, including the Internet, to produce and publish writing and to interact and collaborate with others.

7. Conduct short as well as more sustained research projects based on focused questions, demonstrating understanding of the subject under investigation.

8. Gather relevant information from multiple print and digital sources, assess the credibility and accuracy of each source, and integrate the information while avoiding plagiarism.

9. Draw evidence from literary or informational texts to support analysis, reflection, and research.

10. Write routinely over extended time frames (time for research, reflection, and revision) and shorter time frames (a single sitting or a day or two) for a range of tasks, purposes, and audiences.

11. Develop personal, cultural, textual, and thematic connections within and across genres as they respond to texts through written, digital, and oral presentations, employing a variety of media and genres.

LANGUAGE STANDARDS
GRADES 11/12 (L)

Conventions of Standard English

1. Demonstrate command of the conventions of standard English grammar and usage when writing or speaking.

2. Demonstrate command of the conventions of standard English capitalization, punctuation, and spelling when writing.

Knowledge of Language

3. Apply knowledge of language to understand how language functions in different contexts, to make effective choices for meaning or style, and to comprehend more fully when reading or listening.

Vocabulary Acquisition and Use

4. Determine or clarify the meaning of unknown and multiple meaning words and phrases by using context clues, analyzing meaningful word parts, and consulting general and specialized reference materials, as appropriate.

5. Demonstrate understanding of figurative language, word relationships, and nuances in word meanings.

6. Acquire and use accurately a range of general academic and domain-specific words and phrases sufficient for reading, writing, speaking, and listening at the college and career readiness level; demonstrate independence in gathering vocabulary knowledge when considering a word or phrase important to comprehension or expression.

HOW IS THE REGENTS ELA (COMMON CORE) EXAM SCORED?

WEIGHTING OF PARTS

Each of the three parts of the Regents Examination in English Language Arts (Common Core) has a number of raw score credits associated with the questions/tasks within that part. In order to ensure an appropriate distribution of credits across the test, each part is weighted.

For Part 1, each multiple-choice question is worth one point. The Part 2 essay is scored on a 6-point rubric and then weighted $\times$ 4. The Part 3 Text Analysis is scored on a 4-point rubric and then weighted $\times$ 2.

As you will notice, the Part 2 Argument Essay is the most heavily weighted section.

The table below shows the raw score credits, weighting factor, and weighted score credits for each part of the test. This information will be used to determine each student's scale score (final exam score) through the use of a conversion chart provided by NYSED.

Part	Maximum Raw Score Credits	Weighting Factor	Maximum Weighted Score Credits
Part 1	24	1	24
Part 2	6	4	24
Part 3	4	2	8
			Total 56

The conversion table is determined independently for each administration of the exam. You can find the conversion tables for both forms of the Regents English Exams at *http://www.nysedregents.org*.

SCORING RUBRICS FOR THE REGENTS ELA (COMMON CORE) EXAM

Parts 2 and 3 of the Regents Examination in English Language Arts (Common Core) will be scored using new holistic rubrics. Part 2 will be scored using a 6-credit rubric, and Part 3 will be scored using a 4-credit rubric. Both rubrics reflect the new demands called for by the Common Core Learning Standards for English Language Arts and Literacy through the end of Grade 11.

Appendices

New York State Regents Examination in English Language Arts (Common Core)
Part 2 Rubric
Writing from Sources: Argument

Criteria	6 Essays at this Level	5 Essays at this Level	4 Essays at this Level	3 Essays at this Level	2 Essays at this Level	1 Essays at this Level
Content and Analysis: the extent to which the essay conveys complex ideas and information clearly and accurately in order to support claims in an analysis of the texts	-introduce a precise and insightful claim, as directed by the task -demonstrate in-depth and insightful analysis of the texts, as necessary to support the claim and to distinguish the claim from alternate or opposing claims	-introduce a precise and thoughtful claim, as directed by the task -demonstrate thorough analysis of the texts, as necessary to support the claim and to distinguish the claim from alternate or opposing claims	-introduce a precise claim, as directed by the task -demonstrate appropriate and accurate analysis of the texts, as necessary to support the claim and to distinguish the claim from alternate or opposing claims	-introduce a reasonable claim, as directed by the task -demonstrate some analysis of the texts, but insufficiently distinguish the claim from alternate or opposing claims	-introduce a claim -demonstrate confused or unclear analysis of the texts, failing to distinguish the claim from alternate or opposing claims	-do not introduce a claim -do not demonstrate analysis of the texts
Command of Evidence: the extent to which the essay presents evidence from the provided texts to support analysis	-present ideas fully and thoughtfully, making highly effective use of a wide range of specific and relevant evidence to support analysis -demonstrate proper citation of sources to avoid plagiarism when dealing with direct quotes and paraphrased material	-present ideas clearly and accurately, making effective use of specific and relevant evidence to support analysis -demonstrate proper citation of sources to avoid plagiarism when dealing with direct quotes and paraphrased material	-present ideas sufficiently, making adequate use of specific and relevant evidence to support analysis -demonstrate proper citation of sources to avoid plagiarism when dealing with direct quotes and paraphrased material	-present ideas briefly, making use of some specific and relevant evidence to support analysis -demonstrate inconsistent citation of sources to avoid plagiarism when dealing with direct quotes and paraphrased material	-present ideas inconsistently and/or inaccurately, in an attempt to support analysis, making use of some evidence that may be irrelevant -demonstrate little use of citations to avoid plagiarism when dealing with direct quotes and paraphrased material	-present little or no evidence from the texts -do not make use of citations

Criteria						
Coherence, Organization, and Style: the extent to which the essay logically organizes complex ideas, concepts, and information using formal style and precise language	-exhibit skillful organization of ideas and information to create a cohesive and coherent essay -establish and maintain a formal style, using sophisticated language and structure	-exhibit logical organization of ideas and information to create a cohesive and coherent essay -establish and maintain a formal style, using fluent and precise language and sound structure	-exhibit acceptable organization of ideas and information to create a coherent essay -establish and maintain a formal style, using precise and appropriate language and structure	-exhibit some organization of ideas and information to create a mostly coherent essay -establish but fail to maintain a formal style, using primarily basic language and structure	-exhibit inconsistent organization of ideas and information, failing to create a coherent essay -lack a formal style, using some language that is inappropriate or imprecise	-exhibit little organization of ideas and information -use language that is predominantly incoherent, inappropriate, or copied directly from the task or texts
Control of Conventions: the extent to which the essay demonstrates command of conventions of standard English grammar, usage, capitalization, punctuation, and spelling	-demonstrate control of conventions with essentially no errors, even with sophisticated language	-demonstrate control of the conventions, exhibiting occasional errors only when using sophisticated language	-demonstrate partial control, exhibiting occasional errors that do not hinder comprehension	-demonstrate emerging control, exhibiting occasional errors that hinder comprehension	-demonstrate a lack of control, exhibiting frequent errors that make comprehension difficult	-are minimal, making assessment of conventions unreliable

- An essay that addresses fewer texts than required by the task can be scored no higher than a 3.
- An essay that is a personal response and makes little or no reference to the task or texts can be scored no higher than a 1.
- An essay that is totally copied from the task and/or texts with no original student writing must be scored a 0.
- An essay that is totally unrelated to the task, illegible, incoherent, blank, or unrecognizable as English must be scored as a 0.

Appendices

New York State Regents Examination in English Language Arts (Common Core)
Part 3 Rubric
Text Analysis: Exposition

Criteria	4 Responses at this Level	3 Responses at this Level	2 Responses at this Level	1 Responses at this Level
Content and Analysis: the extent to which the response conveys complex ideas and information clearly and accurately in order to respond to the task and support an analysis of the text	-introduce a well-reasoned central idea and a writing strategy that clearly establish the criteria for analysis -demonstrate a thoughtful analysis of the author's use of the writing strategy to develop the central idea	-introduce a clear central idea and a writing strategy that establish the criteria for analysis -demonstrate an appropriate analysis of the author's use of the writing strategy to develop the central idea	-introduce a central idea and/or a writing strategy -demonstrate a superficial analysis of the author's use of the writing strategy to develop the central idea	-introduce a confused or incomplete central idea or writing strategy and/or -demonstrate a minimal analysis of the author's use of the writing strategy to develop the central idea
Command of Evidence: the extent to which the response presents evidence from the provided text to support analysis	-present ideas clearly and consistently, making effective use of specific and relevant evidence to support analysis	-present ideas sufficiently, making adequate use of relevant evidence to support analysis	-present ideas inconsistently, inadequately, and/or inaccurately in an attempt to support analysis, making use of some evidence that may be irrelevant	-present little or no evidence from the text
Coherence, Organization, and Style: the extent to which the response logically organizes complex ideas, concepts, and information using formal style and precise language	-exhibit logical organization of ideas and information to create a cohesive and coherent response -establish and maintain a formal style, using precise language and sound structure	-exhibit acceptable organization of ideas and information to create a coherent response -establish and maintain a formal style, using appropriate language and structure	-exhibit inconsistent organization of ideas and information, failing to create a coherent response -lack a formal style, using language that is basic; inappropriate, or imprecise	-exhibit little organization of ideas and information -use language that is predominantly incoherent, inappropriate, or copied directly from the task or text -are minimal, making assessment unreliable

Scoring Rubrics for the Regents ELA (Common Core) Exam

Control of Conventions: the extent to which the response demonstrates command of conventions of standard English grammar, usage, capitalization, punctuation, and spelling	-demonstrate control of the conventions with infrequent errors	-demonstrate partial control of conventions with occasional errors that do not hinder comprehension	-demonstrate emerging control of conventions with some errors that hinder comprehension	-demonstrate a lack of control of conventions with frequent errors that make comprehension difficult -are minimal, making assessment of conventions unreliable

- A response that is a personal response and makes little or no reference to the task or text can be scored no higher than a 1.
- A response that is totally copied from the text with no original writing must be given a 0.
- A response that is totally unrelated to the task, illegible, incoherent, blank, or unrecognizable as English must be scored as a 0.

Examination June 2019
English Language Arts

PART 1—Reading Comprehension

Directions (1–24): Closely read each of the three passages below. After each passage, there are several multiple-choice questions. Select the best suggested answer to each question and write its number in the space provided. You may use the margins to take notes as you read.

Reading Comprehension Passage A

     When Marvin was ten years old, his father took him through the long, echoing corridors that led up through Administration and Power, until at last they came to the uppermost levels of all and were among the swiftly growing vegetation of the Farmlands. Marvin liked it here: it was fun
(5) watching the great, slender plants creeping with almost visible eagerness towards the sunlight as it filtered down through the plastic domes to meet them. The smell of life was everywhere, awakening inexpressible longings in his heart: no longer was he breathing the dry, cool air of the residential levels, purged of all smells but the faint tang of ozone. He wished he could
(10) stay here for a little while, but Father would not let him. They went onwards until they had reached the entrance to the Observatory, which he had never visited: but they did not stop, and Marvin knew with a sense of rising excitement that there could be only one goal left. For the first time in his life, he was going Outside.[1]

---

[1]Outside—the part of the Moon outside of Marvin's space habitat

(15)   There were a dozen of the surface vehicles, with their wide balloon tyres [tires] and pressurized cabins, in the great servicing chamber. His father must have been expected, for they were led at once to the little scout car waiting by the huge circular door of the airlock. Tense with expectancy, Marvin settled himself down in the cramped cabin while his father started
(20) the motor and checked the controls. The inner door of the lock slid open and then closed behind them: he heard the roar of the great air-pumps fade slowly away as the pressure dropped to zero. Then the 'Vacuum' sign flashed on, the outer door parted, and before Marvin lay the land which he had never yet entered.

(25)   He had seen it in photographs, of course: he had watched it imaged on television screens a hundred times. But now it was lying all around him, burning beneath the fierce sun that crawled so slowly across the jet-black sky. He stared into the west, away from the blinding splendour of the sun—and there were the stars, as he had been told but had never quite believed.
(30) He gazed at them for a long time, marvelling that anything could be so bright and yet so tiny. They were intense unscintillating[2] points, and suddenly he remembered a rhyme he had once read in one of his father's books:

Twinkle, twinkle, little star,
How I wonder what you are.

(35)   Well, he knew what the stars were. Whoever asked that question must have been very stupid. And what did they mean by 'twinkle'? You could see at a glance that all the stars shone with the same steady, unwavering light. He abandoned the puzzle and turned his attention to the landscape around him.

(40)   They were racing across a level plain at almost a hundred miles an hour, the great balloon tyres sending up little spurts of dust behind them. There was no sign of the Colony: in the few minutes while he had been gazing at the stars, its domes and radio towers had fallen below the horizon. Yet there were other indications of man's presence, for about a mile ahead
(45) Marvin could see the curiously shaped structures clustering round the head of a mine. Now and then a puff of vapour would emerge from a squat smoke-stack and would instantly disperse.

They were past the mine in a moment: Father was driving with a reckless and exhilarating skill as if—it was a strange thought to come into a child's
(50) mind—he was trying to escape from something. In a few minutes they had reached the edge of the plateau on which the Colony had been built. The ground fell sharply away beneath them in a dizzying slope whose lower

---

[2]unscintillating—not sparkling

stretches were lost in shadow. Ahead, as far as the eye could reach, was a jumbled wasteland of craters, mountain ranges, and ravines. The crests of
(55) the mountains, catching the low sun, burned like islands of fire in a sea of darkness: and above them the stars still shone as steadfastly as ever. . . .

And now on the right was a wrinkled, dusty plain, and on the left, its ramparts and terraces rising mile after mile into the sky, was a wall of mountains that marched into the distance until its peaks sank from sight
(60) below the rim of the world. There was no sign that men had ever explored this land, but once they passed the skeleton of a crashed rocket, and beside it a stone cairn[3] surmounted by a metal cross. . . .

The sun was now low behind the hills on the right: the valley before them should be in total darkness. Yet it was awash with a cold white radiance
(65) that came spilling over the crags beneath which they were driving. Then, suddenly, they were out in the open plain, and the source of the light lay before them in all its glory.

It was very quiet in the little cabin now that the motors had stopped. The only sound was the faint whisper of the oxygen feed and an occasional
(70) metallic crepitation[4] as the outer walls of the vehicle radiated away their heat. For no warmth at all came from the great silver crescent that floated low above the far horizon and flooded all this land with pearly light. It was so brilliant that minutes passed before Marvin could accept its challenge and look steadfastly into its glare, but at last he could discern the outlines
(75) of continents, the hazy border of the atmosphere, and the white islands of cloud. And even at this distance, he could see the glitter of sunlight on the polar ice.

It was beautiful, and it called to his heart across the abyss of space. There in that shining crescent were all the wonders that he had never known—the
(80) hues of sunset skies, the moaning of the sea on pebbled shores, the patter of falling rain, the unhurried benison[5] of snow. These and a thousand others should have been his rightful heritage, but he knew them only from the books and ancient records, and the thought filled him with the anguish of exile.

(85) Why could they not return? It seemed so peaceful beneath those lines of marching cloud. Then Marvin, his eyes no longer blinded by the glare, saw that the portion of the disk that should have been in darkness was gleaming faintly with an evil phosphorescence: and he remembered.

---

[3]cairn—memorial
[4]crepitation—crackling sound
[5]benison—blessing

(90) He was looking upon the funeral pyre[6] of a world—upon the radioactive aftermath of Armageddon.[7] Across a quarter of a million miles of space, the glow of dying atoms was still visible, a perennial reminder of the ruined past. It would be centuries yet before that deadly glow died from the rocks and life could return again to fill that silent, empty world....

(95) So, at last, Marvin understood the purpose of this pilgrimage. He [his father] would never walk beside the rivers of that lost and legendary world, or listen to the thunder raging above its softly rounded hills. Yet one day—how far ahead?—his children's children would return to claim their heritage. The winds and the rains would scour the poisons from the burning lands and carry them to the sea, and in the depths of the sea they would (100) waste their venom until they could harm no living things. Then the great ships that were still waiting here on the silent, dusty plains could lift once more into space, along the road that led to home....

—Arthur C. Clarke
excerpted and adapted from "If I Forget Thee, Oh Earth..."
Expedition to Earth, 1999
Orbit

---

[6]pyre—bonfire
[7]Armageddon—a catastrophic battle

1 The images in the first paragraph serve to

   (1) create a sense of solitude
   (2) illustrate the randomness of nature
   (3) create a feeling of anticipation
   (4) illustrate the importance of family   1____

2 Lines 15 through 24 establish

   (1) Marvin's misgivings about going Outside
   (2) the inhospitable conditions of Outside
   (3) Father's fears about traveling Outside
   (4) the unpleasant sensations of Outside   2____

3 The statement "it was a strange thought to come into a child's mind" (lines 49 and 50) signals

   (1) a change in Marvin's understanding
   (2) Marvin's growing embrace of the unknown
   (3) Marvin's objection to his father's behavior
   (4) a chance for Marvin's rescue   3____

4 The phrase "jumbled wasteland of craters, mountain ranges, and ravines" (line 54) reveals the

   (1) futility of the Colony
   (2) desolation of the Outside
   (3) uncertainty of Marvin's future
   (4) loneliness of Marvin's past   4____

5 The "glare" described in lines 74 and 86 represents Marvin's

   (1) romantic vision of the Earth
   (2) obsession with the Earth's past
   (3) vague memory of the Earth
   (4) faith in the Earth's restoration   5____

6 Lines 81 through 84 emphasize Marvin's

   (1) sense of deprivation
   (2) appreciation of his situation
   (3) fear of destruction
   (4) recollection of his childhood   6____

7 The details in lines 86 through 90 confirm the Earth has been damaged by

(1) climate change
(2) cosmic instability
(3) human actions
(4) natural occurences   7_____

8 The images in lines 98 through 100 convey feelings of

(1) fear and disappointment
(2) cleansing and renewal
(3) preservation and protection
(4) confusion and impatience   8_____

9 Which lines best capture Marvin's understanding of his father's perspective?

(1) "Tense with expectancy, Marvin settled himself down in the cramped cabin while his father started the motor and checked the controls" (lines 18 through 20)
(2) "They were intense unscintillating points, and suddenly he remembered a rhyme he had once read in one of his father's books" (lines 31 and 32)
(3) "In a few minutes they had reached the edge of the plateau on which the Colony had been built" (lines 50 and 51)
(4) "He [his father] would never walk beside the rivers of that lost and legendary world, or listen to the thunder raging above its softly rounded hills" (lines 94 through 96)   9_____

Reading Comprehension Passage B

This Life

      My grandmother told me there'd be good days
      to counter the dark ones,
      with blue skies in the heart as far
      as the soul could see. She said
(5) you could measure a life in as many ways
      as there were to bake a pound cake,
      but you still needed real butter and eggs
      for a good one—pound cake, that is,
      but I knew what she meant. She was always
(10) talking around corners like that;
      she knew words carried their treasures
      like a grape clusters around its own juice.
      She loved words; she thought a book
      was a monument to the glory of creation
(15) and a library . . . well, sometimes
      just trying to describe Jubilation
      will get you a bit tongue, so let's
      leave it at that. But my grandmother
      was nobody's fool, and she'd tell anybody
(20) smart enough to listen. Don't let a little pain
      stop you; try as hard as you can
      every minute you're given or else
      sit down and shut-up—though in her opinion,
      keeping quiet in noisy times was a sin
(25) against everything God and democracy
      intended us for. I know she'd like
      where I'm standing right now. She'd say
      a man who could measure his life in deeds
      was larger inside than the vessel that carried him;
(30) she'd say he was a cluster of grapes.
      My grandmother was only four feet ten
      but when she entered a room, even the books
      came to attention. Giants come in all sizes:

Sometimes a moment is a monument;
(35) sometimes an institution breathes—
like a library. Like this halcyon[1] day.

—Rita Dove
from *The Poets Laureate Anthology*, 2010
W. W. Norton & Company, Inc.

---

[1]halcyon—peaceful

10 Lines 1 through 4 establish the grandmother's

 (1) questioning nature
 (2) vivid imagination
 (3) cautious attitude
 (4) optimistic outlook   10____

11 The figurative language in lines 9 and 10 highlights the grandmother's

 (1) desire to avoid conflicts
 (2) tendency to keep secrets
 (3) strategy to impart wisdom
 (4) ability to create humor   11____

12 Which phrase from the poem clarifies the narrator's statement in line 30?

 (1) "there'd be good days" (line 1)
 (2) "smart enough to listen" (line 20)
 (3) "measure his life in deeds" (line 28)
 (4) "sometimes an institution breathes" (line 35)   12____

13 The personification in lines 32 and 33 emphasizes the grandmother's

 (1) small size
 (2) commanding presence
 (3) family history
 (4) successful career   13____

14 The overall tone of the poem can best be described as

 (1) objective   (3) respectful
 (2) skeptical   (4) critical   14____

Reading Comprehension Passage C

Texting isn't the first new technology blamed for ruining communication and common courtesy.

Is text-messaging driving us apart? These days, we talk to each other a lot with our thumbs—mashing out over six billion text messages a day in the United States, and likely a few billion more on services like WhatsApp and Facebook Messenger.

(5) But some worry that so much messaging leads, paradoxically, to less communication. When Sherry Turkle, the MIT clinical psychologist and author, interviewed college students, they said texting was causing friction in their face-to-face interactions. While hanging out with friends they'd be texting surreptitiously at the same time, pretending to maintain eye con-
(10) tact but mentally somewhere else. The new form of communication was fun, sure, but it was colliding with—and eroding—the old one.

"Our texts are fine," as one student said. "It's what texting does to our conversations when we are together that's the problem." . . .

New technologies often unsettle the way we relate to one another,
(15) of course. But social ruptures caused by texting have a strong echo in the arguments we had a hundred years ago. That's when a newfangled appliance gave us a strange new way to contact one another en masse:[1] the telephone. . . .

At first, the telephone was marketed mainly as a tool for business. Physi-
(20) cians and drugstores bought them to process orders, and business owners installed them at home so they could be quickly reached. The phone, proclaimed early ad copy, gave business leaders an ESP-like "sixth sense"[2] of their far-flung operations. . . .

Nonetheless, the telephone quickly gave birth to curious new forms
(25) of socializing. Callers arranged regular weekly "visiting" calls, dialing remote family to catch up on news. "Distance rolls away and for a few minutes every Thursday night the familiar voices tell the little family gossip that both are so eager to hear," a Bell ad cooed in 1921.

Phone companies even boasted that the phone was an improvement over
(30) that stodgy, low-fi communication, the letter. "Correspondence will help for a time, but friendships do not flourish for long on letters alone," a 1931 Bell sales manual noted. "When you can't visit in person, telephone periodically. Telephone calls will keep up the whole intimacy remarkably well."

---

[1] en masse—in a group at the same time
[2] ESP-like "sixth sense"—heightened intuition

(35) Soon, though, social critics began to wonder: Was all this phone chatter good for us? Was it somehow a lesser form of communication than what had come before? "Does the telephone make men more active or more lazy?" wondered the Knights of Columbus in a 1926 meeting. "Does the telephone break up home life and the old practice of visiting friends?"

(40) Others worried that the inverse would occur—that it would be so easy to talk that we'd never leave each other alone. "Thanks to the telephone, motor-car and such-like inventions, our neighbors have it in their power to turn our leisure into a series of interruptions," complained an American professor in 1929. And surely it couldn't be healthy to talk to each other so much. Wouldn't it create Too Much Information [TMI]?

(45) "We shall soon be nothing but transparent heaps of jelly to each other," a London writer moaned in 1897. Others fretted that the telephone sped up life, demanding instant reactions. "The use of the telephone gives little room for reflection," wrote a British newspaper in 1899. "It does not improve the temper, and it engenders a feverishness in (50) the ordinary concerns of life which does not make for domestic happiness and comfort."

Perhaps the strangest thing was being in the room while a friend talked to someone else—someone outside the room. In 1880, Mark Twain wrote "A Telephonic Conversation," transcribing the half-a-conversation as he lis- (55) tened to his wife on the phone. To the observer, as the skit pointed out, a telephone call sounded like disjointed nonsense. Even phone companies worried about whether the device created new forms of rude behavior; a 1910 Bell ad warned about "Dr. Jekyll and Mr. Hyde at the Telephone." ...

Indeed, some believed the phone improved our social behavior, because it (60) forced a listener to pay closer attention to a speaker. Devoid of visual signals, we must be "all ears and memory," a pundit[3] wrote in 1915: "The mind cannot wander." Plus, by eradicating distance, wouldn't the phone reduce misunderstanding? War, even? "Someday we will build up a world telephone system making necessary to all peoples the use of a common language, or common (65) understanding of languages, which will join all the people of the earth into one brotherhood," gushed John J. Carty, AT&T chief engineer, in 1907.

These utopian[4] views, of course, were wildly optimistic. But the gloomy views of pessimists, as [author, Claude] Fischer notes, didn't come true either. Even Emily Post, the etiquette expert, came around to the (70) telephone. By the 1920s, she'd accepted "Hello" as a suitable greeting, and even thought it was acceptable to invite someone to dinner with a call.

---

[3]pundit—an expert who shares opinions with the public
[4]utopian—idealistic

"Custom which has altered many ways and manners has taken away all opprobrium[5] from the message," she shrugged.

Nowadays, the telephone call seems like a quaint throwback to a gentler era. When Jenna Birch, the journalist, started dating a man who insisted on calling her on the phone, she found it warm and delightful—though her friends thought the behavior odd. Phone calls now seem retro.[6]

Academics have observed this shift, too. "My students just do not think of the phone as a mechanism of vocal interaction—they think of that as very rare," says John Durham Peters, a communication professor at the University of Iowa, and author of Speaking Into the Air. He doesn't think the shift to texting has degraded our interactions, though. By the middle of the 20th century, studies found that the telephone appeared not to have eroded social contact—indeed, some research found those with phones wrote more old-fashioned letters than those without. Similarly, modern surveys by the Pew Research Center have found that teenagers who text the most are also those who spend the most time face to face with friends. Communication, it seems, begets more communication, and—as Peters argues—just because talk happens in text doesn't mean it's not meaningful.

"Media scholars," he notes, "have this long romance with 'conversation' as the cure to the disease of media."

Still, it's not hard to be dispirited[7] by the divided attention so many of Turkle's subjects bemoaned in their lives. Indeed, Michéle Martin, of Carleton, thinks we're living through a replay of the telephone, where the things that made it valuable—instant communications—are the same that made it annoying. "People believe they are liberated because they can bring the mobile phone everywhere," Martin says. "But at the same time they are slaves to it."

The poet Carl Sandburg captured that dissonance in a 1916 poem about the telephone. He imagined a telephone wire being aware of the disparate[8] uses to which it was being put—coursing with conversations both deep and frivolous. "It is love and war and money; it is the fighting and the tears, the work and want / Death and laughter of men and women passing through me, carrier of your speech."

—Clive Thompson
excerpted and adapted from "OMG! We've Been Here B4"
Smithsonian, March 2016

---

[5] opprobrium—disgrace
[6] retro—dated
[7] dispirited—discouraged
[8] disparate—varying

15 The first paragraph of the text serves to

   (1) highlight the prevalence of texting
   (2) stress the benefits of texting
   (3) explain the origins of texting
   (4) support the abolition of texting   15____

16 As used in line 9, the word "surreptitiously" most nearly means

   (1) politely   (3) secretively
   (2) boldly   (4) earnestly   16____

17 The details in lines 19 through 23 reveal that the telephone was initially

   (1) associated with the supernatural
   (2) not considered very useful
   (3) often blamed for worker illness
   (4) not used for social purposes   17____

18 The use of the word "cooed" (line 28) implies that telephone advertisers were

   (1) helpful and patient
   (2) strategic and persuasive
   (3) childish and inconsiderate
   (4) sarcastic and relentless   18____

19 Lines 34 through 44 illustrate society's

   (1) enthusiasm about using new technology
   (2) dependence on those proficient in new technology
   (3) grasp of the significance of new technology
   (4) concern about the impact of new technology   19____

20 The figurative language in lines 45 and 46 implies that telephone use would cause people to

(1) lose self-confidence and motivation
(2) lack substance and individuality
(3) attract danger and adversity
(4) become narrow-minded and uninformed   20____

21 The statements from a Bell ad (lines 57 and 58) and the AT&T chief engineer (lines 64 through 66) offer

(1) contrasting perspectives on the potential effects of the telephone
(2) strong support for the growing popularity of the telephone
(3) alternative options for communicating with family members
(4) insightful evaluation of the importance of long-distance conversations   21____

22 The "utopian views" of the early 1900s (line 67) suggested that telephone use could

(1) improve local commerce
(2) encourage language studies
(3) promote global unity
(4) influence community values   22____

23 The information about Emily Post (lines 69 through 73) contributes to a central idea that

(1) rules of proper behavior can be confusing
(2) norms of good conduct are universal
(3) concepts of politeness can evolve over time
(4) conventions of salutation depend on status   23____

24 The quotations in lines 96 through 98 reflect a sense of

(1) bias   (3) suspense
(2) irony   (4) resolution   24____

Examination June 2019

PART 2—Argument Response

Directions: Closely read each of the *four* texts provided on pages 248 through 255 and write a source-based argument on the topic below. You may use the margins to take notes as you read and scrap paper to plan your response. Write your argument on a separate sheet of paper.

> **Topic:** Should pets be allowed in the workplace?

> **Your Task:** Carefully read each of the *four* texts provided. Then, using evidence from at least *three* of the texts, write a well-developed argument regarding whether or not pets should be allowed in the workplace. Clearly establish your claim, distinguish your claim from alternate or opposing claims, and use specific, relevant, and sufficient evidence from at least *three* of the texts to develop your argument. Do *not* simply summarize each text.

Guidelines:

Be sure to

- Establish your claim regarding whether or not pets should be allowed in the workplace.
- Distinguish your claim from alternate or opposing claims.
- Use specific, relevant, and sufficient evidence from at least three of the texts to develop your argument.
- Identify each source that you reference by text number and line number(s) or graphic (for example: Text 1, line 4 or Text 2, graphic).
- Organize your ideas in a cohesive and coherent manner.
- Maintain a formal style of writing.
- Follow the conventions of standard written English.

Texts:

Text 1—Do Pets in the Workplace Improve Morale?
Text 2—Why Pets in the Workplace May Not Be As Great As You Thought
Text 3—Why a Pet-Friendly Office May Be the Key to Employee Satisfaction
Text 4—Don't Bring Your Dog to Work

Text 1

Do Pets in the Workplace Improve Morale?

Human resource managers are always looking for ways to improve morale and create a more appealing workplace culture. The popularity of the recent film release "The Secret Life of Pets" [2016] underscores the love we Americans have for our pets. In fact, around 65 percent of U.S. households are home
(5) to at least one pet. The majority of these are dogs and cats. . . .

The benefits of being around animals have inspired human resource personnel and other business decision makers to allow pets in the workplace. The top motive for making this allowance is the stress-reducing effect that animals bring. Employees who are less stressed at work are more
(10) productive and miss fewer days due to being sick.

Pet-friendly businesses usually focus mainly on allowing dogs in the workplace. However, some allow cats, birds and reptiles. A retail business might have "shop cats" that live on the premises, or smaller animals kept in cages that can become company mascots and offer a source of stress relief for workers.

An Internet giant paves the way with pets in the workplace.
(15) . . .These days, about 2,000 dogs accompany their owners to Amazon each day. Workers and management have embraced the culture, and the pet-friendly policy benefits both owners and those who don't own pets. No matter what the workday brings, Amazon staff members are never far away from a coworker's terrier or spaniel poking its head around a corner.
(20) Any stress they were feeling melts away. . . .

Pet-friendly workplaces rate higher.
Banfield Pet Hospital recently surveyed over 1,000 employees and 200 human resource decision makers for its Pets At Work barometer called "Pet-Friendly Workplace PAWrometer." The goal was to measure worker opinions about pets in the workplace. Those who worked in pet-friendly offices were
(25) found to believe it improves the atmosphere in the workplace significantly.

The majority of workers in pet-friendly workplaces consider the policy to be positive. A full 91 percent of managers and 82 percent of employees felt workers become more loyal to the company with this policy. A large majority felt it made the workplace more productive,
(30) and 86 percent of workers and 92 percent of management reported decreased worker stress levels. Not only do pets in the workplace make the environment less stressful, workers are also less burdened with guilt about leaving a pet at home alone while they are at work. They are then more likely to work longer hours if required.

While pet-friendly businesses improve existing employees' lives, they are also appealing to new applicants. It's a benefit that millennials[1] find appealing and offers a way to draw in a larger talent pool.

So, how do pet-friendly workplaces stack up in terms of pros and cons? Let's take a look:

The benefits of pets in the workplace.

- **Happier, more productive workers.** Both pet owners and non-pet owning employees report lowered stress levels and a higher level of job satisfaction with pets on the premises. This naturally leads to increased productivity.
- **Healthier workers.** In addition to reduced stress levels, being around animals has documented positive effects on blood pressure, cholesterol levels and the immune system.
- **Increased loyalty.** Over half of employees in non-pet-friendly workplaces report they'd be more likely to continue working for a company if they could bring their pet to work.

Potential problems you may encounter by allowing pets in the workplace.

- **Not everyone is an animal lover.** There are people who dislike animals for one reason or another. Allergies, phobias, or a general dislike of animals could cause pets in the workplace to encroach[2] upon productivity and quality of life for these individuals.
- **Hygiene and cleanliness issues.** Even potty-trained pets can have an accident now and then. There is no guarantee this won't happen in the workplace, especially with a high volume of animals brought to work.
- **Interoffice squabbles.** Not all animals get along, so there is the potential for fights between dogs and cats brought to work.

While worker distraction is a concern for some human resource managers considering a pet-friendly policy, the vast majority report that the benefits to morale and overall productivity far outweigh time spent "distracted" by pets in the workplace.

Advocates of allowing pets in the workplace insist that there are ways around the "cons" or risks of pet-friendly workplaces. The key to a successful pet policy is a clear structure....

—excerpted and adapted from "Do Pets in the Workplace Improve Morale?"
https://online.arbor.edu, August 8, 2016

---

[1]millennials—the generation born in the 1980s or 1990s, especially in the U.S.
[2]encroach—intrude

Text 2

Why Pets in the Workplace May Not Be As Great As You Thought

...Study after study has proven how pets have a calming effect on our bodies and minds, how they help children with A.D.D. [Attention Deficit Disorder] focus better, how they reduce blood pressure and lower stress, how pets at the workplace make employees more creative,
(5) productive, and cordial to each other, and how they're such awesome additions to our lives overall.

So it would seem that if we spend the best parts of our waking hours at work, there's no better way to carry forward these wonderful benefits that pets bring into our work lives too, right? Well, unfortunately there are no
(10) simple answers here.

While there is a growing wave of companies led by the usual suspects—Google, Zynga, Ben & Jerry's, and others—that allow employees to take their pets along to the workplace, there's also a growing debate about the practicality of the whole idea. And these voices of concern are not just com-
(15) ing from the minority of pet-haters or pet-neutral folks around. Even pet owners have reservations about bringing their beloved pooch to the office with them on a daily basis. Here's why:

Not in the Pink of Health

...Spare a thought for the millions of your fellow Americans who suffer from pet related allergies. The Asthma and Allergy Foundation of America
(20) pegs the figure of Americans with one form of pet allergy or another at 15% to 30% of the total population. Some of these allergies are so severe that they cause rashes, temporary breathlessness, panic attacks, and even severe respiratory disorders.

In addition to a physical reaction to the presence of pets around them,
(25) you could have coworkers who are genuinely scared of animals and feel stressed out around them. For such individuals a pet in their workplace is not a calming presence, but rather a constant threat to their wellbeing and safety.

Safety First

...Many industries by their very nature are not conducive[1] to having
(30) pets sauntering around. Medical facilities, pharmaceutical companies, chemical laboratories, and food businesses are all sectors where a pet can

---

[1]conducive—favorable

be a serious threat to the quality of the final product or service. In such environments, pets pose a genuine contamination hazard and are best kept out, no questions asked.

(35)   In some cases, it's in your pet's best interest to chill out at home and skip the trip to the workplace. Industries like construction, mining, refineries, and more can be dangerous for your pet's health and well-being. You wouldn't want to put your pet at risk just so you can be happy at work, would you? . . .

Real Costs to the Company

(40)   As any pet owner will tell you, owning their bundle of joy is not cheap. From $1570 for a large dog to $575 for a parakeet per year, pet ownership comes at an ever-increasing price tag. When you turn your office into a pet friendly zone, you are in turn taking on some of the expenses of owning a pet upon yourself. Be prepared to stock your workplace with at least basic
(45)   pet supplies like snacks, water bowls, kitty litter, and chew toys.

If you think your costs end there (or are tangible), you are mistaken. Pets at the workplace also bring with them a built-in deterrent[2] for employees seeking career opportunities at your organization. With the market for talented and qualified workers already so scarce, adding an extra filter to
(50)   your recruitment process may not be the smartest idea from a competitive perspective. . . .

While the benefits that pets bring with them are numerous and the pro-pet lobby gets louder with every passing day, organizations need to also give credence[3] to the real issues that four-legged and feathered guests at work
(55)   bring along with them. . . .

—Rohan Ayyar
excerpted and adapted from "Why Pets in the Workplace May Not Be As Great As You Thought"
www.fastcompany.com, November 14, 2014

---

[2]deterrent—obstacle
[3]credence—support

Text 3

Why a Pet-Friendly Office May Be the Key to Employee Satisfaction

...The pet-friendly office is transforming our current idea of the typical nine-to-five workspace. Although the primary allure appears to be 24/7 cuddles with man's best friend, the actual benefits of a pet-friendly office go much deeper.

(5) Some of the world's biggest companies have proudly joined the ranks of pet-friendly businesses, from Googleplex,[1] to Build-A-Bear Workshop, to hospitals in New Jersey. This shift in office culture has shown that pet-friendly offices can provide unexpected (and positive) results to all varieties of businesses....

Employee Satisfaction and Stress

(10) Employee satisfaction is a constant concern for an engaging and exciting place. Studies have shown that unhappy workers can cause businesses to lose thousands of dollars over time due to sick leave, mediocre work, and destructive behavior. Keeping the office engaging and exciting can be a struggle, and combating organizational stress may be key to improving (15) a company's profits....

Giving employees the option to bring their pet to work could also save them the worry associated with leaving a pet at home. Instead of scrambling through the end of the day to go home and let the dog out, they have the dog with them and can continue to work without rushing. Instead of (20) spending money on a pet daycare on a regular basis, workers can watch their furry friend while in the office.

Pets are also known to be great stress-relievers in general. It's no wonder that Animal-Assisted Therapy is recognized as one of the leading treatments for post-war PTSD [Post-Traumatic Stress Disorder] and is gaining ground (25) as a popular solution for social workers. Multiple studies have shown that simply petting cats or dogs can be extremely beneficial for our health; from lowering blood pressure to increasing bone density.

Attract Millennials

As a millennial, I can assure you: I would choose a pet-friendly office over the majority of other job offers out there. The benefit of bringing my pup to (30) work is a much stronger pull than a larger paycheck or fancy corner office.

Millennials love their pets, and millennials love pet-friendly offices. In fact, you could even argue that millennials are the reason pet-friendly offices

---

[1]Googleplex—Google headquarters

are taking the business world by storm. Being the largest demographic to enter the workforce, they have already brought with them a demand for a new form of workplace flexibility and a break from the traditional office culture of our predecessors. . . .

Improve Communication

If you've ever walked your dog through a park or downtown area, there's a significant chance that you've received more waves, 'hellos', and acknowledgements than if you had been walking by yourself. Walking or even being near a dog is an excellent ice-breaker.

Shifting to a pet-friendly workspace can bring that same level of open and enthusiastic communication into the office. Water cooler conversations[2] will lose some of their awkward chatter, and employees will have the added encouragement of meeting new people in the building through their pets. This can lead to some inspiring brainstorm conversations as well as an increase in camaraderie[3] and trust among workers.

A 2012 study by the Virginia Commonwealth University found that employees that brought their dogs to work were not only less stressed than their pet-free predecessors, but those employees believed they were 50 percent more productive with the presence of their pets. The public relations manager of the company that participated, Lisa Conklin of Replacements Dinnerware, stated after the conclusion of the study:

"The study proved what we always thought: having dogs around leads to a more productive work environment, and people get to know each other through the pets. If you are in a position where something is stressful, seeing that wagging tail and puppy smile brightens the day—it can turn around the whole environment."

Promote Employee Activity

On top of all these benefits, pets can also improve employee activity. Dog owners in the office will most likely have to walk their dog at least once a day, allowing them the opportunity to get away from their computer and into the open air. Workplace wellness has received considerable attention lately and more companies are making this a priority. Pet-friendly offices can inspire a smooth transition to a more 'mobile' office. . . .

—Katie McBeth
excerpted and adapted from "Why a Pet-Friendly Office May Be the Key to Employee Satisfaction"
https://thebossmagazine.com, September 28, 2016

---

[2]water cooler conversations—informal conversation
[3]camaraderie—fellowship

Text 4

Don't Bring Your Dog to Work

If there's a dog in the cubicle next to you, you're hardly alone: About 7 percent of employers now allow pets in the workplace, reports NPR [National Public Radio]. Five years ago, that figure stood at 5 percent. That might not seem like a big jump, but once you remove jobs that don't have
(5) offices from the equation—manufacturing and agriculture, for instance— that's about a 50 percent increase. That rise is a victory for people who tout the benefits of inviting dogs and other furry friends into the office: It lowers the stress of employees, increases morale, produces tangible health benefits, and reduces turnover, all at no cost to the company.
(10) But how do the dogs feel about it?

"Most people do not understand dog body language," said E'Lise Christensen, a board-certified veterinary behaviorist in Colorado. One major concern she has with the rise of pet-friendly work environments is the corresponding increased risk for behavioral problems, especially dog bites.
(15) Since almost no one, not even many dog trainers, knows how to properly interpret dog body language, co-workers might interpret the panting of a dog in the office as a friendly smile, rather than a sign of nervousness. And in dogs, nervousness can lead to bites. "[People] can identify abject[1] fear, and they can identify extreme aggression, but they cannot reliably identify
(20) things in between," said Christensen. It's in that wide middle area where we may not recognize pet discomfort.

Bonnie Beaver, executive director of the American College of Veterinary Behaviorists and a professor at Texas A&M University, said in an email that dog bites are not the only behavioral issues that might present problems.
(25) Generally, dogs are expected to sit still in an office setting, which can be difficult for active dogs, leading to boredom (which, in turn, leads to problem behaviors like chewing up desk legs). These policies are also particularly hard on dogs if they're taken to the office only occasionally, instead of regularly; dogs are big on routines, and uncertainty adds to their
(30) fear and stress.

Once you expand the conversation beyond our most domesticated companion, the prospects get even iffier. "Not all animals are comfortable with a very social setting," said Christensen. Each new animal, like cats or pot-bellied pigs, brings its own social complexities, not to mention the
(35) possibility of contagious disease (it's rare that employers require proof of

---
[1]abject—severe

vaccination). Rabies, ringworm, and parasitic infections like scabies are all potential health risks for humans that come into contact with pets that haven't been properly vetted.²

(40) Of course there's obvious appeal. Many people love dogs. They write whole articles gushing about a furrier workplace. (Dog skeptics, at least vocal ones, are harder to find.) When an employer is on board, the policy is often as informal as a person in charge saying, "Yeah, sure, whatever. Bring your dogs. It'll be great." Little or no oversight is applied to a matter that needs it in order to ensure the environment is conducive³ to pets in the *(45)* workplace.

Christensen said companies should ideally hire an in-house behavioral expert to oversee a pet-at-work policy, especially in the initial stages, "but unless you're Google, I don't see that happening." More realistically, she said, better awareness will go a long way. Employers should take care to *(50)* craft a policy that works for dogs' well-being as well as humans'. This can include requiring proof of vaccinations, as well as providing training for offices on dog behavior (which can be as basic as watching videos).

"It's critical that people with dogs get special education, in at least body language, even if they think they know normal body language," said *(55)* Christensen. Given that most people can't even tell the difference between a relaxed and anxious dog, this advice seems prudent. Before more offices throw open their doors to dogs willy-nilly⁴ and more pets start tagging along on the morning commute, we should learn how better to listen to them. They might be asking to stay at home.

—Matt Miller
excerpted and adapted from "Don't Bring Your Dog to Work"
www.slate.com, August 15, 2016

---

²vetted—examined
³conducive—favorable
⁴willy-nilly—in an unplanned manner

PART 3—Text-Analysis Response

Directions: Closely read the text provided on pages 257 through 259 and write a well-developed, text-based response of two to three paragraphs. In your response, identify a central idea in the text and analyze how the author's use of **one** writing strategy (literary element or literary technique or rhetorical device) develops this central idea. Use strong and thorough evidence from the text to support your analysis. Do *not* simply summarize the text. You may use the margins to take notes as you read and scrap paper to plan your response. Write your response on a separate sheet of paper.

Guidelines:

Be sure to

- Identify a central idea in the text.
- Analyze how the author's use of **one** writing strategy (literary element or literary technique or rhetorical device) develops this central idea. Examples include: characterization, conflict, denotation/connotation, metaphor, simile, irony, language use, point-of-view, setting, structure, symbolism, theme, tone, etc.
- Use strong and thorough evidence from the text to support your analysis.
- Organize your ideas in a cohesive and coherent manner.
- Maintain a formal style of writing.
- Follow the conventions of standard written English.

Text

...There were a number of people out this afternoon, far more than last Sunday. And the band sounded louder and gayer. That was because the Season had begun. For although the band played all the year round on Sundays, out of season it was never the same. It was like some one
(5) playing with only the family to listen; it didn't care how it played if there weren't any strangers present. Wasn't the conductor wearing a new coat, too? She was sure it was new. He scraped with his foot and flapped his arms like a rooster about to crow, and the bandsmen sitting in the green rotunda blew out their cheeks and glared at the music.
(10) Now there came a little "flutey" bit—very pretty!—a little chain of bright drops. She was sure it would be repeated. It was; she lifted her head and smiled.

Only two people shared her "special" seat: a fine old man in a velvet coat, his hands clasped over a huge carved walking-stick, and a big old
(15) woman, sitting upright, with a roll of knitting on her embroidered apron. They did not speak. This was disappointing, for Miss Brill always looked forward to the conversation. She had become really quite expert, she thought, at listening as though she didn't listen, at sitting in other people's lives just for a minute while they talked
(20) round her.

She glanced, sideways, at the old couple. Perhaps they would go soon. Last Sunday, too, hadn't been as interesting as usual. An Englishman and his wife, he wearing a dreadful Panama hat and she button boots. And she'd gone on the whole time about how she ought to wear
(25) spectacles;[1] she knew she needed them; but that it was no good getting any; they'd be sure to break and they'd never keep on. And he'd been so patient. He'd suggested everything—gold rims, the kind that curved round your ears, little pads inside the bridge. No, nothing would please her. "They'll always be sliding down my nose!" Miss Brill had wanted to
(30) shake her.

The old people sat on the bench, still as statues. Never mind, there was always the crowd to watch. To and fro, in front of the flower-beds and the band rotunda, the couples and groups paraded, stopped to talk, to greet, to buy a handful of flowers from the old beggar who had his

---

[1]spectacles—glasses

(35) tray fixed to the railings. Little children ran among them, swooping and laughing; little boys with big white silk bows under their chins, little girls, little French dolls, dressed up in velvet and lace. And sometimes a tiny staggerer came suddenly rocking into the open from under the trees, stopped, stared, as suddenly sat down "flop," until its small high-
(40) stepping mother, like a young hen, rushed scolding to its rescue. Other people sat on the benches and green chairs, but they were nearly always the same, Sunday after Sunday, and—Miss Brill had often noticed—there was something funny about nearly all of them. They were odd, silent, nearly all old, and from the way they stared they looked as though
(45) they'd just come from dark little rooms or even—even cupboards!

Behind the rotunda the slender trees with yellow leaves down drooping, and through them just a line of sea, and beyond the blue sky with gold-veined clouds.

Tum-tum-tum tiddle-um! tiddle-um! tum tiddley-um tum ta! blew the
(50) band....

Oh, how fascinating it was! How she enjoyed it! How she loved sitting here, watching it all! It was like a play. It was exactly like a play. Who could believe the sky at the back wasn't painted? But it wasn't till a little brown dog trotted on solemn and then slowly trotted off, like a
(55) little "theatre" dog, a little dog that had been drugged, that Miss Brill discovered what it was that made it so exciting. They were all on the stage. They weren't only the audience, not only looking on; they were acting. Even she had a part and came every Sunday. No doubt somebody would have noticed if she hadn't been there; she was part of the
(60) performance after all. How strange she'd never thought of it like that before! And yet it explained why she made such a point of starting from home at just the same time each week—so as not to be late for the performance—and it also explained why she had quite a queer, shy feeling at telling her English pupils how she spent her Sunday afternoons. No
(65) wonder! Miss Brill nearly laughed out loud. She was on the stage. She thought of the old invalid gentleman to whom she read the newspaper four afternoons a week while he slept in the garden. She had got quite used to the frail head on the cotton pillow, the hollowed eyes, the open mouth and the high pinched nose. If he'd been dead she mightn't have
(70) noticed for weeks; she wouldn't have minded. But suddenly he knew he was having the paper read to him by an actress! "An actress!" The old head lifted; two points of light quivered in the old eyes. "An actress—

are ye?" And Miss Brill smoothed the newspaper as though it were the manuscript of her part and said gently; "Yes, I have been an actress for
(75) a long time."...

—Katherine Mansfield
excerpted from "Miss Brill"
The Garden Party and Other Stories, 1922
Alfred A. Knopf, Inc.

Examination June 2019
English Language Arts

Answer Key

Part 1

1. 3
2. 2
3. 1
4. 2
5. 1
6. 1
7. 3
8. 2
9. 4
10. 4
11. 3
12. 3
13. 2
14. 3
15. 1
16. 3
17. 4
18. 2
19. 4
20. 2
21. 1
22. 3
23. 3
24. 2

INDEX

Abbreviations, 185
Abstract, 66
   to concrete, 66
Academic language, 128–132
Accept/except, 174
Active voice, 170
Adjectives, 162
   academic language, 130–132
   archaic, 135
   in a series, 190–191
   vocabulary study, 147–148
Adverb, 163
Affect/effect, 174
Aggravate, 175
Allegory, 94
Alliteration, 83, 94
Allusion, 94
Allusion/illusion, 175
Ambiguity, 77, 94
Among/between, 175
Amount/number, 175
Analogy, 66
Analysis, 103
Anecdote, 66, 124
Antecedent, 162
Antecedent-pronoun agreement, 168
Antithesis, 66
Apostrophe, 194–195
   with contractions, 194–195
   with possessive forms of nouns, 195
   with possessive forms of proper names, 195
   with some plurals, 195
Archaic language, 133–135
Argument, 66, 124
As far as . . . is/are concerned, 175
As/if/like, 179–180
Assonance, 81, 94
Atmosphere, 51, 66
Attitude of speaker, 86
Audience, 108, 124
Autobiography. *See also* Biography
   definition of, 66–67
   recommended, 217–218

Bad/badly, 122, 175–176
Ballad, 78, 94
Being as/being that, 176
Biography, 67. *See also* Autobiography

Blank verse, 94
Bracket, 194

Caring, 123
Cause and effect, 59, 103–104
Character, 67, 101
   focus, 106–107
   reading, 51–52
Characterization, 67
Chronological order, 58
Chronology and plot, 48–49
Claim, 3, 32–33
Classification, 62–63, 103
Clauses, 164–165
   comma after introduction, 189
   dependent, 164, 189
   descriptive, 189
   independent, 165, 188
   nonessential, 189
   parallel, 172
   restrictive, 173
   subordinate (dependent), 173
Close reading, 5–6
Coherence, 124
Collective nouns, 168
Colon, 193
Comma, 187
   with adjectives in a series, 190–191
   after introduction clause, 189
   after introductory phrase only when needed, 189
   in dates, 190
   descriptive and nonessential clauses or phrases set off using, 189
   errors involving, 191–192
   before the last item in a series, 188
   with parenthetic and transitional expressions, 190
   quotes set off using, 191
   with some single words and expression, 190
   splice, 188
Common Core Learning Standards, 2
Compare to/compare with, 176
Comparison and contrast, 59–61, 102–103
Composition evaluation, 118
Compound
   elements, 191

Index

expressions, 205
sentences, 187, 192
Conclusions, 108
Concrete, 67
  to abstract, 55–56
Conflict, 67
  external, 48, 67
  internal, 48, 67
  plot and, 47–48
Conjunctions, 163, 187
  coordinating, 163, 187
  subordinating, 163
Connotation, 95, 145–146
Consonants, 198–204
Contractions, 194–195
Controlling idea, 124
Conventions, 124
Coordinating conjunction, 163, 187
Correlatives, 167, 170
Could of/should of (could have/should have), 176
Couplet, 83, 95

Dash, 193
Dates, 190, 195
Declarative sentences, 183
Definition in nonfiction, 62–63
Denotation, 95
Denouement, 67–68
Dependent clauses, 164, 189
Describe/description, 104, 124–125
Descriptive clauses or phrases, 189
Details, 102
Determinism, 68
Development, 125
Diction, 125
Different from (not than), 176
Direct objects, 144
Dramatic monologue, 95
Due to, 123, 176

Effective, 122
Either/or, 167, 170
Elegy, 86, 95
Elements and techniques, 107–108
Ellipsis, 193–194
Emphatic sentences, 192
Endings, 198
End punctuation, 183–187
Epic, 78, 95
Episode, 68

Essay
  definition of, 68
  exam preparation, 119
  formal, 69
  informal, 69
  planning of, 32
  recommended, 217–218
  topics for. *See* Topics for essay
Everybody, somebody, someone, nobody, 177
Examinations. *See also* Regents exams
  compose, 120
  composition evaluation, 118
  edit as you go, 120–121
  essay exams, preparing, 119
  ideas, gathering your, 119–120
  learning standards, 223–227
  organize, 120
  poetry on, 87
  prompt, writing from a, 115
  scoring rubrics, 227–232
  writing on timed, 119–121
Exclamation mark, 184
Exemplification, 104
Explain/show/discuss, 104
Explication, 86
Exposition, 35–38, 68, 125
Extended metaphor, 61–62
External conflict, 48, 67

Farther/further, 177
Fewer/less, 177
Fiction reading, 46–53
Figurative language, 77, 95
First, second..., 177
Flashback, 68
Focus, 125
  character, 106–107
  topic and, 102
Foreshadowing, 68
Form, 69
Formal essay, 69
Fragments for emphasis, 184
Free verse, 95

General to specific, 66
Genre, 69, 103
Gerunds, 169
Good/well, 175–176
Greek prefixes, 141–142
Greek roots, 139

Index

Hang/hanged/hung, 177
Hard/difficult, 123
Him/her/them, 168
Homophones, 205–206
Hopefully, 177–178
However, 178
Hyperbole, 95–96

Iambic pentameter, 96
Identify, 104
If . . . were/if . . . was, 178–179
If/like/as, 179–180
If/whether, 178
Image, 69, 107
Imagery, 77, 96
Imperative sentences, 184
Incredible/incredulous, 179
Independent clauses, 165, 187–188
Infer/imply, 178
Informal essay, 69
Intensifiers (adverbs), 163
Interjection, 163
Internal conflict, 48, 67
Internal punctuation, 187–195
Internal rhyme, 81, 96
Intransitive verbs, 144
Introductory phrase, 189
Ironic, 50, 72
Irony, 69, 82, 88, 96
Italics
  for quotes, 196
  for titles of works of literature, 196
Its/it's, 178

Journal, 69
Just/only, 180

Kind of/sort of/ type of, 179

Language
  academic, 128–132
  archaic, 133–135
  figurative, 95
  fluent and precise, 104–105
  of poetry, 78–83
  unfamiliar, 133–135
Latin prefixes, 140–142
Latin roots, 137–139
Learning standards, 223–227
Lie/lay, 179
Like/as/if, 179–180

Limited omniscient point of view, 50, 70–71
Literacy, 2
Literature. *See also* Reading
  punctuation of titles of works, 196
  on Regents exam, 101–159
  writing about, 101–108
Logical
  comparisons, 172
  modification, 173–174
Lyric, 96
  poetry, 78

Melodrama, 69
Memoir, 69
Metaphor, 77, 96–97
Meter, 75, 97
Monologue, 69
Motivation, 51, 70

Narration in nonfiction, 58
Narrative, 125
  poetry, 78
  point of view, 70
Narrator, 49, 70
Naturalism, 70, 103
Neither/nor, 167
New York State Standards in Literacy
  guide to, 1
  terms for understanding, 2–3
Nobody, everybody, somebody, someone, 177
Nonessential clauses or phrases, 189
Nonfiction. *See also* Reading
  abstract to concrete, 55
  cause and effect, 59
  chronological order, 58
  comparison and contrast, 59–61
  concrete to abstract, 55–56
  definition or classification, 62–63
  extended metaphor, 61–62
  general to specific, 55
  narration, 58
  order of importance, 63–65
  patterns and organization, 54–65
  purpose, 54
  question to answer, 56–58
  reading, 53–66
  recommended, 217–218
  tone, 65–66
Nonrestrictive (nonessential) phrases, 173
Not only/but also, 170
Noun(s), 162

Index

academic language, 130–132
archaic, 134
collective, 168
modifiers of, 164
plurals, 204–205
possessive forms of, 195
vocabulary study, 146–147
Novels, recommended, 215–216

Objective, 50
  point of view, 70
Object of verb, 169–170
Ode, 97
Omniscient, limited, 50
Omniscient narration, 49
Omniscient point of view, 70–71
Only/just, 180
Onomatopoeia, 83, 97
Order of importance, 63–65
Oxymoron, 97

Paradox, 97
Parallelism, 170
Parentheses, 186
Parenthetic expressions, 190
Participial phrase, 173
Participle, 164, 174
Passive voice, 170
Patterns and rules, 197–206
Period, 183–184
Persona, 49, 70–71
Personal narrative, 109
Personification, 82, 97
Persuasive writing, 53, 66, 112
Phrases, 164–165
  descriptive, 189
  nonessential, 189
  nonrestrictive (nonessential), 173
  parallel, 170
  participial, 173
  restrictive, 173
Plays, recommended, 220–221
Plot
  chronology and, 48–49
  conflict and, 47–48
  definition, 71, 104
  story and, 47
  time and, 49
Plurals, 195, 204–205
Poem(s)/poetry
  on examinations, 87

for further reading, 87–93
internal rhyme of, 81
lyric, 78
narrative, 78
prose, 86–87, 97
reading, 75–99
recommended, 218–219
structure and language of, 78–83
theme in, 83–85
tone in, 80, 86
writing about, 86
Poetic justice, 71
Point of view, 49, 71
  limited omniscient, 50, 71
  narrative, 49–51, 70
  objective, 70
  omniscient, 70–71
Position paper, 125
Possessive form, 195
Prefixes, 136, 198, 202–203
Preposition, 163
Presently, 180
Present perfect tense, 171
Present tense, 171
Prologue, 71
Prompt, 115, 125
Pronoun(s), 162, 169–170
Pronoun-antecedent agreement, 168
Proper names, 195
Prose, 71, 86, 97
Protagonist, 71
Punctuation
  end, 183–187
  internal, 187–195
Purpose in nonfiction, 54
Purposely/purposefully, 180

Quatrains, 80, 83, 97
Question, 56–58
Question mark, 184–185
Quotation marks, 185–186
Quotes, 191, 196

Reading. *See also* Literature; Nonfiction
  autobiography, recommended, 217–218
  character, 51–52
  close, 5–6
  essays, recommended, 217–218
  fiction, 46–53
  for information and understanding, 23–30
  narrative point of view, 49–51

Index

nonfiction, 53–66, 217–218
novels, recommended, 215–216
plays, recommended, 220–221
plot
  chronology and, 48–49
  conflict and, 47–48
  story and, 47
  time and, 49
poetry, 75–99, 218–219
setting, 51
short stories, 220
for text analysis, 35–43
theme, 52–53
useful terms, 45–46
Reading comprehension
  close reading, 5–6
  informational passage, 16–21
  poem, 12–15
  questions used in, 6
  sample passages for, 7–21
Realism, 71
Regents exams. *See also* Examinations
  description of, 3
  samples, 233–292
  vocabulary study, 127–159
Restrictive clauses, 173
Restrictive phrases, 173
Rhetoric, 72
Rhetorical question, 72
Rhyme, 80–81, 98
Rhyme scheme, 83, 98
Rhythm, 75, 97
Romance, 72, 103
Roots. *See also* Spelling
  Greek, 136, 139
  Latin, 140–142
  prefixes and, 136–142, 198
Rules and patterns, 197
Run-on sentence, 188

Sad/depressing, 123
Same, 124
Satire, 72, 98
Semicolon, 192–193
Sentence(s)
  complete, 165
  compound, 187, 192
  declarative, 183
  emphatic, 192
  entire, 185–186
  exclamation mark, 184

imperative, 184
  period, 183–184
  question mark, 184–185
  run-on, 188
Series, 188
Setting, 51
Short stories, 72, 220
Significant details, 102
Simile, 77, 98
Simple past tense, 171
So, 180
Soliloquy, 52, 72, 98
Somebody, someone, nobody, everybody, 177
Sonnet, 83, 98
Sort of/type of/kind of, 179
Source-based argument, 31
Speaker, 72, 79–80, 86, 98
Specific to general, 55–56
Spelling. *See also* Roots
  homophones, 205–206
  noun plurals, 204–205
  prefixes and suffixes, 202–203
  rules and patterns, 197–198
  on writing exams, 197
Spelling words
  commonly confused, 206–207
  commonly misspelled, 207–214
  with double letters, 200–202
  ending in silent *e*, 198–199
  ending in *y*, 199–200
  including *ie* or *ei*, 203
Standards, 223
Stanza, 98–99
Story and plot, 47
Structure of poetry, 78–83
Subject and themes, 105
Subject of the participle, 174
Subject of verb, 166, 181–182
Subject-verb agreement, 166–168
Subordinate (dependent) clauses, 173
Subordinating conjunctions, 163
Suffixes, 198, 200, 202–203
Syllable, 198
Symbol, 72, 99
Synonymies, 121–124
Synonyms, 142–143

Tense of verb, 171
Text analysis
  exposition, 35–38
  reading and writing for, 35–43

Index

That/who/which, 181
Themes, 73, 80
  in poetry, 83–85
  reading, 52–53
  subject and, 105
Them/him/her, 168
Thesaurus, 142–143
Thesis, 73
Thesis statement, 3
Time and plot, 49
To cause, 121
To change, 121
To look down upon someone/something, 122
To look upon someone/something, 121
Tone, 73, 125
  definition of, 99
  in poetry, 80, 86
  in writing, 65–66
Topics for essay
  analysis, 103
  classification, 103
  comparison and contrast, 102–103
  details, selecting significant, 102
  developing the, 102–104
  exemplification, 104
  topic and focus, 102
Toward/towards, 181
Tragedy, 103
Transition, 73, 125
Transitional expressions, 190
Transitive verbs, 144–145
Turning point, 73
Type of/kind of/sort of, 179

Underline, 196
Understanding, 101, 107
Understatement, 99
Unity, 125

Verb(s)
  academic language, 128–130
  archaic, 133–134
  definition, 162
  intransitive, 144–145
  object of, 169–170
  subject and, agreement between, 166–168
  subject of, 166, 181–182
  tense of, 171–172
  transitive, 144–145
  vocabulary study of, 143–144

Verisimilitude, 73
Verse
  blank, 94
  free, 95
Vocabulary study, 127–159
  adjectives, 147–148
  from book reviews, 156–159
  nouns, 146–147
  from Op-Ed pages, 152–156
  from Regents exams, 149–152
  verbs, 143–146
Vowels, 197, 200–201, 204–205

When/where, 181
Whether/if, 178
Which/that/who, 181
Who/whom/whoever/whomever, 181–182
Words
  commonly confused, 206–207
  commonly misspelled, 207–214
  with double letters, 200–202
  ending in silent *e*, 198–199
  ending in *y*, 199–200
  Greek prefixes, 141–142
  Greek roots, 136, 139
  including *ie* or *ei*, 203
  Latin prefixes, 140–142
  Latin roots, 137–139
  learning in context, 135
  from Regents exams, 149–159
  roots and prefixes, 136–142, 198
Writing
  audience, 108
  character focus, 106–107
  conclusions, 108
  elements and techniques, 107–108
  essay topics, 101
  on examinations, 109–125
  explication, 86
  fluent and precise, 104–105
  to inform or persuade, 109–115
  literature as focus of, 101–108, 101–159
  personal narrative, 109–111
  persuasive, 109–115
  poetry as focus of, 86
  from prompt, 115–118
  subject and themes, 105
  for text analysis, 35–43
  tone, 65–66

BARRON'S
Regents Exams and Answers

English Revised Edition

CAROL CHAITKIN, M.S.
Former Director of American Studies, Lycée Français de New York
Former English Department Head, Great Neck North High School,
Great Neck, New York

© Copyright 2021, 2020, 2019, 2018, 2017, 2016, 2015, 2014, 2013, 2012, 2011, 2010, 2009, 2008, 2007, 2006, 2005, 2004, 2003, 2002, 2001, 2000, 1999, 1998, 1997, 1996, 1995, 1994, 1993 by Kaplan, Inc., d/b/a Barron's Educational Series

All rights reserved.
No part of this book may be reproduced or distributed in any form or by any means without the written permission of the copyright owner.

Published by Kaplan, Inc., d/b/a Barron's Educational Series
750 Third Avenue
New York, NY 10017
www.barronseduc.com

ISBN: 978-1-5062-6663-3

10 9 8 7 6 5 4 3 2 1

Kaplan, Inc., d/b/a Barron's Educational Series print books are available at special quantity discounts to use for sales promotions, employee premiums, or educational purposes. For more information or to purchase books, please call the Simon & Schuster special sales department at 866-506-1949.

Contents

Introduction   **1**

   The NY State ELA Standards and the Reading and Writing
      We Do in High School English Courses 1
   How Can This Book Help You? 1
   Terms to Help You Understand the English Language Arts Learning
      Standards and the Regents ELA Exam 2
   The Regents ELA Exam—An Overview 3

Strategy and Review for Part 1 of the Regents ELA Exam   **5**

   CHAPTER 1 **Reading Comprehension**

   What Does This Part of the Exam Require? 5
   What Does This Part of the Exam Look Like? 5
   Strategies and Review 19

Strategy and Review for Part 2 of the Regents ELA Exam   **21**

   CHAPTER 2 **Argument**

   What Does This Part of the Exam Require? 21
   What Does This Part of the Exam Look Like? 22
   Looking at the Texts 30
   Know the Rubric 31
   Strategies and Review 35

Strategy and Review for Part 3 of the Regents ELA Exam   37

CHAPTER 3   Text-Analysis Response

What Does this Part of the Exam Require? 37
What Does this Part of the Exam Look Like? 37
Looking at the Text 38
Know the Rubric 41
Strategies and Review 43

Reading and Writing About Literature   45

CHAPTER 4   Reviewing Literary Elements and Techniques

Elements of Fiction and Drama 45
Elements of Nonfiction 51
Elements of Poetry 51

CHAPTER 5   Glossaries of Terms

Structure and Language in Prose 53
Structure and Language in Poetry 61
Terms for Writing 66

A Guide to Proofreading for Common Errors   69

The Basics 69
Punctuation 69
Grammar 70
Spelling 71

Appendices: 73
The New York State Learning Standards for English Language Arts

2017 REVISED ELA STANDARDS FOR READING–Literature and
    Informational Texts (RL and RI)................................. 73
Writing Standards Grades 11/12 (W)................................. 75
Language Standards Grades 11/12 (L) 76
How Is the Regents ELA Exam Scored?............................... 77
Scoring Rubrics for the Regents ELA Exam.......................... 77

Regents ELA Examinations and Answers 83

June 2016 84
August 2016.. 122
June 2017 160
August 2017... 199
June 2018 235
August 2018... 274
June 2019 312
August 2019... 352

Introduction

THE NY STATE ELA STANDARDS AND THE READING AND WRITING WE DO IN HIGH SCHOOL ENGLISH COURSES

Most middle school and high school students in NY State should be familiar with the guidelines for curriculum and instruction in their English courses. These guidelines include the following:

- Students will read both informational texts and literary texts in their English courses. Alignment with the NY State learning standards requires a balancing of the two.
- In all academic subjects, students will be expected to build their knowledge primarily through engaging directly with text.
- Throughout secondary school, students will read texts of increasing complexity and will be expected to develop skills in close reading in all academic subjects.
- Students will be expected to engage in rich and rigorous **evidence-based** conversations/class discussions about text.
- Student writing will emphasize **use of evidence** from sources to express their understanding and to form and develop an argument.
- Students will acquire the academic vocabulary they need to comprehend and respond to grade-level complex texts. This vocabulary is often relevant to more than one subject.

HOW CAN THIS BOOK HELP YOU?

This book provides a detailed guide to the Regents ELA Exam, showing you exactly what each part of the exam looks like. Actual passages and multiple-choice questions, with analysis of the multiple-choice questions and guidelines for composing written responses, are included. The rubrics for the scoring of each section are fully explained. For your review, you will find a chapter on "Reviewing Literary Elements and Techniques" and detailed "Glossaries of Terms" that review structure and language in prose and poetry. There is also

"A Guide to Proofreading for Common Errors." In the Appendix, you will find the New York State Learning Standards for Reading, Writing, and Language. Actual ELA Regents Exams, all with sample essays and answers explained, are also included.

TERMS TO HELP YOU UNDERSTAND THE ENGLISH LANGUAGE ARTS LEARNING STANDARDS AND THE REGENTS ELA EXAM

These are the learning standards in ELA and math, developed and adopted by a consortium of over 40 states. New York State first adopted the CCLS in 2010 and implemented a revised set of standards in 2017. These revisions did not represent significant changes in the expectations for grades 11/12 expressed in the guidelines above.*

CCR—The phrase "**college and career ready**" is widely used in discussion of the curriculum and assessments. This refers to the fundamental principle of the learning standards: to reflect the knowledge and skills that all students need for success in college and careers.

ELA/Literacy—English Language Arts (ELA) refers to skills in reading, writing, speaking, and listening. Courses and exams once identified as "English" may also be identified as ELA. Literacy refers to the ability to read and write and to use language proficiently. The term also identifies the quality of being knowledgeable in a particular subject or field. For example, we often refer to "digital" or "computer literacy."

Assessment—You may hear teachers and other educators using the term **assessment** instead of test or examination. An **assessment** is more than a simple test (in vocabulary, say) because it seeks to measure a number of skills at one time. Although we continue to refer to the English Regents as an exam or a test, its goal is to be a valid **assessment** of a broad range of the reading, thinking, language, and writing skills outlined in the Standards.

Text—Broadly, the term text refers to any written material. The core curriculum uses the term to refer to the great variety of material students are expected to be able to read, understand, analyze, and write about. Texts may include **literary** works of fiction, drama, and poetry; and **informational**, or

---

*See the NY State Education Department's website *www.engageNY.org* for details on all the changes in Standards and Regents Examinations.

nonfiction, including essays, memoirs, speeches, and scientific and historical documents. The learning standards also emphasize the use of **authentic texts**; that is, students will read actual historical documents or scientific essays rather than articles about them.

Close Reading—Skill in close, analytic reading is fundamental to the CCLS and to the ELA Regents exam. The core curriculum focuses student attention on the text itself in order to understand not only what the text says and means, but also how that meaning is constructed and revealed. Close reading enables students to understand central ideas and key supporting details. It also enables students to reflect on the meanings of individual words and sentences, the order in which sentences unfold, and the development of ideas over the course of the text, which ultimately leads students to arrive at an understanding of the text as a whole.

Argument—What is an argument? In academic writing, an argument is usually a central idea, often called a **claim** or **thesis statement**, which is backed up with evidence that supports the idea. Much of the writing high school students do in their English courses constitutes essays of argument, in contrast to personal essays, descriptive pieces, or works of imagination.

Source-Based/Evidence-Based—The ability to compose sound arguments using relevant and specific evidence from a given text is central to the expectations of the learning standards.

Writing Strategy—This is the general term for a literary element, literary technique, or rhetorical device. Examples include: characterization, conflict, denotation/connotation, metaphor, simile, irony, language use, point-of-view, setting, structure, symbolism, theme, tone, etc. (See the Glossaries in this book for definitions and examples of the most widely used terms.)

THE REGENTS ELA EXAM—AN OVERVIEW

This 3-hour examination requires students to read, analyze, and write about both literary and informational texts.

PART 1—READING COMPREHENSION

This part of the exam requires close reading of three texts and will contain a literature passage (prose), a poem, and an informational text, followed by a total of 24 multiple-choice questions.

PART 2—WRITING FROM SOURCES: ARGUMENT

This part of the exam includes close reading of four or five informational texts. Students will compose an essay of argument with a claim based on the sources.

PART 3—TEXT ANALYSIS

Students will do a close reading of one informational or literature text and write a two to three paragraph response that identifies a central idea in the text and analyzes how the author's use of one writing strategy develops that central idea.

Strategy and Review for Part 1 of the Regents ELA Exam

CHAPTER 1
Reading Comprehension

WHAT DOES THIS PART OF THE EXAM REQUIRE?

This part of the exam requires close reading of three texts and will contain at least one prose literature passage, usually from a work of fiction; a poem; and one informational text, which may include a personal narrative, a speech, an account of historical significance, or a discussion of a scientific concept. The prose passages and the poems are sometimes works in translation. These passages are followed by a total of 24 multiple-choice questions. The questions require analysis of different aspects of a text, including: elements of character and plot development, comprehension of a central idea and how it is supported, elements of style, and understanding vocabulary in context. Most of the questions include more than one plausible answer; choosing the correct answer often requires comprehension of the text as a whole.

WHAT DOES THIS PART OF THE EXAM LOOK LIKE?

Sample Passage A and Multiple-Choice Questions

Passage A
Literary Text

It was eleven o'clock that night when Mr. Pontellier returned from Klein's hotel. He was in an excellent humor, in high spirits, and very talkative. His entrance awoke his wife, who was in bed and fast asleep when he came in. He talked to her while he undressed, telling her anecdotes
(5) and bits of news and gossip that he had gathered during the day. From his

trousers pockets he took a fistful of crumpled bank notes and a good deal of silver coin, which he piled on the bureau indiscriminately with keys, knife, handkerchief, and whatever else happened to be in his pockets. She was overcome with sleep, and answered him with little half utterances.

(10) He thought it very discouraging that his wife, who was the sole object of his existence, evinced[1] so little interest in things which concerned him, and valued so little his conversation.

Mr. Pontellier had forgotten the bonbons and peanuts for the boys. Notwithstanding he loved them very much, and went into the adjoining (15) room where they slept to take a look at them and make sure that they were resting comfortably. The result of his investigation was far from satisfactory. He turned and shifted the youngsters about in bed. One of them began to kick and talk about a basket full of crabs.

Mr. Pontellier returned to his wife with information that Raoul had a (20) high fever and needed looking after. Then he lit a cigar and went and sat near the open door to smoke it.

Mrs. Pontellier was quite sure Raoul had no fever. He had gone to bed perfectly well, she said, and nothing had ailed him all day. Mr. Pontellier was too well acquainted with fever symptoms to be mistaken. He assured her the (25) child was consuming[2] at that moment in the next room.

He reproached his wife with her inattention, her habitual neglect of the children. If it was not a mother's place to look after children, whose on earth was it? He himself had his hands full with his brokerage business. He could not be in two places at once; making a living for his family on the street, and (30) staying at home to see that no harm befell them. He talked in a monotonous, insistent way.

Mrs. Pontellier sprang out of bed and went into the next room. She soon came back and sat on the edge of the bed, leaning her head down on the pillow. She said nothing, and refused to answer her husband when he (35) questioned her. When his cigar was smoked out he went to bed, and in half a minute he was fast asleep.

Mrs. Pontellier was by that time thoroughly awake. She began to cry a little, and wiped her eyes on the sleeve of her peignoir.[3] Blowing out the candle, which her husband had left burning, she slipped her bare feet into a (40) pair of satin mules at the foot of the bed and went out on the porch, where she sat down in the wicker chair and began to rock gently to and fro.

It was then past midnight. The cottages were all dark. A single faint light gleamed out from the hallway of the house. There was no sound

---

[1]evinced—clearly showed [2]consuming—wasting away [3]peignoir—dressing gown

abroad except the hooting of an old owl in the top of a water oak, and the (45) everlasting voice of the sea, that was not uplifted at that soft hour. It broke like a mournful lullaby upon the night.

The tears came so fast to Mrs. Pontellier's eyes that the damp sleeve of her peignoir no longer served to dry them. She was holding the back of her chair with one hand; her loose sleeve had slipped almost to the shoulder of (50) her uplifted arm. Turning, she thrust her face, steaming and wet, into the bend of her arm, and she went on crying there, not caring any longer to dry her face, her eyes, her arms. She could not have told why she was crying. Such experiences as the foregoing were not uncommon in her married life. They seemed never before to have weighed much against the abundance of (55) her husband's kindness and a uniform devotion which had come to be tacit[4] and self-understood.

An indescribable oppression, which seemed to generate in some unfamiliar part of her consciousness, filled her whole being with a vague anguish. It was like a shadow, like a mist passing across her soul's summer (60) day. It was strange and unfamiliar; it was a mood. She did not sit there inwardly upbraiding[5] her husband, lamenting at Fate, which had directed her footsteps to the path which they had taken. She was just having a good cry all to herself. The mosquitoes made merry over her, biting her firm, round arms and nipping at her bare insteps.

(65) The little stinging, buzzing imps succeeded in dispelling a mood which might have held her there in the darkness half a night longer.

The following morning Mr. Pontellier was up in good time to take the rockaway which was to convey him to the steamer at the wharf. He was returning to the city to his business, and they would not see him again at (70) the Island till the coming Saturday. He had regained his composure, which seemed to have been somewhat impaired the night before. He was eager to be gone, as he looked forward to a lively week in Carondelet Street.

Mr. Pontellier gave his wife half of the money which he had brought away from Klein's hotel the evening before. She liked money as well as most (75) women, and accepted it with no little satisfaction. . . .

A few days later a box arrived for Mrs. Pontellier from New Orleans. It was from her husband. It was filled with friandises,[6] with luscious and toothsome[7] bits—the finest of fruits, pates, a rare bottle or two, delicious syrups, and bonbons in abundance.

(80) Mrs. Pontellier was always very generous with the contents of such a box; she was quite used to receiving them when away from home. The

---

[4]tacit—not actually stated [5]upbraiding—severely scolding [6]friandises—dainty cakes [7]toothsome—delicious

pates and fruit were brought to the dining-room; the bonbons were passed around. And the ladies, selecting with dainty and discriminating fingers and a little greedily, all declared that Mr. Pontellier was the best husband in the
(85) world. Mrs. Pontellier was forced to admit that she knew of none better.

—Kate Chopin
excerpted from *The Awakening*, 1899

Multiple-Choice Questions

1 The primary purpose of the first paragraph is to

   (1) create a metaphor
   (2) foreshadow an event
   (3) establish a contrast
   (4) present a flashback   1 _____

2 Placed in the context of the rest of the text, Mr. and Mrs. Pontellier's disagreement about Raoul's fever (lines 19–31) reflects

   (1) Mrs. Pontellier's resentment of her husband's night out
   (2) Mr. Pontellier's belief in his authority over his wife
   (3) Mrs. Pontellier's need for her husband's approval
   (4) Mr. Pontellier's concern for his wife's well-being   2 _____

3 In lines 26–31, the author presents Mr. Pontellier as a man who feels

   (1) defeated
   (2) anxious
   (3) distracted
   (4) arrogant   3 _____

4 The author's choice of language in lines 38–46 serves to emphasize Mrs. Pontellier's sense of

   (1) isolation
   (2) boredom
   (3) disbelief
   (4) inferiority   4 _____

5 One major effect of the simile used in lines 45–46 is to emphasize Mrs. Pontellier's

   (1) anger
   (2) distress
   (3) defiance
   (4) exhaustion

6 Lines 52–56 demonstrate Mrs. Pontellier's desire to

   (1) protect her reputation
   (2) question her situation
   (3) abandon her dreams
   (4) disguise her sorrow

7 Lines 73–79 contradict a central idea in the text by describing Mr. Pontellier's

   (1) generosity
   (2) honesty
   (3) sympathy
   (4) humility

8 Based on events in the text, which quotation best reveals the irony of the statement that Mr. Pontellier's wife "was the sole object of his existence" (lines 10–11)?

   (1) "From his trousers pockets he took a fistful of crumpled bank notes" (lines 5–6)
   (2) "Then he lit a cigar and went and sat near the open door to smoke it" (lines 20–21)
   (3) "He assured her the child was consuming at that moment in the next room" (lines 24–25)
   (4) "He was eager to be gone, as he looked forward to a lively week in Carondelet Street" (lines 71–72)

Answers

(1) **3**   (2) **2**   (3) **4**   (4) **1**   (5) **2**   (6) **2**   (7) **1**   (8) **4**

Looking at the Questions

1. *The primary purpose of the first paragraph...*

    This question asks you to analyze the introduction of characters, their interaction and its significance to the development of plot and theme.

2. *Placed in the context, lines 19–31 reflect...*

    This question asks you to understand how the interaction of the two characters develops over the course of the text.

3. *The author presents Mr. Pontellier as a man...*

    This question requires further analysis of how characters are introduced and developed.

4. *The author's choice of language... serves to emphasize*

    Here you must determine the meaning of words and phrases in context and the role of word choice in the passage.

5. *One major effect of the simile...*

    Here you should sense in the metaphor the feelings of both calm and sorrow in the character.

6. *Lines 52–56 demonstrate...*

    This question asks for analysis of what the text says explicitly as well as what can be inferred about the character's feelings.

7. *Lines 73–79 contradict...*

    Here you are asked to determine a central idea and understand its development over the course of the text.

8. *Which quotation best reveals the irony...*

    Here you are expected to recognize the incongruity between what the character says he feels and what he is actually looking forward to.

Sample Passage B
Poem

View with a Grain of Sand

We call it a grain of sand
but it calls itself neither grain nor sand.
It does just fine without a name,
whether general, particular,
(5) permanent, passing,
incorrect or apt.

Our glance, our touch mean nothing to it.
It doesn't feel itself seen and touched.
And that it fell on the windowsill
(10) is only our experience, not its.
For it it's no different than falling on anything else
with no assurance that it's finished falling
or that it's falling still.

The window has a wonderful view of a lake
(15) but the view doesn't view itself.
It exists in this world
colorless, shapeless,
soundless, odorless, and painless.
The lake's floor exists floorlessly
(20) and its shore exists shorelessly.
Its water feels itself neither wet nor dry
and its waves to themselves are neither singular nor plural.
They splash deaf to their own noise
on pebbles neither large nor small.

(25) And all this beneath a sky by nature skyless
in which the sun sets without setting at all
and hides without hiding behind an unminding cloud.
The wind ruffles it, its only reason being
that it blows.

(30) A second passes.
A second second.
A third.
But they're three seconds only for us.

Time has passed like a courier with urgent news.
(35) But that's just our simile.
The character's invented, his haste is make-believe,
his news inhuman.

—Wislawa Szymborska from Polish Poetry of the
Last Two Decades of Communist Rule,
translated by Stanislaw Barańczak and Clare Cavanagh
Northwestern University Press, 1991

Multiple-Choice Questions

1 The statement "Our glance, our touch mean nothing to it" (line 7) helps to establish the concept of

   (1) human resentment of the natural order
   (2) nature's superiority
   (3) human control over the environment
   (4) nature's indifference   1 ____

2 The purpose of lines 14 through 18 is to present

   (1) a contrast with human reliance on the senses
   (2) a focus on the complexity of natural events
   (3) an emphasis on human need for physical beauty
   (4) an appreciation for the role of nature in everyday life   2 ____

3 Lines 30 through 33 contribute to the poem's meaning by

   (1) questioning the finality of death
   (2) commenting on human perception
   (3) revealing the power of anticipation
   (4) describing an unusual phenomenon   3 ____

4 The inclusion of the figurative language in the final stanza serves to
   (1) modify an argument
   (2) stress a value
   (3) reinforce a central idea
   (4) resolve a conflict   4 _____

5 The poem is developed primarily through the use of
   (1) examples
   (2) exaggerations
   (3) cause and effect
   (4) question and answer   5 _____

Answers

(1) **4**   (2) **1**   (3) **2**   (4) **3**   (5) **1**

Looking at the Questions

1. *The statement. . . helps to establish the concept of*

   Reading the entire poem before answering the question helps you to recognize the central theme of the poem in this statement.

2. *The purpose of lines 14 through 18 is to present. . .*

   Here you are expected to notice how specific details and imagery contribute to the development of the central theme.

3. *Lines 30 through 33 contribute to the poem's meaning by. . .*

   This question asks you to identify the tone of the passage and to consider the last line of the stanza as a comment on how humans perceive time.

4. *The inclusion of figurative language in the final stanza serves to. . .*

   Here you are expected to consider how figurative language contributes to the meaning of a poem. In this case, the poet concludes with images of human perception of time as only a simile.

5. *The poem is developed primarily through the use of. . .*

   This question asks you to recognize in the sequence of stanzas the overall structure of the poem as a series of examples.

Sample Passage C
Informational Text

In this excerpt, Andrew Carnegie presents his philosophy regarding how the excess wealth of the rich should be used. Carnegie himself had risen from being an impoverished immigrant to one of the most successful industrialists of the 19th century.

The growing disposition to tax more and more heavily large estates left at death is a cheering indication of the growth of a salutary[1] change in public opinion. The State of Pennsylvania now takes—subject to some exceptions—one-tenth of the property left by its citizens. The budget presented inthe
(5) British Parliament the other day proposes to increase the death-duties; and, most significant of all, the new tax is to be a graduated one. Of all forms of taxation, this seems the wisest. Men who continue hoarding great sums all their lives, the proper use of which for public ends would work goodto the community, should be made to feel that the community, in the form
(10) of the state, cannot thus be deprived of its proper share. By taxing estates heavily at death the state marks its condemnation of the selfish millionaire's unworthy life. . . .

This policy would work powerfully to induce the rich man to attend to the administration of wealth during his life, which is the end that society
(15) should always have in view, as being that by far most fruitful for the people. Nor need it be feared that this policy would sap the root of enterprise and render men less anxious to accumulate, for to the class whose ambition it is to leave great fortunes and be talked about after their death, it will attract even more attention, and, indeed, be a somewhat nobler ambition to have
(20) enormous sums paid over to the state from their fortunes.

There remains, then, only one mode of using great fortunes; but in this we have the true antidote for the temporary unequal distribution of wealth, the reconciliation of the rich and the poor—a reign of harmony—another ideal, differing, indeed, from that of the Communist in requiring
(25) only the further evolution of existing conditions, not the total overthrow of our civilization. It is founded upon the present most intense individualism, and the race is prepared to put it in practice by degrees whenever it pleases. Under its sway we shall have an ideal state, in which the surplus wealth of the few will become, in the best sense, the property of the many, because
(30) administered for the common good, and this wealth, passing through the hands of the few, can be made a much more potent force for the elevation

---

[1] salutary—beneficial

of our race than if it had been distributed in small sums to the people themselves. Even the poorest can be made to see this, and to agree that great sums gathered by some of their fellow-citizens and spent for public (35) purposes, from which the masses reap the principal benefit, are more valuable to them than if scattered among them through the course of many years in trifling amounts....

Poor and restricted are our opportunities in this life; narrow our horizon; our best work most imperfect; but rich men should be thankful (40) for one inestimable boon.[2] They have it in their power during their lives to busy themselves in organizing benefactions from which the masses of their fellows will derive lasting advantage, and thus dignify their own lives. The highest life is probably to be reached, not by such imitation of the life of Christ as Count Tolstoi gives us, but, while animated by Christ's spirit, (45) by recognizing the changed conditions of this age, and adopting modes of expressing this spirit suitable to the changed conditions under which we live; still laboring for the good of our fellows, which was the essence of his life and teaching, but laboring in a different manner.

This, then, is held to be the duty of the man of Wealth: First, to set an (50) example of modest, unostentatious[3] living, shunning display or extravagance; to provide moderately for the legitimate wants of those dependent upon him; and after doing so to consider all surplus revenues which come to him simply as trust funds, which he is called upon to administer, and strictly bound as a matter of duty to administer in the manner which, in his judgment, is best (55) calculated to produce the most beneficial results for the community—the man of wealth thus becoming the mere agent and trustee for his poorer brethren, bringing to their service his superior wisdom, experience and ability to administer, doing for them better than they would or could do for themselves....

(60) Thus is the problem of Rich and Poor to be solved. The laws of accumulation will be left free; the laws of distribution free. Individualism will continue, but the millionaire will be but a trustee for the poor; intrusted for a season with a great part of the increased wealth of the community, but administering it for the community far better than it could or would (65) have done for itself. The best minds will thus have reached a stage in the development of the race in which it is clearly seen that there is no mode of disposing of surplus wealth creditable to thoughtful and earnest men into whose hands it flows save by using it year by year for the general good. This day already dawns. But a little while, and although, without incurring the

---

[2]boon—benefit [3]unostentatious—not showy

(70) pity of their fellows, men may die sharers in great business enterprises from which their capital cannot be or has not been withdrawn, and is left chiefly at death for public uses, yet the man who dies leaving behind many millions of available wealth, which was his to administer during life, will pass away "unwept, unhonored, and unsung," no matter to what uses he leaves the
(75) dross[4] which he cannot take with him. Of such as these the public verdict will then be: "The man who dies thus rich dies disgraced."

Such, in my opinion, is the true Gospel concerning Wealth, obedience to which is destined some day to solve the problem of the Rich and the Poor, and to bring "Peace on earth, among men Good-Will."

—Andrew Carnegie
excerpted from "Wealth," 1889

---

[4]dross—waste

Multiple-Choice Questions

1 The first paragraph (lines 1–12) serves the author's purpose by

 (1) providing examples of alternative tax policies
 (2) contrasting the current taxation system with his proposal
 (3) comparing equal taxation with graduated taxation
 (4) distinguishing estate taxes from income taxes   1 _____

2 The expression "sap the root of enterprise" (line 16) refers to the

 (1) decline in consumer confidence
 (2) reduction in government funding
 (3) discouragement of private business
 (4) harm to international trade   2 _____

3 What evidence from the text best clarifies the author's claim in lines 33–37 ("Even the poorest . . . amounts")?

 (1) lines 38–40 ("Poor and restricted . . . inestimable boon")
 (2) lines 49–50 ("This, then, . . . or extravagance")
 (3) lines 60–61 ("The laws . . . distribution free")
 (4) lines 61–65 ("Individualism . . . for itself")   3 _____

What Does This Part of the Exam Look Like?

4 The author's tone in lines 49–59 can best be described as

  (1) confident
  (2) indifferent
  (3) humble
  (4) sarcastic   4 _____

5 A central idea in the text advocates that the wealthy should

  (1) be rewarded for their generosity to the public
  (2) contribute to the public during their lifetime
  (3) entrust their estates to charitable institutions
  (4) be focused on increasing their institutional worth   5 _____

6 Which statement best reflects a central argument used by the author?

  (1) There is no way to insure fair distribution of earnings.
  (2) People should only be paid what they actually earn.
  (3) Sharing wealth among all would limit large gifts from benefactors.
  (4) Equaling wealth among all would restrict the national tax base.   6 _____

Answers

(1) **1**   (2) **3**   (3) **4**   (4) **1**   (5) **2**   (6) **3**

Looking at the Questions

1. *The first paragraph (lines 1–12) serves the author's purpose by...*

    This question asks you to analyze how an author's ideas are developed in a particular paragraph and to recognize how an author effectively structures an argument.

2. *The expression "sap the root of enterprise" (line 16) refers to the...*

    Here you must recognize the use of figurative language and how it expresses a central claim of the argument.

3. *What evidence from the text best clarifies the author's claim in lines 33–37...?*

    This question requires analysis of a complex set of ideas and how they develop over the course of the text.

4. *The author's tone in lines 49–59 can best be described as...*

    Here you must recognize tone as it is determined in the connotation of words and phrases.

5. *A central idea in the text advocates that the wealthy should...*

    Determining the central idea of a text is a fundamental skill in the learning standards.

6. *Which statement best reflects a central argument used by the author?*

    This question complements the one above because it asks you to identify the author's central argument of the passage as it is developed over the course of the text.

You will notice that the questions in this part of the exam are primarily about:

identifying themes and central ideas and **analyzing** their development
recognizing the significance of tone and point of view
describing the author's use of structure, rhetorical and literary elements
determining the meaning of words and phrases as they are used in the text
understanding figurative language, connotation, and nuances in word meanings

STRATEGIES AND REVIEW

- Remember, close reading means reading to understand <u>what</u> the text says and means as well as to recognize <u>how</u> the meaning is constructed and revealed.
- Be sure to first read through to the end of the passage before trying to answer any of the questions.
- Make your choice of the <u>best</u> answer based on the meaning of the entire passage; there may be more than one plausible choice.
- Recognize the key terms commonly used in the multiple-choice questions.
- Review the Glossaries to support your knowledge and use of literary terms and writing strategies.
- Be confident that the reading, discussion, and writing in your high school courses have prepared you for the exam.
- Review the actual Regents ELA/Exams and the Answers Explained.
- Review the tasks based on a poem in the Regents ELA/exams in the Answers Explained.

Strategy and Review for Part 2 of the Regents ELA Exam

CHAPTER 2
Argument

WHAT DOES THIS PART OF THE EXAM REQUIRE?

First, you must read and comprehend four informational texts. Depending on the topic, these may be examples of literary non-fiction, journalism, scientific publications meant for the general reader, or historical documents. There are no multiple-choice questions in this part of the exam. As in Part 1 of the exam, you must:

- Determine the central ideas of texts, including how ideas within and across texts interact and build on one another.
- Analyze a complex set of ideas and events.
- Determine the meanings of words and phrases as they are used in texts, including figurative, connotative, and technical meanings.

Then, you must take a position on the question and compose an evidence-based argument supported by your analysis of the texts, using valid reasoning and relevant and sufficient evidence from at least three of the texts. An effective essay of argument must clearly establish a claim that can be sufficiently supported with reliable evidence. The organization must be clear and coherent, and the writing is expected to demonstrate command of standard written English. These are reading, research, thinking, and writing skills that high school students are expected to demonstrate across the curriculum.

Argument

WHAT DOES THIS PART OF THE EXAM LOOK LIKE?

The topic is often based on a controversial issue of recent or current interest. Here is an example from the January 2016 Regents ELA exam.

SAMPLE TASK – EVIDENCE-BASED WRITING

Directions: Closely read each of the *four* texts provided on pages 23 through 31 and write a source-based argument on the topic below. You may use the margins to take notes as you read and scrap paper to plan your response.

> **Topic:** Should food be genetically modified?

> **Your Task:** Carefully read each of the *four* texts provided. Then, using evidence from at least *three* of the texts, write a well-developed argument regarding the genetic modification of food. Clearly establish your claim, distinguish your claim from alternate or opposing claims, and use specific, relevant, and sufficient evidence from at least *three* of the texts to develop your argument. Do *not* simply summarize each text.

Guidelines:

Be sure to:

- Establish your claim regarding the genetic modification of food.
- Distinguish your claim from alternate or opposing claims.
- Use specific, relevant, and sufficient evidence from at least three of the texts to develop your argument.
- Identify each source that you reference by text number and line number(s) or graphic (for example: Text 1, line 4 or Text 2, graphic).
- Organize your ideas in a cohesive and coherent manner.
- Maintain a formal style of writing.
- Follow the conventions of standard written English.

Texts:

Text 1—GMOs 101

Text 2—GMO Reality Check

Text 3—GMO Foods: Key Points in the Genetically Modified Debate

Text 4—The Truth about Genetically Modified Food

Text 1

GMOs 101

The six questions on every shopper's mind about the new biotech foods. . . .

1 **What are GMOs [Genetically Modified Organism], and what are they used for?**
    A GMO is created by injecting genetic material from plants, animals, or bacteria into a crop in hopes of creating a new and beneficial trait. For example, one of the most popular genetically modified (GM) crops is a corn plant that's capable of producing its own pesticide, called Bt, which is also
(5) used in spray form by some organic farmers. The idea is to make the plant resistant to insect damage and to limit the amount of harmful pesticides farmers have to spray. Other GM plants, such as Roundup Ready corn, were created to survive the spraying of the herbicide Roundup, which kills weeds and would normally kill the plant, too, says Stephen H. Howell, Ph.D.,
(10) director of the Plant Sciences Institute at Iowa State University.
    Researchers are also using the technology experimentally as a way to nutritionally enhance fruits and vegetables.
    Some GMO supporters say that both applications are necessary to help feed a growing world population, especially in poor countries where drought
(15) and famine are common. But there is very little agreement on whether biotechnology offers a uniform way to address world hunger. "We have plenty of food for the world right now. It's not the deficiency of technology that's a problem for developing countries," says Jane Rissler, Ph.D., a senior staff scientist with the Union of Concerned Scientists, a nonprofit watchdog
(20) group that partners with 80,000 researchers. The international hunger problem, she says, stems from "poverty, corruption, and poor distribution."

2 **What kinds of foods contain GMOs?**
    About 80 percent of the food on grocery-store shelves already contains at least some ingredients made from altered genes. This means that almost any processed food, from salad dressing to snack crackers, could contain
(25) GMOs, unless it has been certified organic (federal regulations explicitly restrict food manufacturers from using the organic seal on products made with GMOs). That's because corn, soy, and canola are the top three GM food crops in the United States, so anything that is produced with corn syrup, high-fructose corn syrup, or soybean or corn oil might include GMOs.
(30)   Very little fresh produce on the market, though, is genetically engineered, with the exceptions of most papaya, some squash, and a few strains of

sweet corn. Meanwhile, we're not the only ones consuming GMOs—animals do, too. GM corn and soybeans are often used in livestock feed, though there's no evidence that GMOs show up in your steak or chops.

3 Should I be concerned about the safety of GM foods?

(35)   Federal agencies like the U.S. Food and Drug Administration (FDA) and the U.S. Department of Agriculture (USDA) say that they are safe, and there have been no documented cases of illness due to consumption of GMOs. The American Medical Association agrees at this point and has encouraged ongoing research in the field. . . .

4 What do GM crops mean for the environment?

(40)   "I think a lot of scientists agree that there are no known environmental problems with the crops that are out there now," says Allison Snow, Ph.D., who studies environmental risk and genetically modified crops as a professor of ecology at Ohio State University. But organic farmers are becoming increasingly concerned about maintaining the integrity of their crops. For (45) example, if Bt corn is planted too close to a neighboring organic-corn crop, crosspollination could occur and contaminate the latter.

Scientists on both sides of the debate also widely agree that insects will eventually become resistant to the Bt crops, Snow says. "It could happen any year now. Then we would be back where we started, and we would have (50) lost a valuable tool for managing insects," Snow says. . . .

5 Is it possible to live completely GMO-free?

Probably not. A study commissioned by the Union of Concerned Scientists and released in February already suggests that seeds that are supposedly non-GMO may be unintentionally tainted. Genetically engineered DNA was found in at least half of the small sample of tested (55) corn and soybean seeds, and about 83 percent of the canola seeds. Even if you buy only certified-organic products, you probably can't avoid GMOs completely. That's because it is also possible for organic food crops to become inadvertently contaminated. . . .

6 What will we see next from the biotech-food market?

Here are some GM foods that might end up on store shelves:
(60)   • The FDA and USDA are currently reviewing safety data on a variety of genetically engineered wheat that would tolerate the herbicide Roundup.

- Researchers are also working on wheat varieties that would resist drought, be less allergenic to those with gluten intolerance, and be *(65)* more nutritious.

Consumers may also start seeing major nutritional benefits in the future:
- Scientists at the University of California, Riverside, announced last year [2003] that they genetically engineered a corn plant to produce up to four times the normal amount of vitamin C by inserting a gene *(70)* from wheat plants. The researchers have filed a patent application and are soliciting companies that might be interested in commercializing the product. . . .
- Other biotech foods that are currently in development include a vitamin A–enhanced rice and a tomato with increased amounts of the *(75)* cancer-fighting antioxidant lycopene.
- Monsanto Co., which is the largest producer of GM seeds, is continuing to tinker with soybeans in hopes of developing a variety that could produce an oil containing few or no saturated and trans fats.

—Alisa Blackwood excerpted and adapted from "GMOs 101" *Health*, May 2004

Text 2

GMO Reality Check

. . . GMO Basics

So what are GMOs? To put it simply, they're plants and seeds created in laboratories. Genetic engineers insert genes from bacteria, viruses, animals, or humans into the DNA of a food crop or animal to create an organism that would never occur in nature. Biotech companies do this for two main *(5)* reasons: to make crops that are tolerant to herbicides such as RoundUp that kill other plants, and to make crops that produce their own insecticides.

The FDA's own scientists actually warned that these never-before-seen foods could create new toxins and new allergens and needed to be more thoroughly tested, but their concerns were largely ignored. Instead, the US *(10)* government took the official position that GM foods were "substantially equivalent" to conventional foods and didn't require safety testing or labeling—in sharp contrast to 40 other countries that require such foods be clearly labeled. Commercial planting of genetically modified seeds in the United States began in 1996, and soon after, food products containing *(15)* GMOs began appearing on store shelves, mostly without our knowledge.

By 2011, 94 percent of all soybeans and 88 percent of all corn grown in the United States was genetically modified. Soy and corn, along with other common GM foods (including canola oil. [sic] cottonseed oil, and sugar from sugar beets), are used as ingredients in countless other products, so (20) many Americans—including health food shoppers—likely have been eating GM foods without realizing it.

No Benefits, Just Risks

What we didn't know about what we were eating may already be harming us. Based on animal research with GM foods, the American Academy of Environmental Medicine (AAEM) says that there are serious (25) health risks associated with eating GM foods, including infertility, immune system problems, accelerated aging, disruption of insulin and cholesterol regulation, gastrointestinal issues, and changes in organs. In 2009, the AAEM urged doctors to prescribe non-GMO diets for all Americans, saying that doctors are probably seeing negative health effects in their patients (30) right now without realizing that GM foods are major contributing factors.

Genetically modified crops pose risks to the environment, too, including the serious threat of GM seeds spreading to and contaminating both organic and conventional crop fields. Plus, the biotech industry claims that genetic engineering reduces the use of pesticides, but research shows otherwise. (35) According to a 2009 report by the Organic Center, overall pesticide use dramatically increased—about 318 million pounds—in the first thirteen years after GM crops were introduced.

Herbicides sprayed in high amounts on GM herbicide-resistant crops have led to the development and spread of so-called "superweeds"—weeds (40) that are able to adapt to and withstand typical herbicides. And the biotech companies' proposed solution to this problem? Create new GM crops that are resistant to ever more toxic chemicals, including 2, 4-D—a major component of Agent Orange.[1] It's a "crazy" idea because weeds would eventually adapt to that herbicide and any others, says Andrew Kimbrell, (45) executive director of the Center for Food Safety and author of *Your Right to Know: Genetic Engineering and the Secret Changes in Your Food*.

The most important thing to know about GM foods is that they benefit only the chemical companies that produce them, says Kimbrell. "[The biotech companies] have yet to produce anything that benefits the consumer. (50) There's no better taste, no better nutrition, no lower price. That's the dirty

---

[1]Agent Orange—chemical used as part of herbicidal warfare programs

little secret that's hardly ever reported. That's why those companies don't want GM foods labeled. They don't want the consumer to be able to have the choice to say, 'I want the same price, less risky version.'" . . .

—Melissa Diane Smith excerpted from "GMO Reality Check"
Better Nutrition, August 2012

Text 3
GMO Foods: Key Points in the Genetically Modified Debate

. . . Safe or Unsafe?

Most studies show genetically modified foods are safe for human consumption, though it is widely acknowledged that the long-term health effects are unknown. The Food and Drug Administration generally recognized these foods as safe, and the World Health Organization has said (5) no ill health effects have resulted on the international market.

Opponents on both sides of the Atlantic say there has been inadequate testing and regulation. They worry that people who eat genetically modified foods may be more prone to allergies or diseases resistant to antibiotics. But they have been hard pressed to show scientific studies to back up those fears.
(10) GM foods have been a mainstay in the U.S. for more than a decade. Most of the crops are used for animal feed or in common processed foods such as cookies, cereal, potato chips and salad dressing.

Europe largely bans genetically engineered foods and has strict requirements on labeling them. They do allow the import of a number of GM
(15) crops such as soy, mostly for animal feed, and individual European countries have opted to plant these types of crops. Genetically engineered corn is grown in Spain, though it amounts to only a fraction of European farmland. . . .

Can GM Food Help Combat World Hunger?

By 2050, the world's population is projected to rise to 9 billion from just over 7 billion currently. Proponents of genetically modified foods say they
(20) are safe and can boost harvests even in bad conditions by protecting against pests, weeds and drought. This, they argue, will be essential to meeting the needs of a booming population in decades to come and avoiding starvation.

However Doug Gurian-Sherman, senior scientist for the food and environment program at the Union of Concerned Scientists, an advocacy
(25) group, said genetic engineering for insect resistance has provided only a modest increase in yields since the 1990s and drought-resistant strains have only modestly reduced losses from drought.

Moreover, he said conventional crossbreeding or cross-pollinating of different varieties for desirable traits, along with improved farming, are getting better results boosting yields at a lower cost. In fact, much of the food Americans eat has been genetically modified by those conventional methods over thousands of years, before genetic engineering came into practice. . . .

Andrea Roberto Sonnino, chief of research at the U.N. food agency, said total food production at present is enough to feed the entire global population. The problem is uneven distribution, leaving 870 million suffering from hunger. He said world food production will need to increase by 60 percent to meet the demands of 9 billion by 2050. This must be achieved by increasing yields, he added, because there is little room to expand cultivated land used for agriculture.

Genetically modified foods, in some instances, can help if the individual product has been assessed as safe, he said. "It's an opportunity that we cannot just miss."

To Label or Not to Label?

Europe requires all GM food to be labeled unless GM ingredients amount to 0.9 percent or less of the total. The U.S. does not require labels on the view that genetically modified food is not materially different than nonmodified food. Opponents of labeling say it would scare consumers away from safe foods, giving the appearance that there is something wrong with them.

U.S. activists insist consumers should have the right to choose whether to eat genetically modified foods and that labeling would offer them that choice, whether the foods are safe or not. They are pushing for labeling at the state and federal level. California voters last year rejected a ballot initiative that would have required GM food labeling. The legislatures of Connecticut and Maine have passed laws to label genetically modified foods, and more than 20 other states are contemplating labeling. . . .

—Marjorie Olster excerpted from "GMO Foods: Key Points in the Genetically Modified Debate" *http://www.huffingtonpost.com*, August 2, 2013

Text 4
The Truth about Genetically Modified Food

... Benefits and Worries

    The bulk of the science on GM safety points in one direction. Take it from David Zilberman, a U.C. Berkeley agricultural and environmental economist and one of the few researchers considered credible by both agricultural chemical companies and their critics. He argues that the
(5) benefits of GM crops greatly outweigh the health risks, which so far remain theoretical. The use of GM crops "has lowered the price of food," Zilberman says. "It has increased farmer safety by allowing them to use less pesticide. It has raised the output of corn, cotton and soy by 20 to 30 percent, allowing some people to survive who would not have without it. If it were more
(10) widely adopted around the world, the price [of food] would go lower, and fewer people would die of hunger." . . .

    Despite such promise, much of the world has been busy banning, restricting and otherwise shunning GM foods. Nearly all the corn and soybeans grown in the U.S. are genetically modified, but only two GM
(15) crops, Monsanto's MON8$_{10}$ maize and BASF's Amflora potato, are accepted in the European Union. Eight E.U. nations have banned GM crops outright. Throughout Asia, including in India and China, governments have yet to approve most GM crops, including an insect-resistant rice that produces higher yields with less pesticide. In Africa, where millions go hungry, several
(20) nations have refused to import GM foods in spite of their lower costs (the result of higher yields and a reduced need for water and pesticides). Kenya has banned them altogether amid widespread malnutrition. No country has definite plans to grow Golden Rice, a crop engineered to deliver more vitamin A than spinach (rice normally has no vitamin A), even though vitamin
(25) A deficiency causes more than one million deaths annually and half a million cases of irreversible blindness in the developing world. . . .

A Clean Record

    . . . Could eating plants with altered genes allow new DNA to work its way into our own? It is theoretically possible but hugely improbable. Scientists have never found genetic material that could survive a trip through the
(30) human gut and make it into cells. Besides, we are routinely exposed to—we even consume—the viruses and bacteria whose genes end up in GM foods. The bacterium *B. thuringiensis*, for example, which produces proteins fatal to insects, is sometimes enlisted as a natural pesticide in organic farming. "We've been eating this stuff for thousands of years," [Robert] Goldberg [a
(35) plant molecular biologist] says.

In any case, proponents say, people have consumed as many as trillions of meals containing genetically modified ingredients over the past few decades. Not a single verified case of illness has ever been attributed to the genetic alterations. Mark Lynas, a prominent anti-GM activist who last year
(40) publicly switched to strongly supporting the technology, has pointed out that every single news-making food disaster on record has been attributed to non-GM crops, such as the *Escherichia coli*—infected organic bean sprouts that killed 53 people in Europe in 2011. . . .

Plenty of other credible groups have arrived at the same conclusion.
(45) Gregory Jaffe, director of biotechnology at the Center for Science in the Public Interest, a science-based consumer-watchdog group in Washington, D.C., takes pains to note that the center has no official stance, pro or con, with regard to genetically modifying food plants. Yet Jaffe insists the scientific record is clear. "Current GM crops are safe to eat and can be grown safely in
(50) the environment," he says. The American Association for the Advancement of Science, the American Medical Association and the National Academy of Sciences have all unreservedly backed GM crops. The U.S. Food and Drug Administration, along with its counterparts in several other countries, has repeatedly reviewed large bodies of research and concluded that GM
(55) crops pose no unique health threats. Dozens of review studies carried out by academic researchers have backed that view. . . .

—David H. Freedman excerpted and adapted
from "The Truth about Genetically Modified Food"
http://www.scientificamerican.com, August 20, 2013

LOOKING AT THE TEXTS

Text 1—GMOs 101: The Six Questions on Every Shoppers Mind About the Bew Biotech Foods. . .

—Alisa Blackwood, excerpted and adapted from "GMOs 101," *Health*, May 2004

This is an article from a popular, generally well-regarded magazine. The question and answer format serves as a good introduction to the topic. The article is rich in information, and details and opinions are documented, which suggests that the sources are reliable. The tone and purpose seem to be objective.

Text 2—GMO Reality Check

—Melissa Diane Smith, excerpted from "GMO Reality Check," *Better Nutrition*, August 2012

This is a good example of a document in which one side of the issue is forcefully expressed. The writer cites sources for much of the information used to support her opposition to the use of GMO foods. This would be an excellent source for the student writer who establishes a claim opposed to the use of GMO foods.

Text 3—GMO Foods: Key Points in the Genetically Modified Debate

—Marjorie Olster, excerpted from "GMO Foods: Key Points in the Genetically Modified Debate," *http://www.huffingtonpost.com*, August 2, 2013

Here is an example of a document that outlines the key points in the debate and offers detailed information both on the development of GMO foods and on how governments in the United States and Europe regulate them. This article acknowledges competing points of view and offers information that could be used to support a variety of arguments.

Text 4—The Truth About Genetically Modified Food

—David H. Freedman, excerpted and adapted from "The Truth about Genetically Modified Food," *http://www.scientificamerican.com*, August 20, 2013

This article presents a very clear opinion on one side of the argument. It is well documented and offers strong evidence for the student writer who establishes a claim for the use of GMO foods.

Note that two of the texts are rich in background information and acknowledge opposing points of view. They can be helpful to the student writer when determining which argument to make. The other two texts offer forceful arguments for one side or the other. All texts include useful information and are documented with reliable sources.

KNOW THE RUBRIC

Here is the information from the chart on pages 80 and 81. The key terms for this part of the exam have been highlighted.

SCORING RUBRIC FOR PART 2

> **Content and Analysis:** The extent to which the essay conveys complex ideas and information clearly and accurately in order to support claims in an analysis of the texts.

Argument

High Scores

6 Essays introduce **a precise and insightful claim**, as directed by the task and demonstrate **in-depth and insightful analysis** of the texts, as necessary to support the claim and to distinguish the claim from alternate or opposing claims.

5 Essays introduce **a precise and thoughtful** claim, as directed by the task and demonstrate **thorough analysis** of the texts, as necessary to support the claim and to distinguish the claim from alternate or opposing claims.

Middle Scores

4 Essays introduce **a precise claim**, as directed by the task and demonstrate **appropriate and accurate analysis** of the texts, as necessary to support the claim and to distinguish the claim from alternate or opposing claims.

3 Essays introduce a **reasonable claim**, as directed by the task and demonstrate **some analysis** of the texts, but **insufficiently distinguish** the claim from alternate or opposing claims.

Low Scores

2 Essays introduce a claim and demonstrate **confused or unclear analysis** of the texts, **failing to distinguish the claim** from alternate or opposing claims.

1 Essays **do not introduce a claim**; do not demonstrate analysis of the texts.

> **Command of Evidence:** The extent to which the essay presents evidence from the provided texts to support analysis.

High Scores

6 Essays **present ideas fully and thoughtfully**, making highly effective use of a **wide range of specific and relevant evidence** to support analysis and demonstrate **proper citation of sources** to avoid plagiarism when dealing with direct quotes and paraphrased material.

5 Essays **present ideas clearly and accurately**, making **effective use of specific and relevant evidence** to support analysis and **demonstrate proper citation** of sources to avoid plagiarism when dealing with direct quotes and paraphrased material.

Middle Scores

4   Essays **present ideas sufficiently**, making **adequate use of specific and relevant evidence** to support analysis and **demonstrate proper citation** of sources to avoid plagiarism when dealing with direct quotes and paraphrased material.

3   Essays **present ideas briefly**, making use of **some specific and relevant evidence** to support analysis and demonstrate **inconsistent citation of sources** to avoid plagiarism when dealing with direct quotes and paraphrased material.

Low Scores

2   Essays **present ideas inconsistently and/or inaccurately**, in an attempt to support analysis, making use of **some evidence that may be irrelevant** and demonstrate **little use of citations** to avoid plagiarism when dealing with direct quotes and paraphrased material.

1   Essays present **little or no evidence** from the texts; do not make use of citations.

> **Coherence, Organization, and Style:** The extent to which the essay logically organizes complex ideas, concepts, and information using formal style and precise language.

High Scores

6   Essays exhibit **skillful organization** of ideas and information to create a **cohesive and coherent essay** and establish and maintain a **formal style**, using **sophisticated language and structure**.

5   Essays exhibit **logical organization** of ideas and information to create a **cohesive and coherent** essay and establish and maintain **a formal style**, using **fluent and precise language and sound structure**.

Middle Scores

4   Essays exhibit **acceptable organization** of ideas and information to create a **coherent essay** and establish and maintain a **formal style**, using **precise and appropriate language and structure**.

3   Essays exhibit **some organization** of ideas and information to create a **mostly coherent essay** and establish but **fail to maintain a formal style**, using primarily **basic language and structure**.

Low Scores

2 Essays exhibit **inconsistent organization** of ideas and information, **failing to create a coherent essay and lack a formal style**, using some **language that is inappropriate or imprecise**.

1 Essays exhibit **little organization** of ideas and information, making assessment unreliable; use language that is **predominantly incoherent, inappropriate, or copied directly** from the task or texts.

> **Control of Conventions:** The extent to which the essay demonstrates command of conventions of standard English grammar, usage, capitalization, punctuation, and spelling.

High Scores

6 Essays demonstrate control of conventions with **essentially no errors, even with sophisticated language**.

5 Essays demonstrate control of the conventions, exhibiting **occasional errors only when using sophisticated language**.

Middle Scores

4 Essays demonstrate **partial control**, exhibiting **occasional errors** that do not hinder comprehension.

3 Essays demonstrate **emerging control**, exhibiting **occasional errors that hinder comprehension**.

Low Scores

2 Essays demonstrate a **lack of control**, exhibiting **frequent errors** that make comprehension difficult.

1 Essays are **minimal**, making assessment of conventions unreliable.

STRATEGIES AND REVIEW

- The reading, writing, and discussion you do in English, social studies, and science classes form the basis of your preparation for this part of the exam.
- There is no "right answer." The topic and the texts provide for a variety of legitimate claims. Your task is to compose a relevant and defensible argument.
- Plan your response. This need not be a formal outline, but take time to articulate clearly what your claim (argument) will be. Then number and underline in the texts three or four passages that you can cite to support your argument. Decide on the most effective order for the examples.
- Review the Glossaries in the chapters that follow in order to recognize literary and rhetorical elements.
- Review the actual ELA/Exams and the Answers Explained for additional examples with essays for Part 2 of the exam.

Strategy and Review for Part 3 of the Regents ELA Exam

CHAPTER 3
Text-Analysis Response

WHAT DOES THIS PART OF THE EXAM REQUIRE?

The Part 3 question is designed to assess reading, writing, and language standards. You will be required to do a close reading of a text (approximately 1,000 words). You will then write a two to three paragraph response that identifies a central idea in the text and analyzes how the author's use of one writing strategy (literary element, literary technique, or rhetorical device) develops this central idea.

There are no multiple-choice questions in this part of the exam.

WHAT DOES THIS PART OF THE EXAM LOOK LIKE?

Your Task: Closely read the text provided and write a well-developed, text-based response of two to three paragraphs. In your response, identify a central idea in the text and analyze how the author's use of one writing strategy (literary element, literary technique, or rhetorical device) develops this central idea. Use strong and thorough evidence from the text to support your analysis. Do *not* simply summarize the text. You may use the margins and scrap paper to take notes as you read and plan your response.

LOOKING AT THE TEXT

The following excerpt is from a speech delivered by suffragist Anna Howard Shaw in 1915.

...Now one of two things is true: either a Republic is a desirable form of government, or else it is not. If it is, then we should have it, if it is not then we ought not to pretend that we have it. We ought at least be true to our ideals, and the men of New York have for the first time in their lives, the rare
(5) opportunity on the second day of next November, of making the state truly a part of the Republic. It is the greatest opportunity which has ever come to the men of the state. They have never had so serious a problem to solve before, they will never have a more serious problem to solve in any future of our nation's life, and the thing that disturbs me more than anything else
(10) in connection with it is that so few people realize what a profound problem they have to solve on November 2. It is not merely a trifling matter; it is not a little thing that does not concern the state, it is the most vital problem we could have, and any man who goes to the polls on the second day of next November without thoroughly informing himself in regard to this subject is
(15) unworthy to be a citizen of this state, and unfit to cast a ballot.

If woman's suffrage[1] is wrong, it is a great wrong; if it is right, it is a profound and fundamental principle, and we all know, if we know what a Republic is, that it is the fundamental principle upon which a Republic must rise. Let us see where we are as a people; how we act here and what
(20) we think we are. The difficulty with the men of this country is that they are so consistent in their inconsistency that they are not aware of having been inconsistent; because their consistency has been so continuous and their inconsistency so consecutive that it has never been broken, from the beginning of our Nation's life to the present time. If we trace our history
(25) back we will find that from the very dawn of our existence as a people, men have been imbued[2] with a spirit and a vision more lofty than they have been able to live; they have been led by visions of the sublimest[3] truth, both in regard to religion and in regard to government that ever inspired the souls of men from the time the Puritans left the old world to come to this country,
(30) led by the Divine ideal which is the sublimest and the supremest ideal in religious freedom which men have ever known, the theory that a man has a right to worship God according to the dictates of his own conscience, without the intervention[4] of any other man or any other group of men. And it was this theory, this vision of the right of the human soul which led men
(35) first to the shores of this country....

---

[1]suffrage—right to vote [2]imbued—inspired [3]sublimest—noblest [4]intervention—interference

Now what is a Republic? Take your dictionary, encyclopedia lexicon or anything else you like and look up the definition and you will find that a Republic is a form of government in which the laws are enacted by representatives elected by the people. Now when did the people of New (40) York ever elect their own representatives? Never in the world. The men of New York have, and I grant you that men are people, admirable people, as far as they go, but they only go half way. There is still another half of the people who have not elected representatives, and you never read a definition of a Republic in which half of the people elect representatives to govern the (45) whole of the people. That is an aristocracy and that is just what we are. We have been many kinds of aristocracies. We have been a hierarchy[5] of church members, than an oligarchy[6] of sex. . . .

Now I want to make this proposition, and I believe every man will accept it. Of course he will if he is intelligent. Whenever a Republic prescribes the (50) qualifications as applying equally to all the citizens of the Republic, when the Republic says in order to vote, a citizen must be twenty-one years of age, it applies to all alike, there is no discrimination against any race or sex. When the government says that a citizen must be a native-born citizen or a naturalized citizen that applies to all; we are either born or naturalized, (55) somehow or other we are here. Whenever the government says that a citizen, in order to vote, must be a resident of a community a certain length of time, and of the state a certain length of time and of the nation a certain length of time, that applies to all equally. There is no discrimination. We might go further and we might say that in order to vote the citizen must be (60) able to read his ballot. We have not gone that far yet. We have been very careful of male ignorance in these United States. I was much interested, as perhaps many of you, in reading the Congressional Record this last winter over the debate over the immigration bill, and when that illiteracy clause was introduced into the immigration bill, what fear there was in the souls of (65) men for fear we would do injustice to some of the people who might want to come to our shores, and I was much interested in the language in which the President vetoed the bill, when he declared that by inserting the clause we would keep out of our shores a large body of very excellent people. I could not help wondering then how it happens that male ignorance is so much less (70) ignorant than female ignorance. When I hear people say that if women were permitted to vote a large body of ignorant people would vote, and therefore

---

[5]hierarchy—order of authority [6]oligarchy—rule by a few

because an ignorant woman would vote, no intelligent women should be allowed to vote, I wonder why we have made it so easy for male ignorance and so hard for female ignorance. . . .

—Anna Howard Shaw
excerpted from "The Fundamental Principle of a Republic"
delivered at Ogdensburg, New York, June 21, 1915
http://www.emersonkent.com

In this excerpted speech, suffragist Anna Howard Shaw uses several techniques to argue for the case of women's right to vote. She employs **repetition** and **rhetorical questioning** while discussing the **definition** of a Republic throughout her speech and a **sarcastic [ironic] tone** when referring to the consistent inconsistencies of men (paragraph 2) and the various requirements to vote in the U.S. (paragraph 3). Shaw's speech is also an excellent example of the use of **logical structure**, leading to her thinking "how it happens that male ignorance is so much less ignorant than female ignorance" (lines 69 and 70).

—*Analysis from "Questions with Annotations," NYSED, June 2014*

KNOW THE RUBRIC

Here is the information from the chart on pages 82 and 83. The key terms for this part of the exam have been highlighted.

SCORING RUBRIC FOR PART 3

> **Content and Analysis:** The extent to which the response conveys complex ideas and information clearly and accurately in order to respond to the task and support an analysis of the text.

4   Essays introduce a **well-reasoned central idea and a writing strategy** that clearly establish the criteria for analysis and demonstrate a **thoughtful analysis** of the author's use of the writing strategy to develop the central idea.

3   Essays introduce a **clear central idea and a writing strategy** that establish the criteria for analysis and demonstrate an **appropriate analysis** of the author's use of the writing strategy to develop the central idea.

2   Essays introduce a **central idea and/or a writing strategy** and demonstrate a **superficial analysis** of the author's use of the writing strategy to develop the central idea.

1   Essays introduce a **confused or incomplete central idea or writing strategy** and/or demonstrate a **minimal analysis** of the author's use of the writing strategy to develop the central idea.

> **Command of Evidence:** The extent to which the response presents evidence from the provided text to support analysis.

4   Essays present ideas **clearly and consistently**, making effective use of **specific and relevant evidence** to support analysis.

3   Essays present ideas **sufficiently**, making **adequate use of relevant evidence** to support analysis.

2   Essays present ideas **inconsistently, inadequately, and/or inaccurately** in an attempt to support analysis, making use of **some evidence that may be irrelevant**.

1   Essays present **little or no evidence** from the text.

> **Coherence, Organization, and Style:** The extent to which the response logically organizes complex ideas, concepts, and information using formal style and precise language.

4   Essays exhibit **logical organization** of ideas and information to create a **cohesive and coherent** response and establish and maintain a **formal style**, using **precise language and sound structure**.

3   Essays exhibit **acceptable organization** of ideas and information to create a **coherent response** and establish and maintain a **formal style**, using **appropriate language and structure**.

2   Essays exhibit **inconsistent organization** of ideas and information, failing to create a coherent response; lack a formal style, using language that is **basic, inappropriate, or imprecise**.

1   Essays exhibit **little organization** of ideas and information; use language that is predominantly **incoherent**, inappropriate, or copied directly from the task or text; or are **minimal**, making assessment unreliable.

> **Control of Conventions:** The extent to which the response demonstrates command of conventions of standard English grammar, usage, capitalization, punctuation, and spelling.

4   Essays demonstrate **control** of the conventions with **infrequent errors**.

3   Essays demonstrate **partial control** of conventions with **occasional errors** that do not hinder comprehension.

2   Essays demonstrate **emerging control** of conventions with **some errors** that **hinder comprehension**.

1   Essays demonstrate a **lack of control** of conventions with **frequent errors** that make comprehension difficult; are **minimal**, making assessment of conventions unreliable.

> Note:
> - A response that is a personal response and makes little or no reference to the task or text can be scored no higher than a 1.
> - A response that is totally copied from the text with no original writing must be given a 0.
> - A response that is totally unrelated to the task, illegible, incoherent, blank, or unrecognizable as English must be scored as a 0.

STRATEGIES AND REVIEW

- Plan your response. This need not be a formal outline, but be sure to articulate clearly which literary element or rhetorical device you choose. List on the blank page provided, and underline in the text itself, three or four passages that convincingly support your topic. Decide on the most effective order for the examples.
- Recognize that the texts for this part are primary sources, often narratives or speeches. They will have distinctive voices and may be of a particular historical context.
- There is no "right answer." The texts will be rich in information and are likely to employ several rhetorical strategies for effect. Choose the one you can discuss most confidently.
- Review the chapter in this book on literary elements and the Glossaries to help you recognize and write about writing strategies.
- Review this part of the exam in the Answers Explained for actual ELA/exams.

Reading and Writing About Literature

CHAPTER 4
Reviewing Literary Elements and Techniques

ELEMENTS OF FICTION AND DRAMA

When we speak of fiction, we are generally speaking of narrative works—works in which events are recounted, are *told*, and which have been imagined and structured by the author. Although not narrative in form, drama shares many of the essential characteristics of fiction.

Plot and Story

The primary pleasure for most readers of narrative fiction is the story. If we become involved in a novel or short story, it is because we want to know how it turns out; we want to know what is going to happen to those characters. An author creates a plot when he or she gives order and structure to the action: in a plot, the **incidents** or **episodes** of the story have a meaningful relationship to one another. A story becomes a plot when we not only understand *what happened* but also *why*. In good fiction we are *convinced* of the causal relationship among incidents and we are convinced by the relationship of characters' motives and feelings to the action.

Plot and Conflict

At the end of any meaningful story, something has *happened*; something is significantly different in the world and lives of the characters from what it was at the beginning. **Conflict** in the most general sense refers to the **forces** that move the action in a plot. Conflict in plot may be generated from a search or pursuit, from a discovery, from a deception or misunderstanding, from opportunities to make significant choices, or from unexpected consequences of an action. Although the term conflict connotes an active struggle between opposing or hostile forces, conflict in fiction may refer to any progression, change, or discovery. The **resolution** of conflict in a plot may be subtle and confined to the inner life of a character or it may be dramatic and involve irreversible change, violent destruction, or death.

Conflict may identify an actual struggle between characters, for anything from dominance or revenge to simple recognition or understanding. A plot may also focus on conflict between characters and the forces of nature or society. These are essentially *external conflicts*. A work may center on *internal conflict*: characters' struggle to know or change themselves and their lives. Most works of fiction and drama contain more than one aspect of conflict.

In Shakespeare's *Romeo and Juliet*, the most dramatic conflicts are external, vivid, and literal: the street brawls between followers of the rival Capulets and Montagues and the fatal fight with Tybalt that leads to Romeo's banishment and the tragic deaths of the young lovers. In *Macbeth*, the primary interest is in the internal conflict between Macbeth's ambitious desires and his understanding of the moral consequences of the actions he takes to achieve those desires.

The action in Edith Wharton's most famous story, "Roman Fever," is ironically serene and pleasant: two middle-age women, long-time friends now both widowed, sit on a terrace overlooking the splendors of Rome and reflect on their common experiences and lifelong friendship. At the end of the conversation—and the story—their actual feelings of rivalry have come to the surface, and one of the two learns something that reveals how little she truly knew her husband or understood her marriage or the life of her friend. The conflict between the two women emerges almost imperceptibly and its meaning is only fully understood in the completely unexpected revelation of the last line.

Structure/Plot and Chronology

Narrative is not necessarily presented in chronological order, but it does have chronology. That is, incidents may be presented out of the order in which they actually occurred, but by the end of the work the reader does understand their order and relationship and appreciates why the story was structured as it was. Plots that are narrated in flashback or from different points of view are common examples.

The Great Gatsby by F. Scott Fitzgerald and *Ethan Frome* by Edith Wharton are novels in which the narrator first introduces himself and his interest in the story, then tells it in a narrative flashback whose full significance to the narrator (and reader) is revealed only at the end. Tennessee Williams's play *The Glass Menagerie* has a similar structure, in which the character of Tom serves both as a narrator in the present and as a principal character in the series of memory scenes that make up the drama. The memory scenes in Arthur Miller's play *Death of a Salesman*, however, are not flashbacks in the same way. Willy Loman relives incidents from the past while the other characters and action of the play continue in the present. As the play progresses, the shifts in time occur only within Willy's mind.

Shakespeare's tragedies are dramas in which normal chronology is preserved, as it is in such familiar novels as William Golding's *Lord of the Flies* and Mark Twain's *Huckleberry Finn*.

Narrative Point of View

The narrator of a work is the character or author's *persona* that tells a story. Point of view is the standpoint, perspective, and degree of understanding from which the narrator speaks. For many students and scholars, the question of how a story is told is one of the most interesting questions. What is the narrative point of view? Is the narration *omniscient,* essentially the point of view of the author? Or, who is the narrator? What is the narrator's relationship to the story? What is the narrator's understanding of the story? How much does the narrator really know? Appreciating how, or by whom, a story is told is often essential to understanding its meaning.

One of the most easily discerned narrative points of view is the **first person** (*I*) in which either the central character or another directly involved in the action tells the story. J. D. Salinger's novel *Catcher in the Rye* is a vivid and popular example of such narration. Fitzgerald's *The Great Gatsby* is also told in the first person. In each of these works, the fundamental meaning of the novel becomes apparent only when the reader understands the character of the narrator. In each of these works, what the narrator experiences and what he learns about himself and the world are the novel's most important themes.

In **first-person narration**, the incidents of the plot are limited to those that the narrator himself experiences. First-person narrators can, however, report what they learn from others. In Wharton's *Ethan Frome*, the engineer who narrates tells us that he has "pieced together the story" from the little he has been able to learn in the town of Starkfield, from his limited conversations with Frome himself, and from his brief visit to the Frome house. Wharton's method, of course, dramatizes Frome's inability to express or fulfill the desires of his heart and reveals the reluctance of the people of Starkfield to fully understand the lives of those around them.

Authors may also use first-person narration to achieve an ironic or satiric effect. In Ring Lardner's story "Haircut," a barber in a small midwestern town narrates a story about a local fellow who kept the town entertained with his practical jokes on people. As the story progresses, the reader understands how cruel and destructive the fellow's pranks were, but the barber does not. The narrative method in this story reveals, indirectly, a story of painful ignorance and insensitivity in the "decent" citizens of a small town. Mark Twain's masterpiece, *Huckleberry Finn*, is told by Huck himself. Through the morally naive observations of Huck, Twain satirizes the evils of slavery, fraud, hypocrisy, and nearly every other kind of corrupt human behavior. Edgar Allan Poe's story "The Tell-Tale Heart" is the confession of a cunning madman.

In **third-person** narration (*he, she, it, they*), a story is reported. The narrative voice may be *omniscient* and, therefore, able to report everything from everywhere in the story and also report on the innermost thoughts and feelings of the characters themselves. In many novels of the eighteenth and nineteenth centuries, the omniscient narrator even speaks directly to the reader, as if taking him or her into the storyteller's confidence. In Nathaniel Hawthorne's *The Scarlet Letter*, the narrator pauses from time to time to share personal feelings with the reader. Nick Carraway, the narrator of *The Great Gatsby* also does this, but the method is not common in contemporary fiction.

A widely used narrative method is the *limited omniscient* point of view. The narrative is in the third person but is focused on and even may represent the point of view of a central character. The actions and feelings of other characters are presented from the perspective of that character. Hawthorne's short story "Young Goodman Brown" is an excellent example.

Some third-person narration is dramatically **objective** and detached; it simply reports the incidents of the plot as they unfold. This narrative method, too, can be used for intensely **ironic** effect. Jackson's "The Lottery" is one of the best examples. The real horror of the story is achieved through the utterly detached, nonjudgmental telling of it.

In some plays, too, there is a character who serves a narrative role: the Chorus in Shakespeare's *Henry V*, the character of Tom in Williams's *The Glass Menagerie*, and the Stage Manager in Thornton Wilder's *Our Town* are familiar examples.

In each of the works discussed here, narrative method is not simply a literary device; it is an intrinsic part of the meaning of the work.

Setting

The setting of a work includes the time and places in which the action is played out; setting may also include significant historical context. In drama, setting may be presented directly in the set, costumes, and lighting. In narrative fiction, setting is usually presented directly through description. In some works, the physical setting is central to the plot and developed in great detail; in other works, only those details necessary to anchor the plot in a time or place will be developed. Regardless of detail, responsive readers re-create images of setting as they read.

In addition to the physical and natural details of the fictional world, setting also includes mood and **atmosphere**. In some works, social or political realities constitute part of the setting. *The Scarlet Letter* is not only set in Puritan Boston, it is also *about* that society; and *The Great Gatsby* presents a vivid picture of life in New York during Prohibition and the roaring twenties.

For some works, the author may create specific details of setting to highlight a theme. In Golding's novel *Lord of the Flies*, the island on which the story takes place has everything essential for basic survival: there is food and water, and the climate is temperate. In order to explore the moral questions of the boys' regression into savagery, Golding carefully establishes a setting in which survival itself is not a primary issue. In *Ethan Frome*, details of the harsh winter and of the isolation of a town "bypassed by the railroad" intensify the story of a man's desperately cold and isolated life.

Character and Characterization

We understand characters in fiction and drama as we do the people in our own lives, by what they say and do, and by what others say about them. Because characters are imagined and created by an author, we can even understand them more reliably and fully than we can many of the people around us. Many students find their greatest satisfaction in reading works about characters to whom they can relate, characters whose struggles are recognizable and whose feelings are familiar.

Understanding character in fiction means understanding a person's values and **motivation**, beliefs and principles, moral qualities, strengths and weaknesses, and degree of self-knowledge and understanding. To fully appreciate a work, the reader must understand what characters are searching for and devoting their lives to.

Literature also seeks to account for the forces outside individuals that influence the direction and outcome of their lives. These "forces" range from those of nature and history to the demands of family, community, and society. The response of characters to inner and outer forces is what literature depicts and makes comprehensible.

In literature courses and on examinations, discussions of character are the most common. That is because any meaningful or convincing plot stems from human thought, motive, and action. Depending on the narrative point of view (see page 47) a character's thoughts and feelings may be presented directly through **omniscient** narrative or first-person commentary. In "Young Goodman

Brown," the narrator tells us directly what the title character is thinking and feeling; in "Roman Fever," the most important revelations of character are discovered by the reader simultaneously with the two central characters. Character in drama is revealed directly in dialogue and action, but it may be expanded through soliloquies and asides. In Shakespeare's *Othello*, for example, the full extent of Iago's evil is revealed through the variety of methods he uses to manipulate different characters and through the soliloquies.

In some works, the author's primary purpose is to reveal character gradually through plot; in others, the author establishes understanding of character from the beginning in order to account for what happens. In the opening pages of *The Great Gatsby*, the narrator, Nick, who is also a character in the novel, introduces himself and declares his judgment of the moral quality of the people and events he is about to narrate. With Nick's own character and motives clearly established, the reader then shares his gradual discovery of the truth about Gatsby and his life.

Theme

The subjects of literature may come from any aspect of human experience: love, friendship, growing up, ambition, family relationships, conflicts with society, survival, war, evil, death, and so on. **Theme** in a work of literature is the understanding, insight, observation, and presentation of such subjects. Theme is what a work *says about* a subject. Themes are the central ideas of literary works.

One way to think about theme is to consider it roughly analogous to the topic or thesis of an expository essay. If the author of a novel, story, or play had chosen to examine the subjects of the work in an essay, what might be the topic assertions of such an essay? The student is cautioned, however, not to overinterpret the analogy. Themes in literature are rarely "morals," such as those found at the end of a fable, but neither are they "hidden meanings." Although scholars and critics often express thematic ideas in phrases, students are often required to express themes in full statements. In the next paragraph are some examples of statements about theme.

Macbeth is a play about the temptation to embrace evil forces and about the power of ambition to corrupt; Macbeth himself makes one of the most important statements of theme in the play when he says, "I do all that becomes a man/ who does more is none." *Ethan Frome* and Lardner's "Haircut" both illustrate that people in small towns do not truly understand the innermost needs and desires of people they think they know. William Golding's novel *Lord of the Flies* illustrates the bleak view that human beings' savage nature will prevail without external forces of authority, that human beings are not civilized in their fundamental natures. In contrast, in *Adventures of Huckleberry Finn*, Twain presents civilization as the source of corruption and finds truly moral behavior only in the runaway slave, Jim, and the ignorant boy, Huck.

ELEMENTS OF NONFICTION

Fiction and nonfiction share many common elements; they also make similar demands and offer comparable rewards to the thoughtful reader. In broad contrast to fiction, where characters and plot are imaginative creations of the author, nonfiction is about actual persons, experiences, and phenomena. Nonfiction also speculates on abstract and philosophical questions of history and politics, ethics and religion, culture and society, as well as the natural world. In biography and autobiography, the writer focuses on what is meaningful and interesting in the life of an individual.

On the Regents ELA exam you will read several examples of nonfiction. In Part 1 Reading Comprehension, you can expect to read one informational text, often on a historical or scientific topic. Part 2 requires reading at least four texts of informed argument and evidence to support a claim; and Part 3 Text Analysis often includes works of nonfiction, personal **narrative**. Authors of literary nonfiction often make imaginative use of **structure**, **chronology**, and **characterization**.

ELEMENTS OF POETRY

Part 1 of the Regents ELA exam will include one poem for close reading. The multiple-choice questions are designed to measure your skill at reading for the meaning. You are also expected to recognize and identify elements of poetry.

Poetry and Experience

In poetry, we are meant to sense a structure and to feel the rhythm (see **meter and rhythm**, page 64). The structure and rhythm of poetry may be formal, informal, even "free." Poetry is also characterized by its directness of effect and by its concentration—ideas and feelings are expressed in relatively few words. Karl Shapiro says, "Poems are what ideas feel like." Where the writer of prose may seek immediate clarity of meaning above all, the poet often seeks **ambiguity**, not to create "confusion," but to offer multiplicity of meaning: in single words, in images, in the meaning of the poem itself.

The experience of poetry is conveyed in vivid **imagery**, which appeals to the mind and to the senses. It is often expressed in **figurative language**; that is, through imaginative use of words and comparisons that are not literal but which create original, vivid, and often unexpected images and associations. (See **metaphor**, page 64, and **simile**, page 65.) Finally, in poetry there is particular significance in the way words and lines sound. The story or experience is enhanced through musical effects. A poem should be heard or felt!

Theme in Poetry

Some poems may assert a belief. Others may be a comment on the nature of human experience—love, death, loss or triumph, mystery and confusion, conflict and peace, on the humorous and the ironic, on the imagined and the unexpected in all its forms. Some poems reflect on the nature of time, of existence. Many poems are about poetry itself. These aspects of human experience are what we refer to as the **themes** of poetry.

Tone

Tone in poetry, as in prose and all forms of human communication, expresses the *attitude* of the speaker toward the reader or listener and toward the subject. Tone in literature is as varied as the range of human experience and feeling it reflects. When we speak of the *mood* of a piece of writing, we are also speaking of tone, of an overall feeling generated by the work.

Here are some terms to help you recognize and articulate **tone** or **mood** (see also Structure and Language in Poetry, beginning on page 61):

ambiguous	insistent	reconciled
amused	**ironic**	reflective
angry	melancholy	regretful
bitter	mournful	reminiscent
celebratory	mysterious	satiric
elegiac	nostalgic	sorrowful
grateful	optimistic	thoughtful
harsh	**paradoxical**	**understated**
humorous	questioning	

Note: Terms in bold are included in the glossary.

Reading and Writing About Literature

CHAPTER 5
Glossaries of Terms

STRUCTURE AND LANGUAGE IN PROSE

abstract In contrast to the *concrete*, abstract language expresses general ideas and concepts apart from specific examples or instances. Very formal writing is characterized by abstract expression. As a noun, *abstract* denotes a brief summary of the key ideas in a scientific, legal, or scholarly piece of writing.

analogy An expression of the similarities between things that are not wholly alike or related. (See *metaphor* in Structure and Language in Poetry, page 64.)

anecdote A very brief, usually vivid story or episode. Often humorous, anecdotes offer examples of typical behavior or illustrate the personality of a character. Writers of biography and autobiography make extensive use of anecdote to reveal the lives of their subjects.

antithesis In formal argument, a statement that opposes or contrasts a *thesis* statement. Informally, we use the term to refer to any expression or point of view completely opposed to another. In literature, even an experience or a feeling may be expressed as the *antithesis* of another. (See also *thesis*.)

argument In persuasive writing or speaking, the development of reasons to support the writer's position; it is the method of reasoning used to persuade. Informally, we may use the term to describe the development of a topic in any piece of expository writing. Historically, it has also denoted a summary of a literary work's plot or main ideas.

atmosphere Closely related to *tone* or mood, it refers to a pervasive feeling in a work. Atmosphere often stems from setting and from distinctive characters or actions. The atmosphere in many of Poe's stories is mysterious, troubling, even sinister. Hawthorne's "Young Goodman Brown" reflects the threatening and morally ambiguous world of its Puritan setting.

autobiography A formally composed account of a person's life, written by that person. Although we must trust, or be skeptical of, the reliability of the account, we often appreciate the firsthand narration of experience. Autobiography is also a rich source of information and insight into a historical period or into literary or artistic worlds. Autobiography, like the novel, has *narrative* and chronology. (See also *journal, memoir.*) We describe literary works that are closely based on the author's life as **autobiographical.** Eugene O'Neill's *Long Day's Journey into Night* and Tennessee Williams's *The Glass Menagerie* are plays that reflect many details of their authors' lives.

biography A narrative, historical account of the life, character, and significance of its subject. Contemporary biography is usually researched in detail and may not always be admiring of its subject. A critical biography of a literary figure includes discussion of the writer's works to show the writer's artistic development and career. Biographies of figures significant in history or public affairs also offer commentary on periods and events of historical importance.

character The imagined persons, created figures, who inhabit the worlds of fiction and drama. E. M. Forster distinguished between *flat* and *round* characters. Flat are those, like stereotypes, who represent a single and exaggerated human characteristic. Round are those whose aspects are complex and convincing, and who change or develop in the course of a work. In good fiction, plot must develop out of character. It is the desires, values, and motives of characters that account for the action and conflict in a plot.

characterization The method by which an author establishes character; the means by which personality, manner, and appearance are created. It is achieved directly through description and dialogue and indirectly through observations and reactions of other characters.

concrete The particular, the specific, in expression and imagery. That which is concrete can be perceived by the senses. Concrete also refers to that which is tangible, real, or actual, in contrast to *abstract*, which is intangible and conceptual.

conflict In the most general sense, it identifies the forces that give rise to a plot. This term may identify an actual struggle between characters, for anything from revenge to simple recognition or understanding. A plot may focus on conflict between characters and the forces of nature or society. These are essentially external conflicts. A work may also center on internal conflicts: characters' struggles to know or change themselves and their lives. Most works of fiction and drama contain more than one aspect of conflict. (See Plot and Conflict, page 45.)

denouement A French term meaning "untying a knot," it refers to the way the complications or conflict of a plot are finally resolved. It also refers to what is called the "falling action" in a drama: that part of the play that follows the dramatic climax and reveals the consequences of the main action for minor characters; it also accounts briefly for what happens in the world of the play after the principal drama is resolved. In Arthur Miller's *Death of a Salesman*, the "Requiem" may be considered a denouement: it accounts for the response to Willy's death of his wife, sons, and only friend. In Shakespeare's *Macbeth*, the climax is in the scene following the death of Lady Macbeth in which Macbeth understands that he has destroyed all capacity for feeling and has rendered his life meaningless; the denouement occurs in the battle scene in which Macbeth understands that he cannot escape the witches' prophecy and is killed by Macduff, thus restoring the throne to the rightful heir, Malcolm.

determinism The philosophical view that human existence is determined by forces over which humans have little or no control. The concept that fate predestines the course of a character's life or a tragic figure's downfall is a form of determinism.

episode A series of actions or incidents that make up a self-contained part of a larger narrative. Some novels are structured so that each chapter is a significant episode. Fitzgerald's *The Great Gatsby* and Mark Twain's *Huckleberry Finn* are good examples. A *scene* in a play is often analogous to an episode in a narrative. Many television series are presented in weekly episodes.

essay Denotes an extended composition, usually expository, devoted to a single topic. Essays may be composed to persuade, to reflect on philosophical questions, to analyze a subject, to express an opinion, or to entertain. As a literary form, the essay dates from the sixteenth century and remains a popular and widely practiced form. The origin of the term is the French word *essai*, which means an attempt, a trying out of something. (See *formal/informal essay.*)

exposition Writing whose purpose is to inform, illustrate, and explain. In literature, exposition refers to those passages or speeches in which setting, offstage or prior action, or a character's background is revealed.

In *The Great Gatsby*, Nick Carraway pauses in the narrative to give the reader additional information about Gatsby's background. The prologue to Shakespeare's *Romeo and Juliet* is an example of exposition.

flashback A presentation of incidents or episodes that occurred prior to the beginning of a narrative itself. When an author or filmmaker uses flashback, the "present" or forward motion of the plot is suspended. Flashback may be introduced through the device of a character's memory, or through the narrative voice itself. William Faulkner's "Barn Burning" and *Light in August* include vivid passages of memory and narrative flashback. Jack Burden's recounting of the Cass Mastern story in Robert Penn Warren's *All the King's Men* is also a form of flashback.

foreshadowing Establishing details or mood in a work that will become more significant as the plot progresses. Thoughtful readers usually sense such details and accumulate them in their memories. In one of the opening scenes of *Ethan Frome*, Ethan and Mattie talk about the dangers of sledding down Starkfield's steepest hill. In the second paragraph of Shirley Jackson's well-known story "The Lottery," the boys stuff their pockets with stones and make piles of them on the edge of the square.

form The organization, shape, and structure of a work. Concretely, form may refer to *genre* (see below); for example, the sonnet form, the tragic form. More abstractly, form also refers to the way we sense inherent structure and shape.

formal/informal essay In contrast to the formal essay, which emphasizes organization, logic, and explication of ideas, the informal essay emphasizes the voice and perspective of the writer. In the informal essay, also called a *personal essay*, the reader is aware of the author's *persona* and is asked to share the author's interest in the subject. Examples of a personal essay might be included in Part 1 Reading Comprehension, among the texts in Part 2 Argument, or in the Part 3 Text Analysis.

genre A type or form of literature. Examples include *novel, short story, epic poem, essay, sonnet,* and *tragedy.*

image Although suggesting something that is visualized, an image is an expression or recreation through language of *any* experience perceived directly through the senses. (See also Structure and Language in Poetry, page 64.)

irony In general, a tone or figure of speech in which there is a discrepancy—a striking difference or contradiction—between what is expressed and what is meant or expected. Irony achieves its powerful effect indirectly: in satire, for example, to ridicule or criticize. We also speak of dramatic irony when the narrator or reader understands more than the characters do.

Structure and Language in Prose 57

journal A diary or notebook of personal observations. Many writers use journals to compose personal reflection and to collect ideas for their works. The journals of many writers have been published. Students are often urged to keep journals as a way to reflect on their reading, compose personal pieces, and practice writing free of concern for evaluation.

melodrama A plot in which incidents are sensational and designed to provoke immediate emotional responses. In melodrama, the "good" characters are pure and innocent and victims of the "bad" ones, who are thoroughly evil. The term refers to a particular kind of drama popular in the late nineteenth century and, later, in silent films and early Westerns. A work becomes melodramatic when it relies on improbable incidents and unconvincing characters for strong emotional effect.

memoir A form of autobiographical writing that reflects on the significant events the writer has observed and on the interesting and important personalities the writer has known. The Regents ELA Exam often includes examples of memoir among the texts for comprehension or analysis.

monologue In a play, an extended expression or speech by a single speaker that is uninterrupted by response from other characters. A monologue is addressed to a particular person or persons, who may or may not actually hear it. In Ring Lardner's short story "Haircut," a barber tells (narrates) the story to a customer (the reader) who is present but does not respond. (See also *dramatic monologue* in Structure and Language in Poetry, page 62.)

motivation The desires, values, needs, or impulses that move characters to act as they do. In good fiction, the reader understands, appreciates, and is convinced that a character's motivation accounts for the significant incidents and the outcome of a plot.

narrative point of view The standpoint, perspective, and degree of understanding from which a work of narrative fiction is told. (See *omniscient point of view, objective point of view*.)

narrator The character or author's *persona* that tells a story. It is through the perspective and understanding of the narrator that the reader experiences the work. In some works, the narrator may inhabit the world of the story or be a character in it. In other works, the narrator is a detached but knowledgeable observer.

naturalism Closely related to *determinism*, naturalism depicts characters who are driven not by personal will or moral principles but by natural forces that they do not fully understand or control. In contrast to other views of human experience, the naturalistic view makes no moral judgments on the lives of the characters. Their lives, often bleak or defeating, simply *are* as they are, determined by social, environmental, instinctive, and hereditary forces. Naturalism was in part a reaction by writers against the nineteenth-century Romantic view of man as master of his own fate. It is important to note, however, that none of the Naturalistic writers in America (Crane, Dreiser, London, Anderson, and Norris chief among them) presented a genuinely deterministic vision. Several of these authors began their careers in journalism and were drawn to the Naturalistic view of life as a result of their own experience and observation of life in America. (See also *realism*.)

objective point of view In fiction or nonfiction, this voice presents a story or information without expressed judgment or qualification. A fundamental principle of journalism is that news *reports* should be objective. Ernest Hemingway's short story "The Killers" is an example of fiction rendered in a completely detached, objective point of view.

omniscient point of view Spoken in third person (*she, he, they*), this is the broadest narrative perspective. The omniscient narrator speaks from outside the story and sees and knows everything about the characters and incidents. Omniscient narration is not limited by time or place. In *limited omniscient* point of view, the author may choose to reveal the story through full understanding of only one character and limit the action to those incidents in which this character is present.

persona A term from the Greek meaning "mask," it refers in literature to a narrative voice created by an author and through which the author speaks. A narrative persona usually has a perceptible, even distinctive, personality that contributes to our understanding of the story. In Nathaniel Hawthorne's *The Scarlet Letter*, the omniscient narrator has a distinctive persona whose attitudes toward Puritan society and the characters' lives are revealed throughout the novel.

plot The incidents and experiences of characters selected and arranged by the author to create a meaningful story. A good plot is convincing in terms of what happens and why.

poetic justice The concept that life's rewards and punishments should be perfectly appropriate and distributed in just proportions. In Ring Lardner's short story "Haircut," Jim Kendall's ironic fate is an example of poetic justice: he is a victim of one of his own crude and insensitive practical jokes. The short story "They Grind Exceeding Small," by Ben Ames Williams, is also a vivid example of what is meant by poetic justice.

point of view In nonfiction, this denotes the attitudes or opinions of the writer. In narrative fiction, it refers to how and by whom a story is told: the perspective of the narrator and the narrator's relationship to the story. Point of view may be *omniscient,* where the narrator knows everything about the characters and their lives; or, it may be *limited* to the understanding of a particular character or speaker. Point of view may also be described as *objective* or *subjective. Third-person* narrative refers to characters as "he, she, they;" *First-person* narrative is from the "I" point of view. J. D. Salinger's *Catcher in the Rye* and Mark Twain's *Huckleberry Finn* are told in the first person. *Second person,* the "you" form, is rare but is found in sermons addressed to a congregation or in essays of opinion addressed directly to a leader or public figure: "You, Mr. Mayor (Madame President), should do the following . . ." Political columnists occasionally write pieces in the second-person voice for the Op-Ed pages of newspapers.

prologue An introductory statement of the dramatic situation of a play. Shakespeare's *Romeo and Juliet* begins with a brief prologue. The first two pages of Fitzgerald's *The Great Gatsby* are a prologue to the story Nick Carraway will tell.

prose Most of what we write is prose, the expression in sentences and phrases that reflect the natural rhythms of speech. Prose is organized by paragraphs and is characterized by variety in sentence length and rhythm.

protagonist A term from ancient Greek drama, it refers to the central character, the hero or heroine, in a literary work.

realism The literary period in America following the Civil War is usually called the Age of Realism. Realism depicts the directly observable in everyday life. Realistic writers seek to *present* characters and situations as they would appear to a careful observer, not as they are imagined or created by the author. After 1865, American writers became increasingly interested in the sources of power and force, and in the means to survival and success, in an increasingly materialistic society. For writers of this period, realism was a literary mode to express a *naturalistic* philosophy. (See also *naturalism, verisimilitude.*)

rhetoric From Ancient Greece, the art of persuasion in speech or writing achieved through logical thought and skillful use of language.

rhetorical question A question posed in the course of an *argument* to provoke thought or to introduce a line of reasoning.

romance A novel or tale that includes elements of the supernatural, heroic adventure, or romantic passion. Hawthorne's *The Scarlet Letter* is a romance, not because it is a love story but because it goes beyond *verisimilitude* in dramatizing elements of demonic and mystical forces in the characters and their lives.

satire A form or style that uses elements of irony, ridicule, exaggeration, understatement, sarcasm, humor, or absurdity to criticize human behavior or a society. All satire is **ironic** (see *irony*) in that meaning or theme is conveyed in the discrepancy between what is said and what is meant, between what is and what should be, and between what appears and what truly is. Although satire is often entertaining, its purpose is serious and meant to provoke thought or judgment. The verses of Alexander Pope and many poems by e. e. cummings are satiric. In prose, much of the writing of Mark Twain is satire; *Huckleberry Finn* is the most striking example. Other American writers of satire include Sinclair Lewis, Edith Wharton, Aldous Huxley, Joseph Heller, Kurt Vonnegut, and Tom Wolfe. Popular television programs such as *The Daily Show*, *South Park*, and *The Simpsons* are also good examples of satire.

short story This form is distinguished from most novels not simply by length but by its focus on few characters and a central, revealing incident. In stories, however, there is as much variety in narrative point of view, subject, and technique as there is in novels. Edgar Allan Poe characterized the short story as "a short prose narrative, requiring from a half-hour to one or two hours in its perusal."

soliloquy A form of *monologue* in which a character expresses thoughts and feelings aloud but does not address them to anyone else or intend other characters in the work to hear them. In essence, the audience for a play is secretly listening in on a character's innermost thoughts. Macbeth's reflection on "Tomorrow, and tomorrow, and tomorrow . . ." is the best-known soliloquy in the play.

speaker The narrative voice in a literary work (see *persona*). Also, the character who speaks in a *dramatic monologue*.

symbol Most generally, anything that stands for or suggests something else. Language itself is symbolic: sounds and abstract written forms may be arranged to stand for virtually any human thought or experience. In literature, symbols are not codes to crack—they are not "hidden meanings." Symbols are real objects and *concrete* images that lead us to *think about* what is suggested. They organize a wide variety of ideas into single acts of understanding. They embody not single "meanings" but suggest whole areas of meaning.

theme Roughly analogous to *thesis* in an essay, this is an observation about human experience or an idea central to a work of literature. The *subject* of a work is in the specific setting, characters, and plot. Theme in a work of fiction is what is meaningful and significant to human experience generally. Themes are the ideas and truths that transcend the specific characters and plot. Shakespeare's *Macbeth* is about an ambitious nobleman who, encouraged by his equally ambitious wife, murders the king of Scotland in order to become king himself. The themes in *Macbeth* include the power of ambition to corrupt even those who are worthy and the mortal consequences of denying what is fundamental to one's nature.

thesis The central point, a statement of position in a formal or logical argument. Also used to refer to the topic or controlling idea of an essay. Use of the term *thesis* implies elaboration by reasons and examples.

tone The attitude of the writer toward the subject and toward the reader. (See the discussion in Chapter 4, page 52, and a glossary of Terms for Writing, page 68.)

transition A link between ideas or sections in a work. In prose arguments, single words such as *first, second, moreover,* and *therefore* or phrases such as *in addition, on the other hand,* and *in conclusion* serve as transitions. In fiction, a brief passage or chapter may serve as a transition. In *The Great Gatsby*, the narrator pauses from time to time to "fill in" the reader and to account for the passage of time between the dramatic episodes that make up the novel's main plot.

turning point In drama and fiction, the moment or episode in a plot when the action is moved toward its inevitable conclusion.

verisimilitude A literal quality in fiction and drama of being "true to life," of representing that which is real or actual. Verisimilitude in fiction is often achieved through specific, vivid description and dialogue; first-person narration also creates the effect of verisimilitude. In drama, it may be achieved through means of set, costumes, and lighting that are realistic in all their details.

STRUCTURE AND LANGUAGE IN POETRY

allegory A narrative, in prose or verse, in which abstract ideas, principles, human values, or states of mind are **personified**. The purpose of the allegory is to illustrate the significance of the ideas by dramatizing them. *Parable* and *fable* are particular kinds of allegory, in which a moral is illustrated in the form of a story.

alliteration The repetition of initial consonant sounds in words and syllables is one of the first patterns of sound a child creates; for example, "ma-ma; pa-pa." The stories of Dr. Seuss are told in alliteration and **assonance**. Poets use alliteration for its rich musical effect: "Fish, flesh, and fowl commend all summer long/Whatever is begotten, born, and dies" (Yeats); for humor: "Where at, with blade, with bloody, blameful blade/He bravely broached his boiling bloody breast" (Shakespeare); and to echo the sense of the lines: "The iron tongue of midnight hath told twelve" (Shakespeare).

allusion A reference to a historical event, to Biblical, mythological, or literary characters and incidents with which the reader is assumed to be familiar. Allusion may, with few words, enrich or extend the meaning of a phrase, idea, or image. Allusion may also be used for ironic effect. In his poem "Out, out . . ." Robert Frost expects the reader to recall from Macbeth's final soliloquy the line, "Out, out brief candle!" Such expressions as "a Pandora's box" or "Achilles heel," are also forms of allusion.

ambiguity Denotes uncertainty of meaning. In literature and especially in poetry, we speak of intentional ambiguity, the use of language and images to suggest more than one meaning at the same time.

assonance The repetition of vowel sounds among words that begin or end with different consonants.

ballads Narrative poems, sometimes sung, that tell dramatic stories of individual episodes and characters.

blank verse Unrhymed *iambic pentameter*, usually in "paragraphs" of verse instead of stanzas. Shakespeare's plays are composed primarily in blank verse. For example, from *Macbeth* (Act I, Scene 5):
>Your face, my Thane, is as a book where men
>May read strange matters. To beguile the time,
>Look like the time; bear welcome in your eye,
>Your hand, your tongue; look like the innocent flower,
>But be the serpent under't . . .

connotation The feelings, attitudes, images, and associations of a word or expression. Connotations are usually said to be "positive" or "negative."

couplet Two lines of verse with similar meter and end ryhme. Couplets generally have self-contained ideas as well, so they may function as stanzas within a poem. In the English (Shakespearean) *sonnet*, the couplet serves as a conclusion. You will also discover that many scenes in Shakespeare's plays end with rhymed couplets: "Away, and mock the time with fairest show/False face must hide what the false heart doth know." (*Macbeth* Act I, Scene 7)

denotation That which a word actually names, identifies, or "points to." Denotation is sometimes referred to as "the dictionary definition" of a word.

dramatic monologue A poem in which a fictional character, at a critical or dramatic point in life, addresses a particular "audience," which is identifiable but silent. In the course of the monologue, we learn a great deal, often ironically, about the character who is speaking and the circumstances that have led to the speech. Robert Browning is the best-known 19th-century poet to compose dramatic monologues; "My Last Duchess" is a famous example. In the 20th century, such poets as Kenneth Fearing, E. A. Robinson, T. S. Eliot ("The Love Song of J. Alfred Prufrock"), Robert Frost, and Amy Lowell composed well-known dramatic monologues.

elegy A meditative poem mourning the death of an individual.

epic A long narrative poem often centering on a heroic figure who represents the fate of a great nation or people. *The Iliad* and *The Odyssey* of Homer, *The Aeneid* of Vergil, and the Anglo-Saxon *Beowulf* are well-known epics. Milton's *Paradise Lost* and Dante's *Divine Comedy* are examples of epic narratives in which subjects of great human significance are dramatized. *Omeros*, by Derek Walcott, is a contemporary example of an epic poem.

figurative language The intentional and imaginative use of words and comparisons that are not literal but that create original, vivid, and often unexpected images and associations. Figurative language is also called *metaphorical language*. (See *metaphor* and *simile*.)

free verse A poem written in free verse develops images and ideas in patterns of lines without specific metrical arrangements or formal rhyme. Free verse is distinguished from prose, however, because it retains such poetic elements as assonance, alliteration, and figurative language. The poetry of Walt Whitman and e. e. cummings offers striking examples. The poem "View with a Grain of Sand" on page 11 is also an example of free verse.

hyperbole An exaggerated expression (also called overstatement) for a particular effect, which may be humorous, satirical, or intensely emotional. Hyperbole is the expression of folktales and legends and, of course, of lovers: Romeo says to Juliet, "there lies more peril in thine eye/Than twenty of their swords." Hyperbole is often the expression of any overwhelming feeling. After he murders King Duncan, Macbeth looks with horror at his bloody hands: "Will all great Neptune's ocean wash this blood/Clean from my hand . . . ?" In her sleepwalking scene, Lady Macbeth despairs that "All the perfumes of Arabia will not sweeten this little hand." And everyone of us has felt, "I have mountains of work to do!"

iambic pentameter The basic meter of English speech: "I think I know exactly what you need/and yet at times I know that I do not." Formally, it identifies verse of ten syllables to the line, with the second, fourth, sixth, eighth, and tenth accented. There is, however, variation in the stresses within lines to reflect natural speech—and to avoid a "sing-song" or nursery rhyme effect. It is the meter in which most of the dialogue in Shakespeare's plays is composed (see *blank verse*).

image Images and imagery are the heart of poetry. Although the term suggests only something that is visualized, an image is the re-creation through language of *any* experience perceived directly through the senses.

internal rhyme A pattern in which a word or words within a line rhyme with the word that ends it. Poets may also employ internal rhyme at irregular intervals over many lines.

irony In general, a tone or figure of speech in which there is a discrepancy—a striking difference or contradiction—between what is expressed and what is meant or expected. Irony may be used to achieve a powerful effect indirectly. In satire, for example, it may be used to ridicule or criticize.

metaphor A form of analogy. Metaphorical expression is the heart of poetry. Through metaphor, a poet discovers and expresses a similarity between dissimilar things. The poet uses metaphor to imaginatively find common qualities between things we would not normally or literally compare. As a figure of speech, metaphor is said to be implicit or indirect, in contrast to simile where the comparison is expressed directly. In his final soliloquy, which begins "Tomorrow, and tomorrow, and tomorrow . . ." Macbeth creates a series of metaphors to express the meaninglessness of his own life: "Life's but a walking shadow, a poor player . . . it is a tale told by an idiot . . ." When we say, "the trip was a nightmare . . . .," or that "the meeting turned into a circus . . .," we are speaking in metaphor.

meter and rhythm Rhythm refers to the pattern of movement in a poem. As music has rhythm, so does poetry. Meter refers to specific patterns of stressed and unstressed syllables. (See *imabic pentameter*.)

ode A meditation or celebration of a specific subject. Traditional odes addressed "elevated" ideas and were composed in elaborate stanza forms. Keats's "Ode to a Nightingale" and "Ode to Autumn" are particularly fine examples. Modern odes may address subjects either serious or personal. One well-known contemporary ode is Pablo Neruda's "Ode to My Socks."

onomatopoeia The use of words whose sound reflects their sense. "Buzz," "hiss," and "moan" are common examples.

oxymoron Closely related to *paradox*, oxymoron is a figure of speech in which two contradictory or sharply contrasting terms are paired for emphasis or ironic effect. Students' favorite examples include "jumbo shrimp" and "army intelligence." Poets have written of the "wise fool," a "joyful sadness," or an "eloquent silence."

paradox An expression, concept, or situation whose literal statement is contradictory, yet which makes a truthful and meaningful observation. Consider the widely used expression, "less is more," for example. Shakespeare's play *Macbeth* opens with a series of paradoxes to establish the moral atmosphere in which "foul is fair." John Donne's famous poem "Death Be Not Proud" ends with the paradox "Death thou shalt die."

personification A form of metaphor or simile in which nonhuman things—objects, plants and animals, forces of nature, abstract ideas—are given human qualities. Examples include "Pale flakes . . . come feeling for our faces . . ." (Owen); "Time . . . the thief of youth," (Milton); and "Blow winds, and crack your cheeks! Rage! Blow!" (Shakespeare).

prose poem This form appears on the page in the sentences and paragraphs of prose yet its effect is achieved through rhythm, images, and patterns of sound associated with poetry. The poetry of Karl Shapiro offers many excellent examples.

quatrain A stanza of four lines. The quatrain is the most commonly used stanza form in English poetry. Quatrains may be rhymed, *abab, aabb, abba,* for example, or they may be unrhymed.

rhyme In general, any repetition of identical or similar sounds among words that are close enough together to form an audible pattern. Rhyme is most evident when it occurs at the ends of lines of metrical verse.

rhyme scheme A regular pattern of end rhyme in a poem. The rhyme scheme in Shakespeare's sonnets, for example, is *abab/cdcd/efef/gg*.

satire A form or style that uses elements of irony, ridicule, exaggeration, understatement, sarcasm, humor, or absurdity to criticize human behavior or a society. All satire is **ironic** in that meaning or theme is conveyed in the discrepancy between what is said and what is meant, between what is and what should be, between what appears and what truly is. Although satire is often entertaining, its purpose is serious and meant to provoke thought or judgment. The verse of Alexander Pope is often extended satire, and many poems by e. e. cummings are satiric.

simile An expression that is a direct comparison of two things. It uses such words as *like, as, as if, seems, appears*. For example, "A line of elms plunging and tossing like horses" (Theodore Roethke); "Mind in its purest play is like some bat" (Richard Wilbur); "I wandered lonely as a cloud" (William Wordsworth).

soliloquy A form of monologue found most often in drama. It differs from a dramatic monologue in that the speaker is alone, revealing thoughts and feelings to or for oneself that are intentionally unheard by other characters. In Shakespeare's plays, for example, the principal characters' reflections on how to act or questions of conscience are revealed in their soliloquies. Hamlet's "To be, or not to be . . ." is probably the most famous of dramatic soliloquies.

sonnet A poem of fourteen lines in *iambic pentameter* that may be composed of different patterns of stanzas and rhyme schemes. The most common forms are the English, or Shakespearean sonnet, which consists of three quatrains and a closing couplet, and the Italian sonnet, which consists of an *octave* of eight lines and a *sestet* of six lines.

speaker The narrative voice in a poem. Also, the character who speaks in a *dramatic monologue*.

stanza The grouping of lines within a poem. A stanza reflects the basic organization and development of ideas, much as paragraphs do in an essay. Many stanza patterns may have a fixed number of lines and a regular pattern of rhyme. Poets, however, often create stanzas of varying length and form within a single poem. A stanza that ends with a period, completing an idea or image, is considered "closed," whereas a stanza that ends with a comma or with no punctuation is called "open," indicating that there should be very little pause in the movement from one stanza to another.

symbol Most generally, anything that stands for or suggests something else. Language itself is symbolic: sounds and abstract written forms may stand for virtually any human thought or experience. Symbols are real objects and *concrete* images that lead us to *think about* what is suggested. Symbols organize a wide variety of ideas into single acts of understanding. They embody not single "meanings" but suggest whole areas of meaning.

understatement Expression in which something is presented as less important or significant than it really is. Understatement is often used for humorous, satiric, or *ironic* effect. Much of the satire in *Huckleberry Finn* stems from Huck's naive and understated observations. One particular form of understatement, actually a double negative, includes such expressions as "I was not uninterested," which really means "I was interested"; or "He was not without imagination," which really means "He had some imagination."

TERMS FOR WRITING

anecdote A brief story or account of a single experience, often biographical, that illustrates something typical or striking about a person. Anecdotes, like parables, are effective as vivid, specific examples of a general observation or quality.

Terms for Writing

argument The development of reasons and examples to support a thesis; narrowly, to outline a position on an issue or problem with the intent to clarify or persuade. Argument is also used in a broad sense to refer to the way a writer develops any topic. See Chapter 2, page 22 for an explanation and examples of Argument, Part 2 of the Regents ELA Exam.

audience For the writer, this term refers to the intended reader. Awareness of an audience determines, for example, what the writer may assume a reader already knows, the level of diction, and the tone.

coherence A piece of writing has coherence when the logical relationship of ideas is evident and convincing. In a coherent discussion, statements and sections follow one another in a natural, even inevitable way. A coherent discussion hangs together; an incoherent one is scattered and disorganized.

description The expression in words of what is experienced by the senses. Good description recreates what is felt, seen, heard—sensed in any way. We also use the term describe to mean *identify, classify, characterize,* even for abstract ideas. Description permits readers to re-create the subject in their own imaginations.

diction Refers to word choice. Diction may be formal or informal, complex or simple, or elegant or modest, depending on the occasion and the audience. The language used in casual conversation is different from the language used in formal writing. The good writer uses language that is varied, precise, and vivid. The good writer has resources of language to suit a wide range of purposes. In the rubrics for the ELA Exam, diction is evaluated as use of "formal style and precise language."

exposition The development of a topic through examples, reasons, and details that explain, clarify, show, and instruct—the primary purpose of exposition is to convey information. Much of the writing assigned to students is referred to as expository writing. Through exposition, you can demonstrate what you have learned, discovered, understood, appreciated. The task for Part 3 of the Regents ELA Exam is a good example of what is meant by expository writing.

focus Refers to the way a writer concentrates and directs all the information, examples, ideas, and reasons in an essay on the specific topic.

narrative Because it tells a story, a narrative has chronological order. The narrative method is commonly used in exposition when examples are offered in a chronological development.

prompt A set of directions for a writing task; may also be a quote or passage meant to stimulate a piece of writing.

tone Refers to the attitude of the writer toward the subject and/or toward the reader. Tone may range from *harsh and insistent* to *gentle and reflective*. There is as much variety of tone in writing as there is in human feeling. Some pieces, essays of opinion for example, usually have a very distinct tone. Other works, especially in fiction or personal expression, may be more subtle and indirect in tone.

transition Words or phrases used to link ideas and sections in a piece of writing. Common transitions include *first, second . . . in addition . . . finally; on the other hand, moreover, consequently, therefore.* Transitions make the development of an argument clear.

unity In the narrowest sense, unity refers to focus: the ideas and examples are clearly related to the topic and to one another. In the largest sense, unity refers to a feature of our best writing. All elements—ideas, form, language, and tone—work together to achieve the effect of a complete and well-made piece.

A Guide to Proofreading for Common Errors

THE BASICS

Review your essays to make sure that you have begun sentences with capital letters and ended them with a period! Carelessness in this basic use of the conventions could lower your score if the test raters feel that you have not mastered this aspect of formal writing.

PUNCTUATION

COMMA USE

There is one general guideline to keep in mind for comma use: The primary function of the comma is to prevent confusion for your reader. The comma shows how separate parts of sentences are related to one another.

Introductory clauses and phrases need a comma. This makes it clear where the introduction ends and the main clause begins. Note the following examples:

> *"Though I have traveled all over the world, it is the smell of the tides and marshes of Beaufort County that identifies and shapes me."*

> *"Because I came to Beaufort County when I was a boy, my novels all smell of seawater."*
>
> —Pat Conroy

Use the comma in compound sentences with coordinating conjunctions *and, but, yet, so, or, for.* A compound sentence joins two or more independent clauses that could be expressed separately as simple sentences. *Note that the comma precedes the conjunction:*

> "I walked slowly, for the detail on the beach was infinite."
> —Ernie Pyle

> "The luncheon hour was long past, and the two had their end of the vast terrace to themselves."
> —Edith Wharton

A final suggestion: Use a comma only where you *hear* a clear need for one.

THE APOSTROPHE

Remember, the most common use of the apostrophe is to show possession.

>   The *novel's* major themes = The major themes **of the novel**
>   Fiction reveals *characters'* motives and actions = The motives **of the characters**
>   Shakespeare dramatizes *Macbeth's* struggle with his conscience and ambition.

Avoid the increasingly common error of using the apostrophe to show the plural.

>   Mark Twain wrote several **novels;** he did not write "novel's."
>   Holden Caulfield spends several **days** (not day's) in New York before going home.
>   Students in New York State are expected to read at least 25 **books** (not book's) per year.

GRAMMAR

SUBJECT/VERB AGREEMENT

Be sure to match subjects and verbs. Agreement is a form of consistency and is one of the most basic elements of grammar. When you learn to conjugate verbs, for example, you are applying the concept of agreement. Singular subjects take singular verbs; plural subjects take plural verbs.

>   He speaks/they speak; One is/many are

PRONOUN/ANTECEDENT AGREEMENT

Because pronouns replace nouns or other pronouns, they must agree with their singular or plural antecedents.

>   *Evelyn* is very grateful to *her parents* for *their* constant support and encouragement.

Most pronoun/antecedent errors arise when we use the indefinite pronouns *anyone, anybody, everyone, everybody, someone, somebody, no one,* and so on. These pronouns are singular because they refer to *individuals:*

Everybody is responsible for *his* own work.
Someone has left *her* books on the floor.
If *anyone* calls while I am out, please tell *him* or *her* that I will call back after lunch.

The common practice of replacing *him/her* with *them,* or *her/his* with *their,* solves the problem of choosing gender, but it is ungrammatical and illogical. The careful writer (and speaker) avoids these errors, or rewrites:

Please tell *anyone who calls* that I will return at noon.
Someone's books have been left on the floor.
Everyone has individual responsibility for the assignments.

SPELLING

You are, of course, expected to spell correctly common words, the key terms of your essay, and the names of authors, titles, and characters. An occasional misspelling in an on-demand piece of writing should not lower your score if all other elements are good.

Be especially careful to proofread for these very common errors—they mar the overall impression that your essay makes on the reader.

accept/except
   To *accept* is to receive, take willingly, agree to:
      I *accept* your offer, apology, invitation
   To *except* is to exclude, to separate out:
      I will *except* you from the requirement.
   Except is also a preposition:
      Everyone *except* him will be leaving on Tuesday.

affect/effect
   To *affect* (v.) means to move, influence, or change.
   To *affect* also means to put on an artificial quality of personality or character; an exaggerated or artificial person may be called *affected.*
   The *effects* (n.) are the consequences or results.
   To *effect* (v.) means to put into action, to complete—a plan or a change, for example.

could of/should of
You mean *could have/should have*.
Do not make this unfortunate confusion in the way words sound!

hear/here
You may put your things *here* on the table.
I cannot *hear* you with all the noise outside.

its/it's
it's = a contraction for *it is*
its = a possessive form; do not add an apostrophe

loose/lose
Be careful not to *lose* your ticket; it cannot be replaced.
The dog ran *loose* when the leash broke.

principal/principle
Lack of effort is often the *principal* reason for failure.
Many consider honesty a fundamental *principle* in their lives.

than/then
My sister is several years younger *than* I am.
You will answer multiple-choice questions, *then* complete your essays.

there/their/they're
There he goes! It is over *there*.
Students should bring *their* books to class everyday.
They're = *they are*

to/too/two
You will have *two* weeks *to* complete the reading assignment; do not put it off until it is *too* late.

who's/whose
Who's (who is) that coming down the hall?
Whose books are these lying on the floor?

Appendices

The New York State Learning Standards for English Language Arts

The following 11/12 grade-specific standards define end-of-year expectations and a cumulative progression designed to enable students to meet college and career readiness (CCR) expectations no later than the end of high school. The ELA/Regents Exam is designed to assess many (but not all) of the standards in each of the categories: Reading Literature, Reading Informational Texts, Writing, and Language. Note that the 2017 Revised Standards now include reading for Literature and reading for Informational Texts in a single set of standards (RL and RI).

2017 REVISED ELA STANDARDS FOR READING–Literature and Informational Texts (RL and RI)

11-12R1: Cite strong and thorough textual evidence to support analysis of what the text says explicitly/implicitly and make logical inferences, including determining where the text is ambiguous; develop questions for deeper understanding and for further exploration. (RI&RL)

11-12R2: Determine two or more themes or central ideas in a text and analyze their development, including how they emerge and are shaped and refined by specific details; objectively and accurately summarize a complex text. (RI&RL)

11-12R3: In literary texts, analyze the impact of author's choices. (RL) In informational texts, analyze a complex set of ideas or sequence of events and explain how specific individuals, ideas, or events interact and develop. (RI)

11-12R4: Determine the meaning of words and phrases as they are used in a text, including figurative and connotative meanings. Analyze the impact of specific word choices on meaning, tone, and mood, including words with multiple meanings. Analyze how an author uses and refines the meaning of technical or key term(s) over the course of a text. (RI&RL)

11-12R5: In literary texts, analyze how varied aspects of structure create meaning and affect the reader. (RL) In informational texts, analyze the impact and evaluate the effect structure has on exposition or argument in terms of clarity, persuasive/rhetorical technique, and audience appeal. (RI)

11-12R6: Analyze how authors employ point of view, perspective, and purpose to shape explicit and implicit messages (e.g., persuasiveness, aesthetic quality, satire, sarcasm, irony, or understatement). (RI&RL)

11-12R7: In literary texts, analyze multiple adaptations of a source text as presented in different formats (e.g., works of art, graphic novels, music, film, etc.), specifically evaluating how each version interprets the source. (RL) In informational texts, integrate and evaluate sources on the same topic or argument in order to address a question or solve a problem. (RI)

11-12R8: Delineate and evaluate an argument in applicable texts, applying a lens (e.g., constitutional principles, logical fallacy, legal reasoning, belief systems, codes of ethics, philosophies, etc.) to assess the validity or fallacy of key arguments, determining whether the supporting evidence is relevant and sufficient. (RI&RL)

11-12R9: Choose and develop criteria to evaluate the quality of texts. Make connections to other texts, ideas, cultural perspectives, eras, and personal experiences. (RI&RL)

WRITING STANDARDS GRADES 11/12 (W)

1. Write arguments to support claims in an analysis of substantive topics or texts, using valid reasoning and relevant and sufficient evidence.
2. Write informative/explanatory texts to examine and convey complex ideas and information clearly and accurately through the effective selection, organization, and analysis of content.
3. Write narratives to develop real or imagined experiences or events using effective technique, well-chosen details, and well-structured event sequences.
4. Produce clear and coherent writing in which the development, organization, and style are appropriate to task, purpose, and audience.
5. Develop and strengthen writing as needed by planning, revising, editing, rewriting, or trying a new approach.
6. Use technology, including the Internet, to produce and publish writing and to interact and collaborate with others.
7. Conduct short as well as more sustained research projects based on focused questions, demonstrating understanding of the subject under investigation.
8. Gather relevant information from multiple print and digital sources, assess the credibility and accuracy of each source, and integrate the information while avoiding plagiarism.
9. Draw evidence from literary or informational texts to support analysis, reflection, and research.
10. Write routinely over extended time frames (time for research, reflection, and revision) and shorter time frames (a single sitting or a day or two) for a range of tasks, purposes, and audiences.
11. Develop personal, cultural, textual, and thematic connections within and across genres as they respond to texts through written, digital, and oral presentations, employing a variety of media and genres.

LANGUAGE STANDARDS GRADES 11/12 (L)

Conventions of Standard English

1. Demonstrate command of the conventions of standard English grammar and usage when writing or speaking.

2. Demonstrate command of the conventions of standard English capitalization, punctuation, and spelling when writing.

Knowledge of Language

3. Apply knowledge of language to understand how language functions in different contexts, to make effective choices for meaning or style, and to comprehend more fully when reading or listening.

Vocabulary Acquisition and Use

4. Determine or clarify the meaning of unknown and multiple meaning words and phrases by using context clues, analyzing meaningful word parts, and consulting general and specialized reference materials, as appropriate.

5. Demonstrate understanding of figurative language, word relationships, and nuances in word meanings.

6. Acquire and use accurately a range of general academic and domain-specific words and phrases sufficient for reading, writing, speaking, and listening at the college and career readiness level; demonstrate independence in gathering vocabulary knowledge when considering a word or phrase important to comprehension or expression.

HOW IS THE REGENTS ELA EXAM SCORED?

WEIGHTING OF PARTS

Each of the three parts of the Regents Examination in English Language Arts has a number of raw score credits associated with the questions/tasks within that part. In order to ensure an appropriate distribution of credits across the test, each part is weighted.

For Part 1, each multiple-choice question is worth one point. The Part 2 essay is scored on a 6-point rubric then weighted × 4. The Part 3 Text Analysis is scored on a 4-point rubric and then weighted × 2.

As you will notice the Part 2 Argument Essay is the most heavily weighted section.

The table below shows the raw score credits, weighting factor, and weighted score credits for each part of the test.

Part	Maximum Raw Score Credits	Weighting Factor	Maximum Weighted Score Credits
Part 1	24	1	24
Part 2	6	4	24
Part 3	4	2	8
			Total 56

A student's final exam score is then determined in the conversion of the weighted score (of up to 56 points) on a scale of 0–100. Here is an example from a recent ELA exam:

SCORING RUBRICS FOR THE REGENTS ELA EXAM

Parts 2 and 3 of the Regents Examination in English Language Arts is scored using holistic rubrics. Part 2 is scored using a 6-credit rubric, and Part 3 is scored using a 4-credit rubric. Both rubrics reflect the demands called for by the Learning Standards for English Language Arts and Literacy through the end of Grade 11.

Regents Examination in English Language Arts—January 2017

Chart for Converting Total Weighted Raw Scores to Final Exam Scores (Scale Scores) (Use for the January 2017 examination only.)

Weighted Raw Score*	Scale Score	Performance Level	Weighted Raw Score*	Scale Score	Performance Level
56	100	5	27	55	2
55	99	5	26	52	1
54	99	5	25	48	1
53	98	5	24	45	1
52	97	5	23	42	1
51	96	5	22	38	1
50	95	5	21	35	1
49	95	5	20	31	1
48	94	5	19	27	1
47	92	5	18	24	1
46	91	5	17	20	1
45	90	5	16	17	1
44	89	5	15	14	1
43	88	5	14	11	1
42	87	5	13	9	1
41	86	5	12	8	1
40	85	5	11	7	1
39	83	4	10	6	1
38	81	4	9	5	1
37	80	4	8	4	1
36	79	4	7	4	1
35	76	3	6	3	1
34	74	3	5	2	1
33	71	3	4	2	1
32	69	3	3	1	1
31	66	3	2	1	1
30	65	3	1	1	1
29	61	2	0	0	1
28	58	2			

The conversion table is determined independently for each administration of the exam. You will find the conversion tables for each exam in the Answers Explained.

Scoring Rubrics for the Regents ELA Exam

New York State Regents Examination in English Language Arts (Common Core)
Part 2 Rubric
Writing from Sources: Argument

Criteria	6 Essays at this Level	5 Essays at this Level	4 Essays at this Level	3 Essays at this Level	2 Essays at this Level	1 Essays at this Level
Content and Analysis: the extent to which the essay conveys complex ideas and information clearly and accurately in order to support claims in an analysis of the texts	-introduce a precise and insightful claim, as directed by the task -demonstrate in-depth and insightful analysis of the texts, as necessary to support the claim and to distinguish the claim from alternate or opposing claims	-introduce a precise and thoughtful claim, as directed by the task -demonstrate thorough analysis of the texts, as necessary to support the claim and to distinguish the claim from alternate or opposing claims	-introduce a precise claim, as directed by the task -demonstrate appropriate and accurate analysis of the texts, as necessary to support the claim and to distinguish the claim from alternate or opposing claims	-introduce a reasonable claim, as directed by the task -demonstrate some analysis of the texts, but insufficiently distinguish the claim from alternate or opposing claims	-introduce a claim -demonstrate confused or unclear analysis of the texts, failing to distinguish the claim from alternate or opposing claims	-do not introduce a claim -do not demonstrate analysis of the texts
Command of Evidence: the extent to which the essay presents evidence from the provided texts to support analysis	-present ideas fully and thoughtfully, making highly effective use of a wide range of specific and relevant evidence to support analysis -demonstrate proper citation of sources to avoid plagiarism when dealing with direct quotes and paraphrased material	-present ideas clearly and accurately, making effective use of specific and relevant evidence to support analysis -demonstrate proper citation of sources to avoid plagiarism when dealing with direct quotes and paraphrased material	-present ideas sufficiently, making adequate use of specific and relevant evidence to support analysis -demonstrate proper citation of sources to avoid plagiarism when dealing with direct quotes and paraphrased material	-present ideas briefly, making use of some specific and relevant evidence to support analysis -demonstrate inconsistent citation of sources to avoid plagiarism when dealing with direct quotes and paraphrased material	-present ideas inconsistently and/or inaccurately, in an attempt to support analysis, making use of some evidence that may be irrelevant -demonstrate little use of citations to avoid plagiarism when dealing with direct quotes and paraphrased material	-present little or no evidence from the texts -do not make use of citations

Coherence, Organization, and Style: the extent to which the essay logically organizes complex ideas, concepts, and information using formal style and precise language	-exhibit skillful organization of ideas and information to create a cohesive and coherent essay -establish and maintain a formal style, using sophisticated language and structure	-exhibit logical organization of ideas and information to create a cohesive and coherent essay -establish and maintain a formal style, using fluent and precise language and sound structure	-exhibit acceptable organization of ideas and information to create a coherent essay -establish and maintain a formal style, using precise and appropriate language and structure	-exhibit some organization of ideas and information to create a mostly coherent essay -establish but fail to maintain a formal style, using primarily basic language and structure	-exhibit inconsistent organization of ideas and information, failing to create a coherent essay -lack a formal style, using some language that is inappropriate or imprecise	-exhibit little organization of ideas and information -are minimal, making assessment unreliable -use language that is predominantly incoherent, inappropriate, or copied directly from the task or texts
Control of Conventions: the extent to which the essay demonstrates command of conventions of standard English grammar, usage, capitalization, punctuation, and spelling	-demonstrate control of conventions with essentially no errors, even with sophisticated language	-demonstrate control of the conventions, exhibiting occasional errors only when using sophisticated language	-demonstrate partial control, exhibiting occasional errors that do not hinder comprehension	-demonstrate emerging control, exhibiting occasional errors that hinder comprehension	-demonstrate a lack of control, exhibiting frequent errors that make comprehension difficult	-are minimal, making assessment of conventions unreliable

- An essay that addresses fewer texts than required by the task can be scored no higher than a 3.
- An essay that is a personal response and makes little or no reference to the task or texts can be scored no higher than a 1.
- An essay that is totally copied from the task and/or texts with no original student writing must be scored a 0.
- An essay that is totally unrelated to the task, illegible, incoherent, blank, or unrecognizable as English must be scored as a 0.

Scoring Rubrics for the Regents ELA Exam

New York State Regents Examination in English Language Arts (Common Core)
Part 3 Rubric
Text Analysis: Exposition

Criteria	4 Responses at this Level	3 Responses at this Level	2 Responses at this Level	1 Responses at this Level
Content and Analysis: the extent to which the response conveys complex ideas and information clearly and accurately in order to respond to the task and support an analysis of the text	-introduce a well-reasoned central idea and a writing strategy that clearly establish the criteria for analysis -demonstrate a thoughtful analysis of the author's use of the writing strategy to develop the central idea	-introduce a clear central idea and a writing strategy that establish the criteria for analysis -demonstrate an appropriate analysis of the author's use of the writing strategy to develop the central idea	-introduce a central idea and/or a writing strategy -demonstrate a superficial analysis of the author's use of the writing strategy to develop the central idea	-introduce a confused or incomplete central idea or writing strategy and/or -demonstrate a minimal analysis of the author's use of the writing strategy to develop the central idea
Command of Evidence: the extent to which the response presents evidence from the provided text to support analysis	-present ideas clearly and consistently, making effective use of specific and relevant evidence to support analysis	-present ideas sufficiently, making adequate use of relevant evidence to support analysis	-present ideas inconsistently, inadequately, and/or inaccurately in an attempt to support analysis, making use of some evidence that may be irrelevant	-present little or no evidence from the text
Coherence, Organization, and Style: the extent to which the response logically organizes complex ideas, concepts, and information using formal style and precise language	-exhibit logical organization of ideas and information to create a cohesive and coherent response -establish and maintain a formal style, using precise language and sound structure	-exhibit acceptable organization of ideas and information to create a coherent response -establish and maintain a formal style, using appropriate language and structure	-exhibit inconsistent organization of ideas and information, failing to create a coherent response -lack a formal style, using language that is basic, inappropriate, or imprecise	-exhibit little organization of ideas and information -use language that is predominantly incoherent, inappropriate, or copied directly from the task or text -are minimal, making assessment unreliable

Control of Conventions: the extent to which the response demonstrates command of conventions of standard English grammar, usage, capitalization, punctuation, and spelling	-demonstrate control of the conventions with infrequent errors	-demonstrate partial control of conventions with occasional errors that do not hinder comprehension	-demonstrate emerging control of conventions with some errors that hinder comprehension	-demonstrate a lack of control of conventions with frequent errors that make comprehension difficult -are minimal, making assessment of conventions unreliable

- A response that is a personal response and makes little or no reference to the task or text can be scored no higher than a 1.
- A response that is totally copied from the text with no original writing must be given a 0.
- A response that is totally unrelated to the task, illegible, incoherent, blank, or unrecognizable as English must be scored as a 0.

Regents ELA Examinations and Answers

Regents ELA Examination June 2016
English Language Arts

PART 1—Reading Comprehension

Directions (1–24): Closely read each of the three passages below. After each passage, there are several multiple-choice questions. Select the best suggested answer to each question and write its number in the space provided. You may use the margins to take notes as you read.

Reading Comprehension Passage A

    ...When the short days of winter came dusk fell before we had well eaten our dinners. When we met in the street the houses had grown sombre. The space of sky above us was the colour of ever-changing violet and towards it the lamps of the street lifted their feeble lanterns. The cold air stung
(5) us and we played till our bodies glowed. Our shouts echoed in the silent street. The career of our play brought us through the dark muddy lanes behind the houses where we ran the gauntlet of the rough tribes[1] from the cottages, to the back doors of the dark dripping gardens where odours arose from the ashpits, to the dark odorous stables where a coach man smoothed
(10) and combed the horse or shook music from the buckled harness. When we returned to the street light from the kitchen windows had filled the areas. If my uncle was seen turning the corner we hid in the shadow until we had seen him safely housed. Or if Mangan's sister came out on the doorstep to call her brother in to his tea we watched her from our shadow peer up
(15) and down the street. We waited to see whether she would remain or go in

---
[1]tribes—gangs

and, if she remained, we left our shadow and walked up to Mangan's steps resignedly. She was waiting for us, her figure defined by the light from the half-opened door. Her brother always teased her before he obeyed and I stood by the railings looking at her. Her dress swung as she moved her body
(20) and the soft rope of her hair tossed from side to side.

Every morning I lay on the floor in the front parlour watching her door. The blind was pulled down to within an inch of the sash so that I could not be seen. When she came out on the doorstep my heart leaped. I ran to the hall, seized my books and followed her. I kept her brown figure always in
(25) my eye and, when we came near the point at which our ways diverged, I quickened my pace and passed her. This happened morning after morning. I had never spoken to her, except for a few casual words, and yet her name was like a summons to all my foolish blood. . . .

At last she spoke to me. When she addressed the first words to me I was
(30) so confused that I did not know what to answer. She asked me was I going to *Araby*. I forget whether I answered yes or no. It would be a splendid bazaar,[2] she said she would love to go.

"And why can't you?" I asked.

While she spoke she turned a silver bracelet round and round her wrist.
(35) She could not go, she said, because there would be a retreat[3] that week in her convent.[4] Her brother and two other boys were fighting for their caps and I was alone at the railings. She held one of the spikes, bowing her head towards me. The light from the lamp opposite our door caught the white curve of her neck, lit up her hair that rested there and, falling, lit up the
(40) hand upon the railing. It fell over one side of her dress and caught the white border of a petticoat, just visible as she stood at ease.

"It's well for you," she said.

"If I go," I said, "I will bring you something."

What innumerable follies laid waste my waking and sleeping thoughts
(45) after that evening! I wished to annihilate the tedious intervening days. I chafed against the work of school. At night in my bedroom and by day in the classroom her image came between me and the page I strove to read. The syllables of the word *Araby* were called to me through the silence in which my soul luxuriated and cast an Eastern enchantment over me. I asked for leave to
(50) go to the bazaar on Saturday night. My aunt was surprised and hoped it was not some Freemason[5] affair. I answered few questions in class. I watched my

---

[2]bazaar—fair
[3]retreat—a time set aside for prayer and reflection
[4]convent—religious school
[5]Freemason—a fraternal organization

master's face pass from amiability to sternness; he hoped I was not beginning to idle. I could not call my wandering thoughts together. I had hardly any patience with the serious work of life which, now that it stood between me and
(55) my desire, seemed to me child's play, ugly monotonous child's play.

    On Saturday morning I reminded my uncle that I wished to go to the bazaar in the evening. He was fussing at the hallstand, looking for the hatbrush, and answered me curtly:

    "Yes, boy, I know." . . .

(60)   At nine o'clock I heard my uncle's latchkey in the halldoor. I heard him talking to himself and heard the hallstand rocking when it had received the weight of his overcoat. I could interpret these signs. When he was midway through his dinner I asked him to give me the money to go to the bazaar. He had forgotten.

(65)   "The people are in bed and after their first sleep now," he said.

    I did not smile. My aunt said to him energetically: "Can't you give him the money and let him go? You've kept him late enough as it is." . . .

    I held a florin[6] tightly in my hand as I strode down Buckingham Street towards the station. The sight of the streets thronged with buyers and glaring
(70) with gas recalled to me the purpose of my journey. I took my seat in a third-class carriage of a deserted train. After an intolerable delay the train moved out of the station slowly. It crept onward among ruinous houses and over the twinkling river. At Westland Row Station a crowd of people pressed to the carriage doors; but the porters moved them back, saying that it was a special
(75) train for the bazaar. I remained alone in the bare carriage. In a few minutes the train drew up beside an improvised wooden platform. I passed out on to the road and saw by the lighted dial of a clock that it was ten minutes to ten. In front of me was a large building which displayed the magical name. . . .

    Remembering with difficulty why I had come I went over to one of the
(80) stalls and examined porcelain vases and flowered tea-sets. At the door of the stall a young lady was talking and laughing with two young gentle men. I remarked their English accents and listened vaguely to their conversation. . . .

    Observing me the young lady came over and asked me did I wish to buy anything. The tone of her voice was not encouraging; she seemed to have
(85) spoken to me out of a sense of duty. I looked humbly at the great jars that stood like eastern guards at either side of the dark entrance to the stall and murmured:

    "No, thank you."

---

[6]florin—coin

The young lady changed the position of one of the vases and went back
(90) to the two young men. They began to talk of the same subject. Once or twice
the young lady glanced at me over her shoulder.

I lingered before her stall, though I knew my stay was useless, to make
my interest in her wares seem the more real. Then I turned away slowly
and walked down the middle of the bazaar. I allowed the two pennies to
(95) fall against the sixpence in my pocket. I heard a voice call from one end
of the gallery that the light was out. The upper part of the hall was now
completely dark.

Gazing up into the darkness I saw myself as a creature driven and
derided by vanity; and my eyes burned with anguish and anger.

—James Joyce
excerpted from "Araby"
Dubliners, 1914
Grant Richards LTD.

1 The description of the neighborhood in lines 1 through 10 contributes to a mood of
   (1) indifference
   (2) gloom
   (3) anxiety
   (4) regret

2 Which quotation from the text best illustrates the narrator's attitude toward Mangan's sister?
   (1) "we watched her from our shadow" (line 14)
   (2) "We waited to see whether she would remain or go in" (line 15)
   (3) "yet her name was like a summons" (lines 27 and 28)
   (4) "She asked me was I going to *Araby*" (lines 30 and 31)

3 Lines 29 through 38 reveal Mangan's sister's
   (1) disinterest
   (2) silliness
   (3) disappointment
   (4) tension

4 Lines 44 through 55 help to develop the idea that the narrator has
   (1) recognized that his priorities have changed
   (2) determined the academic focus of his studies
   (3) eliminated distractions from his daily routine
   (4) reassessed his relationship with his family

5 The description of the narrator's train ride (lines 68 through 76) supports a theme of
   (1) confusion
   (2) isolation
   (3) persecution
   (4) deception

6 The description in lines 83 through 91 suggests that the bazaar symbolizes
   (1) excessive greed
   (2) future wealth
   (3) false promise
   (4) lasting love

7 It can be inferred from the text that the narrator's behavior is most guided by his

(1) school experience
(2) family situation
(3) childhood memories
(4) romantic feelings

7 _____

8 As used in line 99, the word "derided" most nearly means

(1) taunted
(2) restrained
(3) rewarded
(4) flattered

8 _____

9 Based on the text as a whole, the narrator's feelings of "anguish and anger" (line 99) are most likely a result of his having

(1) ignored his opportunities
(2) defended his family
(3) realized his limitations
(4) denied his responsibilities

9 _____

10 Which quotation best reflects a central theme of the text?

(1) "Her brother and two other boys were fighting for their caps" (line 36)
(2) " 'Can't you give him the money and let him go?' " (lines 66 and 67)
(3) "It crept onward among ruinous houses and over the twinkling river" (lines 72 and 73)
(4) "I lingered before her stall, though I knew my stay was useless" (line 92)

10 _____

Reading Comprehension Passage B

Assembly Line

In time's assembly line
Night presses against night.
We come off the factory night-shift
In line as we march towards home.
(5) Over our heads in a row
The assembly line of stars
Stretches across the sky.
Beside us, little trees
Stand numb in assembly lines.

(10) The stars must be exhausted
After thousands of years
Of journeys which never change.
The little trees are all sick,
Choked on smog and monotony,
(15) Stripped of their color and shape.
It's not hard to feel for them;
We share the same tempo and rhythm.

Yes, I'm numb to my own existence
As if, like the trees and stars
(20) —perhaps just out of habit
—perhaps just out of sorrow,
I'm unable to show concern
For my own manufactured fate.

—Shu Ting
from *A Splintered Mirror: Chinese Poetry from the
Democracy Movement*, 1991
translated by Carolyn Kizer
North Point Press

11 In the first stanza, a main idea is strengthened through the poet's use of

(1) repetition
(2) simile
(3) allusion
(4) understatement   11 _____

12 Line 17 contributes to a central idea by pointing out a parallel between

(1) profit and industrialization
(2) humans and nature
(3) recreation and production
(4) sound and motion   12 _____

13 The structure and language of lines 20 and 21 suggests the narrator's

(1) bitterness
(2) determination
(3) selfishness
(4) uncertainty   13 _____

14 The phrase "manufactured fate" (line 23) emphasizes the narrator's

(1) resignation to life
(2) desire for control
(3) hope for change
(4) rejection of nature   14 _____

Reading Comprehension Passage C

....Memory teaches me what I know of these matters. The boy reminds the adult. I was a bilingual child, but of a certain kind: "socially disadvantaged," the son of working-class parents, both Mexican immigrants....

(5) In public, my father and mother spoke a hesitant, accented, and not always grammatical English. And then they would have to strain, their bodies tense, to catch the sense of what was rapidly said by *los gringos*. At home, they returned to Spanish. The language of their Mexican past sounded in counterpoint to the English spoken in public. The words would
(10) come quickly, with ease. Conveyed through those sounds was the pleasing, soothing, consoling reminder that one was at home.

During those years when I was first learning to speak, my mother and father addressed me only in Spanish; in Spanish I learned to reply. By contrast, English (*inglés*) was the language I came to associate with gringos,
(15) rarely heard in the house. I learned my first words of English overhearing my parents speaking to strangers. At six years of age, I knew just enough words for my mother to trust me on errands to stores one block away—but no more.

I was then a listening child, careful to hear the very different sounds
(20) of Spanish and English. Wide-eyed with hearing, I'd listen to sounds more than to words. First, there were English (*gringo*) sounds. So many words still were unknown to me that when the butcher or the lady at the drugstore said something, exotic polysyllabic sounds would bloom in the midst of their sentences. Often the speech of people in public seemed to me very loud,
(25) booming with confidence. The man behind the counter would literally ask, "What can I do for you?" But by being so firm and clear, the sound of his voice said that he was a gringo; he belonged in public society. There were also the high, nasal notes of middle-class American speech—which I rarely am conscious of hearing today because I hear them so often, but could not
(30) stop hearing when I was a boy. Crowds at Safeway or at bus stops were noisy with the birdlike sounds of *los gringos*. I'd move away from them all—all the chirping chatter above me.

My own sounds I was unable to hear, but I knew that I spoke English poorly. My words could not extend to form complete thoughts. And the
(35) words I did speak I didn't know well enough to make distinct sounds. (Listeners would usually lower their heads to hear better what I was trying to say.) But it was one thing for *me* to speak English with difficulty; it was

more troubling to hear my parents speaking in public: their high-whining vowels and guttural[1] consonants; their sentences that got stuck with "eh" (40) and "ah" sounds; the confused syntax; the hesitant rhythm of sounds so different from the way gringos spoke. I'd notice, moreover, that my parents' voices were softer than those of gringos we would meet.

I am tempted to say now that none of this mattered. (In adulthood I am embarrassed by childhood fears.) And, in a way, it didn't matter very (45) much that my parents could not speak English with ease. Their linguistic difficulties had no serious consequences. My mother and father made themselves understood at the county hospital clinic and at government offices. And yet, in another way, it mattered very much. It was unsettling to hear my parents struggle with English. Hearing them, I'd grow nervous, and (50) my clutching trust in their protection and power would be weakened. . . .

But then there was Spanish: *español*, the language rarely heard away from the house; *español*, the language which seemed to me therefore a private language, my family's language. To hear its sounds was to feel myself specially recognized as one of the family, apart from *los otros*.[2] A simple (55) remark, an inconsequential comment could convey that assurance. My parents would say something to me and I would feel embraced by the sounds of their words. Those sounds said: *I am speaking with ease in Spanish. I am addressing you in words I never use with* los gringos. *I recognize you as someone special, close, like no one outside. You belong with us. In the family.* (60) *Ricardo.*

At the age of six, well past the time when most middle-class children no longer notice the difference between sounds uttered at home and words spoken in public, I had a different experience. I lived in a world compounded of sounds. I was a child longer than most. I lived in a magical (65) world, surrounded by sounds both pleasing and fearful. I shared with my family a language enchantingly private—different from that used in the city around us. . . .

If I rehearse here the changes in my private life after my Americanization, it is finally to emphasize a public gain. The loss implies the gain. The (70) house I returned to each afternoon was quiet. Intimate sounds no longer greeted me at the door. Inside there were other noises. The telephone rang. Neighborhood kids ran past the door of the bedroom where I was reading my schoolbooks—covered with brown shopping-bag paper.

---

[1]guttural—throaty
[2]los otros—the others

Once I learned the public language, it would never again be easy for me to
(75) hear intimate family voices. More and more of my day was spent hearing words, not sounds. But that may only be a way of saying that on the day I raised my hand in class and spoke loudly to an entire roomful of faces, my childhood started to end. . . .

—Richard Rodriguez
excerpted from "Aria: A Memoir of a Bilingual Childhood"
The American Scholar, Winter 1981
The Phi Beta Kappa Society

15 The phrase "the boy reminds the adult" in the first paragraph establishes the narrator's

(1) mood
(2) perspective
(3) creativity
(4) disposition   15 _____

16 The use of the word "counterpoint" in line 9 helps to develop a central idea by presenting

(1) differing memories
(2) opposing principles
(3) contrasting cultures
(4) conflicting philosophies   16 _____

17 The use of figurative language in lines 20 and 21 demonstrates the narrator's

(1) eagerness to learn
(2) desire for recognition
(3) frustration with authority
(4) anxiety about adulthood   17 _____

18 The use of the word "public" in line 27 emphasizes the narrator's feeling of

(1) accomplishment
(2) disillusionment
(3) satisfaction
(4) separation   18 _____

19 The description of the narrator speaking English in lines 33 through 37 emphasizes his inability to

(1) communicate effectively
(2) understand the culture
(3) distinguish between languages
(4) express emotions   19 _____

20 In lines 44 through 49 the narrator's reaction to his parents' "linguistic difficulties" (lines 45 and 46) reveals his

(1) low expectations
(2) conflicting feelings
(3) educational concerns
(4) hostile thoughts   20 _____

21 Lines 51 through 60 contribute to a central idea in the text by focusing on the

  (1) narrator's sense of security
  (2) family's economic status
  (3) family's traditional beliefs
  (4) narrator's feeling of confusion   21 _____

22 Which quotation best reflects the narrator's overall experience with language?

  (1) "The words would come quickly, with ease" (lines 9 and 10)
  (2) "I'd listen to sounds more than to words" (lines 20 and 21)
  (3) "My own sounds I was unable to hear, but I knew that I spoke English poorly" (lines 33 and 34)
  (4) "Hearing them, I'd grow nervous" (line 49)   22 _____

23 The phrase "the loss implies the gain" (line 69) contributes to a central idea in the text by indicating that when the narrator speaks English comfortably he is

  (1) disconnected from his family
  (2) distressed by hearing English sounds
  (3) uninterested in his school work
  (4) undeterred from making new friends   23 _____

24 The narrator's tone in lines 75 through 78 suggests

  (1) distrust   (3) confidence
  (2) respect   (4) intolerance   24 _____

PART 2—Argument Response

Directions: Closely read each of the *four* texts on pages 98 through 107 and write a source-based argument on the topic below. You may use the margins to take notes as you read and scrap paper to plan your response. Write your argument on a separate sheet of paper.

> **Topic:** Should celebrities become the voice of humanitarian causes?

> **Your Task:** Carefully read each of the *four* texts provided. Then, using evidence from at least *three* of the texts, write a well-developed argument regarding whether or not celebrities should become the voice of humanitarian causes. Clearly establish your claim, distinguish your claim from alternate or opposing claims, and use specific, relevant, and sufficient evidence from at least *three* of the texts to develop your argument. Do *not* simply summarize each text.

Guidelines:

Be sure to

- Establish your claim regarding whether or not celebrities should become the voice of humanitarian causes.
- Distinguish your claim from alternate or opposing claims.
- Use specific, relevant, and sufficient evidence from at least *three* of the texts to develop your argument.
- Identify each source that you reference by text number and line number(s) or graphic (for example: Text 1, line 4 or Text 2, graphic).
- Organize your ideas in a cohesive and coherent manner.
- Maintain a formal style of writing.
- Follow the conventions of standard written English.

Texts:

Text 1—The Celebrity Solution

Text 2—Ethics of Celebrities and Their Increasing Influence in 21st Century Society

Text 3—Do Celebrity Humanitarians Matter?

Text 4—The Rise of the Celebrity Humanitarian

Text 1

The Celebrity Solution

In 2004, Natalie Portman, then a 22-year-old fresh from college, went to Capitol Hill to talk to Congress on behalf of the Foundation for International Community Assistance, or Finca, a microfinance organization for which she served as "ambassador." She found herself wondering what
(5) she was doing there, but her colleagues assured her: "We got the meetings because of you." For lawmakers, Natalie Portman was not simply a young woman—she was the beautiful Padmé from "Star Wars." "And I was like, 'That seems totally nuts to me,'" Portman told me recently. [*sic*] It's the way it works, I guess. I'm not particularly proud that in our country I can get a
(10) meeting with a representative more easily than the head of a nonprofit can."

Well, who is? But it is the way it works. Stars—movie stars, rock stars, sports stars—exercise a ludicrous influence over the public consciousness. Many are happy to exploit that power; others are wrecked by it. In recent years, stars have learned that their intense presentness in people's daily lives
(15) and their access to the uppermost realms of politics, business and the media offer them a peculiar kind of moral position, should they care to use it. And many of those with the most leverage—Bono and Angelina Jolie and Brad Pitt and George Clooney and, yes, Natalie Portman—have increasingly chosen to mount that pedestal. Hollywood celebrities have become central players
(20) on deeply political issues like development aid, refugees and government-sponsored violence in Darfur.

Activists on these and other issues talk about the political power of stars with a mixture of bewilderment and delight. But a weapon that powerful is bound to do collateral damage. Some stars, like George Clooney, regard the
(25) authority thrust upon them with wariness; others, like Sean Penn or Mia Farrow, an activist on Darfur, seize the bully pulpit with both hands. "There is a tendency," says Donald Steinberg, deputy president of the International Crisis Group, which seeks to prevent conflict around the world, "to treat these issues as if it's all good and evil." Sometimes you need the rallying cry,
(30) but sometimes you need to accept a complex truth. . . .

An entire industry has sprung up around the recruitment of celebrities to good works. Even an old-line philanthropy like the Red Cross employs a "director of celebrity outreach." Oxfam has a celebrity wrangler in Los Angeles, Lyndsay Cruz, on the lookout for stars who can raise the charity's
(35) profile with younger people. In addition to established figures like Colin Firth and Helen Mirren, Oxfam is affiliated with Scarlett Johansson, who has

visited South Asia (where the organization promotes girls' education) and is scheduled to go to Mali. Cruz notes that while "trendy young people" are attracted to the star of "Match Point" and "Lost in Translation," Johansson had "great credibility with an older audience because she's such a great actress."...

Microfinance is a one-star cause. Though for some reason the subject appeals to female royalty, including Queen Rania of Jordan and Princess Maxima of the Netherlands, Natalie Portman is the only member of Hollywood royalty who has dedicated herself to it. Perhaps this is because microfinance is a good deal more complicated than supplying fresh water to parched villages, and a good deal less glamorous than confronting the janjaweed[1] in Darfur. The premise of microfinance is that very poor people should have access to credit, just as the middle class and the rich do. They typically don't have such access because banks that operate in the developing world view the poor as too great a credit risk, and the processing cost of a $50 loan is thought to wipe out much of the potential profit. But small nonprofit organizations found that tiny loans could not only raise the incomes of the rural and small-town poor but also, unlike aid and other handouts, could help make them self-sufficient. And they found as well that if they harnessed the communities' own social bonds to create group support, repayment rates among the very poor could be higher than among the more well-off. (Indeed, commercial banks, apparently having recognized their error, have now begun to extend loans to the poor.) The idea of microfinance is thus to introduce the poor to capitalism. This is not, it's true, star material....

Theres no question that causes do a great deal for the brand identity of the stars and the sponsors who embrace them. But what, exactly, do stars do for causes? They raise money, of course. But that is often less important than raising consciousness, as Natalie Portman has done. John Prendergast, a longtime activist on African issues and the chairman of Enough, an organization that brings attention to atrocities around the world, says: "Celebrities are master recruiters. If you're trying to expand beyond the already converted, there's no better way to do instant outreach than to have a familiar face where people want to know more about what they're doing in their personal lives." People come to see Natalie Portman, and they go away learning about microfinance....

—James Traub
excerpted from "The Celebrity Solution"
www.nytimes.com, March 9, 2008

---

[1]janjaweed—militia

Text 2

Ethics of Celebrities and Their Increasing Influence in 21st Century Society

    The global influence of celebrities in the 21st century extends far beyond the entertainment sector. During the recent Palestinian presidential elections, the Hollywood actor Richard Gere broadcast a televised message to voters in the region and stated,

(5)   Hi, I'm Richard Gere, and I'm speaking for the entire world. (Richard Gere, actor)

    Celebrities in the 21st century have expanded from simple product endorsements to sitting on United Nations committees, regional and global conflict commentators and international diplomacy. The Russian parliament
(10) is debating whether to send a global celebrity to its International Space Station. The celebrities industry is undergoing, "mission creep", or the expansion of an enterprise beyond its original goals.

    There has always been a connection between Hollywood and politics, certainly in the USA. However, global celebrities in the 21st century are
(15) involved in proselytising[1] about particular religions, such as Scientology, negotiating with the Taliban in Afghanistan and participating in the Iraqi refugee crisis. The Hollywood actor, Jude Law's attempt to negotiate with the Taliban in Afghanistan was not successful; but the mere fact that Jude Law tried, and that it was discussed widely over the global internet, shows the
(20) expansion of celebrities' domain in today's society. The global entertainment industry, especially based in Hollywood, has vastly exceeded their original mandate in society. . . .

    How is it that celebrities in the 21st century are formulating foreign aid policy, backing political bills or affecting public health debates? Traditionally,
(25) the economic value or market price of the entertainment industry and its various components was seen as intangible and difficult to measure. Movie stars and films, artists and the quality of art is often seen as difficult to measure in terms of value and price without the role of expert opinions. But global internet-driven 21st century seems to be driven by a general growth
(30) of the idea that celebrity can be measured in a tangible way. . . .

    The 21st century's internet society seems to thrive on a harmonious three-way relationship among celebrities, audiences and fame addiction. The global internet in turns [sic] moulds this three-way relationship and accelerates its dissemination[2] and communication. This in turn allows

---
[1]proselytising—trying to persuade or recruit others
[2]dissemination—wide distribution

(35) celebrities in the 21st century to "mission creep", or expand and accelerate their influence into various new areas of society. This interaction of forces is shown in Figure 1. . . .

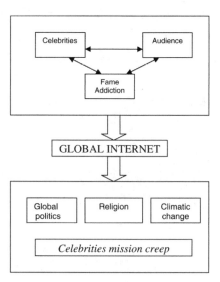

Figure 1. Celebrities' mission creep in the 21st century.

In turn, the global popularity of internet-based social networking sites such as MySpace or individual blogspots all show the need to discuss events, but (40) also things that are famous (Choi and Berger, 2009). Traditionally, celebrities were seen as people that needed to be seen from afar and while keeping one's distance. In this sense, celebrities were similar to art pieces, better to be seen from a distance (Halpern, 2008; Hirsch, 1972; Maury and Kleiner, 2002). This traditional distance has been reduced due to global technologies (45) in communications. Celebrities, and famous people in turn, help to bring people, including adults, together in conversation and social interaction. The global role of the internet in the 21st century society will further accelerate such social and psychological trends throughout today's global knowledge-based society. Global internet communications have increased the availability (50) of "fame" and access to the lives of celebrities, which in turn will further accelerate the global influence of celebrities in the 21st century society. . . .

—Chong Ju Choi and Ron Berger
excerpted from "Ethics of Celebrities and
Their Increasing Influence in 21st Century Society"
Journal of Business Ethics, 2009
www.idc.ac.il

References

Choi, C.J. and R. Berger: 2009, 'Ethics of Internet, Global Community, Fame Addiction', *Journal of Business Ethics* (forthcoming).

Halpern, J.: 2008, *Fame Junkies* (Houghton Mifflin, New York).

Hirsch, P.: 1972, 'Processing Fads and Fashions: An Organisation Set Analysis of Cultural Industry Systems', *American Journal of Sociology* 77 (1), 45–70.

Maury, M. and D. Kleiner: 2002, 'E-Commerce, Ethical Commerce?', *Journal of Business Ethics* 36 (3), 21–32.

Text 3

Do Celebrity Humanitarians Matter?

...Recent years have seen a growth industry for celebrities engaged in humanitarian activities. The website *Look to the Stars* has calculated that over 2,000 charities have some form of celebrity support. UNICEF has dozens of "Goodwill Ambassadors" and "Advocates" such as Angelina Jolie
(5) and Mia Farrow. Celebrities have entered forums for global governance to pressure political leaders: George Clooney has spoken before the United Nations while Bob Geldof, Bono, and Sharon Stone have attended summits like DAVOS[1] and the G8[2] to discuss third world debt, poverty, and refugees. In the U.S. policy arena, [Ben] Affleck joins Nicole Kidman, Angelina Jolie,
(10) and other celebrities who have addressed the U.S. Congress on international issues.[3] The increase in celebrity involvement has spurred debate in academic circles and mainstream media. Celebrity humanitarianism is alternately lauded for drawing media attention and fostering popular engagement and criticized on a number of ethical grounds. According to *Mother Jones*, Africa
(15) is experiencing a "recolonization" as celebrities from the U.S. and UK lay claim to particular countries as recipients of their star power: South Africa (Oprah), Sudan (Mia Farrow), and Botswana (Russell Simmons). As the involvement of American celebrities in humanitarian causes grows, let us consider the activities of Affleck and his Eastern Congo Initiative [ECI].

Celebrity Humanitarians
(20)   Affleck can be considered a "celebrity humanitarian," a celebrity figure who has moved beyond his/her day job as an entertainer to delve into the areas of foreign aid, charity, and development. These activities can involve fundraising, hosting concerts and events, media appearances, and engaging in advocacy. Celebrities are distinguished by their unique ability to
(25) attract and engage diverse audiences ranging from their fan base and the media to political elites and philanthropists. Celebrity humanitarians often play an important bridging role, introducing Northern publics to issues in the developing world. They also use their star power to gain access to policy-making circles to effect social and political change. Since 1980, the U.S.
(30) Congress has seen the frequency of celebrity witnesses double to around

---

[1]DAVOS—an annual meeting of The World Economic Forum, hosted in Davos-Klosters, Switzerland, on global partnership
[2]G8—A group of 8 industrialized nations that hold a yearly meeting to discuss global issues
[3]ProQuest, "Quick Start: Congressional Hearing Digital Collections: Famous (Celebrity) Witnesses," http://proquest.libguides.com/quick_start_hearings/famouscelebs

20 a year with most celebrity appearances taking place before committees addressing domestic issues. Interestingly, fewer than 5 percent of celebrity witnesses testify before committees dealing with foreign relations, where celebrity humanitarians push the United States to address global concerns.[4]

(35) The rise and influence of celebrity humanitarians activate debates on the consequences of their involvement. For some academics and practitioners, celebrities are welcome figures in humanitarianism: educating the public on global issues, raising funds, and using their populist appeal to draw attention to policy-making arenas. For others, celebrity humanitarians (40) are highly problematic figures who dilute debates, offer misguided policy proposals, and lack credibility and accountability. Celebrity humanitarianism privileges and invests the celebrity figure with the responsibility of speaking on behalf of a "distant other" who is unable to give input or consent for their representation. Stakeholders in the developing world unwittingly rely on (45) the celebrity humanitarian as their communicator, advocate, and fundraiser. Finally, celebrities are held to be self-serving, engaging in humanitarian causes to burnish[5] their careers. . . .

Celebrity humanitarians should do their homework to earn credibility while also respecting their bounded roles as celebrity figures. As a celebrity (50) humanitarian, Affleck's proposals are based on serious preparation: spending years to gain an in-depth understanding, consulting with professionals, narrowing his advocacy efforts to a single region, and enduring the scrutiny of the cameras and the blogosphere. Besides this self-education, his credibility is based on ECI's dual mission of re-granting and policymaking. Since ECI (55) has operations and partnerships in the DRC [Democratic Republic of the Congo], the content of Affleck's writings and Congressional testimonies are grounded in the realities of the DRC, peppered with first-hand accounts, and supported by statistics and other research. However, there are limits to his knowledge—Affleck is not a development expert or on-the-ground (60) professional; his day job and main career lie elsewhere. And while the decision to found an organization suggests that Affleck's commitment to the DRC will extend beyond his nascent[6] efforts, rumors that he may seek political office distort this image.

Celebrity humanitarians must find a way to avoid diverting resources (65) and attention. Rather than bring his star power and ample financial support to existing Congolese organizations, ECI furnished a platform for

---

[4]See Demaine, L.J., n.d. Navigating Policy by the Stars: The Influence of Celebrity Entertainers on Federal Lawmaking. *Journal of Law & Politics*, 25 (2), 83–143
[5]burnish—improve or enhance
[6]nascent—beginning

Affleck's advocacy and leadership that amplifies his voice over those of the Congolese. Nor was ECI crafted inside eastern Congo but in the offices of a strategic advisory firm based in Seattle. ECI is privately funded by a
(70) network of financial elites and does not rely on means-tested grant cycles or public support. While Affleck has received multiple awards in the short period he has been a celebrity humanitarian, his star power also distracts us from the people who work in the field of humanitarianism on a daily basis and rarely receive such recognition.[7] And by concentrating attention and
(75) money for Affleck's issue of Eastern Congo, other causes and countries may go unnoticed. . . .

—Alexandra Cosima Budabin
excerpted and adapted from "Do Celebrity Humanitarians Matter?"
www.carnegiecouncil.org, December 11, 2014

---

[7]Marina Hyde, "Angelina Jolie, Paris Hilton, Lassie and Tony Blair: here to save the world," The Guardian, 27 November 2014 *http://www.theguardian.com/lifeandstyle/lostinshowbiz/2014/nov/27/angelina-jolie-paris-hilton-tony-blair-lassie-save-the-childrenaward? CMP=share_btn_fb*

Text 4

The Rise of the Celebrity Humanitarian

    ...One of the most effective methods of attracting a wide, although perhaps not a deep, following is the use of a celebrity humanitarian: An A-Lister who has delved into areas of foreign aid, charity and international development. The United Nations is the leader in this attention getting
(5) ploy, with at least 175 celebrities on the books as goodwill ambassadors[1] for one cause or another. Some celebrities even leverage their star power to promote their very own foundations and philanthropic projects.
    It's a mutually beneficial relationship, really. Hollywood's elite get to wield their unique ability to engage diverse audiences, and the power of
(10) celebrity is put to good use effecting change—whether it's out of the good of their hearts, or because their publicists insist.
    There is some downside that comes with publicly linking a campaign to a celebrity. For some, celebrity humanitarians are problematic figures[2] who dilute debates, offer misguided policy proposals, and lack credibility
(15) and accountability. Take Scarlett Johansson, who became embroiled in a scandal after partnering with soft drink maker SodaStream, which operated a factory in occupied Palestinian territory. This alliance was in direct conflict with her seven-year global ambassador position for Oxfam, which opposes all trade with the occupied territories. In the end, she stepped down from
(20) her role with Oxfam, stating a fundamental difference of opinion.
    Moreover, if the star's popularity takes a hit, it can affect the reception of the cause. For example, when Lance Armstrong's popularity plummeted in the wake of doping allegations, it tarnished the brand of the Livestrong Foundation,[3] the nonprofit he founded to support people affected by cancer.
(25) Livestrong does, however, continue today, after cutting ties with Armstrong and undergoing a radical rebranding.
    Even so, the following big names substantiate the idea that celebrity involvement brings massive amounts of attention and money to humanitarian causes and that, usually, this [sic] is a good thing....
(30)   Bono participates in fundraising concerts like Live 8, and has cofounded several philanthropies, like the ONE Campaign and Product (RED). He also created EDUN, a fashion brand that strives to stimulate trade in Africa

---

[1] Bunting, Madeline. "The Issue of Celebrities and Aid Is Deceptively Complex" http://www.theguardian.com, Dec. 17, 2010
[2] Budabin, Alexandra Cosima. "Do Celebrity Humanitarians Matter?" http://www.carnegiecouncil.org, December 11, 2014
[3] Gardner, Eriq. "Livestrong Struggles After Lance Armstrong's Fall" http://www.hollywoodreporter.com, 7/25/2013

by sourcing production there. He has received three nominations for the Nobel Peace Prize, was knighted by the United Kingdom in 2007, and was (35) named Time's 2005 Person of the Year. . . .

Popular singer Akon may not be as famous for his philanthropic work as Angelina Jolie or Bono, but he is in a unique position to help, as he has deep roots in the areas in which he works: He was raised in Senegal in a community without electricity, which inspired his latest project, Akon (40) Lighting Africa. He also founded the Konfidence Foundation, raising awareness of conditions in Africa and providing underprivileged African youth access to education and other resources. . . .

In weighing the pros and cons of celebrity activism, perhaps [Ben] Affleck himself summed it up best in an essay reflecting on the constraints (45) and possibilities of his own engagement:

"It makes sense to be skeptical about celebrity activism. There is always suspicion that involvement with a cause may be doing more good for the spokesman than he or she is doing for the cause. . .but I hope you can separate whatever reservations you may have from what is unimpeachably (50) important."

—Jenica Funk
excerpted and adapted from "The Rise of the Celebrity Humanitarian"
www.globalenvision.org, January 29, 2015

PART 3—Text-Analysis Response

Your Task: Closely read the text on pages 109 through 111 and write a well-developed, text-based response of two to three paragraphs. In your response, identify a central idea in the text and analyze how the author's use of ***one*** writing strategy (literary element or literary technique or rhetorical device) develops this central idea. Use strong and thorough evidence from the text to support your analysis. Do *not* simply summarize the text. You may use the margins to take notes as you read and scrap paper to plan your response. Write your response on a separate sheet of paper.

Guidelines:

Be sure to

- Identify a central idea in the text.
- Analyze how the author's use of ***one*** writing strategy (literary element or literary technique or rhetorical device) develops this central idea. Examples include: characterization, conflict, denotation/connotation, metaphor, simile, irony, language use, point-of-view, setting, structure, symbolism, theme, tone, etc.
- Use strong and thorough evidence from the text to support your analysis.
- Organize your ideas in a cohesive and coherent manner.
- Maintain a formal style of writing.
- Follow the conventions of standard written English.

Text

It was my father who called the city the Mansion on the River. He was talking about Charleston, South Carolina, and he was a native son, peacock proud of a town so pretty it makes your eyes ache with pleasure just to walk down its spellbinding, narrow streets. Charleston was my father's
(5) ministry, his hobbyhorse, his quiet obsession, and the great love of his life. His bloodstream lit up my own with a passion for the city that I've never lost nor ever will. I'm Charleston-born, and bred. The city's two rivers, the Ashley and the Cooper, have flooded and shaped all the days of my life on this storied[1] peninsula.

(10) I carry the delicate porcelain beauty of Charleston like the hinged shell of some soft-tissued mollusk. My soul is peninsula-shaped and sun-hardened and river-swollen. The high tides of the city flood my consciousness each day, subject to the whims and harmonies of full moons rising out of the Atlantic. I grow calm when I see the ranks of palmetto trees pulling guard duty on the
(15) banks of Colonial Lake or hear the bells of St. Michael's calling cadence[2] in the cicada-filled trees along Meeting Street. Deep in my bones, I knew early that I was one of those incorrigible[3] creatures known as Charlestonians. It comes to me as a surprising form of knowledge that my time in the city is more vocation than gift; it is my destiny, not my choice. I consider it a high
(20) privilege to be a native of one of the loveliest American cities, not a high-kicking, glossy, or lipsticked city, not a city with bells on its fingers or brightly painted toenails, but a ruffled, low-slung city, understated and tolerant of nothing mismade or ostentatious.[4] Though Charleston feels a seersuckered, tuxedoed view of itself, it approves of restraint far more than vainglory.[5]

(25) As a boy, in my own backyard I could catch a basket of blue crabs, a string of flounder, a dozen redfish, or a net full of white shrimp. All this I could do in a city enchanting enough to charm cobras out of baskets, one so corniced and filigreed[6] and elaborate that it leaves strangers awed and natives self-satisfied. In its shadows you can find metalwork as delicate as
(30) lace and spiral staircases as elaborate as yachts. In the secrecy of its gardens you can discover jasmine and camellias and hundreds of other plants that look embroidered and stolen from the Garden of Eden for the sheer love of richness and the joy of stealing from the gods. In its kitchens, the stoves are

---

[1]storied—told of in history
[2]cadence—rhythmic recurrence of sound
[3]incorrigible—cannot be reformed
[4]ostentatious—showy
[5]vainglory—excessive pride
[6]corniced and filigreed—architecturally decorated

lit up in happiness as the lamb is marinating in red wine sauce, vinaigrette is
(35) prepared for the salad, crabmeat is anointed with sherry, custards are baked
in the oven, and buttermilk biscuits cool on the counter.

Because of its devotional, graceful attraction to food and gardens and
architecture, Charleston stands for all the principles that make living well
both a civic virtue and a standard. It is a rapturous, defining place to grow up.
(40) Everything I reveal to you now will be Charleston-shaped and Charleston-
governed, and sometimes even Charleston-ruined. But it is my fault and
not the city's that it came close to destroying me. Not everyone responds
to beauty in the same way. Though Charleston can do much, it can't always
improve on the strangeness of human behavior. But Charleston has a high
(45) tolerance for eccentricity and bemusement.[7] There is a tastefulness in its
gentility[8] that comes from the knowledge that Charleston is a permanent
dimple in the understated skyline, while the rest of us are only visitors. . . .

I turned out to be a late bloomer, which I long regretted. My parents
suffered needlessly because it took me so long to find my way to a place at
(50) their table. But I sighted the early signs of my recovery long before they
did. My mother had given up on me at such an early age that a comeback
was something she no longer even prayed for in her wildest dreams. Yet in
my anonymous and underachieving high school career, I laid the foundation
for a strong finish without my mother noticing that I was, at last, up to some
(55) good. I had built an impregnable castle of solitude for myself and then set
out to bring that castle down, no matter how serious the collateral damage
or who might get hurt.

I was eighteen years old and did not have a friend my own age. There
wasn't a boy in Charleston who would think about inviting me to a party or
(60) to come out to spend the weekend at his family's beach house.

I planned for all that to change. I had decided to become the most
interesting boy to ever grow up in Charleston, and I revealed this secret to
my parents.

Outside my house in the languid[9] summer air of my eighteenth year, I
(65) climbed the magnolia tree nearest to the Ashley River with the agility that
constant practice had granted me. From its highest branches, I surveyed
my city as it lay simmering in the hot-blooded saps of June while the sun
began to set, reddening the vest of cirrus clouds that had gathered along
the western horizon. In the other direction, I saw the city of rooftops and

---

[7]bemusement—bewilderment
[8]gentility—refinement
[9]languid—without energy

(70) columns and gables that was my native land. What I had just promised my parents, I wanted very much for them and for myself. Yet I also wanted it for Charleston. I desired to turn myself into a worthy townsman of such a many-storied city.

Charleston has its own heartbeat and fingerprint, its own mug shots (75) and photo ops and police lineups. It is a city of contrivance,[10] of blueprints; devotion to pattern that is like a bent knee to the nature of beauty itself. I could feel my destiny forming in the leaves high above the city. Like Charleston, I had my alleyways that were dead ends and led to nowhere, but mansions were forming like jewels in my bloodstream. Looking down, (80) I studied the layout of my city, the one that had taught me all the lures of attractiveness, yet made me suspicious of the showy or the makeshift. I turned to the stars and was about to make a bad throw of the dice and try to predict the future, but stopped myself in time.

A boy stopped in time, in a city of amber-colored life, that possessed the (85) glamour forbidden to a lesser angel.

—Pat Conroy
excerpted from *South of Broad*, 2009
Nan A. Talese

---

[10]contrivance—invention

Regents ELA Answers June 2016
English Language Arts

Answer Key

PART 1

1. 2	9. 3	17. 1
2. 3	10. 4	18. 4
3. 3	11. 1	19. 1
4. 1	12. 2	20. 2
5. 2	13. 4	21. 1
6. 3	14. 1	22. 2
7. 4	15. 2	23. 1
8. 1	16. 3	24. 3

PART 2 *See Answers and Explanations*

PART 3 *See Answers and Explanations*

Regents ELA Examination in English Language Arts-June 2016

Chart for Converting Total Weighted Raw Scores to Final Exam Scores (Scale Scores) (Use for the June 2016 examination only.)

Weighted Raw Score*	Scale Score	Performance Level	Weighted Raw Score*	Scale Score	Performance Level
56	100	5	27	60	2
55	99	5	26	57	2
54	98	5	25	55	2
53	97	5	24	51	1
52	96	5	23	47	1
51	95	5	22	44	1
50	94	5	21	40	1
49	93	5	20	37	1
48	93	5	19	33	1
47	92	5	18	29	1
46	91	5	17	25	1
45	90	5	16	22	1
44	89	5	15	18	1
43	88	5	14	15	1
42	87	5	13	11	1
41	86	5	12	9	1
40	85	5	11	8	1
39	83	4	10	7	1
38	82	4	9	6	1
37	81	4	8	5	1
36	79	4	7	4	1
35	78	3	6	3	1
34	76	3	5	3	1
33	74	3	4	2	1
32	72	3	3	2	1
31	70	3	2	1	1
30	67	3	1	1	1
29	65	3	0	0	1
28	62	2			

The conversion table is determined independently for each administration of the exam.

Answers Explained

PART 1—Reading Comprehension

Multiple-Choice Questions

Passage A

1. **2** "gloom." Of the choices, this is the best answer: the houses are "sombre," the light of the street lamps is "feeble," the air is biting cold, and the street is silent.

2. **3** "yet her name was like a summons [to all my foolish blood]." This line concludes the narrator's gradual revelation of his silent attraction to Mangan's sister: he watches for her daily, and when she appears, "my heart leaped." None of the other choices suggests the narrator's feelings.

3. **3** "disappointment." At line 32 Mangan's sister says that "she would love to go" and explains that she must attend a retreat at her school instead. The images of Mangan's sister turning the bracelet on her arm and bowing her head toward the narrator are also subtle indications of her disappointment. This answer best expresses Mangan's sister's feelings.

4. **1** "recognized that his priorities have changed." In this passage, the narrator reveals that he no longer cares to do well in school and that he "had hardly any patience with the serious work of life." What he had considered priorities before he now regards as "ugly, monotonous child's play."

5. **2** "isolation." The narrator takes his seat on the "deserted train" and "remained alone in the bare carriage." These details emphasize how alone the narrator feels on his journey to the bazaar.

6. **3** "false promise." In this passage, the narrator discovers that there is nothing here for him to buy, the young lady at the stand knows he is not a likely customer, and that his stay "was useless." There is no exotic and romantic world to be found in the bazaar; instead, the narrator finds only tea sets and vases he could not possibly afford or even want to buy for Mangan's sister.

7. **4** "romantic feelings." Romantic here refers both to the narrator's attraction to Mangan's sister and to the idea of *Araby* (the bazaar) as a distant place of exotic attraction and escape from the gloom of the Dublin neighborhood where they live.

8. **1** "taunted." Other synonyms for "derided" include "ridiculed," "mocked," and "scorned." The narrator feels foolish and ashamed for acting on his romantic notions. None of the other choices expresses the narrator's feelings here.

9. **3** "realized his limitations." This phrase best expresses the narrator's feelings. This phrase sums up the narrator's recognition of his foolish and naïve behavior cited in the questions above.

10. **4** "I lingered before her stall, though I knew my stay was useless." This line also best expresses the theme of the story. Note how the details cited in questions 6–9 lead to the answer to this question.

Passage B

11. **1** "repetition." The opening line reveals the key metaphor in the poem, but the main idea is strengthened through repetition, notably of "night" and "assembly line." There are no examples of simile, allusion, or understatement in the stanza, and metaphor is not offered as a choice.

12. **2** "humans and nature." The central idea in the second stanza is that "the stars must be exhausted" by years of unchanging work (journeys) and by choking smog and monotony. In line 17, the poet asserts that "We share" the same exhaustion, sickness, and loss of individuality ("their color and shape"). None of the other choices is suggested by the images in this stanza.

13. **4** "uncertainty." In lines 20–21, repetition of the phrases beginning with "perhaps" establishes the sense of uncertainty in the poet's voice. There is also a strong feeling of bitterness and regret in the poem, but the question focuses on the language in these two lines: "uncertainty" is the best answer among these choices.

14. **1** "resignation to life." The images in the last stanza reveal the poet's acceptance of a life that is manufactured and fated: she is numb to her existence and "unable to show concern." None of the other choices is suggested in these lines.

Passage C

15. **2** "perspective." The first sentence establishes Rodriguez's perspective in this passage: the memory of boyhood will "remind the adult" of how through language he grew out of his protected but linguistically limiting childhood.

16. **3** "contrasting cultures." In this paragraph, Rodriguez recalls how his parents struggled in the public world of English speakers but could recover, at home, the ease and comfort that speaking their native Spanish gave them. The contrast here is in cultures, not in memories, principles, or philosophies.

17. **1** "eagerness to learn." "Wide-eyed with hearing" is a lovely metaphor to describe how eager Rodriguez was to distinguish first the differences in sound between English and Spanish and to understand how the sounds of a language conveyed meaning even before he knew the words. The image of one who is wide-eyed conveys a sense of wonder and openness to take in something new.

18. **4** "separation." This paragraph further develops the contrast between the comfort and cultural ease of life at home and the challenges of interactions in the public, English-speaking world. How Rodriguez overcame this "separation" is the key theme of the passage.

19. **1** "communicate effectively." These lines are a vivid description of what it is like to try to communicate before one has sufficient language skills: he could not "form complete thoughts . . . make distinct [English] sounds"; and listeners struggled to hear what he was trying to say. This is the best answer among the choices.

20. **2** "conflicting feelings." The narrator claims at first that "it didn't matter much that my parents could not speak English with ease." "And yet . . . it mattered very much" because he found it unsettling and became nervous about a loss in their "protection and power."

21. **1** "narrator's sense of security." In this paragraph, Rodriguez describes the reassurance he would feel in hearing the sounds of the language of their life in private: he feels "recognized as one of the family . . . *someone special*." He felt "embraced by the sounds of their words." These are all feelings of security. None of the other choices expresses the feelings in this paragraph.

22. **2** "I'd listen to sounds more than to words." Throughout the passage, Rodriguez emphasizes the importance of sounds as he grows up and ultimately learns to speak fluent English. It is the sounds of Spanish that console and reassure him; it is the sounds of English in public that signal a different culture. He tells us toward the end of the passage that, "I lived in a world compounded of sounds." This is the best answer to the question.

23. **1** "disconnected from his family." In the final paragraph, Rodriguez describes the change, the loss, of "intimate sounds" at home: now the sounds are noises from life outside. He is hearing words, the words of public language. The disconnection from his family occurs as "my childhood started to end."

24. **3** "confidence." The act of raising his hand in class and speaking loudly, "to an entire roomful of faces," is a vivid image of the boy confident in expressing himself in the public world of English. None of the other choices captures the significance of what Rodriguez tells us here.

PART 2—Argument Response

Sample Essay Response

In recent years especially, there has been growing concern for conditions in third-world societies and the welfare of their people. Numerous non-profit organizations have been established to address the humanitarian issues in said societies through fundraising and charity. However, these organizations must grab people's attention to raise what they need to help other people in needy situations. What better way to do that than to use celebrities to promote the cause? There is a debate regarding the ethics of using celebrities to promote non-profit organizations, however. While some may believe that celebrities should not be the voice for humanitarian causes, I emphatically believe that celebrities should become the voice of such causes for two compelling reasons.

First, I believe that celebrities should be the voice of humanitarian causes because they can be actively involved by donating their money and their time. According to "The Celebrity Solution," "the premise of microfinance is that very poor people should have access to credit, just as the middle class and the rich do." (Text 1, lines 48–49) The article states that the support of microfinance projects by the actress Natalie Portman means poor people will benefit immensely.

"People come to see Natalie Portman, and they go away learning about microfinance." (Text 1, lines 70–71) According to the article "Do Celebrity Humanitarians Matter?" "celebrities are welcome figures in humanitarianism: educating the public on global issues, raising funds, and using their populist appeal to draw attention to policy-making arenas." (Text 3, lines 37–39) Basically the article is stating that celebrities can be directly involved in promoting and being dedicated to their causes by educating the public and raising money through concerts or other events.

However, "Do Celebrity Humanitarians Matter?" also claims that "For others, celebrity humanitarians are highly problematic figures who dilute debates, offer misguided policy proposals, and lack credibility and accountability." (Text 3, lines 39–41) I disagree with the previous statement because I believe celebrities can easily become educated themselves about a cause through their own research.

Secondly, celebrities have the ability to use their popularity to draw attention to a humanitarian cause. As "The Rise of the Celebrity Humanitarian" puts it, "Hollywood's elite get to wield their unique ability to engage diverse audiences, and the power of celebrity is put to good use effecting change." (Text 4, lines 8–10) Basically the article states that celebrities can influence change by using their popularity. With the use of social media on the rise, celebrities have a powerful means of connecting with the people to promote a cause. According to

"Ethics of Celebrities and Their Increasing Influence in 21st Century Society," "[c]elebrities and famous people in turn, help to bring people, including adults, together in conversation and social interaction." (Text 2, lines 45–46) This means that through the use of the Internet, celebrities can get the public involved in their cause. However, Text 4 also argues, "if the star's popularity takes a hit, it can affect the reception of the cause." (Text 4, lines 21–22) Although this has been known to happen, in the case of Lance Armstrong for example, humanitarian causes can recover from their celebrity spokesperson's decline in popularity and find a new voice for the cause.

I emphatically believe that celebrities should be the voice for humanitarian causes. Celebrities have an uncanny ability to draw attention to a cause, which in turn would undoubtedly benefit those in need.

Analysis

This essay offers a good example of the argument supporting the role of celebrities in humanitarian causes. The opening paragraph outlines the issue and clearly establishes the writer's position: first, with a rhetorical question, "What better way . . . than to use celebrities to promote the cause?" and then with a forceful assertion of the controlling idea: "I emphatically believe that celebrities should become the voice of such causes for two compelling reasons." The reference to a debate over the ethics of using celebrities for humanitarian causes at the beginning establishes that opposing views will be acknowledged.

The argument is organized clearly, with a paragraph devoted to each of the writer's claims. Key points are developed and supported with relevant references to all four texts: some give support to the writer's point of view and some offer opportunities to refute opposing arguments. Development is minimal but adequate; the conclusion is less forcefully expressed than the body of the argument is. The overall strategy of argument is sound, however, and the writer demonstrates control of the conventions. This argument would merit a high score.

(See pages 79–80 for the scoring guidelines.)

PART 3—Text-Analysis Response

Sample Essay Response

    In this passage, the author depicts Charleston, South Carolina, as an understated and beautiful place where anything is possible. The author feels that Charleston has the power to shape people and have an ever-lasting influence on their lives. This idea of Charleston's power is developed through the author's use of figurative language.

    The author is in awe of Charleston's beauty and subtle power. In lines 31–32, imagery is used when Charleston's gardens are described as containing "plants that look embroidered and stolen from the Garden of Eden." This description emphasizes how delicate and cared for Charleston is because embroidery involves delicate and intricate work. Also, by comparing something in Charleston to the Garden of Eden, it is elevated and placed on a holy level. Additionally, the author uses metaphor on lines 46–47 when he states that "Charleston is a permanent dimple in the understated skyline, while the rest of us are only visitors." This emphasizes Charleston's permanence and subtle power. While people may come and go, Charleston is forever. Lastly, Charleston is personified at line 74 when it is given "its own heartbeat and fingerprint."

    By giving Charleston life-like qualities, the author dramatizes the city's power. Charleston is elevated by being compared to a human. The author feels blessed and honored to have grown up in a place like Charleston, and this passage shows its significant and omnipresent force in his life.

Analysis

This richness of language and passionate feelings of the author give students a number of ways to discuss this passage. Point of view is an obvious choice, as are diction, tone, and theme. This writer chose figurative language as a focus for analysis and offers excellent examples of imagery, metaphor, and personification. The essay has a clear plan of development: the opening paragraph expresses the overall theme of the passage and establishes the writer's controlling idea. The second paragraph offers three relevant examples of figurative language, and each is illustrated with an appropriate quote from the passage. Note too that the examples are developed in order of their significance to the overall theme. The final paragraph is a strong statement of how the figurative language supports the author's theme. The writing is clear and demonstrates the writer's control of the conventions. This response would merit a high score.

(See pages 81–82 for the scoring guidelines.)

Regents ELA Examination August 2016
English Language Arts

PART 1—Reading Comprehension

Directions (1–24): Closely read each of the three passages below. After each passage, there are several multiple-choice questions. Select the best suggested answer to each question and write its number in the space provided. You may use the margins to take notes as you read.

Reading Comprehension Passage A

...Three years in London had not changed Richard, although it had changed the way he perceived the city. Richard had originally imagined London as a gray city, even a black city, from pictures he had seen, and he was surprised to find it filled with color. It was a city of red brick and white
(5) stone, red buses and large black taxis, bright red mailboxes and green grassy parks and cemeteries....

Two thousand years before, London had been a little Celtic village on the north shore of the Thames, which the Romans had encountered, then settled in. London had grown, slowly, until, roughly a thousand years later, it
(10) met the tiny Royal City of Westminster immediately to the west, and, once London Bridge had been built, London touched the town of Southwark directly across the river; and it continued to grow, fields and woods and marshland slowly vanishing beneath the flourishing town, and it continued to expand, encountering other little villages and hamlets as it grew, like
(15) Whitechapel and Deptford to the east, Hammersmith and Shepherd's Bush to the west, Camden and Islington in the north, Battersea and Lambeth across the Thames to the south, absorbing all of them, just as a pool of mercury encounters and incorporates smaller beads of mercury, leaving only their names behind.

London grew into something huge and contradictory. It was a good place, and a fine city, but there is a price to be paid for all good places, and a price that all good places have to pay.

After a while, Richard found himself taking London for granted; in time, he began to pride himself on having visited none of the sights of London (except for the Tower of London, when his Aunt Maude came down to the city for a weekend, and Richard found himself her reluctant escort).

But Jessica changed all that. Richard found himself, on otherwise sensible weekends, accompanying her to places like the National Gallery and the Tate Gallery, where he learned that walking around museums too long hurts your feet, that the great art treasures of the world all blur into each other after a while, and that it is almost beyond the human capacity for belief to accept how much museum cafeterias will brazenly charge for a slice of cake and a cup of tea. . . .

Richard had been awed by Jessica, who was beautiful, and often quite funny, and was certainly going somewhere. And Jessica saw in Richard an enormous amount of potential, which, properly harnessed by the right woman, would have made him the perfect matrimonial accessory. If only he were a little more focused, she would murmur to herself, and so she gave him books with titles like *Dress for Success* and *A Hundred and Twenty-Five Habits of Successful Men*, and books on how to run a business like a military campaign, and Richard always said thank you, and always intended to read them. In Harvey Nichols's men's fashion department she would pick out for him the kinds of clothes she thought that he should wear—and he wore them, during the week, anyway; and, a year to the day after their first encounter, she told him she thought it was time that they went shopping for an engagement ring.

"Why do you go out with her?" asked Gary, in Corporate Accounts, eighteen months later. "She's terrifying."

Richard shook his head. "She's really sweet, once you get to know her."

Gary put down the plastic troll doll he had picked up from Richard's desk. "I'm surprised she still lets you play with these." . . .

It was a Friday afternoon. Richard had noticed that events were cowards: they didn't occur singly, but instead they would run in packs and leap out at him all at once. Take this particular Friday, for example. It was, as Jessica had pointed out to him at least a dozen times in the last month, the most important day of his life. So it was unfortunate that, despite the Post-it note Richard had left on his fridge door at home, and the other Post-it note he had placed on the photograph of Jessica on his desk, he had forgotten about it completely and utterly.

(60)   Also, there was the Wandsworth report, which was overdue and taking up most of his head. Richard checked another row of figures; then he noticed that page 17 had vanished, and he set it up to print out again; and another page down, and he knew that if he were only left alone to finish it . . . if, miracle of miracles, the phone did not ring. . . . It rang. He thumbed
(65) the speakerphone.

"Hello? Richard? The managing director needs to know when he'll have the report."

Richard looked at his watch. "Five minutes, Sylvia. It's almost wrapped up. I just have to attach the P & L projection."

(70)   "Thanks, Dick. I'll come down for it." Sylvia was, as she liked to explain, "the MD's PA," [Managing Director's Personal Assistant] and she moved in an atmosphere of crisp efficiency. He thumbed the speaker phone off; it rang again, immediately. "Richard," said the speaker, with Jessica's voice, "it's Jessica. You haven't forgotten, have you?"

(75)   "Forgotten?" He tried to remember what he could have forgotten. He looked at Jessica's photograph for inspiration and found all the inspiration he could have needed in the shape of a yellow Post-it note stuck to her forehead.

"Richard? Pick up the telephone."

(80)   He picked up the phone, reading the Post-it note as he did so. "Sorry, Jess. No, I hadn't forgotten. Seven P.M., at Ma Maison Italiano. Should I meet you there?"

"Jessica, Richard. Not Jess." She paused for a moment. "After what happened last time? I don't think so. You really could get lost in your own
(85) backyard, Richard." . . .

"I'll meet you at your place," said Jessica. "We can walk down together."

"Right, Jess. Jessica—sorry."

"You *have* confirmed our reservation, haven't you, Richard."

"Yes," lied Richard earnestly. The other line on his phone had begun to
(90) ring. "Jessica, look, I. . ."

"Good," said Jessica, and she broke the connection. He picked up the other line.

"Hi Dick. It's me, Gary." Gary sat a few desks down from Richard. He waved. "Are we still on for drinks? You said we could go over the Merstham
(95) account."

"Get off the bloody phone, Gary. Of course we are." Richard put down the phone. There was a telephone number at the bottom of the Post-it note; Richard had written the Post-it note to himself, several weeks earlier. And he *had* made the reservation: he was almost certain of that. But he had not

(100) confirmed it. He had kept meaning to, but there had been so much to do and Richard had known that there was plenty of time. But events run in packs...

Sylvia was now standing next to him. "Dick? The Wandsworth report?"
"Almost ready, Sylvia. Look, just hold on a sec, can you?"
(105) He finished punching in the number, breathed a sigh of relief when somebody answered. "Ma Maison. Can I help you?"
"Yes," said Richard. "A table for three, for tonight. I think I booked it. And if I did I'm confirming the reservation. And if I didn't, I wondered if I could book it. Please." No, they had no record of a table for tonight in the
(110) name of Mayhew. Or Stockton. Or Bartram—Jessica's surname. And as for booking a table...

They had put down the phone.
"Richard?" said Sylvia. "The MD's waiting."
"Do you think," asked Richard, "they'd give me a table if I phoned back
(115) and offered them extra money?"...

—Neil Gaiman
excerpted and adapted from *Neverwhere*, 1997
Avon Books

1 The author most likely includes the description of London in lines 1 through 22 to

   (1) provide reasons for Richard's dislike of the city
   (2) highlight opportunities for Richard's career in the city
   (3) convey a sense of Richard's frustration with the city
   (4) illustrate the nature of Richard's life in the city   1 _____

2 The figurative language used in lines 17 to 19 reinforces the

   (1) growth of the city
   (2) problems with development
   (3) increase in isolation
   (4) history of the towns   2 _____

3 The narrator uses lines 27 through 33 to help the reader understand Richard's

   (1) continuous efforts to save money while on dates
   (2) willingness to tolerate undesirable situations to please others
   (3) overall acceptance of cultural experiences in the city
   (4) affection for newfound experiences when shared with others   3 _____

4 In the context of the text as a whole, which statement regarding lines 47 through 49 is true?

   (1) Gary is jealous of Richard because he has a girlfriend.
   (2) Gary has a moody temperament and hides his feelings.
   (3) Richard has a plan and wishes to keep it a secret.
   (4) Richard is in a state of denial regarding his relationship.   4 _____

5 How do lines 52 through 54 contribute to the characterization of Richard?

   (1) by portraying him as inefficient at organizing his time
   (2) by indicating that he works well under pressure
   (3) by describing him as likely to succeed
   (4) by suggesting that he is unmotivated in his job   5 _____

6 The narrator's description of Sylvia as moving "in an atmosphere of crisp efficiency" (lines 71 and 72) presents a

(1) shift
(2) possibility
(3) contrast
(4) solution

7 Lines 79 through 85 contribute to a central idea by highlighting Jessica's

(1) domineering nature
(2) compassionate side
(3) lack of responsibility
(4) sense of humor

8 The narrator's use of dialogue in lines 79 through 96 enhances a mood of

(1) satisfaction
(2) stress
(3) confidence
(4) remorse

9 Richard's question in lines 114 and 115 reveals his

(1) subtle refinement
(2) suppressed hostility
(3) honest gratitude
(4) quiet desperation

10 Which quote best reflects a central theme in the text?

(1) "London grew into something huge and contradictory . . . and a price that all good places have to pay." (lines 20 through 22)
(2) "Richard checked another row of figures . . . and he set it up to print out again;" (lines 61 and 62)
(3) "Richard looked at his watch. 'Five minutes, Sylvia. It's almost wrapped up. I just have to attach the P & L projection.' " (lines 68 and 69)
(4) "He finished punching in the number, breathed a sigh of relief when somebody answered. 'Ma Maison. Can I help you?' " (lines 105 and 106)

Reading Comprehension Passage B

We Are Many

Of the many men whom I am, whom we are,
I cannot settle on a single one.
They are lost to me under the cover of clothing.
They have departed for another city.

(5) When everything seems to be set
to show me off as a man of intelligence,
the fool I keep concealed on my person
takes over my talk and occupies my mouth.

On other occasions, I am dozing in the midst
(10) of people of some distinction,
and when I summon my courageous self,
a coward completely unknown to me
swaddles[1] my poor skeleton
in a thousand tiny reservations.

(15) When a stately home bursts into flames,
instead of the fireman I summon,
an arsonist bursts on the scene,
and he is I. There is nothing I can do.
What must I do to distinguish myself?
(20) How can I put myself together?

All the books I read
lionize[2] dazzling hero figures,
always brimming with self-assurance.
I die with envy of them;
(25) and, in films where bullets fly on the wind,
I am left in envy of the cowboys,
left admiring even the horses.

---

[1]swaddles—wraps   [2]lionize—glorify

But when I call upon my dashing being,
out comes the same old lazy self,
(30) and so I never know just who I am,
nor how many I am, nor who we will be being.
I would like to be able to touch a bell
and call up my real self, the truly me,
because if I really need my proper self,
(35) I must not allow myself to disappear.

While I am writing, I am far away;
and when I come back, I have already left.
I should like to see if the same thing happens
to other people as it does to me,
(40) to see if as many people are as I am,
and if they seem the same way to themselves.
When this problem has been thoroughly explored,
I am going to school myself so well in things
that, when I try to explain my problems,
(45) I shall speak, not of self, but of geography.

—Pablo Neruda
from *We Are Many*, 1970
translated by Alastair Reid
Grossman Publishers

11 The overall purpose of the figurative language in lines 12 through 14 is to show the narrator's

(1) contempt for self-reliance
(2) desire for adventure
(3) lack of self-confidence
(4) jealousy of writers   11 ____

12 A primary function of the questions in lines 19 and 20 is to

(1) introduce the narrator's biases
(2) challenge the narrator's beliefs
(3) clarify the narrator's dilemma
(4) explain the narrator's decision   12 ____

13 The contradictions presented throughout the poem serve to illustrate the relationship between

(1) society's conflicts and the narrator's reaction
(2) the narrator's sensibilities and his determination
(3) society's expectations and the narrator's possibilities
(4) the narrator's idealism and his reality   13 ____

14 The solution proposed in lines 42 through 45 can best be described as

(1) balanced   (3) inappropriate
(2) universal   (4) unrealistic   14 ____

Reading Comprehension Passage C

...By natural design, dogs' ears have evolved to hear certain kinds of sounds. Happily, that set of sounds overlaps with those we can hear and produce: if we utter it, it will at least hit the eardrum of a nearby dog. Our auditory range is from 20 hertz to 20 kilohertz: from the lowest pitch on
(5) the longest organ pipe to an impossibly squeaky squeak. We spend most of our time straining to understand sounds between 100 hertz and 1 kilohertz, the range of any interesting speech going on in the vicinity. Dogs hear most of what we hear and then some. They can detect sounds up to 45 kilohertz, much higher than the hair cells of our ears bother to bend to. Hence the
(10) power of the dog whistle, a seemingly magical device that makes no apparent sound and yet perks the ears of dogs for blocks around. We call this sound "ultrasonic," since it's beyond our ken,[1] but it is within the sonic range for many animals in our local environment. Don't think for a moment that apart from the occasional dog whistle, the world is quiet for dogs up at those high
(15) registers. Even a typical room is pulsing with high frequencies, detectable by dogs constantly. Think your bedroom is quiet when you rise in the morning? The crystal resonator used in digital alarm clocks emits a never-ending alarm of high-frequency pulses audible to canine ears. Dogs can hear the navigational chirping of rats behind your walls and the bodily vibrations of
(20) termites within your walls. That compact fluorescent light you installed to save energy? You may not hear the hum, but your dog probably can.

    The range of pitches we are most intent on are those used in speech. Dogs hear all sounds of speech, and are nearly as good as we are at detecting a change of pitch—relevant, say, for understanding statements, which end
(25) in a low pitch, versus questions, which in English end in a raised pitch: "Do you want to go for a walk(?)" With the question mark, this sentence is exciting to a dog with experience going on walks with humans. Without it, it is simply noise. Imagine the confusion generated by the recent growth of "up-talking," speech that ends every sentence with the sound of a question?

(30)   If dogs understand the stress and tones—the *prosody*—of speech, does this hint that they understand language? This is a natural but vexed[2] question. Since language use is one of the most glaring differences between the human animal and all other animals, it has been proposed as the ultimate, incomparable criterion for intelligence. This raises serious hackles[3] in some
(35) animal researchers (not thought of as a hackled species, ironically), who have

---

[1]ken—recognition   [2]vexed—problematic   [3]raises serious hackles—arouses anger

set about trying to demonstrate what linguistic ability animals have. Even those researchers who may agree that language is necessary for intelligence have nonetheless added reams of results to the growing pile of evidence of linguistic ability in non-human animals. All parties agree, though, (40) that there has been no discovery of a humanlike language—a corpus[4] of infinitely combinable words that often carry many definitions, with rules for combining words into meaningful sentences—in animals.

This is not to say that animals might not understand some of our language use, even if they don't produce it themselves. There are, for (45) instance, many examples of animals taking advantage of the communicative system of nearby unrelated animal species. Monkeys can make use of nearby birds' warning calls of a nearby predator to themselves take protective action. Even an animal who deceives another animal by mimicry—which some snakes, moths, and even flies can do—is in some way using another (50) species's [sic] language.

The research with dogs suggests that they do understand language—to a limited degree. On the one hand, to say that dogs understand *words* is a misnomer. Words exist in a language, which itself is product of a culture; dogs are participants in that culture on a very different level. Their framework (55) for understanding the application of the word is entirely different. There is, no doubt, more to the words of their world than Gary Larson's *Far Side* comics suggest: eat, walk, and fetch. But he is on to something, insofar as these are organizing elements of their interaction with us: we circumscribe the dog's world to a small set of activities. Working dogs seem miraculously (60) responsive and focused compared to city pets. It is not that they are innately more responsive or focused, but that their owners have added to their vocabularies types of things to do.

One component in understanding a word is the ability to discriminate it from other words. Given their sensitivity to the prosody of speech, dogs do (65) not always excel at this. Try asking your dog on one morning to *go for a walk*; on the next, ask if your dog wants to *snow forty locks* in the same voice. If everything else remains the same, you'll probably get the same, affirmative reaction. The very first sounds of an utterance seem to be important to dog perception, though, so changing the swallowed consonants for articulated (70) ones and the long vowels for short ones—*ma for a polk?*—might prompt the confusion merited by this gibberish. Of course humans read meaning into prosody, too. English does not give the prosody of speech syntactical leverage but it is still part of how we interpret "what has just been said."

---

[4]corpus—collection

If we were more sensitive to the *sound* of what we say to dogs, we might
(75) get better responses from them. High-pitched sounds mean something
different than low sounds; rising sounds contrast with falling sounds. It is
not accidental that we find ourselves cooing to an infant in silly, giddy
tones (called *motherese*)—and might greet a wagging dog with similar baby
talk. Infants can hear other speech sounds, but they are more interested
(80) in motherese. Dogs, too, respond with alacrity[5] to baby talk—partially
because it distinguishes speech that is directed *at* them from the rest of the
continuous yammering above their heads. Moreover, they will come more
easily to high-pitched and repeated call requests than to those at a lower
pitch. What is the ecology behind this? High-pitched sounds are naturally
(85) interesting to dogs: they might indicate the excitement of a tussle or the
shrieking of nearby injured prey. If a dog fails to respond to your reasonable
suggestion that he come *right now*, resist the urge to lower and sharpen
your tone. It indicates your frame of mind—and the punishment that might
ensue for his prior uncooperativeness. Correspondingly, it is easier to get a
(90) dog to *sit* on command to a longer, descending tone rather than repeated,
rising notes. Such a tone might be more likely to induce relaxation, or
preparation for the next command from their talky human. . . .

—Alexandra Horowitz
excerpted from *Inside of a Dog*, 2010
Scribner

---

[5]alacrity—eagerness

15 Lines 1 through 13 introduce the central idea of the passage by

(1) explaining how ear structure affects sound
(2) describing various frequencies dogs hear
(3) explaining various ways humans hear
(4) describing how dog whistle tones differ   15 _____

16 Lines 22 through 26 best support the idea that

(1) dogs cannot learn to obey human signals
(2) human actions are difficult for dogs to interpret
(3) humans can verbally communicate with dogs
(4) dogs can learn complex human language   16 _____

17 Based on lines 22 through 29, humans can possibly confuse dogs by

(1) speaking to dogs in a nonsense language
(2) giving dogs only direct commands
(3) making gestures when speaking to dogs
(4) altering the intonation of familiar words   17 _____

18 Lines 30 through 34 that language use is an indicator of

(1) higher-level thinking
(2) basic survival instinct
(3) increased emotional response
(4) problem-solving skills   18 _____

19 In lines 39 through 42, the author states there is agreement that non-human animals cannot

(1) master complicated directions
(2) duplicate human sound pitches
(3) create human sentence structures
(4) interpret foreign languages   19 _____

20 The primary function of the examples in lines 44 through 50 is to show how some animals can

(1) imitate behavior and sound
(2) foster community and diversity
(3) transform from prey to predator
(4) compromise freedom for safety   20 _____

21 The author uses the term "gibberish" in line 71 to emphasize the

(1) importance of word order
(2) complexity of spoken sounds
(3) relevance of hidden gestures
(4) necessity of voice and movement   21 _____

22 Which sentence best restates a central idea in lines 68 through 76?

(1) High-pitched sounds often cause dogs to become agitated.
(2) How we speak to dogs is more important than what we say.
(3) Dogs must learn to interpret human speech early in life.
(4) Dogs become distressed when they hear baby talk.   22 _____

23 The author's reference to "motherese" (line 78) helps to illustrate a connection between the

(1) combinations of languages and the effects on listeners
(2) volume of speech and possible misperception
(3) importance of word choice and its impact on understanding
(4) styles of spoken communication and likely responses   23 _____

24 The primary purpose of the text is to

(1) explain a popular myth regarding dogs' behavior
(2) promote a new method for working with dogs
(3) educate people about dogs' experience with sound
(4) present an alternative to traditional dog training   24 _____

PART 2—Argument Response

Directions Closely read each of the *four* texts on pages 137 through 145 and write a source-based argument on the topic below. You may use the margins to take notes as you read and scrap paper to plan your response. Write your argument on a separate sheet of paper.

Topic: Should the United States government create strict sugar regulations?

Your Task: Carefully read each of the *four* texts provided. Then, using evidence from at least *three* of the texts, write a well-developed argument regarding whether or not the United States government should create strict sugar regulations. Clearly establish your claim, distinguish your claim from alternate or opposing claims, and use specific, relevant, and sufficient evidence from at least *three* of the texts to develop your argument. Do *not* simply summarize each text.

Guidelines:

Be sure to

- Establish your claim regarding whether or not the United States government should create strict sugar regulations.
- Distinguish your claim from alternate or opposing claims.
- Use specific, relevant, and sufficient evidence from at least *three* of the texts to develop your argument.
- Identify each source that you reference by text number and line number(s) or graphic (for example: Text 1, line 4 or Text 2, graphic).
- Organize your ideas in a cohesive and coherent manner.
- Maintain a formal style of writing.
- Follow the conventions of standard written English.

Texts:

Text 1—FDA Urged to Regulate Sugar in Drinks

Text 2—Sugar Should Be Regulated As Toxin, Researchers Say

Text 3—The Toxic Truth About Sugar

Text 4—Sugar Taxes Are Unfair and Unhealthy

Text 1

FDA Urged to Regulate Sugar in Drinks

   WASHINGTON—The US Food and Drug Administration [FDA] should regulate the amount of added sugars in soda and other sweetened beverages to reverse the obesity epidemic, a Washington-based nutrition activist group urged in a petition signed by Harvard School of Public Health
(5) researchers, the Boston Public Health Commission, and others.
   "The FDA considers sugar to be a safe food at the recommended level of consumption, but Americans are consuming two to three times that much," Michael Jacobson, executive director of the Center for Science in the Public Interest, which filed the petition, said at a press briefing on Wednesday. He
(10) added that the average American consumes 78 pounds of added sugars each year, mostly from high fructose corn syrup prevalent in sugary sodas, sports drinks, and fruit punch. . . .
   Over the past half-century, Americans have dramatically increased their intake of sugary drinks, and research suggests this has contributed to
(15) the obesity epidemic and a rise in related diseases such as type 2 diabetes, heart disease, and a variety of cancers.
   "The evidence is very robust that when we eat more sugar we gain weight and when we eat less, we lose weight," said Dr. Walter Willett, chairman of nutrition at the Harvard School of Public Health, who also spoke at the
(20) briefing. "Each 12-ounce serving of soda a person consumes each day raises type 2 diabetes risk by 10 to 15 percent, and many Americans are consuming five or six servings."
   While the FDA has the authority to set limits on ingredients on its "generally recognized as safe" list, it has not done so for many of them,
(25) including table sugar and high fructose corn syrup.
   Jeffrey Senger, former acting chief counsel of the FDA who is now a partner at the law firm Sidley Austin, said it is unlikely the agency would act to restrict sugar. "Any food, if it's abused, can be unhealthy," he said. "Sugar isn't the same thing as arsenic. It's not a food that's inherently unsafe." . . .
(30)   She [FDA spokeswoman, Shelly Burgess] confirmed that the latest petition was received and would be reviewed by FDA officials, but added that the FDA was not aware of any evidence highlighting added safety risks from high fructose corn syrup compared with other sugars such as honey, table sugar, or molasses.

(35) That suggests that the agency might have a hard time requiring Coke or Pepsi to limit their products to 10 grams of added sugar per serving—what many public health specialists recommend—without also requiring the same limits on cereal, baked goods, and other processed foods.

"To limit the amount of added sugars in beverages, the FDA would (40) need to establish that there is enough scientific evidence to justify limiting these ingredients and to go through a rulemaking process that allows for public comment," said Miriam Guggenheim, a partner in the food and beverage practice at Covington & Burling LLP in Washington, D.C.

Taking a firm position against government regulations to limit added (45) sugars, the American Beverage Association, which represents soft drink manufacturers, pointed out in a statement on its website that companies have already made efforts to reduce sugar in sweetened beverages.

"Today about 45 percent of all non-alcoholic beverages purchased have zero calories," the group said, "and the overall average number of calories (50) per beverage serving is down 23 percent since 1998." . . .

About half of Americans consume sugary beverages on any given day, according to the latest data from the federal Centers for Disease Control and Prevention, and consumption of sugary beverages has increased among children and adults over the past 30 years.

—Deborah Kotz
excerpted and adapted from "FDA Urged to Regulate Sugar in Drinks"
http://www.bostonglobe.com, February 14, 2013

Text 2

Sugar Should Be Regulated As Toxin, Researchers Say

A spoonful of sugar might make the medicine go down. But it also makes blood pressure and cholesterol go up, along with your risk for liver failure, obesity, heart disease and diabetes.
Sugar and other sweeteners are, in fact, so toxic to the human body that
(5) they should be regulated as strictly as alcohol by governments worldwide, according to a commentary in the current issue of the journal Nature by researchers at the University of California, San Francisco (UCSF).
The researchers propose regulations such as taxing all foods and drinks that include added sugar, banning sales in or near schools and placing age
(10) limits on purchases.
Although the commentary might seem straight out of the Journal of Ideas That Will Never Fly, the researchers cite numerous studies and statistics to make their case that added sugar—or, more specifically, sucrose, an even mix of glucose and fructose found in high-fructose corn syrup and in
(15) table sugar made from sugar cane and sugar beets—has been as detrimental to society as alcohol and tobacco.

Sour words about sugar

. . .Many researchers are seeing sugar as not just "empty calories," but rather a chemical that becomes toxic in excess. At issue is the fact that glucose from complex carbohydrates, such as whole grains, is safely metabolized by
(20) cells throughout the body, but the fructose element of sugar is metabolized primarily by the liver. This is where the trouble can begin—taxing the liver, causing fatty liver disease, and ultimately leading to insulin resistance, the underlying causes of obesity and diabetes.
Added sugar, more so than the fructose in fiber-rich fruit, hits the liver
(25) more directly and can cause more damage—in laboratory rodents, anyway. Some researchers, however, remained unconvinced of the evidence of sugar's toxic effect on the human body at current consumption levels, as high as they are.

Economists to the rescue

[Robert] Lustig, a medical doctor in UCSF's Department of Pediatrics, compares added sugar to tobacco and alcohol (coincidentally made from sugar) in that it is addictive, toxic and has a negative impact on society, thus meeting established public health criteria for regulation. Lustig advocates a consumer tax on any product with added sugar.

Among Lustig's more radical proposals are to ban the sale of sugary drinks to children under age 17 and to tighten zoning laws for the sale of sugary beverages and snacks around schools and in low-income areas plagued by obesity, analogous to alcoholism and alcohol regulation.

Economists, however, debate as to whether a consumer tax—such as a soda tax proposed in many U.S. states—is the most effective means of curbing sugar consumption. Economists at Iowa State University led by John Beghin suggest taxing the sweetener itself at the manufacturer level, not the end product containing sugar.

This concept, published last year in the journal Contemporary Economic Policy, would give companies an incentive to add less sweetener to their products. After all, high-fructose corn syrup is ubiquitous[1] in food in part because it is so cheap and serves as a convenient substitute for more high-quality ingredients, such as fresher vegetables in processed foods.

Some researchers argue that saturated fat, not sugar, is the root cause of obesity and chronic disease. Others argue that it is highly processed foods with simple carbohydrates. Still others argue that it is a lack of physical exercise. It could, of course, be a matter of all these issues.

—Christopher Wanjek
excerpted and adapted from "Sugar Should Be Regulated As Toxin, Researchers Say"
http://www.livescience.com, February 1, 2012

---

[1]ubiquitous—present everywhere

Text 3

The Toxic Truth About Sugar

...No Ordinary Commodity

    In 2003, social psychologist Thomas Babor and his colleagues published a landmark book called *Alcohol: No Ordinary Commodity*, in which they established four criteria, now largely accepted by the public-health community, that justify the regulation of alcohol—unavoidability (or
(5) pervasiveness throughout society), toxicity, potential for abuse and negative impact on society. Sugar meets the same criteria, and we believe that it similarly warrants some form of societal intervention.

    First, consider unavoidability. Evolutionarily, sugar as fruit was available to our ancestors for only a few months a year (at harvest time), or as honey, which
(10) was guarded by bees. But in recent years, sugar has been added to virtually every processed food, limiting consumer choice. Nature made sugar hard to get; man made it easy. In many parts of the world, people are consuming an average of more than 500 calories per day from added sugar alone.

    Now, let's consider toxicity. A growing body of epidemiological and
(15) mechanistic[1] evidence argues that excessive sugar consumption affects human health beyond simply adding calories. Importantly, sugar induces all of the diseases associated with metabolic syndrome. This includes: hypertension (fructose increases uric acid, which raises blood pressure); high triglycerides and insulin resistance through synthesis of fat in the liver;
(20) diabetes from increased liver glucose production combined with insulin resistance; and the ageing process, caused by damage to lipids, proteins and DNA [deoxyribonucleic acid] through non-enzymatic binding of fructose to these molecules. It can also be argued that fructose exerts toxic effects on the liver similar to those of alcohol. This is no surprise, because alcohol is
(25) derived from the fermentation of sugar. Some early studies have also linked sugar consumption to human cancer and cognitive decline.

    Sugar also has a clear potential for abuse. Like tobacco and alcohol, it acts on the brain to encourage subsequent intake. There are now numerous studies examining the dependence-producing properties of sugar
(30) in humans. Specifically, sugar dampens the suppression of the hormone ghrelin, which signals hunger to the brain. It also interferes with the normal transport and signalling of the hormone leptin, which helps to produce the

---

[1]epidemiological and mechanistic—evidence based on the study of the causes, incidence, and treatment of diseases

feeling of satiety.[2] And it reduces dopamine signalling in the brain's reward centre, thereby decreasing the pleasure derived from food and compelling
(35) the individual to consume more.

Finally, consider the negative effects of sugar on society. Passive smoking and drink-driving fatalities provided strong arguments for tobacco and alcohol control, respectively. The long-term economic, health-care and human costs of metabolic syndrome place sugar overconsumption in the
(40) same category. The United States spends $65 billion in lost productivity and $150 billion on health-care resources annually for co-morbidities[3] associated with metabolic syndrome. Seventy-five per cent of all US health-care dollars are now spent on treating these diseases and resultant disabilities. Because 75% of military applicants are now rejected for obesity-related reasons, the
(45) past three US surgeons general and the chairman of the US Joint Chiefs of Staff have declared obesity a "threat to national security."

How to Intervene

How can we reduce sugar consumption? After all, sugar is natural. Sugar is a nutrient. Sugar is pleasure. So is alcohol, but in both cases, too much of a good thing is toxic. It may be helpful to look to the many generations of
(50) international experience with alcohol and tobacco to find models that work. So far, evidence shows that individually focused approaches, such as school-based interventions that teach children about diet and exercise, demonstrate little efficacy.[4] Conversely, for both alcohol and tobacco, there is robust evidence that gentle 'supply side' control strategies which stop far short of
(55) all-out prohibition—taxation, distribution controls, age limits—lower both consumption of the product and accompanying health harms. Successful interventions all share a common end-point: curbing availability. . . .

---

[2]satiety—fullness
[3]co-morbidities—diseases that occur simultaneously
[4]efficacy—power to produce an effect

DEADLY EFFECT	
Excessive consumption of fructose can cause many of the same health problems as alcohol.	
Chronic ethanol exposure	**Chronic fructose exposure**
Hematologic disorders	
Electrolyte abnormalities	
Hypertension	Hypertension (uric acid)
Cardiac dilatation	
Cardiomyopathy	Myocardial infarction (dyslipidemia, insulin resistance)
Dyslipidemia	Dyslipidemia (de novo lipogenesis)
Pancreatitis	Pancreatitis (hypertriglyceridemia)
Obesity (insulin resistance)	Obesity (insulin resistance)
Malnutrition	Malnutrition (obesity)
Hepatic dysfunction (alcoholic steatohepatitis)	Hepatic dysfunction (non-alcoholic steatohepatitis)
Fetal alcohol syndrome	
Addiction	Habituation, if not addiction

The Possible Dream

Government-imposed regulations on the marketing of alcohol to young people have been quite effective, but there is no such approach to sugar-
(60) laden products. Even so, the city of San Francisco, California, recently instituted a ban on including toys with unhealthy meals such as some types of fast food. A limit—or, ideally, ban—on television commercials for products with added sugars could further protect children's health. . . .

Ultimately, food producers and distributors must reduce the amount of
(65) sugar added to foods. But sugar is cheap, sugar tastes good, and sugar sells, so companies have little incentive to change. Although one institution alone can't turn this juggernaut[5] around, the US Food and Drug Administration could "set the table" for change. To start, it should consider removing fructose from the Generally Regarded as Safe (GRAS) list, which allows food
(70) manufacturers to add unlimited amounts to any food. Opponents will argue that other nutrients on the GRAS list, such as iron and vitamins A and D, can also be toxic when over-consumed. However, unlike sugar, these substances have no abuse potential. Removal from the GRAS list would send a powerful signal to the European Food Safety Authority and the rest of the world. . . .

—Robert H. Lustig, Laura A. Schmidt, and Claire D. Brindis
excerpted and adapted from "The Toxic Truth About Sugar"
Nature, February 2, 2012

---

[5]juggernaut—powerful force

Text 4

Sugar Taxes Are Unfair and Unhealthy

    If the regulatory discussion about sugar is going to be based on science, rather than science fiction, it needs to move beyond kicking the soda can.
    Conventional wisdom says draconian[1] regulation—specifically, a high tax—on sugary drinks and snacks reduces unhealthy consumption, and
(5) thereby improves public health. There are many reasons, however, why high sugar taxes are at best unsuccessful, and at worst economically and socially harmful.
    Research finds that higher prices don't reduce soda consumption, for example. No scientific studies demonstrate a difference either in aggregate[2]
(10) soda consumption or in child and adolescent Body Mass Index [BMI] between the two thirds of states with soda taxes and those without such taxes.
    The study that did find taxes might lead to a moderate reduction in soda consumption also found this had no effect on adolescent obesity, as
(15) the reduction was completely offset by increases in consumption of other calorific drinks.
    Economic research finds sugar taxes are a futile instrument in influencing the behavior and habits of the overweight and the obese. Why do sugar taxes fail? Those consumers who strongly prefer unhealthy foods
(20) continue to eat and drink according to their individual preferences until such time as it becomes prohibitively expensive to do so.
    Demand for food is largely insensitive to price. A 10 percent increase in price reduces consumption by less than 1 percent. Applied to soda, this means that to reduce consumption by 10 percent, the tax rate on sugary
(25) drinks would need to be 100 percent!
    A sugar tax also has undesirable social and economic consequences. This tax is economically regressive, as a disproportionate share of the tax is paid by low earners, who pay a higher proportion of their incomes in sales tax and also consume a disproportionate share of sugary snacks and drinks.
(30)   Such taxes also have perverse, unintended consequences. Taxes on sugary snacks lead many consumers to replace the taxed food with equally unhealthy foods. Poorer consumers react to higher food prices not by

---

[1] draconian—severe
[2] aggregate—total

changing their diets but by consuming even fewer healthy foods, such as fruits and vegetables, and eating more processed foods. For instance, taxes
(35) levied specifically on sugar content increase saturated fat consumption.

Sugar taxes have failed where they've been tried, and are unfair and unhealthy. Given that there's no compelling evidence they'll improve public health, we can't justify using the tax code to shape the sweetness of our dietary choices.

—Patrick Basham
excerpted and adapted from "Sugar Taxes Are Unfair and Unhealthy"
http://www.usnews.com, March 30, 2012

PART 3—Text-Analysis Response

Your Task: Closely read the text on pages 147 through 149 and write a well-developed, text-based response of two to three paragraphs. In your response, identify a central idea in the text and analyze how the author's use of ***one*** writing strategy (literary element or literary technique or rhetorical device) develops this central idea. Use strong and thorough evidence from the text to support your analysis. Do *not* simply summarize the text. You may use the margins to take notes as you read and scrap paper to plan your response. Write your response on a separate sheet of paper.

Guidelines:

Be sure to

- Identify a central idea in the text.
- Analyze how the author's use of ***one*** writing strategy (literary element or literary technique or rhetorical device) develops this central idea. Examples include: characterization, conflict, denotation/connotation, metaphor, simile, irony, language use, point-of-view, setting, structure, symbolism, theme, tone, etc.
- Use strong and thorough evidence from the text to support your analysis.
- Organize your ideas in a cohesive and coherent manner.
- Maintain a formal style of writing.
- Follow the conventions of standard written English.

Text

    ...In the air now, I feel a new excitement, a slight surge of energy, a new light of a new dawn. This anticipation is like grass in the path of a distant approaching thunderstorm. I feel that the "spirit line" out of our complacencies in art has been drawn. A fresh expression of our passions,
(5) our joys and pains is in the making. A new generation of interpretations of our legends and stories, strengths and weaknesses as Navajo people are replacing the images of stoic[1] tribalism that so pervaded our recent art history. To paraphrase another artist, "realness instead of redness." I feel as do other young fine artists of the northern reservation, that there is much
(10) potential for individual expression of beauty, of power, of mysteries to be created within the perimeter of our culture in this time. But what inspires us young Navajo artists to create these interpretations of our culture? What force drives us to seek fresher means of expression? We all have our reasons and means to do this. It may be money, it may be recognition
(15) or self-satisfaction. For me, it is a means of confronting myself, my fears and mysteries. A means of coming to terms with childhood phobias and a recognition of my strength and weaknesses in this day. In Navajo society, it is necessary to journey that road to self-discovery. To attain a spiritual growth, we will have to go beyond the world we retreat into. We must recognize
(20) and acknowledge this new high tech world, yet still maintain an identity. We must draw a line beyond which we don't venture. Be able to compromise wisely and know how much to expose of ourselves. Know ourselves and our past, yet still have faith in the future. We are a segment of a society that has been thrust into the 20th century all within 30 years. We will not allow
(25) ourselves to become casualties in this collision of cultures. The art that we represent must be flexible and adaptable, like the nature of our grandfather, if it is to survive, lest we become brittle and blow away like shells of dry piñon nuts. The art that we represent, like the role of the medicine man of today, must help in creating a positive evolution into this new era for
(30) our people and those coming after us. It will scream of tomorrow, yet be dressed in the truth of our past. I believe this to be a collective therapy for us, for our culture and our art....

    When I was around four years old, I traveled with my grandmother to the foot of the Sacred Mountain of the West. During this time, she told
(35) me many things. She told me that we are responsible in maintaining and nurturing a good identity with our grandparents every single day. Each day

---

[1]stoic—calm and uncomplaining

before the sun rises, we should greet the new coming day with pollen and re-affirm our relationship with it. To a young piñon tree, we greet *"Yá'áhtééh shima'sáni"* (Hello, my grandmother); to a young juniper tree; *"Yá'áhtééh
(40) shí'cheii"* (hello, my grandfather). In this manner, we bring new light and life to our world. At this age I learned to feel, see and smell my world. I still associate lots of pieces of past experiences, painful and pleasant, to these subtleties. There are few things more pleasant than waking up in the morning to see dew on blades of grass, or to hear rolling of the thunder as dark clouds
(45) gather on spring days. To smell wet sand and hear the raindrops dancing on parched ground. The cornstalks weeping for joy. Forming figures from clay and feeling like a god. The soft crunching sound in the snow as I make my way home with a rabbit or two on moonlit winters [sic] night, or even being momentarily lost in a blizzard. To feel as a tumbleweed rolling across rough
(50) landscape, to see the last ray of sunlight hitting the mesa after an autumn day, light reflecting off a distant passing car makes me feel vulnerable and sad at times. These past feelings and experiences, associated with time and places, I regard as a reservoir of my inspiration.

    Like most young Navajos my age, we spent many winter nights gathered
(55) around our father, listening to stories passed down through generations. We sat in expectation as we journeyed up from the womb of the Mother in creation stories. We sat mesmerized by coyote stories. Laughing at his antics and frightened by his cruelties. We sat in awe as First Man and First Woman brought forth life upon the Fourth World. We journey back from the west,
(60) the home of Changing Woman, into the midst of the Four Sacred Mountains after the creation of our clans. "Slayer of Enemies" and "Born for Water," the hero and savior of the fourth world, came alive for us these nights. I felt the pain of their fathers' testing in the roaring fire of the hearth. Their war with the Monster Gods raged as the snow storm dusted outside our door,
(65) snow sifting through the cracks of the door. Shadows leaping on cribbed wall of the *hooghan*[2] brought to life the animal beings as the shoe game was created. As the nights wore on, the youngest ones of us fell asleep where we sat. My mother's spindle scratching the floor set the tempo of these late night journeys . . . back. From these sources I draw my inspirations. I am
(70) humbled by its beauty and strengthened by its power. With great respect, I relive this in every creation, every all-night Blessingway chant and every vision of glory upon this land. With good intentions, I recreate this in every piece of art: intentions of preserving and passing on, intentions of sharing

---

[2]hooghan—traditional dwelling of the Navajo people

and inviting all good-willed people for the sake of us as American Indians in
(75) general, as Navajos in particular and the beauty of our culture. This culture through art, in whatever form, however expressed, will endure. . . .

—Shonto W. Begay
excerpted from "The View From The Mesa: A Source of Navajo Creativity"
Anii Ánáádaalyaa'Ígíí (Recent ones that are made), 1988
Wheelright Museum of the American Indian

Regents ELA Answers August 2016

English Language Arts

Answer Key

PART 1

1. 4
2. 1
3. 2
4. 4
5. 1
6. 3
7. 1
8. 2
9. 4
10. 1
11. 3
12. 3
13. 4
14. 2
15. 2
16. 3
17. 4
18. 1
19. 3
20. 1
21. 2
22. 2
23. 4
24. 3

PART 2 *See Answers and Explanations*

PART 3 *See Answers and Explanations*

Regents Examination in English Language Arts—August 2016

Chart for Converting Total Weighted Raw Scores to Final Exam Scores (Scale Scores) (Use for the August 2016 examination only.)

Weighted Raw Score*	Scale Score	Performance Level	Weighted Raw Score*	Scale Score	Performance Level
56	100	5	27	55	2
55	99	5	26	52	1
54	99	5	25	49	1
53	98	5	24	45	1
52	97	5	23	42	1
51	96	5	22	38	1
50	96	5	21	35	1
49	95	5	20	31	1
48	94	5	19	27	1
47	93	5	18	24	1
46	92	5	17	20	1
45	91	5	16	17	1
44	90	5	15	13	1
43	89	5	14	10	1
42	88	5	13	9	1
41	87	5	12	8	1
40	85	5	11	7	1
39	84	4	10	6	1
38	82	4	9	5	1
37	81	4	8	4	1
36	79	4	7	4	1
35	77	3	6	3	1
34	74	3	5	2	1
33	72	3	4	2	1
32	69	3	3	1	1
31	67	3	2	1	1
30	65	3	1	1	1
29	61	2	0	0	1
28	58	2			

The conversion table is determined independently for each administration of the exam.

Answers and Explanations

PART 1—Reading Comprehension

Passage A

1. **4** "illustrate the nature of Richard's life in the city." The reader is meant to understand from the description of London that Richard perceives the city as colorful, huge, and contradictory, but he is unchanged by it. We learn in the passage that Richard took the city for granted and made no effort to visit the sights. The images of a vibrant city that has grown and changed over time are meant to contrast with Richard's passive and indifferent nature.

2. **1** "growth of the city." The image in lines 17 through 19, ". . . a pool of mercury encounters and incorporates smaller beads of mercury . . . " reinforces the way London expanded by absorbing what had once been separate small villages and towns.

3. **2** "willingness to tolerate undesirable situations to please others." Richard "learns" from his excursions with Jessica that going to museums means tired feet, boredom, and expensive cafeterias. He tolerates these discomforts because he is "awed by Jessica" and is easily led by her.

4. **4** "Richard is in a state of denial regarding his relationship." Gary thinks that Jessica's behavior is controlling and wonders why Richard puts up with her. Gary says to Richard, "She's terrifying." Richard's panic over the dinner reservation suggests that he may indeed be afraid to disappoint Jessica. None of the other choices is suggested in the text.

5. **1** "by portraying him as inefficient at organizing his time." Richard's feeling that events have a way of piling up and hitting him all at once is a vivid image of what happens to someone who is disorganized and who tends to let things go until the last minute. The text does not suggest that Richard works well under pressure or is likely to succeed. He may be unmotivated by his job, but he seems to be unmotivated by almost everything. These lines best describe Richard's lack of focus and attention to what needs to get done.

6. **3** "contrast." Sylvia's atmosphere of "crisp efficiency" offers a vivid contrast to all that we know about Richard in the text. This is the best answer among the choices.

7. **1** "domineering nature." In these lines, Jessica orders Richard to pick up the phone, insisting that he might have forgotten their date, and correcting him when he calls her "Jess." There is little in this text to suggest compassion, irresponsibility, or a sense of humor in Jessica.

8. **2** "stress." In this passage, Richard is juggling two phone lines and being reminded that, not only has he forgotten to make an important dinner reservation, but he has made a commitment to have drinks and work with Gary that evening. His manager is also waiting for a report due in the next five minutes. "Stressful" best describes this scene.

9. **4** "quiet desperation." Richard has run out of ways to meet Jessica's expectations for that evening. He had obviously forgotten to make the reservation weeks before, and he knows he will pay a heavy price for his failure. None of the other choices captures Richard's state of mind here.

10. **1** "London grew into something huge and contradictory . . . ." These lines from the opening of the passage establish the setting and mood of the story. Richard lives in, " . . . a good place and a fine city," but he is overwhelmed by the variety of forces at work in his life.

Passage B

11. **3** "lack of self-confidence." The image of the narrator's "courageous self" wrapped in self-doubt and hesitation ("reservations") by a cowardly self is best described as a lack of self-confidence. None of the other choices is suggested by that image.

12. **3** "clarify the narrator's dilemma." The narrator's predicament or quandary is in determining which of the many selves, or aspects of character, is his "proper self." The narrator is asking the universal question, "Who am I?" This is a dilemma because he cannot seem to find "my real self, the truly me . . ." The poem reveals little about the narrator's biases or beliefs, and there is no decision revealed in these lines.

13. **4** "the narrator's idealism and his reality." Among these choices, this is the best way to describe the contradictions in the narrator's view of himself. He believes that he has courageous, intelligent, and bold selves (his idealism), but, instead of acting as a man of intelligence, he acts the fool. In situations demanding courage, he is cowardly. He envies heroic figures, but when he needs to be confident and daring, " . . . out comes the same old lazy self (reality)."

14. **2** "universal." Note that in the preceding lines, the narrator declares that his solution will be, " . . . to see if the same thing happens/to other people." The narrator plans a thorough exploration of other people's experiences in order to find a way to explain his problems, to find his "real self."

Passage C

15. **2** "describing various frequencies dogs hear." These lines first outline and compare the range of sounds that can be heard by humans and by dogs. These details support the central idea that, "Dogs hear most of what we hear and then some." These lines are not about *how* dogs and humans hear, but about which range of frequencies each can hear.

16. **3** "humans can verbally communicate with dogs." What these lines establish is that when they hear humans speak, dogs recognize changes in pitch and tone, not necessarily the meaning of specific words. It is that recognition of patterns in sound that allow humans to communicate verbally with dogs. None of the other choices is supported in the passage.

17. **4** "altering the intonation of familiar words." This idea is an elaboration on the ideas in the question above. Because dogs recognize intonation, the pattern in a question for example, they could be confused if something they heard sounded like a familiar question, even when the words were expressing no such thing.

18. **1** "higher-level thinking." These lines include the declaration that language use distinguishes humans from all other animals, and that language use is viewed as an, " . . . incomparable criterion for intelligence." The passage is asserting that language use implies higher-level thinking.

19. **3** "create human sentence structures." This passage acknowledges that there is considerable disagreement among researchers about the extent of linguistic ability in non-human animals, but asserts that, "All parties agree . . ." there is no discovery of the ability in animals to combine " . . . words into meaningful sentences." None of the other choices applies to these lines.

20. **1** "imitate behavior and sound." This passage offers examples of how animals can recognize warning signals in bird cries or can trap prey by using deceptive gestures. These forms of communication are, " . . . in some way using another specie's language."

21. **2** "complexity of spoken sounds." The key term in this answer is "sounds." This section of the text emphasizes the importance of how dogs understand the sound and pattern of what we say more than recognizing specific words. If an utterance sounds familiar but the actual words (sounds) are meaningless (gibberish), the dog may confuse it with an utterance he has understood in the past. This passage does not refer to word order, hidden gestures, or movement.

22. **2** "How we speak to dogs is more important than what we say." The first and last paragraphs of the text do point out how dogs respond to high-pitched sounds, but the central idea in lines 63–71 is that dogs are sensitive to how we speak, to the rhythm and tone of voice in what they hear. The other choices are not supported by the text.

23. **4** "styles of spoken communication and likely responses." The term "motherese" identifies the often babbling, cooing sounds we use in communicating with infants. The author points out that dogs also respond to "baby talk," especially because they perceive that it is actually being directed at them. This passage is further demonstration of the importance of manner and style in spoken communication.

24. **3** "educate people about dogs' experience with sound." Note that the first sentence of the passage establishes dogs' capacity to hear and respond to sounds as the central idea; the examples that follow are illustrations of how dogs perceive the world and human communication through tone, rhythm, and pitch level.

PART 2—Argument Response

Sample Essay Response

Should the government create strict sugar regulations to protect its citizens from serious health problems? I definitely believe the U.S. government has the responsibility to ensure safe food for its people. It must regulate the production, labeling, and availability of sugary foods and drinks.

Critics of the claim say it's not sugar itself that creates health risks but a person's decision to drink and eat sugar-heavy products. As Jeffrey Senger, a former attorney for the FDA remarked, "Sugar isn't the same thing as arsenic. It's not a food that's inherently unsafe." (Text 1, lines 28–29) In addition, an FDA spokesperson placed sugar and high fructose corn syrup in the same category as honey and molasses. (Text 1, lines 33–34) Opponents of regulation, therefore, place blame and responsibility on the people instead of on the companies that produce these sweetened products. This text explains why it would be difficult for the FDA to set limits on sugar.

However, recent scientific research shows just how dangerous sugar in any form is to a person's health, especially since the average person in America consumes 78 pounds of sugar in one year. (Text 1, lines 10–11) Fructose "is metabolized primarily by the liver, . . . taxing the liver, causing fatty liver disease, and ultimately leading to insulin resistance." (Text 2, lines 20–22) The graphic from Text 3 further illustrates the very serious damage that excessive fructose intake creates: "hypertension, pancreatitis, obesity, malnutrition, hepatic dysfunction," and even possible addiction. As the number of potential ill effects of sugar consumption rises, the case for government regulation is strengthened. Text 3 compares the effects of sugar consumption to alcohol and tobacco use in its damaging effects on people. Why wouldn't the government take similar steps to regulate sugar?

Besides being a personal health issue, sugar consumption is having effects on the U.S. economy. As the health of individuals becomes compromised, so are employment, health-care costs, and the military in the U.S. Lost time at work due to sugar-related disease is "$65 billion in lost productivity." Add to that the $150 billion spent on health-care resources for obesity every year. (Text 3; lines 40–41) Sugar is even being called "a threat to national security," because "75% of military applicants are now rejected for obesity-related reasons." (Text 3, lines 44–46)

Clearly, the government must take steps to strictly regulate the consumption of sugar. Sugary drinks and foods must be banned from schools and commercials, taxes should be placed on companies that continue to produce and market high-sugar products, and education about the dangers of excess sugar must be *emphasized. This issue has gone beyond that of personal responsibility; it is having a negative impact on the country as a whole. The U.S. government must take action to protect its citizens from the deadly consequences of high-sugar products.*

Analysis

This response is a good example of an argument developed with evidence from texts. The introduction restates the topic in the form of a rhetorical question, which also suggests the line of reasoning to follow: "Should the government create strict sugar regulations to protect its citizens from serious health problems?" The introduction could be improved if more details to establish the context were included, but the argument that follows is well developed.

The organization is clear. The second paragraph acknowledges one of the key arguments against regulation. The paragraph that follows offers several examples of the health risks of sugar consumption and closes with another effective rhetorical question: "Why wouldn't the government take similar steps to regulate sugar?" The paragraph that follows further develops the argument with examples of economic costs. The conclusion summarizes the argument for regulation, proposes specific regulatory actions, and rejects the opposing view that personal responsibility is a sufficient response. The supporting details come from three of the texts and are accurately cited. This response would merit a high score.

(See pages 79–80 for the scoring guidelines.)

PART 3—Text-Analysis Response

Sample Essay Response

  The central idea of this text is that when two cultures collide, a more primitive culture must adapt to the new culture while maintaining its own cultural identity. This text was written in the perspective of an American Indian artist whose artwork displays the culture of the Navajo people. The artist recognizes the difficulty for the Navajo people to transition and adapt to a new and advanced culture, therefore he uses his artwork to help his people cope with the change. The artist understands that if the Navajo culture is not perpetuated in artwork, it will be lost to a new culture.

  The artist develops this central idea through the literary technique of figurative language. In lines 28 to 30 the artist states, "The art that we represent, like the role of the medicine man of today, must help in creating a positive evolution in this new era for our people and those coming after us." The artist uses a simile to compare contemporary Navajo artwork to the role of a present day medicine man: art that looks to the future yet is "dressed in the truth of our past . . ." is like "a collective therapy." The artwork that is created still incorporates the culture that the Navajo people are accustomed to, making it easier for them to adapt to the new culture while maintaining their own cultural identity. In line 21, the artist states, "We must draw a line beyond which we do not venture." Here, the artist is describing his artwork with a line in the form of a metaphor. This comparison shows a sense of boundary, where the artwork of the Navajo people would show an adaptation to the new culture, but not too much to where they lose their cultural identity. In lines 26 to 28, the artist states, "the art that we represent must be flexible and adaptable . . . if it is to survive, lest we become brittle and blow away like shells of dry pinion nuts." Here, the artist uses a simile to show that the culture of the Navajo people will disappear—blow away like dry shells—if it does not remain true to its own cultural identity as it adapts to the new culture.

Analysis

This passage offers several possibilities for a thoughtful response, including vivid imagery in the author's descriptions of his childhood experiences, effective use of tone, voice, and point of view. This writer chose to analyze the author's use of figurative language in developing the central idea of the passage.

The first paragraph gives an excellent paraphrase of the central idea, outlines the context, and clearly establishes the author's point of view. The significance of figurative language is developed in the second paragraph, with relevant quotes and accurate representations of the author's views. The organization of the essay is clear and the style is appropriately formal, with no significant errors in the conventions. This response would merit a high score.

(See pages 81–82 for the scoring guidelines.)

Regents ELA Examination June 2017
English Language Arts

PART 1—Reading Comprehension

Directions (1–24): Closely read each of the three passages below. After each passage, there are several multiple-choice questions. Select the best suggested answer to each question and write its number in the space provided. You may use the margins to take notes as you read.

Reading Comprehension Passage A

    I received one morning a letter, written in pale ink on glassy, bluelined note-paper, and bearing the postmark of a little Nebraska village. This communication, worn and rubbed, looking as if it had been carried for some days in a coat pocket that was none too clean, was from my uncle Howard,
(5) and informed me that his wife had been left a small legacy by a bachelor relative, and that it would be necessary for her to go to Boston to attend to the settling of the estate. He requested me to meet her at the station and render her whatever services might be necessary. On examining the date indicated as that of her arrival, I found it to be no later than tomorrow. He
(10) had characteristically delayed writing until, had I been away from home for a day, I must have missed my aunt altogether. . . .
    Whatever shock Mrs. Springer [the landlady] experienced at my aunt's appearance, she considerately concealed. As for myself, I saw my aunt's battered figure with that feeling of awe and respect with which we behold
(15) explorers who have left their ears and fingers north of Franz-Joseph-Land,[1]

---

[1]Franz-Joseph-Land—Russian archipelago of 191 islands in the Arctic Ocean

or their health somewhere along the Upper Congo. My Aunt Georgiana had been a music teacher at the Boston Conservatory, somewhere back in the latter sixties [1860s]. One summer, while visiting in the little village among the Green Mountains where her ancestors had dwelt for generations, (20) she had kindled the callow[2] fancy of my uncle, Howard Carpenter, then an idle, shiftless boy of twenty-one. When she returned to her duties in Boston, Howard followed her, and the upshot of this infatuation was that she eloped with him, eluding the reproaches of her family and the criticism of her friends by going with him to the Nebraska frontier. Carpenter, who, (25) of course, had no money, took up a homestead in Red Willow County, fifty miles from the railroad. There they had measured off their land themselves, driving across the prairie in a wagon, to the wheel of which they had tied a red cotton handkerchief, and counting its revolutions. They built a dugout in the red hillside, one of those cave dwellings whose inmates so often (30) reverted to primitive conditions. Their water they got from the lagoons where the buffalo drank, and their slender stock of provisions was always at the mercy of bands of roving Indians. For thirty years my aunt had not been farther than fifty miles from the homestead.

I owed to this woman most of the good that ever came my way in my (35) boyhood, and had a reverential[3] affection for her. During the years when I was riding herd for my uncle, my aunt, after cooking the three meals— the first of which was ready at six o'clock in the morning—and putting the six children to bed, would often stand until midnight at her ironing board, with me at the kitchen table beside her, hearing me recite Latin declensions and (40) conjugations, gently shaking me when my drowsy head sank down over a page of irregular verbs. It was to her, at her ironing or mending, that I read my first Shakspere, and her old text-book on mythology was the first that ever came into my empty hands. She taught me my scales and exercises on the little parlour organ which her husband had bought her after fifteen years (45) during which she had not so much as seen a musical instrument. She would sit beside me by the hour, darning and counting, while I struggled with the "Joyous Farmer." She seldom talked to me about music, and I understood why. Once when I had been doggedly beating out some easy passages from an old score of *Euryanthe* I had found among her music books, she came up

---

[2]callow—naive
[3]reverential—with great honor and respect

(50) to me and, putting her hands over my eyes, gently drew my head back upon her shoulder, saying tremulously, "Don't love it so well, Clark, or it may be taken from you." . . .

At two o'clock the Symphony Orchestra was to give a Wagner program, and I intended to take my aunt; though, as I conversed with her, I grew (55) doubtful about her enjoyment of it. I suggested our visiting the Conservatory and the Common before lunch, but she seemed altogether too timid to wish to venture out. She questioned me absently about various changes in the city, but she was chiefly concerned that she had forgotten to leave instructions about feeding half-skimmed milk to a certain weakling calf, "old Maggie's (60) calf, you know, Clark," she explained, evidently having forgotten how long I had been away. She was further troubled because she had neglected to tell her daughter about the freshly-opened kit of mackerel[4] in the cellar, which would spoil if it were not used directly. . . .

The first number [of the concert] was the *Tannhauser*[5] overture. When (65) the horns drew out the first strain of the Pilgrim's chorus, Aunt Georgiana clutched my coat sleeve. Then it was I first realized that for her this broke a silence of thirty years. With the battle between the two motives,[6] with the frenzy of the Venusberg theme and its ripping of strings, there came to me an overwhelming sense of the waste and wear we are so powerless (70) to combat; and I saw again the tall, naked house on the prairie, black and grim as a wooden fortress; the black pond where I had learned to swim, its margin pitted with sun-dried cattle tracks; the rain gullied clay banks about the naked house, the four dwarf ash seedlings where the dish-cloths were always hung to dry before the kitchen door. The world there was the flat (75) world of the ancients; to the east, a cornfield that stretched to daybreak; to the west, a corral that reached to sunset; between, the conquests of peace, dearer-bought than those of war. . . .

Her lip quivered and she hastily put her handkerchief up to her mouth. From behind it she murmured, "And you have been hearing this ever (80) since you left me, Clark?" Her question was the gentlest and saddest of reproaches. . . .

The deluge of sound poured on and on; I never knew what she found in the shining current of it; I never knew how far it bore her, or past what happy islands. From the trembling of her face I could well believe that (85) before the last number she had been carried out where the myriad graves

---

[4]kit of mackerel—container of fish
[5]*Tannhauser*—an opera by Richard Wagner
[6]motives—recurrent musical phrases

are, into the grey, nameless burying grounds of the sea; or into some world of death vaster yet, where, from the beginning of the world, hope has lain down with hope and dream with dream and, renouncing, slept. . . .

(90) I spoke to my aunt. She burst into tears and sobbed pleadingly. "I don't want to go, Clark, I don't want to go!"

I understood. For her, just outside the concert hall, lay the black pond with the cattle-tracked bluffs; the tall, unpainted house, with weathercurled boards, naked as a tower; the crook-backed ash seedlings where the dish-cloths hung to dry; the gaunt, moulting turkeys picking up refuse about the
(95) kitchen door.

—Willa Cather
excerpted and adapted from "A Wagner Matinée"
Youth and the Bright Medusa, April 1920

1 A primary function of the first paragraph is to
   (1) establish the reason for the meeting
   (2) create an atmosphere of mystery
   (3) identify preferences of the narrator's aunt
   (4) reveal flaws in the narrator's character

2 In lines 1 through 11, the commentary about the letter implies that the narrator believes his uncle is
   (1) uncomfortable with changes
   (2) careless about details
   (3) angry with his wife
   (4) disappointed at his decision

3 The details in lines 16 through 24 suggest that in her youth Aunt Georgiana was
   (1) courageous yet hesitant
   (2) compassionate yet critical
   (3) resourceful yet cautious
   (4) intelligent yet impulsive

4 Lines 32 and 33, "For thirty years my aunt had not been farther than fifty miles from the homestead" reinforces a sense of
   (1) discomfort   (3) isolation
   (2) happiness   (4) affection

5 Which statement from the passage best explains the narrator's "reverential affection" (line 35) for his Aunt Georgiana?
   (1) "It was to her, at her ironing or mending, that I read my first Shakspere" (lines 41 and 42)
   (2) " 'Don't love it so well, Clark, or it may be taken from you' " (lines 51 and 52)
   (3) "Her lip quivered and she hastily put her handkerchief up to her mouth" (line 78)
   (4) "I never knew how far it bore her, or past what happy islands" (lines 83 and 84)

6 Lines 43 through 45 develop a central theme by

(1) recalling the husband's generosity in supporting the narrator's music lessons
(2) suggesting that the narrator resented his music lessons
(3) emphasizing the role of discipline in developing Aunt Georgiana's musical talent
(4) implying that Aunt Georgiana missed having music in her life   6 _____

7 In lines 47 and 48, when the narrator states that he "understood why," he is implying that his Aunt Georgiana

(1) knew little about current musical trends
(2) avoided talking about his musical skills
(3) realized what she has given up
(4) needed some recognition of her ability   7 _____

8 Lines 57 through 63 contribute to a central idea by depicting Aunt Georgiana's

(1) concern for daily responsibilities
(2) desire for cultural experiences
(3) fear of future separations
(4) fixation on painful memories   8 _____

9 The author's choice of how to end the story (lines 89 through 95) places emphasis on Aunt Georgiana's

(1) bleak future   (3) domestic skills
(2) unusual lifestyle   (4) hostile attitude   9 _____

10 Which quotation best reflects the narrator's realization resulting from Aunt Georgiana's visit?

(1) "He requested me to meet her at the station and render her whatever services might be necessary" (lines 7 and 8)
(2) "At two o'clock the Symphony Orchestra was to give a Wagner program, and I intended to take my aunt" (line 53)
(3) "there came to me an overwhelming sense of the waste and wear we are so powerless to combat" (lines 78 and 79)
(4) "sound poured on and on; I never knew what she found in the shining current of it" (lines 82 and 83)   10 _____

Reading Comprehension Passage B

Mi Historia[1]

My red pickup choked on burnt oil
as I drove down Highway 99.[2]
In wind-tattered garbage bags
I had packed my whole life:
(5) two pairs of jeans, a few T-shirts,
and a pair of work boots.
My truck needed work, and through
the blue smoke rising from under the hood,
I saw almond orchards, plums,
(10) the raisins spread out on paper trays,
and acres of Mendota cotton my mother picked as a child.

My mother crawled through the furrows
and plucked cotton balls that filled
the burlap sack she dragged,
(15) shoulder-slung, through dried-up bolls,
husks, weevils, dirt clods,
and dust that filled the air with thirst.
But when she grew tired,
she slept on her mother's burlap,
(20) stuffed thick as a mattress,
and Grandma dragged her over the land
where time was told by the setting sun. . . .

History cried out to me from the earth,
in the scream of starling flight,
(25) and pounded at the hulls of seeds to be set free.
History licked the asphalt with rubber,
sighed in the windows of abandoned barns,

---

[1]Mi Historia—Spanish for "my history"
[2]Highway 99—the highway that runs through California's fertile Central Valley where generations of farmworkers have settled and been employed

slumped in the wind-blasted palms,
groaned in the heat, and whispered its soft curses.
(30) I wanted my own history—not the earth's,
nor the history of blood, nor of memory,
and not the job found for me at Galdini Sausage.
I sought my own—a new bruise to throb hard
as the asphalt that pounded the chassis of my truck.

—David Dominguez
from *Work Done Right*, 2003
The University of Arizona Press

11 The poet's purpose in referencing "Highway 99" in line 2 is most likely to establish

(1) a connection with the narrator's cultural heritage
(2) a criticism of the valley's agricultural economy
(3) an understanding of the narrator's difficult childhood
(4) an emphasis on the region's diverse landscape

12 The second stanza reveals that the narrator's overall point of view is influenced by

(1) his experience working on farms
(2) his nostalgia for farm life
(3) the labor of his relatives
(4) the expectations of his family

13 The personification in lines 23 through 29 stresses history's desire to be

(1) repeated
(2) forgotten
(3) comforted
(4) heard

14 The figurative language in lines 33 and 34 implies the narrator

(1) regrets leaving his past behind
(2) understands that his future will have challenges
(3) anticipates that his new life will be successful
(4) thinks he made a wrong decision

Reading Comprehension Passage C

In 1973, a book claiming that plants were sentient[1] beings that feel emotions, prefer classical music to rock and roll, and can respond to the unspoken thoughts of humans hundreds of miles away landed on the New York Times best-seller list for nonfiction. "The Secret Life of Plants," by
(5) Peter Tompkins and Christopher Bird, presented a beguiling mashup of legitimate plant science, quack experiments, and mystical nature worship that captured the public imagination at a time when New Age thinking was seeping into the mainstream. The most memorable passages described the experiments of a former C.I.A. polygraph expert named Cleve Backster,
(10) who, in 1966, on a whim, hooked up a galvanometer to the leaf of a dracaena, a houseplant that he kept in his office. To his astonishment, Backster found that simply by imagining the dracaena being set on fire he could make it rouse the needle of the polygraph machine, registering a surge of electrical activity suggesting that the plant felt stress. "Could the plant have been
(15) reading his mind?" the authors ask. "Backster felt like running into the street and shouting to the world, 'Plants can think!' " . . .

In the ensuing years, several legitimate plant scientists tried to reproduce the "Backster effect" without success. Much of the science in "The Secret Life of Plants" has been discredited. But the book had made
(20) its mark on the culture. Americans began talking to their plants and playing Mozart for them, and no doubt many still do. This might seem harmless enough; there will probably always be a strain of romanticism running through our thinking about plants. (Luther Burbank and George Washington Carver both reputedly talked to, and listened to, the plants they did such
(25) brilliant work with.) But in the view of many plant scientists "The Secret Life of Plants" has done lasting damage to their field. According to Daniel Chamovitz, an Israeli biologist who is the author of the recent book "What a Plant Knows," Tompkins and Bird "stymied[2] important research on plant behavior as scientists became wary[3] of any studies that hinted at parallels
(30) between animal senses and plant senses." Others contend that "The Secret Life of Plants" led to "self-censorship" among researchers seeking to explore the "possible homologies[4] between neurobiology[5] and phytobiology"[6]; that

---

[1]sentient—conscious
[2]stymied—prevented
[3]wary—cautious
[4]homologies—similarities
[5]neurobiology—the study of the nervous system
[6]phytobiology—the study of plants

is, the possibility that plants are much more intelligent and much more like us than most people think—capable of cognition,[7] communication,
(35) information processing, computation, learning and memory....

Indeed, many of the most impressive capabilities of plants can be traced to their unique existential[8] predicament as beings rooted to the ground and therefore unable to pick up and move when they need something or when conditions turn unfavorable. The "sessile life style," as plant biologists term
(40) it, calls for an extensive and nuanced understanding of one's immediate environment, since the plant has to find everything it needs, and has to defend itself, while remaining fixed in place. A highly developed sensory apparatus is required to locate food and identify threats. Plants have evolved between fifteen and twenty distinct senses, including analogues of our five:
(45) smell and taste (they sense and respond to chemicals in the air or on their bodies); sight (they react differently to various wavelengths of light as well as to shadow); touch (a vine or a root "knows" when it encounters a solid object); and, it has been discovered, sound. In a recent experiment, Heidi Appel, a chemical ecologist at the University of Missouri, found that, when
(50) she played a recording of a caterpillar chomping a leaf for a plant that hadn't been touched, the sound primed the plant's genetic machinery to produce defense chemicals. Another experiment, done in Mancuso's[9] lab and not yet published, found that plant roots would seek out a buried pipe through which water was flowing even if the exterior of the pipe was dry, which
(55) suggested that plants somehow "hear" the sound of flowing water....

Scientists have since found that the tips of the plant roots, in addition to sensing gravity, moisture, light, pressure, and hardness, can also sense volume, nitrogen, phosphorus, salt, various toxins, microbes, and chemical signals from neighboring plants. Roots about to encounter an impenetrable
(60) obstacle or a toxic substance change course before they make contact with it. Roots can tell whether nearby roots are self or other and, if other, kin or stranger. Normally, plants compete for root space with strangers, but, when researchers put four closely related Great Lakes searocket plants (*Cakile edentula*) in the same pot, the plants restrained their usual competitive
(65) behaviors and shared resources.

---

[7]cognition—understanding
[8]existential—relating to existence
[9]Mancuso—Stefano Mancuso, Italian plant physiologist

Somehow, a plant gathers and integrates all this information about its environment, and then "decides"—some scientists deploy the quotation marks, indicating metaphor at work; others drop them—in precisely what direction to deploy its roots or its leaves. Once the definition of "behavior" (70) expands to include such things as a shift in the trajectory[10] of a root, a reallocation of resources, or the emission of a powerful chemical, plants begin to look like much more active agents, responding to environmental cues in ways more subtle or adaptive than the word "instinct" would suggest. "Plants perceive competitors and grow away from them," Rick Karban, a (75) plant ecologist at U.C. Davis, explained, when I asked him for an example of plant decision-making. "They are more leery of actual vegetation than they are of inanimate objects, and they respond to potential competitors before actually being shaded by them." These are sophisticated behaviors, but, like most plant behaviors, to an animal they're either invisible or really, (80) really slow.

The sessile life style also helps account for plants' extraordinary gift for biochemistry, which far exceeds that of animals and, arguably, of human chemists. (Many drugs, from aspirin to opiates, derive from compounds designed by plants.) Unable to run away, plants deploy a complex molecular (85) vocabulary to signal distress, deter or poison enemies, and recruit animals to perform various services for them. A recent study in *Science* found that the caffeine produced by many plants may function not only as a defense chemical, as had previously been thought, but in some cases as a psychoactive drug in their nectar. The caffeine encourages bees to remember a particular (90) plant and return to it, making them more faithful and effective pollinators.

One of the most productive areas of plant research in recent years has been plant signalling. Since the early nineteen-eighties, it has been known that when a plant's leaves are infected or chewed by insects they emit volatile chemicals that signal other leaves to mount a defense. Sometimes (95) this warning signal contains information about the identity of the insect, gleaned from the taste of its saliva. Depending on the plant and the attacker, the defense might involve altering the leaf's flavor or texture, or producing toxins or other compounds that render the plant's flesh less digestible to herbivores. When antelopes browse acacia trees, the leaves produce tannins (100) that make them unappetizing and difficult to digest. When food is scarce and acacias are overbrowsed, it has been reported, the trees produce sufficient amounts of toxin to kill the animals. . . .

---

[10]trajectory—a path

All species face the same existential challenges—obtaining food, defending themselves, reproducing—but under wildly varying circumstances, and so they have evolved wildly different tools in order to survive. Brains come in handy for creatures that move around a lot; but they're a disadvantage for ones that are rooted in place. Impressive as it is to us, self-consciousness is just another tool for living, good for some jobs, unhelpful for others. That humans would rate this particular adaptation so highly is not surprising, since it has been the shining destination of our long evolutionary journey, along with the epiphenomenon of selfconsciousness that we call "free will." . . .

—Michael Pollan
excerpted from "The Intelligent Plant"
The New Yorker, December 23 & 30, 2013

15 The first paragraph conveys a sense of
  (1) caution
  (2) accusation
  (3) excitement
  (4) relief   15 ____

16 The details in the first paragraph serve mainly to establish the
  (1) relationship between plant science and musical trends
  (2) difference between houseplants and wild plants
  (3) importance of forensic science for theories of plant behavior
  (4) impact of early studies of plant behavior on current research   16 ____

17 The author uses the word "But" in line 19 to
  (1) express the controversial nature of "The Secret Life of Plants"
  (2) compare "The Secret Life of Plants" with "What a Plant Knows"
  (3) express the similarities between certain types of plants
  (4) compare the learning ability of particular types of plants   17 ____

18 A primary purpose of the details in lines 43 through 48 is to indicate a connection
  (1) among diverse plant species
  (2) among several independent studies
  (3) between humans and plants
  (4) between predators and prey   18 ____

19 The use of quotation marks in lines 67 and 69 acknowledges the presence of
  (1) deception
  (2) debate
  (3) confusion
  (4) resentment   19 ____

20 Lines 69 through 73 support a central idea suggesting that plants
  (1) resist cooperation
  (2) avoid modification
  (3) produce sound
  (4) possess intent   20 ____

21 The evidence provided in lines 86 through 90 demonstrates that plants may

(1) develop symbiotic relationships
(2) attack weaker organisms
(3) waste essential resources
(4) produce genetic mutations   21 _____

22 The term "plant signalling" (line 92) refers to the way plants

(1) reproduce with similar species
(2) protect themselves from predators
(3) react to human contact
(4) adapt themselves to climate   22 _____

23 The final paragraph contributes to a central idea by suggesting that

(1) humans have acquired superior characteristics
(2) species develop according to their own needs
(3) plants would benefit from having self-awareness
(4) scientists have dismissed important findings   23 _____

24 The text's credibility relies on the author's use of

(1) order of importance
(2) extended comparison
(3) observable evidence
(4) personal anecdotes   24 _____

PART 2—Argument Response

Directions: Closely read each of the *four* texts on pages 176 through 184 and write a source-based argument on the topic below. You may use the margins to take notes as you read and scrap paper to plan your response. Write your argument on a separate sheet of paper.

Topic: Should school recess be structured play?

Your Task: Carefully read each of the *four* texts provided. Then, using evidence from at least *three* of the texts, write a well-developed argument regarding whether or not school recess should be structured play. Clearly establish your claim, distinguish your claim from alternate or opposing claims, and use specific, relevant, and sufficient evidence from at least *three* of the texts to develop your argument. Do *not* simply summarize each text.

Guidelines:

Be sure to

- Establish your claim regarding whether or not school recess should be structured play.
- Distinguish your claim from alternate or opposing claims.
- Use specific, relevant, and sufficient evidence from at least *three* of the texts to develop your argument.
- Identify each source that you reference by text number and line number(s) or graphic (for example: Text 1, line 4 or Text 2, graphic).
- Organize your ideas in a cohesive and coherent manner.
- Maintain a formal style of writing.
- Follow the conventions of standard written English.

Texts:

Text 1—The Crucial Role of Recess in School
Text 2—Why Children Need More Unstructured Play
Text 3—Study Weighs Benefits of Organizing Recess
Text 4—Forget Goofing Around: Recess Has a New Boss

Text 1

The Crucial Role of Recess in School

    ...Structured recess is a recess based on structured play, during which games and physical activities are taught and led by a trained adult (teachers, school staff, or volunteers). Proponents[1] for structured recess note that children often need help in developing games and require suggestions and
(5) encouragement to participate in physical activities. Recently, policy makers and funding organizations have called for more opportunities for daily activity as a means to address childhood obesity. These statements have strengthened the argument to maintain or reinstate recess as an integral component of the school day. Although this new dimension to the recess
(10) debate has increased attention on its role, it also has created tension. Some have promoted recess time as a solution for increasing children's physical activity and combating obesity. If recess assumes such a role, then, like physical education, it will need to be planned and directed to ensure that all children are participating in moderately vigorous physical activity. Pediatric
(15) health care providers, parents, and school officials should be cognizant,[2] however, that in designing a structured recess, they will sacrifice the notion of recess as an unstructured but supervised break that belongs to the child; that is, a time for the child to make a personal choice between sedentary, physical, creative, or social options. However, there are many cited benefits
(20) of structured recess to consider, including:

- Older elementary children may benefit from game instruction and encouragement for total class inclusion.
- Children can be coached to develop interpersonal skills for appropriate conflict resolution.
(25)
- More children can actively participate in regular activity, irrespective of skill level.
- Anecdotally,[3] teachers have reported improved behavior and attention in the classroom after vigorous structured recess.

    To be effective, structured recess requires that school personnel (or
(30) volunteers) receive adequate training so that they are able to address and encourage the diverse needs of all students. One aspect of supervision should be to facilitate social relationships among children by encouraging

---

[1]proponents—those who support
[2]cognizant—aware
[3]anecdotally—based on casual observation

inclusiveness in games. A problem arises when the structured activities of recess are promoted as a replacement for the child's physical education (35) requirement. The replacement of physical education by recess threatens students' instruction in and acquisition of new motor skills, exploration of sports and rules, and a concept of lifelong physical fitness.

There are ways to encourage a physically active recess without necessarily adding structured, planned, adult-led games, such as offering (40) attractive, safe playground equipment to stimulate free play; establishing games/boundaries painted on the playground; or instructing children in games, such as four square or hop-scotch. These types of activities can range from fully structured (with the adult directing and requiring participation) to partly unstructured (with adults providing supervision and initial instruction) (45) to fully unstructured (supervision and social guidance). In structured, partly structured, or unstructured environments, activity levels vary widely on the basis of school policy, equipment provided, encouragement, age group, gender, and race. Consequently, the potential benefits of mandatory participation of all children in a purely structured recess must be weighed (50) against the potential social and emotional trade-off of limiting acquisition of important developmental skills. Whichever style is chosen, recess should be viewed as a supplement to motor skill acquisition in physical education class. . . .

—Council on School Health
excerpted from "The Crucial Role of Recess in School,"
December 31, 2012
http://pediatrics.aapublications.org/

Text 2

Why Children Need More Unstructured Play

      The nature of an average child's free time has changed. For the past 25 years kids have been spending decreasing amounts of time outdoors. The time that our kids do spend outdoors is frequently a part of an organized sports activity. Other activities taking up our children's time include indoor
(5) lessons and organized events such as music, art and dance lessons. Another big indoor activity, taking up to 7.5 hours a day of our children's time according to a Kaiser Family Foundation study, is electronic entertainment. Of course some of these activities bring joy and fulfillment to our kids, but, in return, time for unstructured play has decreased.
(10)   Unstructured play is that set of activities that children create on their own without adult guidance. Children naturally, when left to their own devices, will take initiative and create activities and stories in the world around them. Sometimes, especially with children past the toddler stage, the most creative play takes place outside of direct adult supervision. Unstructured free play
(15) can happen in many different environments, however, the outdoors may provide more opportunities for free play due to the many movable parts, such as sticks, dirt, leaves and rocks which lend themselves to exploration and creation.
      Some parents find it challenging to provide unstructured play time for
(20) their kids. Letting our kids play without constant supervision, especially outside, can be even more difficult. It feels hard to balance reasonable concern, over-vigilance, and the desire to let our kids experience freedom and learn from their own mistakes and experiences. . . .
      Why might we need to loosen up and get over some of our fears in
(25) order to get our kids outdoor unstructured play time? In the January 2005 *Archives of Pediatric and Adolescent Medicine*, Burdette and Whitaker wrote on the importance of free play. They argue that free play promotes intellectual and cognitive growth, emotional intelligence, and benefits social interactions. They describe how play involves problem solving which is one
(30) of the highest executive functions. ["]Children plan, organize, sequence, and make decisions,["] they explain. In addition, play requires attention to the game and, especially in the case of very young children, frequent physical activity. Unstructured play frequently comes from or results in exposure to the outdoors. Surveys of parents and teachers report that children's focus
(35) and attention are improved after outdoor physical activity and free play and some small studies suggest that time spent outdoors improves focus in children with ADHD [Attention Deficit Hyperactivity Disorder].

Socialization and emotional intelligence benefit through shared interactions and physical movement that take place during play. Children (40) must work together to decide which game to play, what agreeable rules are, and how to manage scenarios that invariably involve their differing perspectives. This "work" builds the social qualities that we all wish for our children: empathy, self-awareness, self-regulation, and flexibility. Emotional development is promoted along with physical health when people spend (45) time moving. In adults and older children physical activity has been well documented to decrease stress, anxiety, and depression, and to improve overall mood. Though the research is sparse in younger children, it seems likely that our youngest children benefit as well. Free play in toddlers and young children most frequently involves spurts of gross motor activity over (50) a period of time with multiple episodes of rest in between. Most children are smiling and laughing when they engage in play, and it is reasonable to assume that their mood is improved during and after play. . . .

—Avril Swan, MD
excerpted and adapted from "Why Children Need More
Unstructured Play" *www.kevinmd.com*, July 21, 2011

Text 3

Study Weighs Benefits of Organizing Recess

While an overwhelming number of elementary school principals believe in the power of recess to improve academic achievement and make students more focused in class, most discipline-related problems happen at school when kids cut loose at recess and lunch, according to surveys.

(5) One of the solutions, according to a study released this week [2012] by the Robert Wood Johnson Foundation: more, and well-trained, staff on the playground.

The study examines an approach to creating more-structured recess time that is provided by Playworks, based in Oakland, Calif. It finds that the (10) nonprofit organization's program can smooth the transition between recess and class time—giving teachers more time to spend on instruction—and can cut back on bullying in the schoolyard. Teachers in participating schools also reported that their students felt safer and more included at recess, compared with those at schools without the program. . . .

(15) The most significant finding shows students who participate in a Playworks-structured recess transition from that to schoolwork more quickly than students in traditional recess, said Susanne James-Burdumy, an associate director of research at Mathematica Policy Research. "I think it is an exciting set of findings," Ms. James-Burdumy said. "This is one area (20) where Playworks is aiming to have an impact: specifically trying to improve students' ability to focus on class activities."

The study found that, on average, teachers at participating schools needed about 2.5 fewer minutes of transition time between recess and learning time—a difference that researchers termed statistically significant. (25) Over the course of a school year, that can add up to about a day of class time.

Scaling Up

The Robert Wood Johnson Foundation, also based in Princeton, has been funding Playworks since 2005. It helped the program expand from a few schools in Oakland to more than 300 schools in 23 cities, said Nancy Barrand, the foundation's senior adviser for program development. The goal (30) is to expand into 27 cities and 750 schools.

"We're using a process of scaling where we've identified a successful, evidence-based model," Ms. Barrand said. Playworks "is a pretty common sense approach. It's really about the school environment and how you create a healthy school environment for the children," she continued. "If children (35) are healthy and happy, they learn better."

Playworks founder and chief executive officer, Jill Vialet, said the idea came from a frustrated principal 15 years ago. The principal had been dealing with the same three students daily because of scuffles and mischief at recess that spilled over into their classes.

(40) Ms. Vialet wondered whether creating a little structure at recess could quell some of those ongoing woes. She recalled her own days as a child when a municipal parks and recreation worker named Clarence made sure she—one of the few girls there—was included in the games at a District of Columbia park.

(45) "I wanted to make sure every kid had a Clarence," she said. . . . The coaches map the area where students spend recess, setting boundaries for different activities, such as kickball. They help children pick teams using random measures, such as students' birth months, to circumvent emotionally scarring episodes of being chosen based on skill or popularity.
(50) If conflicts arise, coaches teach simple ways to settle disputes and preempt some quibbles by teaching games including rock-paper-scissors.

Forty percent of the surveyed teachers said students used the rock-paper-scissors game to resolve conflicts or make decisions when they were back in class.

(55) Coaches get involved in the activities, which "makes it possible for kids who don't see themselves as super-sporty to get into the games themselves," Ms. Vialet said. "There's just enough structure for the kids to be successful."

Solving Own Problems

While adults need to be present and ready to intervene at recess if necessary, said Edward Miller, one of the founding partners of the New York
(60) City-based Alliance for Childhood, and Playworks provides that service, children should also have the opportunity for individual and small-group play. . . .

The Mathematica study found Playworks has a mixed effect on behaviors related to bullying: Teachers at schools with the program found that there
(65) was significantly less bullying and exclusionary behavior during recess than teachers at schools without it, but not a reduction in more general aggressive behavior. Playworks has no formal curriculum that addresses the problem, Ms. Vialet noted.

(70) "Our coaches are functioning like the older kids in the play yard used to: teaching kids rules to games, intervening if there is conflict, norming[1] behaviors around inclusion," she said.

However, researchers also found that teachers' and students' perception of aggression and bullying on the playground differed. While teachers observed that there was less name-calling, shoving of classmates, (75) and excluding of some students from games because of Playworks, students didn't, Mathematica's Ms. James-Burdumy said. . . .

—Nirvi Shah
excerpted and adapted from
"Study Weighs Benefits of Organizing Recess"
www.edweek.org, April 17, 2012

---

[1] norming—setting a standard

Text 4

Forget Goofing Around: Recess Has a New Boss

Newark—At Broadway Elementary School here, there is no more sitting around after lunch. No more goofing off with friends. No more doing nothing.

Instead there is Brandi Parker, a $14-an-hour recess coach with a
(5) whistle around her neck, corralling children behind bright orange cones to play organized games. There she was the other day, breaking up a renegade game of hopscotch and overruling stragglers' lame excuses.

They were bored. They had tired feet. They were no good at running.

"I don't like to play," protested Esmeilyn Almendarez, 11.
(10) "Why do I have to go through this every day with you?" replied Ms. Parker, waving her back in line. "There's no choice."

Broadway Elementary brought in Ms. Parker in January out of exasperation with students who, left to their own devices, used to run into one another, squabble over balls and jump-ropes or monopolize the blacktop
(15) while exiling their classmates to the sidelines. Since she started, disciplinary referrals at recess have dropped by three-quarters, to an average of three a week. And injuries are no longer a daily occurrence.

"Before, I was seeing nosebleeds, busted lips, and students being a danger to themselves and others," said Alejandro Echevarria, the principal.
(20) "Now, Coach Brandi does miracles with 20 cones and three handballs."

The school is one of a growing number across the country that are reining in recess to curb bullying and behavior problems, foster social skills and address concerns over obesity. They also hope to show children that there is good old-fashioned fun to be had without iPods and video games. . . .
(25) Although many school officials and parents like the organized activity, its critics say it takes away the only time that children have to unwind. . . .

Dr. Romina M. Barros, an assistant clinical professor at Albert Einstein College of Medicine in the Bronx who was an author of a widely cited study on the benefits of recess, published last year [2009] in the journal *Pediatrics*,
(30) says that children still benefit most from recess when they are let alone to daydream, solve problems, use their imagination to invent their own games and "be free to do what they choose to do."

Structured recess, Dr. Barros said, simply transplants the rules of the classroom to the playground.
(35) "You still have to pay attention," she said. "You still have to follow rules. You don't have that time for your brain to relax." . . .

Ms. Parker, 28, the coach at Broadway Elementary, had worked as a counselor for troubled teenagers in a group home in Burlington, N.C. Besides her work at recess, she visits each class once a week to play games
(40) that teach lessons about cooperation, sportsmanship and respect.

"These are the things that matter in life: who you are as a human being at the core," she said. . . .

There are three 15-minute recesses, with more than 100 children at a time packed into a fenced-in basketball court equipped with nothing more
(45) than a pair of netless hoops.

On a chilly morning, Ms. Parker shoveled snow off the blacktop so that the students could go outside after being cooped up in the cafeteria during recess in the previous week. She drew squares in blue and green chalk for a game called switch, a fast-paced version of musical chairs—without the
(50) chairs. (She goes through a box of chalk a week.) Ms. Parker, who greets students with hugs and a cheerful "hello-hello," keeps the rules simple so that they can focus on playing rather than on following directions. "We're trying to get them to exert energy, to get it all out," she said. "They can be as loud as they want. I never tell them to be quiet unless I'm telling them
(55) something." . . .

—Winnie Hu
excerpted and adapted from "Forget Goofing Around:
Recess Has a New Boss" *www.nytimes.com,* March 14, 2010

PART 3-Text Analysis Response

Your Task: Closely read the text on pages 186 through 188 and write a well-developed, text-based response of two to three paragraphs. In your response, identify a central idea in the text and analyze how the author's use of *one* writing strategy (literary element or literary technique or rhetorical device) develops this central idea. Use strong and thorough evidence from the text to support your analysis. Do *not* simply summarize the text. You may use the margins to take notes as you read and scrap paper to plan your response. Write your response on a separate sheet of paper.

Guidelines:

Be sure to

- Identify a central idea in the text.
- Analyze how the author's use of *one* writing strategy (literary element or literary technique or rhetorical device) develops this central idea. Examples include: characterization, conflict, denotation/connotation, metaphor, simile, irony, language use, point-of-view, setting, structure, symbolism, theme, tone, etc.
- Use strong and thorough evidence from the text to support your analysis.
- Organize your ideas in a cohesive and coherent manner.
- Maintain a formal style of writing.
- Follow the conventions of standard written English.

Text

The following excerpt from the memoir of a South Pole explorer includes quotations from his diary.

...Then came a fateful day—Wednesday, October 27. The position was lat. [latitude] 69° 5′ S., long. [longitude] 51° 30′ W. The temperature was −8.5° Fahr. [Fahrenheit], a gentle southerly breeze was blowing and the sun shone in a clear sky. "After long months of ceaseless anxiety and strain, after
(5) times when hope beat high and times when the outlook was black indeed, the end of the *Endurance* has come. But though we have been compelled to abandon the ship, which is crushed beyond all hope of ever being righted, we are alive and well, and we have stores and equipment for the task that lies before us. The task is to reach land with all the members of the Expedition.
(10) It is hard to write what I feel. To a sailor his ship is more than a floating home, and in the Endurance I had centred ambitions, hopes, and desires. Now, straining and groaning, her timbers cracking and her wounds gaping, she is slowly giving up her sentient[1] life at the very outset of her career. She is crushed and abandoned after drifting more than 570 miles in a north-
(15) westerly direction during the 281 days since she became locked in the ice. The distance from the point where she became beset[2] to the place where she now rests mortally hurt in the grip of the floes[3] is 573 miles, but the total drift through all observed positions has been 1186 miles, and probably we actually covered more than 1500 miles. We are now 346 miles from Paulet
(20) Island, the nearest point where there is any possibility of finding food and shelter. A small hut built there by the Swedish expedition in 1902 is filled with stores left by the Argentine relief ship. I know all about those stores, for I purchased them in London on behalf of the Argentine Government when they asked me to equip the relief expedition. The distance to the nearest
(25) barrier west of us is about 180 miles, but a party going there would still be about 360 miles from Paulet Island and there would be no means of sustaining life on the barrier. We could not take from here food enough for the whole journey; the weight would be too great.

---

[1]sentient—conscious
[2]beset—hemmed in
[3]floes—ice sheets

"This morning, our last on the ship, the weather was clear, with a gentle south-southeasterly to south-south-westerly breeze. From the crow's-nest there was no sign of land of any sort. The pressure was increasing steadily, and the passing hours brought no relief or respite[4] for the ship. The attack of the ice reached its climax at 4 p.m. The ship was hove[5] stern up by the pressure, and the driving floe, moving laterally across the stern, split the rudder and tore out the rudder-post and stern-post. Then, while we watched, the ice loosened and the *Endurance* sank a little. The decks were breaking upwards and the water was pouring in below. Again the pressure began, and at 5 p.m. I ordered all hands on to the ice. The twisting, grinding floes were working their will at last on the ship. It was a sickening sensation to feel the decks breaking up under one's feet, the great beams bending and then snapping with a noise like heavy gunfire. The water was overmastering the pumps, and so to avoid an explosion when it reached the boilers I had to give orders for the fires to be drawn[6] and the steam let down. The plans for abandoning the ship in case of emergency had been made well in advance, and men and dogs descended to the floe and made their way to the comparative safety of an unbroken portion of the floe without a hitch. Just before leaving, I looked down the engineroom skylight as I stood on the quivering deck, and saw the engines dropping sideways as the stays and bed-plates gave way. I cannot describe the impression of relentless destruction that was forced upon me as I looked down and around. The floes, with the force of millions of tons of moving ice behind them, were simply annihilating the ship." . . .

"To-night the temperature has dropped to −16° Fahr., and most of the men are cold and uncomfortable. After the tents had been pitched I mustered all hands and explained the position to them briefly and, I hope, clearly. I have told them the distance to the barrier and the distance to Paulet Island, and have stated that I propose to try to march with equipment across the ice in the direction of Paulet Island. I thanked the men for the steadiness and good morale they have shown in these trying circumstances, and told them I had no doubt that, provided they continued to work their utmost and to trust me, we will all reach safety in the end. Then we had supper, which the cook had prepared at the big blubber stove, and after a watch[7] had been set all hands except the watch turned in." For myself, I could not sleep.

---

[4]respite—rest
[5]hove—heaved
[6]drawn—closed
[7]watch—crewman who stays awake on guard all night

The destruction and abandonment of the ship was no sudden shock. The disaster had been looming ahead for many months, and I had studied my
(65) plans for all contingencies[8] a hundred times. But the thoughts that came to me as I walked up and down in the darkness were not particularly cheerful. The task now was to secure the safety of the party, and to that I must bend my energies and mental power and apply every bit of knowledge that experience of the Antarctic had given me. The task was likely to be long and
(70) strenuous, and an ordered mind and a clear programme were essential if we were to come through without loss of life. A man must shape himself to a new mark directly the old one goes to ground. . . .

—Sir Ernest Shackleton
excepted and adapted from *South*, 1920
The MacMillan Company

---

[8]contingencies—possibilities

Regents ELA Answers June 2017

English Language Arts

Answer Key

PART 1

1. **1**	9. **1**	17. **1**
2. **2**	10. **3**	18. **3**
3. **4**	11. **1**	19. **2**
4. **3**	12. **3**	20. **4**
5. **1**	13. **4**	21. **1**
6. **4**	14. **2**	22. **2**
7. **3**	15. **3**	23. **2**
8. **1**	16. **4**	24. **3**

PART 2 *See Answers and Explanations*

PART 3 *See Answers and Explanations*

Regents Examination in English Language Arts—June 2017

Chart for Converting Total Weighted Raw Scores to Final Exam Scores (Scale Scores) (Use for the June 2017 examination only.)

Weighted Raw Score*	Scale Score	Performance Level	Weighted Raw Score*	Scale Score	Performance Level
56	100	5	27	52	1
55	99	5	26	47	1
54	99	5	25	43	1
53	99	5	24	39	1
52	98	5	23	36	1
51	97	5	22	32	1
50	96	5	21	28	1
49	95	5	20	24	1
48	94	5	19	21	1
47	92	5	18	18	1
46	91	5	17	14	1
45	90	5	16	11	1
44	88	5	15	9	1
43	87	5	14	8	1
42	86	5	13	7	1
41	85	5	12	6	1
40	83	4	11	5	1
39	82	4	10	5	1
38	80	4	9	4	1
37	79	4	8	3	1
36	76	4	7	3	1
35	74	3	6	2	1
34	72	3	5	2	1
33	69	3	4	1	1
32	66	3	3	1	1
31	65	3	2	1	1
30	60	2	1	1	1
29	57	2	0	0	1
28	55	2			

The conversion table is determined independently for each administration of the exam.

Answers Explained

PART 1—Reading Comprehension

Multiple-Choice Questions

Passage A

1. **1** "establish the reason for the meeting." In this paragraph, the narrator describes the letter he received from his uncle and the request that he assist his aunt when she comes to Boston to receive a small inheritance. This passage is factual and straightforward in tone and reveals little about the narrator or his aunt.

2. **2** "careless about details." The narrator tells us that the letter showed signs of being carried in a pocket for several days, and that it arrived only the day before his aunt was to arrive. These details suggest that the uncle neglected to mail the letter in a timely way. None of the other choices is suggested in this paragraph.

3. **4** "intelligent yet impulsive." We learn in these lines that the narrator's aunt had been an accomplished music teacher in Boston when she met and eloped with the young Howard, ". . . an idle, shiftless [lacking ambition] boy of twenty-one." These lines indicate that both her parents and her friends were deeply opposed to this relationship. Aunt Georgiana's actions suggest that she was not very critical, hesitant, or cautious in her youth.

4. **3** "isolation." This passage describes a life with no money on a nearly barren prairie homestead of primitive conditions, which is ". . . fifty miles from the railroad." This detail at line 26 strongly suggests that Aunt Georgiana had been physically and emotionally isolated in the thirty years since she first arrived in Nebraska.

5. **1** "It was to her, at her ironing or mending, that I read my first Shakespere." In this section of the story, we learn that Aunt Georgiana gave the narrator his early encounters with classical education, coaching him in Latin, arithmetic, and music. The passage strongly implies that it was because of his aunt that the narrator had a life of possibilities beyond a Nebraska boyhood.

6. **4** "implying that Aunt Georgiana missed having music in her life." The image in these lines strongly suggests how important music once was in her life as she urges the narrator as a young boy to develop musical ability himself. None of the other choices are suggested in these lines.

7. **3** "realized what she has given up." Here the narrator indicates that he understood even as a boy how deeply his aunt felt the loss of music in her life. Among the choices, this is the most convincing description of the narrator's understanding.

8. **1** "concern for daily responsibilities." This passage describes the aunt's reluctance to visit various places in Boston because, before the concert, she is ". . . chiefly concerned about . . . a weakling calf . . . ," and a container of fish in the basement at home.

9. **1** "bleak future." The author closes the story with images of the life Aunt Georgiana will return to: "the tall, unpainted house . . . ," wash-cloths drying on the seedlings of trees, and gaunt turkeys pecking at, " . . . refuse about the kitchen door."

10. **3** "there came to me an overwhelming sense of the waste and wear we are so powerless to combat." The first two choices are simple statements of fact, and the fourth is a statement about what the narrator does not fully understand. What he does feel is the sense of loss—of "waste and wear"—in his aunt's life.

Passage B

11. **1** "a connection with the narrator's cultural heritage." The footnote identifies Highway 99 as the main route through California's Central Valley, where for generations migrant farm workers—historically from Mexico—have picked the crops. The poem ends with the poet's assertion that he will seek his own, and a different, life history. Note here how the title, "Mi Historia," contributes to the meaning of the poem.

12. **3** "the labor of his relatives." The second stanza of the poem offers vivid images of what that life was like for his mother and grandmother. Close reading reveals that his mother was picking cotton as a young child, who, ". . . when she grew tired/. . . slept on her mother's burlap." The grandmother is also in the field picking cotton. It is this "history" that the poet is determined not to live.

13. **4** "heard." The images in these lines are of the sounds the poet hears when, "History cried out to me . . . and pounded . . . sighed in the windows . . . groaned in the heat, and whispered its soft curses." None of the other choices describes the effect of the personification in these lines.

14. **2** "understands that his future will have challenges." The poet says his new life, will be a ". . .bruise to throb hard as the asphalt . . . ." His new "history" may be a life as hard as the one of his ancestors, but it will be of his own choice. The tone of voice in the last five lines does not suggest that the poet feels regret at leaving or that he has made a wrong decision, nor does he express confidence that he will necessarily be successful.

Passage C

15. **3** "excitement." This paragraph, about a once popular belief that plants had thoughts and emotions, closes with a description of Clive Backster's thrilling belief that he had proved, "Plants can think!" He is so excited, ". . . he felt like running into the street and shouting to the world . . . ."

16. **4** "impact of early studies of plant behavior on current research." The author describes the claims of a popular book on "The Secret Life of Plants" as " . . . a mashup of legitimate plant science, quack experiments, and mystical nature worship . . . ." Because this kind of thinking, "was seeping into the mainstream . . . ," many legitimate scientists later tried to reproduce Backster's experiment, but without success.

17. **1** "express the controversial nature of 'the Secret Life of Plants.'" Because "The Secret Life of Plants" "had made its mark on the culture" and people were "talking to their plants and playing Mozart for them," many plant scientists later believed that the book had "done lasting damage to their field." Because the science in Tompkins and Bird's work was formally discredited, later researchers were reluctant to explore any "parallels between animal senses and plant senses."

18. **3** "between humans and plants." This passage outlines the scientific view that plants have evolved " . . . between fifteen and twenty distinct senses, including analogues of our five . . . ." None of the other choices accurately describes the purpose of this passage.

19. **2** "debate." The terms "decides" and "behavior" are in quotes because they attribute human intentional acts to plants. This passage indicates that some scientists prefer to use these terms as metaphors, while others drop the quotation marks and describe plants as "active agents" in their behavior.

20. **4** "possess intent." In the preceding paragraphs, the author outlines a number of ways in which plants actively respond to their environment: they can emit chemicals to defend from insects; they can ". . . somehow 'hear' the sound of flowing water . . ." and they will "share or compete for resources" with neighboring plants.

21. **1** "develop symbiotic relationships." This item is an example of how the Regents Exam indirectly assesses vocabulary. The term "symbiotic" refers to a mutually beneficial relationship between or among plants and animals. These lines describe, for example, how the caffeine produced by many plants as a defense mechanism also ". . . encourages bees to remember [them] . . . , making [the bees] more faithful and effective pollinators."

22. **2** "protect themselves from predators." This paragraph presents examples of how, when chewed or infected, plants can "emit volatile chemicals that signal other leaves to mount a defense." Some plants or trees can produce "toxins or other compounds that render [them] . . . less digestible," even poisonous. None of the other choices accurately refers to the term "plant signalling."

23. **2** "species develop according to their own needs." This paragraph concludes with the observation that, "All species face the same existential challenges . . . , but under wildly varying circumstances, and so they have evolved wildly different tools in order to survive." This is the best choice to describe a central idea of the article, which is about the evolutionary adaptability of plants, not about the importance of brains and self-consciousness in humans.

24. **3** "observable evidence." The author cites "several legitimate plant scientists" and reliable, published research to support each illustration of the plant world's "impressive capabilities."

PART 2—Argument Response

Sample Essay Response

 Elementary school is a pivotal time for the development of children. A child's brain, emotions, and skills are very rapidly developing. With all of the structure and classroom education forced into children at that age, a time to unwind and grow interpersonally is crucial. Recess is a very important part of child development and should be a time for free, unlimited expression—not structured play.

 Anyone who watches children play freely can see that they are completely capable of creating games and physical activities on their own. Students have shown that during this free playing time, "intellectual and cognitive growth, emotional intelligence, and benefits social interactions" are all benefited and promoted (Text 2, lines 28–29). At a time when the brain is most delicate and moldable, these experiences are crucial. On the other hand, structured play forces a burden onto children who may not enjoy or feel comfortable in group sports and games. At one school practicing structured recess, the children would claim they, "were bored . . . had tired feet . . . were no good at running" (Text 4, line 8). In these programs, children are told they have "no choice" and are thus apt to develop negative attitudes toward physical activity and group play if they are forced to participate. Unstructured recess allows children a period of time to make their own choices and freely express themselves in a safe environment, while structured play takes away from this freedom and restricts the developing minds of young children.

 Although structured recess shows potential benefits, there is contradictory and negative evidence. Supporters of structured recess claim that "significantly less bullying and exclusionary behavior" occurs during recess with structured play programs (Text 3 line 65). However, there is no shown reduction in more general aggressive behavior. The lower aggression levels solely during recess will remain only during that period of time. Children will still find a way to bully and hurt others. Therefore, a simple reduction in immediate bullying is not worth further taking away from the freedom and creative expression of children. Reducing child obesity is another objective on the minds of supporters. However, children in elementary school are already offered a physical education class, which they regularly attend. The option to pursue more physical activities should then be left up to the students, and not miserably forced upon them.

 Structured recess is an unnecessary stressor on young children. This form of play takes away from children's creative expression and initial exposure to freedom. Children should be allowed freedom at recess time, and schools should not force structured play upon them.

Analysis

This is a good response to the task. The writer establishes a clear and thoughtful position in the opening paragraph: "Recess is a very important part of child development and should be a time for free, unlimited expression—not structured play." The argument is then briefly, but adequately, developed in the body of the essay and supported with relevant references to the texts. The argument is logical, coherent, and generally well written. The final sentence of the second paragraph is an especially strong assertion of the writer's argument: "Unstructured recess allows children a period of time to make their own choices and freely express themselves in a safe environment, while structured play takes away from this freedom and restricts the developing minds of young children."

An even stronger response to this part of the exam would offer a more extensive discussion, with additional examples and citations from the wide range of evidence in the texts. This response, however, reflects understanding of the main issue and offers a strong argument on one side of the issue. This response would merit a high score.

(See pages 79–80 for the scoring guidelines.)

PART 3—Text-Analysis Response

Sample Essay Response

    The South Pole explorer develops an important and central theme throughout this memoir, excerpted from his diary. The explorer conveys that the destruction of the Endurance, the ship that was more than just his "floating home," was heartbreaking. The explorer states that it was in the ship that he had "centred ambitions, hopes, and desires." At several points, the explorer declares that he finds it difficult to put into words his true feelings about the demise of the Endurance. He explains that even though he had planned for the possible disaster and that the end of the ship was "looming ahead for many months," he was profoundly disturbed by the loss. The explorer recounts this devastating loss in vivid language and images.

    The South Pole explorer, Edwin Shackleton, develops this central theme through the use of figurative language, primarily personification. He gives the ship human qualities to illustrate the importance of the Endurance in his life and heart. The most vivid example of personification is, "Now straining and groaning . . . her wounds gaping, she is slowly giving up her sentient life. . . ." This personification shows how Shackleton feels the pain of his ship "dying." He also personifies the cause of destruction, the floes in which the ship is breaking up, "mortally hurt," as "the attack of the ice." The explorer also uses a simile in describing the breaking up of the Endurance, which was "snapping with a noise like heavy gunfire." For Shackleton, it was as if a loved one was being gunned down. This South Pole explorer successfully conveys his profound loss to the reader in beautiful and moving figurative language.

Analysis

This writer recognizes the author's powerful use of figurative language to describe a central incident in this passage, an account that is otherwise composed in the language of factual detail and scientific observation. The first paragraph explains the significance of the event to the author and establishes the central idea of the response. In the second paragraph, this writer illustrates, with relevant quotes, how Shackleton conveys the heartbreak of the loss of his ship. The significance of the examples is presented clearly and convincingly, with skillful use of complex sentence structures. There are no significant errors in the conventions. This response would merit a high score.

(See pages 81–82 for the scoring guidelines.)

Regents ELA Examination August 2017
English Language Arts

PART 1—Reading Comprehension

Directions (1–24): Closely read each of the three passages below. After each passage, there are several multiple-choice questions. Select the best suggested answer to each question and write its number in the space provided. You may use the margins to take notes as you read.

Reading Comprehension Passage A

In this passage, Dora-Rouge, a Native American Indian elder, is traveling back to her homeland by canoe with a small group of women.

...As we traveled, we entered time and began to trouble it, to pester it apart or into some kind of change. On the short nights we sat by firelight and looked at the moon's long face on water. Dora-Rouge would lie on the beaver blankets and tell us what place we would pass on the next day. She'd
(5) look at the stars in the shortening night and say, "the Meeting Place," or "God Island." True to her word, the next day we reached those places....
   Now, looking back, I understand how easily we lost track of things. The time we'd been teasing apart, unraveled. And now it began to unravel us as we entered a kind of timelessness. Wednesday was the last day we called by
(10) name, and truly, we no longer needed time. We were lost from it, and lost in this way, I came alive. It was as if I'd slept for years, and was now awake. The others felt it, too. Cell by cell, all of us were taken in by water and by land, swallowed a little at a time. What we'd thought of as our lives and being on earth was gone, and now the world was made up of pathways of its own
(15) invention. We were only one of the many dreams of earth. And I knew we were just a small dream.

But there was a place inside the human that spoke with land, that entered dreaming, in the way that people in the north found direction in their dreams. They dreamed charts of land and currents of water. They dreamed where food animals lived. These dreams they called hunger maps and when they followed those maps, they found their prey. It was the language animals and humans had in common. People found their cures in the same way. . . .

For my own part in this dreaming, as soon as I left time, when Thursday and Friday slipped away, plants began to cross my restless sleep in abundance. A tendril reached through darkness, a first sharp leaf came up from the rich ground of my sleeping, opened upward from the place in my body that knew absolute truth. It wasn't a seed that had been planted there, not a cultivated growing, but a wild one, one that had been there all along, waiting. I saw vines creeping forward. Inside the thin lid of an eye, petals opened, and there was pollen at the center of each flower. Field, forest, swamp. I knew how they breathed at night, and that they were linked to us in that breath. It was the oldest bond of survival. I was devoted to woods the wind walked through, to mosses and lichens. Somewhere in my past, I had lost the knowing of this opening light of life, the taking up of minerals from dark ground, the magnitude of thickets and brush. Now I found it once again. Sleep changed me. I remembered things I'd forgotten, how a hundred years ago, leaves reached toward sunlight, plants bent into currents of water. Something persistent nudged me and it had morning rain on its leaves.

Maybe the roots of dreaming are in the soil of dailiness, or in the heart, or in another place without words, but when they come together and grow, they are like the seeds of hydrogen and the seeds of oxygen that together create ocean, lake, and ice. In this way, the plants and I joined each other. They entangled me in their stems and vines and it was a beautiful entanglement. . . .

Some mornings as we packed our things, set out across water, the world was the color of copper, a flood of sun arrived from the east, and a thick mist rose up from black earth. Other mornings, heating water over the fire, we'd see the world covered with fog, and the birdsongs sounded forlorn and far away. There were days when we traveled as many as thirty miles. Others we traveled no more than ten. There were times when I resented the work, and days I worked so hard even Agnes' liniment and aspirin would not relax my aching shoulders and I would crave ice, even a single chip of it, cold and

shining. On other days I felt a deep contentment as I poled[1] inside shallow
(55) currents or glided across a new wide lake.

We were in the hands of nature. In these places things turned about and were other than what they seemed. In silence, I pulled through the water and saw how a river appeared through rolling fog and emptied into the lake. One day, a full-tailed fox moved inside the shadows of trees, then
(60) stepped into a cloud. New senses came to me. I was equal to the other animals, hearing as they heard, moving as they moved, seeing as they saw.

One night we stayed on an island close to the decaying, moss-covered pieces of a boat. Its remains looked like the ribs of a large animal. In the morning, sun was a dim light reaching down through the branches of trees.
(65) Pollen floated across the dark water and gathered, yellow and lifegiving, along the place where water met land. . . .

One evening it seemed cooler. The air had a different feel, rarefied, clean, and thin. Wolves in the distance were singing and their voices made a sound that seemed to lie upon the land, like a cloud covering the world from
(70) one edge of the horizon to the other. We sat around the fire and listened, the light on our faces, our eyes soft. Agnes warmed her hands over the flames.

There was a shorter time of darkness every night, but how beautiful the brief nights, with the stars and the wolves. . . .

Sometimes I felt there were eyes around us, peering through trees
(75) and fog. Maybe it was the eyes of land and creatures regarding us, taking our measure. And listening to the night, I knew there was another horizon, beyond the one we could see. And all of it was storied land, land where deities[2] walked, where people traveled, desiring to be one with infinite space.

(80) We were full and powerful, wearing the face of the world, floating in silence. Dora-Rouge said, "Yes, I believe we've always been lost," as we traveled through thick-grown rushes, marsh, and water so shallow our paddles touched bottom.

The four of us became like one animal. We heard inside each other
(85) in a tribal way. I understood this at once and was easy with it. With my grandmothers, there was no such thing as loneliness. Before, my life had been without all its ears, eyes, without all its knowings. Now we, the four of us, all had the same eyes, and when Dora-Rouge pointed a bony finger and said, "This way," we instinctively followed that crooked finger.

---

[1]poled—propelled a boat with a pole
[2]deities—gods

(90)   I never felt lost. I felt newly found, opening, like the tiny eggs we found in a pond one day, fertile and transparent. I bent over them. The life was already moving inside them, like an eye or heartbeat. One day we passed alongside cliff walls that bore red, ancient drawings of moose and bear. These were said to have been painted not by humans, but by spirits. . . .

—Linda Hogan
excerpted from "Solar Storms," 1995
Scribner

1 In lines 3 through 6, the narrator portrays Dora-Rouge as
   (1) compassionate
   (2) detached
   (3) knowledgeable
   (4) misguided

   1 _____

2 In lines 15 and 16, the narrator compares people's lives to dreams in order to illustrate the idea of
   (1) resourcefulness
   (2) individuality
   (3) vulnerability
   (4) insignificance

   2 _____

3 Which phrase from the text best illustrates the meaning of "tendril" as used in line 25?
   (1) "I saw vines creeping forward" (line 29)
   (2) "there was pollen at the center" (line 30)
   (3) "Field, forest, swamp" (lines 30 and 31)
   (4) "woods the wind walked through" (line 35)

   3 _____

4 The imagery in lines 29 through 33 can best be described as
   (1) amusing
   (2) threatening
   (3) confusing
   (4) enlightening

   4 _____

5 The description in lines 56 through 61 creates a sense of
   (1) transformation
   (2) isolation
   (3) division
   (4) vindication

   5 _____

6 The phrase, "We were full and powerful, wearing the face of the world," (line 80) suggests that the group
   (1) believed they were something they were not
   (2) developed a kinship with the environment
   (3) became outwardly proud and aggressive
   (4) adopted a casual attitude toward nature

   6 _____

7 The language use in lines 90 through 94 serves to
   (1) link the past with the future
   (2) continue an ongoing struggle
   (3) present a cultural dilemma
   (4) clarify the need for cooperation   7 _____

8 The passage is primarily developed through the use of
   (1) rhetorical questions
   (2) comparison and contrast
   (3) parallel structure
   (4) personal narrative   8 _____

9 The passage as a whole supports the theme that with
   (1) approval of society comes cultural freedom
   (2) clarity of mind comes connection of spirit
   (3) support of others comes environmental change
   (4) passage of time comes acceptance of nature   9 _____

10 Which quotation best supports a central idea of the passage?
   (1) "Maybe the roots of dreaming are in the soil of dailiness" (line 40)
   (2) "On other days I felt a deep contentment as I poled inside shallow currents or glided across a new wide lake" (lines 54 and 55)
   (3) "The air had a different feel, rarefied, clean, and thin" (lines 67 and 68)
   (4) "And listening to the night, I knew there was another horizon, beyond the one we could see" (lines 76 and 77)   10 _____

Reading Comprehension Passage B

I Am Vertical

    But I would rather be horizontal.
    I am not a tree with my root in the soil
    Sucking up minerals and motherly love
    So that each March I may gleam into leaf,
(5) Nor am I the beauty of a garden bed
    Attracting my share of Ahs and spectacularly painted,
    Unknowing I must soon unpetal.
    Compared with me, a tree is immortal
    And a flower-head not tall, but more startling,
(10) And I want the one's longevity and the other's daring.

    Tonight, in the infinitesimal[1] light of the stars,
    The trees and flowers have been strewing their cool odors.
    I walk among them, but none of them are noticing.
    Sometimes I think that when I am sleeping
(15) I must most perfectly resemble them—
    Thoughts gone dim.
    It is more natural to me, lying down.
    Then the sky and I are in open conversation,
    And I shall be useful when I lie down finally:
(20) Then the trees may touch me for once, and the flowers
    have time for me.

—Sylvia Plath
from *Uncollected Poems*, 1965
Turret Books

---

[1]infinitesimal—very small

11 The word "unpetal" in line 7 suggests

   (1) inspiration
   (2) invisibility
   (3) isolation
   (4) impermanence   11 ____

12 Lines 11 through 13 reveal the narrator's awareness of

   (1) the limited time people exist on earth
   (2) the unexpected changes that affect one's life
   (3) her anxiety over the shifting of seasons
   (4) her insignificance in the eyes of nature   12 ____

13 In lines 14 through 16, the narrator suggests that

   (1) consciousness is a barrier to connecting with nature
   (2) nature's ability to impress surpasses human's imagination
   (3) the future depends on natural forces beyond human control
   (4) nature's cruelty causes one to feel helpless   13 ____

14 Throughout the poem, the tone can best be described as

   (1) envious
   (2) hostile
   (3) skeptical
   (4) indignant   14 ____

Reading Comprehension Passage C

Jian Lin was 14 years old in 1973, when the Chinese government under Mao Zedong recruited him for a student science team called "the earthquake watchers." After a series of earthquakes that had killed thousands in northern China, the country's seismologists[1] thought that if they augmented[2] their
(5) own research by having observers keep an eye out for anomalies like snakes bolting early from their winter dens and erratic[3] well-water levels, they might be able to do what no scientific body had managed before: issue an earthquake warning that would save thousands of lives.

In the winter of 1974, the earthquake watchers were picking up some
(10) suspicious signals near the city of Haicheng. Panicked chickens were squalling and trying to escape their pens; water levels were falling in wells. Seismologists had also begun noticing a telltale pattern of small quakes. "They were like popcorn kernels," Lin tells me, "popping up all over the general area." Then, suddenly, the popping stopped, just as it had before a
(15) catastrophic earthquake in 1966 that killed more than 8,000. "Like 'the calm before the storm,' " Lin says. "We have that exact same phrase in Chinese." On the morning of February 4, 1975, the seismology bureau issued a warning: Haicheng should expect a big earthquake, and people should move outdoors.
(20) At 7:36 p.m., a magnitude 7.0 quake struck. The city was nearly leveled, but only about 2,000 people were killed. Without the warning, easily 150,000 would have died. "And so you finally had an earthquake forecast that did indeed save lives," Lin recalls. "People were excited. Or, you could say, uplifted. *Uplifted* is a great word for it." But uplift turned to heartbreak
(25) the very next year, when a 7.5 quake shattered the city of Tangshan without so much as a magnitude 4 to introduce it. When the quake hit the city of 1.6 million at 3:42 a.m., it killed nearly 250,000 people, most of whom were asleep. "If there was any moment in my life when I was scared of earthquakes, that was it," Lin says. "You think, what if it happened to you?
(30) And it could. I decided that if I could do anything—*anything*—to save lives lost to earthquakes, it would be worth the effort."

Lin is now a senior scientist of geophysics at Woods Hole Oceanographic Institution, in Massachusetts, where he spends his time studying not the scurrying of small animals and fluctuating electrical current between trees
(35) (another fabled warning sign), but seismometer readings, GPS coordinates,

---

[1]seismologists—people who study earthquakes   [2]augmented—added to   [3]erratic—unpredictable

and global earthquake-notification reports. He and his longtime collaborator, Ross Stein of the U.S. Geological Survey, are champions of a theory that could enable scientists to forecast earthquakes with more precision and speed.

(40) Some established geophysicists[4] insist that all earthquakes are random, yet everyone agrees that aftershocks are not. Instead, they follow certain empirical laws. Stein, Lin, and their collaborators hypothesized that many earthquakes classified as main shocks are actually aftershocks, and they went looking for the forces that cause faults to fail.

(45) Their work was in some ways heretical:[5] For a long time, earthquakes were thought to release only the stress immediately around them; an earthquake that happened in one place would decrease the possibility of another happening nearby. But that didn't explain earthquake sequences like the one that rumbled through the desert and mountains east of Los (50) Angeles in 1992. The series began on April 23 with a 6.2 near the town of Joshua Tree; two months later, on June 28, a 7.3 struck less than 15 miles away in the desert town of Landers. Three and a half hours after that, a 6.5 hit the town of Big Bear, in the mountains overlooking the Mojave. The Big Bear quake was timed like an aftershock, except it was too far off the Landers (55) earthquake's fault rupture. When Lin, Stein, and Geoffrey King of the Paris Geophysical Institute got together to analyze it, they decided to ignore the distance rule and treat it just as a different kind of aftershock. Their ensuing report, "Static Stress Changes and the Triggering of Earthquakes," became one of the decade's most-cited earthquake research papers.

(60) Rocks can be subject to two kinds of stresses: the "clamping" stress that pushes them together, and the "shear" stress they undergo as they slide past each other. Together, these stresses are known as Coulomb stress, named for Charles-Augustin de Coulomb, an 18th-century French physicist. Coulomb calculations had been used for years in engineering, to find the failure points (65) of various building materials, but they'd never been applied properly to faults. It turned out, though, that faults in the ground behave much like rocks in the laboratory: they come unglued when shear stress exceeds the friction and pressure (the clamping stress) holding them together. When Stein, Lin, and King applied the Coulomb model to the California sequence, (70) they found that most of the earthquakes had occurred in areas where the shifting of the ground had caused increased stress.

---

[4]geophysicists—people who study the physics of the earth and its environment, including seismology
[5]heretical—against the opinion of authorities

In 1997, Stein and two other geologists using the model found that there was a 12 percent chance that a magnitude 7 or greater would hit near Izmit, Turkey, within 30 years; two years later, on August 17, 1999, a magnitude 7.4 destroyed the city, which wasn't designed to withstand such a tremor. A Turkish geologist named Aykut Barka quickly wrote up a paper warning that Coulomb stress from the Izmit quake could trigger a similar rupture near Düzce, a town roughly 60 miles east. His work persuaded authorities there to close school buildings damaged during the Izmit shaking. On November 12, a segment of the North Anatolian Fault gave way, in a magnitude 7.2. The empty school buildings collapsed.

Lin and Stein both admit that Coulomb stress doesn't explain all earthquakes. Indeed, some geophysicists, like Karen Felzer, of the U.S. Geological Survey, think their hypothesis gives short shrift[6] to the impact that dynamic stress—the actual rattling of a quake in motion—has on neighboring faults.

In the aftermath of the disastrous March 11 Tohoku quake, both camps are looking at its well-monitored aftershocks (including several within 100 miles of Tokyo) for answers. Intriguingly, it was *preceded* by a flurry of earthquakes, one as large as magnitude 7.2, that may have been foreshocks, although no one thought so at the time; the researchers are trying to determine what those early quakes meant.

When I ask Lin whether California, where I live, is next, he laughs. "I understand that the public now thinks that we've entered a global earthquake cluster. Even my own mother in China thinks that. But there's no scientific evidence whatsoever to suggest that the earthquake in New Zealand triggered the earthquake in Japan, or Japan will trigger one in California." Still, Lin and his colleagues do wonder whether Tohoku has pushed neighboring faults closer to rupture. "I am particularly interested in how this earthquake might have changed the potential of future earthquakes to the south, even closer to Tokyo," Lin tells me. "There, even a much smaller earthquake could be devastating."

—Judith Lewis Mernit
"Is San Francisco Next?"
The Atlantic, June 2011

---

[6]short shrift—little consideration

15 As used in line 5, the word "anomalies" most nearly means

(1) seasonal changes
(2) odd occurrences
(3) dangerous incidents
(4) scheduled events   15 _____

16 The first paragraph contributes to a central idea in the text by

(1) contributing historical facts
(2) contrasting early theories
(3) comparing two philosophies
(4) challenging cultural beliefs   16 _____

17 The figurative language in lines 13 and 14 conveys a sense of

(1) disbelief
(2) disappointment
(3) apathy
(4) urgency   17 _____

18 The contrast drawn between the Haicheng and Tangshan earthquakes (lines 9 through 31) contributes to a central idea that earthquakes are

(1) preceded by reliable signs
(2) controlled by observable factors
(3) not always predictable
(4) not often studied   18 _____

19 The purpose of lines 32 through 36 is to emphasize that Jian Lin

(1) relied on his past experience to identify earthquakes
(2) modified his methods of observing earthquakes
(3) changed his understanding about the causes of earthquakes
(4) disagreed with his co-researcher on the measurement of earthquakes   19 _____

20 The word "champions" as used in line 37 most nearly means
   (1) advisers
   (2) adaptors
   (3) supporters
   (4) survivors

21 Which statement reflects a long-held belief disproved by Lin, Stein, and King?
   (1) "many earthquakes classified as main shocks are actually after-shocks" (lines 42 and 43)
   (2) "an earthquake that happened in one place would decrease the possibility of another happening nearby" (lines 46 and 47)
   (3) "Rocks can be subject to two kinds of stresses" (line 60)
   (4) "faults in the ground behave much like rocks in the laboratory" (lines 66 and 67)

22 According to lines 60 through 71, seismologists realized that the California sequence of earthquakes happened because
   (1) shear stress forced rocks to fuse together
   (2) clamping stress caused rocks to move apart
   (3) shear stress was greater than clamping stress
   (4) clamping stress balanced the shear stress

23 Throughout the text, the author portrays Jian Lin as
   (1) satisfied
   (2) cautious
   (3) superstitious
   (4) dedicated

24 Jian Lin's research regarding earthquakes can best be described as
   (1) flawed by inconsistent methodology
   (2) concurrent with prior theories
   (3) challenged by conflicting findings
   (4) important to future studies

PART 2—Argument Response

Directions: Closely read each of the *four* texts on pages 213 through 221 and write a source-based argument on the topic below. You may use the margins to take notes as you read and scrap paper to plan your response. Write your argument on a separate sheet of paper.

Topic: Should self-driving cars replace human drivers?

Your Task: Carefully read each of the *four* texts provided. Then, using evidence from at least *three* of the texts, write a well-developed argument regarding whether or not self-driving cars should replace human drivers. Clearly establish your claim, distinguish your claim from alternate or opposing claims, and use specific, relevant, and sufficient evidence from at least *three* of the texts to develop your argument. Do *not* simply summarize each text.

Guidelines:

Be sure to

- Establish your claim regarding whether or not self-driving cars should replace human drivers.
- Distinguish your claim from alternate or opposing claims.
- Use specific, relevant, and sufficient evidence from at least *three* of the texts to develop your argument.
- Identify each source that you reference by text number and line number(s) or graphic (for example: Text 1, line 4 or Text 2, graphic).
- Organize your ideas in a cohesive and coherent manner.
- Maintain a formal style of writing.
- Follow the conventions of standard written English.

Texts:

Text 1—How Google's Self-Driving Car Will Change Everything

Text 2—Google's Driverless Cars Run Into Problem: Cars With Drivers

Text 3—Autonomous Vehicles Will Replace Taxi Drivers, But That's Just the Beginning

Text 4—Along for the Ride

Text 1

How Google's Self-Driving Car Will Change Everything

Imagine getting in your car, typing or speaking a location into your vehicle's interface, then letting it drive you to your destination while you read a book, surf the web or nap. Self-driving vehicles—the stuff of science fiction since the first roads were paved—are coming, and they're going to
(5) radically change what it's like to get from point A to point B.

Basic Technology Already In Use

...The first big leap to fully autonomous[1] vehicles is due in 2017, when Google Inc. (GOOG) said it would have an integrated system ready to market. Every major automotive manufacturer is likely to follow by the early 2020s, though their systems could wind up being more sensor-based, and rely less
(10) on networking and access to map information. Google probably wont [sic] manufacture cars. More likely, it'll license the software and systems.

A Drastic Change

As with the adoption of any new revolutionary technology, there will be problems for businesses that don't adjust fast enough. Futurists estimate that hundreds of billions of dollars (if not trillions) will be lost by automakers,
(15) suppliers, dealers, insurers, parking companies, and many other car-related enterprises. And think of the lost revenue for governments via licensing fees, taxes and tolls, and by personal injury lawyers and health insurers.

Who needs a car made with heavier-gauge steel and eight airbags (not to mention a body shop) if accidents are so rare? Who needs a parking spot
(20) close to work if your car can drive you there, park itself miles away, only to pick you up later? Who needs to buy a flight from Boston to Cleveland when you can leave in the evening, sleep much of the way, and arrive in the morning?

Indeed, Google's goal is to increase car utilization from 5–10% to 75%
(25) or more by facilitating sharing. That means fewer cars on the road. Fewer cars period, in fact. Who needs to own a car when you can just order a shared one and it'll drive up minutes later, ready to take you wherever you want?...

---

[1]autonomous—self-directed

Changing Oil Demand

If you're in the business of finding, extracting, refining and marketing
(30) hydrocarbons,[2] such as Exxon Mobil Corp. (EOX), Chevron Corp. (CVX) or BP plc (BP), you could see your business fluctuate as use changes.

"These vehicles should practice very efficient eco-driving practices, which is typically about 20% better than the average driver," said [Robin] *Chase*[3] [sic] "On the other hand, if these cars are owned by individuals, I see a huge rise in
(35) the number of trips, and vehicle miles traveled. People will send out their car to run errands they would never do if they had to be in the car and waste their own time. If the autonomous cars are shared vehicles and people pay for each trip, I think this will reduce demand, and thus (vehicle miles traveled)."

Safety Dividend

. . ."Over 90% of accidents today are caused by driver error," said
(40) Professor Robert W. Peterson of the Center for Insurance Law and Regulation at Santa Clara University School of Law. "There is every reason to believe that self-driving cars will reduce frequency and severity of accidents, so insurance costs should fall, perhaps dramatically."

"Cars can still get flooded, damaged or stolen," notes Michael Barry,
(45) the v.p. [vice president] of media relations at the Insurance Information Institute. "But this technology will have a dramatic impact on underwriting[4]. A lot of traditional underwriting criteria will be upended."

Barry said it's too early to quantify exactly how self-driving vehicles will affect rates, but added that injured parties in a crash involving a selfdriving
(50) car may choose to sue the vehicle's manufacturer, or the software company that designed the autonomous capability. . . .

Risks, Hurdles and the Unknown

There are regulatory and legislative obstacles to widespread use of selfdriving cars, and substantial concerns about privacy (who will have access to any driving information these vehicles store?). There's also the question
(55) of security, as hackers could theoretically take control of these vehicles, and are not known for their restraint or civic-mindedness.

---

[2]hydrocarbons—organic compounds that are chief components of petroleum and natural gas
[3]Robin Chase—founder and CEO of Buzzcar
[4]underwriting—risk determination

The Bottom Line

However it plays out, these vehicles are coming—and fast. Their full adoption will take decades, but their convenience, cost, safety and other factors will make them ubiquitous[5] and indispensable. Such as with any (60) technological revolution, the companies that plan ahead, adjust the fastest and imagine the biggest will survive and thrive. And companies invested in old technology and practices will need to evolve or risk dying.

—Joseph A. Dallegro
excerpted and adapted from "How Google's
Self-Driving Car Will Change Everything"
www.investopedia.com, 2015

---

[5]ubiquitous—everywhere

Text 2

Google's Driverless Cars Run Into Problem: Cars With Drivers

Google, a leader in efforts to create driverless cars, has run into an odd safety conundrum:[1] humans.

Last month, as one of Google's self-driving cars approached a crosswalk, it did what it was supposed to do when it slowed to allow a pedes trian to
(5) cross, prompting its "safety driver" to apply the brakes. The pedestrian was fine, but not so much Google's car, which was hit from behind by a human-driven sedan.

Google's fleet of autonomous test cars is programmed to follow the letter of the law. But it can be tough to get around if you are a stickler for
(10) the rules. One Google car, in a test in 2009, couldn't get through a fourway stop because its sensors kept waiting for other (human) drivers to stop completely and let it go. The human drivers kept inching forward, looking for the advantage—paralyzing Google's robot.

It is not just a Google issue. Researchers in the fledgling[2] field of auton
(15) omous vehicles say that one of the biggest challenges facing automated cars is blending them into a world in which humans don't behave by the book. "The real problem is that the car is too safe," said Donald Norman, director of the Design Lab at the University of California, San Diego, who studies autonomous vehicles....

(20) Traffic wrecks and deaths could well plummet in a world without any drivers, as some researchers predict. But wide use of self-driving cars is still many years away, and testers are still sorting out hypothetical risks—like hackers—and real world challenges, like what happens when an autonomous car breaks down on the highway.

(25) For now, there is the nearer-term problem of blending robots and humans. Already, cars from several automakers have technology that can warn or even take over for a driver, whether through advanced cruise control or brakes that apply themselves. Uber is working on the self-driving car technology, and Google expanded its tests in July to Austin, Tex[as].

(30) Google cars regularly take quick, evasive maneuvers or exercise caution in ways that are at once the most cautious approach, but also out of step with the other vehicles on the road....

Since 2009, Google cars have been in 16 crashes, mostly fenderbenders, and in every single case, the company says, a human was at fault. This
(35) includes the rear-ender crash on Aug. 20, and reported Tuesday by Google.

---

[1]conundrum—difficult problem [2]fledgling—new and inexperienced

The Google car slowed for a pedestrian, then the Google employee manually applied the brakes. The car was hit from behind, sending the employee to the emergency room for mild whiplash.

Google's report on the incident adds another twist: While the safety driver did the right thing by applying the brakes, if the autonomous car had been left alone, it might have braked less hard and traveled closer to the crosswalk, giving the car behind a little more room to stop. Would that have prevented the collision? Google says it's impossible to say.

There was a single case in which Google says the company was responsible for a crash. It happened in August 2011, when one of its Google cars collided with another moving vehicle. But, remarkably, the Google car was being piloted at the time by an employee. Another human at fault. . . .

On a recent outing with *New York Times* journalists, the Google driverless car took two evasive maneuvers that simultaneously displayed how the car errs on the cautious side, but also how jarring that experience can be. In one maneuver, it swerved sharply in a residential neighborhood to avoid a car that was poorly parked, so much so that the Google sensors couldn't tell if it might pull into traffic.

More jarring for human passengers was a maneuver that the Google car took as it approached a red light in moderate traffic. The laser system mounted on top of the driverless car sensed that a vehicle coming the other direction was approaching the red light at higher-than-safe speed. The Google car immediately jerked to the right in case it had to avoid a collision. In the end, the oncoming car was just doing what human drivers so often do: not approach a red light cautiously enough, though the driver did stop well in time.

Courtney Hohne, a spokeswoman for the Google project, said current testing was devoted to "smoothing out" the relationship between the car's software and humans. For instance, at four-way stops, the program lets the car inch forward, as the rest of us might, asserting its turn while looking for signs that it is being allowed to go.

The way humans often deal with these situations is that "they make eye contact. On the fly, they make agreements about who has the right of way," said John Lee, a professor of industrial and systems engineering and expert in driver safety and automation at the University of Wisconsin.

"Where are the eyes in an autonomous vehicle?" he added. . . .

—Matt Richtel and Conor Dougherty
excerpted and adapted from
"Google's Driverless Cars Run Into Problem: Cars With Drivers"
www.nytimes.com, Sept. 1, 2015

Text 3

Autonomous Vehicles Will Replace Taxi Drivers, But That's Just the Beginning

...According to the Bureau of Labor Statistics [BLS] there are about 178,000 people employed as taxi drivers or chauffeurs in the United States. But once driverless technology advances to the point that vehicles can be fully autonomous—without the need for any human behind the wheel in case
(5) of emergencies—professional drivers will become a thing of the past. Bus drivers, whether they're for schools, cities, or long-distance travel, would be made obsolete. Once cars drive themselves, food deliveries will be a matter of restaurants filling a car with orders and sending it off, eliminating the need for a delivery driver. Each of these professions employ more people
(10) and are better paid than taxi drivers, as shown in the table below.

Occupation	Average annual wage	Number of jobs	Total annual wages
Taxi drivers & chauffeurs	$25,690	178,260	$4,579,499,400
Bus drivers – transit & intercity	$39,410	158,050	$6,228,750,500
Driver / sales workers (delivering food, newspapers)	$27,720	405,810	$11,249,053,200
Bus drivers – school or special client	$29,910	499,440	$14,938,250,400
Postal service mail carriers	$51,790	307,490	$15,924,907,100
Light truck or delivery services drivers (UPS, FedEx)	$33,870	797,010	$26,994,728,700
Heavy and tractor-trailer truck drivers	$41,930	1,625,290	$68,148,409,700
TOTAL	$35,760.00	3,971,350	$148,063,599,000.00

Source: Bureau of Labor Statistics

Some of these may be a bit surprising, like postal carriers. But once fully autonomous vehicles are commonplace it would make sense for the Postal Service to make use of the technology to deliver mail, especially in areas where curbside mailboxes are standard and it would be rather simple
(15) for a mechanical arm to deposit and retrieve mail directly. Drivers of delivery trucks for companies like UPS and FedEx may also face extinction, if they're not replaced by Amazon's delivery drones first—or perhaps they'll

develop a combined system where self-driving trucks bring packages from the warehouse to their destination, and a drone delivers them the last few yards from curbside to doorstep.

Despite their importance for the economy, each of these professions pale [sic] in comparison to heavy and tractor-trailer truck drivers. This field employs the most by far—nine times as many people work as truckers than as taxi drivers, and it's the most common job in a whopping 29 states— and is also better paid than most, with an average salary of about $42,000. When considering the total amount of wages paid to each of the seven occupations in the table above, truck drivers make up nearly half, while taxi drivers & chauffeurs only account for 3%. The development of self-driving tractor-trailers won't be far behind automated taxi cabs, with companies like Daimler already testing out partially-automated trucks in Nevada.

While there may be other driving-focused jobs not included in these BLS statistics, there are certainly many more industries that will be impacted by the replacement of humans with self-driving vehicles. If this technology leads to a sharp decline in car ownership like many predict, insurance companies will have far fewer customers and may not need as many employees to service them. The same goes for mechanics and auto part manufacturers, who could face a massive drop in demand. Fewer human truckers on the road means fewer motel stays and rest stop visits, and cheaper trucking could take business away from freight trains or even oil pipelines. Vehicles programmed to obey traffic laws won't need nearly as much policing, which also means fewer traffic tickets and less revenue for municipalities. The full scale of these economic shifts will be impossible to understand until they're upon us, but the one thing we can know for sure is that they'll touch almost every aspect of society. . . .

—Sam Tracy
excerpted and adapted from "Autonomous Vehicles Will Replace Taxi Drivers, But That's Just the Beginning"
www.huffingtonpost.com, June 11, 2015

Text 4

Along for the Ride

...Automotive designers have a good incentive to get human drivers out from behind the wheel: public safety. In 2012, according to the most recent figures from the National Highway Traffic Safety Administration (NHTSA), 33,561 people were killed in car crashes in the United States, and an estimated 2.36 million were injured. According to NHTSA, a number of major crash studies have found that human error caused more than 90 percent of those crashes. In a perfect world, technology would take driver error out of the equation....

But before society can reap those benefits, experts caution there are important problems to solve. Namely, since people interact with technology in unexpected ways, how will each individual driver engage with an automated car?

For some people, automation might lead to complacency,[1] says Nicholas Ward, PhD, a human factors psychologist in the department of mechanical and industrial engineering at Montana State University. Drivers who put too much trust in automation may become overly reliant on it, overestimating what the system can do for them....

Information overload may be another concern, says Neville Stanton, PhD, a psychologist at the University of Southampton in the United Kingdom, who studies human performance in technological systems. While automated systems are designed to take pressures off the driver, he's found that they may add complexity in some cases. In an automated system, drivers may feel compelled to monitor the behavior of the system as well as keep an eye on the driving environment. That extra pressure might increase stress and error....

Given a nearly infinite combination of driver personalities, road conditions and vehicle technologies, the answer is anything but straightforward. In a study using a driving simulator, for example, Stanton found that adaptive cruise control—in which a car maintains a safe following distance from the vehicle ahead of it—can reduce a driver's mental workload and stress levels. However, that technology also caused a reduction in drivers' situational awareness. And while a lower mental workload may be a good thing in tricky traffic jams, it could cause problems if drivers totally tune out.

---

[1] complacency—a feeling of security, often while unaware of potential dangers

(35)	Indeed, driver disengagement is a serious concern for automated-car designers. Users in such vehicles are expected to tune out. After all, the appeal of such cars is that they can transport us to and fro without our having to do the hard work. But that presents a problem for our busy brains. . . .

Detached from the activity of driving, most people soon begin to (40) experience "passive fatigue," says Gerald Matthews, PhD, a psychologist at the Applied Cognition and Training in Immersive Virtual Environments Lab at the University of Central Florida. That cognitive muddling can be a big problem, Matthews says, if the driver has to take back control of the vehicle (when leaving a highway "platoon" of automated cars to re-enter city streets, (45) for instance—or, in a worst-case scenario, if automated systems fail). . . .

Like it or not, though, carmakers are pressing forward with automated systems, and psychologists can play a role in making them as safe as possible. One important issue, says Pradhan,[2] is how drivers of different ages, personalities, experience levels and cognitive abilities will deal with such (50) systems. "There is no average driver. The field is so new, we're still asking a lot of fundamental questions—and there are very few people looking at driver characteristics," he says. "Automation has to be designed for everybody." . . .

—Kirsten Weir
excerpted from "Along for the Ride"
www.apa.org, January 2015

---

[2]Anuj K. Pradhan, PhD—a research scientist who studies driver behavior and injury prevention at the University of Michigan Transportation Research Institute

PART 3—Text-Analysis Response

Your Task: Closely read the text on pages 223 through 225 and write a well-developed, text-based response of two to three paragraphs. In your response, identify a central idea in the text and analyze how the author's use of *one* writing strategy (literary element or literary technique or rhetorical device) develops this central idea. Use strong and thorough evidence from the text to support your analysis. Do *not* simply summarize the text. You may use the margins to take notes as you read and scrap paper to plan your response. Write your response on a separate sheet of paper.

Guidelines:

Be sure to
- Identify a central idea in the text.
- Analyze how the author's use of *one* writing strategy (literary element or literary technique or rhetorical device) develops this central idea. Examples include: characterization, conflict, denotation/connotation, metaphor, simile, irony, language use, point-of-view, setting, structure, symbolism, theme, tone, etc.
- Use strong and thorough evidence from the text to support your analysis.
- Organize your ideas in a cohesive and coherent manner.
- Maintain a formal style of writing.
- Follow the conventions of standard written English.

Text

The following excerpt is taken from a novel set in France during the World War II era.

Sixteen paces to the water fountain, sixteen back. Forty-two to the stairwell, forty-two back. Marie-Laure draws maps in her head, unreels a hundred yards of imaginary twine, and then turns and reels it back in. Botany smells like glue and blotter paper and pressed flowers. Paleontology
(5) smells like rock dust, bone dust. Biology smells like formalin and old fruit; it is loaded with heavy cool jars in which float things she has only had described for her: the pale coiled ropes of rattlesnakes, the severed hands of gorillas. Entomology smells like mothballs and oil: a preservative that, Dr. Geffard explains, is called naphthalene. Offices smell of carbon paper,
(10) or cigar smoke, or brandy, or perfume. Or all four.

She follows cables and pipes, railings and ropes, hedges and sidewalks. She startles people. She never knows if the lights are on.

The children she meets brim with questions: Does it hurt? Do you shut your eyes to sleep? How do you know what time it is?
(15) It doesn't hurt, she explains. And there is no darkness, not the kind they imagine. Everything is composed of webs and lattices and upheavals of sound and texture. She walks a circle around the Grand Gallery, navigating between squeaking floorboards; she hears feet tramp up and down museum staircases, a toddler squeal, the groan of a weary grandmother lowering
(20) herself onto a bench.

Color—that's another thing people don't expect. In her imagination, in her dreams, everything has color. The museum buildings are beige, chestnut, hazel. Its scientists are lilac and lemon yellow and fox brown. Piano chords loll in the speaker of the wireless in the guard station, projecting rich blacks
(25) and complicated blues down the hall toward the key pound.[1] Church bells send arcs of bronze careening off the windows. Bees are silver; pigeons are ginger and auburn and occasionally golden. The huge cypress trees she and her father pass on their morning walk are shimmering kaleidoscopes, each needle a polygon of light.
(30) She has no memories of her mother but imagines her as white, a soundless brilliance. Her father radiates a thousand colors, opal, strawberry red, deep russet, wild green; a smell like oil and metal, the feel of a lock tumbler sliding home, the sound of his key rings chiming as he walks. He is

---

[1] key pound—the office of her father, the museum locksmith

an olive green when he talks to a department head, an escalating series of
(35) oranges when he speaks to Mademoiselle Fleury from the greenhouses, a
bright red when he tries to cook. He glows sapphire when he sits over his
workbench in the evenings, humming almost inaudibly as he works, the tip
of his cigarette gleaming a prismatic blue.

She gets lost. Secretaries or botanists, and once the director's assistant,
(40) bring her back to the key pound. She is curious; she wants to know the
difference between an alga and a lichen, a *Diplodon charruanus* and a
Diplodon delodontus. Famous men take her by the elbow and escort her
through the gardens or guide her up stairwells. "I have a daughter too,"
they'll say. Or "I found her among the hummingbirds."

(45)   "*Toutes mes excuses*,"[2] her father says. He lights a cigarette; he plucks
key after key out of her pockets. "What," he whispers, "am I going to do with
you?"

On her ninth birthday, when she wakes, she finds two gifts. The first is
a wooden box with no opening she can detect. She turns it this way and that.
(50) It takes her a little while to realize one side is spring-loaded; she presses it
and the box flips open. Inside waits a single cube of creamy Camembert that
she pops directly into in [sic] her mouth.

"Too easy!" her father says, laughing.

The second gift is heavy, wrapped in paper and twine. Inside is a massive
(55) spiral-bound book. In Braille.

"They said it's for boys. Or very adventurous girls." She can hear him
smiling.

She slides her fingertips across the embossed[3] title page. *Around. The.
World. In. Eighty. Days.* "Papa, it's too expensive."
(60)   "That's for me to worry about."

That morning Marie-Laure crawls beneath the counter of the key
pound and lies on her stomach and sets all ten fingertips in a line on a page.
The French feels old-fashioned, the dots printed much closer together than
she is used to. But after a week, it becomes easy. She finds the ribbon she
(65) uses as a bookmark, opens the book, and the museum falls away.

Mysterious Mr. Fogg lives his life like a machine. Jean Passepartout
becomes his obedient valet. When, after two months, she reaches the novel's
last line, she flips back to the first page and starts again. At night she runs
her fingertips over her father's model: the bell tower, the display windows.
(70) She imagines Jules Verne's characters walking along the streets, chatting in

---

[2]toutes mes excuses—my apologies   [3]embossed—a stamped, molded or carved design

shops; a half-inch-tall baker slides speck-sized loaves in and out of his ovens; three minuscule burglars hatch plans as they drive slowly past the jeweler's; little grumbling cars throng the rue⁴ de Mirbel, wipers sliding back and forth. Behind a fourth-floor window on the rue des Patriarches, a miniature (75) version of her father sits at a miniature workbench in their miniature apartment, just as he does in real life, sanding away at some infinitesimal⁵ piece of wood; across the room is a miniature girl, skinny, quick-witted, an open book in her lap; inside her chest pulses something huge, something full of longing, something unafraid.

—Anthony Doerr
excerpted from *All the Light We Cannot See*, 2014
Scribner

---

⁴rue—street ⁵infinitesimal—very small

Regents ELA Answers August 2017
English Language Arts

Answer Key

PART 1

1. 3	9. 2	17. 4
2. 4	10. 4	18. 3
3. 1	11. 4	19. 2
4. 4	12. 4	20. 2
5. 1	13. 1	21. 2
6. 2	14. 1	22. 3
7. 1	15. 2	23. 4
8. 4	16. 1	24. 4

PART 2 *See Answers and Explanations*

PART 3 *See Answers and Explanations*

Regents Examination in English Language Arts—August 2017

Chart for Converting Total Weighted Raw Scores to Final Exam Scores (Scale Scores) (Use for the August 2017 examination only.)

Weighted Raw Score*	Scale Score	Performance Level	Weighted Raw Score*	Scale Score	Performance Level
56	100	5	27	52	1
55	99	5	26	48	1
54	99	5	25	45	1
53	99	5	24	41	1
52	99	5	23	38	1
51	98	5	22	34	1
50	98	5	21	31	1
49	97	5	20	27	1
48	96	5	19	24	1
47	94	5	18	21	1
46	92	5	17	17	1
45	91	5	16	14	1
44	89	5	15	12	1
43	88	5	14	10	1
42	87	5	13	8	1
41	85	5	12	8	1
40	84	4	11	7	1
39	82	4	10	6	1
38	80	4	9	5	1
37	79	4	8	4	1
36	76	3	7	4	1
35	74	3	6	3	1
34	72	3	5	2	1
33	69	3	4	2	1
32	67	3	3	1	1
31	65	3	2	1	1
30	61	2	1	1	1
29	58	2	0	0	1
28	55	2			

The conversion table is determined independently for each administration of the exam.

Answers and Explanations

PART 1—Reading Comprehension
Multiple-Choice Questions

Passage A

1. **3** "knowledgeable." In this introductory scene, the character of Dora-Rouge would look at the stars and, ". . . tell us what place we would pass on the next day." The narrator tells us that the next day they did reach those places.

2. **4** "insignificance." In this passage, the narrator illustrates how the characters enter a sense of timelessness and leave behind their lives on earth; they become, ". . . just a small dream among the . . . many dreams of earth." "Insignificance" best describes these feelings.

3. **1** "I saw vines creeping forward." A tendril is a vine or stem. The meaning of the word is revealed in the images of a leaf and flowers reaching up through darkness to reveal a truth, ". . . that had been there all along . . . ." None of the other choices expresses the feeling in these images.

4. **4** "enlightening." In this passage, the narrator describes how she recovers a lost knowledge, "the oldest bond of survival . . . this opening light of life . . . ." This passage does not suggest feelings of confusion, amusement, or threat.

5. **1** "transformation." Here the narrator tells us that, "New senses came to me." In becoming equal to other animals (transformed), she moves, ". . . as they moved, seeing as they saw."

6. **2** "developed a kinship with the environment." For the women in this story, the experience of their journey is one of recovering an ancestral relationship with the natural world. Among the choices, this answer best expresses the meaning of their experience.

7. **1** "link the past with the future." Toward the end of the passage, the narrator tells us that she, ". . . felt newly found . . . ." Before recovering a lost relationship with nature and her ancestral past, she felt her life had been, ". . . without all its knowings." Looking forward, she says, "Now we, the four of us, all had the same eyes, ..."

8. **4** "personal narrative." This passage, from a novel, is a vivid example of a first-person narrative of a significant experience.

9. **2** "[with] clarity of mind comes connection of spirit." This statement best describes the spiritual journey of the narrator and her companions. The other choices express themes that might reliably fit other contexts but are not central to this passage.

10. **4** "And listening to the night, I knew there was another horizon, beyond the one we could see." This quote best supports the central idea of rediscovery and spiritual enlightenment in the passage. It recalls both the experience of the journey and suggests its meaning for the women in the future.

Passage B

11. **4** "impermanence." The poet creates her own verb to describe what happens as flowers wither and die: they lose their petals. None of the other choices is suggested in this stanza.

12. **4** "her insignificance in the eyes of nature." In these lines, the poet remarks that, ". . . none of [The trees and flowers] are noticing [her]" as she walks among them. This best describes what the narrator is feeling in these lines.

13. **1** "consciousness is a barrier to connecting with nature." The narrator expresses the feeling that she, ". . . most perfectly resembles" the trees and flowers, ". . . when I am sleeping . . . ." The poet and the sky are, ". . . in open conversation," only with, "Thoughts gone dim." None of the other choices expresses these ideas in this poem.

14. **1** "envious." In the first stanza, the narrator tells us that she does not, "gleam into leaf . . ." like a tree, or dazzle with beauty like a flower. She wishes she had (envies) the tree's longevity and the flower's daring.

Passage C

15. **2** "odd occurrences." The meaning of "anomalies" is clarified in the examples that follow: snakes that leave their winter dens early and erratic (unpredictable) well-water levels are best described as odd occurrences.

16. **1** "contributing historical facts." The article begins with a reference to a decision by the Chinese government, after a series of devastating earthquakes in 1973, to recruit young students to be "earthquake watchers." The article is developed and uses historical and scientific facts throughout.

17. **4** "urgency." The sense of urgency is felt when, suddenly, ". . . the popping stopped, just as it had before a catastrophic earthquake in 1966 that killed more than 8,000."

18. **3** "not always predictable." The contrast between the two earthquakes in this passage are (1) the warnings were effective and saved many lives, and (2) the quake hit without warning and ". . . killed nearly 250,000 people, most of whom were asleep." None of the other choices is an accurate statement about earthquakes.

19. **2** "modified his methods of observing earthquakes." This paragraph reports on how as a scientist Jian Lin no longer observes odd behavior in snakes but, instead, uses sophisticated scientific methods to observe earthquakes. This section of the article focuses on how his methods of study changed.

20. **2** "supporters." The meaning of "champions" as supporters and advocates is clarified in the context of the sentence and in the subsequent information about how the scientists presented their theories to other scientists.

21. **2** "an earthquake that happened in one place would decrease the possibility of another happening nearby." This long-held belief about earthquakes failed to explain a sequence of quakes in Los Angeles in 1992; further analysis by Lin, Stein and King ignored this belief and showed them to be a series of aftershocks. Their work became "one of the decade's most-cited earthquake research papers." Review of the text will show that each of the other choices is reported as reliable.

22. **3** "shear stress was greater than clamping stress." Determining the answer to this question requires careful reading of the paragraph to understand the two kinds of stress and how they account for earthquakes. The seismologists determined that, ". . . most of the earthquakes [in the Los Angeles series] had occurred in areas where the shifting of the ground had caused increased stress." None of the other choices is consistent with the information in the passage.

23. **4** "dedicated." As a young man, Jian Lin experienced a devastating earthquake in China: ". . . I was scared of earthquakes . . . . I decided that if I could do anything—*anything*—to save lives lost to earthquakes, it would be worth the effort." None of the other choices adequately describes his character and determination.

24. **4** "important to future studies." Throughout the article, there are references to the ways in which Lin's work has supported further research. At the end, we understand that Lin and other seismologists continue their research to find ways to reliably predict earthquakes and to save lives.

PART 2—Argument Response

Sample Essay Response

 As technology advances, innovations are introduced to society on a regular basis. One of these innovations, which humans may see in the near future, is a self-driving car. Although this idea may seem promising, many disadvantages come along with it. Self-driving cars should not replace human drivers, despite how beneficial they sound.

 A primary reason to oppose self-driving cars is that many people would lose their jobs. At present, autonomous cars usually have a person in the driver's seat in case of a problem. However, once the cars can function safely without human intervention, professional drivers will no longer be needed. Heavy truck and tractor-trailer drivers have "the most common job in a whopping 29 states." (Text 3, line 24) In addition to the 1,625,290 heavy and tractor-trailer drivers who would lose their jobs, other workers, such as taxi drivers, bus drivers, and mail carriers, might face unemployment. (Text 3, graphic)

 Another concern about self-driving cars is the risk of confusion that can occur between drivers and robots. This is not a good idea, "blending [self-driving cars] into a world in which humans don't behave by the book." (Text 2, line 16) One example of this confusion is when a Google car, "sensed that a vehicle coming the other direction was approaching the red light at a higher-than-safe speed." (Text 2, lines 56–57) In response, the Google car immediately veered to the side in anticipation of a crash; however, the driver of the other car stopped in plenty of time. Although challenging driving situations may occur on a regular basis, "the way humans often deal with these situations is that, "they make eye contact." (Text 2, lines 67–68) This interaction is not possible between a self-driving car and a human. An automated reaction could result in otherwise avoidable crashes.

 A third issue with self-driven cars is privacy. Just as home computers and other technology can be hacked, the same applies for the software in a self-driving car. For example, "who will have access to any driving information these vehicles store?" (Text 1, lines 53 and 54) If the vehicle stores a person's payment information or a record of places the person usually goes, a hacker might have access to significant personal and financial information of someone who rides in a self-driving car.

 Supporters of self-driving cars argue that self-driving cars are safer. They explain that, "Over 90% of accidents today are caused by driver error." (Text 1, line 39) However, that does not prove that self-driving cars will be safer. Humans make errors, but technology can malfunction. Errors and accidents can still occur, whether they are caused by a human or by a computer.

The idea of self-driving cars is exciting, but the truth is that technology is never 100% reliable. Self-driving cars, once they become part of everyday life, could bring about a loss of jobs, confusion between human and automated drivers, and concerns about privacy. Although the immediate attraction is that self-driving cars are safer than human drivers, the reality is this world is not ideal or perfect. These two worlds—realistic and idealistic—will never mesh. Too many risks are at stake here, with little to no benefits.

Analysis

This argument represents a good response to the task. The first paragraph identifies the context and establishes a claim that is distinguished from opposing claims. The argument is clearly organized, and each section begins with an appropriate transition: "A primary reason . . . Another concern . . . A third issue . . . ." The writer's claim is supported by relevant evidence in the texts. Development is adequate, but the argument would be stronger if the fifth paragraph, refuting the claim that self-driving cars are safer, were more fully developed with evidence from Text 4. The conclusion appropriately acknowledges the appeal of self-driving cars but forcefully urges the need for caution. The writing is clear and free of significant errors in the conventions. This response would merit a high score.

(See pages 79–80 for the scoring guidelines.)

PART 3—Text-Analysis Response

Sample Essay Response

    The story centers around a young girl who, after losing her sense of sight, compensates for it by heightening the strength of her imagination and other senses. Through the vivid, colorful things that she imagines on a morning walk, such as the image of "huge cypress trees" that "are shimmering kaleidoscopes, with each needle a polygon of light," the character, Marie-Laure, is able to construct her own vision of the world even though she cannot see with her eyes. The author intends to express to the reader that there are no limitations to what a human can do. A person with a disability such as Marie-Laure's can function nearly as well as anyone, and can even go beyond seeing and feeling what other people normally can. Some people who lose a sense can develop a creativity that cannot be mimicked and is entirely unique to themselves.

    The author uses imagery to convey the point of the story. He answers questions such as, "How does Marie-Laure feel being blind?" and, "How exactly is she able to live in the world without sight?" We understand that Marie-Laure must have had vision at one time: "In her imagination, in her dreams, everything has color." When other children are curious and ask her what it is like, she assures them that it does not hurt, and it is not all darkness. She says, ". . . everything is composed of webs and lattices and upheavals of sound and texture."

    The author chose to use images to create a visual in the reader's mind, where Marie has color in her imagination, where "museum buildings are beige, chestnut, hazel," and its scientists are "lilac and lemon yellow and fox brown." She describes bees as silver and "pigeons are ginger and auburn and occasionally gold." The author's use of vivid imagery gives the reader a clear sense of the girl's experiences and her imaginative way of seeing her world.

Analysis

This response (edited for clarity) is especially good in the way the central idea is expressed as answers to a series of questions: "How does Marie-Laure feel being blind?" and, "How exactly is she able to live in the world without sight?" The analysis is supported through extensive use of relevant quotes and skillful use of the language of vision, seeing, and imagery. The response is brief but clearly organized in two paragraphs. The writing is appropriately formal and demonstrates control of complex sentence structures and the conventions. This response would merit a high score.

(See pages 81–82 for the scoring guidelines.)

Regents ELA Examination June 2018
English Language Arts

PART 1—Reading Comprehension

Directions (1–24): Closely read each of the three passages below. After each passage, there are several multiple-choice questions. Select the best suggested answer to each question and write its number in the space provided. You may use the margins to take notes as you read.

Reading Comprehension Passage A

    "That woman's art-jargon[1] tires me," said Clovis to his journalist friend. "She's so fond of talking of certain pictures as 'growing on one,' as though they were a sort of fungus."
    "That reminds me," said the journalist, "of the story of Henri Deplis.
(5) Have I ever told it [to] you?"
    Clovis shook his head.
    "Henri Deplis was by birth a native of the Grand Duchy of Luxemburg. On maturer reflection he became a commercial traveller. His business activities frequently took him beyond the limits of the Grand Duchy, and
(10) he was stopping in a small town of Northern Italy when news reached him from home that a legacy[2] from a distant and deceased relative had fallen to his share.
    "It was not a large legacy, even from the modest standpoint of Henri Deplis, but it impelled him towards some seemingly harmless extravagances.
(15) In particular it led him to patronise local art as represented by the tattoo-

---

[1] art-jargon—language specific to the art world
[2] legacy—inheritance

needles of Signor Andreas Pincini. Signor Pincini was, perhaps, the most brilliant master of tattoo craft that Italy had ever known, but his circumstances were decidedly impoverished, and for the sum of six hundred francs he gladly undertook to cover his client's back, from the collarbone down to the waistline, with a glowing representation of the Fall of Icarus.[3] The design, when finally developed, was a slight disappointment to Monsieur Deplis, who had suspected Icarus of being a fortress taken by Wallenstein in the Thirty Years' War, but he was more than satisfied with the execution of the work, which was acclaimed by all who had the privilege of seeing it as Pincini's masterpiece.

"It was his greatest effort, and his last. Without even waiting to be paid, the illustrious craftsman departed this life, and was buried under an ornate tombstone, whose winged cherubs would have afforded singularly little scope[4] for the exercise of his favourite art. There remained, however, the widow Pincini, to whom the six hundred francs were due. And thereupon arose the great crisis in the life of Henri Deplis, traveller of commerce. The legacy, under the stress of numerous little calls on its substance,[5] had dwindled to very insignificant proportions, and when a pressing wine bill and sundry[6] other current accounts had been paid, there remained little more than 430 francs to offer to the widow. The lady was properly indignant, not wholly, as she volubly explained, on account of the suggested writing-off of 170 francs, but also at the attempt to depreciate the value of her late husband's acknowledged masterpiece. In a week's time Deplis was obliged to reduce his offer to 405 francs, which circum stance fanned the widow's indignation into a fury. She cancelled the sale of the work of art, and a few days later Deplis learned with a sense of consternation[7] that she had presented it to the municipality of Bergamo, which had gratefully accepted it. He left the neighbourhood as unobtrusively as possible, and was genuinely relieved when his business commands took him to Rome, where he hoped his identity and that of the famous picture might be lost sight of.

"But he bore on his back the burden of the dead man's genius. On presenting himself one day in the steaming corridor of a vapour bath, he was at once hustled back into his clothes by the proprietor, who was a

---

[3]Fall of Icarus—In Greek mythology Icarus wore wings made of wax and feathers so he could fly. However, because of his excessive pride and carelessness he flew too close to the sun. His wings melted and he plunged to his death in the sea.
[4]scope—opportunity
[5]little calls on its substance—withdrawals from the inheritance
[6]sundry—various
[7]consternation—alarmed amazement

North Italian, and who emphatically refused to allow the celebrated Fall of Icarus to be publicly on view without the permission of the municipality of Bergamo. Public interest and official vigilance increased as the matter became more widely known, and Deplis was unable to take a simple dip in the sea or river on the hottest afternoon unless clothed up to the collarbone in a substantial bathing garment. Later on the authorities of Bergamo conceived the idea that salt water might be injurious to the masterpiece, and a perpetual injunction[8] was obtained which debarred[9] the muchly harassed commercial traveller from sea bathing under any circumstances. Altogether, he was fervently thankful when his firm of employers found him a new range of activities in the neighbourhood of Bordeaux. His thankfulness, however, ceased abruptly at the Franco-Italian frontier. An imposing array of official force barred his departure, and he was sternly reminded of the stringent law, which forbids the exportation of Italian works of art.

"A diplomatic parley ensued between the Luxemburgian and Italian Governments, and at one time the European situation became overcast with the possibilities of trouble. But the Italian Government stood firm; it declined to concern itself in the least with the fortunes or even the existence of Henri Deplis, commercial traveller, but was immovable in its decision that the Fall of Icarus (by the late Pincini, Andreas) at present the property of the municipality of Bergamo, should not leave the country. . . .

"Meanwhile, the unhappy human background fared no better than before, and it was not surprising that he drifted into the ranks of Italian anarchists. Four times at least he was escorted to the frontier as a dangerous and undesirable foreigner, but he was always brought back as the Fall of Icarus (attributed to Pincini, Andreas, early Twentieth Century). And then one day, at an anarchist congress at Genoa, a fellow-worker, in the heat of debate, broke a phial full of corrosive liquid over his back. The red shirt that he was wearing mitigated[10] the effects, but the Icarus was ruined beyond recognition. His assailant was severely reprimanded for assaulting a fellow-anarchist and received seven years' imprisonment for defacing a national art treasure. As soon as he was able to leave the hospital Henri Deplis was put across the frontier as an undesirable alien.

---

[8]injunction—restraint
[9]debarred—prevented
[10]mitigated—lessened

"In the quieter streets of Paris, especially in the neighbourhood of the Ministry of Fine Arts, you may sometimes meet a depressed, anxious-looking man, who, if you pass him the time of day, will answer you with a slight Luxemburgian accent. He nurses the illusion that he is one of the lost arms of the Venus de Milo,[11] and hopes that the French Government may be persuaded to buy him. On all other subjects I believe he is tolerably sane."

—H.H. Munro ("Saki")
excerpted and adapted from "The Background"
The Chronicles of Clovis, 1912
John Lane, The Bodley Head

---

[11]Venus de Milo—a famous statue of the goddess Venus

1 Lines 13 through 16 and lines 29 through 35 reveal that Henri Deplis

   (1) invests wisely
   (2) behaves impulsively
   (3) avoids confrontation
   (4) resists change   1 _____

2 The municipality of Bergamo owns the artwork on Henri Deplis's back as a result of

   (1) a harmless misunderstanding
   (2) widow Pincini's vengeance
   (3) a fair exchange
   (4) Henri Deplis's pride   2 _____

3 As used in line 43, the word "unobtrusively" most nearly means

   (1) reluctantly
   (2) indecisively
   (3) rebelliously
   (4) inconspicuously   3 _____

4 The figurative language in line 46 implies that Henri Deplis feels

   (1) the tattoo is a curse to him
   (2) responsible for the artist's death
   (3) the tattoo is a thing of beauty
   (4) obligated to display the artwork   4 _____

5 Lines 59 through 62 indicate that Henri Deplis's situation causes him to become

   (1) successful
   (2) powerless
   (3) manipulative
   (4) respected   5 _____

6 It can be inferred that Henri Deplis joins the "Italian anarchists" (lines 71 and 72) because he

(1) is afraid for his future
(2) desires wealthy friends
(3) is unconcerned with international politics
(4) seeks gainful employment   6 _____

7 Lines 78 through 81 support a central idea that

(1) people can achieve their personal goals
(2) governments often choose stability over change
(3) societies often value objects above individuals
(4) governments can develop reasonable regulations   7 _____

8 The phrase "nurses the illusion" (line 85) reveals that Henri Deplis is

(1) fulfilling his ambitious dream
(2) searching for anonymity
(3) struggling with reality
(4) enjoying his freedom   8 _____

9 The subject of Henri Deplis's tattoo implies a parallel to his

(1) social ignorance
(2) economic worth
(3) sense of humility
(4) loss of control   9 _____

Reading Comprehension Passage B

Carmel Point

    The extraordinary patience of things!
    This beautiful place defaced with a crop of surburban houses —
    How beautiful when we first beheld it,
    Unbroken field of poppy and lupin[1] walled with clean cliffs;
(5) No intrusion but two or three horses pasturing,
    Or a few milch[2] cows rubbing their flanks on the outcrop[3] rock-heads —
    Now the spoiler has come: does it care?
    Not faintly. It has all time. It knows the people are a tide
    That swells and in time will ebb, and all
(10) Their works dissolve. Meanwhile the image of the pristine[4] beauty
    Lives in the very grain of the granite,
    Safe as the endless ocean that climbs our cliff. — As for us:
    We must uncenter our minds from ourselves;
    We must unhumanize our views a little, and become confident
(15) As the rock and ocean that we were made from.

—Robinson Jeffers
The Collected Poetry of Robinson Jeffers, Volume Three, 1991
Stanford University Press

---

[1] poppy and lupin—brightly colored wildflowers
[2] milch—milk
[3] outcrop—protruding
[4] pristine—pure, unspoiled

10 The word "defaced" (line 2) suggests that the narrator is
   (1) suspicious
   (2) confused
   (3) worried
   (4) critical

11 The description in lines 3 through 6 creates a mood of
   (1) despair
   (2) amusement
   (3) tranquility
   (4) negativity

12 The metaphor in lines 8 through 10 suggests that
   (1) humanity's impact is beneficial
   (2) nature's power is limited
   (3) humanity's influence is temporary
   (4) nature's significance is exaggerated

13 The words "uncenter" (line 13) and "unhumanize" (line 14) suggest that people should
   (1) become more tolerant
   (2) recognize their superiority
   (3) uphold their values
   (4) become less egocentric

14 The narrator implies that humans are
   (1) protective of their environment
   (2) unaware of their insignificance
   (3) perplexed by their surroundings
   (4) satisfied with their indifference

Reading Comprehension Passage C

Learning to Love Volatility[1]

Several years before the financial crisis descended on us, I put forward the concept of "black swans": large events that are both unexpected and highly consequential. We never see black swans coming, but when they do arrive, they profoundly shape our world: Think of World War I, 9/11, the
(5) Internet, the rise of Google.

In economic life and history more generally, just about everything of consequence comes from black swans; ordinary events have paltry[2] effects in the long term. Still, through some mental bias, people think in hindsight that they "sort of" considered the possibility of such events; this gives
(10) them confidence in continuing to formulate predictions. But our tools for forecasting and risk measurement cannot begin to capture black swans. Indeed, our faith in these tools make it more likely that we will continue to take dangerous, uninformed risks.

Some made the mistake of thinking that I hoped to see us develop
(15) better methods for predicting black swans. Others asked if we should just give up and throw our hands in the air: If we could not measure the risks of potential blowups, what were we to do? The answer is simple: We should try to create institutions that won't fall apart when we encounter black swans— or that might even gain from these unexpected events.

(20) Fragility is the quality of things that are vulnerable to volatility. Take the coffee cup on your desk: It wants peace and quiet because it incurs more harm than benefit from random events. The opposite of fragile, therefore, isn't robust or sturdy or resilient—things with these qualities are simply difficult to break.

(25) To deal with black swans, we instead need things that gain from volatility, variability, stress and disorder. My (admittedly inelegant) term for this crucial quality is "antifragile." The only existing expression remotely close to the concept of antifragility is what we derivatives traders[3] call "long gamma," to describe financial packages that benefit from market volatility.
(30) Crucially, both fragility and antifragility are measurable.

As a practical matter, emphasizing antifragility means that our private and public sectors should be able to thrive and improve in the face of disorder. By grasping the mechanisms of antifragility, we can make better

---

[1]volatility—the amount of uncertainty or risk about the size of changes in investment values
[2]paltry—insignificant
[3]derivative traders—financial professionals who work buying and selling stock options, futures, and other contracts

decisions without the illusion of being able to predict the next big thing. We can navigate situations in which the unknown predominates[4] and our understanding is limited.

Herewith are five policy rules that can help us to establish antifragility as a principle of our socioeconomic life.

Rule 1: Think of the economy as being more like a cat than a washing machine.

We are victims of the post-Enlightenment view that the world functions like a sophisticated machine, to be understood like a textbook engineering problem and run by wonks.[5] In other words, like a home appliance, not like the human body. If this were so, our institutions would have no self-healing properties and would need someone to run and micromanage them, to protect their safety, because they cannot survive on their own.

By contrast, natural or organic systems are antifragile: They need some dose of disorder in order to develop. Deprive your bones of stress and they become brittle. This denial of the antifragility of living or complex systems is the costliest mistake that we have made in modern times. Stifling natural fluctuations masks real problems, causing the explosions to be both delayed and more intense when they do take place. As with the flammable material accumulating on the forest floor in the absence of forest fires, problems hide in the absence of stressors, and the resulting cumulative harm can take on tragic proportions. . . .

Rule 2: Favor businesses that benefit from their own mistakes, not those whose mistakes percolate into the system.

Some businesses and political systems respond to stress better than others. The airline industry is set up in such a way as to make travel safer after every plane crash. A tragedy leads to the thorough examination and elimination of the cause of the problem. The same thing happens in the restaurant industry, where the quality of your next meal depends on the failure rate in the business—what kills some makes others stronger. Without the high failure rate in the restaurant business, you would be eating Soviet-style cafeteria food for your next meal out.

These industries are antifragile: The collective enterprise benefits from the fragility of the individual components, so nothing fails in vain. These

---

[4]predominates—exerts control or influence
[5]wonks—experts

businesses have properties similar to evolution in the natural world, with a well-functioning mechanism to benefit from evolutionary pressures, one error at a time. . . .

Rule 3: Small is beautiful, but it is also efficient.

Experts in business and government are always talking about economies of scale. They say that increasing the size of projects and institutions brings cost savings. But the "efficient," when too large, isn't so efficient. Size produces visible benefits but also hidden risks; it increases exposure to the probability of large losses. Projects of $100 million seem rational, but they tend to have much higher percentage overruns than projects of, say, $10 million. Great size in itself, when it exceeds a certain threshold, produces fragility and can eradicate all the gains from economies of scale. To see how large things can be fragile, consider the difference between an elephant and a mouse: The former breaks a leg at the slightest fall, while the latter is unharmed by a drop several multiples of its height. This explains why we have so many more mice than elephants. . . .

Rule 4: Trial and error beats academic knowledge.

Things that are antifragile love randomness and uncertainty, which also means—crucially—that they can learn from errors. Tinkering by trial and error has traditionally played a larger role than directed science in Western invention and innovation. Indeed, advances in theoretical science have most often emerged from technological development, which is closely tied to entrepreneurship.[6] Just think of the number of famous college dropouts in the computer industry.

But I don't mean just any version of trial and error. There is a crucial requirement to achieve antifragility: The potential cost of errors needs to remain small; the potential gain should be large. It is the asymmetry between upside and downside that allows antifragile tinkering to benefit from disorder and uncertainty. . . .

America has emulated this earlier model, in the invention of everything from cybernetics[7] to the pricing formulas for derivatives. They were developed by practitioners in trial-and-error mode, drawing continuous feedback from reality. To promote antifragility, we must recognize that there is an inverse relationship between the amount of formal education that a culture supports and its volume of trial-and-error by tinkering. Innovation doesn't require theoretical instruction, what I like to compare to "lecturing birds on how to fly."

---

[6]entrepreneurship—new business development and ownership
[7]cybernetics—related to computer networks

Rule 5: Decision makers must have skin in the game.

At no time in the history of humankind have more positions of power been assigned to people who don't take personal risks. But the idea of incentive in capitalism demands some comparable form of disincentive. In the business world, the solution is simple: Bonuses that go to managers whose firms subsequently fail should be clawed back, and there should be additional financial penalties for those who hide risks under the rug. This has an excellent precedent[8] in the practices of the ancients. The Romans forced engineers to sleep under a bridge once it was completed.

Because our current system is so complex, it lacks elementary clarity: No regulator will know more about the hidden risks of an enterprise than the engineer who can hide exposures to rare events and be unharmed by their consequences. This rule would have saved us from the banking crisis, when bankers who loaded their balance sheets with exposures to small probability events collected bonuses during the quiet years and then transferred the harm to the taxpayer, keeping their own compensation.

In these five rules, I have sketched out only a few of the more obvious policy conclusions that we might draw from a proper appreciation of antifragility. But the significance of antifragility runs deeper. It is not just a useful heuristic[9] for socioeconomic matters but a crucial property of life in general. Things that are antifragile only grow and improve under adversity. This dynamic can be seen not just in economic life but in the evolution of all things, from cuisine, urbanization and legal systems to our own existence as a species on this planet. . . .

—Nassim Nicholas Taleb
excerpted from "Learning to Love Volatility"
The Wall Street Journal, November 16, 2012

---

[8]precedent—established example
[9]heuristic—formula

15 The author believes that "black swans" (line 2) are

(1) used to anticipate failures
(2) unimportant setbacks
(3) unpredictable occurrences
(4) used to guarantee benefits   15 _____

16 What is the tone of lines 17 through 19?

(1) insistent   (3) reverent
(2) sarcastic   (4) pessimistic   16 _____

17 The reference to "long gamma" (lines 28 and 29) serves to

(1) introduce a political theory
(2) provide a relevant example
(3) oppose a previous argument
(4) support a scientific proposal   17 _____

18 It can be inferred from lines 45 through 53 that stressors

(1) should be seen as signals of faulty systems
(2) can be expected to occur in predictable cycles
(3) must be carefully managed to avoid instability
(4) should be viewed as opportunities to improve performance   18 _____

19 Lines 54 through 61 contribute to a central idea by emphasizing the

(1) role of government in quality management
(2) dismissal of progressive practices
(3) importance of setbacks to industry success
(4) consequences of ignoring standards   19 _____

20 Rule 3 suggests the most "efficient" way to manage projects is to

(1) have an economic plan
(2) resist unnecessary growth
(3) encourage fragile economics
(4) revise corporate regulation   20 _____

21 As used in line 91, the word "emulated" most nearly means
   (1) imitated
   (2) discredited
   (3) accelerated
   (4) ignored

22 The comparison drawn in lines 96 through 98 illustrates that innovation
   (1) can be instinctive
   (2) relies on education
   (3) can be rigid
   (4) depends on technology

23 The phrase "clawed back" (line 103) implies that some managers
   (1) are intolerant of traditional rules
   (2) should be open to constructive criticism
   (3) are wary of unconventional ideas
   (4) should be accountable for careless decisions

24 Which statement best reflects a central idea about disorder?
   (1) "Things that are antifragile love randomness and uncertainty, which also means—crucially—that they can learn from errors" (lines 79 and 80)
   (2) "There is a crucial requirement to achieve antifragility: The potential cost of errors needs to remain small; the potential gain should be large" (lines 86 through 88)
   (3) "At no time in the history of humankind have more positions of power been assigned to people who don't take personal risks" (lines 99 and 100)
   (4) "No regulator will know more about the hidden risks of an enterprise than the engineer who can hide exposures to rare events" (lines 108 through 110)

PART 2—Argument Response

Directions: Closely read each of the *four* texts on pages 250 through 259 and write a source-based argument on the topic below. You may use the margins to take notes as you read and scrap paper to plan your response. Write your argument on a separate sheet of paper.

Topic: Is graffiti vandalism?

Your Task: Carefully read each of the *four* texts provided. Then, using evidence from at least *three* of the texts, write a well-developed argument regarding whether or not graffiti is vandalism. Clearly establish your claim, distinguish your claim from alternate or opposing claims, and use specific, relevant, and sufficient evidence from at least *three* of the texts to develop your argument. Do *not* simply summarize each text.

Guidelines:

Be sure to

- Establish your claim regarding whether or not graffiti is vandalism.
- Distinguish your claim from alternate or opposing claims.
- Use specific, relevant, and sufficient evidence from at least *three* of the texts to develop your argument.
- Identify each source that you reference by text number and line number(s) or graphic (for example: Text 1, line 4 or Text 2, graphic).
- Organize your ideas in a cohesive and coherent manner.
- Maintain a formal style of writing.
- Follow the conventions of standard written English.

Texts:

Text 1—What Is Street Art? Vandalism, Graffiti or Public Art—Part I

Text 2—Graffiti Vandals Cost Public Millions

Text 3—Is Urban Graffiti a Force for Good or Evil?

Text 4—Art or Vandalism: Banksy, 5Pointz and the Fight for Artistic Expression

Text 1

What Is Street Art? Vandalism, Graffiti or Public Art—Part I

What is Street Art?

There is as yet no simple definition of street art. It is an amorphous[1] beast encompassing art which is found in or inspired by the urban environment. With anti-capitalist and rebellious undertones, it is a democratic form of popular public art probably best understood by seeing it in situ.[2] It is not
(5) limited to the gallery nor easily collected or possessed by those who may turn art into a trophy.

Considered by some a nuisance, for others street art is a tool for communicating views of dissent,[3] asking difficult questions and expressing political concerns.
(10) Its definition and uses are changing: originally a tool to mark territorial boundaries of urban youth today it is even seen in some cases as a means of urban beautification and regeneration.

Whether it is regarded as vandalism or public art, street art has caught the interest of the art world and its lovers of beauty.

Is street art vandalism?

(15) In an interview with the Queens Tribune, New York City's Queens Museum of Art Executive Director Tom Finkelpearl said public art "is the best way for people to express themselves in this city." Finkelpearl, who helps organize socially conscious art exhibitions, added, "Art gets dialogue going. That's very good." However, he doesn't find graffiti to be art, and
(20) says, "I can't condone vandalism... It's really upsetting to me that people would need to write their names over and over again in public space. It's this culture of fame. I really think it's regrettable that they think that's the only way to become famous."

Is street art illegal?

The legal distinction between permanent graffiti and art is permission,
(25) but the topic becomes even more complex regarding impermanent, nondestructive forms of graffiti (yarn bombing, video projection, and street installation).

---

[1]amorphous—hard to define
[2]in situ—in its original place
[3]dissent—differing opinion

With permission, traditional painted graffiti is technically considered public art. Without permission, painters of public and private property (30) are committing vandalism and are, by definition, criminals. However, it still stands that most street art is unsanctioned, and many artists who have painted without permission, (Banksy, Shepard Fairey) have been glorified as legitimate and socially conscious artists. . . .

Broken Window Theory: Vandalism vs. Street Art
Vandalism is inexcusable destruction of property, and has been shown (35) to have negative repercussions on its setting. It has also been observed by criminologists to have a 'snowball effect' of generating more negativity within its vicinity. Dr. James Q. Wilson and Dr. George Kelling studied the effects of disorder (in this case, a broken window) in an urban setting, and found that one instance of neglect increases the likelihood of more broken (40) windows and graffiti will appear. Then, there is an observable increase in actual violent crime. The researchers concluded there is a direct link between vandalism, street violence, and the general decline of a society.

Their theory, named the Broken Window Theory and first published in 1982, argues that crime is the inevitable result of disorder, and that if neglect (45) is present in a place, whether it is disrepair or thoughtless graffiti, people walking by will think no one cares about that place, and the unfavorable damage is therefore acceptable.

Street Art and Gentrification[4]
Thoughtful and attractive street art, however, has been suggested to have regenerative effects on a neighborhood. In fact, the popular street artist (50) Banksy, who has catapulted his guerilla[5] street art pastime into a profitable career as an auctionable contemporary artist, has come under criticism for his art contributing to the gentrification of neighborhoods. Appropriate Media claims that:

> "Banksy. . . sells his lazy polemics[6] to Hollywood movie stars
> (55) for big bucks. . . . Graffiti artists are the performing spraycan
> monkeys for gentrification. In collusion with property developers,
> they paint deprived areas bright colours to indicate the latest

---

[4]gentrification—the process of renovation and revival of deteriorated urban neighborhoods that results in the displacement of lower income residents by higher income residents
[5]guerilla—combative
[6]polemics—criticisms

funky inner city area ripe for regeneration. Pushing out low income families in their wake, to be replaced by middle class metrosexuals with their urban art collections." [Times Online] . . .

Video Projection

Digitally projecting a computer-manipulated image onto a surface via a light and projection system.

Street Installation

Street installations are a growing trend within the 'street art' movement. Whereas conventional street art and graffiti is done on surfaces or walls, 'street installations' use 3-D objects and space to interfere with the urban environment. Like graffiti, it is non-permission based and once the object or sculpture is installed it is left there by the artist. . . .

Yarn Bombing

Yarn Bombing is a type of street art that employs colourful displays of knitted or crocheted cloth rather than paint or chalk. The practice is believed to have originated in the U.S. with Texas knitters trying to find a creative way to use their leftover and unfinished knitting projects, but has since spread worldwide. While other forms of graffiti may be expressive, decorative, territorial, socio-political commentary, advertising or vandalism, yarn bombing is almost exclusively about beautification and creativity.

—Erin Wooters Yip
excerpted from "What Is Street Art? Vandalism,
Graffiti or Public Art—Part I"
http://artradarjournal.com, January 21, 2010

Text 2

Graffiti Vandals Cost Public Millions

There is a certain rhythm to Michael Parks' job. He paints, they tag, he paints, they tag. ...

It's a silent tango between those who scrawl graffiti and those who are paid to remove it. The dance pauses briefly when one side gives up. Maybe a
(5) tagger gets bored—or caught. Maybe a painter moves on to something else.

For now, that won't be Parks. He shows up as a "graffiti ranger" for Seattle Public Utilities (SPU) every day, just as he has for the past six years, in a white uniform and orange vest. He and a partner roam Seattle neighborhoods in a city-owned truck, their solvent cans, brushes and paint
(10) drums clanging in the back.

They stop at stairwells, bridges, trash cans, postal boxes, retaining walls. Graffiti disappears. And it all comes back the next week. ...

In Seattle, rangers are only one faction. The parks department, Seattle's Department of Transportation, King County Metro Transit and Sound
(15) Transit all pay workers to erase the mess. For years, Seattle police even had a "graffiti detective," but he retired in 2007 and the position never was filled.

The effort is expensive. Seattle Public Utilities spent about $1 million last year for graffiti enforcement, removal, education and outreach, while King County Metro Transit spent $734,000 last year to rid buses, tunnels,
(20) park and rides and bus shelters of graffiti.

Add it all up and, overall, city and county agencies are spending millions in tax dollars a year trying to combat the ubiquitous[1] squiggles, tags, gang symbols and drawings that mar public property.

Its persistence creates headaches for private-property owners required to
(25) get rid of it, and anxiety from residents worried about neighborhood blight. ...

No centralized front

It's hard for officials to talk with any certainty about graffiti trends. Because so many city agencies deal with it, no one keeps a centralized database of complaints.

And there are a lot.

(30) Seattle Public Utilities has averaged about 7,300 a year since 2008, said Linda Jones, manager of the graffiti-rangers team. Some are divvied up among the six rangers. The rest are handed off to other city agencies, she said.

---

[1]ubiquitous—found everywhere

The rangers erased or painted out 445,000 square feet of graffiti in 2009. That's almost eight football fields.
(35) Hate messages take first priority; those have to be gone in 24 hours. Everything else is tackled within six to 10 days, Jones said. . . .
 Certainly, graffiti seems to tattoo all urban landscapes. Look around Seattle and you'll find it everywhere: billboards, construction sites, businesses and homes.
(40) Overhead highway signs and train cars hold particular appeal, evidence of the adrenaline rush—and grudging respect of other taggers—that go along with the crime, officials say.
 In some cities, such as Los Angeles, these signs are wrapped with barbed wire to prevent vandalism. But that's not the case in Washington, said Jamie
(45) Holter, spokeswoman for the Washington state Department of Transportation.
 To clean a freeway sign, workers have to shut down a lane at night, get in a truck and raise a boom.[2] . . .
 Last year, a 28-year-old Miami man made national news after he fell to his death while tagging a sign on the Palmetto Expressway. In 1997, one
(50) prolific Seattle tagger severed a foot while tagging a train in Golden Gardens. But that didn't stop him. Records show he pleaded guilty for tagging again in 1999 and 2000. . . .

Hard to catch . . .
 Arrest numbers fluctuate wildly year to year. For instance, Seattle police made 234 graffiti-related arrests in 2008. That number fell to 41 last year.
(55) "Usually [taggers] are on foot, so they can just drop the stuff and run," police spokesman Mark Jamieson said.
 And property owners are left to clean it up.
 Under the city's Graffiti Nuisance Ordinance, if private businesses or homes get tagged and owners don't act promptly, SPU sends a letter asking
(60) them to remove it within 10 days. Ignore the notice, and property owners could face fines of $100 per day with a maximum of $5,000.
 SPU sent 1,392 first-time warnings to property owners last year. About 75 percent complied, Jones said. After a second warning, nearly all got rid of the graffiti, she said. . . .

—Sonia Krishnan
excerpted from "Graffiti Vandals Cost Public Millions"
www.seattletimes.com, April 25, 2010

---

[2]boom—a maneuverable arm of a truck used to lift workers for aerial work

Text 3

Is Urban Graffiti a Force for Good or Evil?

   Ban it, legalise it, put it behind glass . . . no matter what city councils do, graffiti remains the scapegoat for all manner of urban ills, from burglary on one extreme to gentrification on the other. But it may have another effect on cities entirely.

(5)   In the spring of 2008, the Tate Modern opened the world's first major public museum display of graffiti and street art, inviting six international artists to decorate its facade[1] with enormous, eye-catching murals.

   Meanwhile, just down the riverbank at Southwark crown court, eight members of London's well-known DPM crew[2] were tried for an estimated (10) £1m[3] in graffiti-related damages across the country, and sentenced to a total of 11 years in prison—the biggest prosecution for graffiti that the UK [United Kingdom] has ever seen. . . .

   Since its contemporary birth in 1960s Philadelphia, city leaders have tended to condemn graffiti as mindless vandalism. Policing later began (15) leaning towards the "broken window" theory, which argues that if petty crime like graffiti is visibly ignored, suggesting general neglect, it could inspire more serious offences. The UK spends £1bn[4] on graffiti removal each year.

   But as cities seek to "clean up", could graffiti's ephemeral[5] role within the urban environment actually be good for cities?

(20)   For Ben Eine, a graffiti artist whose work was gifted to Barack Obama by David Cameron,[6] graffiti leads not to drug deals and robberies, as the broken windows theory suggests, but to something very different. "If they [councils] stopped painting over them, they would get tagged and then they'd do silver stuff over it. And then eventually, people would do nice (25) paintings over it . . . The natural evolution of graffiti is that it will just turn out looking nice," he told the recent Graffiti Sessions academic conference. . . .

   Embracing graffiti's cultural value can do wonders for a city's tourism industry, too. In Bristol, the 2012 See No Evil festival saw 50,000 people flock to the streets; in Stavanger, Norway, the city walls are transformed into a canvas for (30) the highly successful annual NuArt festival. Even without a dedicated event, for every painted wall in a city there is most likely a tour to go with it. A three-hour

---

[1] facade—front of a building
[2] DPM crew—graffiti gang
[3] £1m—one million British pounds
[4] £1bn—one billion British pounds
[5] ephemeral—short-lived
[6] David Cameron—British Prime Minister 2010–2016

graffiti walk around the streets of Shoreditch could set you back £20, and in colourful Buenos Aires a tour of the decorated walls can cost $25 (£16).

Buenos Aires is a particularly fascinating example of a city where the walls talk, telling tales of a turbulent past. Here, graffiti has been continuously harnessed as a tool of political communication, resistance and activism by citizens caught up in a cycle of military dictatorship, restored democracy and economic collapse. Although there are laws prohibiting graffiti, the city has gained worldwide recognition for its urban art. Now a new bill proposes to assign a registry of graffiti artists to designated spots in Buenos Aires, with the aim of decreasing undesirable markings elsewhere.

A similar approach has been adopted in Toronto, where a Graffiti Management Plan sees that "graffiti vandalism" is removed by city staff, while "graffiti art and other street art that adds vibrancy" may remain if commissioned by the building's owner. Toronto council has even assigned an official panel of specialists to judge the value of graffiti, deciding whose markings are artistically worthy to grace the city's bricks. . . .

Legal or not, as graffiti seeps into the fabric of neighbourhoods, it becomes a natural fact of everyday life in the city, a cultural practice appreciated and legitimised by young urban dwellers. Simultaneously, it is harnessed by local authorities and property owners as a method of cultural branding, to create the sort of "poor but sexy" neighbourhoods that work so well for cities like Berlin. Active curation[7] of street art really got into full swing in pre-Olympic London when the work of a local crew was scrubbed from the walls of the River Lea Navigation to make way for street art by several international artists, specially commissioned by the Olympic legacy's public art body. . . .

From its roots as a means of visual communication for disenfranchised[8] youth to both hide and be seen, graffiti has developed into a bona fide art form, a legitimate force for economic, cultural and social good—and, as we continue to shift towards increasingly sanitised urban environments, one of the few remaining ways we have to respond to our surroundings in an expressive, public way. "Good" v "bad" graffiti might continue to be disputed between fervid councillors,[9] but Eine says the public have moved on. "The whole world is covered in graffiti. No one cares. It's just part of urban noise."

—Athlyn Cathcart-Keays
excerpted and adapted from "Is Urban Graffiti a Force for Good or Evil?"
www.theguardian.com, January 7, 2015

---

[7]curation—to organize for presentation
[8]disenfranchised—marginalized or powerless
[9]fervid councillors—passionate community representatives

Text 4

Art or Vandalism: Banksy, 5Pointz and the Fight for Artistic Expression

In 1974, Norman Mailer wrote, *The Faith of Graffiti*, one of the first literary works that looked at the origins and importance of graffiti in modern urban culture. Mailer's belief was not widespread with many opponents looking at graffiti as no more than vandalism. The battle between those two
(5) camps[1] has waged ever since, although the graffiti artists, (now given the more politically correct name of street artist), have slowly begun to win the battle.

Artists like Banksy and Mr. Brainwash have actually made the public salivate with anticipation as they await their next creative exploits. While
(10) often unsanctioned, street art allows the artist to bypass the confines of the formal art world where only the elite can participate. Communicating directly with the public allows street artists to present socially relevant content while at the same time beautifying the bleak sprawl of urban decay.

Whether graffiti is art or crime has an implication in protecting the
(15) integrity of a street artist's work. If considered art, the creative works might be shielded under the Visual Arts Rights Act (VARA). VARA protects the work of visual art, from intentional distortion, mutilation or other modification. As a crime, these works can be washed away without further consideration, as has been the fate of many.

(20)   *"It's a very frustrated feeling you get when the only people with good photos of your work are the police department."*

       —Banksy

Street artists across the country have been fighting back using the VARA argument. 5Pointz, an outdoor art exhibit space in Long Island City, New
(25) York, is considered to be the world's premiere "graffiti Mecca." Since 1993, with the property owner's permission, artists have been creating unique artistic works on numerous walls of a 200,000-square-foot factory. 5Pointz has now become a tourist attraction, with hundreds visiting each week. Now, the building is supposed to be razed to make way for a luxury apartment
(30) complex. Sixteen artists have sued to preserve the space citing VARA. They are currently seeking a temporary injunction.[2]

---

[1] camps—groups
[2] injunction—a judicial order that restrains a person from beginning or continuing an action that threatens the legal rights of another

Los Angeles, often on the forefront of intellectual property issues, recently passed a new murals ordinance making street art legal if you pay for a permit, get permission from the location, and publicly post your (35) intentions. Shepard Fairey, best known for his Obama Hope poster and his Obey campaign, has teamed up with renowned graffiti artist, Risk to create a major piece in Skid Row. Another work will be painted in the Arts District by culture-jamming contemporary artist, Ron English.

Other artists thrive on the illegality of their work. Banksy recently (40) hit New York City, creating 17 works throughout various neighborhoods. Despite their aesthetic value, the NYPD's Vandal Squad want to question him in connection with the vandalism, and if they catch him, he will be charged. The vandal squad is currently combing through hours of surveillance footage looking for clues to Banksy's whereabouts. Mayor Bloomberg said that any (45) Banksy works on public property will be removed. . . .

So, while the battle rages on, it at least seems for the time being that street artists are gaining public support and it may only be a matter of time before laws like the one in L.A. are the norm.

—Steve Schlackman
excerpted from "Art or Vandalism: Banksy, 5Pointz and the Fight for Artistic Expression"
http://artlawjournal.com, October 26, 2013

PART 3—Text-Analysis Response

Your Task: Closely read the text on pages 261 through 263 and write a well-developed, text-based response of two to three paragraphs. In your response, identify a central idea in the text and analyze how the author's use of *one* writing strategy (literary element or literary technique or rhetorical device) develops this central idea. Use strong and thorough evidence from the text to support your analysis. Do *not* simply summarize the text. You may use the margins to take notes as you read and scrap paper to plan your response. Write your response on a separate sheet of paper.

Guidelines:

Be sure to
- Identify a central idea in the text.
- Analyze how the author's use of *one* writing strategy (literary element or literary technique or rhetorical device) develops this central idea. Examples include: characterization, conflict, denotation/connotation, metaphor, simile, irony, language use, point-of-view, setting, structure, symbolism, theme, tone, etc.
- Use strong and thorough evidence from the text to support your analysis.
- Organize your ideas in a cohesive and coherent manner.
- Maintain a formal style of writing.
- Follow the conventions of standard written English.

Text

He always feels hot, I always feel cold. In the summer when it really is hot he does nothing but complain about how hot he feels. He is irritated if he sees me put a jumper[1] on in the evening.

He speaks several languages well; I do not speak any well. He manages— (5) in his own way—to speak even the languages that he doesn't know.

He has an excellent sense of direction, I have none at all. After one day in a foreign city he can move about in it as thoughtlessly as a butterfly. I get lost in my own city; I have to ask directions so that I can get back home again. He hates asking directions; when we go by car to a town we don't (10) know he doesn't want to ask directions and tells me to look at the map. I don't know how to read maps and I get confused by all the little red circles and he loses his temper.

He loves the theatre, painting, music, especially music. I do not understand music at all, painting doesn't mean much to me and I get bored (15) at the theatre. I love and understand one thing in the world and that is poetry.

He loves museums, and I will go if I am forced to but with an unpleasant sense of effort and duty. He loves libraries and I hate them.

He loves travelling, unfamiliar foreign cities, restaurants. I would like (20) to stay at home all the time and never move. . . .

He tells me I have no curiosity, but this is not true. I am curious about a few, a very few, things. And when I have got to know them I retain scattered impressions of them, or the cadence[2] of phrase, or a word. But my world, in which these completely unrelated (unless in some secret fashion unbeknown (25) to me) impressions and cadences rise to the surface, is a sad, barren place. His world, on the other hand, is green and populous and richly cultivated; it is a fertile, well-watered countryside in which woods, meadows, orchards and villages flourish.

Everything I do is done laboriously, with great difficulty and uncertainty. (30) I am very lazy, and if I want to finish anything it is absolutely essential that I spend hours stretched out on the sofa. He is never idle, and is always doing something; when he goes to lie down in the afternoons he takes proofs to correct or a book full of notes; he wants us to go to the cinema, then to a reception, then to the theatre—all on the same day. In one day he succeeds (35) in doing, and in making me do, a mass of different things, and in meeting extremely diverse kinds of people. If I am alone and try to act as he does I

---

[1]jumper—sweater
[2]cadence—rhythm

get nothing at all done, because I get stuck all afternoon somewhere I had meant to stay for half an hour, or because I get lost and cannot find the right street, or because the most boring person and the one I least wanted to meet drags me off to the place I least wanted to go to. . . .

I don't know how to dance and he does.

I don't know how to type and he does.

I don't know how to drive. If I suggest that I should get a licence too he disagrees. He says I would never manage it. I think he likes me to be dependent on him for some things. . . .

And so—more than ever—I feel I do everything inadequately or mistakenly. But if I once find out that he has made a mistake I tell him so over and over again until he is exasperated. I can be very annoying at times. . . .

When he was a young man he was slim, handsome and finely built; he did not have a beard but long, soft moustaches instead, and he looked like the [British] actor Robert Donat. He was like that about twenty years ago when I first knew him, and I remember that he used to wear an elegant kind of Scottish flannel shirt. I remember that one evening he walked me back to the *pensione*[3] where I was living; we walked together along the *Via Nazionale*.[4] I already felt that I was very old and had been through a great deal and had made many mistakes, and he seemed a boy to me, light years away from me. I don't remember what we talked about on that evening walking along the *Via Nazionale*; nothing important, I suppose, and the idea that we would become husband and wife was light years away from me. Then we lost sight of each other, and when we met again he no longer looked like Robert Donat, but more like Balzac [French writer]. When we met again he still wore his Scottish shirts but on him now they looked like garments for a polar expedition; now he had his beard and on his head he wore his ridiculous crumpled woollen hat; everything about him put you in mind of an imminent[5] departure for the North Pole. Because, although he always feels hot, he has the habit of dressing as if he were surrounded by snow, ice and polar bears; or he dresses like a Brazilian coffee-planter, but he always dresses differently from everyone else.

If I remind him of that walk along the *Via Nazionale* he says he remembers it, but I know he is lying and that he remembers nothing; and I sometimes ask myself if it was us, these two people, almost twenty years ago

---

[3]pensione—boarding house
[4]Via Nazionale—a grand boulevard
[5]imminent—upcoming or about to occur

on the *Via Nazionale*; two people who conversed so politely, so urbanely,[6] as the sun was setting; who chatted a little about everything perhaps and (75) about nothing; two friends talking, two young intellectuals out for a walk; so young, so educated, so uninvolved, so ready to judge one another with kind impartiality; so ready to say goodbye to one another for ever, as the sun set, at the corner of the street.

—Natalia Ginzburg
excerpted and adapted from "He and I"
The Little Virtues, 1962 Arcade Publishing

---

[6]urbanely—elegantly

Regents ELA Answers June 2018
English Language Arts

Answer Key

PART 1

1. 2	9. 4	17. 2
2. 2	10. 4	18. 4
3. 4	11. 3	19. 3
4. 1	12. 3	20. 2
5. 2	13. 4	21. 1
6. 1	14. 2	22. 1
7. 3	15. 3	23. 4
8. 3	16. 1	24. 1

PART 2 *See Answers and Explanations*

PART 3 *See Answers and Explanations*

Regents Examination in English Language Arts—June 2018

Chart for Converting Total Weighted Raw Scores to Final Exam Scores (Scale Scores) (Use for the June 2018 examination only.)

Weighted Raw Score*	Scale Score	Performance Level
56	100	5
55	99	5
54	99	5
53	99	5
52	99	5
51	98	5
50	97	5
49	96	5
48	94	5
47	92	5
46	91	5
45	89	5
44	88	5
43	87	5
42	86	5
41	85	5
40	83	5
39	81	4
38	80	4
37	79	4
36	76	4
35	73	3
34	71	3
33	69	3
32	66	3
31	65	3
30	60	3
29	57	2
28	55	2
27	52	2
26	48	1
25	45	1
24	42	1
23	38	1
22	35	1
21	32	1
20	29	1
19	25	1
18	22	1
17	19	1
16	16	1
15	13	1
14	11	1
13	9	1
12	8	1
11	7	1
10	6	1
9	6	1
8	54	1
7	4	1
6	3	1
5	3	1
4	2	1
3	2	1
2	1	1
1	1	1
0	0	1

The conversion table is determined independently for each administration of the exam.

Answers Explained

PART 1—Reading Comprehension
Multiple-Choice Questions

Passage A

1. **2** "behaves impulsively." The narrator tells us that Deplis "was impelled" to spend nearly all of his small inheritance (his modest legacy) on having a local tattoo master, Signor Andreas Pincini, cover his back with the representation of a painting.

2. **2** "widow Pincini's vengeance." The narrator reports that following the sudden death of her husband and Deplis's failure to pay her what was owed, the widow Pincini canceled the sale and presented the art work (the tattoo) as a gift to the municipality.

3. **4** "inconspicuously." Here, both terms mean "unnoticeably, discreetly, and quietly." In other words, Deplis left Bergamo without drawing attention to himself. Deplis was hoping that "his identity and that of the famous picture might be lost sight of."

4. **1** "the tattoo is a curse to him." The details in the paragraph that contains lines 47–64 reveals situations in which the tattooed painting on his back prevents Deplis from taking a "simple dip in the sea" or from traveling outside of Italy. None of the other choices suggests the feeling of a burden or a curse that Deplis comes to experience.

5. **2** "powerless." These lines illustrate how "official force . . . [and] stringent law" deny Deplis the opportunity to take on "a new range of activities" in Bordeaux (France). The passage reveals the ways in which Deplis has become powerless to change or improve his life. None of the other choices expresses Deplis's increasingly unhappy condition.

6. **1** "is afraid for his future." Joining up with Italian anarchists suggests that Deplis becomes desperate about how his life will continue. None of the other choices is supported by the text.

7. **3** "societies often value objects above individuals." Following the incident in which Deplis is attacked by a fellow anarchist, we are told that "his assailant was severely reprimanded [criticized, scolded] for attacking a fellow-anarchist" and sentenced to seven years in prison for defacing the (tattooed) painting, "a national art treasure." Now that the tattoo was no longer a pristine work of art, "Henri Deplis was put across the frontier as an undesirable alien."

8. **3** "struggling with reality." The end of the story reveals that Deplis inhabits the streets of Paris near the Ministry of Fine Arts, telling passersby that he is actually "one of the lost arms" of a famous ancient Greek statue. He hopes the French government will buy him! None of the other choices accurately describes Deplis's state of mind.

9. **4** "loss of control." Footnote 3 (at line 20) reminds the reader of the story of Icarus: the young man who, in pride and recklessness, flies too close to the sun and plunges to his death. Deplis's choice of the painting of Icarus as the subject of his tattoo is an ironic parallel to the consequences of Deplis's own impulsiveness.

Passage B

10. **4** "critical." *To deface* means "to mar, ruin, or disfigure." The critical tone in the speaker's voice, however, becomes evident only in the poem as a whole. This question reveals the importance of understanding an entire passage before determining the meaning of many specific details.

11. **3** "tranquility." The images in these lines evoke feelings of quiet and calm beauty; there is "no intrusion" of noise or human disruption. None of the other choices suggests the tone of this passage.

12. **3** "humanity's influence is temporary." The beautiful place the poet is addressing, "Knows the people are a tide . . . and [that] all/Their works dissolve." The central idea of the poem is that nature, in its pristine beauty, is patient and will endure in "rock and ocean." The "spoiler" of human activity will come and go as do the tides.

13. **4** "become less egocentric." Line 13 offers a clear and vivid definition of what it means to be "egocentric." To "unhumanize" our views means to think beyond human concerns, to recognize the ageless source of life in "rock and ocean."

14. **2** "unaware of their insignificance." The poet is urging us to "uncenter our minds" and to "unhumanize our views" because we fail to understand that humans are only a small part of the natural world.

Passage C

15. **3** "unpredictable occurrences." The author defines the term *black swans* as "large events that are both unexpected [unpredictable] and highly consequential [very important]." None of the other choices accurately explains what the author means.

16. **1** "insistent." This word best describes the author's tone in answering the rhetorical question "what were we to do?" The author insists that "we should try to create institutions that won't fall apart." The tone is positive, assertive, and practical; it is not sarcastic, reverent, or pessimistic.

17. **2** "provide a relevant example." The term "long gamma" is offered as an example of what the author means by "antifragility."

18. **4** "should be viewed as opportunities to improve performance." In lines 46–54, the author develops further the concept of "antifragility," leading to the central idea established in item 19 below.

19. **3** "importance of setbacks to industry success." Note that Rule 2 argues that "businesses . . . benefit from evolutionary pressures, one error at a time. . . ."

20. **2** "resist unnecessary growth." Rule 3 explains both that small is efficient and that unnecessarily large businesses or political systems become fragile and fail to gain from "economies of scale." None of the other choices supports the author's views on efficient ways to manage projects.

21. **1** "imitated." The sentence that starts in line 91 says that in the invention of cybernetics and pricing formulas, America has used, copied, or adopted an "earlier model" of trial and error. This question is an example of understanding vocabulary in context.

22. **1** "can be instinctive." In Rule 4, the author argues that formal education and theoretical instruction actually work against, or have an inverse relationship to, trial-and-error tinkering. Trying things and seeing what works or doesn't is, in the author's view, central to Western invention and innovation. Innovation may use technology, but the author would not say that innovation depends on technology.

23. **4** "should be accountable for careless decisions." The author says very forcefully that managers of failed companies should give back any bonuses they received and should even pay additional penalties. None of the other choices conveys the meaning of the expression "clawed back."

24. **1** "Things that are antifragile love randomness and uncertainty, which also means—crucially—that they can learn from errors (lines 79 and 80)." Among the choices, this best expresses the author's central idea about disorder, namely that, "things that are antifragile only grow and improve under adversity" (line 118).

PART 2—Argument Response

Sample Essay Response

Graffiti on public or private urban buildings has been a problem for decades. In recent years, many have jumped to the defense of graffiti artists by passing legislation and using the softer label "street artists." Nevertheless, graffiti is still nothing more than brightly colored vandalism.

Graffiti is, by its nature, selfish. Most graffiti is just covering others' buildings with the so-called artist's name in eye-catching fonts (Text 1, line 21). Many are doing it for attention, and they do it at the expense of property owners and taxpayers. In one year, for example, the city of Seattle spent $1 million getting rid of graffiti on public buildings and vehicles, catching and punishing perpetrators, and attempting to prevent future crimes (Text 2, lines 17–20). In the UK, the figure is about £1 billion on graffiti removal a year (Text 3, line 17). This does not include the burden put on private property owners, who have to remove their unwanted graffiti under risk of fines (Text 2, lines 60–61). Graffiti artists who don't bother to get permission from the city or from building owners are just creating a financial burden on taxpayers and property owners.

Another major problem of graffiti is described by the broken window theory. According to this theory, if the public sees crime go unpunished, such as a broken window left in full view or graffiti not removed or covered, there is an increased likelihood that more crimes of similar natures will be committed (Text 1, lines 37–42). This can escalate. For example, graffiti of a person's name left out in the open can encourage graffiti of profanity, hate messages, and symbols and, finally, more active violent forms of vandalism. Unpunished graffiti encourages more crime.

Legislation has been passed to protect the so-called street art, but it is misguided. The Visual Arts Rights Act (VARA) protects public art as long as it is done with permission (Text 4, lines 15 and 16). However, VARA has also been used to protest the renovation of a building in New York. Several graffiti artists decorated a private factory's exterior with permission; the factory has since been sold and the new owner wants to change the exterior. Although the new owners can do whatever they please with their building, 16 artists are seeking an injunction to prevent destruction of their work. Legislation such as VARA will only reinforce graffiti artists' notion that they have the right to vandalize their cities. In the end, no matter how attractive the art is, property rights should come first.

Graffiti art is always vandalism unless done with explicit permission of the building's owner, which is rarely the case. Efforts to excuse or protect graffiti will only further harm the victims of the crime.

Analysis

This is a clear and forcefully developed argument that demonstrates understanding of a complex subject. This writer accepts the proposition that all graffiti is vandalism and supports that view with appropriate citations from all four texts. The argument is also strengthened by granting, briefly, the distinction between so-called street art and vandalism. The former is acceptable if done with permission. The latter is a violation of property rights and often creates a financial burden.

This essay is well organized. Each paragraph concludes with a strong assertion of the main idea. "Graffiti is still nothing more than brightly colored vandalism." "Graffiti artists who don't bother to get permission . . . are just creating a financial burden on taxpayers and property owners." "Unpunished graffiti encourages more crime." "In the end, no matter how attractive the art is, property rights should come first." Each is an example of a "precise and insightful claim."

This writer demonstrates skill in varying sentence structures and shows command of the conventions. (Minor errors in punctuation or usage have been edited.) This essay would merit a high score.

(See pages 79–80 for the scoring guidelines.)

PART 3—Text-Analysis Response

Sample Essay Response

From the first line of the text, the author is already shaping the two characters through the use of juxtaposition. By using simple comparisons at first, like hot and cold, the author gradually develops the comparisons to be much more insightful. For example, she compares her world as a sad, empty wasteland to his world, which is lavish, abundant, and beautiful. Through these comparisons, the author is able to characterize herself and her husband as two completely different people. Placing these contrasting characteristics right next to each other actually further pushes the two figures to opposite ends of the spectrum, dramatically developing the idea that people grow and evolve over time.

Although one might interpret these opposing qualities to mean that the narrator and her husband balance out each other, this is clearly not the central idea she is trying to get across. At the end of the passage, the author offers an anecdote about how she and her husband walked along the Via Nazionale when they first met twenty years before. She likens their earlier selves to those of friends and intellectuals, similar in their likes and interests. This part of the passage, juxtaposed with the stark contrasts in the characters they have become, shows how significantly they have evolved as people and as a couple over the years. Once similar, their personalities not only oppose now but also clash. In the larger context, these images of opposition and evolution over time illustrate important ideas about marriage and other human relationships.

Analysis

This text is developed as a series of dramatic, unsentimental assertions about the differences in the lives and personalities of the author and her husband. Many writers focused on the author's effective use of parallel construction and repetition; some commented on the use of a first person point of view. This essay successfully demonstrates how the juxtaposition of ideas and details serves the author's purpose.

    The essay is brief, insightful, and generally well written. The first sentence reveals the writer's understanding of how Ginzburg's method and subject are complementary, "From the first line of the text, the author is already shaping the two characters through the use of juxtaposition." The essay is further developed to show how the method of juxtaposition not only tells us about the characters but also dramatizes the larger theme of how people change and how marriages evolve over time. The writer demonstrates command of sentence variety and of the conventions. This essay would merit a high score.

(See pages 81–82 for the scoring guidelines.)

Regents ELA Examination August 2018
English Language Arts

PART 1—Reading Comprehension

Directions (1–24): Closely read each of the three passages below. After each passage, there are several multiple-choice questions. Select the best suggested answer to each question and write its number in the space provided. You may use the margins to take notes as you read.

Reading Comprehension Passage A

    When my mother found out that the large mirror in the living room was inhabited, we all gradually went from disbelief to astonishment, and from this to a state of contemplation, ending up by accepting it as an everyday thing.
(5)   The fact that the old, spotted mirror reflected the dear departed in the family was not enough to upset our life style. Following the old saying of "let the house burn as long as no one sees the smoke," we kept the secret to ourselves since, after all, it was nobody else's business.
    At any rate, some time went by before each one of us would feel
(10) absolutely comfortable about sitting down in our favorite chair and learning that, in the mirror, that same chair was occupied by somebody else. For example, it could be Aurelia, my grandmother's sister (1939), and even if cousin Natalie would be on my side of the room, across from her would be the almost forgotten Uncle Nicholas (1927). As could have been expected,
(15) our departed reflected in the mirror presented the image of a family gathering almost identical to our own, since nothing, absolutely nothing in the living-room—the furniture and its arrangement, the light, etc.—was changed in the mirror. The only difference was that on the other side it was them instead of us.

(20) I don't know about the others, but I sometimes felt that, more than a vision in the mirror, I was watching an old worn-out movie, already clouded. The deceased's efforts to copy our gestures were slower, restrained, as if the mirror were not truly showing a direct image but the reflection of some other reflection.

(25) From the very beginning I knew that everything would get more complicated as soon as my cousin Clara got back from vacation. Because of her boldness and determination, Clara had long given me the impression that she had blundered into our family by mistake. This suspicion had been somewhat bolstered by her being one of the first women dentists in the (30) country. However, the idea that she might have been with us by mistake went away as soon as my cousin hung up her diploma and started to embroider sheets beside my grandmother, aunts and other cousins, waiting for a suitor who actually did show up but was found lacking in one respect or another—nobody ever really found out why.

(35) Once she graduated, Clara became the family oracle,[1] even though she never practiced her profession. She would prescribe painkillers and was the arbiter[2] of fashion; she would choose the theater shows and rule on whether the punch had the right amount of liquor at each social gathering. In view of all this, it was fitting that she take one month off every year to go to the (40) beach....

Naturally, the idea of moving the mirror to the dining-room was hers. And so was its sequel: to bring the mirror near the big table, so we could all sit together for meals.

In spite of my mother's fears that the mirror people would run away (45) or get annoyed because of the fuss, everything went fine. I must admit it was comforting to sit every day at the table and see so many familiar faces, although some of those from the other side were distant relatives, and others, due to their lengthy—although unintentional—absence, were almost strangers. There were about twenty of us sitting at the table every (50) day, and even if their gestures and movements seemed more remote than ours and their meals a little washed-out, we generally gave the impression of being a large family that got along well....

For a while we ate all together, without further incidents or problems. We mustn't forget Clara, however, whom we had allowed to sit at the (55) frontier between the two tables, the equator separating what was from what was not. Although we paid no attention to the situation, we should have.

---

[1] oracle—a person who gives wise or authoritative opinions
[2] arbiter—judge

Compounding our regrettable oversight was the fact that lethargic[3] Eulalia sat across from her so that one night, with the same cordiality with which she had addressed Gus [a family member], Clara asked Eulalia to pass the salad. (60) Eulalia affected the haughty disdain[4] of offended royalty as she passed the spectral[5] salad bowl, filled with dull lettuce and grayish semi-transparent tomatoes which Clara gobbled up, smiling mischievously at the novelty of it all. She watched us with the same defiance in her eyes that she had on the day she enrolled in a man's subject. There was no time to act. We (65) just watched her grow pale, then her smile faded away until finally Clara collapsed against the mirror.

Once the funeral business was over and we sat back down at the table again, we saw that Clara had taken a place on the other side. She was between cousin Baltazar (1940) and a great-uncle whom we simply called "Ito."

(70) This *faux pas*[6] dampened our conviviality[7] somewhat. In a way, we felt betrayed; we felt that they had grievously abused our hospitality. However, we ended up divided over the question of who was really whose guest. It was also plain that our carelessness and Clara's irrepressible inquisitiveness had contributed to the mishap. In fact, a short time later we realized that (75) there wasn't a great deal of difference between what Clara did before and what she was doing now, and so we decided to overlook the incident and get on with things. Nevertheless, each day we became less and less sure about which side was life and which its reflection, and as one bad step leads to another, I ended up taking Clara's empty place.

(80) I am now much closer to them. I can almost hear the distant rustle of the folding and unfolding of napkins, the slight clinking of glasses and cutlery, the movement of chairs. The fact is that I can't tell if these sounds come from them or from us. I'm obviously not worried about clearing that up. What really troubles me, though, is that Clara doesn't seem to behave (85) properly, with either the solemnity or with the opacity owed to her new position; I don't know how to put it. Even worse, the problem is that I— more than anybody else in the family—may become the target of Clara's machinations,[8] since we were always joined by a very special affection, perhaps because we were the same age and had shared the same children's (90) games and the first anxieties of adolescence. . . .

---

[3] lethargic—sluggish
[4] disdain—contempt
[5] spectral—ghostly
[6] *faux pas*—social mistake
[7] conviviality—liveliness
[8] machinations—schemes

As it happens, she is doing her best to get my attention, and ever since last Monday she has been waiting for me to slip up so she can pass me a pineapple this big, admittedly a little bleached-out, but just right for making juice and also a bit sour, just as she knows I like it.

—María Elena Llano
excerpted and adapted from "In the Family"
Short Stories by Latin American Women: The Magic and the Real, 1990
translated by Beatriz Teleki
Arte Público Press

1 Lines 1 through 8 introduce the family's

(1) tendency to gossip
(2) experience with loss
(3) process of adaptation
(4) attempt to socialize

1 _____

2 The description in lines 9 through 19 reinforces the

(1) isolation of the deceased relatives
(2) strangeness of the family's situation
(3) fearfulness of the insecure relatives
(4) tension of the family's interaction

2 _____

3 The statement, "The only difference was that on the other side it was them instead of us" (lines 18 and 19) emphasizes a central idea of the

(1) rivalry among different generations
(2) continuity between life and death
(3) conflict between tradition and change
(4) respect among distant relatives

3 _____

4 The use of the word "However" (line 30) signals a change in

(1) the narrator's perception of Clara's place in the family
(2) Clara's understanding of the narrator's submission to the family
(3) the narrator's resentment of Clara's profession
(4) Clara's rejection of the family's eccentricities

4 _____

5 Clara's title of "family oracle" (line 35) is most likely a result of her

(1) assertive personality
(2) disciplined character
(3) warm demeanor
(4) generous spirit

5 _____

6 Lines 44 through 49 suggest that the mirror people are

(1) an inconvenience to the living family
(2) curious about the living family
(3) welcomed by the living family
(4) disturbed by the living family

6 _____

7 The phrases "regrettable oversight" (line 57) and "funeral business" (line 67) imply that the narrator's reaction to her cousin's death can best be described as

(1) indifferent
(2) irritated
(3) impulsive
(4) irrational

7 ____

8 Lines 91 through 94 suggest that the narrator

(1) loses her identity
(2) dislikes intrusions
(3) distrusts her cousin
(4) resents routines

8 ____

9 Which detail best reveals Clara's character?

(1) "been with us by mistake" (line 30)
(2) "waiting for a suitor" (line 32)
(3) "gobbled up, smiling mischievously" (line 62)
(4) "collapsed against the mirror" (line 66)

9 ____

10 Which quotation best reflects a central idea in the text?

(1) "the idea of moving the mirror to the dining-room was hers" (line 41)
(2) "There were about twenty of us sitting at the table every day" (lines 49 and 50)
(3) "We just watched her grow pale, then her smile faded away" (lines 64 and 65)
(4) "we became less and less sure about which side was life and which its reflection" (lines 77 and 78)

10 ____

Reading Comprehension Passage B

Pears, Unstolen

I was stopped on the sidewalk by pears
glowing on their tree like antique ornaments
with flaking paint, a green metallic shimmer,
hinting at yellow, mottled with a few flecks of red.

(5) As light flickered over them, they seemed
to flutter like candles in the leaves.
But no—they were pears, and probably hard,
I told myself, probably inedible and holding

their juices tight, if they had juices at all.
(10) Besides, something was pitting[1] them like brass,
splotching, as if trying to spoil. Still, I wanted them.
I wanted that September light fingering each fruit,

so it seemed lit from without and within,
a fleshy tallow. I wanted the season's clock
(15) stopped before the next strike, stopped
in this amber afternoon, my walk halfway,

the shiny leaves just starting to curl,
but still far from falling, and the pears
half hidden among them like birds singing
(20) so sweetly you step closer, peer in,

careful, careful, wanting to touch that song,
but not spoil it. I stood there wanting
to hoard time, a thief trying to steal
a song I couldn't hear, a fool believing

(25) there's something sweet that won't disappoint,
that pears in the hand could be anything
like pears dreamed in the mind, or a moment
stopped could be kept from rotting.

---

[1] pitting—scarring

But what's so bad, a thief will ask: How is
(30) plucking a piece of fruit worse than worms
tunneling in, or bees sating themselves
on that honeyed light, or mold blotching it?

Surely a saint has an answer to that,
something about how too much sweetness spoils,
(35) or there's another sweetness that grows within.
For weeks I went back and forth, stopping

at the tree, watching first one pear let go
of its limb, then many begin to fall,
flickering briefly like coals in the grass
(40) before they shrivel, letting their seeds slip out.

"That's the way it goes," mutters the thief.
"As scripture says they must," muses the saint,
while a few last pears glow on their brittle stems,
and the wind-strummed boughs bend toward earth.

—Betsy Sholl
from *www.imagejournal.org*, Issue 66

11 The description of the pears in lines 1 through 11 helps to illustrate the

(1) balance between stability and change
(2) difficulty of recognizing imperfection
(3) difference between perception and reality
(4) importance of overcoming obstacles   11 ____

12 The word "sating" as used in line 31 is closest in meaning to

(1) indulging   (3) sunning
(2) blinding   (4) endangering   12 ____

13 The narrator's conflict in lines 36 through 42 is resolved through

(1) understanding the nature of humans
(2) posing philosophical arguments
(3) accepting the cycle of the seasons
(4) questioning religious beliefs   13 ____

14 The narrator in the poem can best be described as

(1) hopeful and excited
(2) dejected and alienated
(3) impulsive and carefree
(4) reflective and resigned   14 ____

Reading Comprehension Passage C

    I had a farm in Africa, at the foot of the Ngong Hills. The Equator runs across these highlands, a hundred miles to the North, and the farm lay at an altitude of over six thousand feet. In the day-time you felt that you had got high up, near to the sun, but the early mornings and evenings were limpid[1] and
(5) restful, and the nights were cold....
    We grew coffee on my farm. The land was in itself a little too high for coffee, and it was hard work to keep it going; we were never rich on the farm. But a coffee-plantation is a thing that gets hold of you and does not let you go, and there is always something to do on it: you are generally just a
(10) little behind with your work....
    Coffee-growing is a long job. It does not all come out as you imagine, when, yourself young and hopeful, in the streaming rain, you carry the boxes of your shining young coffee-plants from the nurseries, and, with the whole number of farm-hands in the field, watch the plants set in the regular rows
(15) of holes in the wet ground where they are to grow, and then have them thickly shaded against the sun, with branches broken from the bush, since obscurity is the privilege of young things. It is four or five years till the trees come into bearing, and in the meantime you will get drought on the land, or diseases, and the bold native weeds will grow up thick in the fields,—
(20) the black-jack, which has long scabrous[2] seed-vessels that hang on to your clothes and stockings. Some of the trees have been badly planted with their tap-roots bent; they will die just as they begin to flower. You plant a little over six hundred trees to the acre, and I had six hundred acres of land with coffee; my oxen dragged the cultivators up and down the fields, between
(25) the rows of trees, many thousand miles, patiently, awaiting coming bounties.
    There are times of great beauty on a coffee-farm. When the plantation flowered in the beginning of the rains, it was a radiant sight, like a cloud of chalk, in the mist and the drizzling rain, over six hundred acres of land. The coffee-blossom has a delicate slightly bitter scent, like the black-thorn
(30) blossom. When the field reddened with the ripe berries, all the women and the children, whom they call the Totos, were called out to pick the coffee off the trees, together with the men; then the waggons and carts brought it down to the factory near the river. Our machinery was never quite what it should have been, but we had planned and built the factory ourselves
(35) and thought highly of it. Once the whole factory burned down and had to

---

[1] limpid—clear
[2] scabrous—rough

be built up again. The big coffee-dryer turned and turned, rumbling the coffee in its iron belly with a sound like pebbles that are washed about on the sea-shore. Sometimes the coffee would be dry, and ready to take out of the dryer, in the middle of the night. That was a picturesque moment, with
(40) many hurricane lamps in the huge dark room of the factory, that was hung everywhere with cobwebs and coffee-husks, and with eager glowing dark faces, in the light of the lamps, round the dryer; the factory, you felt, hung in the great African night like a bright jewel in an Ethiope's ear. Later on the coffee was hulled, graded, and sorted by hand, and packed in sacks sewn up
(45) with a saddler's needle. . . .

    My farm was a little too high up for growing coffee. It happened in the cold months that we would get frost on the lower land and in the morning the shoots of the coffee-trees, and the young coffee-berries on them, would be all brown and withered. The wind blew in from the plains, and even in
(50) good years we never got the same yield of coffee to the acre as the people in the lower districts of Thika and Kiambu, on four thousand feet.

    We were short of rain, as well, in the Ngong country, and three times we had a year of real drought, which brought us very low down. In a year in which we had fifty inches of rain, we picked eighty tons of coffee, and in a
(55) year of fifty-five inches, nearly ninety tons; but there were two bad years in which we had only twenty-five and twenty inches of rain, and picked only sixteen and fifteen tons of coffee, and those years were disastrous to the farm.

    At the same time coffee-prices fell: where we had got a hundred pounds
(60) a ton we now got sixty or seventy. Times grew hard on the farm. We could not pay our debts, and we had no money for the running of the plantation. My people at home, who had shares in the farm, wrote out to me and told me that I would have to sell. . . .

    Our real trouble was that we were short of capital, for it had all been
(65) spent in the old days before I took over the running of the farm. We could not carry through any radical improvements, but had to live from hand to mouth,—and this, in the last years, became our normal mode of living on the farm. . . .

    When I had no more money, and could not make things pay, I had to
(70) sell the farm. A big Company in Nairobi bought it. They thought that the place was too high up for coffee, and they were not going in for farming. But they meant to take up all the coffee-trees, to divide up the land and lay out roads, and in time, when Nairobi should be growing out to the West, they meant to sell the land for building-plots. That was towards the end of
(75) the year.

Even as it was then, I do not think that I should have found it in me to give up the farm if it had not been for one thing. The coffee-crop that was still unripe upon the trees belonged to the old owners of the farm, or to the Bank which was holding a first mortgage in it. This coffee would not (80) be picked, handled in the factory and sent off, till May or later. For such a period I was to remain on the farm, in charge of it, and things were to go on, unaltered to the view. And during this time, I thought, something would happen to change it all back, since the world, after all, was not a regular or calculable place. . . .

—Karen Blixen
excerpted from *Out of Africa,* 1948
Putnam

15 The second paragraph introduces a central idea of
 (1) security in the farm's abundance
 (2) perseverance in spite of obstacles
 (3) trust in the crop's profitability
 (4) success in spite of inexperience   15 ____

16 The language in lines 11 through 17 suggests that new coffee plants require
 (1) isolation   (3) irrigation
 (2) fertilization   (4) protection   16 ____

17 The words "black-jack" (line 20) and "tap-roots" (line 22) provide evidence of the
 (1) narrator's knowledge
 (2) workers' responsibility
 (3) farm's prosperity
 (4) trees' hardiness   17 ____

18 The imagery in lines 26 through 30 highlights the farm's
 (1) diversity   (3) appeal
 (2) routine   (4) history   18 ____

19 The figurative language in lines 36 through 38 reinforces the
 (1) power of the ocean   (3) heat of the dryer
 (2) rattle of the machine   (4) noise of the night   19 ____

20 The purpose of lines 46 through 51 is to explain the
 (1) impact of the farm's elevation
 (2) benefits of the farm's size
 (3) fragility of the immature berries
 (4) success of the annual harvests   20 ____

21 The details in lines 52 through 58 demonstrate that the

(1) growing conditions are beneficial
(2) natural events are unpredictable
(3) excessive rain lowers coffee prices
(4) careful records improve crop yields   21 _____

22 The phrase "hand to mouth" (lines 66 to 67) most likely means

(1) using unusual resources
(2) enjoying occasional luxuries
(3) covering basic necessities
(4) ignoring financial problems   22 _____

23 The statement in lines 82 through 84 reflects the narrator's

(1) sympathy   (3) ignorance
(2) indifference   (4) optimism   23 _____

24 Which statement best represents a central idea of the text?

(1) "Our machinery was never quite what it should have been, but we had planned and built the factory ourselves" (lines 33 and 34)
(2) "That was a picturesque moment, with many hurricane lamps in the huge dark room of the factory" (lines 39 and 40)
(3) "But they meant to take up all the coffee-trees, to divide up the land and lay out roads" (lines 72 and 73)
(4) "Even as it was then, I do not think that I should have found it in me to give up the farm" (lines 76 and 77)   24 _____

PART 2—Argument Response

Directions: Closely read each of the *four* texts provided on pages 289 through 297 and write a source-based argument on the topic below. You may use the margins to take notes as you read and scrap paper to plan your response. Write your argument on a separate sheet of paper.

> **Topic:** Should shark netting be used on coastal beaches?

> **Your Task:** Carefully read each of the *four* texts provided. Then, using evidence from at least *three* of the texts, write a well-developed argument regarding whether or not shark netting should be used on coastal beaches. Clearly establish your claim, distinguish your claim from alternate or opposing claims, and use specific, relevant, and sufficient evidence from at least *three* of the texts to develop your argument. Do *not* simply summarize each text.

Guidelines:

Be sure to:
- Establish your claim regarding whether or not shark netting should be used on coastal beaches.
- Distinguish your claim from alternate or opposing claims.
- Use specific, relevant, and sufficient evidence from at least *three* of the texts to develop your argument.
- Identify each source that you reference by text number and line number(s) or graphic (for example: Text 1, line 4 or Text 2, graphic).
- Organize your ideas in a cohesive and coherent manner.
- Maintain a formal style of writing.
- Follow the conventions of standard written English.

Texts:

Text 1 – Shark Nets

Text 2 – Shark Nets: A Tangled Web of Destruction

Text 3 – Nick Carroll on: Beyond the Panic, the Facts about Shark Nets

Text 4 – Sharing the Sea with Sharks

Text 1

Shark Nets

... For over 70 years, shark nets have been protecting Australian swimmers from a death almost too awful to contemplate. Since their introduction in 1936, not one fatal shark attack has been recorded at beaches where nets have been installed.
(5)   But a growing body of scientific evidence suggests that shark nets remove more than just big-fanged predators from our beaches.
   Protected species such as whales, dolphins and manta rays also get trapped in these nets. Ironically, another protected species, the majestic but terrifying Great White Shark is regularly caught in shark nets in significant numbers. No
(10) one really knows what removing such a high level predator from the marine food chain will do. ...
   Shark nets are used on open ocean beaches, and are simply a straight, rectangular piece of net suspended in the water column between buoys. The mesh holes are 50 cm wide, small enough to entangle sharks and other
(15) large marine species, while leaving smaller fish alone.

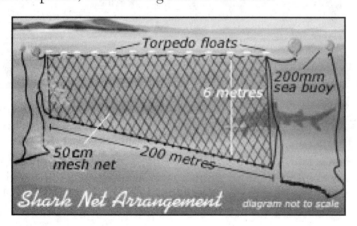

   Most shark nets stretch about 200 metres along the beach and down to a depth of six metres. Lines of torpedo floats at the top and sinkers at the bottom keep the net upright in the water. They are anchored at either end, usually about 200 metres from shore in roughly 10 metres of water. The nets
(20) are not intended to form a complete barrier, and sharks can still get through. The Queensland Shark Control Program uses another technique in addition to nets: hooks baited with fresh fish suspended from buoys to catch the sharks. In a typical 20 km stretch of coastal surf beach, a strip of net will be set up every couple of kilometres along the beach.

(25)   Shark enclosures, on the other hand, are more rigid constructions used on harbour beaches, and offer an unbroken barrier against incoming predators. The mesh in enclosures is much smaller than shark nets, and doesn't usually entangle any living creatures. These enclosures can't be easily built on open ocean beaches because experience has shown that the
(30) energy of the waves will eventually tear them to pieces. And like all beach constructions, they can also cause major sand erosion. When, for example, a temporary volleyball stadium was built on Bondi Beach for the Sydney Olympics a new surfing wave was created, dubbed the 'Olympic Lefts' by local surfers.

(35)   Now certain sections of the public and conservation groups such as the WWF (World Wide Fund for Nature) are calling for shark nets (the ones used at ocean beaches) to be completely removed. Not only do nets kill protected marine species, they argue, they don't guarantee protection for swimmers either. But how much more risk would we face without the nets?
(40) What if they were removed, would governments face big liability claims if a shark attack were to then occur on a previously protected beach? . . .

To net or not to net?

Weighing the benefits of the reduced risk of shark attack against the relatively unknown environmental impact of shark meshing is complicated by several highly emotive[1] issues. The impact on the marine ecology of removing large
(45) predatory sharks is not completely known, and protected species such as

---

[1] emotive—emotional

dolphins, turtles, and whales can also fall victim to the nets. For instance, in May 2001, a humpback whale calf became entangled in the nets off the Gold Coast[2] and died while its 20 plus tonne mother looked on. As a result of this and other incidents, there is increasing pressure on the NSW [New South Wales] and Queensland governments, which administer nets, to cease the practice.

Our fear of sharks

. . .It is true that shark meshing was introduced as a response to a perceived public demand almost seventy years ago. But a report submitted by the government appointed 'Shark Menace Advisory Committee' in 1935 is remarkably rational for its time. The document shows that the media's obsession with sharks probably dates back to well before the film 'Jaws', which has received much of the blame for sparking widespread white shark killings. In the absence of fatal attacks since meshing began, it is difficult to know whether the public reaction would be significantly different today if the nets were removed and fatalities returned. . . .

—Ruben Meerman
excerpted and adapted from "Shark Nets"
www.abc.net.au, January 16, 2009

---

[2] Gold Coast—an Eastern coastal area of Australia, between the states of New South Wales and Queensland

Text 2

Shark Nets: A Tangled Web of Destruction

... Throughout the world, people get into the water without shark deterrents; the extremely slim chance of even encountering a shark—much less being bitten—does not weigh heavily in their decision-making. Nor does it merit unnecessarily killing a threatened or harmless animal. In the last 100 years, (5) there were over 4 times more shark bites in the United States than in Natal [South Africa]. And, there have never been nets in the U.S., including in the "shark bite capital" of the world, Volusia County, Florida. Even there, the risk of shark bite is so low that many more stitches are administered as the result of shell and glass lacerations than shark bites. ...

(10) True, if one takes the nets at face value, there are far more destructive practices occurring worldwide. The nets are currently responsible for the deaths of between 500–700 sharks yearly, a very small percentage of the total number of sharks killed worldwide—or even in Southern Africa. Over one hundred million sharks will be killed this year. That's 11,432 every hour. (15) With some regional populations down 90%, we could witness the extinction of [shark] species during our lifetimes.

However, it is the mere existence of the nets that is the most damaging due to their impact on our collective psyches.[1] Their installation reinforces our misguided and irrational fears of sharks, providing a very real example (20) that our concerns are valid. This in turn fuels the biggest issue faced in shark conservation: the public's apathy or even loathing towards sharks. The media-created and shark-net reinforced image of sharks makes it difficult for many people to understand why sharks are worth saving—let alone take measures to do so.

(25) The frightening reality is, like them or not, we need sharks on this planet. Remove the apex predators from the oceans, and we are tampering with elements essential to our survival and the livelihoods of the 400 million that rely on the oceans for their income. Sharks are a critical component in an ecosystem that controls our planet's temperature and weather, (30) provides 1/3 of the world with food, and generates more oxygen than all the rainforests combined. Recent studies indicate that regional elimination of sharks caused disastrous effects including the collapse of fisheries and the death of coral reefs.

---

[1] collective psyches—shared understanding

Fortunately, there are many other options to the archaic practice of killing sharks with nets and drumlines,[2] many of which have been implemented successfully in other locations—including the other coast of South Africa. Other methods of harmless deterrents such as electrical current, alloys, and chemicals are also being developed. If we can put a man on the moon, we certainly can determine a method to ensure sharks and humans can peacefully coexist in the shark's domain. Programs like the Shark Spotters in the Western Cape prove that there are viable alternatives to shark nets and also, that education and awareness go far. . . .

The days of killing animals out of fear are over. And one only need to look at Yellowstone Park, in the U.S., as a prime example[3] as to the far-reaching impacts of these short-sighted acts. South Africa—a country whose environmental policies, fueled by booming eco-tourism, should be setting precedence for the world. At a time when we are racing through our natural resources at unsustainable rates, destroying wild animals simply because we can, or because of irrational fears fueled by a lack of knowledge, is no longer acceptable. . . .

—Shark Angels
excerpted and adapted from "Shark Nets:
A Tangled Web of Destruction"
http://sharkangels.org, 2011

---

[2] drumlines—hooks baited with fresh fish, suspended from buoys

[3] prime example—Yellowstone's wolf-elimination program drastically altered the park's ecosystem by allowing elk to flourish and overgraze on vital flora. Since the wolves were reintroduced in 1995 there has been a steady rebuilding of balance in the ecosystem.

Text 3

Nick Carroll on: Beyond the Panic, the Facts about Shark Nets

    Last week, after two shark attacks in ten days off Ballina's [Australia] beaches, NSW [New South Wales] Premier Mike Baird announced a six-month trial of meshing this suddenly very dangerous piece of coastline.
    The announcement came on top of other measures, "smart" drumlines,[1] tagging,[2] and sonar buoys,[3] in a further attempt to reduce a dramatic increase in attacks on local surfers and swimmers.
    It inspired relief among many of Ballina's surfers and businesspeople, who've been dreading the news of another fatal attack and its potential effect on the town—yet it also raised angst[4] among green-thinking people, who dislike the idea of sharks and other sea life dying in human-laid traps.
    Indeed, the whole idea of "shark nets" seems to press some serious buttons for everyone.
    But beyond the relief and the angst: what *is* meshing? What does it do? What are its effects on marine life, and on human encounters with big sharks? . . .
    Both NSW and Queensland's programs are a lot more sophisticated than they used to be. Queensland's program is a lot bigger, and more expensive: 83 beaches are meshed compared with NSW's current 51, and Queensland also employs numerous drumlines, from the Snapper Rocks area all the way up to Cairns. As a result, Queensland's shark catch is way bigger—in 2015 alone, for instance, it captured 297 tiger sharks, mostly in northern waters, and mostly on drumlines, which are considered more effective in catching large sharks than meshing. (Meshing is pretty effective against bull sharks in turbid[5] water, which might help a bit at Lighthouse.) . . .
    What does seem obvious is when it comes to separating humans and large sharks, meshing works. In the years from 1900 to 1937, 13 people were killed off NSW surf beaches by sharks; over the next 72 years, the death rate fell to eight, only one of which was at a meshed beach. This in a period when the NSW human population rose from 1.4 million to seven million—and way more people began going to the beach.

---

[1] drumlines—hooks baited with fresh fish, suspended from buoys
[2] tagging—attachment of identification tags for monitoring sharks
[3] sonar buoys—buoys with sound receivers and radio transmitters
[4] angst—anxiety
[5] turbid—cloudy

Similar figures can be seen elsewhere. In Dunedin, New Zealand, between 1964 and 1968, three fatal great white shark attacks occurred off a series of local beaches. Local authorities took a look at the NSW meshing program, and nets were laid off those beaches; nobody has since been attacked in the area while the nets were set. . . .

Then there is the emotionally loaded, and occasionally very visible, issue of bycatch.[6] It's one reason why the authorities have been so cautious about meshing Ballina's beaches—the idea that the nets kill a lot more than just sharks.

The records make it clear they do—but perhaps not nearly as much as you'd suspect. Meshing is supported by pingers[7] designed to alert marine mammals to their existence, and by and large they seem to work. In NSW, the meshing averages one humpback whale every two years; the whale is almost always released alive. In Queensland in 2015, the bycatch included one bottlenose and seven common dolphins (one released alive), 11 catfish, eight cow-nose rays, nine eagle rays, 13 loggerhead turtles, five manta rays (all but one survived), eight shovelnose rays, three toadfish, four tuna, and a white spotted eagle, which was safely released. . . .

Oh and here's something else the records make clear. If you're worried about sharks' survival, or sea-life bycatch in general, you're way better off looking offshore. Australia's commercial shark fishing industry is taking over 1200 tonne of shark out of our various fisheries each year: everything from gummy shark to mako, and very likely a few white sharks as well. The NSW prawn trawling[8] industry alone results in 64 tonne of shark as bycatch each year. Six percent of what's caught in the tuna longline fisheries in northern Australia is shark. . . .

Next to that action, as the figures show, surf zone protective meshing is a minnow in a very big pond.

—Nick Carroll
excerpted and adapted from "Nick Carroll on:
Beyond the Panic, the Facts about Shark Nets"
www.coastalwatch.com, October 21, 2016

---

[6] bycatch—the capture of non-target species
[7] pingers—devices that transmit short, high-pitched signals
[8] trawling—a method of fishing that drags nets behind a boat

Text 4

Sharing the Sea with Sharks

... In 1937, when the first shark nets were installed off Sydney beaches, on Australia's east coast, sea-bathing was still a relatively new pastime—prior to 1903, daylight ocean bathing had been banned as improper. At the time the nets were introduced, the state's beaches were experiencing, on average, one
(5) fatal shark bite every year. The government felt that it needed to be seen as proactive, and nets were one of the least hawkish measures proposed; suggestions made during a 1935 public-submissions process included mounting machine guns on headlands and setting explosives. From the outset, the purpose of the nets was to catch and kill sharks.
(10)   Almost eighty years later, the nets are still installed off the New South Wales coast. They go in at the start of September, the beginning of the warm-weather season, and are removed at the end of April. At each of the fifty-one participating beaches, nets are installed for fourteen days of the month. They do not act as a total barrier: they are generally only a hundred and fifty
(15) metres long and six metres wide, and are set beneath the surface in ten to twelve metres of water, five hundred metres out from the shore. They're anchored to the sea floor, but there is significant space above and below them. (A study of a similar shark-net program in South Africa found that thirty-five percent of the catch was "on the shoreward side of the nets"—in
(20) other words, sharks are often caught on their way out to sea.) ...

The most controversial aspect of shark-net programs is whether it has been scientifically proven that shark nets reduce shark bites. Some researchers who have worked for government shark-meshing programs over a long period wholeheartedly believe that they do. Since the start of the
(25) KwaZulu-Natal Sharks Board netting program[1]—which uses much larger nets, for a longer period, than the New South Wales program—there have been "only two attacks, both non-fatal ... at protected beaches ... over the past three decades." And the New South Wales government reports that since "the NSW shark meshing program was put in place in Sydney in 1937,
(30) there has only been one fatal attack on a meshed beach." ...

---

[1] KwaZulu-Natal Sharks Board netting program—South African program

Either way, nets and drumlines[2] are increasingly painted as crude, antiquated[3] shark-culling[4] tools. Shark scientists and entrepreneurs are now starting to direct their energies toward finding a technological solution that could keep both humans and sharks safe. The KwaZulu–Natal Sharks Board, in response to growing opposition to shark nets, aims to come up with a "non-lethal alternative." It has been researching electronic shark-deterrent technologies since the nineteen-nineties, based on findings that a shark's electroreception system—clusters of nerve fibres in gel-filled canals, visible as dark pores on a shark's head—may be sensitive to changes in electrical fields. The board recently began testing a hundred-metre cable that emits a low-frequency pulsed electronic signal designed to repel sharks. . . .

Most of the shark scientists I spoke to believe public education is still the best method of protecting oceangoers and marine animals, especially while a technological solution is still years off. Many cite Cape Town's [South Africa] Shark Spotters program as a gold standard because of its emphasis on observation and education: community members on beachside cliffs use flags and alerts to keep the public informed of shark sightings. "As an effective approach, education is number one," [Robert] Hueter, the Florida-based shark expert, said. "Most people here have embraced the idea that this is the sharks' home, their natural habitat, we're going into their space. . . . People respond to a shark-bite incident differently now. It's a tragedy, yes, but it's accepted as something out of our control, like being struck by lightning." . . .

—Ceridwen Dovey
excerpted and adapted from "Sharing the Sea with Sharks"
www.newyorker.com, April 26, 2015

---

[2] drumlines—hooks baited with fresh fish, suspended from buoys
[3] antiquated—outdated
[4] culling—killing

PART 3—Text-Analysis Response

Your Task: Closely read the text provided on pages 299 through 301 and write a well-developed, text-based response of two to three paragraphs. In your response, identify a central idea in the text and analyze how the author's use of **one** writing strategy (literary element or literary technique or rhetorical device) develops this central idea. Use strong and thorough evidence from the text to support your analysis. Do *not* simply summarize the text. You may use the margins to take notes as you read and scrap paper to plan your response. Write your response on a separate sheet of paper.

Guidelines:

Be sure to:
- Identify a central idea in the text.
- Analyze how the author's use of **one** writing strategy (literary element or literary technique or rhetorical device) develops this central idea. Examples include: characterization, conflict, denotation/connotation, metaphor, simile, irony, language use, point of view, setting, structure, symbolism, theme, tone, etc.
- Use strong and thorough evidence from the text to support your analysis.
- Organize your ideas in a cohesive and coherent manner.
- Maintain a formal style of writing.
- Follow the conventions of standard written English.

Text

The following excerpt is from the 2013 Duke University commencement address, given by Melinda Gates, co-founder of the Bill & Melinda Gates Foundation.

....The people who say technology has disconnected you from others are wrong. So are the people who say technology automatically connects you to others. Technology is just a tool. It's a powerful tool, but it's just a tool. Deep human connection is very different. It's not a tool. It's not a means to
(5) an end. It is the end—the purpose and the result of a meaningful life—and it will inspire the most amazing acts of love, generosity, and humanity.

In his famous speech "Remaining Awake Through a Great Revolution," Martin Luther King Jr. said, "Through our scientific and technological genius, we have made of this world a neighborhood and yet we have not had
(10) the ethical commitment to make of it a brotherhood."...

What does it mean to make of this world a brotherhood and a sisterhood? That probably sounds like a lot to ask of you as individuals, or even as a graduating class. I'm pretty sure none of you will respond to the annoying question "What are you going to do after graduation?" by saying "I plan to
(15) have the ethical commitment to make of this world a brotherhood."

But you can change the way you think about other people. You can choose to see their humanity first—the one big thing that makes them the same as you, instead of the many things that make them different from you....

(20) Paul Farmer, the Duke graduate I admire most, is a testament to the deep human connection I'm talking about. As many of you know, Paul, who's here today, is a doctor and global health innovator. For years, he travelled back and forth from Boston, where he is a professor of medicine, to Haiti, where he ran a health clinic giving the highest quality care to the poorest
(25) people in the world. Now, he lives mostly in Rwanda, where he's working on changing the country's entire health care system.

I first met Paul in 2003, when I went to see him in Haiti. It took us forever to walk the 100 yards from our vehicle to the clinic because he introduced me to every single person we met along the way. I am not
(30) exaggerating. Every single person.

As we moved along, he introduced each person to me by first and last name, wished their families well, and asked for an update about their lives. He hugged people when he greeted them and looked them in the eyes throughout each conversation. If you believe love plays a role in healing,
(35) there was healing happening at every step of that journey....

Of course, not everybody is Paul Farmer. Not everybody is going to dedicate their whole life to connecting with the poorest people in the world. But just because you don't qualify for sainthood doesn't mean you can't form deep human connections—or that your connections can't make a difference (40) in the world.

That's where technology comes in. If you make the moral choice to connect deeply to others, then your computer, your phone, and your tablet make it so much easier to do.

Today, there are 700 million cell phone subscribers in Africa. I (45) travelled to Kenya recently and spent a day in Kibera, which many people consider the largest slum in Africa. One image that sticks with me is all the cell phones piled up in a small kiosk where locals paid to recharge their batteries. Most people in Kibera don't have electricity—even the cell phone charging businesses steal it from the city's power grid—but everywhere (50) I looked young people were on their phones. And guess what they were doing? Exactly what you do. . . they were texting.

You and they can share your stories directly with each other, with literally billions of people, because you're all using the same technology. . . .

When my husband Bill [Gates] and I started our foundation, we didn't (55) know much about global health at all. I read the academic literature and talked to experts in the field. But most of what I learned was expressed in morbidity[1] and mortality rates, not in flesh and blood. So in 2001, I took my first foundation learning trip, to India and Thailand, to meet with people and find out what their lives were really like behind the veil of statistics. . . .

(60) Late in the afternoon, one of the women who'd been showing me around invited me into her home. We went inside and she produced two lawn chairs that were hanging from a nail in her kitchen. They were the aluminum folding kind with the itchy fabric seat you've sat on a million times, quite possibly when you were tenting in Krzyzewskiville.[2] When I (65) was growing up in Dallas, we had the same chairs. On Sunday nights in the summer, my parents and my siblings and I used to set them up on our back patio and gaze up into the sky together as a family.

It turned out my host wanted to show me her stunning view of the Himalayas, and as we sat and contemplated the planet's highest peaks, we (70) talked about our children and the future. Our aspirations were basically the same. We wanted our children to fulfill their potential. We wanted the love

---

[1] morbidity—the rate at which an illness occurs
[2] Krzyzewskiville—the annual tent city that is erected in celebration of the Duke versus UNC basketball game

and respect of family and friends. We wanted meaningful work. The biggest difference between us was not what we dreamt about, but how hard it was for her to make her dreams come true.

(75) Some people assume that Bill and I are too rich to make a connection with someone who's poor, even if our intentions are good. But adjectives like rich and poor don't define who any of us truly are as human beings. And they don't make any one individual less human than the next. The universe is like computer code in that way. Binary. There is life, and there is everything (80) else. Zeroes and ones. I'm a one. You're a one. My friend in the Himalayas is a one.

Martin Luther King was not a computer programmer, so he called this concept a brotherhood. His hope was that college students could bring a brotherhood into being. Dr. King thought the world had shrunk as much as (85) it was going to shrink—in his words, we'd "dwarfed distance and placed time in chains." So the fact that people still didn't treat each other like brothers and sisters was, to him, an ethical failure.

I take a slightly different view. I believe we are finally creating the scientific and technological tools to turn the world into a neighborhood. And (90) that gives you an amazing ethical opportunity no one has ever had before.

You can light up a network of 7 billion people with long-lasting and highly motivating human connections. . . .

I hope you will use the tool of technology to do what you already had it in your heart to do. . . To connect. . . To make of this world a brotherhood. (95) . . and a sisterhood. . .

I can't wait to see what it looks like when you do. . . .

—Melinda Gates
excerpted and adapted from "Melinda Gates:
Duke Commencement 2013"
www.gatesfoundation.org, 2013

Regents ELA Answers August 2018
English Language Arts

Answer Key

PART 1

1. 3	9. 3	17. 1
2. 2	10. 4	18. 3
3. 2	11. 3	19. 2
4. 1	12. 1	20. 1
5. 1	13. 3	21. 2
6. 3	14. 4	22. 3
7. 1	15. 2	23. 4
8. 3	16. 4	24. 4

PART 2 *See Answers and Explanations*

PART 3 *See Answers and Explanations*

Regents Examination in English Language Arts—August 2018
Chart for Converting Total Weighted Raw Scores to Final Examination Scores (Scaled Scores)

Weighted Raw Score	Scale Score	Performance Level	Weighted Raw Score	Scale Score	Performance Level
56	100	5	27	49	1
55	99	5	26	45	1
54	99	5	25	42	1
53	99	5	24	39	1
52	98	5	23	36	1
51	97	5	22	32	1
50	96	5	21	29	1
49	95	5	20	26	1
48	94	5	19	23	1
47	93	5	18	20	1
46	92	5	17	17	1
45	90	5	16	14	1
44	89	5	15	12	1
43	87	5	14	10	1
42	86	5	13	9	1
41	85	5	12	8	1
40	83	4	11	7	1
39	81	4	10	6	1
38	79	4	9	5	1
37	77	3	8	5	1
36	75	3	7	4	1
35	72	3	6	3	1
34	70	3	5	3	1
33	67	3	4	2	1
32	65	3	3	2	1
31	61	2	2	1	1
30	58	2	1	1	1
29	55	2	0	0	1
28	52	1			

Answers Explained

PART 1—Reading Comprehension

Passage A

1. **3** "process of adaptation" The narrator outlines the family's gradual movement from disbelief that the mirror was inhabited to "accepting it as an everyday thing." She goes on to say that this was "not enough to upset our life style."

2. **2** "strangeness of the family's situation" The narrator remarks that it took a while for the family to feel "absolutely comfortable" with the arrangement, for example, in learning that the chair one sat in was occupied by someone else "on the other side." The feeling of strangeness is the best among the choices to describe the tone of this paragraph.

3. **2** "continuity between life and death" The narrator explains that the image of the departed in the mirror was "almost identical to our own [family gathering]." Nothing else "was changed in the mirror." This passage does not suggest feelings of rivalry or conflict, nor does it suggest the idea of respect among distant relatives.

4. **1** "the narrator's perception of Clara's place in the family" The narrator reveals that her first impression of Clara was that "she had blundered into our family by mistake." At lines 30 to 31, the idea that Clara was in the family by mistake "went away as soon as my cousin hung up her diploma." The narrator's perception is completely changed when Clara takes up traditional tasks with the other women in the family, in preparation for a suitable marriage. The narrator doesn't claim understanding of what has happened, she just observes it; and there is no sense of rejection or resentment in what the narrator describes.

5. **1** "assertive personality" Among the choices, this phrase best captures the effect Clara has on the family: it is Clara who prescribes medications and who dictates choices in fashion, entertainment, and hospitality for the family; and it is Clara, of course, whose idea it is to move the mirror to the dining room.

6. **3** "welcomed by the living family" This section of the story begins with the narrator telling us that, despite her mother's fears, "everything went fine" as the living family and the mirror people began to share meals. It was "comforting. . . and gave the impression of being a large family that got along well." The narrator does not suggest they felt disturbed or inconvenienced, nor does she mention that they felt especially curious.

7. **1** "indifferent" This is the best option among the answer choices, given the description of Clara's death and the family's reaction to it. The narrator tells us they just weren't paying attention when Clara was "allowed to sit at the frontier between the two tables. . . separating what was from what was not." The living family "just watched" as Clara was pulled into the world of the mirror people. There is a feeling of indifference in the way the narrator reports that "once the funeral business was over" the family "sat back down at the table again." The narrator does not say that the family acted irritated or irrational; Clara's actions may have been impulsive and led to her own death, but the tone in the narrator's reaction is almost without feeling.

8. **3** "distrusts her cousin" The narrator says that Clara has been trying to get her attention and is waiting for her to "slip up." Remember that what happened to Clara was the consequence of a "regrettable oversight" on the part of the family and Clara's own defiant curiosity. The narrator senses that Clara wants to pull her into the other side by tempting her to make juice from a pineapple that is "a little bleached-out." None of the other choices is supported by the story.

9. **3** "gobbled up, smiling mischievously" This phrase best describes the Clara who sits at the table, eagerly sharing the salad passed from the other side, and the Clara we see at the end, mischievously trying to get the narrator to accept the pineapple she offers.

10. **4** "we became less and less sure about which side was life and which its reflection" Among the choices, this is the only statement that suggests a theme. As the story progresses, the narrator reports that Clara's behavior in the mirror is no different from her behavior before; she also reports that the family became "divided over the question of who was really whose guest." The narrator comes to feel closer to the mirror people than to the living people, and by the end of the story she is trying to resist becoming part of the mirror people as Clara has.

Passage B

11. **3** "difference between perception and reality" In the first two stanzas, the narrator describes in *simile* what she sees (her perception): the pears are "like antique ornaments. . .they seemed/to flutter like candles in the leaves." Then she sees that they are pears.

12. **1** "indulging" The images of worms and bees feeding on the fruit best support this answer among the choices.

13. **3** "accepting the cycle of the seasons" These lines describe the experience of the narrator as she walks by the tree over a period of weeks and observes how "first one pear let go/of its limb, then many begin to fall." The images in these lines are of the end of summer (September) as the pears gradually fall, shrivel, and let "their seeds slip out." The image in the final line of the poem anticipates the coming of winter.

14. **4** "reflective and resigned" This answer best describes how the narrator's feelings develop over weeks on her walks: she is resigned to the fact that she cannot stop the season's clock, that she cannot "hoard time" or prevent the fruit from rotting. She is reflective when she considers what a thief would say and what a saint might answer.

Passage C

15. **2** "perseverance in spite of obstacles" This is the best answer among the choices. The narrator explains that, even though "the land was. . .a little too high for coffee" and "it was hard work to keep it going," the coffee plantation "gets hold of you. . .and there is always something to do." The narrator's voice does not suggest feelings of security, profitability, or guaranteed success in these lines.

16. **4** "protection" The work described here is of farm-hands carefully planting and shading the young coffee plants, which need to mature over several years before they bear fruit.

17. **1** "narrator's knowledge" This entire paragraph offers the narrator's detailed description of both the plants themselves and the care they require over several years before harvesting. Informative throughout, the passage also details various risks and hazards, such as drought, disease, and weeds, which can threaten the plantation's success.

18. **3** "appeal" The images of "great beauty" in these lines offer vivid contrast in the narrator's description of the hard work and many challenges of running a coffee farm.

19. **2** "rattle of the machine" In these lines, the narrator is describing the noise of the beans in the coffee-dryer: "rumbling. . .with a sound like pebbles that are washed about on the sea-shore." This is the most precise answer among the choices.

20. **1** "impact of the farm's elevation" The first sentence establishes the topic of this paragraph: "My farm was a little too high up for growing coffee." The narrator then offers examples of the effects of higher elevation on the crop. There is reference to the effects of cold on the immature berries (choice 3), but the main idea is that the narrator's farm "never got the same yield" as farms at lower elevations would.

21. **2** "natural events are unpredictable" In this brief paragraph, the narrator shows how lack of adequate rain affected the crop yield; the range, from drought to years in which there was adequate rain, illustrates how vulnerable farmers are to unpredictable weather patterns.

22. **3** "covering basic necessities" To live from hand to mouth is a common expression used to describe how those who are poor, or have no money other than what is in their pockets, live from day to day. The narrator tells us that "our real trouble was that we were short of capital." In other words, there was no saved money available to make repairs or to cover expenses in the years when the farm had a small yield or when coffee prices fell.

23. **4** "optimism" This is the best among the choices. Despite years of struggle against natural and economic forces and the fact that the farm itself had been mortgaged, the narrator thought "something would happen to change it all back."

24. **4** "Even as it was then, I do not think that I should have found it in me to give up the farm" This expresses the narrator's central idea: her love for this farm is a hold that will not let her go. This theme is established at the beginning of the passage in lines 7–12.

PART 2—Argument Response

Sample Essay Response

Since the appearance of shark netting in the 1930s, its use has been widely debated. The world has developed a near universal fear of shark attacks, and many feel that the most effective preventive action is the installation of shark netting around coastal beaches. While netting may reduce shark attacks significantly, it comes with great literal and figurative costs. I believe officials at costal beaches should refrain from utilizing shark netting, because it has the potential to capture other sea life and to disrupt the food chain; overall, there are better and safer options.

While netting prevented numerous attacks in Australia during the 1900s, it removed more than just sharks from the water. For example, "Protected species such as whales, dolphins and manta rays also get trapped in these nets...the majestic but terrifying Great White Shark is regularly caught in shark nets in significant numbers. No one really knows what removing such a high level predator from the marine food chain will do." (Text 1, lines 7–11) Not only does shark netting create a high risk for the loss of important creatures such as great white sharks, which regulate the food chain, smaller creatures such as whales, dolphins and turtles often face the dangers of the nets as well. Ultimately, even though shark netting seems to be the best answer to widespread panic over shark attacks, shark netting poses great danger to other sea life as their "homes" are invaded.

The effectiveness of shark netting is debatable. As stated in an article titled "Sharing the Sea with Sharks": "The most controversial aspect of shark-net programs is whether it has been scientifically proven that shark nets reduce shark bites." (Text 4, lines 21–22) There are researchers who truly believe that nets are effective, while others do not. However, according to a KwaZulu-Natal Sharks Board program, the nets prevented all but two non-fatal attacks to occur in three decades. (Text 4, lines 25–28) This proves Nick Carroll somewhat wrong; he stated that "what does seem obvious is when it comes to separating humans and large sharks, meshing works." (Text 3, lines 25–26) If nets were truly as effective as Carroll and other researchers claim, then attacks would be all but impossible in netted areas.

There are, however, several more promising options for preventing shark attacks. Since the installation of nets only validates the world's collective fear of sharks, it is important that other preventive measures be taken. (Text 2, lines 17–20) One other possible method for preventing shark bites is the use of "harmless deterrents such as electrical current, alloys, and chemicals." (Text 2, lines 37–38) These methods can help keep sharks far away while protecting their safety. Yet another method is simply educating the world. Many scientists believe public education is the best method for protecting humans and sharks alike. (Text 4, lines 42–44) By educating humans, sharks can easily be protected and also avoided at almost no cost at all.

Ultimately, shark attacks can be prevented in a variety of ways. Though many argue that netting is, in fact, the most effective, the benefits do not outweigh the negative effects. By using shark netting, habitats are invaded and food chains are harmed. Other safe options are rejected, and other sea life is harmed.

> **Analysis**
>
> This is a good response because it presents a reasoned argument to support the writer's position on the use of shark netting. The opening paragraph effectively states the issue and acknowledges why it is controversial. The paragraph closes with a clear and forceful statement of the writer's central idea. Supported with multiple references to three of the four texts, the argument is developed clearly and coherently. The first sentence of each paragraph both signals the topic and clarifies the development of the overall argument: "While netting prevented numerous attacks. . ."; "The effectiveness. . .is debatable"; "There are. . .more promising options"; "Ultimately, shark attacks can be prevented in a variety of ways."
>
> The writing is clear and appropriately formal, with no significant errors in diction or usage. This essay would merit a high score. (See the Scoring Rubric.)

(See pages 79–80 for the scoring guidelines.)

PART 3—Text-Analysis Response

Note: Many successful responses for this part emphasized effective use of point of view, personal anecdote, or optimistic tone. Some developed the concept that the speech is structured around the central theme of a famous speech by MLK cited at the beginning and then recalled toward the end. The response below is a good example of how point of view supports the author's central idea.

Sample Essay Response

Authors use different writing strategies to develop the central idea of their texts. The author of this text, who happens to be Bill Gates's wife, uses her personal experiences to show how technology connects people all around the world. In this text, which was a university commencement speech, she tells these stories in a first-person point of view to connect with her audience on a more personal level.

In one example, the author describes her visit to Kibera, a large slum in Kenya. To her surprise, there were young people on their phones everywhere, texting just like we do. She connects this personal story with her main point that technology allows us to communicate and connect with people all over. She tells her listeners, "You and they can share your stories directly with each other, with literally billions of people, because you're all using the same technology."

The author also shares a story about her trip to the Himalayas. While she was there, she met a family and went to their home. On this visit, they did not share any technology; they learned about each other's lives just by talking. She understands from her travels that people everywhere share many of the same hopes and desires for the future. The connections she makes around the world show her and the audience that people, rich or poor, are still people, and that technology allows us to reach out and make bonds with these people.

The author shares personal experiences to emphasize how important human connections are and how technology can improve these connections. She shares these experiences using first-person point of view to make her stories feel real to the audience, allowing her to connect with them on a personal level.

Analysis

Point of view is a logical choice of topic for this text, a commencement speech, and the writer of this response clearly establishes the central idea in the first paragraph: "she tells these stories in a first-person point of view to connect with her audience on a more personal level." The essay is adequately developed with two examples of the author's experiences, and the final two sentences are especially effective in expressing both the central theme of the speech and the effective use of first-person point of view to support that central theme.

The organization in four brief paragraphs is logical; the writing is clear and free of any significant errors in usage. This response would merit a high score. (See the Scoring Rubric.)

(See pages 81–82 for the scoring guidelines.)

Regents ELA Examination June 2019
English Language Arts

PART 1—Reading Comprehension

Directions (1–24): Closely read each of the three passages below. After each passage, there are several multiple-choice questions. Select the best suggested answer to each question and write its number in the space provided. You may use the margins to take notes as you read.

Reading Comprehension Passage A

  When Marvin was ten years old, his father took him through the long, echoing corridors that led up through Administration and Power, until at last they came to the uppermost levels of all and were among the swiftly growing vegetation of the Farmlands. Marvin liked it here: it was fun
(5) watching the great, slender plants creeping with almost visible eagerness towards the sunlight as it filtered down through the plastic domes to meet them. The smell of life was everywhere, awakening inexpressible longings in his heart: no longer was he breathing the dry, cool air of the residential levels, purged of all smells but the faint tang of ozone. He wished he
(10) could stay here for a little while, but Father would not let him. They went onwards until they had reached the entrance to the Observatory, which he had never visited: but they did not stop, and Marvin knew with a sense of rising excitement that there could be only one goal left. For the first time in his life, he was going Outside.[1]
(15) There were a dozen of the surface vehicles, with their wide balloon tyres [tires] and pressurized cabins, in the great servicing chamber. His father must have been expected, for they were led at once to the little scout

---

[1]Outside—the part of the Moon outside of Marvin's space habitat

car waiting by the huge circular door of the airlock. Tense with expectancy, Marvin settled himself down in the cramped cabin while his father started (20) the motor and checked the controls. The inner door of the lock slid open and then closed behind them: he heard the roar of the great air-pumps fade slowly away as the pressure dropped to zero. Then the 'Vacuum' sign flashed on, the outer door parted, and before Marvin lay the land which he had never yet entered.

(25) He had seen it in photographs, of course: he had watched it imaged on television screens a hundred times. But now it was lying all around him, burning beneath the fierce sun that crawled so slowly across the jet-black sky. He stared into the west, away from the blinding splendour of the sun—and there were the stars, as he had been told but had never quite believed. He (30) gazed at them for a long time, marvelling that anything could be so bright and yet so tiny. They were intense unscintillating[2] points, and suddenly he remembered a rhyme he had once read in one of his father's books:

Twinkle, twinkle, little star,
How I wonder what you are.

(35) Well, he knew what the stars were. Whoever asked that question must have been very stupid. And what did they mean by 'twinkle'? You could see at a glance that all the stars shone with the same steady, unwavering light. He abandoned the puzzle and turned his attention to the landscape around him.

They were racing across a level plain at almost a hundred miles an hour, (40) the great balloon tyres sending up little spurts of dust behind them. There was no sign of the Colony: in the few minutes while he had been gazing at the stars, its domes and radio towers had fallen below the horizon. Yet there were other indications of man's presence, for about a mile ahead Marvin could see the curiously shaped structures clustering round the head of a (45) mine. Now and then a puff of vapour would emerge from a squat smokestack and would instantly disperse.

They were past the mine in a moment: Father was driving with a reckless and exhilarating skill as if—it was a strange thought to come into a child's mind—he was trying to escape from something. In a few minutes (50) they had reached the edge of the plateau on which the Colony had been built. The ground fell sharply away beneath them in a dizzying slope whose lower stretches were lost in shadow. Ahead, as far as the eye could reach, was a jumbled wasteland of craters, mountain ranges, and ravines. The crests of the mountains, catching the low sun, burned like islands of fire in a sea of (55) darkness: and above them the stars still shone as steadfastly as ever. . . .

---

[2]unscintillating—not sparkling

And now on the right was a wrinkled, dusty plain, and on the left, its ramparts and terraces rising mile after mile into the sky, was a wall of mountains that marched into the distance until its peaks sank from sight below the rim of the world. There was no sign that men had ever explored
(60) this land, but once they passed the skeleton of a crashed rocket, and beside it a stone cairn[3] surmounted by a metal cross. . . .

The sun was now low behind the hills on the right: the valley before them should be in total darkness. Yet it was awash with a cold white radiance that came spilling over the crags beneath which they were driving. Then,
(65) suddenly, they were out in the open plain, and the source of the light lay before them in all its glory.

It was very quiet in the little cabin now that the motors had stopped. The only sound was the faint whisper of the oxygen feed and an occasional metallic crepitation[4] as the outer walls of the vehicle radiated away their
(70) heat. For no warmth at all came from the great silver crescent that floated low above the far horizon and flooded all this land with pearly light. It was so brilliant that minutes passed before Marvin could accept its challenge and look steadfastly into its glare, but at last he could discern the outlines of continents, the hazy border of the atmosphere, and the white islands of
(75) cloud. And even at this distance, he could see the glitter of sunlight on the polar ice.

It was beautiful, and it called to his heart across the abyss of space. There in that shining crescent were all the wonders that he had never known—the hues of sunset skies, the moaning of the sea on pebbled shores, the patter
(80) of falling rain, the unhurried benison[5] of snow. These and a thousand others should have been his rightful heritage, but he knew them only from the books and ancient records, and the thought filled him with the anguish of exile.

Why could they not return? It seemed so peaceful beneath those
(85) lines of marching cloud. Then Marvin, his eyes no longer blinded by the glare, saw that the portion of the disk that should have been in darkness was gleaming faintly with an evil phosphorescence: and he remembered. He was looking upon the funeral pyre[6] of a world—upon the radioactive aftermath of Armageddon.[7] Across a quarter of a million miles of space, the
(90) glow of dying atoms was still visible, a perennial reminder of the ruined past.

---

[3]cairn—memorial
[4]crepitation—crackling sound
[5]benison—blessing
[6]pyre—bonfire
[7]Armageddon—a catastrophic battle

It would be centuries yet before that deadly glow died from the rocks and life could return again to fill that silent, empty world. . . .

So, at last, Marvin understood the purpose of this pilgrimage. He [his father] would never walk beside the rivers of that lost and legendary world, or listen to the thunder raging above its softly rounded hills. Yet one day—how far ahead?—his children's children would return to claim their heritage. The winds and the rains would scour the poisons from the burning lands and carry them to the sea, and in the depths of the sea they would waste their venom until they could harm no living things. Then the great ships that were still waiting here on the silent, dusty plains could lift once more into space, along the road that led to home. . . .

—Arthur C. Clarke
excerpted and adapted from "If I Forget Thee, Oh Earth. . ."
Expedition to Earth, 1999
Orbit

1 The images in the first paragraph serve to
   (1) create a sense of solitude
   (2) illustrate the randomness of nature
   (3) create a feeling of anticipation
   (4) illustrate the importance of family   1 _____

2 Lines 15 through 24 establish
   (1) Marvin's misgivings about going Outside
   (2) the inhospitable conditions of Outside
   (3) Father's fears about traveling Outside
   (4) the unpleasant sensations of Outside   2 _____

3 The statement "it was a strange thought to come into a child's mind" (lines 48 and 49) signals
   (1) a change in Marvin's understanding
   (2) Marvin's growing embrace of the unknown
   (3) Marvin's objection to his father's behavior
   (4) a chance for Marvin's rescue   3 _____

4 The phrase "jumbled wasteland of craters, mountain ranges, and ravines" (line 53) reveals the
   (1) futility of the Colony
   (2) desolation of the Outside
   (3) uncertainty of Marvin's future
   (4) loneliness of Marvin's past   4 _____

5 The "glare" described in lines 73 and 86 represents Marvin's
   (1) romantic vision of the Earth
   (2) obsession with the Earth's past
   (3) vague memory of the Earth
   (4) faith in the Earth's restoration   5 _____

6 Lines 80 through 83 emphasize Marvin's
   (1) sense of deprivation
   (2) appreciation of his situation
   (3) fear of destruction
   (4) recollection of his childhood   6 _____

7 The details in lines 85 to 89 confirm the Earth has been damaged by
   (1) climate change
   (2) cosmic instability
   (3) human actions
   (4) natural occurences   7 _____

8 The images in lines 97 through 99 convey feelings of
   (1) fear and disappointment
   (2) cleansing and renewal
   (3) preservation and protection
   (4) confusion and impatience   8 _____

9 Which lines best capture Marvin's understanding of his father's perspective?
   (1) "Tense with expectancy, Marvin settled himself down in the cramped cabin while his father started the motor and checked the controls" (lines 18 through 20)
   (2) "They were intense unscintillating points, and suddenly he remembered a rhyme he had once read in one of his father's books" (lines 31 and 32)
   (3) "In a few minutes they had reached the edge of the plateau on which the Colony had been built" (lines 49 through 51)
   (4) "He [his father] would never walk beside the rivers of that lost and legendary world, or listen to the thunder raging above its softly rounded hills" (lines 93 through 95)   9 _____

Reading Comprehension Passage B

This Life

    My grandmother told me there'd be good days
    to counter the dark ones,
    with blue skies in the heart as far
    as the soul could see. She said
(5) you could measure a life in as many ways
    as there were to bake a pound cake,
    but you still needed real butter and eggs
    for a good one—pound cake, that is,
    but I knew what she meant. She was always
(10) talking around corners like that;
    she knew words carried their treasures
    like a grape clusters around its own juice.
    She loved words; she thought a book
    was a monument to the glory of creation
(15) and a library . . . well, sometimes
    just trying to describe Jubilation
    will get you a bit tongue, so let's
    leave it at that. But my grandmother
    was nobody's fool, and she'd tell anybody
(20) smart enough to listen. Don't let a little pain
    stop you; try as hard as you can
    every minute you're given or else
    sit down and shut-up—though in her opinion,
    keeping quiet in noisy times was a sin
(25) against everything God and democracy
    intended us for. I know she'd like
    where I'm standing right now. She'd say
    a man who could measure his life in deeds
    was larger inside than the vessel that carried him;
(30) she'd say he was a cluster of grapes.
    My grandmother was only four feet ten
    but when she entered a room, even the books
    came to attention. Giants come in all sizes:

Sometimes a moment is a monument;
(35) sometimes an institution breathes—
like a library. Like this halcyon[1] day.

—Rita Dove
from *The Poets Laureate Anthology*, 2010
W. W. Norton & Company, Inc.

---

[1] halcyon—peaceful

10 Lines 1 through 4 establish the grandmother's

   (1) questioning nature
   (2) vivid imagination
   (3) cautious attitude
   (4) optimistic outlook   10 _____

11 The figurative language in lines 9 and 10 highlights the grandmother's

   (1) desire to avoid conflicts
   (2) tendency to keep secrets
   (3) strategy to impart wisdom
   (4) ability to create humor   11 _____

12 Which phrase from the poem clarifies the narrator's statement in line 30?

   (1) "there'd be good days" (line 1)
   (2) "smart enough to listen" (line 20)
   (3) "measure his life in deeds" (line 28)
   (4) "sometimes an institution breathes" (line 35)   12 _____

13 The personification in lines 32 and 33 emphasizes the grandmother's

   (1) small size
   (2) commanding presence
   (3) family history
   (4) successful career   13 _____

14 The overall tone of the poem can best be described as

   (1) objective
   (2) skeptical
   (3) respectful
   (4) critical   14 _____

Reading Comprehension Passage C

Texting isn't the first new technology blamed for ruining communication and common courtesy.

    Is text-messaging driving us apart? These days, we talk to each other a lot with our thumbs—mashing out over six billion text messages a day in the United States, and likely a few billion more on services like WhatsApp and Facebook Messenger.

(5)   But some worry that so much messaging leads, paradoxically, to less communication. When Sherry Turkle, the MIT clinical psychologist and author, interviewed college students, they said texting was causing friction in their face-to-face interactions. While hanging out with friends they'd be texting surreptitiously at the same time, pretending to maintain eye contact (10) but mentally somewhere else. The new form of communication was fun, sure, but it was colliding with—and eroding—the old one.

    "Our texts are fine," as one student said. "It's what texting does to our conversations when we are together that's the problem." . . .

    New technologies often unsettle the way we relate to one another, (15) of course. But social ruptures caused by texting have a strong echo in the arguments we had a hundred years ago. That's when a newfangled appliance gave us a strange new way to contact one another en masse:[1] the telephone. . . .

    At first, the telephone was marketed mainly as a tool for business. (20) Physicians and drugstores bought them to process orders, and business owners installed them at home so they could be quickly reached. The phone, proclaimed early ad copy, gave business leaders an ESP-like "sixth sense"[2] of their far-flung operations. . . .

    Nonetheless, the telephone quickly gave birth to curious new forms of (25) socializing. Callers arranged regular weekly "visiting" calls, dialing remote family to catch up on news. "Distance rolls away and for a few minutes every Thursday night the familiar voices tell the little family gossip that both are so eager to hear," a Bell ad cooed in 1921.

    Phone companies even boasted that the phone was an improvement (30) over that stodgy, low-fi communication, the letter. "Correspondence will help for a time, but friendships do not flourish for long on letters alone," a 1931 Bell sales manual noted. "When you can't visit in person,

---

[1] en masse—in a group at the same time
[2] ESP-like "sixth sense"—heightened intuition

telephone periodically. Telephone calls will keep up the whole intimacy remarkably well."

(35) Soon, though, social critics began to wonder: Was all this phone chatter good for us? Was it somehow a lesser form of communication than what had come before? "Does the telephone make men more active or more lazy?" wondered the Knights of Columbus in a 1926 meeting. "Does the telephone break up home life and the old practice of visiting (40) friends?"

Others worried that the inverse would occur—that it would be so easy to talk that we'd never leave each other alone. "Thanks to the telephone, motor-car and such-like inventions, our neighbors have it in their power to turn our leisure into a series of interruptions," complained an American (45) professor in 1929. And surely it couldn't be healthy to talk to each other so much. Wouldn't it create Too Much Information [TMI]?

"We shall soon be nothing but transparent heaps of jelly to each other," a London writer moaned in 1897. Others fretted that the telephone sped up life, demanding instant reactions. "The use of the telephone (50) gives little room for reflection," wrote a British newspaper in 1899. "It does not improve the temper, and it engenders a feverishness in the ordinary concerns of life which does not make for domestic happiness and comfort." Perhaps the strangest thing was being in the room while a friend talked to someone else—someone outside the room. In 1880, (55) Mark Twain wrote "A Telephonic Conversation," transcribing the half-a-conversation as he listened to his wife on the phone. To the observer, as the skit pointed out, a telephone call sounded like disjointed nonsense. Even phone companies worried about whether the device created new forms of rude behavior; a 1910 Bell ad warned about "Dr. Jekyll and (60) Mr. Hyde at the Telephone." . . .

Indeed, some believed the phone improved our social behavior, because it forced a listener to pay closer attention to a speaker. Devoid of visual signals, we must be "all ears and memory," a pundit[3] wrote in 1915: "The mind cannot wander." Plus, by eradicating distance, wouldn't the phone (65) reduce misunderstanding? War, even? "Someday we will build up a world telephone system making necessary to all peoples the use of a common language, or common understanding of languages, which will join all the people of the earth into one brotherhood," gushed John J. Carty, AT&T chief engineer, in 1907.

---

[3]pundit—an expert who shares opinions with the public

These utopian[4] views, of course, were wildly optimistic. But the gloomy views of pessimists, as [author, Claude] Fischer notes, didn't come true either. Even Emily Post, the etiquette expert, came around to the telephone. By the 1920s, she'd accepted "Hello" as a suitable greeting, and even thought it was acceptable to invite someone to dinner with a call. "Custom which has altered many ways and manners has taken away all opprobrium[5] from the message," she shrugged.

Nowadays, the telephone call seems like a quaint throwback to a gentler era. When Jenna Birch, the journalist, started dating a man who insisted on calling her on the phone, she found it warm and delightful—though her friends thought the behavior odd. Phone calls now seem retro.[6]

Academics have observed this shift, too. "My students just do not think of the phone as a mechanism of vocal interaction—they think of that as very rare," says John Durham Peters, a communication professor at the University of Iowa, and author of *Speaking Into the Air*. He doesn't think the shift to texting has degraded our interactions, though. By the middle of the 20th century, studies found that the telephone appeared not to have eroded social contact—indeed, some research found those with phones wrote more old-fashioned letters than those without. Similarly, modern surveys by the Pew Research Center have found that teenagers who text the most are also those who spend the most time face to face with friends. Communication, it seems, begets more communication, and—as Peters argues—just because talk happens in text doesn't mean it's not meaningful.

"Media scholars," he notes, "have this long romance with 'conversation' as the cure to the disease of media."

Still, it's not hard to be dispirited[7] by the divided attention so many of Turkle's subjects bemoaned in their lives. Indeed, Michéle Martin, of Carleton, thinks we're living through a replay of the telephone, where the things that made it valuable—instant communications—are the same that made it annoying. "People believe they are liberated because they can bring the mobile phone everywhere," Martin says. "But at the same time they are slaves to it."

The poet Carl Sandburg captured that dissonance in a 1916 poem about the telephone. He imagined a telephone wire being aware of the disparate[8]

---

[4]utopian—idealistic
[5]opprobrium—disgrace
[6]retro—dated
[7]dispirited—discouraged
[8]disparate—varying

(105) uses to which it was being put—coursing with conversations both deep and frivolous. "It is love and war and money; it is the fighting and the tears, the work and want/Death and laughter of men and women passing through me, carrier of your speech."

—Clive Thompson
excerpted and adapted from "OMG! We've Been Here B4"
Smithsonian, March 2016

15 The first paragraph of the text serves to

   (1) highlight the prevalence of texting
   (2) stress the benefits of texting
   (3) explain the origins of texting
   (4) support the abolition of texting   15 _____

16 As used in line 9, the word "surreptitiously" most nearly means

   (1) politely
   (2) boldly
   (3) secretively
   (4) earnestly   16 _____

17 The details in lines 19 through 23 reveal that the telephone was initially

   (1) associated with the supernatural
   (2) not considered very useful
   (3) often blamed for worker illness
   (4) not used for social purposes   17 _____

18 The use of the word "cooed" (line 28) implies that telephone advertisers were

   (1) helpful and patient
   (2) strategic and persuasive
   (3) childish and inconsiderate
   (4) sarcastic and relentless   18 _____

19 Lines 35 to 46 illustrate society's

   (1) enthusiasm about using new technology
   (2) dependence on those proficient in new technology
   (3) grasp of the significance of new technology
   (4) concern about the impact of new technology   19 _____

20 The figurative language in 47 and 48 implies that telephone use would cause people to

(1) lose self-confidence and motivation
(2) lack substance and individuality
(3) attract danger and adversity
(4) become narrow-minded and uninformed   20 _____

21 The statements from a Bell ad (lines 59 and 60) and the AT&T chief engineer (lines 65 through 69) offer

(1) contrasting perspectives on the potential effects of the telephone
(2) strong support for the growing popularity of the telephone
(3) alternative options for communicating with family members
(4) insightful evaluation of the importance of long-distance conversations   21 _____

22 The "utopian views" of the early 1900s (line 70) suggested that telephone use could

(1) improve local commerce
(2) encourage language studies
(3) promote global unity
(4) influence community values   22 _____

23 The information about Emily Post (lines 72 through 76) contributes to a central idea that

(1) rules of proper behavior can be confusing
(2) norms of good conduct are universal
(3) concepts of politeness can evolve over time
(4) conventions of salutation depend on status   23 _____

24 The quotations in lines 100 through 102 reflect a sense of

(1) bias
(2) irony
(3) suspense
(4) resolution   24 _____

PART 2—Argument Response

Directions: Closely read each of the *four* texts provided on pages 328 through 337 and write a source-based argument on the topic below. You may use the margins to take notes as you read and scrap paper to plan your response. Write your argument on a separate sheet of paper.

Topic: Should pets be allowed in the workplace?

Your Task: Carefully read each of the *four* texts provided. Then, using evidence from at least *three* of the texts, write a well-developed argument regarding whether or not pets should be allowed in the workplace. Clearly establish your claim, distinguish your claim from alternate or opposing claims, and use specific, relevant, and sufficient evidence from at least *three* of the texts to develop your argument. Do *not* simply summarize each text.

Guidelines:

Be sure to:
- Establish your claim regarding whether or not pets should be allowed in the workplace.
- Distinguish your claim from alternate or opposing claims.
- Use specific, relevant, and sufficient evidence from at least *three* of the texts to develop your argument.
- Identify each source that you reference by text number and line number(s) or graphic (for example: Text 1, line 4 or Text 2, graphic).
- Organize your ideas in a cohesive and coherent manner.
- Maintain a formal style of writing.
- Follow the conventions of standard written English.

Texts:

Text 1—Do Pets in the Workplace Improve Morale?
Text 2—Why Pets in the Workplace May Not Be As Great As You Thought
Text 3—Why a Pet-Friendly Office May Be the Key to Employee Satisfaction
Text 4—Don't Bring Your Dog to Work

Text 1

Do Pets in the Workplace Improve Morale?

  Human resource managers are always looking for ways to improve morale and create a more appealing workplace culture. The popularity of the recent film release "The Secret Life of Pets" [2016] underscores the love we Americans have for our pets. In fact, around 65 percent of U.S.
(5) households are home to at least one pet. The majority of these are dogs and cats. . . .
  The benefits of being around animals have inspired human resource personnel and other business decision makers to allow pets in the workplace. The top motive for making this allowance is the stress-reducing effect that
(10) animals bring. Employees who are less stressed at work are more productive and miss fewer days due to being sick.
  Pet-friendly businesses usually focus mainly on allowing dogs in the workplace. However, some allow cats, birds and reptiles. A retail business might have "shop cats" that live on the premises, or smaller animals kept in
(15) cages that can become company mascots and offer a source of stress relief for workers.

An Internet giant paves the way with pets in the workplace.
  . . .These days, about 2,000 dogs accompany their owners to Amazon each day. Workers and management have embraced the culture, and the pet-friendly policy benefits both owners and those who don't own pets. No
(20) matter what the workday brings, Amazon staff members are never far away from a coworker's terrier or spaniel poking its head around a corner. Any stress they were feeling melts away. . . .

Pet-friendly workplaces rate higher.
  Banfield Pet Hospital recently surveyed over 1,000 employees and 200 human resource decision makers for its Pets At Work barometer called
(25) "Pet-Friendly Workplace PAWrometer." The goal was to measure worker opinions about pets in the workplace. Those who worked in pet-friendly offices were found to believe it improves the atmosphere in the workplace significantly.
  The majority of workers in pet-friendly workplaces consider the policy
(30) to be positive. A full 91 percent of managers and 82 percent of employees felt workers become more loyal to the company with this policy. A large majority felt it made the workplace more productive, and 86 percent of workers and 92 percent of management reported decreased worker stress

levels. Not only do pets in the workplace make the environment less
(35) stressful, workers are also less burdened with guilt about leaving a pet at
home alone while they are at work. They are then more likely to work
longer hours if required.

While pet-friendly businesses improve existing employees' lives, they
are also appealing to new applicants. It's a benefit that millennials[1] find
(40) appealing and offers a way to draw in a larger talent pool.

So, how do pet-friendly workplaces stack up in terms of pros and cons?
Let's take a look:

The benefits of pets in the workplace.

- **Happier, more productive workers.** Both pet owners and non-pet owning employees report lowered stress levels and a higher level of job
(45) satisfaction with pets on the premises. This naturally leads to increased productivity.
- **Healthier workers.** In addition to reduced stress levels, being around animals has documented positive effects on blood pressure, cholesterol levels and the immune system.
(50) - **Increased loyalty.** Over half of employees in non-pet-friendly workplaces report they'd be more likely to continue working for a company if they could bring their pet to work.

Potential problems you may encounter by allowing pets in the workplace.

- **Not everyone is an animal lover.** There are people who dislike animals for one reason or another. Allergies, phobias, or a general dislike of
(55) animals could cause pets in the workplace to encroach[2] upon productivity and quality of life for these individuals.
- **Hygiene and cleanliness issues.** Even potty-trained pets can have an accident now and then. There is no guarantee this won't happen in the workplace, especially with a high volume of animals brought to work.
(60) - **Interoffice squabbles.** Not all animals get along, so there is the potential for fights between dogs and cats brought to work.

While worker distraction is a concern for some human resource
managers considering a pet-friendly policy, the vast majority report that

---

[1]millennials—the generation born in the 1980s or 1990s, especially in the U.S.
[2]encroach—intrude

the benefits to morale and overall productivity far outweigh time spent
(65) "distracted" by pets in the workplace.

Advocates of allowing pets in the workplace insist that there are ways around the "cons" or risks of pet-friendly workplaces. The key to a successful pet policy is a clear structure. . . .

—excerpted and adapted from "Do Pets in the
Workplace Improve Morale?"
https://online.arbor.edu, August 8, 2016

Text 2

Why Pets in the Workplace May Not Be As Great As You Thought

    ... Study after study has proven how pets have a calming effect on our bodies and minds, how they help children with A.D.D. [Attention Deficit Disorder] focus better, how they reduce blood pressure and lower stress, how pets at the workplace make employees more creative, productive, and
(5) cordial to each other, and how they're such awesome additions to our lives overall.
    So it would seem that if we spend the best parts of our waking hours at work, there's no better way to carry forward these wonderful benefits that pets bring into our work lives too, right? Well, unfortunately there are no
(10) simple answers here.
    While there is a growing wave of companies led by the usual suspects—Google, Zynga, Ben & Jerry's, and others—that allow employees to take their pets along to the workplace, there's also a growing debate about the practicality of the whole idea. And these voices of concern are not just
(15) coming from the minority of pet-haters or pet-neutral folks around. Even pet owners have reservations about bringing their beloved pooch to the office with them on a daily basis. Here's why:

Not in the Pink of Health
    ... Spare a thought for the millions of your fellow Americans who suffer from pet related allergies. The Asthma and Allergy Foundation of America
(20) pegs the figure of Americans with one form of pet allergy or another at 15% to 30% of the total population. Some of these allergies are so severe that they cause rashes, temporary breathlessness, panic attacks, and even severe respiratory disorders.
    In addition to a physical reaction to the presence of pets around them,
(25) you could have coworkers who are genuinely scared of animals and feel stressed out around them. For such individuals a pet in their workplace is not a calming presence, but rather a constant threat to their wellbeing and safety.

Safety First
    ... Many industries by their very nature are not conducive[1] to having
(30) pets sauntering around. Medical facilities, pharmaceutical companies,

---

[1] conducive—favorable

chemical laboratories, and food businesses are all sectors where a pet can be a serious threat to the quality of the final product or service. In such environments, pets pose a genuine contamination hazard and are best kept out, no questions asked.

(35) In some cases, it's in your pet's best interest to chill out at home and skip the trip to the workplace. Industries like construction, mining, refineries, and more can be dangerous for your pet's health and well-being. You wouldn't want to put your pet at risk just so you can be happy at work, would you? . . .

Real Costs to the Company

As any pet owner will tell you, owning their bundle of joy is not cheap.
(40) From $1570 for a large dog to $575 for a parakeet per year, pet ownership comes at an ever-increasing price tag. When you turn your office into a pet friendly zone, you are in turn taking on some of the expenses of owning a pet upon yourself. Be prepared to stock your workplace with at least basic pet supplies like snacks, water bowls, kitty litter, and chew toys.
(45) If you think your costs end there (or are tangible), you are mistaken. Pets at the workplace also bring with them a built-in deterrent[2] for employees seeking career opportunities at your organization. With the market for talented and qualified workers already so scarce, adding an extra filter to your recruitment process may not be the smartest idea from a competitive
(50) perspective. . . .

While the benefits that pets bring with them are numerous and the pro-pet lobby gets louder with every passing day, organizations need to also give credence[3] to the real issues that four-legged and feathered guests at work bring along with them. . . .

—Rohan Ayyar
excerpted and adapted from "Why Pets in the Workplace
May Not Be As Great As You Thought"
www.fastcompany.com, November 14, 2014

---

[2]deterrent—obstacle
[3]credence—support

Text 3

Why a Pet-Friendly Office May Be the Key to Employee Satisfaction

... The pet-friendly office is transforming our current idea of the typical nine-to-five workspace. Although the primary allure appears to be 24/7 cuddles with man's best friend, the actual benefits of a pet-friendly office go much deeper.

(5) Some of the world's biggest companies have proudly joined the ranks of pet-friendly businesses, from Googleplex,[1] to Build-A-Bear Workshop, to hospitals in New Jersey. This shift in office culture has shown that pet-friendly offices can provide unexpected (and positive) results to all varieties of businesses....

Employee Satisfaction and Stress

(10) Employee satisfaction is a constant concern for an engaging and exciting place. Studies have shown that unhappy workers can cause businesses to lose thousands of dollars over time due to sick leave, mediocre work, and destructive behavior. Keeping the office engaging and exciting can be a struggle, and combating organizational stress may be key to improving a (15) company's profits....

Giving employees the option to bring their pet to work could also save them the worry associated with leaving a pet at home. Instead of scrambling through the end of the day to go home and let the dog out, they have the dog with them and can continue to work without rushing. Instead of spending (20) money on a pet daycare on a regular basis, workers can watch their furry friend while in the office.

Pets are also known to be great stress-relievers in general. It's no wonder that Animal-Assisted Therapy is recognized as one of the leading treatments for post-war PTSD [Post-Traumatic Stress Disorder] and is gaining ground (25) as a popular solution for social workers. Multiple studies have shown that simply petting cats or dogs can be extremely beneficial for our health; from lowering blood pressure to increasing bone density.

Attract Millennials

As a millennial, I can assure you: I would choose a pet-friendly office over the majority of other job offers out there. The benefit of bringing my (30) pup to work is a much stronger pull than a larger paycheck or fancy corner office.

---

[1]Googleplex—Google headquarters

Millennials love their pets, and millennials love pet-friendly offices. In fact, you could even argue that millennials are the reason pet-friendly offices are taking the business world by storm. Being the largest demographic to (35) enter the workforce, they have already brought with them a demand for a new form of workplace flexibility and a break from the traditional office culture of our predecessors. . . .

Improve Communication

If you've ever walked your dog through a park or downtown area, there's a significant chance that you've received more waves, 'hellos', and (40) acknowledgements than if you had been walking by yourself. Walking or even being near a dog is an excellent ice-breaker.

Shifting to a pet-friendly workspace can bring that same level of open and enthusiastic communication into the office. Water cooler conversations[2] will lose some of their awkward chatter, and employees (45) will have the added encouragement of meeting new people in the building through their pets. This can lead to some inspiring brainstorm conversations as well as an increase in camaraderie[3] and trust among workers.

A 2012 study by the Virginia Commonwealth University found that (50) employees that brought their dogs to work were not only less stressed than their pet-free predecessors, but those employees believed they were 50 percent more productive with the presence of their pets. The public relations manager of the company that participated, Lisa Conklin of Replacements Dinnerware, stated after the conclusion of the study:

(55) "The study proved what we always thought: having dogs around leads to a more productive work environment, and people get to know each other through the pets. If you are in a position where something is stressful, seeing that wagging tail and puppy smile brightens the day—it can turn around the whole environment."

Promote Employee Activity

(60) On top of all these benefits, pets can also improve employee activity. Dog owners in the office will most likely have to walk their dog at least once a day, allowing them the opportunity to get away from their computer and into the open air. Workplace wellness has received considerable attention lately and more companies are making this a

---

[2]water cooler conversations—informal conversation
[3]camaraderie—fellowship

(65) priority. Pet-friendly offices can inspire a smooth transition to a more 'mobile' office. . . .

—Katie McBeth
excerpted and adapted from "Why a Pet-Friendly Office May Be the Key to Employee Satisfaction"
https://thebossmagazine.com, September 28, 2016

Text 4

Don't Bring Your Dog to Work

If there's a dog in the cubicle next to you, you're hardly alone: About 7 percent of employers now allow pets in the workplace, reports NPR [National Public Radio]. Five years ago, that figure stood at 5 percent. That might not seem like a big jump, but once you remove jobs that
(5) don't have offices from the equation—manufacturing and agriculture, for instance—that's about a 50 percent increase. That rise is a victory for people who tout the benefits of inviting dogs and other furry friends into the office: It lowers the stress of employees, increases morale, produces tangible health benefits, and reduces turnover, all at no cost to
(10) the company.

But how do the dogs feel about it?

"Most people do not understand dog body language," said E'Lise Christensen, a board-certified veterinary behaviorist in Colorado. One major concern she has with the rise of pet-friendly work environments is the
(15) corresponding increased risk for behavioral problems, especially dog bites. Since almost no one, not even many dog trainers, knows how to properly interpret dog body language, co-workers might interpret the panting of a dog in the office as a friendly smile, rather than a sign of nervousness. And in dogs, nervousness can lead to bites. "[People] can identify abject[1] fear,
(20) and they can identify extreme aggression, but they cannot reliably identify things in between," said Christensen. It's in that wide middle area where we may not recognize pet discomfort.

Bonnie Beaver, executive director of the American College of Veterinary Behaviorists and a professor at Texas A&M University, said in
(25) an email that dog bites are not the only behavioral issues that might present problems. Generally, dogs are expected to sit still in an office setting, which can be difficult for active dogs, leading to boredom (which, in turn, leads to problem behaviors like chewing up desk legs). These policies are also particularly hard on dogs if they're taken to the office only occasionally,
(30) instead of regularly; dogs are big on routines, and uncertainty adds to their fear and stress.

Once you expand the conversation beyond our most domesticated companion, the prospects get even iffier. "Not all animals are comfortable with a very social setting," said Christensen. Each new animal, like cats

---

[1]abject—severe

(35) or pot-bellied pigs, brings its own social complexities, not to mention the possibility of contagious disease (it's rare that employers require proof of vaccination). Rabies, ringworm, and parasitic infections like scabies are all potential health risks for humans that come into contact with pets that haven't been properly vetted.[2]

(40) Of course there's obvious appeal. Many people love dogs. They write whole articles gushing about a furrier workplace. (Dog skeptics, at least vocal ones, are harder to find.) When an employer is on board, the policy is often as informal as a person in charge saying, "Yeah, sure, whatever. Bring your dogs. It'll be great." Little or no oversight is applied to a matter that (45) needs it in order to ensure the environment is conducive[3] to pets in the workplace.

Christensen said companies should ideally hire an in-house behavioral expert to oversee a pet-at-work policy, especially in the initial stages, "but unless you're Google, I don't see that happening." More realistically, she (50) said, better awareness will go a long way. Employers should take care to craft a policy that works for dogs' well-being as well as humans'. This can include requiring proof of vaccinations, as well as providing training for offices on dog behavior (which can be as basic as watching videos).

"It's critical that people with dogs get special education, in at least (55) body language, even if they think they know normal body language," said Christensen. Given that most people can't even tell the difference between a relaxed and anxious dog, this advice seems prudent. Before more offices throw open their doors to dogs willy-nilly[4] and more pets start tagging along on the morning commute, we should learn how better to listen to them.
(60) They might be asking to stay at home.

—Matt Miller
excerpted and adapted from "Don't Bring Your Dog to Work"
www.slate.com, August 15, 2016

---

[2]vetted—examined
[3]conducive—favorable
[4]willy-nilly—in an unplanned manner

PART 3—Analysis Response

Your Task: Closely read the text provided on pages 339 and 340 and write a well-developed, text-based response of two to three paragraphs. In your response, identify a central idea in the text and analyze how the author's use of **one** writing strategy (literary element or literary technique or rhetorical device) develops this central idea. Use strong and thorough evidence from the text to support your analysis. Do *not* simply summarize the text. You may use the margins to take notes as you read and scrap paper to plan your response. Write your response on a separate sheet of paper.

Guidelines:

Be sure to:
- Identify a central idea in the text.
- Analyze how the author's use of **one** writing strategy (literary element or literary technique or rhetorical device) develops this central idea. Examples include: characterization, conflict, denotation/connotation, metaphor, simile, irony, language use, point-of-view, setting, structure, symbolism, theme, tone, etc.
- Use strong and thorough evidence from the text to support your analysis.
- Organize your ideas in a cohesive and coherent manner.
- Maintain a formal style of writing.
- Follow the conventions of standard written English.

Text

   ... There were a number of people out this afternoon, far more than last Sunday. And the band sounded louder and gayer. That was because the Season had begun. For although the band played all the year round on Sundays, out of season it was never the same. It was like some one playing
(5) with only the family to listen; it didn't care how it played if there weren't any strangers present. Wasn't the conductor wearing a new coat, too? She was sure it was new. He scraped with his foot and flapped his arms like a rooster about to crow, and the bandsmen sitting in the green rotunda blew out their cheeks and glared at the music. Now there came a little "flutey" bit—very
(10) pretty!—a little chain of bright drops. She was sure it would be repeated. It was; she lifted her head and smiled.

   Only two people shared her "special" seat: a fine old man in a velvet coat, his hands clasped over a huge carved walking-stick, and a big old woman, sitting upright, with a roll of knitting on her embroidered apron. They did
(15) not speak. This was disappointing, for Miss Brill always looked forward to the conversation. She had become really quite expert, she thought, at listening as though she didn't listen, at sitting in other people's lives just for a minute while they talked round her.

   She glanced, sideways, at the old couple. Perhaps they would go soon.
(20) Last Sunday, too, hadn't been as interesting as usual. An Englishman and his wife, he wearing a dreadful Panama hat and she button boots. And she'd gone on the whole time about how she ought to wear spectacles;[1] she knew she needed them; but that it was no good getting any; they'd be sure to break and they'd never keep on. And he'd been so patient. He'd suggested
(25) everything—gold rims, the kind that curved round your ears, little pads inside the bridge. No, nothing would please her. "They'll always be sliding down my nose!" Miss Brill had wanted to shake her.

   The old people sat on the bench, still as statues. Never mind, there was always the crowd to watch. To and fro, in front of the flower-beds and the
(30) band rotunda, the couples and groups paraded, stopped to talk, to greet, to buy a handful of flowers from the old beggar who had his tray fixed to the railings. Little children ran among them, swooping and laughing; little boys with big white silk bows under their chins, little girls, little French dolls, dressed up in velvet and lace. And sometimes a tiny staggerer came
(35) suddenly rocking into the open from under the trees, stopped, stared, as suddenly sat down "flop," until its small high-stepping mother, like a young

---

[1]spectacles—glasses

hen, rushed scolding to its rescue. Other people sat on the benches and green chairs, but they were nearly always the same, Sunday after Sunday, and—Miss Brill had often noticed—there was something funny about (40) nearly all of them. They were odd, silent, nearly all old, and from the way they stared they looked as though they'd just come from dark little rooms or even—even cupboards!

Behind the rotunda the slender trees with yellow leaves down drooping, and through them just a line of sea, and beyond the blue sky with gold- (45) veined clouds.

Tum-tum-tum tiddle-um! tiddle-um! tum tiddley-um tum ta! blew the band. . . .

Oh, how fascinating it was! How she enjoyed it! How she loved sitting here, watching it all! It was like a play. It was exactly like a play. Who could (50) believe the sky at the back wasn't painted? But it wasn't till a little brown dog trotted on solemn and then slowly trotted off, like a little "theatre" dog, a little dog that had been drugged, that Miss Brill discovered what it was that made it so exciting. They were all on the stage. They weren't only the audience, not only looking on; they were acting. Even she had a part and (55) came every Sunday. No doubt somebody would have noticed if she hadn't been there; she was part of the performance after all. How strange she'd never thought of it like that before! And yet it explained why she made such a point of starting from home at just the same time each week—so as not to be late for the performance—and it also explained why she had (60) quite a queer, shy feeling at telling her English pupils how she spent her Sunday afternoons. No wonder! Miss Brill nearly laughed out loud. She was on the stage. She thought of the old invalid gentleman to whom she read the newspaper four afternoons a week while he slept in the garden. She had got quite used to the frail head on the cotton pillow, the hollowed (65) eyes, the open mouth and the high pinched nose. If he'd been dead she mightn't have noticed for weeks; she wouldn't have minded. But suddenly he knew he was having the paper read to him by an actress! "An actress!" The old head lifted; two points of light quivered in the old eyes. "An actress—are ye?" And Miss Brill smoothed the newspaper as though it (70) were the manuscript of her part and said gently; "Yes, I have been an actress for a long time." . . .

—Katherine Mansfield
excerpted from "Miss Brill"
The Garden Party and Other Stories, 1922
Alfred A. Knopf, Inc.

Regents ELA Answers June 2019

English Language Arts

Answer Key

PART 1

1. **3**
2. **2**
3. **1**
4. **2**
5. **1**
6. **1**
7. **3**
8. **2**
9. **4**
10. **4**
11. **3**
12. **3**
13. **2**
14. **3**
15. **1**
16. **3**
17. **4**
18. **2**
19. **4**
20. **2**
21. **1**
22. **3**
23. **3**
24. **2**

PART 2 *See Answers and Explanations*

PART 3 *See Answers and Explanations*

Regents Examination in English Language Arts—June 2019
Chart for Converting Total Weighted Raw Scores to Final Exam Scores (Scale Scores)

Weighted Raw Score*	Scale Score	Performance Level	Weighted Raw Score*	Scale Score	Performance Level
56	100	5	27	55	2
55	99	5	26	52	1
54	99	5	25	50	1
53	99	5	24	47	1
52	98	5	23	45	1
51	97	5	22	42	1
50	96	5	21	40	1
49	95	5	20	37	1
48	93	5	19	34	1
47	92	5	18	31	1
46	90	5	17	28	1
45	89	5	16	25	1
44	88	5	15	22	1
43	86	5	14	19	1
42	85	5	13	16	1
41	84	4	12	13	1
40	82	4	11	10	1
39	80	4	10	9	1
38	79	4	9	8	1
37	77	3	8	6	1
36	75	3	7	5	1
35	72	3	6	4	1
34	70	3	5	3	1
33	68	3	4	3	1
32	66	3	3	2	1
31	65	3	2	1	1
30	61	2	1	1	1
29	59	2	0	0	1
28	57	2			

The conversion table is determined independently for each administration of the exam.

Answers Explained

PART 1—Reading Comprehension
Multiple-Choice Questions

Passage A

1. **3** "create a feeling of anticipation." The images in this paragraph describe the narrator being led through levels of what we gradually understand to be a created environment, a Colony on the moon perhaps, where humans now live after life on Earth has been destroyed by nuclear Armageddon. The narrator, a ten-year-old child, wants to linger at various levels. However, the Father rushes ahead insistently, and the boy experiences "a sense of rising excitement." Note that the questions are best understood and answered after you read the entire story.

2. **2** "the inhospitable conditions of Outside." The description of vehicles with pressurized cabins exiting through airlocks establishes that the environment outside the Colony does not support human life. This question is also an example of how, on the ELA Regents, knowledge of vocabulary is assessed in context. None of the other choices is supported by the text.

3. **1** "a change in Marvin's understanding." At this point, the boy only senses something "strange" in his father's behavior. At the end of the story, though, Marvin reveals how he finally "understood the purpose of this pilgrimage."

4. **2** "desolation of the Outside." The grim barrenness (desolation) of the landscape further reveals the inhospitable conditions of the Outside. (See also question 2.)

5. **1** "romantic vision of the Earth." Once Marvin could see Earth through the brilliant glare, "It was beautiful, and it called to his heart across the abyss of space." (line 77) *Romantic* here refers to a view that is characterized by intense emotion and an idealized appreciation of nature. Marvin dreams that one day, succeeding generations of humans may return to the beautiful, "lost and legendary world" of Earth.

6. **1** "sense of deprivation." Marvin feels that life on a beautiful Earth "should have been his rightful heritage." Marvin feels denied (deprived) of that possibility because he will know the beauties of Earth only through books and ancient records.

7. **3** "human actions." Images of "evil phosphorescence . . . radioactive aftermath . . . [and] glow of dying atoms" establish that in this story, life on Earth was destroyed by human actions—nuclear war. This was often a theme in 20th-century literature, especially after the use of atom bombs at end of the World War II.

8. **2** "cleansing and renewal." These lines offer images of winds and rains that would "scour [scrub clean] the poisons" and where the seas would "waste their [the poisons'] venom," making possible the return (renewal) of human life on Earth. The feelings offered in the other choices are not suggested in lines 98 through 100.

9. **4** "He [his father] would never walk beside the rivers of that lost and legendary world, or listen to the thunder raging above its softly rounded hills" (lines 93 through 95). These lines best capture Marvin's understanding of his father's profound feelings of loss and of his father's knowledge that he will never return to Earth. None of the other choices reflects details of the father's understanding.

Passage B

10. **4** "optimistic outlook." The images of "good days/to counter the dark ones" and of "blue skies in the heart" are expressions of the grandmother's confidence that life offers positive and hopeful things to balance pain or discouragement. Optimism best characterizes the tone in these lines.

11. **3** "strategy to impart wisdom." The images in the previous lines and the metaphor of baking a cake to measure a life represent the grandmother's use of language as a tactical way (strategy) to give valuable advice and guidance (wisdom) to her grandchild. Lines 9 and 10 include no significant expression of conflict, secrets, or humor.

12. **3** "measure his life in deeds" (line 28). Just as words "carried their treasures/like a grape clusters around its own juice," a person whose life is measured in how well he or she has acted can be seen as a cluster of meaningful deeds. None of the other choices expresses what the grandmother would admire in the life of her grandchild.

13. **2** "commanding presence." *Commanding* denotes something or someone who is impressive, strong, and demands obedience. The image of "even the books" coming "to attention" vividly expresses the powerful influence the grandmother had on those around her.

14. **3** "respectful." This is the best answer among the choices, even if it somewhat understates the admiration and appreciation the poet has for the grandmother.

Passage C

15. **1** "highlight the prevalence of texting." These lines report on the frequency, popularity, and widespread use (*prevalence*) of texting. The paragraph cites "six billion text messages a day in the United States, . . . and a few billion more on" worldwide services. These details do not directly stress the benefits, explain the origins, or support the abolition of texting.

16. **3** "secretively." This is the familiar image of an individual hanging out with friends in a café while also holding his or her phone under the table to check messages and pretending to be fully engaged with the friends who are present.

17. **4** "not used for social purposes." This brief paragraph offers examples of how at first the telephone was seen "as a tool for business." Lines 19 through 23 offer no examples of telephones being used for social purposes.

18. **2** "strategic and persuasive." The word *cooed* is used here to identify the gentle, quiet manner in which one—a mother soothing a baby, for example—speaks calmly and reassuringly to persuade another to do something. Choice (1), "helpful and patient," seems at first to be a good answer because it expresses the tone and feeling of cooing. However, the telephone advertisers are actually using this as a strategy to persuade customers that frequent phone calls are the most meaningful way to stay in touch with family and friends. Choice (2) is the best answer.

19. **4** "concern about the impact of new technology." These two paragraphs offer several examples of concern expressed in the 1920s by critics, scientists, and social groups, who began to wonder, "Was all this phone chatter good for us?"

20. **2** "lack substance and individuality." Among the choices, this phrase best describes the image of telephone users as "transparent heaps of jelly." Each of the other choices describes strong and specific feelings, which do not suggest "heaps of jelly."

21. **1** "contrasting perspectives on the potential effects of the telephone." The Bell ad from 1910 warned that phone use might create "new forms of rude behavior." In contrast, in 1907 the chief engineer at AT&T had proclaimed that the advent of the telephone could promote a "common understanding of languages" and a universal brotherhood, thereby preventing misunderstandings and even war.

22. **3** "promote global unity." The idealistic vision of the AT&T engineer cited in question 21 is an example of the "utopian views" of the 1900s. These views suggested that misunderstanding and distrust among nations could be overcome when people could speak directly to one another through telephone communication. This passage does not consider the benefits to local commerce, language studies, or the influence on community values.

23. **3** "concepts of politeness can evolve over time." Even though choices (1) and (4) offer statements that could be true, the reference to Emily Post and *etiquette*—standards of correct (polite) behavior in social situations—makes this the best answer. In Emily Post's time, she offered guidelines for good manners and acceptable behavior. As the world changed, Emily Post's "rules" changed as well.

24. **2** "irony." The mobile phone is convenient and annoying at the same time. The ironic contradiction expressed here is that people feel liberated in being able to take a phone with them everywhere, but "at the same time they are slaves to it." None of the other choices expresses the intended irony in the quotations.

PART 2—Argument Response

Sample Essay Response

    The modern workplace is the center of many debates. Sexual harassment, racism, and the encroachment of technology on jobs are all topics that have come up in the working world. Compared to these, the discussion over whether or not pets should be allowed in the workplace might be noncontroversial to the point of being dull. However, many people have clashing opinions over whether and how the growing practice of bringing one's pets to work should continue. Although there should be some adjustments or limits to the current practice, I believe it would be beneficial if some workplaces allowed their employees to bring pets to work.

    A key reason for bringing pets to work is in the psychological benefits. Having a parakeet to chat with or a fluffy friend to hug creates a more positive atmosphere, which in turn increases loyalty to and productivity for the company. One study showed that "86 percent of workers and 92 percent of management reported decreased worker stress levels" following the implementation of the policy. (Text 1, lines 32–34) Having pets around also improves worker communication by giving people topics of discussion and shared interest since "walking or even being near a dog is an excellent ice-breaker." (Text 3, lines 40–41) The presence of pets in the workplace can lead to closer emotional bonds or even valuable brainstorms among workers.

    Having pets around can leave workers and, by extension, their employers much more satisfied and stress-free. Besides the pleasant psychological effects, having pets around can also have a positive impact on one's physical well-being. Petting a cat or a dog can have healthy side effects, which can range from "lowering blood pressure to increasing bone density." (Text 3, line 27) Pets can also increase employee activity since walking dogs or feeding cats requires workers to move around more than they would when just sitting at their computers. Younger workers, who represent a large percentage of the workforce, are especially attracted to workplaces that permit pets. For employers, this can be a way to attract millennials as new workers. (Text 3, lines 32–37) Finally, workers of all ages are less likely to rush through work or request shorter hours when they don't need to worry about caring for house-bound pets.

    Of course, having pets in a workplace is not all cuddles and birdsong. There are legitimate concerns about workers who have harmful physical or psychological reactions to having animals around. For example, 15% to 30% of the total American population has some kind of pet allergy (Text 2, lines 19–21), and there are people who are genuinely uneasy in the presence of animals. Contact between humans and pets may even pose the risk of spreading parasitic infections such as ringworm. *(Text 4, lines 37–39)*

Moreover, pets themselves may fare badly in a workplace setting. Restrictive spaces or erratic schedules may lead dogs, a favorite American pet, to suffer psychologically and display bad behavior in the workplace. One writer argues that there is a general human illiteracy in the intricacies of dog body language, leading people to interpret "the panting of a dog in the office as a friendly smile, rather than a sign of nervousness." *(Text 4, lines 17–19)* These are all valid concerns and need to be taken seriously. However, many difficulties can be addressed by educating pet owners about how to identify physical or psychological discomfort in fellow workers

I believe that a policy that welcomes pets would be beneficial to many workplaces. Pets have positive psychological and physical effects on the humans around them. They can even support hiring and worker productivity. Pets need to be protected from dangerous environments, and only well-trained and healthy pets should be permitted in the workplace. These measures would not make the office pets movement welcome everywhere, but they would help smooth the way.

Analysis

Unlike many of the topics presented in Part 2 of the Regents ELA exam, this topic leaves room for a qualified position. This essay meets the requirement to present an argument in support of a particular position, allowing pets in the workplace, but accepts the need for exceptions as well. This writer presents a precise and thoughtful argument, which is balanced with both claims and counterclaims.

The essay is well organized. It opens with an introductory paragraph to outline the issue and establish the writer's position. The information is then developed, with clear exposition of relevant ideas and with specific evidence from the texts to represent alternative points of view. The conclusion appropriately restates the writer's position, which is strengthened by including guidelines to meet many of the concerns of those who may not agree. The use of language is fluent and often sophisticated. "Of course, having pets in a workplace is not all cuddles and birdsong" is a particularly pleasant way to recognize the concerns of those who are not comfortable with pets in the workplace. There are no significant errors in usage or conventions. This essay would merit a high score.

(See pages 79–80 for the scoring guidelines.)

PART 3—Text-Analysis Response

Sample Essay Response

 Through the use of characterization, the author expertly crafts the idea that life is like one big play and that everyone is merely acting out their own parts while simultaneously observing as the audience. The author recounts all of the little details Miss Brill notices about those around her, while the other characters' quirks, mannerisms, or actions create the image of life in this town as action in a play.

 Miss Brill is characterized as an actor playing a role in her own life. As a member of the audience, "she had become really quite expert, she thought, at listening as though she didn't listen, at sitting in on other people's lives . . . while they talked round her." (lines 16–18) As a listener or watcher, Miss Brill always observes the people around her. On this afternoon, though, they are less interesting. The people sitting on the benches appear "nearly always the same." (line 38) Each Sunday, she is at the performance of the band: "How she loved . . . watching it all. It was like a play!" (lines 48–49) She is both listening to the music and taking part in the performance herself. Someone would notice if she was absent from her role. Although she never thought about it that way before, "it explained why she made such a point of starting from home at just the same time each week—so as not be late for the performance." (lines 57–59) The author shows how Miss Brill now understands that she is acting out her own part in the play of life by attending the little band concerts each week. To those around her, she is a character in the play and they are her audience. The events—the drama—of this particular day in Miss Brill's life lead her to the realization that she is "an actress!" (line 67) Miss Brill is no longer just an observer but an actress on the stage of the life around her.

Analysis

This response clearly introduces a central theme from the text: life is a play in which people are both actors/players and audience. The discussion effectively shows how the author's characterization of Miss Brill dramatizes how that life is lived. With specific references to the text and appropriate quotations, the essay shows how the author's strategy is to recount "all of the little details Miss Brill notices" and to reveal the pleasure Miss Brill takes in both listening to and seeing herself as part of the performance.

This response is logically organized. The opening paragraph establishes the central idea and the writing strategy for analysis. The second paragraph contains details from the story that are presented sequentially to reveal the character's own growing understanding of herself and her life. The language and style are appropriately formal and demonstrate control of the conventions. This response would merit a high score.

(See pages 81–82 for the scoring guidelines.)

Regents ELA Examination August 2019
English Language Arts

PART 1—Reading Comprehension

Directions (1–24): Closely read each of the three passages below. After each passage, there are several multiple-choice questions. Select the best suggested answer to each question and write its number in the space provided. You may use the margins to take notes as you read.

Reading Comprehension Passage A

Brooklyn

  Eilis Lacey, sitting at the window of the upstairs living room in the house on Friary Street, noticed her sister walking briskly from work. She watched Rose crossing the street from sunlight into shade, carrying the new leather handbag that she had bought in Clerys in Dublin [Ireland] in the
(5) sale. Rose was wearing a cream-coloured cardigan over her shoulders. Her golf clubs were in the hall; in a few minutes, Eilis knew, someone would call for her and her sister would not return until the summer evening had faded.
  Eilis's bookkeeping classes were almost ended now; she had a manual on her lap about systems of accounting, and on the table behind her was a
(10) ledger where she had entered, as her homework, on the debit and credit sides, the daily business of a company whose details she had taken down in notes in the Vocational School the week before.
  As soon as she heard the front door open, Eilis went downstairs. Rose, in the hall, was holding her pocket mirror in front of her face. She was
(15) studying herself closely as she applied lipstick and eye make-up before glancing at her overall appearance in the large hall mirror, settling her hair. Eilis looked on silently as her sister moistened her lips and then checked herself one more time in the pocket mirror before putting it away.

Their mother came from the kitchen to the hall. . . .

(20)　　Rose reached into her handbag and took out her purse. She placed a one-shilling piece on the hallstand. "That's in case you want to go to the pictures," she said to Eilis.

"And what about me?" her mother asked.

"She'll tell you the story when she gets home," Rose replied. . . .

(25)　　All three laughed as they heard a car stop outside the door and beep its horn. Rose picked up her golf clubs and was gone.

Later, as her mother washed the dishes and Eilis dried them, another knock came to the door. When Eilis answered it, she found a girl whom she recognized from Kelly's grocery shop beside the cathedral.

(30)　　"Miss Kelly sent me with a message for you," the girl said. "She wants to see you."

"Does she?" Eilis asked. "And did she say what it was about?"

"No. You're just to call up there tonight.". . . .

Miss Kelly slowly came down the stairs into the hallway and turned on (35) a light.

"Now," she said, and repeated it as though it were a greeting. She did not smile. . . .

"I hear you have no job at all but a great head for figures."

"Is that right?"

(40)　　"Oh, the whole town, anyone who is anyone, comes into the shop and I hear everything.". . . .

"And we are worked off our feet every Sunday here. Sure, there's nothing else open.

And we get all sorts, good, bad and indifferent. And, as a rule, I open (45) after seven mass,[1] and between the end of nine o'clock mass until eleven mass is well over, there isn't room to move in this shop. I have Mary here to help, but she's slow enough at the best of times, so I was on the lookout for someone sharp, someone who would know people and give the right change. But only on Sundays, mind. The rest of the week we can manage (50) ourselves. And you were recommended. I made inquiries about you and it would be seven and six a week, it might help your mother a bit.". . .

"Well?" Miss Kelly asked.

Eilis realized that she could not turn down the offer. It would be better than nothing and, at the moment, she had nothing. . . .

---

[1] seven mass—church service at 7 A.M.

(55) Rose, at thirty, Eilis thought, was more glamorous every year, and, while she had had several boyfriends, she remained single; she often remarked that she had a much better life than many of her former schoolmates who were to be seen pushing prams[2] through the streets. Eilis was proud of her sister, of how much care she took with her appearance and how much care she put
(60) into whom she mixed with in the town and the golf club. She knew that Rose had tried to find her work in an office, and Rose was paying for her books now that she was studying bookkeeping and rudimentary accountancy, but she knew also that there was, at least for the moment, no work for anyone in Enniscorthy, no matter what their qualifications.
(65) Eilis did not tell Rose about her offer of work from Miss Kelly; instead, as she went through her training, she saved up every detail to recount to her mother, who laughed and made her tell some parts of the story again.

"That Miss Kelly," her mother said, "is as bad as her mother and I heard from someone who worked there that that woman was evil incarnate.[3] And
(70) she was just a maid in Roche's before she married. And Kelly's used to be a boarding house as well as a shop, and if you worked for her, or even if you stayed there, or dealt in the shop, she was evil incarnate. Unless, of course, you had plenty of money or were one of the clergy."

"I'm just there until something turns up," Eilis said.
(75) "That's what I said to Rose when I was telling her," her mother replied. "And don't listen to her if she says anything to you." . . .

One day at dinnertime Rose, who walked home from the office at one and returned at a quarter to two, mentioned that she had played golf the previous evening with a priest, a Father Flood, who had known their father
(80) years before and their mother when she was a young girl. He was home from America on holidays, his first visit since before the war. . . .

"Anyway," Rose said, "I invited him in for his tea when he said that he'd like to call on you [the mother] and he's coming tomorrow." . . .

Father Flood was tall; his accent was a mixture of Irish and American.
(85) Nothing he said could convince Eilis's mother that she had known him or his family. His mother, he said, had been a Rochford.

"I don't think I knew her," her mother said. "The only Rochford we knew was old Hatchethead."

Father Flood looked at her solemnly. "Hatchethead was my uncle," he
(90) said. "Was he?" her mother asked. Eilis saw how close she was to nervous laughter. . . . Rose poured more tea as Eilis quietly left the room, afraid that if she stayed she would be unable to disguise an urge to begin laughing.

---

[2] prams—baby carriages
[3] incarnate—in bodily form

When she returned she realized that Father Flood had heard about her job at Miss Kelly's, had found out about her pay and had expressed shock at how low it was. He inquired about her qualifications.

"In the United States," he said, "there would be plenty of work for someone like you and with good pay." . . .

"In Brooklyn, where my parish is, there would be office work for someone who was hard-working and educated and honest."

"It's very far away, though," her mother said. "That's the only thing." . . .

"It would be a great opportunity, especially if you were young," Father Flood said finally. . . .

Eilis felt like a child when the doctor would come to the house, her mother listening with cowed respect. It was Rose's silence that was new to her; she looked at her now, wanting her sister to ask a question or make a comment, but Rose appeared to be in a sort of dream. As Eilis watched her, it struck her that she had never seen Rose look so beautiful. And then it occurred to her that she was already feeling that she would need to remember this room, her sister, this scene, as though from a distance. In the silence that had lingered, she realized, it had somehow been tacitly arranged that Eilis would go to America. Father Flood, she believed, had been invited to the house because Rose knew that he could arrange it. . . .

—Colm Tóibín
excerpted and adapted from *Brooklyn*, 2009
Scribner

1 The first three paragraphs serve to introduce
   (1) a contrast between the sisters
   (2) Rose's condescension toward her sister
   (3) the competition between the sisters
   (4) Eilis's concern about her sister

2 Lines 20 through 24 show Rose's
   (1) impatience with her mother
   (2) restlessness in her home
   (3) satisfaction with her work
   (4) thoughtfulness toward her sister

3 The dialogue in lines 36 through 41 depicts Miss Kelly as
   (1) indecisive   (3) jealous
   (2) abrupt   (4) bitter

4 The statement "And we are worked off our feet" (line 42) illustrates that Miss Kelly's shop is
   (1) disorderly   (3) bankrupt
   (2) bustling   (4) treasured

5 Eilis's attitude toward Rose in lines 55 through 60 can best be described as
   (1) protective   (3) admiring
   (2) critical   (4) indifferent

6 The phrase "no work for anyone in Enniscorthy, no matter what their qualifications" (lines 63 and 64) supports a central idea about Eilis's
   (1) respect for Miss Kelly's successful business
   (2) incentive to accept any employment
   (3) pressure to pursue further education
   (4) envy of Rose's comfortable situation

7 The author's choice of the word "mentioned" (line 78) as well as Father Flood's comments (lines 98 and 99) most likely indicate that Rose is

(1) afraid that her mother will object to Father Flood's visit
(2) anticipating that Eilis will help her with the meal
(3) careful about ensuring that Father Flood feels welcomed
(4) subtle about putting her plan for Eilis in motion   7 _____

8 The recognition that a job "had somehow been tacitly arranged" (line 111) suggests that

(1) an agreement was made without Rose's permission
(2) actions were taken to deceive Eilis's family
(3) an agreement was made without Eilis's knowledge
(4) actions were taken to limit Father Flood's influence   8 _____

9 Which quotation best reflects a central idea in the passage?

(1) "All three laughed as they heard a car stop outside the door and beep its horn" (line 25)
(2) " 'Miss Kelly sent me with a message for you,' the girl said. 'She wants to see you' " (lines 30 and 31)
(3) "Rose, at thirty, Eilis thought, was more glamorous every year, and, while she had had several boyfriends, she remained single" (lines 55 and 56)
(4) " 'In the United States,' he said, 'there would be plenty of work for someone like you and with good pay' " (lines 96 and 97)   9 _____

Reading Comprehension Passage B

Slam, Dunk, & Hook

    Fast breaks. Lay ups. With Mercury's[1]
    Insignia on our sneakers,
    We outmaneuvered to footwork
    Of bad angels. Nothing but a hot
(5) Swish of strings like silk
    Ten feet out. In the roundhouse
    Labyrinth our bodies
    Created, we could almost
    Last forever, poised in midair
(10) Like storybook sea monsters.
    A high note hung there
    A long second. Off
    The rim. We'd corkscrew
    Up & dunk balls that exploded
(15) The skullcap of hope & good
    Intention. Lanky, all hands
    & feet. . .sprung rhythm.
    We were metaphysical[2] when girls
    Cheered on the sidelines.
(20) Tangled up in a falling,
    Muscles were a bright motor
    Double-flashing to the metal hoop
    Nailed to our oak.
    When Sonny Boy's mama died
(25) He played nonstop all day, so hard
    Our backboard splintered.
    Glistening with sweat,
    We rolled the ball off
    Our fingertips. Trouble
(30) Was there slapping a blackjack
    Against an open palm.
    Dribble, drive to the inside,
    & glide like a sparrow hawk.
    Lay ups. Fast breaks.
(35) We had moves we didn't know

---

[1] Mercury—Roman god who acted as a messenger to the gods
[2] metaphysical—superhuman

We had. Our bodies spun
On swivels of bone & faith,
Through a lyric slipknot
Of joy, & we knew we were
(40) Beautiful & dangerous.

—Yusef Komunyakaa
"Slam, Dunk, & Hook"
from *Pleasure Dome: New and Collected Poems*, 2004
Wesleyan University Press

10 The images in lines 6 through 12 create a sense of

  (1) youth ending
  (2) anxious movement
  (3) time stopping
  (4) imaginative strategy   10 _____

11 In the context of the poem as a whole, lines 24 through 26 present

  (1) an example of the players' excitement with the game
  (2) a shift in the players' expectations
  (3) a contrast to the players' feelings of invincibility
  (4) an illustration of the players' skill   11 _____

12 Lines 32 through 36 most clearly reflect the players'

  (1) competition   (3) insecurity
  (2) agility   (4) devotion   12 _____

13 In the context of the poem as a whole, the mythological allusions best reflect the players' sense of being
  (1) popular
  (2) extraordinary
  (3) competent
  (4) successful

14 Which quotation best reflects a central idea of the poem?
  (1) "We'd corkscrew/Up & dunk balls that exploded" (lines 13 and 14)
  (2) "We were metaphysical when girls/Cheered on the sidelines" (lines 18 and 19)
  (3) "Glistening with sweat/We rolled the ball off/Our fingertips" (lines 27 through 29)
  (4) "Of joy, & we knew we were/Beautiful & dangerous" (lines 39 and 40)

Reading Comprehension Passage C
How We Make Sense of Time

"What is the difference between yesterday and tomorrow?" The Yupno man we were interviewing, Danda, paused to consider his answer. A group of us sat on a hillside in the Yupno Valley, a remote nook high in the mountains of Papua New Guinea.[1] Only days earlier we had arrived on a single-engine
(5) plane. After a steep hike from the grass airstrip, we found ourselves in the village of Gua, one of about 20 Yupno villages dotting the rugged terrain. We came all the way here because we are interested in *time*—in how Yupno people understand concepts such as past, present and future. Are these ideas universal, or are they products of our language, our culture and our
(10) environment?

As we interviewed Danda and others in the village, we listened to what they said about time, but we paid even closer attention to what they did with their hands as they spoke. Gestures can be revealing. Ask English speakers about the difference between yesterday and tomorrow, and they
(15) might thrust a hand over the shoulder when referring to the past and then forward when referring to the future. Such unreflective movements reveal a fundamental way of thinking in which the past is at our backs, something that we "leave behind," and the future is in front of us, something to "look forward" to. Would a Yupno speaker do the same?

(20) Danda was making just the kinds of gestures we were hoping for. As he explained the Yupno word for "yesterday," his hand swept backward; as he mentioned "tomorrow," it leaped forward. We all sat looking up a steep slope toward a jagged ridge, but as the light faded, we changed the camera angle, spinning around so that we and Danda faced in the opposite direction,
(25) downhill. With our backs now to the ridge, we looked over the Yupno River meandering[2] toward the Bismarck Sea. "Let's go over that one more time," we suggested.

Danda obliged, again using his hands to enliven his explanation. But as we expected, his gestures had changed. As he referred to "yesterday," he now
(30) gestured, not backward, but forward. As he explained "tomorrow," he gestured back over his shoulder, up toward the ridge. Inconsistent as these movements may seem, Danda was not confused. His gestures expressed the Yupno way of understanding time, one in which the future is not something in front of you—it is uphill. By having interviewees change sitting positions, we were able to
(35) show that it does not matter whether the slope is in front of you, behind you, to

---
[1] Papua New Guinea—an oceanic country, north of Australia
[2] meandering—winding

your left or to your right. The Yupno conception of time is not anchored to the body, as the Western one is, but to the world and its contours. By investigating cases such as these, we and other researchers are starting to piece together an answer to a question that has puzzled thinkers for centuries: How are human (40) beings able to make sense of time?

    Humans, like creatures ranging from amoebas and bees to mockingbirds and elephants, come with built-in equipment for perceiving some aspects of time, such as the rhythms of night and day, the waxing and waning of the moon, and the turning of the seasons. What separates humans from other (45) animals is that we do not stop at merely sensing time's passage. We tackle time head-on—or at least we try. We dice it into units, even ones that go beyond what is perceivable, such as milliseconds, or that transcend our life span, such as millennia. We depict time graphically, talk about it ceaselessly and even make gestural models of it in the air as we talk. In short, humans (50) everywhere create and rely on time concepts—ideas about the nature of time that allow us to make plans, follow recipes, share memories and discuss possible futures.

    But what are our time concepts made of? What is going on in the mind of a speaker of Yupno, or English for that matter, when answering our (55) question about the difference between yesterday and tomorrow? Recent research in cognitive science[3] is uncovering a surprising answer. Across cultures, human time concepts depend, in large part, on metaphor—in particular, on what cognitive scientists call conceptual metaphor, in which we think about something, in this case time, in terms of something else, (60) in this case space. Thus, we build our understanding of duration, of time's passage and of sequences of events out of familiar spatial ideas such as size, movement and location. The latest findings reveal that this basic "time is like space" metaphor appears to be universal around the world—yet it also takes strikingly different forms from one culture to the next. . . .

(65)   We sometimes imagine ourselves inside the sequence of events, with past, present and future conceptualized as locations where we once were, currently are and will be. This internal perspective on time motivates English expressions such as "the week ahead of us." When we take the external perspective, however, we view the succession of events from the (70) outside, much like watching a lineup of people all moving in one direction. This external perspective motivates phrases such as "a reception follows the ceremony."

---

[3] cognitive science—the study of the mind and its processes

These basic ideas about time are expressed spatially[4] in a dazzling variety of unrelated languages, across cultures that differ in every way imaginable. The idea that temporal[5] sequences are like queues[6] of people is found, for example, in Tamil (India), Maori (New Zealand), Greenlandic (Greenland) and Sesotho (South Africa), where the idea that "spring follows winter" can be expressed as "spring is in the footprints left by winter."

But now we come to a wrinkle. Even as people of all cultures lean on spatial concepts for understanding time, exactly *which* spatial metaphors they use can vary. Take the internal perspective, future-in-front metaphor mentioned earlier, found in English and many other languages. This metaphor was long thought to be universal, but in 2006 members of our team investigated a striking counterexample in South America. In Aymara, a language spoken high in the Andes, many phrases suggest the opposite metaphor is at work. For example, the expression "a long time ago" could be loosely rendered in Aymara as "a lot of time in front." Analysis of video-recorded interviews with 30 speakers showed conclusively that Aymara speakers gesture according to this future-behind, past-in-front metaphor. The pattern is especially strong among older speakers who do not speak Spanish, which has the future-in-front metaphor common to English and most European languages. . . .

The human reliance on spatial metaphors for abstract thinking may have deep evolutionary roots and is not likely to change any time soon. The particular metaphors we lean on, however, are a product of culture—not of biological evolution—and are much more malleable.[7] Literacy is a recent and rapid achievement in the scope of the human saga, but it already has had profound consequences for how people conceptualize[8] time. New spatial metaphors for our dearest abstract concepts will almost certainly enter the picture as our culture evolves. E-mail in-boxes show the most recent items at the top, but text messages go the other way, with the newest at the bottom. And so we must wonder: Which way will time flow next?

—Kensy Cooperrider and Rafael Núñez
excerpted from "How We Make Sense of Time"
Scientific American Mind, November/December 2016

---

[4] spatially—with gestures
[5] temporal—relating to time
[6] queues—lines of people
[7] malleable—adaptable
[8] conceptualize—form ideas about

15 A primary function of the first paragraph is to introduce
  (1) a challenge to the author's research
  (2) the goals of the author's research
  (3) an ease of accessing the Yupno villages
  (4) the hardness of life in the Yupno villages   15 _____

16 As used in line 16, the word "unreflective" most nearly means
  (1) unreliable   (3) unconscious
  (2) unnatural   (4) uncertain   16 _____

17 The details in lines 25 through 29 show that the author
  (1) wanted to influence the way Danda would react
  (2) had a theory about how Danda would respond
  (3) needed to complete the interview with Danda before dark
  (4) had difficulty in communicating instructions to Danda   17 _____

18 Lines 36 and 37 support a central idea by demonstrating
  (1) a contrast between small and large societies
  (2) the difference in interpretation between cultures
  (3) the relationship between language and customs
  (4) a change in behavior adapted over time   18 _____

19 Which statement best summarizes the information in lines 41 through 44?
  (1) Nature interferes with creatures' awareness of time.
  (2) All creatures align their behavior to lunar cycles.
  (3) Physical size inhibits creatures' adaptations to seasonal change.
  (4) All creatures have some awareness of time.   19 _____

20 The statements "We tackle time head-on" and "We dice it into units" (lines 45 and 46) emphasize human attempts to
  (1) enjoy the passage of time
  (2) structure the concept of time
  (3) control the speed of time
  (4) make efficient use of time   20 _____

21 Which word helps clarify the meaning of "transcend" (line 47)?

(1) "beyond" (line 47)
(2) "milliseconds" (line 47)
(3) "span" (line 48)
(4) "depict" (line 48)

22 Researchers found that humans can best understand time (lines 48 through 64) through

(1) examination of philosophical explanations of change
(2) observation of the regularity in daily schedules
(3) using figurative language to express complex ideas
(4) recording the beginning, ending, and duration of events

23 The text is developed primarily through the use of

(1) point counterpoint
(2) detailed examples
(3) parallel structure
(4) chronological sequence

24 Which quotation reflects a central idea of the text?

(1) "By having interviewees change sitting positions, we were able to show that it does not matter whether the slope is in front of you, behind you, to your left or to your right" (lines 34 through 36)
(2) "Recent research in cognitive science is uncovering a surprising answer" (lines 55 and 56)
(3) "The latest findings reveal that this basic 'time is like space' metaphor appears to be universal around the world—yet it also takes strikingly different forms from one culture to the next" (lines 62 through 64)
(4) "New spatial metaphors for our dearest abstract concepts will almost certainly enter the picture as our culture evolves" (lines 98 through 100)

PART 2—Argument Response

Directions: Closely read each of the *four* texts provided on pages 367 through 374 and write a source-based argument on the topic below. You may use the margins to take notes as you read and scrap paper to plan your response. Write your argument on a separate sheet of paper.

> **Topic:** Should plastic shopping bags be banned?

> **Your Task:** Carefully read each of the *four* texts provided. Then, using evidence from at least *three* of the texts, write a well-developed argument regarding whether or not plastic shopping bags should be banned. Clearly establish your claim, distinguish your claim from alternate or opposing claims, and use specific, relevant, and sufficient evidence from at least *three* of the texts to develop your argument. Do *not* simply summarize each text.

Guidelines:

Be sure to:
- Establish your claim regarding whether or not plastic shopping bags should be banned.
- Distinguish your claim from alternate or opposing claims.
- Use specific, relevant, and sufficient evidence from at least *three* of the texts to develop your argument.
- Identify each source that you reference by text number and line number(s) or graphic (for example: Text 1, line 4 or Text 2, graphic).
- Organize your ideas in a cohesive and coherent manner.
- Maintain a formal style of writing.
- Follow the conventions of standard written English.

Texts:

Text 1 – The Right Chemistry: Ban Plastic Bags? It's Not So Simple

Text 2 – The Effects of Plastic Bags on Environment

Text 3 – Should Cities Ban Plastic Bags?

Text 4 – The Economic Effect of Plastic Bag Bans

Text 1

The Right Chemistry: Ban Plastic Bags? It's Not So Simple

...There's no question that plastic bags are a symbol of our throw-away culture and are an inviting target for scorn, because they are a visible sign of pollution. They can be seen fluttering from trees, floating in that much publicized patch of plastic detritus[1] in the middle of the Pacific Ocean and
(5) clogging sewers in parts of Asia. But the bags don't dive into the ocean, jump into sewers or take flight without help. Human help. We are the real problem. With proper recycling, reuse or disposal, benefits can outweigh risks.
    What then are the perceived risks? Arguments usually revolve around
(10) the bags being made from oil, a non-renewable resource, the plastic being non-biodegradable,[2] the bags taking up space in landfills, the bags being unnecessary because of ready replacement by paper or reusable bags, and the bags leaving a large carbon footprint.[3] Disposable bags are made of high-density polyethylene, which is manufactured from ethylene derived either
(15) from petroleum or natural gas. In Canada, the source is usually ethylene made from ethane, a component of natural gas that otherwise is commonly burned off.
    Plastic bags do not biodegrade in a landfill, as we are often told. This is true, but modern landfills are designed to have a low oxygen environment
(20) to prevent biodegradation that would result in the formation of methane, a greenhouse gas. The purpose of a landfill is to seal in the contents and prevent substances from leaching[4] out. Since plastic bags are highly compressible, they take up very little volume in landfills. In any case, plastic shopping bags are estimated to make up less than 1 percent of litter.
(25)   Paper shopping bags do not biodegrade in a landfill either and because of their greater mass they are a greater burden on the waste stream. Paper manufacture is an energy intensive process and requires the use of many chemicals. Cradle to grave calculations generally show that plastic bags have a lower carbon footprint than paper bags. "Biodegradable" bags are a
(30) marketing scheme; they don't degrade under normal conditions.
    But why should we make an issue of plastic versus paper? Why not rely on reusable bags? Here too, the issue is not as simple as it seems.

---

[1] detritus—debris
[2] non-biodegradable—unable to break down
[3] carbon footprint—the amount of greenhouse gas associated with a product
[4] leaching—leaking

A cotton bag would have to be used about 130 times in order to have a carbon footprint that is less than that of a plastic bag. Growing cotton requires more
(35) pesticides than most crops and processing and transport require a great deal of energy. If the plastic bag is reused to line your garbage can, a cotton bag would have to be used over 300 times to have a lower global warming potential.

Reusable plastic bags are often made of laminated plastics and are
(40) not recyclable. Depending on the type of plastic, whether low density polyethylene, or non-woven polypropylene, a reusable bag would have to be used at least 10–20 times before it becomes more environmentally friendly than a disposable bag. There is also the issue of contamination if reusable bags are not cleaned properly. A warm trunk is an excellent incubator for
(45) bacteria originating from that trace of meat juice left in the bag.

If not reused for that next trip to the grocery store, or for lining garbage bins, or for collecting garbage in a car, or for picking up after pets, or for covering food in the fridge, disposable plastic bags are eminently recyclable into plastic lumber, trash cans, containers and new plastic bags.
(50) Many municipalities[5] and even countries have banned the giveaway of plastic bags or have introduced fees for them. That has resulted in the use of more paper bags, not an environmental plus, and an increase in the sales of plastic bags for garbage bins. . . .

—Joe Schwarcz
excerpted from "The Right Chemistry: Ban Plastic Bags? It's Not So Simple"
http://montrealgazette.com, March 25, 2016

---

[5] municipalities—communities

Text 2

The Effects of Plastic Bags on Environment

    ...There is no way to strictly limit the effects of plastic bags on the environment because there is no disposal method that will really help eliminate the problem. While reusing them is the first step, most people either don't or can't based on store policies. They are not durable enough to
(5) stand up to numerous trips to the store so often the best that citizens can do is reuse them when following pooper scooper laws.
    The biggest problem with this is that once they have been soiled, they end up in the trash which then ends up in the landfill or burned. Either solution is very poor for the environment. Burning emits toxic gases that
(10) harm the atmosphere and increase the level of VOCs[1] [Volatile Organic Compounds] in the air while landfills hold them indefinitely as part of the plastic waste problem throughout the globe.
    Even when citizens try to manage their plastic bag disposal, wind plays a role in carrying them away as litter. This litter is not biodegradable and
(15) thus where it lands it tends to stay for a long period of time. A bag that is eventually ripped to shreds from high winds or other factors doesn't disappear but instead is spread in smaller amounts throughout the area. This can cause more problems as these smaller pieces are carried away through storm drains and often end up in the waterways....
(20)   One of the greatest problems is that an estimated 300 million plastic bags end up in the Atlantic Ocean alone. These bags are very dangerous for sea life, especially those of the mammal variety. Any hunting mammal can easily mistake the size, shape, and texture of the plastic bag for a meal and find its airway is cut off. Needless deaths from plastic bags are increasing every year....
(25)   The environmental balance of the waterways is being thrown off by the rate of plastic bags finding their way into the mouths and intestinal tracts of sea mammals. As one species begins to die off at an abnormal rate, every other living organism in the waterway is impacted. There are either too many or too few and changes within the environment continue to kill off yet
(30) more organisms.
    The indefinite period of time that it takes for the average plastic bag to break down can be literally hundreds of years. Every bag that ends up in the woodlands of the country threatens the natural progression of wildlife. Because the breakdown rate is so slow the chances that the bag

---

[1] VOCs—carbon-based chemicals that easily become a vapor or gas at room temperature

(35) will harmlessly go away are extremely slim. Throughout the world plastic bags are responsible for suffocation deaths of woodland animals as well as inhibiting soil nutrients.

    The land litter that is made up of plastic bags has the potential to kill over and over again. It has been estimated that one bag has the potential to (40) unintentionally kill one animal per every three months due to unintentional digestion or inhalation. If you consider the number of littered plastic bags ranges from 1.5 million to 3 million depending on location, this equals a lot of ecosystem-sustaining lives lost. . . .

    While it's a noble thought to place the plastic bags in the recycling bin (45) every week, studies have proven that there are very few plants that actually recycle them. Most municipalities either burn them or send them off to the landfill after sorting. This is because it can be expensive to recycle this type of plastic. It doesn't melt down easily and is often not realistically able to be reused from its original form without considerable overhaul to the (50) facility.

    The premise of recycling these bags is nice. Yet funding for the upgrades just has not happened and thus less than 1% of all bags sent to recycling plants worldwide end up in the recycling project. Most are left to become a pollution problem in one way or another. . . .

—Jamey Wagner
excerpted and adapted from
"The Effects of Plastic Bags on Environment"
www.healthguidance.org, 2017

Text 3

Should Cities Ban Plastic Bags?

This excerpt from a Wall Street Journal article includes a journalist's introduction to the plastic bag ban issue and the viewpoints of an environmental expert, Todd Myers, against the ban.

Plastic bags are one of the most common items in everyday life. And they are at the heart of a fight raging in municipalities world-wide.

Many cities around the globe have already banned the ubiquitous[1] bags from stores, and activists are pushing for bans elsewhere. They argue that
(5) cities must spend vast sums to clean up the bags and the damages caused by them, money that's better spent elsewhere. Not to mention that plastic bags are a blight on the environment, polluting waterways and other natural areas and killing off animals. Banning plastic bags, the activists say, will redirect funds to infrastructure[2] and spur entrepreneurial[3] efforts to come up with
(10) alternatives to plastic. . . .

But there's no evidence that banning bags helps the environment—and plenty of evidence that it may actually hurt. Bans yield little benefit to wildlife while increasing carbon emissions[4] and other unhealthy environmental effects.

Little Harm to Wildlife

(15)   Let's go through the arguments for banning bags. Ban backers cite impacts on marine life, but they consistently sidestep the actual data. The National Oceanic and Atmospheric Administration, for one, says there are currently no published studies about how many marine mammals die because of marine debris. Meanwhile, other sources of marine debris, such
(20) as discarded fishing gear, are recognized as a danger to sea life. Why the frenzy over *one* source—plastic bags—in the absence of evidence?

As for the pollution caused by plastic bags, consider a study by Ospar, the European organization working to protect the marine environment. The study found plastic shopping bags represented less than 3% of marine litter
(25) on European beaches, a figure that includes scraps of plastic from shredded bags.

---

[1] ubiquitous—found everywhere
[2] infrastructure—fundamental facilities and structures, such as roads, bridges, and power supplies
[3] entrepreneurial—business leadership
[4] carbon emissions—greenhouse gases released into the atmosphere

Meanwhile, the claim that municipalities spend a substantial amount of their trash budget, let alone millions of dollars, on picking up plastic bags is hard to believe. In many cases, these claims are guesses by advocates instead of data based on actual studies, and cost is often thrown in as a justification after bans are enacted for political reasons. . . .

Some ban supporters claim plastics harm human health, even when studies from organizations like the Environmental Protection Agency, the Centers for Disease Control and Prevention, and Pacific Northwest National Labs show these claims are false or exaggerated.

Consider a study from the U.K. Environment Agency that found plastic grocery bags have the lowest environmental impact in "human toxicity" and "marine aquatic toxicity" as well as "global-warming potential" even after paper bags are used four times and reusable cotton bags are used 173 times. Why? Largely because paper and cotton bags come from crops that require fertilizer, pesticides, herbicides and the like.

Environmental Effects

Critics also say that ban opponents ignore the environmental impact of bags over the course of their lifetime. But many studies do just that. The U.K. Environment Agency's study, for instance, compared the energy expended in creating, using and disposing of plastic, paper and reusable bags to arrive at its figures. Consumers would have to use a cotton bag 173 times before they match the energy savings of one plastic bag, assuming 40% of bags are reused—a percentage that's actually *lower* than the rate in some cities.

Some critics say we need to ban bags because voluntary take-back programs don't work. But the point of the programs is simply to reuse bags, and consumers *already* reuse bags to hold garbage or pick up after pets.

As for the idea that plastic bags cost consumers more, the reason grocery stores use plastic instead of paper or other bags is that they cost less and hold more. Reusable bags are even more expensive.

Let's Be Honest

. . .Weighing the costs and benefits makes it clear that banning plastic bags yields little benefit at very high cost. Unfortunately, the political symbolism of banning the bags is powerful. It is often easier to ignore the science that indicates such bans may actually harm the environment than to make an honest effort to weigh these issues. All of this is why plastic-bag bans are more about environmental image than environmental benefit.

—excerpted from "Should Cities Ban Plastic Bags?"
www.wsj.com, October 8, 2012

Text 4

The Economic Effect of Plastic Bag Bans

    A study from the National Center for Policy Analysis [NCPA] claims that a ban on plastic bags used by grocers and retailers can negatively impact sales in the ban area and increase sales among stores just outside the bag ban region....

(5)   During a one-year period, before and after the ban, the majority of stores surveyed in areas with a ban reported an overall average sales decline of nearly 6%. While the majority of respondents surveyed in areas without a ban reported an overall average sales growth of 9%....

    The NCPA survey said that stores under the bag ban also experienced
(10) a 10% reduction in employment, while employment in stores outside of the ban slightly increased. [NCPA senior fellow, Pamela] Villarreal said that was particularly "alarming."

"We often hear about the environmental effects of plastic bags, but the economic effects are generally ignored," she said. "When you think about
(15) the unemployment rate in this country, any negative impact on employment is something to take notice of."

    The U.S. plastic bag manufacturing and recycling sector employs more than 30,000 workers in 349 communities across the nation, according to the American Progressive Bag Alliance, an organization representing the plastic
(20) bag manufacturing and recycling sector....

Leila Monroe, staff attorney for the oceans program at the Natural Resources Defense Council (NRDC), looks at the impact on jobs in a different way. She said bag bans provide an opportunity for the industry to innovate.

"They can pull together and look at how they can design better products that are
(25) truly durable and easily recyclable," Monroe said. "I have no doubt that if the industry put in the time and investment to retool operations, they can ensure there aren't job losses, but instead work on ways to move the industry forward."

Plastic bag alternatives

    As paper bags are starting to also get listed on the ban list, more attention is now focused on reusable bags. Reusable shopping bags can be
(30) made from fabric, woven synthetic fibers, or even polypropylene.

    Vincent Cobb, founder of Reuseit.com, first launched the site in 2003 to offer alternatives to single-use plastic shopping bags. The site then expanded to include all types of reusable products....

    Brad Nihls, VP [Vice President] of operations for Reuseit.com, said the
(35) company is all too aware that the reusable bag market is flooded with cheap

quality, green-washing[1] products. He said the company warns customers about looking out for cheaply made reusable shopping bags.

"One item of concern with reusable shopping bags are the very cheap reusables that are often given away during promotions or selling at grocery (40) stores for 99 cents," he said. "The concern here is that while they are marketed as reusable shopping bags, they really are just a glorified disposable bag, which we feel is even more damaging than the single-use plastic shopping bags.". . .

When it comes to plastic shopping bag bans, Nihls said the company doesn't view bans as a big "windfall" for the company. . . .

(45) Some reports state that plastic bags are responsible for less than 1% of all litter. For instance, litter audit data from major Canadian municipalities show that plastic shopping bags are less than 1% of litter. In San Francisco, surveyors found that plastic bags consisted of 0.6% of the city's litter before a local ban was enacted.

(50) What can be lost in the debate between bans, taxes and consumer choice at the checkout, is the fact that plastic shopping bags are fully recyclable, when disposed of properly.

Still, a study conducted by Boustead Associates found that only 5.2% of plastic bags are recycled. . . .

(55) However, plastic bag recycling requires a different type of infrastructure than plastic bottles and containers. It's been reported that when people put plastic bags in their curbside bin, it has the potential to clog machines at the recycling facilities.

"The problem with plastic bags is that they are extremely difficult, if (60) not almost impossible, to recycle," Monroe said. "At municipality recycling facilities, plastic bags have to be removed because the lightweight thin film can impact the recycling process.". . .

Recycling plastic bags can be turned into raw materials for fencing, decking, building and construction products, shopping carts and new bags, (65) according to the American Chemistry Council.

Monroe points out that the 5% recycling of bags is still the current and, potentially, future reality.

"There's just a large number of bags available where there is no incentive really to recycle them," she said. "In contrast when bag bans and fees are put (70) in place, they show it's working to reduce waste.". . .

—Heather Caliendo
excerpted and adapted from "The Economic Effect of Plastic Bag Bans"
www.npr.com, February 6, 2013

---

[1] green-washing—falsely claiming that a product is environmentally friendly

PART 3—Text-Analysis Response

Your Task: Closely read the text provided on pages 376 through 378 and write a well-developed, text-based response of two to three paragraphs. In your response, identify a central idea in the text and analyze how the author's use of **one** writing strategy (literary element or literary technique or rhetorical device) develops this central idea. Use strong and thorough evidence from the text to support your analysis. Do *not* simply summarize the text. You may use the margins to take notes as you read and scrap paper to plan your response. Write your response on a separate sheet of paper.

Guidelines:

Be sure to:
- Identify a central idea in the text.
- Analyze how the author's use of **one** writing strategy (literary element or literary technique or rhetorical device) develops this central idea. Examples include: characterization, conflict, denotation/connotation, metaphor, simile, irony, language use, point-of-view, setting, structure, symbolism, theme, tone, etc.
- Use strong and thorough evidence from the text to support your analysis.
- Organize your ideas in a cohesive and coherent manner.
- Maintain a formal style of writing.
- Follow the conventions of standard written English.

Text

The Edge of the Sea

     The edge of the sea is a strange and beautiful place. All through the long history of Earth it has been an area of unrest where waves have broken heavily against the land, where the tides have pressed forward over the continents, receded, and then returned. For no two successive days is the shore line
(5) precisely the same. Not only do the tides advance and retreat in their eternal rhythms, but the level of the sea itself is never at rest. It rises or falls as the glaciers melt or grow, as the floor of the deep ocean basins shifts under its increasing load of sediments, or as the earth's crust along the continental margins warps up or down in adjustment to strain and tension. Today a little
(10) more land may belong to the sea, tomorrow a little less. Always the edge of the sea remains an elusive and indefinable boundary.
     The shore has a dual nature, changing with the swing of the tides, belonging now to the land, now to the sea. On the ebb tide it knows the harsh extremes of the land world, being exposed to heat and cold, to wind,
(15) to rain and drying sun. On the flood tide it is a water world, returning briefly to the relative stability of the open sea.
     Only the most hardy and adaptable can survive in a region so mutable, yet the area between the tide lines is crowded with plants and animals. In this difficult world of the shore, life displays its enormous toughness and
(20) vitality by occupying almost every conceivable niche. Visibly, it carpets the intertidal rocks; or half hidden, it descends into fissures and crevices, or hides under boulders, or lurks in the wet gloom of sea caves. Invisibly, where the casual observer would say there is no life, it lies deep in the sand, in burrows and tubes and passageways. It tunnels into solid rock and bores
(25) into peat and clay. It encrusts weeds or drifting spars[1] or the hard, chitinous[2] shell of a lobster. It exists minutely, as the film of bacteria that spreads over a rock surface or a wharf piling; as spheres of protozoa, small as pinpricks, sparkling at the surface of the sea; and as Lilliputian[3] beings swimming through dark pools that lie between the grains of sand.
(30)   The shore is an ancient world, for as long as there has been an earth and sea there has been this place of the meeting of land and water. Yet it is a world that keeps alive the sense of continuing creation and of relentless

---

[1] spars—pieces of wood
[2] chitinous—tough, protective
[3] Lilliputian—tiny

drive of life. Each time that I enter it, I gain some new awareness of its beauty and its deeper meanings, sensing that intricate fabric of life by which (35) one creature is linked with another, and each with its surroundings. . . .

The flats took on a mysterious quality as dusk approached and the last evening light was reflected from the scattered pools and creeks. Then birds became only dark shadows, with no color discernible. Sanderlings scurried across the beach like little ghosts, and here and there the darker forms of the (40) willets stood out. Often I could come very close to them before they would start up in alarm—the sanderlings running, the willets flying up, crying. Black skimmers flew along the ocean's edge silhouetted against the dull, metallic gleam, or they went flitting above the sand like large, dimly seen moths. Sometimes they "skimmed" the winding creeks of tidal water, where (45) little spreading surface ripples marked the presence of small fish.

The shore at night is a different world, in which the very darkness that hides the distractions of daylight brings into sharper focus the elemental realities. Once, exploring the night beach, I surprised a small ghost crab in the searching beam of my torch. He was lying in a pit he had dug just (50) above the surf, as though watching the sea and waiting. The blackness of the night possessed water, air, and beach. It was the darkness of an older world, before Man. There was no sound but the all-enveloping, primeval sounds of wind blowing over water and sand, and of waves crashing on the beach. There was no other visible life—just one small crab near the sea. I have seen (55) hundreds of ghost crabs in other settings, but suddenly I was filled with the odd sensation that for the first time I knew the creature in its own world— that I understood, as never before, the essence of its being. In that moment time was suspended; the world to which I belonged did not exist and I might have been an onlooker from outer space. The little crab alone with the sea (60) became a symbol that stood for life itself—for the delicate, destructible, yet incredibly vital force that somehow holds its place amid the harsh realities of the inorganic world. . . .

Looking out over the cove I felt a strong sense of the interchangeability of land and sea in this marginal world of the shore, and of the links between (65) the life of the two. There was also an awareness of the past and of the continuing flow of time, obliterating much that had gone before, as the sea had that morning washed away the tracks of the bird. . . .

There is a common thread that links these scenes and memories—the spectacle of life in all its varied manifestations as it has appeared, evolved, (70) and sometimes died out. Underlying the beauty of the spectacle there is meaning and significance. It is the elusiveness of that meaning that haunts us, that sends us again and again into the natural world where the key to the

riddle is hidden. It sends us back to the edge of the sea, where the drama of life played its first scene on earth and perhaps even its prelude; where the
(75) forces of evolution are at work today, as they have been since the appearance of what we know as life; and where the spectacle of living creatures faced by the cosmic realities of their world is crystal clear.

—Rachel Carson
excerpted from *The Edge of the Sea*, 1955
Houghton Mifflin Company

Regents ELA Answers August 2019
English Language Arts

Answer Key

PART 1

1. **1**
2. **4**
3. **2**
4. **2**
5. **3**
6. **2**
7. **4**
8. **3**
9. **4**
10. **3**
11. **3**
12. **2**
13. **2**
14. **4**
15. **2**
16. **3**
17. **2**
18. **2**
19. **4**
20. **2**
21. **1**
22. **3**
23. **2**
24. **3**

PART 2 *See Answers and Explanations*

PART 3 *See Answers and Explanations*

Regents Examination in English Language Arts—August 2019
Chart for Converting Total Weighted Raw Scores to Final Exam Scores
(Scale Scores)

Raw	Scale	Perf.	Raw	Scale	Perf.
56	100	5	27	55	2
55	98	5	26	53	1
54	97	5	25	50	1
53	96	5	24	47	1
52	95	5	23	45	1
51	94	5	22	42	1
50	93	5	21	39	1
49	91	5	20	36	1
48	90	5	19	33	1
47	89	5	18	31	1
46	88	5	17	28	1
45	87	5	16	24	1
44	86	5	15	21	1
43	85	5	14	18	1
42	84	5	13	15	1
41	83	5	12	12	1
40	82	5	11	10	1
39	81	4	10	9	1
38	79	4	9	8	1
37	77	4	8	6	1
36	76	4	7	5	1
35	74	3	6	4	1
34	72	3	5	4	1
33	69	3	4	3	1
32	67	3	3	2	1
31	65	3	2	1	1
30	63	3	1	1	1
29	60	2	0	0	1
28	58	2			

Answers Explained

PART 1—Reading Comprehension

Multiple-Choice Questions

Passage A

1. **1** "a contrast between the sisters." These first paragraphs introduce the sisters and reveal how different their daily lives are. We learn that Rose is popular, outgoing, and attentive to her overall appearance. Eilis, on the other hand, is at home, silently observing her lively sister. Eilis, we learn, is going to vocational school, studying to become a bookkeeper. The attitudes offered in the other choices are not suggested in the first three paragraphs.

2. **4** "thoughtfulness toward her sister." Rose, who is picking up her golf clubs and about to go out again for the rest of the day, makes a point of leaving money for Eilis to "go to the pictures [movies]." This passage reveals that Eilis has no money for herself, nor does she have a social life like her sister's.

3. **2** "abrupt." In this brief interview, Miss Kelly doesn't even greet Eilis. Instead, Miss Kelly immediately and unexpectedly announces what she knows about Eilis and lists all the reasons she has decided Eilis will be the best person for a job helping in her store. Nothing in lines 36 through 41 suggests Miss Kelly is indecisive, jealous, or bitter; she is simply "all business." This question is an example of how knowledge of vocabulary is assessed indirectly.

4. **2** "bustling." This term best describes a store that is crowded and hurriedly busy. At certain times on Sunday mornings, Miss Kelly and her employees are "worked off our feet." (This question is an example of how knowledge of vocabulary is assessed indirectly)

5. **3** "admiring." In the opening paragraphs (question 1), we have little sense of how Eilis feels about her sister. In lines 55 through 60, however, we learn that Eilis is proud of her sister in the way Rose takes care of her appearance, chooses friends wisely, and values her independence. Eilis also appreciates the way her sister is supporting Eilis's own efforts to gain employment and have a life for herself.

6. **2** "incentive to accept any employment." This is clearly the best answer to the question. Where Eilis lives, there simply is no work, even for people with qualifications. Eilis accepts the job at Miss Kelly's because it is a rare opportunity to earn a bit of money to help her mother.

7. **4** "subtle about putting her plan for Eilis in motion." These lines reveals Rose's clever and indirect (subtle) way of arranging, through Father Flood, a plan for Eilis to go to America, to Brooklyn, in fact, where, "there is plenty of work for someone like you with good pay." Rose is careful about ensuring that her mother will welcome Father Flood, choice (3) but the significance of these lines is in what it reveals about Rose's plan.

8. **3** "an agreement was made without Eilis's knowledge." This paragraph describes Eilis's feelings as she gradually realizes, especially in observing Rose's silence, that a tacit (unspoken) arrangement had been made without her knowledge. She also realizes that, unknown to her, Father Flood had made inquiries about her job and pay at Miss Kelly's.

9. **4** "'In the United States,' he said, 'there would be plenty of work for someone like you and with good pay'" (lines 96 and 97). Each incident in the passage leads to the final scene, which in turn reflects this reality for many in the Ireland of the early 1950s. (Note that Colm Tóibín's lovely and much-celebrated novel *Brooklyn* tells the story of how Eilis makes a new life for herself in America.)

Passage B

10. **3** "time stopping." The images of players ". . . poised in midair . . . hung there / A long second" capture those instants, within the "fast breaks and lay ups" of the game, when players seem suspended in air and time.

11. **3** "a contrast to the players' feelings of invincibility." This sudden insertion of the image of Sonny Boy's grief and anger over the death of his mother is a reminder of the boys' world just beyond the sidelines of their game.

12. **2** "agility." These images of the boys' swift and nimble (agile) moves on the court are a further reflection of the energy in the opening lines and of the poem's title, "Slam, Dunk, & Hook."

13. **2** "extraordinary." The boys believed ". . . we could almost / Last forever . . . Like storybook sea monsters. . . . We were metaphysical . . . We had moves we didn't know / We had." The word "extraordinary" best expresses the boys' feelings.

14. **4** "Of joy, & we knew we were / Beautiful & dangerous" (lines 39 and 40). These lines complete the theme expressed in the lines cited in Question 13 and conclude the poem with a declaration of the central idea. The other choices are examples of the vivid details that develop this theme in the body of the poem.

Passage C

15. **2** "the goals of the author's research." The last three lines of the first paragraph state clearly that the researchers are "interested in time—in how the Yupno people understand concepts [of time]," and whether concepts of time are universal or are products of language, culture, and environment.

16. **3** "unconscious." We are meant to understand in context here that "unreflective movements" are spontaneous and natural, done without the need for serious thought or contemplation (reflection).

17. **2** "had a theory about how Danda would respond" In lines 28 and 29, the author reveals that after Danda is facing in the opposite direction, "his gestures had changed" and that this was "as we expected." This passage reveals how the researchers carefully planned their experiment to confirm their theory. By only suggesting casually that Danda change position, the researchers seek to avoid influencing his behavior in any way. None of the other choices are supported by these lines.

18. 2 "the difference in interpretation between cultures." Lines 36 and 37 assert a clear difference between the Yupno conception of time, which is "anchored to the . . . world," and the Western concept of time, which is "anchored to the body." This is the most precise answer among the choices.

19. **4** "all creatures have some awareness of time." This is the best answer among the choices. The range of creatures mentioned, from amoebas to elephants, implies that the researchers believe all creatures have some awareness of time. The article continues by illustrating how humans go beyond awareness to ". . . tackle time head-on." (See question 20.)

20. **2** "structure the concept of time." This point is developed further when, in lines 45 and 46, the authors outline how human ideas about time ". . . allow us to make plans, follow recipes, share memories and discuss possible futures." The emphasis here is on how humans *attempt to structure* ideas about time.

21. **1** "beyond." Millennia are periods of thousands of years. They represent periods of time far beyond the human life span. In other words, humans have concepts of time that far exceed our ability to experience those lengths of time.

22. **3** "using figurative language to express complex ideas." Lines 48 through 64 develop the researchers' observation that in nearly all cultures, understanding of time is expressed in metaphor—thinking about something in terms of something else by using in figurative language.

23. **2** "detailed examples." This article is developed through a series of examples of how time is understood, in concept and metaphor, in different cultures. None of the other choices accurately describes the structure of this article.

24. **3** "The latest findings reveal that this basic 'time is like space' metaphor appears to be universal around the world—yet it also takes strikingly different form from one culture to the next" (lines 62 through 64). This is the most comprehensive statement of the central idea here. Choices (1) and (2) offer specific details, and choice (4) states a conclusion.

PART 2—Argument Response

Sample Essay Response

    The argument over whether or not to ban plastic shopping bags from use in stores is a very heated issue. Those who have not researched the other options, or actually looked at the harm they create, may say that banning plastic shopping bags is a good step in the right direction for saving our planet. However, the damage that banning plastic bags can create may be greater than the current damage caused by using plastic bags. There is convincing evidence that plastic bags should not be banned, because the alternative options often create an even bigger problem.

    Plastic shopping bags are both economical and good for the economy. They are often reused by customers, which saves them money by not having to buy bags for other purposes. One recent article lists the many secondary uses for plastic bags, showing that they can be "reused for that next trip to the grocery store, or for lining garbage bins, or for collecting garbage in a car, or for picking up after pets, or for covering food in the fridge." (Text 1, lines 46–48) This list shows some of the many other uses of plastic bags that cannot simply be replaced by paper or reusable bags. Besides customers saving money by reusing them, plastic bags are also good for both business owners and employees. They are cheap and easy for store owners to buy, and when stores were surveyed before and after a ban, most of the stores with the ban lost up to 6% of sales while those "in areas without a ban reported an overall average sales growth of 9%." (Text 4, lines 5–8) The use of plastic bags supports employment as well: "The U.S. plastic bag manufacturing and recycling sector employs more than 30,000 workers in 349 communities across the nation." (Text 4, lines 17–18)

On the other hand, many activists argue that overuse of plastic bags causes serious harm to the environment; they demand a ban on plastic bags and insist on the exclusive use of reusable or paper bags. As persuasive as this may seem, these alternatives are not better for the environment and may create more harm to the ecosystem than plastic bags do. One report indicates that "paper shopping bags do not biodegrade in a landfill either and because of their greater mass they are a greater burden on the waste stream." (Text 1, lines 25–26) Reusable bags are not a realistic fix either: "Consumers would have to use a cotton bag 173 times before they match the energy saving of one plastic bag." (Text 3, lines 46–47) Since reusable bags need to be cleaned often and may rip, it is unreasonable to expect that every customer uses their reusable bag almost 200 times before losing it, breaking it, or getting a new one. Overall, plastic bags generally have the same or less of an impact than some of the alternatives.

Despite the evidence presented by those opposed to banning plastic bags, some may still believe that plastic bags are harmful to animals and people. A study from a U.K. Environment Agency found, however, that "plastic grocery bags have the lowest environmental impact in 'human toxicity' and 'marine aquatic toxicity' as well as 'global warming potential.'" (Text 3, lines 36–38) This same study also disputes the argument that plastic bags are harmful to animals when it reports that the U.S. National Oceanic and Atmospheric Administration says, "There are currently no published studies about how many marine mammals die because of marine debris." (Text 3, lines 17–19) As for plastic bags being harmful to people, "the U.S. Environmental Protection Agency, the Centers for Disease Control and Prevention, and Pacific Northwest National Labs show these claims are false or exaggerated." (Text 3, lines 34–35)

Overall, plastic shopping bags should not be banned, because the cost of the ban is greater than the reward. Plastic bags have many uses besides holding groceries, many of which cannot be replaced by paper or cotton bags. In addition, recent evidence suggests that plastic bags are less harmful to wildlife and humans than we thought.

Analysis

This is an excellent response to the task. In the first paragraph, the writer identifies the topic and opposing positions and then establishes a clear and forceful claim: "There is convincing evidence that plastic bags should not be banned, because the alternative options often create an even bigger problem." The argument is well developed, with several supporting examples from the texts, relying most heavily on the one that supports the writer's position. The argument is coherent in its focus on the claim, restated in the conclusion: "Overall, plastic shopping bags should not be banned, because the cost of the ban is greater than the reward." The essay does not consistently identify the issue as plastic *shopping* bags, but the context makes this sufficiently clear.

The argument might be even more effective if it were balanced in acknowledging some additional details from the opposing view; however this is not required in the task. The writing is clear and appropriately formal, with no significant errors in the conventions. This essay would merit a high score.

(See pages 79–80 for the scoring guidelines.)

Part 3—Text-Analysis Response

Sample Essay Response

A central idea of this passage focuses on the recognition of the sea and its shoreline as an ever-changing and vital force. The author effectively uses diction in the observations of this "spectacle" of the meeting of these two natural elements. Through the use of selective and vivid word choice, the author relates both the variations and the energy created in this meeting.

The author's effective use of diction to portray this scene is evident in the various descriptions that focus on its vitality. The shore is described as being a "relentless drive of life," (lines 32–33) whose inhabitants display "enormous toughness and vitality." (line 19–20) One of these creatures, a little crab, is viewed as a "delicate, destructible, yet incredibly vital force that somehow holds its place." (lines 60–61) Words like "relentless" and "toughness" are not ones that would ordinarily be associated with a shoreline and its creatures. As used here, however, they make the reader aware of the true energy and drive that exist within them.

Diction also plays an important role in helping the reader to understand that this "meeting place" between land and sea is ever changing. The word "mutable" (line 17) to describe this region immediately allows the reader to recognize that nothing stays the same here. When speaking of the shore's dual nature, the author describes it as "changing with the swing of the tides, belonging now to the land, now to the sea." (lines 12–13) Using an expression like "the swing of" emphasizes the constant ebb and flow of the water as it alters the landscape of the shoreline, helping the reader to not only visualize, but also feel, the rhythm of the phenomenon. The author goes on further to describe this "meeting of land and water" (line 31) as "a world that keeps alive the sense of continuing creation," (line 32) and the link of land and sea as "an awareness of the past and of the continuing flow of time." (lines 65–66) The repetition of the word "continuing," when coupled with the word "flow" in the latter example, serves to complete an image of an ongoing progression of life, over time and space, and its ever changing nature.

Analysis

The richness of language and imagery in this passage makes "diction" a good choice of writing strategy for this task. This passage also presents a significant challenge to the student writer: how to find appropriate language of one's own to discuss how good prose is achieved. This writer succeeds in appreciating not only the beauty of the passage but also the power of language itself to convey a complex natural phenomenon.

This response is brief but coherent. The first paragraph establishes the central idea of the text and the writer's choice of diction for analysis. The second paragraph discusses the power of the language to portray the scene "in the various descriptions that focus on its vitality." The third paragraph demonstrates how the language helps the reader understand ". . . this meeting place between land and sea." The discussion is well developed, with a variety of relevant examples to illustrate how diction supports the central idea. This writer demonstrates command of the conventions and notable skill in quoting phrases within sentences. This response to the task would merit a high score.

(See pages 81–82 for the scoring guidelines.)